OUTSOURCING CONTRACTS – A PRACTICAL GUIDE

OUTSOURCING CONTRACTS – A PRACTICAL GUIDE

Amanda Lewis
Denton Wilde Sapte LLP

Third Edition

City & Financial Publishing

City & Financial Publishing
8 Westminster Court, Hipley Street
Old Woking
Surrey GU22 9LG
United Kingdom
Tel: 00 44 (0)1483 720707 Fax: 00 44 (0)1483 727928
Web: www.cityandfinancial.com

ISBN 978 1905 121 373

British Library Cataloguing-in-Publication Data. A catalogue record for this book is available from the British Library.

Typeset by Cambrian Typesetters, Camberley and printed and bound in Great Britain by the MPG Books Group, Bodmin and King's Lynn

Contents

Foreword to the third edition

First of all, I would like to say how grateful I am that as outstanding an expert as Amanda Lewis has asked me to write this foreword.

Focusing now on the content, I would like to thank Amanda for writing a book that will be of great assistance to all experts who advise on outsourcing arrangements, particularly bearing in mind the outstanding usefulness, importance and topicality of the book's coverage.

Currently, the business trend throughout Europe is for there to be an increase in outsourcing, in particular business process outsourcing. Outsourcing agreements in Europe involve numerous technical issues that require a specialised knowledge of a variety of topics, including contract, employment, pensions, data protection, finance, property, competition and insolvency law. And this is where the usefulness of the book lies. Amanda's book has been structured and written so that all of these complicated issues can easily be understood.

The book is comprehensive, setting out the possible reasons why a customer may want to outsource, to ensure a better understanding of the business context of the outsourcing arrangement. It then covers key business and legal issues relevant for each of the stages of procuring, managing and ultimately terminating outsourcing arrangements, from both the customer's and the supplier's perspectives. It also includes specialist information on certain sectors.

All of us who advise on outsourcing agreements within Europe, whether members of the ItechLaw Association or otherwise, will find in this book many situations and problems that are familiar to us. It is clear that the book has been written by a person who knows what she is writing about, who has dealt with the problems she is writing about and knows how to manage them and, more importantly, how to prevent them.

In view of all of the above, nothing remains except for me to congratulate Amanda once more for writing this highly recommended book and to encourage her to continue to be the great professional she is.

Enrique J. Batalla
Former President of ItechLaw Association
December 2008

Foreword to the second edition

Amanda Lewis and Berwin Leighton Paisner have long been stalwart supporters of the National Outsourcing Association (NOA) and I was understandably pleased to be asked to write a foreword for Amanda's "Outsourcing Contacts – A Practical Guide".

Really I should say no more, because this book's title says it all. It really is a practical guide to outsourcing partially aimed at senior management and legal counsel. A quick look through will show you that all stages are comprehensively covered in a handy accessible way. You can either start at the beginning and read through or dip into the sections as and when you need them. Not only is it an excellent primer but a great reference book that can be used time and time again.

One thing that you wouldn't expect to read in the book, but as a "foreword" writer I should tell you, is that I have been at many of the presentations that Amanda has given. Whereas often the legal aspects of outsourcing come over as dry and dull, Amanda injects life and enthusiasm into the subject and shows how essential the correct legal stance must be. She does this by drawing on her personal experience of many years in industry and literally hundreds of outsourcing contracts in which she has been involved. This comes through in the book in terms of the examples, advice and warnings that she gives; this has all been hard won and makes the book of tremendous value to the reader.

As the Chairman of the NOA, I've been challenged many times on how long this outsourcing "phenomenon" will last. Is it just a new management fad to go the way of many? Well, the NOA (www.noa.co.uk) has been going since 1987, and we don't see any end on the horizon; in fact there is a growing European Outsourcing Association (EOA) to boot. Laws change of course, and Amanda has incorporated recent changes in those that affect outsourcing. What does seem to be changing is that outsourcing "principles" are being applied to internal company supply, which gives this book another purpose as you may well not have a legal contract but the best practice inherent here is just as essential internally as externally for a successful relationship.

In conclusion, if you want a comprehensive guide, based on many years of practical experience in the business of outsourcing, aimed at helping you build a successful outsourcing relationship, then I have no hesitation in recommending it to you.

Plus, of course, congratulating Amanda on a job well done!

Martyn Hart
Chairman National Outsourcing Association
Clermont-Ferrand, France
25 April 2006

Foreword to the first edition

Outsourcing has been the dominant feature of the business landscape in recent years. While other methods for business performance improvement have briefly hogged the limelight, outsourcing has continued to grow and evolve – from simple data centre outsourcing to more recent innovations such as business process and offshore outsourcing. Outsourcing remains high on the business agenda – in research conducted by PA Consulting Group in 2003,[1] an overwhelming majority of CEOs said that outsourcing offered considerable business advantage. And yet, in the same research, over 60 per cent of organisations stated that they had not realised the expected benefits of outsourcing.

At first sight, these results seem contradictory – if organisations find the result disappointing, why is the market growing? Outsourcing will inevitably continue to be a popular option as long as the potential benefits are large and well documented. The drive to outsource is no longer a straightforward question of cost reduction (although that remains an important factor in many decisions). Increasingly, businesses are seeking very different outcomes from outsourcing, including:

(a) the ability to react rapidly to market changes;
(b) improving time to market;
(c) accessing true industry best practice;
(d) delivering global services; and
(e) promoting innovation.

These are challenging targets – maybe it is not so surprising that organisations often fail to achieve them. So what are the obstacles that need to be overcome? Is there a magic formula?

Of course the answer is no. But there are some practical steps that an organisation can take to improve their chance of achieving the expected benefits. The fundamental principles of good practice have remained constant, in spite of the changing technology and business landscape. Best practice suggests that successful outsourcing deals occur when:

(a) the organisation's sourcing strategy is clear and unambiguous;
(b) the ability of the outsourcing supply market to provide the required services is understood;

1 "Outsourcing: mindset switch - moving from cost control to managing for flexibility and benefits realization." Outsourcing survey results 2002, PA Consulting Group 2003.

(c) in-house capability to deliver the same services has been properly assessed and evaluated;
(d) the risks and rewards of the deal are understood by customer and supplier; and
(e) the transition path is well defined and embedded in the contract.

It sounds simple, but, as with many things, the details of a matter are often the most problematic part. Which brings us to this Guide.

One of the most important steps that an organisation can take is to learn from the experience of others. In this Guide the author has compressed a vast amount of practical advice covering the key areas that will concern the prospective outsourcer, from business strategy to termination. Two things come across very clearly – one is that Amanda is, above all, a practitioner, not a theorist, and her advice is based on hard won experience. The other is that Amanda is genuinely enthusiastic about her subject, as anyone who has heard her present on the subject will attest.

Although the focus of the Guide is on constructing the deal, its strength is that it places this in the wider context of the entire outsourcing process. Without this broad perspective, my experience is that an outsourcing deal is doomed to failure. This Guide will help you understand how to make the outsourcing deal work for you.

Greg Jones
PA Consulting Group

Preface

Intended audience

This Guide is aimed at in-house legal counsel, finance directors and senior management at both customer and supplier organisations, government legal departments who are dealing with outsourcing projects and commercial lawyers and accountants who advise outsourcing customers or suppliers.

Business and legal issues

I initially wrote the Guide because I felt that there was inadequate guidance for parties entering into outsourcing arrangements with regard to business and legal issues. Books on the business issues relating to outsourcing often omitted important legal issues which could have profound business implications. Legal textbooks were not designed for business people and did not put legal issues in the business context.

In addition, legal textbooks usually failed to address all of the different legal issues particularly relevant for outsourcing agreements. For outsourcing agreements usually involve contract, employment, pensions, data protection, property law, corporate, finance and insolvency issues. They may also, however, involve many other areas of law.

All of the legal issues described are set out in simple terms which should be clear to non-lawyers. Strategic issues are dealt with in the main text of chapters whilst detailed legal and business issues are set out in separate tables. Senior business people can read the main text of the book to understand the strategic issues without being bogged down in details in the tables. As the Guide is intended as a practical handbook and not a legal textbook, it contains summaries of relevant legal issues, not detailed expositions. Cases and statutes are not referred to unless they are useful to illustrate the points being made.

There are highlights of some of the more general taxation issues that could arise in England and Wales. However, both customers and suppliers are strongly recommended to obtain specialist taxation advice on specific outsourcing projects both prior to and during the negotiation of the outsourcing arrangement, and indeed where substantial variations to existing transactions are proposed.

The Guide reflects the legal position as at the end of March 2009.

Best practice

Another reason I initially wrote the Guide was because I wanted to describe best practice with regard to different types of outsourcing services and in different sectors, so that best practice could be applied by outsourcing customers and suppliers with regard to other services or sectors – I certainly find this very helpful in practice in assisting me to find creative solutions to business issues. For this reason, for example, the chapters in the Guide on the public, utility and financial services sectors address the question as to what customers and suppliers in other sectors can learn from the experience and regulations in that sector. For example, the FSA guidance on practical steps which can be taken by financial firms to deal with data security may also be helpful for other types of businesses.

Changes in the third edition

The continuing desire to ensure that the Guide comprehensively covers the various different legal and business issues relevant for outsourcing agreements has meant substantial changes in the third edition of the Guide. I have reviewed the whole of the Guide and updated all sections, including, in particular:

(a) updating the Guide to ensure that it covers best practice in outsourcing to cut costs during a recession, an area which presents particular challenges;
(b) updating the Guide to provide advice on what to do if your outsourcing supplier (or customer) experiences financial difficulties;
(c) re-writing the chapters on financial services, public sector and utilities and adding a new chapter on PFI/PPP;
(d) extending the Guide to cover competition, state aid and environmental issues;
(e) including an entire chapter on pensions issues;
(f) rewriting the chapter on data protection and security and strengthening the other sections in the Guide on data protection and security to reflect the importance of these topics;
(g) including a section on the recent use of adjudication in outsourcing agreements;
(h) updating the Guide in the light of recent cases, in particular *Quest 4 Finance* v *Maxfield, Crystal Decisions (UK) Limited* v *Vedatech, MAN Nuzfahrzeuge AG and others* v *Freightliner Limited and others, David Philip Hawley* v *Luminar Leisure Limited, Golden Strait Corporation* v *Nippon Yusen kubishka Kaisha and Regus (UK) Ltd* v *Epcot Solutions Ltd, Seatbooker Sales Limited* v *Southend United Football Club Limited; Transfield Shipping Inc.* v *Mercator Shipping Inc.* and *Steria LTD* v *Sigma Wireless Communications Ltd* and *Internet Broadcasting Corporation Ltd (t/a NETTV) and NETTV Hedge Funds Ltd (formerly MARHedge TV Ltd)* v *MAR LLC (t/a MARHedge)*;
(i) adding an explanation of proposals for reform relating to the law on unfair contract terms;
(j) covering new types of outsourcing, such as legal process outsourcing and knowledge process outsourcing;

(k) extending the section of the Guide on ITIL and the balanced scorecard and including a section on the contract scorecard;
(l) adding details of best practice in construction outsourcing, facilities management outsourcing and fund administration outsourcing, so that customers and suppliers can decide whether they want to apply similar principles to their transactions;
(m) rewriting the chapter on software development to explain the implications of using waterfall and agile development methodologies;
(n) rewriting the sections on benchmarking, step in joint ventures, service bonuses and alternatives to service credits;
(o) updating the chapters on due diligence by the customer and the supplier, in the light of recent experience; and
(p) adding a section on shared service centres.

European law and best practice

In the third edition of the Guide, I have extended my mission to describe relevant legal issues, business issues and best practice in different service industries and sectors in England and Wales to cover legal issues, business issues and best practice in the major European countries. This is particularly important with the growth of outsourcing in Europe.

This has meant fundamental changes in the nature of the Guide. In the third edition, the main chapters are based on the legal system in England and Wales only and have been amended to describe the relevant EU directives and their implementation in England and Wales. Many of the issues raised relate to business principles and best practice that will be relevant in other countries, and these sections have been amended (where relevant) to deal with business issues and best practice in other EU countries.

The Guide then includes additional chapters describing the legal position in major EU countries. These chapters cover employment, pensions, data protection, insolvency, financial services regulation and competition law issues in these countries – note that these issues will be relevant whether the outsourcing contract is governed by English law or not. In addition, the chapters deal with contract law, which will be relevant where the parties have agreed that the relevant local law will apply to the outsourcing contract. Lastly, the chapters cover public sector and utilities regulation, which will apply to public bodies and utilities in the relevant country. The contents of these chapters will be indispensable for customers and suppliers entering into outsourcing (or indeed other types of contract) affecting these key EU countries.

The chapters on other European countries have been written by experts in law firms in each of the jurisdictions concerned, with me acting as editor. I am extremely grateful to all of them for their contributions. In particular I would like to thank:

(a) Germany – Dr. Stephan Witteler, Partner, Beiten Burkhardt;
(b) Spain – Jose Ramon Morales, Partner, Garrigues;
(c) France – Thierry Bernard, Partner, and Mary-Daphné Fishelson, Partner, Lefèvre Pelletier & Associés;

(d) Netherlands – Serge Zwanen, Partner, Loyens and Loeff;
(e) Italy – Gabriele Capecchi, Partner, Legance;
(f) Scandinavia – Jörgen Axelsson, Partner, Setterwalls;
(g) Switzerland – Michele Bernasconi, Partner and Nicola Bernardoni, Associate, Bär & Karrer AG; and
(h) Ireland – Anne-Marie Bohan, Partner, Matheson Ormsby Prentice.

In addition, due to the popularity of outsourcing to India and China, I have added chapters on the specific issues involved with outsourcing to these destinations and I would like to thank the following for their contributions in writing these chapters:

(a) India – Sajai Singh, Partner, J.Sagar Associates; and
(b) China – Dominic Hui, Partner, Vivien Chan & Co.

In writing the third edition of this Guide, I have also taken the opportunity to consult more widely with other experts who work in the outsourcing industry. There is a lot of knowledge about outsourcing and strategic sourcing which has not been included previously in any written articles and books on outsourcing. I would like to thank, in particular: Ian Reeves of Gartner Consulting; Tony Rawlinson of EquaTerra; Tony Dyhouse of QinetiQ; Alan Baxter of the Highways Agency; Mike Whay of RSRL; Chris Peacock of the London Borough of Hackney; Linda Bonner and Dean Francis of the London Borough of Enfield; Steve Alexander and Les Bond of Southern Water; Nigel Annett of Welsh Water; Mark Richards of EDF Energy; Andrew Phillips and Dave Copeland of Wessex Water; Heather Rogers of Centrica; Ian Seagrave of Deutsche Bank; Jeremy Barden of HBOS; John Roome of Chubb Insurance of Europe; Lulu O'Leary of Blue Moon; John Rixon of Prudential; Mandy Caller of Svenske Handelsbanken; Peter Higgins of PD Consult; David King of Boots; Jane Kimberlin of Domino Pizzas; Tim Cowen of BT; and Martin Hobbs of Morse.

I would like to thank all of my former colleagues at Berwin Leighton Paisner who have helped me with this Guide, including in particular Adrian Magnus and Simon Albert, who wrote the new chapter on competition law and Alexandra Davidson, Martha Quinn, Carol Mulcahy, Katherine Calder, Gary Richards, David Harrison, Jennifer McEwan, Katherine Ollerhead, Kiran Arora, Barry Gross, John Hurdley, William Bateman and James Palmer.

Lastly, I would like to thank my publisher, Nick Bliss, for his help and support.

If you have any comments on the Guide, you can contact me at 020 7242 1212 or amanda.lewis@dentonwildesapte.com.

Amanda Lewis
Partner,
Denton Wilde Sapte
March 2009

Part One – Introduction

Chapter 1

Defining Successful Outsourcing

1.1 Outline

This chapter contains a definition of outsourcing and an explanation of the different types of outsourcing. It also describes the purpose of the Guide and outlines what constitutes successful outsourcing and why customers outsource. Lastly, it explains the difference between contracting for business outcomes, services outputs or inputs, a distinction that will be used throughout the Guide.

There are references to "suppliers" and "customers"; the intention is that the Guide should assist both public and private sector customers and also suppliers. Customers of the customer are referred to as "clients".

1.2 What is outsourcing?

The Financial Services Authority ("FSA") provides a useful definition of outsourcing, defining outsourcing as "the use of a person to provide customised services to a firm".[1] It also defines outsourcing as "any third party dependency".[2]

This approach reflects that there are two different elements of outsourcing. First, outsourcing involves the provision of a service. Second, the service is not a commodity service (unlike, for example, the provision of standard stationery) which the customer can turn on and off at will. There is a level of dependency upon the supplier. This could arise, for example, because people or assets needed for the provision of the service are transferred to the outsourcing supplier. It could also arise because elements of the service are tailored specifically for the customer.

From the supplier's perspective, there is a level of interdependency between the parties as the supplier depends upon the customer's ability to pay the supplier its fees. In addition, if the customer is satisfied with the supplier's performance, it is more likely to increase the services outsourced to the supplier. Lastly, if the customer's business or reputation suffers in the market, this may affect the supplier's business.

---

1 *See* page 130 of the FSA's Handbook.

2 *See* the FSA's comments on the feedback on CP142 in Policy Statement Operational Risk Systems and Controls. The FSA's comments were superseded by the "near-final" text for its Policy Statement on Prudential Risks, Systems and Controls, which adopts the definition of outsourcing in the Handbook but states that guidance on outsourcing should apply to all third-party dependencies.

This definition of outsourcing covers an extremely wide variety of transactions. It includes some arrangements that are designated as "managed services", "strategic partnerships" or "partnering arrangements".[3] It also covers non-traditional outsourcing models, which are predicted to gain in popularity[4] (including application service provider ("ASP"), utility computing, software on demand, software as a service ("SAAS"), cloud computing[5] and business process utility ("BPU") models) under which software or services are made available to the customer as a commoditised service, on a rental basis.

As outsourcing is a business tool which is used to achieve specific business objectives, the character of outsourcing changes as market conditions develop. It also evolves to reflect an individual customer's requirements and circumstances. Thus a major characteristic of outsourcing is that no two arrangements will be exactly the same.

1.3 Classification of outsourcing

1.3.1 Sector

One way of classifying the wide variety of outsourcing arrangements is by sector. There are specific laws and regulations that apply to customers entering into outsourcing transactions in certain sectors, notably the public sector, utilities and financial services sectors. For example, firms regulated by the FSA will be subject to its guidance on outsourcing. Chapter 33 covers some of the regulations that relate to the financial services sector. Chapters 34 to 36 describe some of the laws, policies and guidance which apply to the public sector. Chapter 37 deals with the regulations affecting the utilities sector. All three chapters also highlight lessons that bodies which are not in these sectors can learn from the purpose and nature of the regulations.

1.3.2 Nature of the service

A second way of classifying outsourcing initiatives is by the nature of the service being provided, as listed in Table 1.

This Guide deals with the key issues relevant to all of the listed types of outsourcing (for example services and charging). It does not describe in detail specific issues relating to one particular service (for example telecommunications regulatory issues).

---

3 For example, the arrangements described by the Strategic Partnering Taskforce. *See* the Final Report of the Taskforce, which can be found at http://www.communities.gov.uk/publications/localgovernment/strategicpartneringtaskforce or, more recently, HM Treasury's report "Infrastructure procurement: delivering long term value" March 2008 found at www.hm-treasury.gov.uk/d/bud08_procurement_533.pdf. For details of sector specific models in the public sector *See* the website of the Public Private Partnerships Programme (4Ps) at www.4ps.gov.uk.

4 In September 2008, the Gartner Group stated that it anticipates that, by 2012, 25 per cent of IT will be delivered through non-traditional models.

5 Where services are provided over the internet the services are referred to as "cloud computing".

Table 1 *Classification of outsourcing initiatives*

Category of outsourcing	*Subcategories*	*Examples*
IT and telecommunications	IT Telecommunications	
Business process outsourcing	Back office and middle office	Human resources Finance and accounting Mortgage processing Cheque processing Life policy administration Local authority revenue and benefits processing
	Sales and front office	Call centres Sales
Knowledge process outsourcing		Sales research Market research services Drug trial data management
Legal process outsourcing	Core legal services	Due diligence Legal research Discovery and litigation support Contract review
	Legal support services	Document management Paralegal support
Facilities and property	Facilities Property[6]	

1.3.3 Commercial structure

Outsourcing projects can be classified by commercial structure. Thus, outsourcing projects can be distinguished depending upon whether, for example, they are executed by way of a services agreement between the customer and supplier or whether they involve the parties entering into a strategic partnership or joint venture. Commercial structures for outsourcing agreements are discussed in Chapter 17.

---

6 In practice, property outsourcing includes three distinct types of arrangement:

(a) property management;
(b) serviced accommodation, which operates like hotel accommodation; and
(c) "total property solutions" in which a supplier takes over a customer's property portfolio and then makes premises available to the customer.

1.3.4 Onshore/offshore

Outsourcing transactions can be divided into those that are onshore and those that are offshore. Most of the chapters in this Guide are applicable to both types of outsourcing. Chapter 38 deals with some of the additional issues that are relevant for offshore outsourcing transactions and Chapters 39 and 40 deal specifically with issues affecting outsourcing to India and China (respectively).

1.3.5 Value

Lastly, outsourcing can be distinguished by value. A low-value transaction will often be simpler than one that is high value. Accordingly, some of the issues raised by this Guide may not be relevant for a low-value project.

1.4 Purpose of this Guide

Despite the differences between the various types of outsourcing projects, many of the fundamental challenges presented by them are similar. The aim of this Guide is to give the reader an insight into a range of tested solutions so as to enable the parties to an outsourcing arrangement to find the most appropriate solution for their particular set of circumstances. It will accordingly enable best practice in one area to be applied in other areas. Chapters 2 to 32 describe the general issues that arise in most types of outsourcing transactions (for example service descriptions and charging) and possible ways of dealing with them.

This Guide also describes the key commercial and legal success factors relevant to the various types of outsourcing. In order to keep the Guide short and readable, it is not designed to cover all relevant provisions that need to go into an outsourcing agreement, but it focuses on fundamental issues that the parties will need to consider in order to ensure that their outsourcing project is successful.

1.5 What does it mean to be successful?

An outsourcing project can only be regarded as successful if it satisfies the business objectives of the party entering into the outsourcing arrangement.

1.5.1 Customer's perspective

From the customer's perspective, the outsourcing arrangement must satisfy the following three types of objectives:

(a) it must satisfy the customer's original business objectives;

(b) it must fulfil the customer's future business objectives, which the customer needs to satisfy during the term of the agreement; therefore, the agreement must include adequate change management measures;

(c) it must satisfy the customer's objectives on termination. On termination, the customer may want the flexibility to migrate the service back in-house or to an alternative supplier; it will not want to be locked in to receiving the services from the previous supplier.

1.5.2 Supplier's perspective

From a supplier's perspective, the outsourcing project will be successful mainly if it is (or can contribute towards) the supplier obtaining a profitable piece of business.[7] In practice, an outsourcing contract is unlikely to be successful from the customer's perspective if the outsourcing supplier is not making any profit, as, in this situation, the supplier will be tempted to cut corners and the service will suffer.

In addition, even if an outsourcing contract is profitable for the supplier, if it is unsuccessful from the customer's perspective, then the supplier may find itself the subject of unfavourable publicity, particularly if the customer is in the public sector or has a public profile. This may cause damage to the supplier's reputation and adversely affect its ability to win new profitable business.

1.5.3 Advantages of understanding the other side's perspective

It is an advantage for each side to understand the other side's perspective.

If the customer has a greater understanding of the supplier's viewpoint, then it is likely to prepare its initial outsourcing offering in a manner which is attractive to suppliers. This will avoid the need to modify the offering in order to attract sufficient levels of interest from suppliers, thus saving time and money. If the customer can increase the attractiveness of its project to outsourcing suppliers, then it will improve its bargaining power.

If the supplier has a greater understanding of the customer's perspective, this should enable it to make itself more attractive to customers in what is an increasingly competitive marketplace. Thus, for example, suppliers endeavouring to break into the public sector or utilities market need to understand the specific needs of public sector and utility customers, as described in Chapters 34 to 37.

It is in both parties' interests to understand the other side's concerns so that contractual negotiations proceed smoothly and efficiently. Therefore, this guide presents both the customer and the supplier perspectives.

1.6 Why customers outsource

The success of the outsourcing project has been defined in terms of satisfying the different business objectives of the supplier and customer.

The supplier's business objectives are discussed in greater detail in Chapter 6, which describes the preparation that the supplier will need to carry out before it enters into an outsourcing arrangement.

7 *See* Chapter 6, which describes other possible business objectives of the supplier.

There are various different business objectives that motivate customers to enter into outsourcing agreements. The reasons for outsourcing evolve to fit the times. In the early 1990s there was a focus on outsourcing in order to downsize and save costs. However, in the late 1990s as the economy boomed, outsourcing was used to support growth by providing access to scarce skills. In the early 2000s, customers in the financial services sector were particularly interested in exploiting the cost efficiencies which can result from offshore outsourcing. Customers in the utilities sector, tied to infrastructure investment needs and caps on charges, sought to boost returns to shareholders by using outsourcing to beat efficiency targets. Outsourcing by customers in the public sector was, to some extent, required by government by virtue of the Local Government Act 1999 which established the statutory responsibility to ensure continuous improvement and "Best Value". This was boosted by the Gershon report[8] which has been followed up most recently by the Operational Efficiency Programme.[9]

This Guide does not cover the validity or appropriateness of different reasons for outsourcing. There are plenty of books on this subject. For example, in his book *Strategic Outsourcing – a structured approach to outsourcing decisions and initiatives*, Maurice F Greaver II[10] highlights various reasons for outsourcing. These are listed in Table 2.

Table 2 *Possible business objectives*[11]

Reduce costs through superior provider performance and the provider's lower cost structure
Generate cash by transferring assets (such as equipment or premises) to the provider
Turn fixed costs into variable costs
Commercially exploit the existing skills[12]
Increase flexibility to meet changing business conditions, demand for products, services and technologies
Improve risk management

8 The Gershon report in the summer of 2004 committed the public sector to reducing public sector jobs by over 100,000 and to achieving savings of £15 billion a year.

9 For an overview of the Programme *see* "Operational Efficiency Programme: prospectus" July 2008 at www.hm-treasury.gov.uk/vfm_operational_efficiency.htm.

10 Amacom 1999.

11 The situation regarding local authorities is particularly interesting because, under Section 3 of the Local Government Act 1999, they have a duty to ensure best value. Thus they have a duty to secure continuous improvements in delivery of their services, focusing on economy, efficiency and effectiveness. This means that the local authorities have statutory objectives and targets that they must satisfy. Central government also has imposed upon itself a significant efficiency saving target of £30 billion for 2010/11. *See* www.hm-treasury.gov.uk.

12 The customer may have special industry knowledge relating to how a particular business process is carried out (e.g. cheque processing). It may want to exploit that knowledge to provide similar services to other companies in its sector. By entering into a joint venture with an outsourcing supplier, it may be able to gain the marketing support needed to market its skill.

Improve management and control

Improve operating performance

Enhance effectiveness by focusing on what you do best

Increase commitment and energy in non-core areas

Improve credibility and image by associating with superior providers

Enhance product and service value, customer satisfaction and shareholder value

Transform the organisation

Acquire innovative ideas

Give employees a stronger career path

Gain market access and business opportunities through the provider's network

Accelerate expansion by tapping in to the provider's capacity, processes and systems

Expand sales and production capacity during periods when such expansion

could not be financed

Obtain expertise, skills and technologies that would not otherwise be available

It will be clear from the variety of business objectives that the customer may be seeking to achieve, that different approaches will need to be taken and different issues will need to be dealt with in the individual outsourcing project, depending upon the customer's specific business objectives. This Guide deals with the key legal and commercial issues that the parties will need to consider to ensure that business objectives such as those listed above are achieved. In the current recession, most outsourcing is motivated by a desire to cut costs.

1.7 Risk allocation[13]

Paragraph 1.6 explains that outsourcing projects can be classified by reference to the business objectives that the customer is seeking to achieve. Outsourcing projects can also be categorised by reference to the extent to which the supplier will be responsible for the achievement of the customer's business goal. A major function of an outsourcing agreement is to allocate risk between the customer and the supplier, and a major risk that needs to be apportioned between the parties is the risk that the customer's business aims will not be met. Depending upon the extent to which the supplier will be responsible for the achievement of the customer's business objective, the outsourcing project may include "business outcome", "service output" or "input" elements. These terms are defined below.

13 A similar distinction is made in the OGC Guidance Successful Delivery Toolkit which can be found on www.ogc.gov.uk.

1.7.1 Business outcome

The outsourcing project will be business outcome based if the supplier accepts a level of responsibility for the achievement by the customer of its business goal. For many business objectives, it will not be appropriate to pass on the risk of their achievement to the supplier. For example, if the customer's business is to sell motor cars and it outsources its human resources function with the aim of enhancing its own effectiveness by focusing on what it does best, the outsourcing supplier will be reluctant to accept any risk that the customer is unable to sell more motor cars.

In other circumstances, it may be appropriate for the supplier to accept some risk of the customer's business aim not being achieved. Suppliers will not usually accept responsibility for the achievement of business objectives unless they have control over the manner in which the business goal is to be achieved. Therefore, the approach may be appropriate if, for example, the outsourcing arrangement involves the implementation of new software (developmental outsourcing) or the provision of business process re-engineering services (transformational outsourcing), where the purpose of the project is for the supplier to implement specified changes designed to improve the customer's operating performance.[14] In these circumstances, the supplier may be willing to accept some risk that the particular improvement in the customer's operating performance is not satisfied. It may also be appropriate if the supplier is providing training services. For example, if the supplier takes over responsibility for training soldiers and there is some guarantee of the calibre of the people being submitted for training, the supplier may be able to contract to provide a certain number of trained soldiers.

The manner in which the supplier will accept responsibility for the business objective will usually be through a risk/reward charging mechanism. This risk/reward charging mechanism, and the problems involved in using such a charging regime, are discussed in Chapter 18. The business outcome based nature of the project may also be reflected in the service levels and service credits – these are discussed in Chapters 9 and 19. Business outcome transactions are often termed "partnering" arrangements.

1.7.2 Service output

In the past, it has been more common for outsourcing projects to be "service output" based rather than "business outcome" based. Service output based liability is where the supplier is responsible for the provision of the specified service, the service output, but the customer is responsible for ensuring that the provision of the service satisfied its business objective. To describe it in another way, the customer is responsible for ensuring that the service description describes the outsourcing service that it needs. The supplier's role is limited to providing the service described in the service description.

Suppliers will not usually accept responsibility for the provision of the services unless they have sufficient control over the manner in which the services are to be provided. This issue is discussed in greater detail in Chapter 8.

14 Transformational and developmental outsourcing arrangements are discussed in greater detail in Chapter 21.

Lastly, the customer must bear in mind that it cannot entirely transfer over to a supplier the risk that the outsourced services will be provided. The customer must have adequate business continuity arrangements to cover a failure by the supplier to meet its obligations under the outsourcing agreement.

1.7.3 Input[15]

If the liability profile is "input" based, the supplier's responsibility is limited to the provision of certain resources, for example man days of consultancy. The customer is responsible for directing the consultant as to what to do and hence is responsible for the result of the consultancy services.

1.7.4 Hybrid

In practice, most outsourcing arrangements will be a hybrid of business outcome, service output and input liability arrangements, with individual service elements being either business outcome, service output or input based. For example, the outsourcing project may involve the supplier providing a desktop maintenance service as requested by the customer (service output based) but with the supplier being asked to prepare an annual service improvement plan explaining how the services can be improved so that they satisfy the customer's business objectives (business outcome based).

The distinction between business outcomes, service outputs and inputs will be used throughout this Guide to explain the risk profile of individual elements of the outsourcing transaction.

15 If the supplier is going to provide the services in whole or in part from Spain or France, then see Chapter 42 or Chapter 43 before signing an input-based outsourcing agreement.

Part Two – Preparation

Chapter 2

Preparation by the Customer

2.1 Outline

This chapter describes the first stage of the outsourcing process, which involves the customer clarifying its business objectives.

The customer must define its business objectives and support them with a business case. It needs to carry out due diligence to ensure that the business case stands up to scrutiny. It also needs to review the business case on an ongoing basis to ensure that key performance indicators are being met and that the objectives and the outsourcing arrangements themselves are changed, where necessary, when the customer's business changes. The customer should prepare a risk register and use it to manage risk during the outsourcing project.

2.2 Focus on business objectives

A lack of focus on the business objectives that the customer is attempting to achieve by entering into the outsourcing arrangement is a major reason why outsourcing transactions fail.[1] There has been a tendency, in particular in IT outsourcing transactions, for the customer to see the implementation of particular technology as an end in itself, for example to see the outsourcing deal as "the implementation and maintenance of a new finance system". It is more helpful to see IT systems and services as a means to an end, for example implementing a new finance system to enable more efficient billing.

Focusing on business goals, however, is not a straightforward task. It may involve the customer prioritising or seeking a satisfactory balance between the various aims of different departments or factions within the customer organisation. It may involve the customer balancing different types of business aims, for example satisfying a short-term goal such as reducing costs, and ensuring that it does not cause long-term problems of inflexibility. It may also involve the customer analysing how quickly its current business objectives are likely to change and how important it is that its business can respond quickly to commercial opportunities.[2]

In practice, any decision about what the customer's business aims are and how they can be achieved is reached in the context of the individual politics of the specific organisation, and external advisers

---

1 Good business objectives should be specific, measurable, appropriate, realistic and time bound ("SMART").

2 This may determine the optimum term of the outsourcing arrangement. *See* 23.2 below for a more detailed discussion of issues relating to the optimum term for an outsourcing arrangement.

advising the customer organisation, in particular, need to be aware of this. For example, in the case of a human resources outsourcing project, the chief finance officer may initiate the outsourcing project as a way of cutting costs. The chief executive officer may support the project if he feels that it will improve the company's share price. The human resources director may resent the outsourcing project and attempt to undermine it if he feels that it will decrease his importance within the organisation, for example if some of his staff will be transferred out of the company to the supplier under the Acquired Rights Directive ("ARD"). He may also feel that he is letting his staff down if he recruited them and now participates in a course of action which will lead to them being transferred to another company.

2.3 Business case

The customer's business objectives must be reflected in and supported by a business case which proves that, out of the various options open to the customer (such as keeping the service in-house, moving to a shared service or outsourcing), outsourcing is the best way to satisfy the specific goal the customer is endeavouring to achieve. As the outsourcing project will only be regarded as successful if it satisfies the customer's business aims over the term of the agreement, the business case should endeavour to address anticipated costs and benefits over this period.

This Guide does not describe how to prepare a business case. There is various guidance on this issue, both in the private[3] and the public[4] sectors.

2.4 Due diligence

The quality of the customer's business case and ultimately the success of the outsourcing arrangement will depend upon the thoroughness of the customer's due diligence in exploring and establishing the facts and assumptions underlying its business case. Table 3 gives examples of factors that a customer may need to check.

Table 3 *Factors to be considered in due diligence*

Business objectives

What are the customer's business objectives?

What are the possible ways that the customer could achieve its objectives?

Is outsourcing the best way of achieving its goals, or could its goals be achieved, for example, by improving performance?

3 *See*, for example, "Successful IT Outsourcing – strategies, tactics and management approaches for effective strategic sourcing", *Executive Report*, Gartner Press, 2003.

4 *See* the OGC guidance "Successful Delivery toolkit" at www.ogc.gov.uk. *See* also the report "From Vision to Outline Business Case" (ODPM, 2003). For project specific guidance for local government *see* the Public Private Partnership Programme's (4Ps) guidance for preparing "Outline Business Case" and "Final Business Case" at its website www.4ps.gov.uk.

What are the customer's competitors doing?

Will the proposed transaction affect other strategic aims, whether related to sourcing decisions or otherwise, for example the anticipated sale of part of the business?

How are the customer's business objectives likely to change over time?

Will the outsourcing project result in favourable or unfavourable publicity for the organisation?

Stakeholder support[5]

Do stakeholders in senior management agree with the business requirements and support the outsourcing initiative?

Will users and customers affected by the outsourcing arrangement support any resulting change in the services they receive?

If the success of the outsourcing project is dependent upon users or clients of the customer using the new services, will they use them?

Current services

What services are currently being provided?

What are the strengths and weaknesses of the current method of providing the services?

What are the stakeholders satisfied with and what are they dissatisfied with?

How are the services being provided?

From which locations or countries are the services being provided?

What service levels are being achieved?

What service levels are being achieved by the customer's competitors?

What volume of services is being provided?

To which locations are services being provided?

What trends are there regarding the volume of services?

Are the services being provided to other members of the customer's group or to external organisations?

Future service requirements

In what ways do the outsourced services and service levels need to be different from the current services, taking into account the customer's business requirements?

Can the customer's business requirements be satisfied by providing the services offshore?

5 Stakeholders include all individuals or groups of individuals who can impact or who will be impacted by the project. They include, for example, the individuals or groups who use the services or who select or pay for them and also those individual whose jobs depend upon the services.

Can suppliers suggest alternative ways of satisfying the customer's business requirements?

What steps are needed to effect a transition from the existing arrangements and the existing agreements?

Is any business process re-engineering required and if so, when should it be carried out, as part of the outsourcing project or before it?

What management services will the customer need to provide during the term of the agreement?

What are the customer's possible future service requirements, taking into account its overall business objectives?

What assistance from the supplier will the customer require on termination?

Current data protection and security requirements[6]

What are the current security risks?

What current security measures are taken to protect the customer's assets and data?

What security policies and standards have been implemented?

Future data protection and security requirements

What sensitive and critical data will be affected by the outsourcing arrangement?

Is there an accurate inventory of these?

What security risks will arise as a result of the outsourcing arrangement?

What security measures should be taken by the customer and the supplier to deal with the security risks under the outsourcing arrangement? What security policies and standards should be implemented?

What steps will need to be taken to ensure compliance with data protection legislation?

What transitional measures will be necessary to implement the new security requirements?

Assets or premises with regard to which the services are provided (e.g. outsourcing of maintenance of equipment or premises)

Where relevant, what assets or premises are covered by the outsourcing arrangements?

Are these listed in an accurate asset register?

Operational risk

Are the services to be outsourced critical to the customer's business?

What are the operational risks involved in the transition?

What are the operational risks involved in outsourcing the services?

6 *See* Chapter 32 for an explanation of the laws on data protection.

What are the operational risks involved in transferring the services back in house or to a successor supplier on termination?

What are the security implications of outsourcing, including the initial transition and the transition on termination (including the implications of termination for insolvency of the supplier[7])?

If the customer is regulated by the Financial Services Authority, will the outsourcing agreement adversely affect its ability to comply with its regulatory obligations?[8]

Costs and charges

What are the costs of the current service?

What will be the whole-life costs of the outsourcing transaction?

What costs will be incurred in procuring the outsourced services?

What costs and expenses will be incurred as a result of the transition to the new arrangements?

What charges will be payable for the outsourcing services?

What costs will be incurred as a result of managing the new arrangement?

What costs will be incurred on expiry or termination of the new arrangement?

What are the tax implications (particularly VAT) of the proposed project?

What are the exchange rate risks and who will bear them?

What are the inflation risks and who will bear them?

Funding and structuring the arrangement

What are the alternative ways to fund or structure the new transaction and which is the best way?[9]

Staff and contractors

What staff and contractors currently provide the services?

Will employees transfer from the customer to the new supplier under ARD?

What are the relevant terms and conditions of employment of the transferring staff?

Will employees transfer from the customer's existing suppliers to the new supplier?[10]

What rights to information and other protections does the customer have under its agreement with the existing supplier?

---

7 *See* Chapter 26 for a more detailed discussion of insolvency issues relating to outsourcing projects.
8 *See* Chapter 33 for an explanation of the regulation affecting outsourcing in the financial services sector.
9 *See* Chapter 17 for a description of different outsourcing structures.
10 *See* Chapter 27 for an explanation of relevant staffing issues.

Assets

What assets are used to provide the services?

Does the customer own or lease the assets?

Does the customer have an asset register?

Is the database up to date?

Third-party licences and permissions

Will the customer need to obtain permission from its software licensors for the outsourcing supplier to use its software licences and, if so, will the software licensors demand a fee for granting permission?[11]

Can the customer's current supplier agreements be transferred to the supplier where required?[12]

Will the customer need permission from its landlord or mortgagees to grant licences or subleases relating to relevant premises?[13]

Client relationships

If the outsourcing relates to services provided to the customer's clients, is the customer restricted by its contract with its clients from entering into an outsourcing arrangement?

Will the customer breach its confidentiality obligations to its clients if it outsources the services?

Will the outsourcing arrangement damage the relationship of the customer with its clients?

Regulatory requirements

Does the customer require the approval of any relevant regulator before it can outsource the services? Are there any other regulatory requirements?[14]

If the customer is in the public sector, does it have the power or "vires" to enter into the outsourcing arrangement?

Environmental issues[15]

Do the services require inputs or result in outputs which are subject to environmental obligations such as those on substances, emissions and pollutants, packaging or other waste law?

Is there a risk of any environmental liability arising?

---

11 For an explanation of issues relating to open source software, *see* Heather J. Meeker, *The Open Source Alternative: Understanding Risks and Leveraging Opportunities*, John Wiley & Sons Inc., 2008.

12 *See* Chapter 14 for a discussion of software licence and other supplier issues.

13 *See* Chapter 15 for further information on property issues.

14 *See* Chapter 37 for further information about regulatory requirements in the financial services sector.

15 In the public sector, *see* the Government's Green Action Plan published in March 2007. The plan identifies how government departments should ensure that environmental factors are factored into their procurement decisions.

How will any corporate and social responsibility concerns and legal obligations relating to sustainability be met?

Could the customer face responsibility for any administrative or criminal sanctions for breaches of environmental law?

How will the outsourcing project affect the carbon footprint of the customer? Will the carbon footprint of the outsourced service cease to be included in the carbon footprint of the customer?

If environmental taxes are introduced, how will this affect the outsourcing arrangement?

Culture and training

How will the project affect the morale of employees providing the services who will transfer to the outsourcing supplier?

Are there cultural differences between the customer's organisation and the proposed supplier?

What skills will the customer need to manage the new arrangement?

Procurement process

What is the most appropriate procurement process for negotiating the outsourcing arrangement?

What is the desired timetable?

Is the desired timetable realistic?

Does the timetable need to be speeded up to ensure the quick achievement of the customer's business objectives?

If so, what are the risks of a truncated procurement procedure?

2.5 Updating the business case

After the customer has carried out its initial due diligence and prepared a first draft of its business case, it will need to update the business case and the due diligence as the procurement progresses to ensure that the underlying assumptions in the business case continue to be correct, in particular if details of the outsourcing arrangement (e.g. the exact services to be outsourced) change.

Once the agreement has been signed, the business case should be used as a tool for monitoring progress in achieving the business objectives, for example when changes to the services are proposed.[16]

16 *See* for example, the OGC Gateway Review process which must be followed by central government authorities.

It should also be updated to reflect changes in the customer's business goals. The McCartney Report[17] gives an interesting example of a company that failed to review changes in its business aims. An insurance company in the US conducted a 30-person project to improve the sales of a particular insurance product. The development took three years to complete, against an original estimate of one year. When it was finished, the customer found that the company had stopped selling the insurance product more than a year before.[18]

The subject of changing business objectives is covered in greater detail in Chapter 22.

2.6 Risk register and risk management

The quality of the customer's business case depends upon the level of due diligence carried out, so, if the customer decides that in order to achieve a business objective it does not have time or resources to investigate certain factors, it should be aware of the risks it is taking. It may be appropriate to list in a risk register these and any other risks that may affect the project and consider ways in which they may be mitigated.

The risk register should list the individual risk, the likelihood it will occur, the effect of it occurring and the mitigation strategy. It may also be useful to specify who will be responsible for managing the risk, as between the customer and the supplier.[19] The parties should bear in mind the principle that allocation of risk to the party who is best able to manage it tends to provide the most economically advantageous solution.

Like the business case, the risk register should be monitored throughout the term of the outsourcing arrangement and should be updated to reflect changes in the risk profile. The parties should review the risk register regularly throughout the project, so that they can consider appropriate steps that should be taken to manage the risks.

2.7 Feedback from suppliers

Before initiating a procurement process, as well as understanding its own business objectives and risk profile, the customer may also want to investigate whether there are suppliers who can provide the necessary services. If there are suppliers available, the customer may (in the private sector[20]) want to decide which ones will be most suitable – this may involve the customer profiling the supplier market, the key players and the drivers affecting the market.

The customer may also want to investigate the suppliers' potential business objectives and risk profile. This will help the customer to understand whether suppliers will be interested in providing

17 Details of the McCartney Report can be found on the OGC's website at www.ogc.gov.uk.
18 Standish Group.
19 *See* Robert White and Barry James, *The Outsourcing Manual*, Gower Publishing Ltd, 1996 for a more detailed discussion of risk registers. In the public sector see the OGC guidance on risk registers which can be found under the section "Successful Delivery Toolkit" on the OGC's website at www.ogc.gov.uk.
20 *See* Chapters 34 and 37 for an explanation of the Procurement Directives which apply to the public and utilities sectors.

the services that the customer requires (taking into account whether demand for outsourced services exceeds supply or vice versa, at the relevant time).

It may also help the customer decide how to package the outsourced services (e.g. by aggregating services or dividing them up) to attract suppliers and maximise its bargaining power.

Lastly, it may provide the customer with an understanding of the suppliers' perspective that will prevent the customer preparing an offering to suppliers that undermines the suppliers' potential business benefit from the project, hence resulting in limited or no response to the offering.

Chapter 3

A Competitive Procurement Process

3.1 Outline

Chapter 2 describes the first stage in an outsourcing project, namely the customer's preparation for the outsourcing transaction. The next stage involves the customer procuring the outsourcing services, and that is the subject of this chapter. The chapter describes different procurement approaches, depending upon whether or not the procedure involves an element of competition between the different suppliers. It also gives practical hints for preparing an invitation to tender.

3.2 Procurement process

Once the customer has completed its due diligence and come to the conclusion that the evidence supports the business case for outsourcing, the customer will need to decide how to procure the outsourcing services.

3.2.1 Public and utilities sectors

In the public and utilities sectors, the procurement process used by the customer will be dictated by the applicability (or not, as the case may be) of the EU Consolidated Procurement Directive 2004 or the EU Utilities Procurement Directive 2004 ("Procurement Directives") which have been incorporated into UK law by the Public Contracts Regulations 2006 and the Public Utilities Regulations 2006 respectively ("Procurement Regulations"). If they apply, the relevant Procurement Regulations set out the procedural framework that the authority or utility must follow and lay down principles for the selection of the outsourcing supplier. (*See* Chapters 34 and 37 for a more detailed discussion of the application and implications of the Procurement Directives and Procurement Regulations.)

The interesting point about the procedures set out in the Procurement Regulations is that they are all highly competitive and highly structured. Only two procedures are suitable for high-value and/or relatively complex contracts, the "competitive dialogue procedure" and the "negotiated procedure". The former is now recommended by the government to be used on all PFI/PPP contracts unless they are particularly innovative, complex and of high value. Both procedures require that authorities should continue to "dialogue" or "negotiate" (as applicable) with more than one supplier until the parties have agreed all of the key commercial issues.[1] In the private

---

1 *See* "The Competitive Dialogue Procedure 2008 – OGC/HM Joint Guidance" at www.hm-treasury.gov.uk and similar sector-specific guidance for local government at www.4ps.gov.uk.

sector, following a tender process, customers often select one preferred supplier or a restricted panel.

3.2.2 Private sector

So, in the private sector, what are the advantages and disadvantages of adopting a procurement procedure that involves competition between different suppliers? From the supplier's perspective the position is clear. Suppliers, not unnaturally, prefer customers to negotiate exclusively with them, so that they know that they are likely to be awarded the contract and do not waste time and money negotiating contracts that are then awarded to another supplier.

From the customer's perspective, the situation is more complex. Table 4 lists some advantages and disadvantages of a competitive procurement process.

Table 4 *Advantages and disadvantages of competition for the customer*

Advantages of competition

Cheaper charges

Suppliers may be more aggressive in their charging and may charge a lower margin if they know that they are in competition.

Better terms

Suppliers may be more amenable to agreeing commercial and legal terms which suit the customer if they are competing for the business.

More thorough examination of the possible solutions

Negotiating with more than one supplier may mean that the customer examines its business requirements more thoroughly and considers possible alternative solutions. (However, customers should be careful not to breach confidentiality obligations agreed by the parties by disclosing elements of one supplier's solution to other bidders. *See* 3.5 below for a more detailed discussion of confidentiality issues relating to suppliers' proposals.)

Innovative solutions

Suppliers may be incentivised through the competitive process to come up with innovative means to provide the services.

Disadvantages of competition

Suppliers drop out

Suppliers may drop out of the procurement process if they do not think that they are likely to win.

Charges uneconomic for supplier

In some high-value outsourcing arrangements, where negotiations with two suppliers can continue for two years or more, it has been argued that this can lead to a situation where suppliers have invested so much time and money in the procurement that they feel they cannot afford to lose. Accordingly, or so it is argued, they have been forced to quote extremely low charges to ensure they win. There is a concern that this can lead to suppliers being forced to cut corners in providing the services, so that ultimately the customer suffers. In addition, competition is not the only way of ensuring a reasonable price; *see* Chapter 20 for a description of other ways of ensuring value for money.

Cost of negotiating with different suppliers

Negotiating with more than one supplier will clearly involve more management time and, if external advisers are being engaged to handle part of the negotiations, more fees being paid to the advisers. The customer will need to weigh up the possible reduction in the charges and improvement in terms resulting from exerting competitive pressure upon suppliers against the cost of running more than one set of negotiations.

Emphasis on charges

It is sometimes argued that running a competitive procurement procedure results in a particular emphasis in the negotiations on the fees charged by different suppliers rather than, for example, the quality of the different suppliers' solutions or other commercial terms (e.g. risk allocation). An extreme example of this is where an outsourcing supplier is selected by using an e-auction, where, once the suppliers satisfy certain minimum quality criteria, the preferred supplier is selected entirely on the basis of cost. This may or may not be appropriate, depending upon, in particular, whether:

(a) the services are commodity services which can be defined clearly;
(b) the charges can be determined by reference to a defined service description, without the need to negotiate them to establish the best balance between service quality and price; and
(c) sufficient suppliers are willing to participate in an e-auction.

Quality of the supplier's proposal

If suppliers know that there are several suppliers being asked to respond to the customer's request for proposals ("RFP"), and hence that their efforts may be in vain, they may be reluctant to commit substantial amounts of time to developing their proposal. The customer needs to manage this situation to encourage suppliers to invest in the procurement, perhaps by limiting the number of suppliers asked to respond to the tender to two or three, or (in exceptional circumstances) by offering to contribute towards the bid costs of the bidders.

Delay

Negotiating with more than one supplier may delay the commencement of the services. If the outsourcing arrangement is designed to reduce the cost of running the services, then the customer may be reluctant to allow any delay in signing the agreement. The customer may feel that any reduction in the charges resulting from exerting competitive pressure upon the supplier will be offset by the money lost as a result of the delay.

Sensitive information

Negotiating with more than one supplier may increase the number of organisations that will have to be given confidential information about the customer's organisation.

Secrecy

The customer may not want its employees to know about the outsourcing transaction until it is clear that there is a business case supporting the outsourcing proposition. Therefore, it may want to restrict the number of people who know about the project.

Looking at the advantages and disadvantages of competitive procurement procedures, as described in Table 4, it can be suggested that in many cases the most appropriate procurement procedure will be one that reaches a balance which ensures that some of the advantages of competition are achieved without too many of the disadvantages. For example, the customer could maintain a dialogue with two suppliers so that there is a competitive tension between the two, whilst in practice concentrating efforts in negotiating with one particular supplier if it was clear that supplier was more likely to achieve the customer's business objectives. The customer would not formally select a preferred supplier until the key commercial issues had been agreed.

However, ultimately, like so many other issues in an outsourcing arrangement, the most appropriate procurement procedure will depend upon the customer's business objectives.

3.3 Preparing the request for proposals ("RFP")

If the customer decides to adopt a procurement procedure that initially involves negotiating with more than one supplier, it may need to draft a document (commonly called a request for proposals, invitation to tender, invitation to negotiate, request for information or other similar title) to send out to suppliers.

The customer may break down the procurement process into different stages with an initial request for information. This is designed to obtain feedback from suppliers on the customer's proposed procurement and to enable the customer to select appropriate suppliers who will then receive the RFP.[2]

Table 5 includes a description of information which the customer should consider including in its RFP.

2 In the public or utilities sectors, if the Procurement Directives apply, information which can be requested for the purposes of the initial shortlisting is strictly limited. *See* Chapters 32 and 37 for further information.

Table 5 *Checklist for RFP*

Background on the customer

What is the relevant background information on the customer's organisation (such as its history, recent events that have affected it, its culture, size and organisational structure)?

Customer's business objectives

What is the customer's exact business objective?

How important is it that the supplier is flexible in agreeing changes to the arrangement?

How important is it that the supplier assists with a smooth transition on termination?

Benefit for the supplier

What will the supplier find attractive about the customer's project? (This issue is particularly important if the outsourcing market is such that there are many opportunities for the suppliers at the time.)

Multisourcing/prime contractor

Does the customer reserve the right to divide the services up and appoint different suppliers to provide different services?[3]

Current services

What services are currently being provided to the customer?

How are they being provided?

Where available, what service levels are being met?

What volume of services is being provided?

What are the trends regarding the volume of services?

Are services being provided to other members of the customer's group or to external organisations?

Are there any specific problems or challenges currently being faced or which the supplier will need to deal with?

Future service requirements

How would the customer like the services and the service levels to be changed, both after the initial transition period and throughout the rest of the agreement? (The customer may want to give the supplier an opportunity to suggest ways in which the customer's objectives can best be achieved, rather than being too prescriptive.)

What service management and service reporting is the customer expecting the supplier to provide?

3 *See* Chapter 17 for a discussion of the implications of multisourcing versus single-sourcing strategies.

What services are excluded from the scope of the outsourcing project?

Is there any potential for the customer to give the supplier additional work?

Are there any quality processes and accreditation that the customer expects the supplier to have?[4]

Would the customer be willing to move to a more standardised or commoditised service?

Current security requirements

What security measures are currently taken by the customer or an incumbent supplier?

Future security requirements

What additional security measures will the supplier have to take?

Assets or premises with regard to which the services are provided

Where relevant, what assets or premises are covered by the services?

Operational risk

What are the major perceived risks and how will the risks be allocated between the parties?

Staff

What are the current resourcing arrangements for the provision of the services?

On what basis should the supplier prepare its proposal, regarding the application of TUPE?[5]

Assets

Are there any assets that the customer intends to provide to the supplier so that it can provide the services?

Are there any costs and liabilities that the customer intends to transfer to the supplier?

It will be apparent that many of the topics in Table 5 reflect those listed in Table 3 as areas where the customer will need to carry out due diligence before it issues the RFP. Failure to carry out effective due diligence of these areas may make it difficult for the customer to provide sufficient information in its RFP and accordingly undermine the suppliers' ability to provide meaningful proposals.

4 For example, the customer may want the supplier to hold an ISO 9001 or ISO 9002 certificate. Such a certificate proves that the supplier has an adequate quality system whose effectiveness is regularly assessed by an independent auditor. The certificate does not guarantee the quality of the services provided, although it is an indication that the supplier takes quality assurance seriously. The ISO 9000 series of standards, ISO-9000-2000 emphases the ability of the supplier to learn from experience and to implement continuous quality improvement. For offshore outsourcing transaction the customer may want to refer to Six Sigma qualifications or ask suppliers to carry out STAR audits.

5 *See* Chapter 27 for a detailed discussion of TUPE. If the customer is advised by its legal advisers that TUPE will apply and that certain employees will transfer to the supplier from the customer, then the customer may want to include general details about the employees transferring, including the number of employees and their salaries and other benefits, so that the supplier can include these costs in its charges. The customer will need to ensure that it does not breach data protection law in disclosing information about staff. *See* Chapter 32 for a description of data protection law.

3.4 Procurement process

The customer should specify in the RFP what information it will need the supplier to provide in its proposal so that the customer can ascertain whether the supplier meets its evaluation criteria. This will include the general information in Table 6.

Table 6 *Information that the supplier must provide in its proposal*

Background on supplier

What is the supplier's management structure?

What is its customer base?

How large is the supplier's organisation?

How long has the supplier been in business?

Service requirements

What is the supplier's solution?

From where will the services be provided?

How will it manage the services?

What key personnel would be used to provide the services?

What is the staff attrition rate?

What subcontractors will it use?

How is it intending to implement the transition towards the new services?

What experience does it have of providing similar services?

What experience does it have of providing services in the customer's industry sector?

Can it provide references from other customers?

What is the supplier's track record?

Is any litigation against the supplier existing, pending or threatened?

Is the supplier the subject of any investigation, enquiry or enforcement proceedings by any governmental, administrative or regulatory body?

What history of involvement with relevant regulators does the supplier have?

Has the supplier complied with its obligations under agreements with other customers?

Security requirements

Can the supplier comply with the customer's security requirements?

Operational risk

How will the supplier manage those risks allocated to it?

Commitment

What is the relative size of the services to the supplier's overall business?

Are there any other factors which influence how important the customer will be to the supplier?

Quality

What quality processes and accreditation does the supplier have?

Environment

Is the supplier's solution environmentally friendly? (This will be particularly relevant for certain public sector bodies and corporates who want to be included in the "FTSE 4 Good Index".[6])

Charges

What are the supplier's charges?[7]

The customer will also need the supplier's proposal to include any other specific information required to enable the customer to evaluate whether the supplier satisfies the concerns specified in Table 6, where relevant.

The customer may want to summarise relevant evaluation criteria in the RFP, and may want to specify whether the supplier can submit variant bids which, for example, represent better value for the customer than the standard bid.

The customer may want to specify the intended procurement process, with details of the procurement team. It may want to explain at what stage it envisages the supplier carrying out its due diligence. If the customer has sufficient information to formulate a draft or outline project plan, it may want to include this as well. Where relevant, the customer will need to specify the procedure by which the suppliers may raise queries on the RFP, the dates on which the supplier will be able to make a presentation (explaining its solution), the date for submission of proposals, together with the number of copies of the proposal required and how they should be submitted. It is advisable for the customer to specify that the suppliers' proposals must follow a particular format so as to facilitate comparison between different suppliers.

6 The FTSE 4 Good Index lists companies which meet criteria in three areas: working towards environmental sustainability, developing positive relationships with stakeholders and upholding and supporting human rights. For further information, *see* http://www.ftse.com/Indices/FTSE4Good_Index_Series/index.jsp.

7 The customer will need sufficient information about the charging structure and a breakdown of the charges to enable it to determine its final requirements. *See* Chapter 18 for a discussion of charging issues.

3.5 Confidentiality[8]

The RFP should make clear which of the information that it contains is confidential from the customer's perspective.

It should set out how it proposes to deal with confidential information made available by individual suppliers. If the customer states that it will not disclose details of one supplier's proposal to other suppliers, then the suppliers will be more willing to disclose original suggestions about how the services can be improved. If the customer states that information made available by one supplier may be made available to other suppliers so that they can provide quotes for providing that solution, then suppliers will be reluctant to suggest novel solutions to the customer's requirements.

A similar concern can arise with regard to questions asked by suppliers. Customers sometimes feel that they will be regarded as acting unfairly unless they give all suppliers the same information. However, if the customer states that all information provided in answer to a question by a particular supplier will be copied to other suppliers, this may deter a supplier from raising questions that indicate the innovative solutions it is intending to propose. A possible compromise is for the customer to state that it will copy answers to all suppliers, unless there is a reason not to do so. It will then explain, when a question is raised, whether it proposes copying the response to other bidders, giving the supplier raising the question the opportunity to withdraw it if it considers that this will be prejudicial.

The approach taken by public sector procurers is slightly different. Due to requirements to comply with the public procurement principles of transparency and equality of treatment, a public authority will share all clarification questions with other bidders unless the bidder raising the query specifically marks the question as confidential and provides sound reasons why revealing the question to others would give away commercially sensitive information particular to that bidder. However, bidders can take comfort that, once the dialogue begins in earnest, the public sector customer is prohibited from sharing one bidder's "solution" with others under the Procurement Regulations.

3.6 Legal terms and conditions

Within the RFP, the customer will need to explain its commercial requirements, for example how long the outsourcing arrangement will be.

3.6.1 Full set of draft terms and conditions

If the nature and structure of the outsourcing arrangement is not likely to be fundamentally varied at a later stage, there may be an advantage to the customer in including a full set of draft terms and conditions in the RFP. This will establish that any negotiations will start from the customer's

8 In certain sectors, the customer will need to ensure that suppliers' staff who have access to the RFP have appropriate security clearance. *See* Chapter 32 for a discussion of security issues relevant in outsourcing agreements.

draft terms and conditions and not those of the supplier. It may also mean that the customer can negotiate the terms and conditions from a position of strength before selection of a preferred supplier.

3.6.2 Heads of terms

If the customer is giving the RFP to several suppliers and it is not practical to include a full agreement, it may be possible to include heads of terms, key clauses or key principles and request suppliers to agree to or comment on these so that the supplier is aware of the customer's desired approach to key commercial and legal issues.

3.6.3 Supplier's response

If the customer does include terms and conditions or key principles, it should explain how the supplier is expected to respond to these. In either situation, the customer may want to indicate if certain terms and conditions are non-negotiable. The customer should explain whether the supplier must include in its proposal general comments on the agreement or a detailed mark up the agreement. Marking up an agreement involves a substantial investment of time by the supplier and suppliers are often reluctant to commit to such an investment at a stage where several suppliers are being asked to bid for the work. (*See* Chapter 4 for a more detailed discussion on selecting a preferred supplier.) Equally, from the customer's perspective, it may not want to spend time reviewing a detailed mark up of the agreement from suppliers until it has short-listed the final two or three suppliers.

3.7 Legal protections

The customer will usually want to clarify the following points in its RFP:

(a) that it does not guarantee the accuracy of information provided in the RFP;
(b) that it reserves the right to amend the RFP document and the RFP process at any time;
(c) that it reserves the right to disqualify bidders who collude[9] with each other or who submit non-compliant bids or for other reasons;
(d) that it is not obliged to proceed with the outsourcing negotiations, so that it can abandon the process if it becomes apparent that the customer's business objective will not be achieved or for any other reason;
(e) that it will not pay the supplier's costs, whether these relate to the supplier preparing and submitting its proposal, undertaking any tests, demonstrations or meetings as part

9 Suppliers should note that collusive tendering is a serious breach of competition law, which could result in fines of up to 10 per cent of turnover; unenforceability of the agreement; action for damages by third parties; directors' disqualification; and imprisonment of individuals involved. *See* Chapter 29 for a detailed description of competition law and its implication for outsourcing. In a decision relating to the roofing industry, the Office of Fair Trading noted that "there is no reason why undertakings invited to participate in a ... competitively tendered process would need to communicate with one another in relation to the tender before returning their bids" (Case CE/3344-03, 8 July 2005, paragraph 121).

of the negotiations, participating in the RFP process, participating in the negotiation process or preparing for the provision of the services;

(f) that it may accept the supplier's proposal in parts (where relevant); and

(g) that it reserves the right to select whichever supplier it regards as appropriate, and not necessarily the cheapest supplier.[10]

3.8 Disclosure of information in the RFP

On the one hand, the customer will need to include sufficient information on the matters specified in Table 5 to ensure that suppliers can submit meaningful proposals. It will need to ensure that it attracts the right suppliers and that the supplier will not withdraw from the process as and when they fully understand the requirements. For example, some suppliers will not tender for public sector private finance initiative ("PFI") work and so, if the tender does not clarify that it involves a PFI approach, the customer may find that suppliers respond to the tender only to withdraw at a later stage when the nature of the proposed transaction becomes clear. This is particularly important in the public sector or utilities sector, as a failure to describe the scope of the requirements adequately in the RFP or the call for competition could constitute a breach of the Procurement Directives where they apply.

On the other hand, the customer must ensure that it does not disclose in the RFP any information about its organisation that is sensitive, that is in breach of confidentiality obligations (e.g. in its supply or client agreements), competition law or the Data Protection Act 1998. (*See* Chapter 32 for a description of data protection law.)

In addition, before the customer provides the suppliers with any information about its possible outsourcing project, it must ensure that they sign a non-disclosure agreement agreeing not to disclose any information made available to them. This is particularly important if the customer has not made public the fact that it is considering outsourcing and especially if there is a risk that staff will be made redundant as part of the outsourcing arrangement. To safeguard confidentiality, the customer may want to specify that the supplier may discuss the negotiations only with specified members of the customer's negotiation team.

In practice, once a customer commences the outsourcing procurement process, it must recognise the risk that this fact will become known publicly or by its staff, and should make contingency plans for dealing with the possible implications. In some jurisdictions, national laws relating to information and consultation with employees (e.g. where there are Works Councils) have an impact on the timing of this process.

10 A public sector or utility customer will be constrained in the basis upon which it may select a supplier (*see* Chapters 34 and 37).

Chapter 4

Selecting a Preferred Supplier

4.1 Outline

Chapter 3 describes the customer's preparation of an RFP. The next stage is the selection of a preferred supplier or preferred suppliers. This chapter deals with the criteria for selecting a preferred supplier and how the selection or evaluation criteria should be reflected in the outsourcing agreement.

4.2 Evaluation criteria

Whether the customer has decided to negotiate with several suppliers before selecting a preferred supplier or to negotiate with only one supplier, it will need to decide upon the evaluation criteria that will assist it in choosing a supplier.

As mentioned at 3.2 above, for public sector transactions covered by the Procurement Directives, the evaluation criteria will need to comply with the requirements set out in those directives. These are described in greater detail in Chapter 34. Subject to these constraints, the evaluation criteria should ultimately flow from the business objectives which the customer wants to achieve and so will depend upon the individual facts of the case.

Examples of issues that may be relevant in selecting a preferred supplier are listed in Table 7.

Table 7 *Selecting a preferred supplier*

Business objectives

Does the supplier understand the customer's business objectives and business strategy?

Does the supplier's solution support the achievement of the customer's business objectives?

Does the supplier's suggested method of structuring the outsourcing transaction achieve the customer's business objectives?

Does the supplier's track record demonstrate that its solution will achieve the customer's business objectives?

Commitment

Is the supplier committed to achieving the customer's business objectives?

Where relevant, has the supplier shown commitment by its senior management to the transaction?

What commitment does the supplier have to the provision of the services in the future?

Is the provision of the services the supplier's core business?

How important is the customer's industry sector to the supplier?

How important will the customer be to the supplier?

Will it be one of the supplier's key clients?

Stakeholder support

Does senior management within the customer organisation approve of the supplier?

Do users within the customer organisation approve of the supplier?

Service requirements

Is the supplier's solution sufficient to satisfy the customer's business objectives?

Do the supplier's staff have sufficient skills and experience to provide the solution?

Does the supplier's track record demonstrate that the supplier and its staff have the ability to implement the supplier's solution?

Security requirements

Is the supplier's solution sufficient to satisfy the customer's future security requirements?

Do the supplier's staff have sufficient security skills and experience?

Does the supplier's track record demonstrate that it has sufficient security skills and experience? Has the supplier been the subject of any investigation by the Information Commissioner? If so, was an adverse finding made or enforcement action taken by the Information Commissioner?

Does the supplier's solution result in any additional security risks, for example because of the location of the supplier's premises?

What additional security measures will need to be taken to deal with these additional risks?

Operational risk

Is the supplier's proposal for managing risk adequate?

Does the supplier conform to recognised security standards such as BS7799?

Does the supplier have an adequate security policy?

How does the supplier ensure business continuity?

Supplier's resources

Does the supplier have the resources to provide the services?

If the outsourcing agreement is a substantial one, are there pressures on the supplier's resources due, for example, to it recently winning other business?

Supplier's other customers

Does the supplier provide services for competitors of the customer?

Does it provide services to those customers from the same site or using the same personnel who would be used for the provision of services to the customer?

Does this cause confidentiality, security or other problems?

Charges

What charging assumptions has the supplier made?

How do the supplier's charges compare with its competitors' charges?

How carefully has the supplier checked its charges?

Will the supplier commit to price protection schemes such as benchmarking or maximum margin?

Have customers of the supplier said that the supplier has been reasonable in agreeing the charge for changes requested by the customer after signature of the agreement?

Flexibility and innovation

Can the supplier provide services that may be required in the future?

Do the references indicate that the supplier takes a flexible approach to agreeing changes in the charges?

Do the references indicate that the supplier expects to increase its margin by levying substantial charges for changes to the services?

Are there any grounds for believing that the supplier will not be flexible about agreeing changes to the agreement?

If required, has the supplier demonstrated that it keeps pace with cutting edge technology and is continually innovative in the services it offers to its clients?

Configuration management

Does the supplier have adequate configuration management processes?

Staff

What is the track record of the supplier regarding managing the transfer of employees from customers?

What opportunities will transferring employees have working for the supplier?

What experience does the supplier have of dealing with the transfer of staff under TUPE?

How does the supplier treat its staff?

Does the supplier invest in training its staff?

What are the supplier's staff turnover levels?

How will the project affect the morale of employees, including any staff transferring to the outsourcing supplier?

Independence

If the services are to include consultancy services or the provision of advice, will the supplier be able to provide independent, impartial advice or does it have exclusive arrangements with specific suppliers?

Will the supplier commit to informing the customer of any commissions it receives for recommending certain suppliers?

Termination

What is the supplier's approach to helping the customer ensure a smooth transition on termination?

Can the supplier give examples where it has assisted other customers to effect a smooth transition to a new supplier on termination of the agreement?

Are there any grounds for believing that the supplier will not assist in a smooth transition on termination?

Culture

What is the supplier's culture? For example, have the supplier's customers said that it has behaved in a trustworthy manner and with integrity?

Are the cultures of the two organisations compatible?

Commitment to customer satisfaction

What is the supplier's culture with regard to emphasis of short-term aims (e.g. maximising profit for the relevant quarter) over long-terms aims (e.g. whether the customer will extend the agreement when it expires in five years' time)?

Is the supplier committed to achieving customer satisfaction?

Is the supplier good at establishing and maintaining longer-term relationships with its customers?

Financial stability

Is the supplier financially stable?

How long has it been in business?

What is the financial standing and credit rating of the supplier?

Is it unduly reliant upon certain outsourcing contracts or specific markets?

Is the supplier aware of any pending or threatened claims against it?

Does the customer need to require the supplier to provide additional comfort, in the form of a parent company guarantee or a performance bond?

Management structure

How stable is the supplier's management structure likely to be? Is the company a likely target for a takeover?

Legal terms and conditions

Where the customer has supplied terms and conditions, how do the supplier's comments on the agreement compare with comments from other suppliers?

What do the supplier's comments on the terms and conditions show about its confidence in its ability to provide the services and its confidence that it can achieve any cost savings expected by the customer?

What do the comments show about the commercial prudence of the supplier organisation?

Is it being prudent in protecting its commercial interests?

4.3 Recording the selection process

The customer may want to ensure that its evaluation criteria are objective by listing them in a table and weighting them. The customer will also need to ensure that, in comparing the prices of different suppliers, it is comparing like with like. It will be easier for the customer to do this if it has provided in the RFP a charges template for the suppliers to complete. Some suppliers may state that aspects of the services will be provided at an additional charge and the customer should be aware if this is the case.

In the public and utility sectors, the customer will be required to keep records of how it selected the supplier and provide feedback to the unsuccessful suppliers.[1] In the financial services sector, the customer may want to show that it has considered issues set out in the FSA Handbook, relevant to outsourcing.[2] Customers outside the public, utility or financial services sectors may also want to keep records of selection processes to demonstrate the probity of the process followed.[3]

1 *See* Chapters 32 and 37 for an explanation of the Procurement Directives applying to the public and utility sectors.

2 *See* Chapter 33 for a description of the regulations affecting the financial services sector.

3 Companies listed in New York will also need to comply with the US Sarbanes-Oxley Act 2002. This requires that the principal executive and principal financial officer of SEC-registered firms sign a statement declaring that procedures and controls are in place and working effectively to ensure accuracy in asset disposals, transactions and internal reporting processes. In short, they must pledge that their company's accounts are "truly presented". If any accounting irregularities are found subsequently, executives face substantial fines and jail terms of up to 20 years. However, a violation of this section must be knowing and intentional to give rise to liability. This Act will apply to any asset disposals relating to outsourcing arrangements.

4.4 Due diligence

Before the customer selects a suitable supplier, it will need to carry out sufficient due diligence to ensure that it has collected adequate evidence to show that the supplier can satisfy the customer's evaluation criteria. This due diligence exercise may involve the customer taking account of the sources of information listed in Table 8.

Table 8 *Due diligence of supplier*

The supplier's proposal including information about the supplier's track record.
A report by accountants on the reliability of the supplier's financial model.
The results of security audits.
Presentations given by the supplier's team who would be responsible for providing the services.
Site visits to the supplier's premises.
The supplier's annual accounts.
Industry reports relating to the supplier or the outsourced services.
Searches for newspaper articles relating to the supplier.
Reports of litigation against the supplier.
Case studies provided by the supplier.
References provided by the supplier.
Feedback obtained from other customers of the supplier as a result of reference site visits.

4.5 Reflecting the evaluation criteria in the contract

When the customer selects its outsourcing supplier, it will usually have selected it on the basis of various information about the supplier. As stated in 4.4 above, the information may have been contained in the supplier's proposal, or in correspondence, or it may have been revealed during discussions with the supplier (where relevant). The customer must ensure that it can rely upon this information. There are various ways in which it can ensure this.

4.5.1 Warranties

The customer can suggest that the supplier warrants the accuracy of every statement that it has made in writing or possibly even in conversation before the agreement is made. For the warranty to be useful, the customer will need the supplier to warrant that these statements are still accurate as at the date of signature of the agreement. There are two problems with this approach:

(a) it may be difficult for the customer to prove what the supplier has said; and
(b) the supplier is unlikely to agree to a provision that does not list the specific representations relied upon as it will need to check that they are still accurate when the agreement is signed.

4.5.2 Attaching documentation to the agreement

The supplier will usually prefer that the customer focuses on the statements that are important and that all of the statements relied upon by the customer are set out or cross-referenced in the agreement. It will want to exclude representations and state that documentation not attached to the agreement is to be superseded by the terms of the agreement.[4] The supplier will therefore want to exclude all representations or warranties other than those set out in the agreement.[5] This exclusion will be enforceable at law if it is reasonable.[6] Therefore, the parties should consider having someone present at the negotiations who can record minutes of everything that has been agreed. The minutes can then be circulated to the other side for approval. Once agreed, the minutes can be circulated to any legal or commercial advisers who were not present at the meeting, to ensure that any important promises made by either party are actually incorporated into the agreement.

4 Entire agreement clauses must be drafted with some care – *see*, for example, *Quest 4 Finance* v *Maxfield* [2007] EWHC 2313 (QB), *Crystal Decisions (UK) Limited* v *Vedatech* [2007] EWHC 1062 (Ch), *The Inntrepreneur Pub Co (GL)* v *East Crown Limited* [2000] 2 Lloyd's Rep 611 and *Deepak* v *ICI* [1999] 1 Lloyd's Rep 387.

5 Representations and warranties are different at law. Representations are statements which may induce the person to whom they are made to act in reliance upon them in some manner. Representations which are untrue may give rise to a variety of legal consequences, depending upon the particular circumstances. Fraudulent misrepresentations may create a right to action in the tort of deceit. Negligence misrepresentation may create a right of action in tort for negligent misstatement. Any representations which induce the entry of a contract may give rise to rights to rescind the contract or to recover damages, the availability of these remedies being governed by common law in the case of fraudulent misrepresentation and by common law as modified by the Misrepresentation Act 1967 in the case of negligence or innocent misrepresentations. Rescission of a contract for misrepresentation is conceptually quite different from termination for breach of contract. Rescission amounts to setting the contract aside for all purposes, so as to restore, as far as practicable, the parties to their pre-contract position. The measure of damages recoverable for a misrepresentation may differ from that recoverable for breach of a warranty in identical terms to the misrepresentation. Damages for misrepresentation will be based on the "reliance" measure of loss, that is, the loss suffered by the customer relying upon the representation. A warranty has two meanings: (a) a term of the contract, the breach of which may give rise to a claim for damages but not to a right to treat the contract as repudiated. The use of the word "warranty" in this sense is reserved for the less important terms of the contract, or for those which are collateral to the main purpose of the contract, the breach of which by one party does not entitle the other to treat his obligations as discharged. The amount recoverable is the sum required to put the innocent party in the position which it would have been in had the warranty not been breached; or (b) in the context of commercial contracts, (such as outsourcing agreements), "warranty" usually refers to particular statements that are incorporated as contractual terms in the agreement, which are identified as being "warranted" by one party and made subject to a special regime. Damages for breach of warranties will usually be based upon the "contractual" measure of damages, as described in chapter 30. *See MAN Nuzfahrzeuge AG and others* v *Freightliner Ltd and others* [2007] EWCA Civ 910.

6 Section 3 Misrepresentation Act 1967. The test of reasonableness is referred to in Section 11(1) Unfair Contract Terms Act 1977. Provisions excluding liability for fraudulent misrepresentations will not be regarded as reasonable.

Chapter 5

The Project Plan

5.1 Outline

This chapter explains how the submission of the RFP and the selection of the preferred supplier fit in with the general project plan for the procurement. The chapter describes the benefits of preparing a project plan for the procurement of outsourcing services and provides an example plan. It also highlights the importance of appointing a project manager to manage the project plan.

5.2 Advantages of a project plan

One of the concerns felt by customers is that the negotiation of the outsourcing arrangement, particularly if it is a competitive process similar to that described in the previous chapters, will incur excessive amounts of time and (particularly where external advisers are involved) money. For this and other reasons, it may be useful to prepare a project plan and timetable setting out how the negotiations will proceed and issuing an agenda for each meeting on the project plan. Table 9 lists the advantages of working to a project plan.

Table 9 *Advantages of a project plan*

Realistic timetable

Listing all of the activities that will need to be completed before the agreement can be concluded may assist the parties to determine a realistic deadline for contract signature, together with a realistic assessment of the resources that they will need to dedicate to the project to ensure that the deadline is met.

Good preparation

Establishing a time when certain issues are to be discussed may assist both parties to focus on the negotiations and to turn up to meetings well prepared and with the correct negotiating team for that particular meeting. Separating out different issues to be covered at different meetings may avoid a situation where service managers, financial advisers, human resources or legal advisers attend meetings only to find that many of the issues discussed are not relevant to them.

Discourages renegotiation

Setting aside a particular meeting to discuss a specific issue, which is then resolved at the meeting, may discourage the other side from re-opening issues already discussed and agreed.

Heightens competitive tension

From the customer's perspective, structuring a project plan so that it is clear that the same issue will be discussed consecutively with different suppliers may serve to heighten competitive tension between the different suppliers.

Indication of commitment

From the supplier's perspective, preparation by the customer of a project plan may be seen as a positive step, explaining to the supplier the negotiation procedure that will be followed until contract signature. It may serve as an indication to the supplier of the commitment of the customer to the outsourcing strategy. For this reason, once a project plan has been finalised, it is important that the customer keeps to it, or, where this is impractical, communicates changes to the plan and the reasons for the changes.

5.3 Example project plan

Table 10 shows an example project plan for a private sector customer. Paragraph 3.2 mentioned that, for public sector outsourcing projects, the procedural framework that the authority must follow is covered by the Procurement Directives.

Table 10 *Example procurement project plan*

Date	*Action*
	Establish internal team and project manager
	Customer to carry out due diligence described in Chapter 2
… to …	Prepare RFP
	RFP sent out
	Date by which suppliers must submit any questions on the RFP
	Date by which proposals must be submitted by suppliers
	Clarification meetings with various suppliers (including presentations by the suppliers if required)
	Customer's due diligence on supplier
	Shortlisting of two suppliers

	First day of negotiation of service description with supplier 1
	First day of negotiation of service description with supplier 2
	First day of negotiation of charges with supplier 1
	First day of negotiation of charges with supplier 2
	First day of negotiation of legal terms with supplier 1
	First day of negotiation of legal terms with supplier 2
	First TUPE meeting with supplier 1
	First TUPE meeting with supplier 2
... to ...	Suppliers' due diligence
	Discussion of the supplier's due diligence findings and agreement of changes to the service description or the charges.
	Second etc. day of negotiation of service description with supplier 1
	Second etc. day of negotiation of service description with supplier 2
	Second etc. day of negotiation of charges with supplier 1
	Second etc. day of negotiation of charges with supplier 2
	Second etc. day of negotiation of legal terms with supplier 1
	Second etc. day of negotiation of legal terms with supplier 2
	Second etc. TUPE meeting with supplier 1
	Second etc. TUPE meeting with supplier 2 etc.
	Best and final offers submitted by suppliers
	Selection of preferred supplier
	Consultation with employees, election of employee representatives and holding of consultation meetings
	Final negotiation of service description (including transition plan and service management)
	Final negotiation of charges
	Final negotiation of legal terms
	Final TUPE meeting
	Signature of the contract and press release
	Presentation by the lawyers summarising key terms of the contract
	Commencement of transition
	Commencement of service delivery

5.4 Project manager

The customer will also need to appoint a project manager, either from the customer's staff or an external consultant, who will be responsible for ensuring that the deadlines in the project plan are met, that sufficient resources are dedicated to the project and that delays are managed. The project manager's role is fundamental to the success of the outsourcing and it is therefore important to ensure that the project manager has appropriate experience and authority.

5.5 Project team

As well as appointing a project manager, the customer will need to appoint other relevant members of the project team to form a cross-functional team who will be able to work together to ensure that the project is successful. This will usually include procurement, finance, operational and legal experts. The outsourcing arrangement is more likely to succeed if the members of the project team work together to ensure that all members are aware of relevant financial, operational and legal issues, rather than individual members of the team working in silos.

The project plan should be prepared taking into account a realistic view of the commitment required from and availability of the relevant members of the project team.

5.6 Communication plan

The project team will need to inform the stakeholders within the customer's organisation of progress with the outsourcing project. For this reason it is usually useful for the project plan to include a communication plan.

Chapter 6

Preparation by the Supplier

6.1 Outline

Chapters 2, 3, 4 and 5 describe the preparation that the customer will need to carry out for the outsourcing project. This chapter covers the supplier's preparation. It explains how the supplier prepares its business case. It also discusses the due diligence that the supplier will need to carry out and the issues surrounding the question of when the supplier should complete its due diligence.

6.2 Preparation of business case

The information provided by the customer in the RFP (as described in Chapter 3) will be used by the supplier to assist it in preparing its own business case supporting a decision to bid for the work. The business case may include the issues in Table 11.

Table 11 *Supplier's business case*

Supplier's business strategy

How will the outsourcing deal fit in with the supplier's business strategy regarding the size of the contract, the types of services it wants to provide, the location at which it wants to operate and the types of customers to whom it wants to provide services?

Will the arrangement provide the supplier with a reference site in a sector it is targeting?

Profitability

What will be the supplier's estimated revenue, expenditure and resulting profit over the term of the agreement?

Can the supplier maximise its margin by "sweating the assets" namely using the staff, assets and premises to provide services to other customers?

What are the prospects of receiving additional business from the customer?

Service requirements

What are the customer's service requirements and how confident is the supplier that it can satisfy them?

What service credits are payable if it fails to meet the service levels?

Security requirements

What are the customer's security requirements and how confident is the supplier that it can satisfy them?

Customer's financial standing

What is the customer's financial position?

Will the supplier require guarantees from the customer?

Risks and key legal terms and conditions

What risks is the supplier expected to manage?

How will it be able to mitigate them?

Can it charge a risk premium for accepting the risks?

Bid strategy

What is the supplier's bid strategy?

How likely is the supplier to win the business?

Is there an incumbent supplier?

Is the customer asking for a quotation from the supplier merely so that it can renegotiate the charges payable to the incumbent supplier in line with market rates?

What costs will the supplier need to incur before selection of a preferred supplier?

The supplier's business case will usually need to be approved by the supplier's management before the supplier submits its proposal. The business case will then be updated from time to time until final approval for signature of the agreement is granted by the supplier's management and the agreement is signed.

The supplier will usually update the profit and loss account for the project throughout the term of the agreement, in particular to ensure that it is making a profit on the individual outsourcing deal.

6.3 Types of due diligence by the supplier

Just as the customer needs to carry out due diligence regarding its business objectives and its requirements (as described in Chapter 2) and the supplier's experience and financial standing (as described in Chapter 4), the supplier will need to carry out due diligence to substantiate its business objectives, the details of its solution and its charges. Table 12 provides examples of the type of due diligence which the supplier may need to carry out.

Table 12 *Due diligence by the supplier*

Customer's business requirements

What are the customer's business requirements?

Can the supplier suggest an alternative way to satisfy the customer's goals?

Current services

What services are currently being provided?

How are the services being provided?

What service levels are being achieved?

How confident is the supplier that the information given about the current services and service levels is accurate?

Does the information provided by the customer show service levels over a full period (e.g. a financial year)?

Is there a backlog where services have not been provided as a result of the impending outsourcing arrangement?

Future service requirements

Is the service description clear?

How will the new services differ from the current services?

What improvements in the service levels are required?

What will the supplier need to do to achieve the improved service levels?

Is the supplier confident that it can provide the services to the service levels required?

What is the risk of it failing to provide the services to the required service levels?

What volumes of services (e.g. number of users using the service) are required by the customer?

Are the volumes likely to rise or fall considerably, for example due to external events?

Current security requirements

What security measures are currently being taken?

Future security requirements

Are the security requirements clear?

How will the new security measures differ from the current security measures?

What improvements in the security measures are required?

What will the supplier need to do to satisfy the improved security measures?

Is the supplier confident that it can satisfy the security measures?

Assets or premises with regard to which the services are provided

Where relevant, what assets or premises are covered by the services?

Is there an accurate list of these?

How much further due diligence is required on, for example, the state of the assets or the premises?

Risks

What are the major perceived risks?

Will the supplier be able to manage those risks allocated to it?

How will it manage them?

Charges

What assumptions has the supplier made in calculating its charges?

Which of these assumptions have been tested and which are still subject to due diligence?

Are all of the assumptions listed in the proposal?

What opportunities are there for the supplier to provide additional services?

How is the risk of different tax consequences allocated between supplier and customer?

Employees

General

Does the supplier agree that the relevant staff will transfer under TUPE?

Which staff does the customer or incumbent supplier maintain will transfer to the supplier under ARD?

Staff profile

How many employees are there?

How long have the staff been employed?

Are there any other employees who are assigned to the business but are on long-term absence or maternity leave and who would transfer under TUPE?

What are the employees' ages?

Are any of the employees approaching retirement age?

Have they transferred recently?

Where did they transfer from and what pension entitlements did they have immediately before the transfer?

Organisational

How much of the time of the relevant employees is dedicated to providing the services to be outsourced?

At which sites are the employees based?

Will the supplier need to relocate them?

Staff benefits

Has the customer notified the supplier of the salaries and other benefits received by the employees?

Has the customer notified the supplier of any other terms and conditions of the transferring employees (including pension arrangements, special redundancy entitlements, notice period, overtime payments, loans, company car arrangements or parking spaces entitlement)?

Have any variations to the terms and conditions been agreed?

Will the supplier need to change the terms and conditions of the transferring staff and, if so, has it checked whether it is legally able to do so?

Do their terms and conditions allow for any potential relocation?

What is the normal retirement age under the employees' terms and conditions?

Could any of the employees potentially qualify for enhanced pension benefits during the contract term or at the end of the contract term?

Potential liabilities

Do the employees belong to a trade union? If so, has any industrial action been taken or threatened in the previous two years?

Are there any current claims, or is the customer aware of any possible future claims against it by staff?

What payments have been made over the last 12 months in overtime payments?

What accrued holiday entitlements are owing?

What details are available of performance monitoring arrangements?

What are the staff sickness levels over the previous 12 months?

Are any of the staff subject to disciplinary proceedings?

Have any of the staff raised a grievance in the previous two years?

Staffing and contractors

Is the number and quality of the staff and contractors sufficient to provide the services?

Are specific members of the customer's staff or contractors key to the supplier's ability to provide the services?

Are the key staff transferring?

Are the key contractors willing to work for the supplier?

Is the customer (or incumbent supplier) intending to transfer staff out of the business so that they will not transfer to the supplier?

Is the supplier aware of any staff intending to resign?

What skills transfer will the supplier need and what training will need to be provided to staff or contractors who will provide the services?

Does the customer expect the supplier to change the staff who provide the services?

Assets and premises used to provide the services

What assets and premises would transfer to the supplier?

Will the customer warrant the condition of the assets or premises?

If not, has the supplier been able to check the condition of the assets or premises?

Will the customer warrant that the transferring assets or premises are all of the assets or premises currently employed to provide the services?

If not, has the supplier been able to check the adequacy of the assets or premises?

Will the assets and premises be suitable for providing the services or does work need to be done to make them suitable?

What technology refresh will be required for the assets?

Are there any additional security or health and safety measures that need to be taken at the premises?

Can the assets or premises be used to provide services to other customers?

Are any of the assets required held by an incumbent supplier?

Is the incumbent supplier willing to make these available to the supplier and, if so, on what conditions (financial and otherwise)?

Legal and regulatory requirements

Does the supplier need to comply with any specific legislation or regulations in providing the services?[1]

1 For example, if the supplier is to provide call centre services, then the supplier may need to comply with the Data Protection Act 1998 (*see* Chapter 32), Privacy and Electronic Communications (EC Directive) Regulations 2003, Consumer Protection (Distance Selling) Regulations 2000, Telephone Preference Service, Emailing Preference Service, Fax Preference Service and Mailing Preference Service. If the supplier is required to dispose of electronic or electrical goods, the customer may also want to clarify that such disposal must comply with the Waste Electrical and Electronic Equipment Directive ("WEEE Directive"). The directive was implemented in the United Kingdom in the WEEE Regulations, which came into force on 1 July 2007. The Directive seeks to address the growing impact of electrical and electronic goods on the environment by making producers liable for financing the collection, treatment and recovery of waste equipment. The most common and practical means of compliance for suppliers is to join a distributor "take back scheme" which has been set up by the government to establish a network of designated collection facilities for consumers to dispose of their electrical and electronic waste.

Does the customer or the supplier require the approval of any relevant regulator before it can enter into the outsourcing arrangement?

Will the supplier be prevented by any laws from providing the services as it proposes?

Software licences and other supply agreements

What software licences and other intellectual property rights are needed to provide the services?

Is any open source software used?[2]

How can the supplier obtain the necessary rights?

Will the supplier need the customer to license it to use software owned by the customer?

Will the supplier need the customer to ensure that it is licensed to use bespoke software created by the previous supplier?

Will the supplier need the customer to ensure that it is licensed to use other third-party software?

What licences, subcontracts and other supply agreements will the supplier need to take out?

Liabilities transferring to supplier

What third-party contracts does the customer want to transfer to the supplier?

What are the terms of the relevant third-party contracts?

Do the terms of the third-party agreements permit transfer or are there costs involved in obtaining third-party consents?

Are the terms of the third-party contracts acceptable?

Is the performance of the third-party suppliers acceptable and compatible with the supplier meeting the service levels?

If not, how can the supplier terminate the third-party contracts?

Property leases/licences

From which site will the services be provided?

Will the customer make accommodation available to the supplier free of charge?

What will be the terms of any leases or licences between the parties?

Will the supplier need to amend the software licences to use the software at the new location?

2 For an explanation of issues relating to open source software, *see* Heather J. Meeker, "*The Open Source Alternative: Understanding Risks and Leveraging Opportunities*", John Wiley & Sons Inc., 2008.

Service dependencies

Is the supplier dependent upon the customer carrying out certain actions so that it can provide the services?[3]

Supplier's other customers

Does the supplier provide services for competitors of the customer?

Is the supplier prevented from providing services for the customer by its agreements with its other customers?

Will providing services to the customer cause confidentiality, security or other problems with its relationships with its existing clients?

Financial standing

What is the financial standing of the customer?

Cultural

What is the customer's culture?

Are the cultures of the two organisations compatible?

Until the supplier has completed its due diligence, it will need to protect itself in any correspondence with the customer by stating that any information it provides is subject to due diligence or subject to specific assumptions which will need to be investigated at a later stage.

The result of the due diligence may lead the supplier to propose variations in the customer's requirements or the charges or may lead to suggestions as to actions that should be taken to minimise risks revealed by the due diligence. In extreme cases, it may lead the supplier to the decision that the project is unviable or not suitable for the supplier, and hence prompt a withdrawal from the process.

6.4 Warranties

The amount of due diligence required by the supplier will depend upon the thoroughness of the customer's due diligence. This is evident from the similarity between Table 2 and Table 13.

It will also depend upon whether the customer is willing to warrant information that it provides to the supplier. Table 13 lists the type of warranties commonly requested by suppliers.

3 *See* Chapter 12 for a discussion of customer responsibilities.

Table 13 *Customer warranties*

Sufficiency of assets and contracts

That the assets, properties and contracts are all that is required to provide the services in the same manner and at the same level as for the 12 months prior to the signature of the outsourcing agreement.

Condition of assets and contracts

That the assets and properties are in a suitable condition to provide the services.

Title of assets to be sold

That the customer is the legal and beneficial owner of the assets and properties and sells them with full title guarantee free from encumbrances other than those agreed and those existing in the ordinary course of trading.

Information about charges due

That any information provided by the customer about the charges due under the leases, licences and supply agreements is correct.

Information about the customer's premises

That, where the services are to be provided on site, at a customer site, the premises are suitable for the provision of the services, do not have any latent defects, and all appropriate consents have been obtained.

Information about employees

See Chapter 27 for a discussion of people issues relating to TUPE.

Laws and regulations

That there are no laws or regulations which the supplier will need to comply with in providing the services.[4]

General warranties

That the customer has disclosed all material information that could reasonably have been expected to affect the supplier's willingness to enter into the outsourcing agreement.

If the customer agrees to provide the warranties requested by the supplier, then the customer is taking the risk that its due diligence has not been thorough and that the information that it is warranting is not accurate. The customer will often therefore be unwilling to provide general warranties, such as the last warranty in Table 13. The customer may want to give some warranties "to the best of its knowledge or belief" or subject to the contents of a disclosure letter.

4 The supplier may be particularly anxious to obtain this warranty if it is an offshore supplier, unfamiliar with the legal system in the customer's jurisdiction.

The customer may also be reluctant to provide warranties where the supplier has an alternative course of action open to it. For example, it may refuse to grant warranties about the sufficiency or condition of customer assets, preferring the supplier to check the assets, unless there are specific circumstances that mean that it is unreasonable to expect the supplier to rely upon its own due diligence. This may mean that the customer will not provide any warranties other than those relating to information about employees transferring to the supplier, title of assets transferring to the supplier or specific contractual liabilities transferring to the supplier.

If the supplier agrees to rely upon its own due diligence, then it is taking the risk that its due diligence has not been thorough and that it has made mistakes. It may be reluctant to accept this risk where it cannot verify information provided by the customer, for example (as explained in the previous paragraph) relating to charges due under supply agreements transferring to it, or information about employees transferring from the customer or an incumbent supplier to the supplier.

6.5 Timing of due diligence

In circumstances where the customer is reluctant to provide warranties and where the supplier has to rely upon its own due diligence, the issue arises as to when the supplier should carry out its due diligence.

6.5.1 Advantages of carrying out due diligence early

The customer may prefer suppliers tendering for an outsourcing project to carry out their due diligence as early as possible, so that the customer has a reliable view of the charges proposed by the suppliers and their solutions and hence will be able to clarify whether the outsourcing arrangement will satisfy its business objectives.

6.5.2 Disadvantages of carrying out due diligence early

Alternatively, the customer may want to restrict the number of suppliers who carry out due diligence if the exercise involves the customer's staff in dedicating time and effort to assisting the customer or if the due diligence will interfere with the customer's operation. It may also want to restrict the disclosure of sensitive information so that it is disclosed to only one supplier. Therefore, it may want to delay the supplier's due diligence until it has selected a preferred supplier.

The supplier may also want to delay due diligence. It may need to spend substantial amounts of money and time in carrying out due diligence of its solution and its charges. Therefore, it may also prefer not to invest in due diligence until it has been selected as preferred supplier and is confident that the customer will sign an agreement with it or until it has received some reassurance of the customer's commitment. The reassurance may be in the form of heads of agreement, or a letter confirming the customer's intention to proceed, or a lock out agreement in which the customer agrees not to negotiate with other suppliers for a specified period.

Even once the supplier has been selected as preferred supplier, it may be impractical for it to carry out a full due diligence exercise. Thus, if the due diligence effort required is substantial (e.g.

the services involve numerous assets at numerous sites), the supplier may suggest that it would be more economical for it to carry out due diligence at each site after signature of the contract, when it rolls out the outsourcing services to each site. Carrying out a separate due diligence and roll-out exercise may involve duplicating costs that the supplier will endeavour to pass on to the customer. The supplier's due diligence may also interfere with the carrying out by the customer of its business or operations.

6.5.3 Disadvantages of delaying due diligence

The problem with postponing due diligence until after contract signature, from the customer's perspective, is clear in that the customer will not be certain that the solution or charges will not be changed once the supplier has completed its due diligence. It may also be concerned that, when it comes to negotiate these changes, its bargaining power may have weakened following signature of the contract. At its worst, it could mean that the customer would be entering into the outsourcing agreement in order to achieve certain business objectives but without sufficient clarity that its goals will be achieved.

For example, the customer could enter into the agreement to achieve certain cost savings that it believes it will achieve. Because the customer is anxious to sign the agreement as soon as possible, it does not want to delay signature of the agreement so that the supplier can carry out due diligence. The parties sign the contract on the basis of certain pricing assumptions that the supplier agrees to confirm during the first six months of the agreement. Once the contract has been signed, the due diligence exercises carried out by the supplier indicate that some of the pricing assumptions were incorrect and the customer is forced to agree increases in the charges which undermine the benefit which it anticipated receiving.

Accordingly, the customer should think very carefully about signing outsourcing agreements or other commitments to the supplier until it is certain that the outsourcing arrangement will satisfy its business objectives. In most cases, unless there are exceptional circumstances, this will mean the customer insisting that the supplier carry out its due diligence before contract signature so that charges and service commitments included in the agreement are guaranteed and not subject to renegotiation. The supplier may also prefer to have certainty before signature of the agreement as to the charges it will be paid.

6.5.4 Possible solution – customer carries out due diligence

It will usually be sensible for the customer to endeavour to carry out substantial amounts of due diligence itself (anticipating the due diligence which the suppliers will need to carry out) to collate the information and to make it available in an electronic or physical data room. For example, this process could be applied in relation to asset or property-related surveys, which can be extremely costly and disruptive to existing operations and can readily be carried out by an independent third party.[5]

5 The OGC suggests that local authorities may want to prepare a comprehensive information pack or "seller's brief" for prospective suppliers. *See* the "Successful Delivery Toolkit" at www.ogc.gov.uk.

The customer can either bear the cost of this due diligence or the costs could be shared equally between the suppliers, possibly with the unsuccessful suppliers being reimbursed by the successful supplier once selected. The first option may be simpler, bearing in mind that the successful supplier is likely to build any resulting cost into its charges for the outsourcing agreement.

6.5.5 Possible solution – customer pays for due diligence

If the supplier cannot agree a fixed charge or finalise its solution because the customer has not carried out adequate due diligence and is unable to provide sufficient information to the supplier, then the customer may agree to pay the costs of the due diligence exercise if the outsourcing project is ultimately abandoned. Otherwise, it may see the costs as part of the supplier's cost of doing business.

6.5.6 Possible solution – agree variation mechanism

In exceptional circumstances, where due diligence cannot be carried out before contract signature, the customer may want to consider agreeing exactly how the charges will be adjusted to reflect the findings of the due diligence exercise so that the supplier is not given the opportunity to reopen the negotiations. An example of this would be where the parties agree that, as part of the outsourcing arrangement, the customer will transfer to the supplier certain third-party supplier agreements. The customer provides the supplier with information relating to the charges payable under these agreements but the customer cannot be certain that the information is up to date. The customer is accordingly unwilling to warrant the information relating to the contracts. The parties may agree to attach a schedule to the agreement showing what the customer believes to be the correct charges payable under the contracts. The supplier is given six months to check that the information is correct. The parties then agree a specific adjustment to the charges so that if the information is incorrect, whether too low or, for that matter, too high, the annual charges payable under the outsourcing contract will be adjusted to reflect the exact change in the annual charges payable under the third-party contracts.

Part Three – Services

Chapter 7

The Service Description

7.1 Outline

Chapters 2 to 6 describe the procurement process by which the customer will select an outsourcing supplier. Chapters 7 to 10 cover the services to be provided by the outsourcing supplier. This chapter includes a summary of the purpose of the service description and some practical hints for drafting service descriptions. It also discusses whether suppliers should have a duty to advise the customer of weaknesses in the service description.

In this Guide, the phrase "service description" is used to describe any documents that describe the services, including "service requirement", "service levels agreements", "customer requirements", "statement of work", "scope of services" or any other similar term.

7.2 Purpose of the service description

The business objectives and the business plan referred to in Chapter 2 must feed into a detailed service description. In this way, the customer must communicate to the supplier what its business and service objectives are with regard to the outsourcing.

It is no exaggeration to say that the service description is the key document in the outsourcing arrangement and that failure to prepare a clear service description is a major reason why disputes between the customer and supplier occur.[1]

The service description must satisfy various requirements.

7.2.1 Support business objectives

It must support the customer's business objectives. For example, if the customer wants to reduce costs, it may consider ways in which it can reduce the service hours without affecting the operation of its business. The customer cannot outsource to the supplier the responsibility for deciding what the customer's business objectives should be. The customer must define its business goals and decide when these need to be modified or superseded during the term of the agreement, although the supplier may be able to advise on alternative ways of achieving the customer's business aims.

---

1 "Whether or not the service fulfils the expectations [of the customer] depends primarily on how effectively the deliverables were agreed upon in any dialogue with the customer, rather than on how well the supplier provides the service." *IT Service Management based on ITIL – an introduction*, *it*SMF, May 2005.

7.2.2 Describe services

The service description must communicate to the supplier, on a practical level, the services that the customer expects to receive.

7.2.3 Describe services covered by fixed charge

If the charges for providing the services are to be calculated on a fixed-price basis, then the service description will also serve the function of defining what the customer gets for its money and what the supplier is obliged to provide in return for receiving payment of the charges. (*See* Chapter 18 for an explanation of possible charging mechanisms.) Therefore, if the boundaries of the service description are unclear, this is likely to lead to a dispute between the parties, as neither customer nor supplier will be certain as to what is or is not covered by the fixed charge.

7.2.3.1 Supplier concerns – vague or open-ended service descriptions
From the supplier's perspective, if it accepts a service description that is vague or open ended, it can find that it has given what is, in effect, a blank cheque to the customer. The supplier will therefore need to ensure that the services are sufficiently clearly defined for it to be able to price them accurately.

For some services, for example some facilities management services, it may be helpful for the supplier to prepare detailed and clear service descriptions for its service offerings, which the customer can use to save both parties time and effort. It may be necessary to include flexibility in the service descriptions (e.g. gold, silver and platinum levels of service) so that the customer can select which level of service particularly meets its requirements.

Unfortunately, this solution will not be practical for services which vary considerably between customers or which are competitively tendered by the customer in circumstances where the customer will expect to go out to tender with a description of its requirements.

7.2.3.2 Customer concerns – incomplete service descriptions
From the customer's perspective, if it drafts a service description which omits elements of the services, it may enter into the outsourcing transaction assuming that the charges will be cheaper than its previous service, only to find that the supplier can make additional charges for providing the omitted services and that the end result is that the outsourced services are more expensive than the in-house solution.

7.2.3.3 Solution to customer's concern – wide drafting
The risk to the customer may also be mitigated by drafting the service description widely, bearing in mind, however, that the supplier will calculate its price on the basis of this service description so that, if the service description implies a broader level of service than the customer requires, the charges may be higher.

An alternative approach, where staff are transferring to the supplier, is to state that the service description is intended to include all of the services previously provided by the employees transferring to the supplier, although this may have an impact upon the price that the supplier charges to the customer if it means that the supplier includes all of the staff costs of the transferring employees in the outsourcing charges, rather than assuming that staff can be partly deployed in providing services to other clients.

7.2.3.4 Solution to customer's concern – due diligence

Neither of the above solutions to customer concerns about having omitted elements of the services is ideal, as they may lead to the customer paying more for the services than is necessary. The ideal solution is for the customer to carry out adequate due diligence exercises, as stressed in Chapter 2, so that it has an accurate view of the services being provided prior to the outsourcing arrangement and of the changes that will need to be made in these services so that they will reflect the customer's current business objectives and service requirements.

7.2.3.5 Solution to customer's concern – ITIL

The IT Infrastructure Library ("ITIL") can help the customer carry out due diligence and draft complete service descriptions in several different ways. ITIL was developed by the Central Computer and Telecommunications Agency ("CCTA"), now part of the Office of Government Commerce ("OGC"). It was designed to codify best practice in the IT services industry. However, some of the concepts may be helpful for business process outsourcing ("BPO") agreements, particularly those involving a substantial IT element. ITIL is used extensively within Europe, the US and Japan.

ITIL emphasis on documentation

ITIL emphasises the importance of documenting key aspects of how IT services are provided. For example, ITIL includes detailed descriptions of documentation which should be maintained as part of configuration management.

An outsourcing customer who has adopted ITIL is less likely to find that it has little or no relevant documentation showing the services it is currently receiving.

However, the costs of providing an ITIL-compliant IT service (whether in-house or outsourced) may increase because of the level of documentation required and some companies feel that the ITIL approach is too bureaucratic for their business.

Use of ITIL as checklist

ITIL includes a detailed description of IT processes and services which will usually need to be carried out as part of IT service management. A customer entering into IT outsourcing agreements can use this information as a checklist to ensure that its service descriptions are comprehensive, even if the specific details of its services and the manner in which they provide the services are different from those suggested by ITIL. For example, ITIL clarifies that business continuity involves consideration of capacity management, availability management, business continuity plan management, risk management and risk analysis.

Use of ITIL to reflect best practice

As ITIL is intended to reflect best practice in IT service management, a customer entering into an IT outsourcing agreement can also use ITIL to consider ways in which its IT management can be improved. For example, ITIL suggests that it is good practice to distinguish between "incident management" and "problem management". Incident management is designed to restore normal service operation as quickly as possible by dealing with the immediate issues causing service failures. Problem management is designed to resolve the root cause of incidents, reduce the number and severity of incidents, minimise the adverse impact of incidents and prevent the recurrence of incidents.

7.2.3.6 Solution to customer's concern – value for money

Where the customer is entering into an outsourcing arrangement to cut its costs, its due diligence will need to be sufficient for it to have a detailed understanding of the services required to support its business so that it can distinguish between service or levels of service which are essential for it to carry out its business and services or levels of services which are desirable but not necessary. It may be useful for the customer to collaborate with the supplier to gain an accurate understanding of the charging structure for the services and ways in which the charges for the services can be reduced without affecting critical elements of the services. The customer will then be able to make an informed decision as to what services and levels of services it requires.

Unfortunately this may not be practical in all cases, for example if the due diligence would involve considerable amounts of time or if the customer wants to keep the outsourcing arrangement confidential until it has decided that it is likely that outsourcing will satisfy its business objectives.

7.2.3.7 Standardisation of services

Another factor which the customer will need to consider, in particular if it is endeavouring to reduce its costs under an outsourcing agreement, is the extent to which it can standardise or harmonise the services it requires so that all parts of the customer organisation require the same or similar (e.g. gold, silver and platinum) services.

For IT outsourcing agreements, implementing ITIL[2] may assist the standardisation of relevant services and hence help reduce costs. Clearly this will not be so, however, if the standard of service previously required by the customer was considerably lower than that required by ITIL.

Another way that the customer may standardise its services is to accept a commoditised service from the supplier. Non-traditional outsourcing models (including application service provider ("ASP"), utility computing, software on demand, software as a service ("SAAS"), cloud computing and business process utility ("BPU") models) under which IT or business process services are made available to the customer, on a rental basis, usually involve the provision of a commoditised service by the supplier. These types of arrangement are expected to grow in popularity, in particular as a result of any recession, as they may be cheaper than traditional outsourcing models. In these types of arrangement, the customer needs to clarify and document its service requirements and evaluate which supplier's offering best meets its requirements, but the customer ultimately contracts on the basis of the supplier's standard service offering (although not necessarily on the supplier's standard terms and conditions).

2 *See* 7.2.3.5 for an explanation of the background to ITIL.

7.2.4 Legal document

The service description is an important legal document. It must set out the division of responsibility between the customer and supplier. In some cases this may involve describing the boundary between the responsibility of the customer and that of the supplier (e.g. in a telecommunications outsourcing service, that the supplier is responsible for the network up to a specific point on that network).

It also involves defining terms used in the service description. ITIL[3] may be useful in this context for IT and BPO outsourcing agreements as it defines key terms relevant for service management, for example "incident" and "problem". This provides a common technical language for the parties to the outsourcing arrangement. This is particularly useful for offshore or near-shore outsourcing agreements, where the ability to rely upon a common understanding of relevant terms may assist communication between the parties.

Lastly, it is important, particularly to the customer, that the service description is drafted so that it is legally enforceable. It must state clearly who is responsible for what action (project plans which include lists of actions without stating who is responsible for carrying out the specific action are particularly unhelpful). The customer will want the service description to be drafted in the form of obligations (e.g. "The supplier will ..."). It is desirable that a lawyer checks the service description to ensure that it is legally enforceable.

7.2.5 Tax considerations

The description of the services will be important in establishing whether the services (e.g. certain financial services) are regarded as falling within any exemption from VAT. This will be critical for customers who cannot recover all of the VAT charged on the services. While technically the legal issue is what services are supplied, not what label is applied to them, the correct description may in practice reduce the likelihood of a challenge from the tax authorities.

7.3 Timing of agreement of the service description

7.3.1 Problems agreeing the service description

Sometimes customers find it difficult to define the services before the agreement is signed. If the customer cannot document the services to be provided, and as a result it is not certain that the parties have a shared understanding of the services to be provided, then it is difficult to avoid the conclusion that the agreement should be input based, with the supplier being obliged to provide resources only or that signature of the agreement should be postponed until these issues can be clarified, as none of the objectives of the service description have been satisfied.

3 *See* 7.2.3.5 for an explanation of the background to ITIL.

7.3.2 Problems documenting the services

The situation is more difficult if the parties have problems documenting the services to be provided in the time available before contract signature but feel that they are clear what services are to be provided. Theoretically, it would appear that one of the functions of the service description has been satisfied in this situation, namely that the supplier understands on a practical level the services that the customer expects to receive. In practice, as anyone who has experience of negotiating service descriptions will confirm, parties often assume that they have the same view of the services to be provided but subsequent negotiations show that each party has made different assumptions as to the exact service to be provided.

However, if the parties do have a mutual understanding of the services to be provided, perhaps because the services are not complex or because they reflect services currently being provided by the customer, then the question arises as to whether the charges can similarly be calculated and agreed. If the charges can be agreed, then the parties will need to decide whether they want to take the risk of starting provision of the services without the agreement of a binding legal document. In the short term, the parties may be willing to take this risk if they feel that both parties have an interest in getting the details of the services documented as soon as possible after signature. Naturally, lawyers will usually advise against taking this risk.

7.4 Contents of the service description

Because the service description must communicate to the supplier on a practical level the services that the customer expects to receive, it must address all of the issues mentioned in Table 14.

Table 14 *Contents of the service description*

Nature of services

What services are to be provided by the supplier?

What is the scope of the services? Are there any particular exclusions from the scope of the services?

What are the boundaries of the services and the handover points, where services are provided by other suppliers of the customer? (This will be particularly important where the customer has adopted a multi-sourcing approach, as described in Chapter 17.)

Application of services

Where relevant, if the services involve the support or maintenance of assets or premises, is there a list of those assets or premises?

Are any assets or premises specifically excluded?

Recipients

Which parts of the customer's organisation are to receive the services?

Are the services also provided to clients of the customer or any external organisations?

Will this change over the term of the arrangement?

What will happen if there are changes in the customer's organisation, for example a purchase or a sale?

Customer dependencies

What assistance will need to be provided by the customer's organisation so that the services can be provided?[4]

What assistance will need to be provided by the customer's other suppliers so that the services can be provided? (This will be particularly important where the customer has adopted a multisourcing approach, as described in Chapter 17.)

Transition

Will the services be provided in a different manner during an initial transition period?

Does the supplier have additional tasks that it must carry out during the transition period to ensure that it can provide the services to the contracted service levels?

Can the supplier commit to carrying out these activities in accordance with a detailed project plan?

What are the acceptance criteria which must be satisfied before the end of the transition?

Changes in the services

Can the customer foresee any changes in the services?

Are the services to improve during the term of the arrangement and, if so, how is the required improvement described and how will it be measured?

Will the customer want to benchmark the level of services against the level of services provided at that time in the market?

Will the supplier be obliged to inform the customer of, or make available, new technology?

How will this affect the charges?

Seasonal variations

Is a different service to be provided at certain times, for example the customer's year end?

For how long will the special service be provided, for example 30 days prior to year end?

Term

Are all of the services to be provided during the full term of the agreement?

4 *See* Chapter 12 for a discussion of customer dependencies.

If a particular service is to be provided for a shorter term, will a replacement service be provided when that service ceases (e.g. mainframe services replaced by mid-range service)?

Is the replacement service specified in the service description or will it be agreed through change control, in which case does the business case take into account the fact that additional charges will be payable for the replacement services?

Service hours

During what service hours will the services be provided?

If the service hours are not 24 hours a day, seven days a week, can the customer extend the service hours?

If so, is a particular notice period required and is the extension at an additional charge?

Location

Are the services being provided in respect of assets at particular locations? Do the services need to be provided on site or can they be provided remotely? Can they be provided offshore?

Quality

What quality procedures will the supplier need to comply with?

What quality procedures must be followed to ensure version control of documents?

What inspection, testing and approvals will be needed before new systems are implemented into a production environment?

Industry codes of practice

Will the supplier be required to follow relevant industry codes of practice?[5]

5 Here are a few examples of codes of practice which may be relevant in England and Wales:

(a) Intellect's IT Supplier Code of Best Practice may be relevant for IT outsourcing arrangements. For more information about Intellect, *see* www.intellectuk.org;

(b) the Call Centre Association's Standard Framework for Best Practice may be relevant for call centre outsourcing arrangements. For more information about the CCA, *see* www.cca.org.uk;

(c) the Direct Marketing Association's Code of Practice and relevant best practice guidelines may be relevant if the services involve direct marketing campaigns. For more information about the DMA, *see* www.dma.org.uk;

(d) the International Chamber of Commerce's International Code of Advertising Practice may be relevant if the services include advertisements for the promotion of goods or services. For more information about the ICC, *see* www.iccwbo.org;

(e) the International Committee for the Supervision of Standards of Telephone Information Services Code of Practice may apply if the services include the provision of premium-rate services to customers within the UK. For further information, *see* www.icstis.org.uk;

(f) the Finance and Leasing Association's Codes of Conduct may be relevant for outsourcing of leasing collection services.

Legislation

Will the supplier need to comply with relevant legislation?[6]

Policies and procedures

Will the supplier need to follow the customer's policies in providing the services (e.g. security or health and safety policies)?

Disaster recovery/contingency?

What force majeure events could affect the services?

How likely are they?

What would be their impact if they did occur?

What measures (including disaster recovery and business continuity services) will the supplier need to take to deal with force majeure events?

What measures should the customer take to deal with force majeure events?

Training

Will the supplier need to train the customer's users to ensure that they can take full advantage of the supplier's services?

7.5 Multinational outsourcing arrangements

If the customer is a company comprising various different divisions or group companies or is a multinational group of companies, then there may be additional issues that will need to be considered in the service description.

The customer may need to decide the extent to which the service and the service levels will be mandated centrally so as to allow standardisation of the services received throughout the group, or whether the services may be customised to fit local requirements. For example, where the service comprises a telecommunications service, the customer may decide that members of the group must accept a certain minimum level of service, but that group companies will be free to decide that they need (and want to pay for) a higher level of service where appropriate for their particular business.

6 For example, if the services involve the provision of a call centre in England or Wales, the supplier may need to comply with the Data Protection Act 1998, Privacy and Electronic Communications (EC Directive) Regulations 2003 and Consumer Protection (Distance Selling) Regulations 2000. To give another example, if the services being outsourced are personnel services, then it is a fundamental part of the services that the supplier will comply with all relevant employment law.

7.6 Stages in drafting a service description

Table 15 provides a checklist of stages that can be followed in drafting service descriptions.

Table 15 *Checklist of stages in drafting service descriptions*

Stage 1 – list service elements.

Stage 2 – consider service elements that need to be included in the service description.

Stage 3 – consider appropriate names for the service elements.

Stage 4 – decide which documents are going to make up the service description.

Stage 5 – draft an introduction to the service description listing the different service elements.

Stage 6 – draft the detailed description of each service element, using precedents where available and appropriate.

Stage 7 – add the customer's responsibilities.

Stage 8 – add definitions not defined elsewhere in the agreement.

Stage 9 – list (and draft, if necessary) documents to be attached to the service description (e.g. lists of assets or premises to be maintained) if not in the rest of the agreement.

Stage 10 – consider the term during which the services will be provided.

Stage 11 – add details of service hours.

Stage 12 – add details of service management.

Stage 13 – add service levels and service credits.

Stage 14 – proofread.

As the service description defines what the customer receives in return for paying the charges, the service description and the charging schedule must be drafted so that they are consistent. The structure of the service description must be consistent with the structure of the charging schedule. (See Chapter 18 for a discussion of charging regimes.) The customer may want a description of each service element, with a breakdown of the charges for the service elements, so that it can understand the charging implications of changes in the services.

7.7 Supplier's duty to warn

A final issue relating to service descriptions is whether the supplier should be required to inform the customer if the customer has included in its service description requirements that the supplier knows will not lead to the satisfaction of the customer's business objectives or to the provision of an efficient service. This is a way in which the supplier may be asked to accept some form of liability for achievement of the customer's business objectives. This has been referred to, in Chapter 1, as acceptance by the supplier of the business outcome risk rather than the service output risk, and it may or may not be appropriate depending upon the circumstances.

7.7.1 No general obligation

The situation at law is that the courts in England and Wales will not imply a general duty for the supplier to warn the customer about problems with the services,[7] although there may be circumstances in which the supplier's implied obligation to act with reasonable skill and care may imply such a duty.

7.7.2 Supplier to advise customer at commencement

Therefore, it will be in both parties' interests for them to clarify exactly what the supplier's responsibility will be in this regard and to document it clearly in the agreement. For example, if the customer has specifically asked the supplier to advise on how its business objectives can best be achieved, then the parties should document this.

7.7.3 Supplier to advise customer on continuing basis

A more difficult situation arises where the customer expects the supplier to warn it on a continuing basis if the customer instructs the supplier to do something or itself does something that may adversely affect the provision of the services or the achievement of the customer's business objectives.

Instructions as to how to provide the services are limited. It will also be helpful if there is a procedure (such as the change control procedure) that will be followed to ensure that the supplier considers the impact of the customer's instructions upon the services and the customer's business objectives. The procedure should ensure that the customer documents the precise nature of its instructions and that the supplier responds within a specified period of time, notifying the customer of any identifiable problems with the instructions.

The supplier will also need to ensure that agreeing to the obligation will not constitute a blank cheque and that it can evaluate the amount of effort needed to comply with the obligation or make an additional charge for complying with the provision.

---

7 *See* Richard Stephens, "Is there a duty to warn", *C&L Computer and Law*, June/July 2003.

Chapter 8

Control Over How the Services are Provided

8.1 Outline

Chapter 7 provides some practical guidance on preparing service descriptions. This chapter deals with the issue of whether the customer should have some control over how the services are provided, including, for example, whether the customer should have the right to instruct the supplier how to provide the services.

8.2 Reasons for allowing the supplier control

8.2.1 Supplier is responsible for the services

It may make sense to permit the supplier to control how the services are provided because the supplier will not usually accept responsibility for the services (i.e. the service output risk, as described in Chapter 1) unless it has sufficient control over the manner in which they are to be provided.

It is arguable that allowing the customer to control how the services are provided can undermine the supplier's clear responsibility for the services. If there is no clear division of responsibility between the customer and supplier, this increases the likelihood that any failure in providing the services will lead to a long and costly dispute between the parties.

8.2.2 Supplier is an expert in providing the services

It may also make sense to allow the supplier to control how the services are provided, because the supplier, assuming that it is an expert in providing the services, may be best placed to decide how they should be provided and may be able to suggest improvements in the services. This is particularly relevant for IT and telecommunications outsourcing projects if the outsourcing supplier is a leading IT or telecommunications provider. The situation may be more complex in business process outsourcing projects, where the customer may have more expertise in providing the services than the supplier and the supplier may be dependent upon a knowledge transfer from the customer or the transfer to the supplier of the customer's skilled workforce.

8.2.3 Services will be more flexible

In addition, focusing on the service outputs to be delivered by the supplier will mean that the services will be more flexible and that the parties will not need to change the service description when the manner in which the services is provided changes.

8.2.4 Customer benefits from fixed price

If the customer attempts to control how the services are provided, by insisting that changes in how the services are provided are agreed through the change control procedure, this can undermine the benefit of the customer having agreed a fixed price with the supplier. By agreeing that changes in how the services are provided will be approved under the change control procedure, the customer may (intentionally or inadvertently) accept the risk that consequently the charges will have to be increased.

8.3 Reasons for allowing the customer control

However, in some circumstances the customer may want control over how the services are provided. These circumstances are described in the following paragraphs. In addition, Chapter 33 describes specific guidance on this issue from the FSA, which is relevant for firms regulated by the FSA.

Ultimately, with regard to all of the situations described in the following paragraphs relating to the customer concerns, the parties will usually need to find a compromise that provides sufficient reassurance for the customer without unduly restricting the supplier's ability to control how it provides the services. The supplier may need to be informed of the proposed restrictions before it can agree the service levels and the charges.

If the customer concludes that it needs substantial control over how the services are provided, then this begs the question as to whether the customer should enter into an input-based outsourcing arrangement (where the supplier provides resources only) or should set up a joint venture with the supplier for the provision of the services (*see* Chapter 17 for a discussion of joint ventures). In some cases, it may also beg the question as to whether outsourcing is the appropriate course of action or whether the customer should be providing the services in-house.

8.4 Service requirement includes how the services are to be provided

In general, if it is not important to the customer how the services are provided, they should be defined in terms of the services to be provided. If it is important to the customer how the services are provided, then the customer must seek to control the inputs. For example:

(a) if the customer wants the supplier to ensure that call centre staff are polite, then the customer should specify this in the service description; and

(b) the customer may want to control or approve the technical architecture and may dictate standards or policies with which the supplier will need to comply. *See* 22.15 below regarding the implications of changes in the customer's policies.

8.5 Inability to operate business

The customer may want to control how the services are provided so that it has the power to act before its business suffers. The customer cannot pass on to the supplier the risk of it being unable to operate its business as a result of the supplier's failure to provide the services. Claiming damages from the supplier after the event may be an inadequate remedy.

8.5.1 Employees[1]

The customer may want the supplier to warrant that it will provide suitably qualified staff to provide the services. In some situations (e.g. where the outsourcing is resource based or is a knowledge process outsourcing arrangement) the customer may want to specify the specific qualifications, skills and experience which the staff must have. It may also need staff to satisfy security vetting procedures.[2]

In certain circumstances, the customer may want a further guarantee that there will be sufficient staff engaged in providing the services or may want the supplier to commit that employees will be exclusively engaged in providing the services. This latter restriction is usually not helpful because:

(a) it will prevent the supplier from employing specialists to provide parts of the services;
(b) it may have cost implications if the employees could otherwise have been used to provide services to other customers; and
(c) it may also restrict the supplier's ability to deal with changes in the services (e.g. reductions in volumes) where the employees must continue to be engaged exclusively in providing the services even if this only takes up part of their time.

The customer may want the ability to instruct the supplier to remove any employees or certain listed key employees from the provision of the services, even if the supplier is not yet in breach of the agreement. The supplier will usually want to avoid abuse of this provision by defining the circumstances in which it applies and stating that the customer must act reasonably and explain why it is relying upon the provision. The supplier may also need notice of the exercise of this right in order to give it sufficient time to arrange for the provision of the services by alternative employees. Lastly, the supplier should ensure that it acts in accordance

1 If the supplier is going to provide the services in whole or in part from Spain or France, then *see* Chapter 42 or 43 before including provisions allowing the customer control over the employees.
2 *See* Chapter 32 for more information on security requirements.

with its employment contract with the employee and that the employee will not have a claim against it as a result of the supplier complying with the customer's instructions.[3]

8.5.2 Subcontractors

The customer may want the right:

(a) to approve the supplier's subcontractors; or
(b) to instruct the supplier to stop the subcontractors providing the services.

The first right is less problematic from the supplier's perspective, particularly if it can obtain the customer's approval of the subcontractor before the agreement is signed.

The second provision is more problematic from the supplier's perspective and may mean that the supplier will need to include in its agreement with its subcontractor a right to terminate the subcontract if the customer exercises its right to instruct the supplier to stop providing services to the customer. The supplier will usually want to avoid abuse of the provision by defining the circumstances in which it applies and stating that the customer must act reasonably. If the customer is unable to define the circumstances in which it will need to rely upon this right the agreement will be less attractive to the subcontractor, who may treat the contract as being potentially short term. This may mean that the subcontractor's charges may be more expensive than they would otherwise have been.

The customer may also insist upon the supplier including certain clauses in its subcontracts (e.g. regarding confidentiality, the customer's audit rights or the customer's right to step in to the relationship with the supplier).

Lastly, if the subcontractor is key to the provision of the services by the supplier, the customer may want a direct agreement with the subcontractor so that it can step in to the agreement with that subcontractor.[4]

8.5.3 Change of control

The customer may want the right to terminate the agreement if there is a change of control in the supplier. This may be resisted by the supplier as, in any sale of the supplier company, any long-term outsourcing agreements are likely to form valuable assets which increase the value of the company and the ability of the customer to terminate the agreements may have a seriously

---

3 In the case of *Viasystems (Tyneside) Ltd* v *Thermal Transfer (Northern) Ltd and others* the court of appeal broadened the potential scope of vicarious liability to hold that more than one entity may be vicariously liable for the acts of an employee. Following this decision, the customer may want to consider whether it requires an indemnity from the supplier for any liability it may have for the negligent acts of the supplier's employees. *See* also *David Philip Hawley* v *Luminar Leisure Limited* [2006] EWCA Civ 18. In this case *Viasystems* was distinguished because there had been effectively and substantially a transfer of control and responsibility from one entity to the other.

4 *See* Chapter 24 for a description of direct agreements designed to protect the customer if the supplier becomes insolvent.

adverse impact upon the value of the supplier company. This issue is discussed in greater detail in 23.3 below.

8.5.4 Location and relocation

The customer may want the right to approve the location from which services are to be provided if the location may have an impact upon the provision of the services, for example if the services involve staff of the supplier travelling from the supplier's location to the customer's site to provide on-site services, or if the customer wants to be aware of any offshore outsourcing activities. It may also need to approve the location if, for example, the services are being provided by the supplier using customer systems which are made available to the customer or maintained under third-party contracts which restrict the location of the equipment or software.

The customer may also want the supplier to agree that it will not relocate the services after the date of signature of the agreement without agreeing an implementation plan for the move with the customer.

Lastly, the customer may want the supplier to bear any costs associated with the relocation, for example any increased third-party maintenance costs resulting from systems being relocated. The supplier will need to ensure that it includes these costs in its business case.

8.6 Rights other than termination

The customer may want to have other rights to affect the way that the services are provided short of terminating the agreement.

8.6.1 Step in

The customer may want to have the right to step in and take over the provision of the services itself or via a third-party supplier.

8.6.1.1 Application of step-in rights
Step-in rights are often drafted to apply in circumstances where the supplier is unable to provide the services as a result of it being in breach of the agreement. If the failure of the supplier to provide the services could have serious implications for the customer's business, it is more logical for the step-in provision to apply whenever the supplier is unable to provide the services, whether this is as a result of a supplier breach or a force majeure, assuming that the force majeure event affecting the supplier would not prevent the customer or another supplier from providing the services.

8.6.1.2 Step-in costs
The financial implications of the two situations described above would, however, be different:

(a) If the customer needs to step in because of a supplier breach, then it would normally expect to deduct the step-in costs from any charges due to the supplier for the relevant period. If the charges are automatically reduced when the customer steps in, for example because the payment of the charges depends upon the supplier providing the services, then compensation to the customer should take into account any sums the customer is saving as a result of this reduction. The supplier will be concerned about incurring liability for costs over which it has no control and may either, as a result, refuse to agree to the customer having step-in rights at all or ensure that it is only liable for reasonable costs. The supplier may also want reassurance that the customer will "step out" as soon as practicable.

(b) If the customer steps in because of a force majeure event, then the supplier will not expect to be liable for the step-in costs and may argue that it should be paid for any step-in assistance it provides. *See* Chapter 30 for a description of the affect of a force majeure event upon the charges due to the supplier.

8.6.1.3 Responsibility for the services

The supplier should not be responsible for services being provided by the customer or a third-party supplier. The supplier may be concerned about ensuring that the customer or third party has not caused problems with the services when they stepped in, for which the supplier will be responsible once they step out and allow the supplier to resume provision of the services. This may result in the supplier refusing to agree to the step-in right at all or ensuring that the customer or third party cannot step out until the supplier is happy to take back responsibility for the services.

The supplier may also be concerned about the customer exercising a right to step in regarding part of the services, in case this undermines the supplier's provision of other services. Where the supplier is providing part of the services and the customer is providing another part of the services, this may undermine the clear division of responsibilities between the parties, unless the services are clearly severable.

8.6.1.4 Conditions for exercise of step-in right

As described above, step in raises various concerns for the supplier, in particular because it undermines the supplier's control over the services. Therefore the supplier may suggest that the customer does not have the right to step in until the supplier has been given an opportunity to demonstrate that it can correct the problems with the services. In appropriate cases, the supplier may suggest that it has the right to correct the problems itself or by using third parties. The supplier may use this right to ensure that, where a third party needs to correct problems with the services, the supplier enters into an agreement with the third party instead of the customer. In practice this can be a satisfactory solution for both parties, as the supplier retains control over and the liability for the services and the costs involved in remedying the problems with the services.

Any use of third parties would need to be subject to any relevant provisions in the agreement regarding customer approval of subcontractors or material subcontractors.

8.6.1.5 Step-in assistance

In practice, exercising a step-in right may be difficult, and its success may depend upon the step-in assistance that the supplier provides. The customer may need the supplier to cooperate with the party stepping in to provide the services and to make available to it any necessary assets and information.

The supplier may be reluctant to make certain information or assets available if the party stepping in is a third-party competitor of the supplier and the parties may need to decide what information and assets will be made available and in what circumstances. For example, the supplier may want the third party to comply with confidentiality and security obligations or may refuse to allow the customer or the third party direct access to its premises and may agree to grant them remote access to its systems only.

Lastly, the supplier may be restricted from making certain assets available to the customer or a third-party supplier, for example third-party software licences, without the consent of the third party.

On termination of the step-in right, the supplier will usually want the customer to ensure that the customer and any third party employed by the customer cooperate with the supplier in ensuring a smooth transfer of the services back to the supplier.

8.6.2 Requirement for certain actions

Instead of stepping in to provide the services itself or via a third party, the customer may want the right to require the supplier to implement reasonable actions necessary to deal with a supplier default. This remedy would enable the customer to interfere directly with how the supplier is providing the services and so is likely to be resisted by suppliers. Nevertheless, it may be appropriate in certain circumstances, for example where the customer is a public sector body and the action has been required by the authority's auditors or the customer is subject to another regulator (e.g. the FSA or the Water Services Regulatory Authority).

In this situation, the parties will need to agree who will pay for the implementation of the change and whether the supplier will be responsible for the effect of the change.

8.7 Ensure smooth termination

The customer may want control over how the services are provided in order to ensure a smooth transition on termination.

8.7.1 Technology refresh

The customer may want the supplier to commit to carrying out a technology refresh, so that equipment used in the outsourcing services will not need to be replaced the day after expiry. Another way of achieving a similar result is for the customer to specify that the assets transferring to it on termination must be capable of providing the services for another, say, six months after termination. The customer should bear in mind that the supplier will increase its charge in order to comply with these requirements.

8.7.2 Exclusive assets

The customer may want to specify which assets used to provide the services are to be used exclusively for the provision of services to it, so that they can be transferred to it on termination. This issue is discussed in greater detail in Chapter 16.

8.7.3 Control over nature of assets used

The customer may want to ensure that the supplier does not make it difficult for the customer to move to another supplier on termination, for example by incorporating into the supplier's services proprietary products owned by the supplier. This issue is discussed in greater detail in Chapter 25.

8.8 Should service descriptions be objective or subjective?

Sometimes a customer includes subjective wording in service descriptions, for example, "The Supplier will provide a service to the reasonable satisfaction of the Customer". The wording is subjective because it does not describe the level of service that will satisfy the customer but leaves it up to the subjective judgment of the customer as to what level of service will be acceptable.

The customer tends to rely upon subjective wording when it is not confident that the service description fully describes its requirements and wants to change the service description once the requirements are clarified.

From a supplier's perspective, subjective wording is unhelpful for various reasons which are specified in Table 16.

Table 16 *Reasons for avoiding subjectively worded obligations*

Enables control over how the services are provided

They may give the customer the ability to instruct the supplier on how to provide the services.

Not descriptive

They do not tell the supplier what it needs to do to satisfy the customer and so, to that extent, they defeat one of the fundamental purposes of the service description.

Unilateral variation

They may allow the customer to attempt to vary the service description unilaterally, instead of agreeing amendments in accordance with the agreed change control procedure.

Retrospective variation

They may allow the customer to vary the service description retrospectively and hence put the supplier in breach of the agreement.

Idiosyncratic behaviour

They may leave the supplier at risk should the party making the decisions behave in an idiosyncratic manner.

8.9 Should the service description include the supplier's proposal?

In some negotiations, the procurement procedure involves the customer preparing a RFP (as described in Chapter 3), which includes a description of the required services. The supplier then responds to the request with its proposal. The question arises as to whether the supplier's proposal should be attached to the contract and form part of the service description. This may sound like a minor issue, but in fact it may have serious ramifications for the outsourcing project.

8.9.1 Inconsistent documents

Problems with this approach arise where the proposal appears to differ from the RFP. For example:

(a) the supplier may not be able to satisfy a particular element of the service description;
(b) the supplier may propose an enhancement to the service description; or
(c) the customer's service requirements may have changed and the supplier's proposal may be more up to date.

Including both the service description and the supplier's proposal in the contract can lead to a situation where the description of the services is contained in two inconsistent documents. This will be extremely difficult to manage on a daily basis and stating that, in the event of conflict, one overrides the other does not solve the problem.

8.9.2 Sales document

Other problems with including the supplier's proposal in the service description may arise where the supplier's proposal is a sales document, which includes vague promises, which the supplier is reluctant to include in the contract.

In both of the situations described above, the ideal solution is for the parties to amend the service description so that it contains a comprehensive, up-to-date and clear description of the services. The process of agreeing this comprehensive document may in itself be helpful in enabling the supplier to understand the customer's requirements and the customer to understand the supplier's proposal.

8.9.3 Documents serve different functions

The situation will be different where the service description and the supplier's proposal deal with different issues, the service description describing the services and the supplier's proposal containing its solution, explaining how the supplier will provide the services. In this situation, it may be helpful, from the customer's perspective, to include both documents in the agreement. However, both parties should ensure that the service description and proposal are up to date as at the date of signature of the agreement, in particular if they were written several months previously.

The customer may want to clarify that the supplier's proposal does not undermine the supplier's obligation to provide the services and to achieve the customer's business objectives.

Also, the customer may want to clarify that the supplier will not be able to make an additional charge for changing how the services are provided, unless this results from a change in the customer's service description.

8.9.4 Controlling changes to the supplier's proposal

The customer may want to clarify that the supplier may not change its solution without the customer's consent. In this way, including the supplier's proposal in the service definition is another method by which the customer may seek to control how the services are provided (assuming that the proposal describes how they will be provided).

From the supplier's perspective, this may undermine its flexibility to change how the services are to be provided during the term of the agreement or impose an unwanted bureaucratic requirement that it will need to satisfy before changing how the services are provided. Accordingly the supplier may need to check the details contained in the proposal to ensure that they are likely to apply throughout the term of the agreement and are not unduly restrictive. It may also want to state that the customer will act reasonably in approving changes to the proposal. Lastly, the supplier may want to restrict the areas where approval will be required. For example, it could restrict the areas to those which:

- (a) are crucial to the delivery of the services and hence were taken into account by the customer in selecting the supplier;
- (b) will result in additional expenditure for the customer; or
- (c) would result in a change in the customer's requirements.

Ideally, the supplier should take into account the fact that, when it prepares its proposal, the customer may regard the proposal as a contractual document. However, if the supplier is in a competitive tendering situation, it may see the proposal as first and foremost a sales document.

Chapter 9

Service Levels or Key Performance Indicators

9.1 Outline

Chapter 8 provides some practical guidance on preparing service descriptions. This chapter discusses the use of service levels and key performance indicators. It applies the distinction between business outcome, service output and input-based outsourcing arrangements explained in Chapter 1, by analysing the manner in which service levels support a business outcome, service output or input-based risk profile. It includes examples of different service level regimes and analyses the behaviour that they encourage. It discusses exclusions of liability and remedies for failure to meet service levels.

9.2 The need for service levels

Except where the agreement says otherwise, the law obliges the supplier to provide the services with reasonable skill and care.[1] The customer may want to document this obligation in the agreement and state that the supplier must provide the services in accordance with good or best industry practice, or similar wording.[2]

Unless the outsourcing arrangement is low value, however, the customer will not usually want to rely solely upon this general obligation and will want to ensure that the service description includes specific service levels (sometimes known as key performance indicators) that set out the precise level at which the service must be provided. It may also want to include service credits that are payable by the supplier if those minimum service levels are not met.[3] In circumstances where service management is regarded as particularly important, the customer may want to include service levels and service credits for failure to comply with key service management obligations.

---

1 Supply of Goods and Services Act 1982.

2 The general obligation to provide the services with reasonable skill and care and in accordance with good or best industry practice can, from the customer's perspective, act as a "catch all" provision, designed to imply obligations which are not expressly covered by the service description. *See* the interesting case of *Vertex Data Science Limited* v *Powergen* [2006] 2 Lloyd's Rep. 591, in which the judge suggested that the requirement that the supplier provide the services with reasonable skill and care and in accordance with best industry practice could be relied upon to imply a level of service which exceeded that required by the service levels: "It is perfectly possible that the terms of the SLA permit a level of performance which is, objectively, unsatisfactory."

3 *See* Chapter 19 for a discussion of service credits.

9.3 Relationship with the customer's business objectives

The service levels that customers put in their service descriptions should support the customer's business objectives and should be consistent with, although probably at a lower level than, those that they have in their strategic plans.

9.3.1 Background to the balanced scorecard

One of the most common ways of translating strategic plans into measurement is through the balanced scorecard. The balanced scorecard was introduced by Kaplan and Norton in the early 1990s, originally as a means to encourage companies to include non-financial measurement in their accounting.

> "The balanced scorecard retains traditional financial measures. But financial measures tell the story of past events ... These financial measures are inadequate ... for guiding and evaluating the journey that information age companies must make to create future value through investment in customers, suppliers, employees, processes, technology, and innovation."

Since it was developed, the balanced scorecard has been extensively adopted by companies within Europe.

9.3.2 Balanced scorecard as a strategic management tool

In practice, the customer may use the balanced scorecard to define critical success factors, upon which the future success of the company's business strategy depends.

The principle behind the use of the balanced scorecard is that these critical success factors should not be limited to financial measures but should also include other measures, such as the relationship between the company and its customers, the efficiency of its internal business processes and its ability to learn and change.

It is interesting that the balanced scorecard was developed during the early 1990s recession as a way of enabling companies to understand the types of critical success factors which would be relevant in a turbulent economy, such as the ability to learn and change and the efficiency of their internal processes. As a result, the balanced scorecard seems particularly relevant in today's economy.

9.3.3 Use of balanced scorecard to define key performance indicators

Using the balanced scorecard, companies define key performance indicators ("KPIs") which measure how successful the company is at achieving the critical success factors referred to above, and hence how successful it is in achieving its business strategy and objectives.

9.3.4 Balanced scorecard in the service level regime

In practice, if a customer uses the balanced scorecard to measure its performance, it will be helpful if its strategic outsourcing service level agreements are drafted in the light of and in support of the relevant business key performance indicators, such as those relating to the efficiency of internal processes. This will align the customer's strategy with its day-to-day requirements and operations. It will ensure that the supplier understands the customer's business objectives and hence ensure that the outsourcing agreement supports achievement of the customer's business objectives. Where relevant, key performance indicators can be used by customers entering into outsourcing agreements directly as the basis for contractual service levels, to ensure that the contractual service levels support the company's business objectives.

9.3.5 Contract scorecard

Leslie Willcocks and Sara Cullen[4] have suggested that, rather than using service levels which flow down from the balanced scorecard in outsourcing agreements, customers should prepare a "contract scorecard". The contract scorecard is based on the same objective as the balanced scorecard in stating that performance measurement should involve more than financial measures. It should evaluate performance in a holistic and balanced manner, to encourage organisations to think more strategically. They argue that it should involve measurement of the following:

(a) financial measures – these will usually be dealt with in the charging schedule to the agreement;
(b) service quality – these will usually be set out in the service level agreement;
(c) relationship – these may be included in a schedule to the contract setting out the relationship charter or code of conduct; and
(d) strategy – these may be set out in a separate schedule to the agreement.

The contract scorecard is designed to articulate the goals of the contract in a measurable form, providing clear explanations as to what is driving the deal.

The contents of the contract scorecard are set out in Table 17.

Table 17 *Contract scorecard – quadrants and contents*

Service quality	*Relationship*
Effectiveness – the degree to which the services produce an end result. For example utilisation, vacancy levels, call reduction and customer retention. **Precision** – the degree to which services are error free. KPIs include accuracy rates, compliance, fit to specification and completeness. **Reliability** – the degree to which services are consistently dependable. KPIs include	**Communication** – the degree to which the parties communicate frequently and honestly. **Creative solutions** – the degree to which the parties continuously search for better ways of doing things. **Conflict resolution** – the degree to which there is a focus on solving problems, not apportioning blame. **Fairness** – the degree to which the

4 *See* Sara Cullen and Leslie Willcocks, "Measuring Success", *The FD's Guide to Outsourcing*, REALFD, 2007.

availability, abandon rates, failure rate, rework and deadlines. **Speed** – KPIs include response rates, queue time, processing time or volumes, turnaround time and backlog clearing. **Satisfaction** – the extent to which customers, users or other stakeholders are pleased with the services.	parties act fairly towards each other. **Integration** – the degree to which the suppliers' value chain appears seamless to the end customer. **Positive interaction** – the degree to which the parties enjoy working together and have respect for one another. **Proactivity** – the degree to which the parties are proactive with each other. **Time investment** – the degree to which the parties provide management time and focus for each other.
Financial	*Strategy*
Historical/baseline – current cost compared to previous periods. KPIs include maintaining costs to a percentage under the historical baseline, ongoing annual reductions or indexation. **Budget/target** – current costs compared to planned expenditure. KPIs are percentage under/over budget/target. **Competitiveness** – current costs compared to the current benchmarked market rates. **Total cost of ownership** ("TCO") – influence upon the cost of the entire supply chain.	**Objective achievement** – the degree to which the strategic reason for the outsourcing has been achieved. **Innovation** – the degree to which better practices and assets have been introduced. **Business contribution** – the degree to which the parties have achieved more out of the deal than the fundamental exchange of money for services. KPIs include level of knowledge transfer provided, number of mutual business initiatives created and implemented and royalties earned. **Alignment to customer's business practices** – the extent to which the supplier conducts business in line with the customer's broader corporate goals. KPIs include safety, use of SMEs, employment created, positions filled by minorities and environmental benefits.

Willcocks and Cullen state that the intention is that the contract scorecard will be used for drafting the contract documentation, selecting the right supplier and monitoring the success of the outsourcing arrangement.

9.4 Relationship with the risk profile

Ideally, the service levels and service credits should support the level of risk that the supplier is accepting.

9.4.1 Business outcome-based service levels

If the supplier accepts responsibility for the achievement of the customer's business outcome (business outcome risk), then the service levels will reflect achievement of the specific business objectives.

9.4.2 Service output-based service levels

Service output-based service levels are usually more powerful than input-based service levels because they relate to the end service being provided to the customer, for example the availability of the services to the customer or end user or the time taken to fix problems. However, care should be taken in drafting the service levels in order to ensure that they encourage the appropriate behaviour. For example, imposing upon the supplier an obligation to ensure that, measured on a monthly basis, all defects are corrected within eight hours, could encourage the supplier to refrain from carrying out preventative maintenance so that small defects arise which the supplier can correct quickly, thus improving the average statistics for the time to fix defects. In this situation, the customer could include additional supporting service levels which ensure that the supplier carries out the corrective maintenance on a regular basis, as agreed, or ensure that there are no more than a specified maximum number of defects per period, if this is acceptable to the supplier.

The supplier may be unwilling to commit to meeting service output-based service levels if it does not have sufficient control over whether the service levels are achieved, for example, if the achievement of the service levels is dependant upon the customer's behaviour or is dependant upon the cooperation of other suppliers of the customer (unless all of the suppliers set up a supplier joint venture to provide services to the customer). If the customer were to insist upon the supplier guaranteeing service levels in this situation, with service credits applying for any service level failure, then the supplier might decide that it was prudent to increase its charges by the amount of the relevant service credits. In this situation, the service credits would encourage the supplier to meet the service levels, as the service credits would operate as a bonus payable to the extent to which the service levels were met.

In an extreme situation, however, where the supplier is unable to influence whether the service levels are met or not, it is difficult to see how the service credits could serve any useful purpose.

In other circumstances, the supplier may be unable to achieve service levels requested by the customer without making substantial changes to the assets used to provide the services. For example, to guarantee certain levels of system availability, it may need to provide a parallel system on which the customer's application will run if the main server is unavailable. It is important in this situation for the customer to be aware of the implications of its decisions. It may be that it is critical to the customer's business that the service levels are achieved, so that the service levels are achieving exactly the desired business objective, namely ensuring that the supplier changes how the services are provided so as to improve performance.

In many cases, however, the customer will need to find a balance between the level of service that it wants the supplier to guarantee and the charges it is willing to pay.

9.4.3 Input-based service levels

If the supplier cannot commit to service output-based service levels, then input-based service levels on their own may be helpful. For example if the supplier cannot commit to rectifying defects in a complex application within a certain amount of time, it may be able to commit to commencing work on rectifying the problem within a specified time frame.

In addition, even if the supplier is able to guarantee the service output-based service levels, some of the input-based service levels may be useful where the customer wants reassurance that the inputs will be satisfied. For example the customer may want to ensure that the obligation to fix defects in the services does not encourage the supplier to refrain from carrying out preventative maintenance (as mentioned above).

9.5 Examples of service levels

There are various types of service levels that can be included in a service description. *See* Table 18 for examples of service levels that can be included in outsourcing contracts.

Table 18 *Types of service levels*

Service levels that are business outcome based

These will depend upon the specific business objective that the customer is endeavouring to satisfy. For example, if the customer's objective is to improve the speed of its billing process, then the service levels may relate to the time taken to prepare and send out bills.

Service levels that are service output based

Availability: For example availability (or uptime) of a system or service. The parties will need to define when the service will be regarded as being available. The supplier may insist that the services are not regarded as being unavailable during periods of scheduled down-time or scheduled maintenance.

Reliability: For example downtime duration or downtime frequency.

Response times: For example the response time of a system will not exceed a specified number of seconds. This will show how quickly the system is working. If it is slow, it may be unworkable. The supplier may be required to achieve the response time in all cases or in a specified percentage of cases.

Time to fix (resolution time): For example, time within which the supplier will fix incidents, whether measured for all incidents or by the priority of the incidents. The parties will need to decide when the clock starts ticking and when it stops ticking. The customer will not want the period to end when the supplier decides to close the call unless the incident has been resolved. If the customer's representative who reported the fault is unavailable, the supplier will not want the period to continue until the customer confirms that the incident has been resolved.

Capacity management: For example:

(a) the number of incidents due to capacity issues; or
(b) the ability of the supplier to meet the customer's demand.

Security: For example:

(a) the number of security violations;
(b) the number of situations in which security is not monitored including where events are not detected and logged; or
(c) the number of situations in which physical access controls or logical security is not maintained.

Backups: For example, all backups are taken as agreed.

Configuration management: For example:

(a) the number of observed differences between the records and the situation found during an audit;
(b) the number of occasions on which a recorded configuration could not be located;
(c) the time needed to process a request for recording information.

Change management: For example:

(a) the rate at which changes are implemented;
(b) the number of incidents resulting from changes;
(c) the number of back outs related to changes;
(d) the number of changes within resource and time estimation.

Service levels which are input based

Help desk or call centre phone answered: For example, the number of times the phone rings or the number of seconds it takes before the phone is answered by the supplier's help desk. The supplier may be required to achieve the service level in all cases or in a specified percentage of cases. The customer should consider whether the service level will discourage call centre staff from dealing with calls thoroughly if they can see that other calls are waiting.

Fault logging: For example, the number of calls not logged by the supplier's help desk. The supplier will usually be required to log all calls.

Time to respond: The time taken from when the supplier becomes aware of an incident or from when the incident is reported to the supplier's help desk until the supplier takes substantial action to correct the incident. This service level may be useful if the supplier cannot guarantee to fix incidents by a certain time.

Call to site: The time taken from when the supplier becomes aware of an incident or from when the incident is reported to the supplier's help desk until the supplier attends the customer's site to fix an incident. This service level may be useful if the supplier cannot guarantee to fix incidents by a certain time.

Utilisation not to exceed specified percentages or cache memory available/unused hard disk capacity to exceed specified percentages: For example, utilisation of the central processing unit ("CPU") of hardware or of a telecommunications network over a specified period. This service level may be useful if the supplier cannot guarantee a response time for the system or network.

Service levels to incentivise reductions in repeat calls

Repeat problems: For example, the number of successful security or virus breaches that are exploiting a security or virus weakness previously identified.

Service levels to incentivise first fixes

First fixes: The percentage of calls resolved whilst the caller is still on the line. The customer should consider whether this service level will encourage the supplier to refrain from preventing minor faults occurring so that it can remedy them when the faults are reported to the help desk.

Service levels measuring "soft" factors

Customer satisfaction: Customer satisfaction will often be a key element of the services and the customer may want to measure the level of customer satisfaction as part of the service levels by distributing questionnaires to users. If the users are employees of the customer, however, the supplier may be reluctant to accept the payment of service credits if customer satisfaction falls, because it will be concerned that the customer may be able to influence its employees. In this situation, the supplier may suggest the payment of a bonus for high levels of customer satisfaction. If the services are being provided to members of the public then the results of any customer satisfaction survey or "mystery shopper" survey may be regarded as being more reliable.

Service levels which can be business outcome, service output or input based

Completion of specified actions within a specified period: For example, acknowledgment of faxes or emails to the supplier's help desk, notification of security problems to the customer, preparation of accurate and complete management reports, printing of documents, updating the asset register, retrieving tapes and restoring data from backups, implementing changes, removal of access to a system, grant of access to a system, completion of monthly financial accounts etc.

Classification: For example, the number of incidents initially classified correctly by the supplier.

Routing: For example, the number of incidents routed correctly by the supplier.

9.6 Defining the service levels

For all service levels, the parties will need to agree how these will operate. Service levels need to be SMART, that is, specific, measurable, achievable, real and time bound. Defining the service levels will involve considering the factors specified in Table 19.

Table 19 *Definition and operation of service levels*

Definition of the service levels

How is the specific service level defined, for example, what is regarded as availability and where is it measured?

Period

Over what period will the service levels be measured: weekly, monthly, eight-week running periods, quarterly or annually? (If the service levels are to be calculated as an average over this period, then calculating the service levels over a longer period will mean it is possible that the services will be extremely bad for a short period and yet that the supplier will still meet the overall service levels.)

Service hours

During what hours will the service levels be measured: over a 24-hour, seven-days-a-week basis or only during specified service hours?

Transition period

Will service levels apply from the commencement of the services or will there be a transition period during which the service levels will not apply or different service levels will apply?

Will the service levels vary during the term of the agreement, for example gradually improving?

Measurement

How will achievement of the service levels be measured?

9.7 Customer due diligence

Before the customer is able to define its desired service levels, it will usually need to carry out a detailed due diligence exercise, as stressed in Chapter 2. The due diligence exercise should cover the details of the service levels being achieved prior to the outsourcing arrangement and of the changes that will need to be made in these service levels so that they will reflect the customer's business objectives and service requirements. Lastly, the customer may want to benchmark the service levels it is achieving against those being achieved by its competitors (if the relevant information is available) to ensure that the customer's business will remain competitive.

9.8 Supplier due diligence and agreement of service levels

The supplier will need to satisfy itself that it can provide the services in accordance with the service levels before it commits to meeting them. If the supplier's acceptance of the service levels is dependent upon an understanding that the customer or previous supplier is meeting certain service levels, then the supplier has two options.

9.8.1 Warranty

The supplier may request that the customer provide a warranty that it has been meeting the service levels. However, the customer may be reluctant to provide warranties of this nature because it means that it is taking the risk that the information is incorrect.

9.8.2 Due diligence

Alternatively, the supplier can rely upon its own due diligence, which means that the supplier takes the risk that its due diligence has been inadequate and that it will not be able to provide the services to the specified service levels.

9.8.3 Advantages for supplier of agreeing service levels after signature

The supplier may prefer to enter into an agreement when the services are defined but the service levels and service credits are not, with an agreement that it will carry out due diligence after signature of the agreement.[5] In some situations, this may be a reasonable stance based upon the difficulty that the parties have in ascertaining what service levels the customer or previous supplier was actually achieving. Deferring agreement of the service levels, from the supplier's perspective, may be ideal as it means that the supplier does not need to take the risk that its due diligence has been inadequate and that it will not be able to provide the services to the specified service levels. It means that the supplier does not have to commit to achieving specific service levels until it has taken over provision of the services and has accurate statistics of the service levels it is achieving in practice.

9.8.4 Disadvantages for customer of agreeing service levels after signature

From the customer's perspective, however, this approach is rarely to be recommended. The disadvantage of delaying agreement of the service levels and service credits until after signature of the agreement is that the customer's bargaining power may have eroded after signature and it may be negotiating from a position of weakness. The customer will be dependent upon the supplier to agree to any service levels or service credits and the supplier does not benefit from agreeing any service levels or credits.

The situation is different from that mentioned in Chapter 7, where the supplier starts to provide the services before the detailed service description is agreed, because, in that case, both parties

---

5 The parties should also consider whether failure to agree the service levels will mean that there is no binding agreement between the parties due to a failure to agree a fundamental issue. *See Willis Management (Isle of Man) Ltd & Willis UK Ltd* v *Cable & Wireless Plc & Pender Insurance Ltd* [2005] EWCA Civ 806.

have an interest in ensuring that the service description is agreed. The situation is different here, in that the supplier may be happy to be a party to an agreement that does not impose any service levels or credits upon it and agreements to agree the service levels after signature of the agreement are not sufficiently precise to be enforceable at law. In practice, where service levels and service credits are not agreed before signature, in many cases they are never agreed, and the customer is left without any commitment from the supplier as to the level of service to be provided. It is possible for the customer to reserve certain rights, for example to terminate the agreement, if the service levels are not agreed within a certain period, but the cost and inconvenience of terminating the agreement will usually discourage the customer from exercising the right.

9.8.5 A compromise

Where the customer has not documented the service levels it has been achieving but would like the supplier to commit to achieving the same service levels (where perhaps the customer's objective is to enter into the agreement speedily on the basis that the supplier will provide similar services but at a cheaper price), the parties may be able to agree the principles surrounding the contractual service levels without agreeing the exact availability percentage etc. to be reached. This would be achieved by documenting the types of service levels to be measured (e.g. availability) and stating that the contractual service levels will be those achieved by the customer during the period of months after contract signature or prior to contract signature, if this will be ascertainable after signature (e.g. 97 per cent). The parties can specify dispute resolution procedures that will be followed if the parties cannot agree what the service levels were. This approach can be avoided if the customer has been able to carry out the due diligence specified in Chapter 2.

9.9 Transitional service levels

Even where the parties have been able to define and agree suitable service levels in the agreement, the supplier may not be able to commit to meeting the service levels from the first day of the agreement. It may need to make changes to the manner in which the services are provided, for example if the service levels are more exacting than those previously being met. The supplier may suggest that the service levels do not apply during this transition period. An alternative approach may be for the customer to suggest that the supplier maintains the services at the levels previously being achieved by the customer, until the improvements are made, to avoid a situation in which no service levels apply. The acceptability of this proposal to the supplier will depend upon the exact details of the transition.

The length of any transition period will depend upon the time that the supplier will need to implement improvements in the services.

Where the supplier is initially providing the services using legacy third-party supplier contracts entered into by the customer, the supplier may suggest that the transition period ties in with the period of notice required to terminate the legacy agreements with relevant third-party suppliers and replace them. If the customer is unwilling to agree to this, then the supplier may need to calculate its charges on the basis of a period of overlap between the legacy suppliers and the replacement third-party suppliers. In either case, the customer should understand the charging implications of the different options open to it.

9.10 Restrictions on liability

The supplier will want to ensure that it is not responsible for failure to provide the services or meet the service levels as a result of a force majeure event. (*See* Chapter 30 for a more detailed discussion of force majeure events.)

In addition, the supplier should consider any actions that it needs the customer to carry out in order that it can provide the services to the service levels. The supplier will not expect to be liable if it is unable to provide the services where this results from the customer's failure to comply with its responsibilities. (*See* Chapter 12 for a more detailed discussion of the customer's obligations.)

Lastly, the supplier may want to exclude liability for meeting the service levels if the volume of services exceeds specified limits, for example in a telecommunications outsourcing agreement if the traffic exceeds the allocated bandwidth or the number of queries to the call centre exceeds a specified number. Where appropriate, taking into account the nature of the services, the customer may want the supplier to take responsibility for monitoring volumes or capacity and anticipating demand, so that sufficient volume or capacity can be provided before the service levels are affected. For other types of services, it may be appropriate for the customer to be obliged to notify the supplier if it takes steps that are likely to increase the volume of services. For example, if the supplier is providing a call centre which takes orders for the customer's products, the supplier may want the customer to notify it if it is planning a marketing campaign which is designed to increase demand for its products.

9.11 Remedies for failure to meet service levels

If the supplier fails to meet the service levels, the customer will want the supplier to commit to correcting the failure, at no additional charge, where the failure can be remedied and to correct the reason for the failure so that the problem does not recur.

The customer may also want the supplier to commit to paying service credits if it fails to meet the service levels. Service credits are discussed in greater detail in Chapter 19.

Some customers feel that service credits are an unhelpful remedy as any reduction in the supplier's revenue is likely to reduce the sums of money which the supplier has available to invest in correcting problems with the services. As a result, they seek creative solutions as to how to incentivise suppliers to meet the service levels. One solution is for customers to define contracted service levels and "performance targets" which measure the extent to which the supplier is supporting achievement of the customer's business objectives, as reviewed and updated by the customer on a regular basis. The supplier is contractually obliged to meet the service levels but not the performance targets. However, if the supplier meets the service levels and the performance targets, it is awarded an automatic extension to the term of the outsourcing contract, unless the customer's business objectives make this undesirable. This approach formalises and clarifies the extension process, taking into account that, in any event, the customer is likely to extend the agreement if the supplier is providing a good service and supporting the customer's business objectives. An interesting variation to this approach includes a process for automatically reducing the term of the outsourcing agreement if service levels are not met. This approach presents problems for suppliers who have intended to spread their fixed costs over the term of the outsourcing agreement, taking one step further as it does the right of the customer to terminate the agreement if the supplier fails to meet relevant service levels.

Lastly, the customer will want the supplier to be committed to meeting the service levels so that any failure to meet them will constitute a breach of the agreement, and the customer may want the right to terminate the agreement if certain levels of service are not achieved over a specific period or if there are persistent minor breaches of the service levels. Termination rights are discussed in greater detail in Chapter 23.

Chapter 10

Governance

10.1 Outline

Chapters 7, 8 and 9 cover the services that the supplier must provide and the service levels that the supplier must meet in providing the services. This chapter describes the management of the outsourcing arrangement. Adequate governance of the outsourcing arrangement is a key success factor.

10.2 Managing the transition

It is important that the transition process between the previous services and the outsourced services is managed correctly. This will be particularly important for developmental or transformational outsourcing arrangements where considerable change may occur during the transition. Transitional and transformational outsourcing arrangements are defined and described in Chapter 21.

Managing the transition will usually entail the customer and supplier appointing a transition team who will be responsible for ensuring a smooth transition.

It will also entail them agreeing and maintaining a detailed project plan describing:

(a) the obligations of the members of the transition team;
(b) the interrelationship between each party's obligations;
(c) the key deliverables which will be delivered as part of the transition process; and
(d) the dates by which the deliverables should be completed by the relevant party.

Agreeing a detailed transition plan will ensure that everyone knows what they need to do to ensure a successful transition and by when. It will help each side to allocate the appropriate resources to the tasks for which they are responsible.

One party will need to be responsible for project managing the transition. This will usually be the supplier. If, however, the customer has adopted a multisourcing approach (where different services are provided by different suppliers as described in Chapter 17), the customer will usually be responsible for managing the integration of services provided by the different suppliers.

The project manager will need to monitor achievement against the project plan so that he can see where the problem areas are and ensure that any necessary correctional action is taken promptly.

10.3 Communicating the customer's business objectives

Another important aspect of managing the transition involves communicating the customer's business objectives. This may involve the customer preparing and implementing a communications policy which details how it will communicate the customer's business objectives to staff, users and other stakeholders. Chapter 27 discusses in greater detail the issues relating to the transfer of staff from the customer to the supplier and the importance of consulting with them.

The customer will also need to manage the expectation of users. For example, if the customer's business objective is to reduce costs and hence the arrangement requires the supplier to achieve service levels that are lower than those previously being achieved in practice by the customer or its previous supplier, then unless this is explained carefully to users, they will usually conclude that the supplier is providing a poor service and that the outsourcing initiative is a failure.

In appropriate circumstances, the communications policy should also cover how the customer is going to explain its outsourcing strategy to the press. This is particularly important, for example, if one of the customer's business objectives is to improve its share price.

10.4 Managing the services

10.4.1 Appointment of managers

The parties will usually want to agree how the supplier will manage the services on an ongoing basis, after transition. This may involve the supplier appointing certain individuals to manage aspects of the services, for example a service manager, project manager, programme manager or account development manager. The customer may want some control over the identity of the individuals appointed to these roles. The customer may also want the supplier to commit to giving a specified period of notice before it replaces the key individuals. Lastly, the customer may want the supplier to commit to maintaining continuity of services when the key individuals are replaced.

The controls mentioned above relating to the key individuals are all interferences with *how* the supplier provides the services. Nevertheless, they are not usually contentious from the perspective of the supplier. In practice, the customer is unlikely to be satisfied with the services if it is not impressed with the supplier's key personnel and so it is in both parties' interests that the supplier's key personnel are respected by and able to work with the customer.

The supplier may be concerned primarily to see that the right cannot be abused (e.g. by stating that the customer must act reasonably in approving or rejecting a candidate for a key role, and must notify the supplier of its reasons for accepting or rejecting a candidate in writing). Second, the supplier will need to ensure that, from a practical and legal perspective, it can comply with the provisions. Therefore, it will want to make it clear that it is not required to give a period of advance notice of the replacement of the key individual if, for example, he is injured.

10.4.2 Reports

The supplier will usually be obliged to produce reports summarising its performance over the previous month or quarter and comparing performance with previous periods, so that the customer can audit the provision of the services by the supplier. The sort of information that may be required by the customer is specified in Table 20.

Table 20 *Supplier's performance*

Problems

Any problems affecting the services reported to the supplier's help desk including the nature of the problem, the name of the person reporting the problem, the date and time when the problem was reported, the cause of the problem, the action taken to correct the problem and the time and date when the problem was corrected.

Complaints

Complaints made about the services, including the nature of the complaint, the name of the person making the complaint, the date and time when it was received, the action taken to remedy the complaint and the date and time when the remedy was completed. This information may be maintained in a complaints register.

Service levels

The service levels achieved by the supplier and any service credits payable by the supplier.

The reports may be collated automatically by the supplier's management systems and the customer may be given online access to the information. The parties will usually meet at regular service review meetings to discuss the service reports.

The customer may want to apply service levels and service credits to the delivery of service management reports by the supplier.

10.5 Managing problems

The supplier may use the reports to analyse the cause of problems proactively and hence prevent their recurrence. For example, the reports may show a need for the supplier to improve the training it has given to users.

ITIL, which describes best practice in IT service management[1] makes a distinction between "incident management" and "problem management". The intention behind the terminology is to distinguish between rapid return of service and identifying and remedying the cause of the incident.

1 *See* 7.2.3.4 for an explanation of ITIL.

10.5.1 Incident management

Incidents include any interruption or reduction in the quality of a service.

Incident management aims to resolve the incident and restore the provision of services speedily. It includes recording, classifying and allocating incidents to appropriate specialists. Incident progress is then monitored; incidents are resolved and closed.

10.5.2 Problem management

Problems include undesirable situations indicating the unknown root cause of one or more existing or potential incidents.

If a problem is suspected, problem management aims to identify the underlying cause and prevent incidents from recurring. Problem management includes reactive and proactive activities. Reactive activities aim to identify the root cause of past incidents and present proposals for improvement or rectification. Proactive problem management aims to prevent incidents from recurring by identifying weaknesses in the infrastructure and making proposals to eliminate them.

10.6 Managing future requirements

The reports produced by the supplier may also be used to carry out trend analysis. Thus the customer may want the supplier to take responsibility for analysing trends in usage by the customer (e.g. an increase in calls to a customer call centre), forecasting future requirements by the customer and proposing appropriate amendments to the services.

10.7 Encouraging innovation

Lastly, the reports produced by the supplier may be used to show areas where the services should be changed or improved so as to improve the quality of the services or reduce the charges.

The supplier may be required to produce a regular service improvement plan (e.g. quarterly or annual). Where appropriate, the supplier may be asked to include in its charges the cost of carrying out a survey of up-to-date technology that may be used to improve the operation of the services and to include recommendations for incorporating the technology in its service improvement plan.

It may be useful for the supplier to be required to carry out a customer or user satisfaction survey before it prepares the service improvement plan, and to use any feedback obtained from the survey and any feedback obtained from the complaints procedure to suggest relevant improvements to the services. The customer may also want to suggest specific concerns that it has, to assist the supplier to focus its attention. Lastly, the customer may also want to benchmark the services against other services available in the marketplace to see if there are ways that they can be improved.

From the supplier's perspective, it is important that any changes to the services recommended by the supplier or proposed by the customer should constitute changes to the services to be agreed by the parties under the change control procedure, so that that supplier has an opportunity to make additional charges for improvements in the services. Assuming that this principle is agreed by the customer, the supplier will often be willing to prepare the service improvement plan itself at no additional charge to the customer, either because the charge is already included in the charges for the outsourced services or because it sees the preparation of the plan as an opportunity to interest the customer in investing further sums of money in the services.

Change management is dealt with in greater detail in Chapter 22.

10.8 Managing the customer's business objectives

The customer must also manage the outsourcing arrangement at a strategic level to ensure that it continues to satisfy the customer's business objectives.

10.8.1 Achievement of current objectives

This involves the customer monitoring the arrangement to ensure that it is satisfying its current business objective. In circumstances where the customer is not achieving its business aims, it will want to analyse the reasons for this and what correctional steps will need to be taken to remedy the situation, for example whether training is required to ensure that users take full advantage of the improved services.

10.8.2 Changed business objectives

It also involves the customer recognising when its business objectives change and modifying the outsourcing arrangement to ensure that it supports the changed business objectives.

It is important that the customer realises that it cannot outsource responsibility for deciding upon its business strategy and objectives, although the supplier may be able to assist by providing advice.

10.8.3 Relationship between technical developments and changed business objectives

In practice, the processes described in 10.7 and 10.8.2 above interrelate, with the supplier explaining how new technology and new working practices can bring business benefit to the customer and the customer deciding upon its desired business goals in the light of what is achievable bearing in mind the new technology.

10.8.4 Partnership board

The customer may want to establish procedures for ensuring that strategic issues relating to the outsourcing arrangement are considered, for example by setting up a joint partnership or partnering board with the supplier.[2]

2 It is common to refer to the board as a "partnership" board to embody the concept that the parties will be working together to ensure the success of the arrangement. The parties should be aware that "partnership" has a specific legal meaning in English law. A partnership is defined in Section 1(1) Partnership Act 1890 as "the relation which subsists between persons carrying on a business in common with a view of profit". Therefore, the outsourcing agreement will not be a partnership in the strict legal sense.

10.9 Managing the customer's obligations

Just as the supplier will need to manage its responsibilities under the arrangement, if the customer has substantial responsibilities, for example in an IT or business process outsourcing arrangement, then it will need to manage these. Sometimes the supplier will suggest that, just as the customer has a right to approve the supplier's key individuals, it should have a right to approve the customer's key representative, on the basis that, if the outsourcing arrangement is to be a success, both parties will need to be able to work together.

10.10 Managing security

The customer will want to monitor the compliance by the supplier with its security obligations. It will also need to ensure that its security requirements are reviewed and updated as changes in security risks and solutions occur. Security issues are dealt with in greater detail in Chapter 32.

10.11 Managing risk

Chapter 2 explains the importance of the parties preparing a risk register. The parties will need to review the risk register on a regular basis to ensure that any risks which may affect the outsourcing arrangement are mitigated by the party best able to deal with them.

10.12 Managing integration

If the customer has adopted a multisourcing approach (*see* Chapter 17 for an explanation of this approach), it will need to manage the integration of the supplier's services with services provided by other suppliers. It may want the supplier to commit to cooperating with its other suppliers.

10.13 Managing value for money

The customer will also need to manage the financial aspects of the transaction to ensure that it continues to provide value for money. This issue is addressed in Chapter 20.

10.14 Audit rights

The customer will want the supplier to carry out audits to ensure that its staff are complying with the agreement and (where relevant taking into account the services) are not committing any fraudulent or inappropriate actions.

The customer will also want to reserve the right to audit the supplier's performance and charges.[3]

10.14.1 Who needs the right to audit?

The customer and its auditors will need audit rights.

If the customer is in a regulated sector (e.g. the public sector, utilities or the financial services sector) then the customer's regulator will also need audit rights. Customers in regulated sectors must ensure that they have all necessary audit rights under their outsourcing agreements – this may include sector-specific requirements not mentioned in 10.14.2 to 10.14.8 below.

10.14.2 What audit rights will the customer need?

The customer will usually need the right to audit:

- (a) compliance with the terms of the agreement;
- (b) the quality of the services provided by the supplier (e.g. by using a mystery caller to review how the supplier's staff deal with calls to its call centre);
- (c) the assets used to provide the services;
- (d) any charges payable by the customer; and
- (e) any charges proposed by the supplier for additional services or changes to the services.

3 Various issues arise in relation to audit rights in a dispute situation where both parties will want to see documents held by the other party for the purposes of establishing or defeating a claim. In practice, a party with audit rights, in addition to relying on available court procedures, may seek to use audit rights to gain access to documentation. The question arises as to whether this leads to an uneven playing field. A litigation pre-action protocol, introduced in April 2003, provides that both parties to a dispute in England must, by exchange of correspondence, provide full details of claims and defences, together with documentation relied upon. Each party is also entitled to ask the other party for documents within that party's possession which they consider to be relevant to the issues in dispute. The object of this procedure is to facilitate early consideration by both parties of the strengths and weaknesses of their position with a view to encouraging early settlement and the avoidance of court proceedings. A further opportunity to obtain disclosure of documents from the other party will arise during the course of any litigation subsequently issued in the event that a settlement cannot be reached. In general terms, each party will be obliged to disclose to the other party documents which adversely affect its own case or support the other party's case, in addition to documents upon which it relies. In theory, therefore, this means that each party should be operating on equal terms. However, a contractual right of access to documentation may give the party with the rights an advantage in that it will be able to see some or all or the other party's documents in advance of the litigation procedures referred to above. Although court procedures do permit applications for pre-action disclosure, the circumstances in which this will be permitted are very limited. In addition, following the introduction of the Woolf Reforms in April 1999, a party has the right to argue during the course of litigation that an exhaustive search for documents that would normally fall within the scope of the disclosure obligation would be unreasonable, perhaps for reasons of cost. If this argument is accepted by the court, the extent of disclosure ordered may be reduced or restricted. In such circumstances, a party with audit rights may have an advantage that it will attempt to exploit. This situation is one that the parties may wish to address at the drafting stage, perhaps by making clear that the right of audit is to be limited to particular circumstances or perhaps that the right of access should be a mutual one.

The customer, its third-party auditors and any relevant regulators may also need the right to investigate whether the customer is complying with relevant regulations.

10.14.3 What would the audit involve?

The customer will want the supplier to:

(a) maintain relevant records and grant access to them;
(b) grant the customer access to the assets, premises and staff used to provide the services; and
(c) cooperate with the audit and provide reasonable assistance in carrying it out.

10.14.4 Audit costs

The supplier, at no additional charge, may be able to provide access to:

(a) existing records; or
(b) records which it is notified before the agreement is signed that it will need to maintain.

It may be willing to provide reasonable access and cooperation if the audit arises out of problems with the supplier's service. Otherwise, it will usually want to charge for any additional costs of complying with the audit.

The customer will not want to pay for the audit if it relates to a failure by the supplier to comply with its obligations.

10.14.5 Confidentiality

The supplier may want to be reassured that any information disclosed during the audit will be confidential and that the audit will not (where this is a possibility because of the nature of the services) be carried out by a competitor of the supplier.

It may want to restrict access to its proprietary materials or to information relating to how its charges are broken down (so-called "open book information").

10.14.6 Interruption to supplier's business

The supplier may have security and operational issues which may mean that it will need to restrict the access that it is able to give to its sites. Even where it is able to grant access, it may want the customer to fix a convenient appointment before it turns up at a site and requests access. If the outsourcing services are such that the supplier or its employees may have an opportunity to defraud the customer (e.g. outsourcing of a payroll service, a billing service, a collections service or a local authority revenues and benefits service), then the customer will need special rights if there is a real suspicion of fraud, including the right to demand records and access without notice. If the customer is regulated by the FSA, the FSA will also want the right to gain access to the supplier's premises without notice.

10.14.7 Enhanced audit rights

In certain cases, the customer may want the right to require the supplier to implement reasonable actions necessary to deal with a supplier default. This remedy would enable the customer to interfere directly with how the supplier is providing the services and so is likely to be resisted by suppliers. Nevertheless, it may be appropriate in certain circumstances, for example where the customer is a public sector body and the action has been required by the National Audit Office (for central government) the Audit Commission (for local authority and non-Crown bodies) or the customer is subject to another regulator (e.g. the FSA) who has required the action.

10.14.8 Material breach

From the customer's perspective, cooperation with reasonable audit requirements (particularly if the customer is in a regulated industry), may be seen as being central to the relationship between the parties, and the customer may want to specify that refusal by the supplier to cooperate with audits may constitute a remediable material breach of the agreement which would entitle the customer to terminate the agreement. (*See* Chapter 23 for a discussion of rights of termination.)

Chapter 11

Dealing with Disputes

11.1 Outline

Chapter 11 deals with day-to-day aspects of managing the services. Service management should also cover the management of disputes relating to the outsourcing. This involves two aspects. First, it involves each party ensuring that it maintains all relevant documentation including change controls, correspondence, complaints, formal notices etc. relating to the outsourcing arrangement. Each party may want to maintain a central repository for the documentation. It will also need to document any disputes with the other side, so that, for example, if the service is suffering as a result of the customer failing to comply with its obligations, then the supplier can later prove by reference to contemporaneous documents that this is the case.

The second aspect involves procedures that may be used to resolve disputes between the parties. These are dealt with in this chapter. It includes a brief description of escalation, alternative dispute resolution procedures and litigation.

11.2 Internal escalation procedure

Escalating disputes within the customer and supplier organisations can be one of the most useful ways of resolving them. Outsourcing arrangements often last several years, with both supplier and customer investing considerable time, effort and money in the arrangement. If there is a dispute, both parties usually have an incentive to work together to resolve differences between them. Escalation may involve, for example, copying the service delivery reports referred to in Chapter 10 to senior management or requiring senior management on both sides to attend services meetings to resolve problems. Where the problems relate to problems with service provision, this will usually involve senior management agreeing and monitoring the implementation of a correction plan which sets out how any service failures are to be corrected.

In practice, in dispute situations, it can sometimes be helpful to agree a swap of personnel so that employees of the supplier and customer have an opportunity to gain a greater understanding of the other side's concerns and needs. If the customer agrees a swap of personnel, it should ensure that this will not undermine the supplier's liability for any service failures.

11.3 Alternative dispute resolution

If internal escalation fails, the parties may want to move on to "alternative" dispute resolution procedures (so called because they are alternatives to litigation).

The most frequently used of these (mediation, early neutral evaluation, mini trial, expert determination and arbitration) are described in 11.4 to 11.8 below. All can be extremely valuable in the right circumstances. However, an important distinction to bear in mind when considering the various forms of ADR is the distinction between those that are aimed at assisting the parties to reach agreement and those that result in a binding and enforceable determination by a third party.

11.4 Mini trial/executive tribunal

In most forms of mini trial or executive tribunal, lawyers or other advisers for each party present a "mini" version of their case to a panel made up of a senior executive of their client and of the other party. A neutral third party is sometimes invited to chair the panel. The objective of the process is to provide a useful starting point from which the parties can attempt to negotiate a resolution. The presentation enables the senior executives to get to grips with the issues in the dispute, and the strengths and weaknesses on each side. The involvement of senior executives in the negotiation process brings an element of detachment that may not be present between the representatives on each side actually involved in the dispute at an operational level. Provision for a mini trial or executive tribunal is becoming more common as part of an escalation procedure in commercial agreements.

11.5 Mediation

Mediation is a consensual process where representatives of each party come together for an agreed period (usually one day) and, with the assistance of a trained third party (the mediator), attempt to reach a settlement of the dispute. If terms are agreed, a settlement agreement is drawn up and signed. If the parties cannot reach agreement, they are free to revert to other forms of process. All of the discussions or negotiations that take place during mediation remain confidential and may not be disclosed to a third party.

Mediation is generally considered to be of considerable value in relation to disputes arising in a long-term commercial relationship. If the parties need to work together for several more years there is an obvious incentive to finding a solution without resorting to the courts. Another feature of mediation which makes it particularly suitable where the parties are in an ongoing relationship is the fact that a mediator, in trying to establish some common ground upon which a settlement can be reached, will often try to explore with the parties factors outside the dispute itself to see if there are commercial matters not directly connected with the dispute but which may assist the parties in reaching a commercial compromise acceptable on both sides. For example, if the dispute is about whether the supplier is due an additional payment for the services, a settlement in which the amount paid is significantly less than that claimed but where the customer will also commit itself to placing an order for additional services may well be acceptable to both parties and may allow the parties to preserve the relationship more or less intact.

Mediation clauses in commercial agreements are now extremely common. For example, central government has made it clear that, where the other party agrees, they should be included in public sector contracts.

Even if the contract does not contain a mediation clause there is no reason why one of the parties should not suggest mediation. Mediation is now accepted as a commercial and pragmatic approach to a dispute. In addition, should one of the parties to the outsourcing arrangement later have to litigate, the court can impose costs sanctions on a party if it is deemed to have acted unreasonably in refusing to mediate.

11.6 Early neutral evaluation

Early neutral evaluation ("ENE") is not a procedure for which specific provision is often made in agreements, but it is an option that it may be appropriate to consider if there is a dispute in relation to a particular question or issue. ENE is a process by which the parties agree to refer a particular dispute or issue to a third party (often a lawyer) for an opinion on the merits, i.e. which of the parties has the better case. The opinion is not binding in any way and the parties remain free to take the matter to litigation or another form of dispute resolution process. As a matter of practice, however, the opinion obtained can be very persuasive in causing the "losing" party to rethink its position.

11.7 Expert determination

Essentially, an expert determination is where the parties agree to refer the dispute to a third party with a particular technical expertise. In many cases, the expert will have no formal legal background. The exercise is very often done on paper without any oral presentation of the arguments. Each party will provide the expert with written submissions setting out its case and supported by relevant documents. There may be an opportunity for each party to reply to the submissions made by his opponent and the expert will then make his decision. With some limited exceptions, the decision of the expert is final and binding – there is no appeal.

The advantages of this process are that, because of the procedure adopted, the cost and, perhaps more importantly, the delay involved is likely to be significantly less than most other forms of dispute resolution.

Expert determination is appropriate if the dispute is concerned solely with a technical issue – for example, did work performed comply with a specification or has a financial calculation been undertaken correctly? However, it is important to ensure that the expert has the appropriate skills to decide the specific dispute. The expert may be, for example, an IT expert or an accountant. The expert may indeed be a lawyer if, for example, the dispute concerns the proper meaning to be given to a particular contractual provision; in such circumstances, it may be helpful to appoint a senior barrister to act as an expert to give a decision on the correct reading of the clause.

11.8 Adjudication

Adjudication is a form of hybrid procedure. It provides for an independent third party (the adjudicator) to decide the dispute within a very short time frame. The adjudicator's decision is binding, but only for an interim period – perhaps until conclusion of the contract and/or until review of the decision by way of arbitration. It is most commonly used in the construction industry following the introduction of compulsory statutory adjudication by the Housing Grants, Construction and Generation Act 1996. The acknowledged advantage of adjudication in a construction dispute is to obtain a quick interim decision and thereby limit the potential for the dispute to hold up progress on the wider project. In this sense, adjudication is effective in producing a fast "rough and ready" result that meets operational needs. In a significant number of cases, parties decide to live with the adjudicator's decision, that is, they do not exercise their right to challenge it by way of arbitration. This is seen as another of its advantages. Although still a relatively novel approach, some form of adjudication process is now sometimes included in outsourcing agreements. The parallels with a construction contract are obvious: the parties are often working together on a long-term project with a number of critical deadlines for completion of work product. The obtaining of a quick interim decision on a dispute can often prevent time and effort being diverted away from the project.

11.9 Arbitration

If the parties become involved in a full-blown dispute which it appears can only be resolved by a full judicial process that will result in a binding determination, then the parties may want to consider arbitration as an alternative to litigation. If the outsourcing arrangement involves parties from different jurisdictions they may well have already made provision in their contract for disputes to be dealt with by way of arbitration rather than litigation. Arbitration permits the choice of a neutral venue for the dispute and, very importantly, provides a regime for enforcement of awards in foreign jurisdictions that, in many cases, offers significant advantages to the regimes available in relation to court judgments. There are also other factors that may be important in particular circumstances. For example, although there will be extra cost involved because the parties have to pay the arbitrator, the process may offer some advantages in the context of an ongoing relationship. The first of these is that it is a private process. For the most part, the dispute will not be aired in public in the same way as it might were it to be dealt with through the courts. This factor alone may help the parties maintain some sort of working relationship.

The other advantage is that, with the right arbitrator, it is possible to have the dispute dealt with within a much shorter timescale. If the parties are intending to continue to work together, the sooner they can have the dispute resolved and move on to other things the better for all concerned.

If the outsourcing arrangement is a multinational one with a number of subsidiary companies holding separate contracts under the umbrella of a framework agreement, then any arbitration agreement will need to be drafted with care. For example, the parties may wish to provide for similar disputes arising under one or more of the subsidiary contracts to be dealt with by the same arbitral tribunal.

11.10 Litigation

Like arbitration, litigation should, as a general rule, be the process of last resort in a long-term commercial relationship. It will cost considerable sums of money, will involve a very significant period of delay before the dispute is resolved and is likely to cause irreparable harm to the relationship between the parties. The weight each party gives to these factors will clearly depend upon what is at stake in the dispute and the extent to which the party needs or values the services provided by or to the other party.

On the other hand, in circumstances where the contract is at an end or the party is no longer concerned with preserving a relationship, there may be little choice but to address the dispute in this way. Where the parties are from different jurisdictions (and assuming that arbitration has not been chosen in preference to litigation) a well-drafted contract will make clear which courts are to deal with any disputes that arise. An express provision confirming the right to seek urgent interim assistance from any appropriate jurisdiction should be considered.

11.11 Settlement payments

The tax treatment (e.g. whether the payments are liable to VAT and whether they are taxable or tax deductible) of payments made under a settlement of litigation, or as damages, needs to be considered by both supplier and customer under the appropriate jurisdictional regime.

Chapter 12

Customer Dependencies

12.1 Outline

Chapters 7, 8 and 9 describe the supplier's responsibility for providing the services. This chapter describes customer dependencies. It discusses, first, whether the outsourcing agreement should include the customer's responsibilities and, if so, how these should be drafted. Second, it discusses the contractual effect of failure by the customer to comply with its obligations.

12.2 Inclusion of customer responsibilities

It is useful to consider whether, from the customer's perspective, the agreement should include a comprehensive list of customer obligations. The customer sometimes assumes that the agreement will be onerous if it imposes too many detailed obligations upon it. Some customers are also concerned that their inclusion will provide the supplier with an opportunity to evade liability under the agreement by blaming the customer. For both of these reasons, customers sometimes prefer not to include customer obligations in the agreement.

However, to ensure that the parties have a clear understanding of what they need to do in order that the services can be provided successfully, the agreement needs to include responsibilities of both the supplier and the customer. This area is often given less attention than negotiating the services to be provided by the supplier and yet, if the services are to be successfully provided, both issues need to be considered carefully. In addition, if the agreement does not clearly specify the customer's obligations, then the English courts may imply obligations (*see, e.g.*, *Anglo Group plc* v *Winther Brown & Co Limited*).[1] For both of these reasons, it is better to include customer responsibilities.

12.3 Defining customer responsibilities

The customer's concern that the agreement will be onerous if its obligations are included or that the supplier will exploit customer obligations to evade its responsibility under the agreement can be dealt with by ensuring that customer obligations are clearly defined so that the customer knows what is expected of it and can ensure that it can comply. The customer will not want to accept vague obligations.

---

1 QBD (T&CC) Technology & Construction Court, 1 March 2000.

From the supplier's perspective, however, it is essential that all customer dependencies are covered thoroughly in the agreement, so that the supplier is not in breach of the agreement as a result of acts or omissions of the customer. The supplier should check each aspect of the services in this regard. In appropriate cases it may be helpful to set the service description out in a series of tables listing the supplier and customer responsibilities for each part of the service, side by side.

The supplier may need the customer to commit to providing specific data, information or documentation in accordance with agreed service levels in order that the supplier can meet its service levels.

Just as customers are sometimes uncertain as to whether they have defined all aspects of the services and may want to include catch-all phrases to describe the services (as mentioned in 7.2 above), so suppliers may be concerned that they have not anticipated every customer dependency and seek to include general exclusions of liability, for example that the supplier will not be responsible for a failure to provide the services as a result of an act or omission of the customer. The supplier may also seek to include customer obligations that are widely drafted, for example that the customer will cooperate with the supplier or provide all necessary assistance. Whether or not these approaches are reasonable depends upon the particular circumstances of the arrangement and, in particular, whether the supplier can reasonably be expected to predict all customer dependencies and what liability the supplier is accepting.

12.4 Obligation to notify the customer of breach

The customer may want to state that the supplier must notify it promptly if it becomes aware that a failure by the customer to comply with its obligations under the agreement might have a detrimental effect on the supplier's ability to deliver the services. This notification procedure serves two purposes:

(a) It ensures that, where possible, the customer's contract manager is informed if customer obligations have not been carried out and is given an opportunity to ensure that they are carried out before too much damage is caused to the services. If the supplier is to be responsible for managing the overall provision of the services, then it may be reasonable to regard this obligation as including the responsibility to manage customer dependencies.

(b) It means that the supplier must promptly raise arguments that problems with the services are caused by the customer. This reduces the risk that the supplier will raise such arguments for the first time many months after the problems with the services occurred, in circumstances where it is difficult for the customer to prove what happened at the relevant time.

The supplier will want to ensure that any notification obligation imposed upon it is reasonable, so that it does not lose its right to rely upon a breach of the customer's obligations because it notifies the customer of the problem late. It may want to ensure that it has a procedure for ensuring that it complies with the notification requirement, for example by stating that the supplier must notify the customer of problems at the next service management meeting.

12.5 Service output or input-based arrangement

If the customer responsibilities are so extensive that it is difficult to detail them all, or it is difficult to define the boundaries of the supplier's responsibility, then it may be that the customer will find it difficult to hold the supplier responsible for the services and that the type of service is not appropriate for outsourcing, or the outsourcing arrangement should be for the provision of resources only (an input-based outsourcing arrangement, as described in Chapter 1).

12.6 The effect of non-compliance

If the customer fails to comply with its obligations, then the supplier will want to ensure that it is not liable for any resulting failure by it to provide the services. The supplier will also usually want the customer to compensate it for any additional costs it has incurred (or, in appropriate cases, damages it has suffered) as a result of the customer breach.

The supplier may want the right to terminate the agreement if the customer fails to comply with its obligations. Whether this is appropriate depends upon the circumstances. This issue is discussed in Chapter 23.

Part Four – Structure

Chapter 13

Existing Equipment

13.1 Outline

Chapter 12 discusses whether customer dependencies should be included in the agreement and if so, how. This chapter deals with one of the major customer dependencies, namely the provision of assets from the customer to the supplier, usually so that the supplier can provide the services.

Prior to the outsourcing arrangement, various assets may have been used by the customer for the provision of its services. The supplier may need these for the provision of the services. Even if the supplier does not need them for the provision of the services, if the customer does not need them after it has entered into the outsourcing arrangement, the outsourcing arrangement may provide for the supplier to acquire them and use them to provide services to its other customers, thus reducing the charge to the customer.

Chapters 13, 14 and 15 discuss the various ways of dealing with the assets. This chapter covers equipment, hardware, and supply and maintenance contracts. Chapter 14 discusses intellectual property rights. Chapter 15 deals with land.

Chapters 13 to 15 point out that some ways of dealing with the assets may be considerably more cost effective than other ways. In particular, this chapter includes a very brief, UK-focused list of some of the more important taxation issues. If the outsourcing arrangement involves the transfer, lease or license of substantial amounts of assets, all parties will need to take specialist taxation advice. These issues will need to be considered both at the time of any initial transfer and also on any transfer of assets, or replacement assets, by the supplier to the customer at the end of the outsourcing arrangement. If the outsourcing arrangement is multinational, then the parties will also need to take advice on local law. In particular, for customers in England and Wales, if there is a cross-border element or the transaction involves procurement on behalf of individual entities, the way in which the transaction is structured may have a significant impact on tax, including VAT costs. This will particularly be the case with effect from 1 January 2010, when almost all supplies of services cross-border will be subject to the reverse charge, that is, the customer will charge itself VAT calculated at the rate applicable in the country in which the customer is based, and not where the supplier is based.

Where the customer has previously outsourced the relevant services and the current outsourcing arrangement constitutes the transfer of the services from one outsourcing supplier to another, then the customer and supplier will need to negotiate with the incumbent supplier to obtain the assets that they require (*see* Chapter 25 for a discussion of the relevant issues).

In addition, the customer and the supplier may want to consider the implication of transferring assets from the customer to the supplier or from an incumbent supplier to the new supplier to the application of the Acquired Rights Directive ("ARD"). This is because transferring assets may increase the likelihood that the courts will decide that the transfer of a business has occurred and that staff employed in the business will also transfer. *See* Chapter 27 for a discussion of ARD.

13.2 Recommended approach

In deciding between the various options, it is recommended that the simplest and cheapest option that achieves the parties' business objectives should be adopted, unless there are good reasons for adopting another course of action.

13.3 Equipment owned by the customer

Where physical assets to be used by the supplier in the provision of the services to the customer are owned by the customer, there are a number of options. The customer may sell them, lease them or loan them to the supplier.

13.3.1 Selling the equipment

The advantages and disadvantages to the customer of selling the equipment to the supplier are explained in Table 21.

Table 21 *Selling the equipment*

Advantages

The customer may receive a cash payment for the assets.

Even if the purchase price is recovered as part of the supplier's cost base for providing the outsourced services, the customer will obtain a cash-flow benefit if the cash payment for the equipment is made in advance or over the first few months of the arrangement and the service charges are spread over the term of the agreement.

The equipment may cease to be on the customer's balance sheet.

A sale may be more appropriate if the supplier is to be responsible for upgrading the equipment at its own cost, and the upgrades are specific to the equipment, so that it makes sense for the same company to own both the equipment and the upgrades.

Disadvantages

If the equipment is to be used to provide the services to the customer, the supplier will usually recover the purchase price of the equipment from the customer in the charges.

The sale of equipment may give rise to a liability for corporation tax. The nature and extent of any liability will depend upon the specific equipment in question, for example disposals of plant and machinery will normally give rise to adjustments to the transferor's capital allowances position. In some cases, a clawback of capital allowances could give rise to an immediate tax charge, although it is more likely to result in a reduction in the expenditure on which tax relief can be obtained in future years.

In England and Wales, VAT is potentially chargeable on a transfer of equipment unless the transfer to the supplier can be categorised as a transfer of a business or part of a business as a going concern. (This treatment is unlikely to apply where the activities and assets transferred have previously been used in house as part of the transferor's activities.)

In a UK context, stamp duty will not apply, although transfer tax may be relevant in other jurisdictions, and stamp duty land tax ("SDLT") may be chargeable to the extent to which the equipment has become a fixture in buildings to be transferred to the supplier.

On expiry of the agreement, the equipment (assuming that it is needed for the provision of the services by the customer or the successor supplier) will be owned by the supplier. The customer will need to protect its position by ensuring that, if the supplier has included the purchase price of the equipment in the charges, so that the customer has paid for the equipment, the customer (or the successor supplier) has an option to purchase the equipment for a nominal amount.

On early termination of the agreement, the equipment will be owned by the supplier. The customer will need to pay to get it back if it is needed for the provision of the services by the customer or the successor supplier. The customer may already have paid part or all of the purchase price of the equipment in the charges. The customer will need to protect itself by including in the agreement a right for it (or the successor supplier) to purchase the equipment for a price which takes into account the extent to which the customer has already paid for the equipment. Thought will need to be given to the taxation consequences of such a retransfer. The customer will also need to protect itself against the possibility that the equipment has not been maintained adequately. (*See* Chapter 25, which covers this issue in greater detail.)

The supplier may create security over the equipment, for example by executing a debenture in favour of its financiers. In these circumstances, it may be necessary to have the equipment carved out of any security given by the supplier. The customer may also want a negative pledge in relation to the equipment. This is particularly important where the customer has the option to buy back the equipment.

There is a risk that the supplier will become insolvent and the customer will find that key equipment it needs to provide the outsourced services is owned by the supplier. (*See* Chapter 26 for a discussion of insolvency related issues.)

13.3.2 Leasing or loaning the equipment

The customer can lease or loan the equipment to the supplier. The advantage of this approach is that it is a simpler, cheaper option. The term of the lease or loan should match the term of the outsourcing agreement so that, on termination, the equipment will return to the customer. The disadvantage is that the supplier may have to ensure that it has an asset register detailing where the equipment is, so that it can be returned on termination.

13.3.3 Recommended approach

As stated above, in deciding between the various alternatives, it is recommended that the simplest and cheapest option should be adopted unless there are good reasons for adopting another course of action. Therefore, the customer should loan the equipment to the supplier unless there is a good reason for selling it or leasing it to the supplier.

13.4 Equipment leased by the customer

Where equipment to be used by the supplier for the provision of services to the customer is leased to the customer by a third-party lessor then, where necessary, the lease could be novated to the supplier. Alternatively, the customer could obtain the lessor's consent for the supplier to use the equipment. In practice, the customer's options will depend upon the precise terms of the lease with the lessor and the extent to which the lessor is willing to agree to changes in the lease.

In any event, as the outsourcing agreement is between the customer and the supplier, the customer will need to either negotiate changes in the arrangements with the lessor or assist the supplier in negotiating with the lessor.

13.4.1 Transferring the lease

The advantages and disadvantages of transferring the lease (from the perspective of the customer) are explained in Table 22.

Table 22 *Novation of the lease*

Advantages

The leased equipment may cease to be on the customer's balance sheet (if it ever was).

Disadvantages

The parties will need to obtain the consent of the lessor to a novation of the lease. This may take time to obtain. The lease may have been granted to the customer on favourable terms due to the financial standing of the customer and hence may not be transferable to the supplier on the same terms unless a customer guarantee is produced. The customer may find that the only alternative would be to terminate the lease, exposing it to the possibility of financial penalties.

The assignment of a lease may give rise to a supply for VAT purposes, unless it is part of a transfer of a going concern to the supplier. Even if the transaction is a transfer of a going concern, if the supplier is a member of a partly exempt VAT group, the supplier will be deemed to supply the asset to itself, which may result in a VAT charge which the supplier will want to pass on to the customer in the charges for the outsourcing services.

On termination of the agreement, the leased equipment (assuming that it is needed for the provision of the services by the customer or the successor supplier) will be in the supplier's name. The customer must endeavour to protect itself by ensuring that the lease can be further novated back to the customer, or to the successor supplier or the equipment can be purchased by the customer or the successor supplier in these circumstances. Transfer of the equipment to the successor supplier would have the added advantage of keeping the asset off the customer's balance sheet. Thought will need to be given to the taxation consequences of such a retransfer. The supplier may be anxious to transfer the lease to the customer or the successor supplier, so that it is not responsible for making the payments under the lease.

There is a risk that the supplier will become insolvent. The customer may want to protect itself by agreeing a direct agreement with the lessor. (*See* Chapter 26 for a discussion of insolvency related issues.)

There is a risk also that the lessor may become insolvent and, in circumstances where the supplier leases equipment for the provision of the services, it is worthwhile for the customer to consider the creditworthiness of equipment lessor.

13.4.2 Obtaining consent for use

The advantage of obtaining the lessor's consent for the supplier to use the equipment (from the perspective of the customer) is that it is a simpler option. The disadvantage is that it still requires the lessor's consent, although such consent may be easier to obtain than consent for the transfer of the lease, depending upon the terms of the lease.

13.4.3 Recommended approach

In practice, the parties will usually decide that the customer will obtain a right for the supplier to use the leased equipment, unless there is a good reason for transferring the lease to the supplier.

13.5 Access to equipment

If the supplier will need access to other equipment, whether owned or leased to the customer, which will continue to be used by the customer (for example computer equipment to be maintained by the supplier), then the customer will usually grant the supplier rights of access or a licence to use the relevant equipment. The customer should check the terms of its lease to see whether it needs the lessor's consent before allowing the supplier access to leased hardware.

13.6 Supply or maintenance contracts

Supply or maintenance agreements are not usually personal to the customer and so the customer will have the option of:

(a) transferring them to the supplier; or
(b) retaining them in its name and providing for the supplier to manage the third-party supply agreement. This may include the supplier acting as paying agent for the third-party supply agreements by making payments to the third-party supplier on the customer's behalf and recovering the payments as part of the outsourcing charges.

13.6.1 Transferring the agreements

The advantages and disadvantages of transferring the agreements to the supplier (from the perspective of the customer) are explained in Table 23.

Table 23 *Transferring the agreements*

Advantages

The supplier may be able to take advantage of corporate arrangements with the third-party supply agreements under which it obtains preferential rates such as volume discounts.

The supplier may be willing to take more responsibility for the actions of the third-party suppliers if it is a party to the agreements and has the right to terminate the agreements if it is dissatisfied with the suppliers' performance.

Unless the agreement specifies otherwise, if the charges payable to the third-party supplier increase, the supplier will pay these.

Disadvantages

The parties may need to obtain the consent of the third party. This may take time to obtain. The third party may be unwilling to agree to the transfer, for example if the financial standing of the supplier is worse than that of the customer. Until the third party's consent has been obtained, the customer may be in breach of confidentiality obligations in the agreement if it discloses details of the third-party agreement.

On termination, the third-party supply agreements (assuming that they are needed for the provision of the services by the customer or the successor supplier) will be in the supplier's name. The customer may require the supplier to use reasonable endeavours to transfer them to the customer. If the supplier has a corporate arrangement with the third-party supplier, then the charges may incorporate volume discounts which will not be transferable to the customer. This may not be a problem if the successor supplier has similar discount arrangements with appropriate third-party suppliers.

Unless the agreement specifies otherwise, if the supplier decides that it does not need the supply agreement and terminates it, the supplier receives the benefit of the cost saving.

13.6.2 Retaining the agreements

The advantages and disadvantages of retaining the agreements in the customer's name (from the perspective of the customer) are explained in Table 24.

Table 24 *Retaining the agreements in the customer's name*

Advantages

It is a simpler option – the parties may not need to agree a variation to the supply agreement if the supplier is merely to manage the third-party supplier.

Unless the agreement specifies otherwise, if the parties decide that the supply agreement is not needed and the customer terminates it, the customer will receive the benefit of the cost saving.

Disadvantages

Unless the agreement specifies otherwise, if the charges payable to the third-party supplier increase, the customer will pay these.

13.7 Defining the equipment

Apart from deciding how the equipment will be dealt with, the customer and the supplier will also need to resolve how the equipment will be defined or identified. In some outsourcing arrangements, including simpler arrangements, the customer may have a comprehensive list of all the equipment, perhaps in the form of an asset register.

In other cases, the customer may have an asset register but it may be unclear whether it is up to date or complete. The customer and the supplier may need to decide whether the customer will grant a warranty regarding the asset register, whether the supplier will be expected to rely upon its own due diligence or whether the supplier will get a limited period during which it will not be responsible for problems in the services resulting from assets which are on the asset register not being transferred (for example because they have been destroyed or damaged).

The customer may also agree that, if equipment has been omitted from the asset register that is needed for the provision of the services, then, assuming it is still held by the customer, the parties will amend the asset register so that it is added to it and transferred or made available to the supplier together with the other equipment.

13.8 State aid

Public sector customers must ensure that any assets transferred to the supplier are sold or leased at market value or above in order to comply with the EU state aid rules. The state aid rules are designed to prevent suppliers from receiving public assets at an undervalue. The purchase price can be received either as a separate cash payment or incorporated within the overall deal. Where the price is incorporated as part of the overall deal, it is recommended that this be documented.

Where the total value of the assets in question is less than €200,000, it may be possible to take advantage of an exemption under the state aid rules, provided that the total of any state aid received by the supplier does not exceed that figure over a rolling three-year period. If reliance is being placed on this exemption, certain reporting requirements apply and reference should be made to the exemption in the transfer documents.

Chapter 14

Existing Software and Intellectual Property Rights

14.1 Outline

Chapter 13 describes the options for dealing with one type of assets, namely equipment. This chapter deals with another type of assets – software and intellectual property rights. It describes the various ways of dealing with software and intellectual property rights that are owned by or licensed to the customer.

14.2 Intellectual property rights owned by the customer

Where the customer owns intellectual property rights ("IPR") used to provide the services (e.g. bespoke software developed by the customer), the customer may decide to sell them to the supplier or to license them to the supplier. Thus, the options are similar to those for physical equipment, even if the implications are slightly different for IPR.

14.2.1 Selling the IPR

The advantages and disadvantages (from the perspective of the customer) of selling the IPR to the supplier are described in Table 25.

Table 25 *Selling IPR owned by the customer*

Advantages

The customer may receive a cash payment for the IPR.

Even if the purchase price is recovered as part of the supplier's cost base for providing the outsourced services, the customer will obtain a cash-flow benefit if the cash payment for the IPR is paid in advance or over the first few months of the arrangement and the purchase price is spread over the term of the agreement.

The IPR may cease to be on the customer's balance sheet.

The supplier may be able to exploit the IPR by licensing them to other customers (although this could also be achieved by allowing the supplier to sub-license the IPR).

Disadvantages

The supplier may recover the cash payment from the customer in the charges, unless the supplier has an opportunity to license the IPR to other customers. This may be unlikely if the IPR constitutes software that has been developed for the customer's specific requirements.

Corporation tax liabilities may arise on sales of IPR. Different tax consequences may apply to IPR created after 1 April 2002 when the intangibles legislation[1] was introduced.

On expiry of the agreement, the IPR (assuming that they are needed for the provision of the services by the customer or the successor supplier) will be owned by the supplier. The customer will need to protect its position, for example by ensuring that it receives a royalty-free licence to use the IPR for the provision of the services by it and a successor supplier.

On early termination of the agreement, the IPR (assuming that they are needed for the provision of the services by the customer or the successor supplier) will be owned by the supplier. The customer will need to ensure that it can continue to use them. The customer may have already paid part of the purchase price of the IPR in the charges. The customer will need to protect itself, for example by including in the agreement a licence for it to use the IPR for the provision of the services by it and a successor supplier. The parties may need to agree a charging mechanism for calculating what licence fee is payable by the customer if it has not compensated the supplier for the purchase price of the IPR. Thought will also need to be given to the taxation consequences of such a retransfer.

There is a risk that the supplier will become insolvent and the customer will find that key IPR needed by it to provide the outsourced services are owned by the supplier. (*See* Chapter 26 for a discussion of insolvency related issues.)

14.2.2 Licensing the IPR

The advantages of licensing the IPR to the supplier are that it is a simpler option. In practice, the parties will usually decide that the customer will license the supplier to use the customer's bespoke software, unless there is a good reason for selling it to the supplier.

14.2.3 Taxation consequences

If the IPR are either sold or licensed to the customer for a capital sum, then tax issues, varying depending on whether the IPR pre-date or are subject to the intangibles legislation,[2] may arise and so the parties should take specialist taxation advice on this point.

1 Schedule 29 Finance Act 2002.
2 Schedule 29 Finance Act 2002.

14.3 IPR licensed to the customer[3]

Where software or other IPR are licensed to the customer, in theory:

(a) the licences could be transferred to the supplier;
(b) the supplier could rely upon the customer's licences (with the parties obtaining the licensor's consent for the supplier to use the software or other rights, where necessary, if the licence does not already cover an outsourcing supplier); or
(c) the customer could terminate its licences and the supplier could be responsible for ensuring that the appropriate licences are obtained.

In practice, the options open to the parties will depend upon the precise terms of the licence with the licensor and what the parties can agree with the licensor.[4]

14.3.1 Transferring the licences

The advantages and disadvantages of the licences being transferred to the supplier (from the perspective of the customer) are described in Table 26.

Table 26 *Transferring the licences*

Advantages

The supplier may be able to take advantage of corporate arrangements with licensors under which it obtains preferential rates when licences are transferred to it.

The licensor may want to transfer the licence so that it has a contractual relationship with the supplier, thus making it easier to sell other products to the supplier.

Disadvantages

The licensor may charge a fee for transferring the licences, but not if the licences stay in the customer's name. The parties will need to agree who will pay the fee.

Signing an agreement to transfer the licence may involve more administrative effort than merely obtaining the licensor's approval for the supplier to use them.

On termination of the agreement, the licences (assuming that they are needed for the provision of the services by the customer or the successor supplier) will be in the supplier's name. The customer must endeavour to protect itself by ensuring that any

3 For an explanation of issues relating to open source software, *see* Heather J. Meeker, *The Open Source Alternative: Understanding Risks and Leveraging Opportunities*, John Wiley & Sons Inc., 2008.

4 In addition, if the licences are not to remain with the customer, there are two options: the licences can be assigned to the supplier, or they can be novated to the supplier. An assignment is a transfer of part or all of the benefit of a contract. The other party will still be able to enforce the contract against the original party. Novation replaces the contract so that another party takes the place of the transferring party. Unless the agreement provides otherwise, assignment of the benefit of a contract can take place without the consent of the customer but novation can only take place if supplier and customer agree.

licences transferred to the supplier can be transferred back on termination without any transfer charge. The situation will be more complex if the supplier has merged the licences in with other corporate arrangements that it has. Before the agreement is signed the customer should check if the supplier will be able to carve the licences out of the corporate arrangement on termination. Usually the customer will not be able to benefit from the supplier's corporate discounts after termination.

14.3.2 Obtaining the licensor's consent

The advantages and disadvantages of the customer obtaining the licensor's consent for the supplier to use the software or other rights (from the perspective of the customer) are described in Table 27.

Table 27 *Obtaining licensor's consent to a right to use*

Advantages

The licensor may want to retain the agreement in the customer's name so that it continues to have a relationship with the customer, thus making it easier to sell other products to the customer.

On termination of the agreement, the licences (assuming that they are needed for the provision of the services by the customer or the successor supplier) will already be in the customer's name.

Disadvantages

The licensor may charge a fee for granting the right to use. Note that this could be prevented in the future by the customer ensuring that all new software licences allow use of the IPR by an outsourcing supplier to provide outsourced services to the customer. The licence may also be restricted to the use of the software at certain locations. Therefore, if the supplier is intending to relocate the provision of the services, the parties may need to obtain the consent of the licensor for use of the software at the new location. The parties will need to check whether any additional charges are payable for obtaining the consent of the licensor to the use of the software by the supplier or at the new premises, and will need to document whether these will be paid by the customer or whether they are already included in the supplier's charges.

The customer will be liable to the licensor for actions taken relating to the licence, whether by it or by the supplier. Therefore, the customer will need the supplier to commit to complying with the terms of the licence and indemnify it against breaches of the licence by the supplier.

As any IPR licences will be between the customer and the licensor, if the parties decide to adopt either of the above two options, the customer will need to either negotiate changes in the arrangement with the licensor or assist the supplier to negotiate with the licensor.

14.3.3 Taking out new licences

The advantages and disadvantages of the supplier taking out new licences (from the perspective of the customer) are described in Table 28.

Table 28 *Supplier taking out new licences*

Advantages

The supplier may be able to take advantage of corporate arrangements with licensors under which it obtains preferential rates.

Disadvantages

If the licence fees for the software are payable in one lump sum for a perpetual licence, then taking out new licences will mean the parties paying for licences which the customer has already paid for.

On termination, the licences (assuming that they are needed for the provision of the services by the customer or the successor supplier) will be in the supplier's name.

Before deciding to adopt this course of action, the customer should check with the licensor whether it will agree that the licences will be transferable to the customer on termination. If the licensor will not approve the transfer on termination, in a worst-case scenario, the customer may have to take out new licences or find another supplier who has the relevant licences. If the supplier has a corporate arrangement with the licensor, then even if the licences are transferable, usually the customer will not be able to benefit from the supplier's corporate discounts after termination.

14.4 Problems with software licences

14.4.1 Ensuring all relevant parties are licensed

In considering how to deal with software in an outsourcing arrangement, it is easy for the parties to concentrate on the fact that the supplier will need to use the software to provide the services, and to ignore the fact that the customer may also need to continue to use the software to take advantage of the services or that the licences will need to cover any disaster recovery arrangements.

14.4.2 Breach of copyright

Failing to ensure that software licences cover all parties who will need to use the software is a serious mistake to make. Software is protected by copyright. A party will be in breach of copyright to the extent to which it uses software without a proper licence. Software licence agreements may state that software is licensed for use by a specified party, at a specified location, on specified hardware and even by specified listed individuals. Any use outside the specific scope of the licence will be in breach of copyright.

Remedies for copyright infringement include:

(a) a right to damages awarded on the basis of the gross proceeds received by the defendant (not the net profit derived from the infringement);
(b) an account of profits;
(c) an order for delivery up of infringing copies;
(d) an injunction to restrain further or expected infringements; and
(e) prosecution for a criminal act.

For this reason, not only must the parties ensure that any use of the software is properly licensed, but any legal adviser will recommend that they ensure that they take out the proper licences before the supplier starts to use the software.

14.4.3 Due diligence

Before the agreement is signed, the parties may also want to know whether the licensor will be unwilling to grant its consent or will require the payment of exorbitant fees in return for granting its consent to the required use of the software. This is particularly important where it is possible that this will undermine the business case for entering into the outsourcing arrangement or may mean that the parties will have to change the services to be outsourced or how they will be provided, for example if it is possible to avoid situations where the supplier uses the software.

Chapter 15

Property Aspects

15.1 Outline

Chapters 13 and 14 deal with the transfer of equipment, software and IPR from the customer to the supplier. This chapter deals with property issues relating to the outsourcing arrangement. If the outsourced services are to be provided from the customer's site, then the customer can either sell the premises to the supplier or grant it a licence or a lease in respect of the relevant premises.

15.2 Selling the premises

Table 29 explains the advantages and disadvantages (from the customer's perspective) of the customer selling the premises to the supplier.

Table 29 *Sale*

Advantages

Sale is appropriate where the supplier will be the only party using the premises.

The customer may receive a cash payment for the premises.

The premises (if leasehold, and therefore a liability) may cease to be on the customer's balance sheet.

Disadvantages

If the premises are to be used to provide the services to the customer, the supplier will almost certainly include part of the cost of purchasing the premises in the charges for the outsourced services.

If the property is leasehold, the landlord's consent is likely to be required.

The sale of land may attract corporation tax on chargeable gains, in which case the parties will need to consider what, if any, tax reliefs are available to the parties (e.g. tax reliefs relating to reinvesting in other business premises).

Stamp Duty Land Tax is likely to be payable by the supplier, and so detailed consideration will need to be given as to what interest in the property is transferred and whether any relief is available on the land (e.g. sale and leaseback relief).

A liability for VAT may occur, depending on the nature of the property and whether an election to charge VAT has been made by the transferee. If the customer is exempt or partially exempt (i.e. it does not recover all of the VAT charged to it), transferring the property to a supplier who recovers the cost of the purchase by increasing fees to the customer over the life of the contract may increase the customer's irrecoverable VAT.

The customer and supplier will need to consider what will happen on termination of the agreement.

15.3 Leasing or licensing the premises

The customer will need to take specialist property and taxation advice on what is more appropriate, a lease or a licence.

15.3.1 Lease

Generally, if the supplier is to be granted exclusive rights to use an entire building, or part of a building, then a lease will usually be appropriate. If the customer does decide to grant the supplier a lease of the premises, then the customer will have to take specialist legal advice to ensure that the lease is excluded from the Landlord and Tenant Act 1954 (as amended) so that the supplier does not obtain security of tenure. This is now a relatively straightforward process.

15.3.2 Specific licence

A licence will be more appropriate if the supplier is to provide the services from part or parts of the customer's premises, shared with the customer, rather than taking over an entire building or defined area from the customer. To be enforceable as a licence, the licence will need to grant the supplier non-exclusive access to the relevant premises and not reserve the customer a right of entry to the relevant premises (which are both characteristics of a lease not a licence). Care must also be taken in ensuring what rights are actually given to the supplier in practice, as whether a supplier is granted a licence or a lease will depend upon the facts of the situation, not just the wording of the agreement. Therefore, whilst a customer may prefer a licence as a simpler document, if exclusive possession is in fact given to the supplier, this could result in the supplier acquiring security of tenure.

15.3.3 General licence

In addition, the supplier may need temporary non-exclusive access to the customer's premises solely to carry out the services. For example, it may need to enter the customer's premises to maintain customer equipment at the premises.

The customer will usually grant the supplier a general licence to enter any of its premises to the extent necessary to provide the outsourcing services.

15.3.4 Landlord's consent

If the customer is not the freehold owner of the premises, then, depending on the terms of its lease, it will need the consent of the landlord to a licence or sublease. The terms of the lease under which the customer occupies the premises will need to be checked to ensure the customer can grant the sublease or licence. Also, the customer should factor into its project plan for the procurement the fact that obtaining this permission may take some considerable time (or, indeed, consent may not be forthcoming).

15.4 Terms of the licence or lease

Once the parties have decided upon the desired approach, they will need to decide upon the appropriate terms of the lease or licence. *See* Table 30 for a list of issues that may need to be considered in the lease or licence.

Table 30 *Licence or lease terms*

Outgoings

The parties will need to decide whether the supplier will be responsible for the outgoings (in respect of electricity, telephone, water etc. and the maintenance of the premises) and if so, whether the supplier will be entitled to charge these amounts back to the customer or whether they are already included in the charges payable by the customer. The customer will be reluctant to pay all of the outgoings if the premises are to be used for the provision of services to other customers of the supplier.

Furniture and other facilities

The parties will need to agree whether the customer will make available to the supplier at the premises any furniture or office, parking, meeting-room or canteen facilities.

Security

The parties will need to decide who will be responsible for the security of the premises. They will also need to decide whether the premises satisfy the security requirements necessary to provide the services and if not, whether the supplier's charges already include the cost of improving the premises or whether the supplier will be able to make an additional charge to cover these costs.

Health and safety

The supplier may need to commit to complying with the customer's health and safety, security and access and other regulations at the premises.

Access hours

The supplier will need to know the hours during which it will be able to gain access to the premises and will need to compare this with the service hours during which it must provide the services to the customer.

Non-interference

If the supplier is to be given non-exclusive access to the premises, then the customer may want the supplier to commit to not interfering with the carrying on by the customer of its normal business activities.

Damage to the premises

The parties will want to clarify who will be responsible for insuring the premises and in what circumstances the supplier will be responsible for damage to the premises.

Relocation

If the supplier is relocating the services to alternative premises, the customer and supplier should check if this will result in any additional expenditure and will need to decide who will be responsible for this. An example of a potential problem area is where the supplier is relocating a mainframe computer but the lease for the mainframe hardware and software is remaining with the customer. In this situation, the hardware lessor may make an additional charge under the lease for the relocation of the mainframe.

All of these issues can also affect whether, as a matter of law, the relationship between the customer and the supplier is one of landlord–tenant or licensor–licensee.

15.5 State aid

The transfer of any publicly owned land to a supplier is subject to the EU state aid rules. Under these rules, the transfer of land should be at market value or above. Market value can be determined either on the basis of an unconditional bidding procedure or in accordance with an independent valuation. The valuation should take into account conditions attached to the land (such as, e.g., restrictions on use) but not other factors (such as, e.g., other elements of the outsourcing transaction).

Where the transfer is part of an overall outsourcing transaction which has been procured under the EU Public Procurement Directives, the purchase price for the land can form part of the overall package.

Chapter 16

Treatment of Assets During Term

16.1 Outline

Chapters 12, 13 and 14 discuss options for transferring to the supplier at the beginning of the outsourcing arrangement the assets or rights in the assets previously used by the customer. This chapter deals with issues relating to the treatment of assets during the term of the arrangement. It covers how the customer ensures that it has obtained value for money if it has sold assets to the supplier. It also describes the issues regarding whether the supplier should be able to use the assets for the provision of services to its other customers. It goes on to discuss the replacement of the assets and the funding of new assets.

16.2 Ensuring value for money

16.2.1 Resale of the assets

If the customer decides to sell assets to the supplier, whether physical assets or intangible IPR, it will want to ensure that it obtains value for money from the transaction. For example, it may check the value of the assets and the price payable by the supplier or include a clawback provision whereby it receives, for example, a share of the proceeds of sale if the supplier sells the assets within a certain period of time for more than it paid the customer.

16.2.2 Use of the assets to provide services to other customers

If the supplier includes the cost of acquiring the assets in its charges to the customer, then the customer may want to ensure that it obtains a reduction in the charges if the assets are later used for the provision of services to the supplier's other customers. Therefore, it may restrict the supplier from using the assets for the provision of services to other customers until the supplier has satisfied the customer that it has received a reasonable reduction in the charges to reflect the benefit that the supplier is obtaining. There are two ways that the parties can deal with this situation.

16.2.3 Approval on a case-by-case basis

The customer can require the supplier to obtain its approval each time it wants to use the assets for the provision of services to its other customers. The customer can then receive a fixed percentage of the profits (e.g. 50 per cent) or the profits can be distributed in a reasonable manner designed to reflect each party's investment in enabling the acquisition of the new customer. This mechanism can be used, for example, to reward the customer for assisting the supplier in marketing the services to other customers.

This approach will usually be overly bureaucratic unless the amount of money involved is substantial. Even if the amount of money involved is substantial, the supplier will be reluctant to disclose to the customer confidential information relating to its agreements with other customers. In addition, unless the other customers are being granted a licence to use the IPR previously owned by the customer, the contracts with the other customers will not usually involve a separate payment for the use of the specific assets and so it will be difficult to measure the exact benefit that the supplier is obtaining.

16.2.4 General approval

In most cases it will be more realistic for the customer to allow the supplier to use the assets generally for the provision of services to other customers subject to ensuring that the customer has received a reasonable reduction in the charges in return for granting this right. This may be the only option regarding premises leased or licensed to the supplier. For, if the supplier is providing the services from the customer's premises, the only way it can guarantee that the premises will not be used for the provision of services to other customers will be if all of the employees and contractors who work at the premises are dedicated to providing services to the customer. This may introduce a level of inflexibility that will undermine the supplier's ability to provide the services in the most cost-effective manner.

16.2.5 Residual value

In appropriate circumstances, even where the supplier is using the assets exclusively to provide services to the customer during the term of the arrangement, the customer may take the view that the supplier should not include the full cost of acquiring the assets in its charges to the customer if the assets will still be valuable on expiry of the outsourcing arrangement. This is because, on termination, the supplier will still own the assets and will be able to sell them or use them to provide services to other customers after termination. A similar argument may apply where the supplier develops assets specially for the customer if the assets can be used by other customers after termination. The parties will need to negotiate and agree issues surrounding residual value and who retains that value.

16.3 Use of the assets and premises

Ensuring value for money is not the only consideration arising out of the supplier's use of assets transferred to it by the customer for the provision of services to its other customers.

16.3.1 Services not adversely affected

From the customer's perspective, if the assets or premises are to be used for the provision of services to it and to other customers, it will want to be reassured that the services to it are not adversely affected. The supplier may argue that it should have control over how it provides the services and that it is sufficient for it to have an obligation to meet the service levels. In some cases the supplier may use the assets or premises for the provision of services to its other customers and not to the customer. This issue has been discussed in Chapter 8.

16.3.2 Third-party agreements

The customer will need to ensure that it is not breaching any third-party agreements by allowing the supplier to use the assets for the provision of services to third parties. For example, software licences covering the customer and a supplier providing outsourcing services to it will not enable the supplier to provide services to other customers.

16.3.3 Smooth transition on termination

Lastly, it will want to ensure that the use of the assets by third parties does not adversely affect the smooth transition of the services back in-house or to the successor supplier on termination of the outsourcing arrangement. This topic is discussed in Chapter 23.

16.4 Maintenance

In establishing an outsourcing arrangement, the customer and the supplier usually remember to deal with how the different assets are to be made available to the supplier so that it can provide the services. However, the parties also need to consider ongoing issues relating to the assets.

16.4.1 Damage to the assets

The parties need to decide who will be responsible for damage to the assets and who will be responsible for insuring them. They will need to consider the implications if the customer's users or clients damage the assets and, in particular, who will be responsible for paying any increased insurance premiums and insurance excesses. The parties need to agree the nature of their interests under any insurance policy, and whether they are to be co-insured under it. This may involve consideration of which parties have an insurable interest in the assets in question.

16.4.2 Maintenance and customisation

The parties will also need to decide who will be responsible for maintaining the assets or modifying them so that they are suitable to provide the services.

16.4.3 Replacement of the obsolete assets

The parties will need to decide who will be responsible for replacing obsolete assets used to provide the services if they can no longer be used for that purpose. If the customer retains this responsibility, then it must take this into account in anticipating its expenditure over the term of the arrangement and in building its business case. If the supplier takes over the responsibility, then clearly it will need to include the expenditure in its business case.

16.5 New or replacement assets

If the customer does not have the assets needed to provide the outsourced services or its assets need to be replaced, either on the commencement of the outsourcing of the services or at a later time, the customer and the supplier will need to decide how to acquire and fund the new assets. There are various options. The most common options are set out below:

(a) The customer may buy or lease the assets from a third-party lessor, in which case the issues in 13.3 and 13.4 above will be relevant. The customer may wish to make the supplier responsible for the selection and suitability of the equipment.

(b) The supplier can buy the assets or lease them from a third-party lessor. The customer may prefer the supplier to be responsible for acquiring the assets so that it takes the risk as to their suitability for the provision of the services.

(c) If the assets will be used exclusively for the provision of services to the customer, it may be possible to secure cheaper funding for the assets if the supplier acquires the assets and leases them to the customer on the basis of a UK tax-based lease coterminous with the outsourcing agreement.

The parties will need to take specialist taxation, accounting and insolvency advice before deciding upon the most appropriate course of action. Dealing with the various options is outside the scope of this Guide as the issues are not specific to outsourcing arrangements.

Chapter 17

Different Supplier Models

17.1 Outline

Chapters 13 to 16 deal with how equipment and premises, which have been previously used by the customer as part of the services, can be made available to the supplier so that it can provide the outsourced services. This chapter deals with various ways of structuring the outsourcing relationship including multisourcing, prime contractor, consortium and joint venture models. Lastly, it includes some hints on how to deal with the outsourcing of shared services centres.

17.2 Relationship between different suppliers

When a customer decides to outsource a particular service or function, it will often find that the service or function will need to be provided by various different suppliers. Equally, when the supplier responds to the customer's RFP, it may conclude that it needs to work with other suppliers to provide all aspects of the services. The question arises as to how the different relationships should be structured.

17.2.1 Types of relationship

There are various different approaches that can be adopted:

(a) the customer can enter into multiple agreements with the various different suppliers ("multisourcing");
(b) the customer can enter into one agreement with a prime contractor who then enters into subcontracts with the other suppliers ("multisourcing");[1]
(c) the customer can enter into an agreement with two or more suppliers ("consortium"); and
(d) several suppliers can form a joint venture and the customer can enter into an agreement with the joint venture ("joint venture").

17.2.2 Factors to take into account

Table 31 describes the different factors to be taken into account in deciding which approach to adopt. In the private sector, there is a trend towards multisourcing, for the reasons highlighted in

1 A PFI contract will generally fall within this category, although the "prime contractor" in such contracts is usually a special purpose vehicle. *See* Chapter 35 for a description of this approach.

the table, although it will be interesting to see whether this trend will be reversed during the downturn, as customers entering into outsourcing agreements to cut costs concentrate their spend with a smaller number of suppliers to achieve volume discounts.

In public/private outsourcing arrangements, the trend is towards contracting with a prime contractor or a consortium in order to ensure the risk of full integration and seamless provision of all of the services is transferred to the private sector.[2] Where a public body intends to multi-source services it will likely advertise the contracts under separate notices in the Official Journal of the European Union ("OJEU").

There are additional considerations which need to be taken into account if the parties are considering entering into a joint venture and these are described in 17.3.

Table 31 *Multisourcing, prime contractor, consortium or joint venture*

Total cost

On the one hand, multisourcing may be cheaper for the customer if it avoids a prime contractor charging a margin on the subcontractors' services and charging for managing the subcontractors. On the other hand, it may be more expensive if it reduces the opportunities for the suppliers to exploit economies of scale or results in one supplier having to test or confirm the quality of a deliverable produced by another supplier.

Multisourcing may enable the customer to obtain better value for money for additional services if they can obtain competitive quotations for the services from the different outsourcing suppliers (although, if a best-of-breed approach has been employed, the other suppliers may not be able to provide the additional services).

Alternatively, under a prime contractor arrangement, the prime contractor may be able to obtain better discounts from its suppliers for bulk purchasing than the customer could achieve in entering into agreements directly with the suppliers.

A consortium or joint venture arrangement may be more expensive because of the additional set up and management costs (*see* 17.3).

Transparency of charges

In a prime contractor or consortium model, the customer will not know the subcontractor's or supplier's charges unless a specific open-book arrangement is agreed. *See* Chapter 20 for a discussion of open-book arrangements. In the multisourcing arrangement, it will know the charges of the different suppliers.

Risk of increases in subcontractor charges

In a prime contractor model, the charges may be calculated on the basis of a fixed price, in which case the prime contractor will take the risk of managing its supply chain including the risk that subcontractors increase their charges to the prime contractor. In a consor-

2 *See* for example HM Treasury's "Managing Risks with Delivery Partners" at www.ogc.gov.uk/documents

tium model, the customer will also be able to negotiate a fixed price which means that it will not take the risk of increases in the suppliers' charges.

Responsibility

In multisourcing, it may be difficult to allocate responsibility for specific faults between the various suppliers. In all of the other arrangements, responsibility for service delivery will be clearer (except that, in the case of the joint venture, the liability of the joint venture may be clearer but the fact that the joint venture has been set up by the supplier and the customer serves to undermine the customer's rights and remedies in the event of a service failure (*see* 17.3)).

In a prime contractor relationship, the supplier will usually expect the subcontractor to enter into a back-to-back agreement. The subcontractor may, however, want to cap its liability at a level that is fixed by reference to the value of the subcontract rather than the value of the entire agreement, which will leave the supplier with a residual liability for the actions of the subcontractor. If the subcontractor is an existing supplier of the customer or has been selected by the customer, additional issues arise and these are discussed in Chapter 30.

In consortium arrangements, each supplier will also usually accept joint and several liability vis-a-vis the customer and enter into direct agreements with the other suppliers under which they agree to compensate the other suppliers for losses caused as a result of their actions.

Limitations of liability

Under a consortium arrangement, in theory the parties may be able to use the limited liability joint venture company to limit their liability. However, if the joint venture company lacks the financial standing of its shareholder companies, the customer will usually demand a guarantee from the suppliers.[3]

Setting up the arrangements

In multisourcing there will be more work for the customer in negotiating the various arrangements with suppliers.

In a prime contractor model, the supplier will negotiate back to back contracts with its subcontractors.

In a consortium the suppliers will negotiate agreements between each other.

Joint ventures can be particularly complicated to set up. The parties will need to negotiate shareholders' agreements and subcontracts – *see* 17.3.

Ongoing management

In all of the different models, someone needs to be responsible for managing the integration of the different suppliers.

3 This is not the case with PFI, which is a "limited recourse" arrangement. The special purpose vehicle will not offer parental guarantees to the procuring authority but other contractual protections are put in place, not least the comfort that the senior lender will step in to avoid the project collapsing.

In a multisourcing arrangement, the customer will be responsible for managing the different suppliers and (in particular) the integration between the various suppliers unless it appoints one of the suppliers to act as a systems integrator and manage the integration process between the other suppliers.

In a prime contractor model the customer outsources the management and integration of the subcontractors to the prime contractor and the prime contractor is responsible for seamless service delivery.

In a consortium arrangement the members of the consortium manage the integration of their individual services.

Joint ventures may be more complex to manage. There will be additional legal, administrative and audit expenses involved in running the joint venture (*see* 17.3); however, this should not be an issue for the customer provided the overall price remains competitive.

Integration risk

In multisourcing, the customer may retain responsibility for integrating the solutions of the different suppliers (unless it appoints one of the suppliers to act as systems integrator – *see* above).

In a prime contractor or consortium model, the supplier/suppliers may accept the integration risk, provided that the customer does not attempt to control how the services are provided.

For comments on the liability situation in a joint venture – *see* 17.3.

Flexibility

Multisourcing may be more flexible than the other options if it means that the customer can replace one supplier without affecting the agreements with the other suppliers. It may also be more flexible if the customer is able to request one supplier to provide services previously provided by the other supplier, or to ask either of them to bid for new additional services. Therefore, it may be argued that the arrangement avoids dependence upon a single outsourcing supplier. This could be a particular advantage in situations such as those prevailing at the time of writing where there is an heightened risk of supplier insolvency.

Multisourcing arrangements will, however, not be more flexible if the suppliers are each specialists in specific fields.

In a contract with a prime contractor, the customer may be more dependent upon the prime contractor but can still ensure that it has flexibility with regard to the subcontractors. Thus the contract with the prime contractor can be drafted to allow the customer to direct the prime contractor to replace a subcontractor which is repeatedly failing. It may also include a mandatory market testing of subcontractors on a regular basis (e.g. every five years under a typical PFI), with a replacement of subcontractors who cannot compete on price or quality with others in the market.

Quality

In multisourcing, the customer can select suppliers who are the leading specialists in providing the individual services. However, individual suppliers may be less willing to invest in understanding the customer's business if the value of the individual contracts is less.

In a prime contractor arrangement the prime contractor may subcontract elements of the services to specialist subcontractors.

A consortium may be established between different leading specialists.

Relationship with end provider

A prime contractor model may result in the customer feeling distanced from the end provider of goods or services, but this can be managed by including regular liaison provisions in the contract.

Variety

In appropriate circumstances, a multisourcing option may provide users with a variety of suppliers to choose from, which may increase support for the outsourcing process by users if they feel that they have a choice.

Control

In a prime contractor model, the customer will not have control over the subcontractors unless specifically agreed. *See* Chapter 8 for ways in which the customer may control subcontractors.

In the other models, the customer has a direct relationship with the various suppliers and will be able to decide to replace any unsatisfactory supplier (provided that it has the right to terminate the agreement with the relevant supplier).

Staff and asset transfer

Where there are multiple suppliers, under TUPE the customer's staff may transfer to more than one supplier and the assets used by the customer for the provision of the services may need to be transferred to more than one supplier. *See* Chapter 27 for a discussion of staff issues and Chapter 15 for a discussion of asset transfer issues.

17.3 Joint venture between supplier and customer

17.3.1 Structure of joint venture

If the supplier and the customer decide to set up a joint venture with each other, this will usually involve the following:

(a) The supplier and customer will set up a separate company or a partnership (either incorporated as a Limited Liability Partnership or unincorporated) if there are tax benefits to this.

(b) The customer will transfer the assets (or rights relating to assets) previously used to provide the services to the joint venture vehicle.
(c) Employees will be transferred under TUPE or seconded to work for the joint venture vehicle either from the customer and/or the supplier.
(d) The customer will enter into a services agreement with the joint venture vehicle.
(e) The supplier may contribute additional assets and investment and may also enter into a services agreement with the joint venture vehicle.
(f) Both parties will have shares in the joint venture and will agree how any investment will be funded. Funding may take the form of equity (i.e. shares) and/or debt (i.e. loans to the joint venture vehicle).
(g) In addition to delivering the services to each of the partners, the joint venture vehicle will also then be free to trade and sell services to third parties in order to make a profit for its member partners.

Whether a joint venture will be appropriate will depend upon various factors which are described in the following paragraphs.

17.3.2 Combining strengths

Joint ventures are particularly appropriate for business process outsourcing arrangements in which both sides have skills to contribute. For example, the customer may have an understanding and experience of a sector in which the supplier wants to provide business process outsourcing services and may have a recognised brand in the relevant sector. The supplier may be able to provide technical IT or business process re-engineering skills and the commercial skills required to sell outsourcing services to other customers. In practice, these situations are rare.

Unless the customer is contributing special knowledge or experience to the joint venture, the joint venture vehicle, which lacks its parent company's track record, may find it more difficult to win additional third-party business than the supplier unless it is able to also use the supplier's branding.

The parties will need to agree whether the supplier can tender for third-party service contracts in competition with the joint venture vehicle:

(a) If the supplier can tender in competition with the joint venture, then this may undermine the ability of the joint venture to win other business and hence its value to the customer.
(b) If the supplier is prevented from bidding for work in competition with the joint venture, then there will have to be clear agreement as to what type of work the joint venture will tender for in order to avoid a situation where the joint venture fails to win the business and the supplier may have had a better chance of winning the business but is prevented from bidding.

This explains why the arrangement is more likely to be successful if the customer has contributed some special skill or sector-specific knowledge that gives the joint venture an advantage over the supplier bidding on its own. Competition law advice will need to be taken in relation to any restrictions on the activities of either the shareholder or the joint venture and as to any merger control or other competition issues which the creation or operation of the joint venture may raise.

17.3.3 Termination arrangements

The parties will need to decide what happens on termination. On expiry or in the event of any dispute, the customer may want the right to buy the shares of the supplier. However, this right may undermine the motivation of the supplier to invest in the joint venture. The supplier may want the right to buy the customer out in certain circumstances, for example if third-party revenue increases.

17.3.4 Cost

Joint ventures are more expensive to establish than a straightforward outsourcing contract as they will involve the negotiation and agreement of a members agreement and, if the vehicle is a company, its memorandum and articles of association. Additional legal, administrative and audit expenses will also be incurred in running the joint venture, but this cost will depend on the existing resource and infrastructure which the parties can offer to the joint venture, for example if seconded staff and existing office space is used, costs can be kept to a minimum.

The value-for-money argument in participating in a joint venture will also, of course, depend on the strength of the joint venture's business plan and the anticipated annual return to each of the partners. Profits are unlikely to be distributed until all of the vehicle costs and overheads have been met.

The parties will need to agree the percentage of profit which will accrue to each depending upon the investment each makes to the joint venture.

If the customer is VAT exempt, it may have been able in the past to avoid paying VAT on the charges for the services if the joint venture was set up as part of the user's VAT group. However, the VAT grouping rules have been changed to preclude VAT grouping in most cases, unless the supplier and customer are in a parent/subsidiary relationship determined by accounting standards rather than the definitions in the Companies Act 1985.

17.3.5 Business outcome-based charging[4]

A joint venture approach may enable the parties to link the success of the joint venture business to the service charge which the customer pays to the joint venture for the services that it receives. For example, the customer may extract its profit share from the joint venture by way of an annual reduction in the services charge. However, this can become complicated and it would be advisable to keep the joint venture arrangement and the customer's service contract with the joint venture vehicle at arm's length to avoid conflicts of interest as customer and shareholder. This is more important where the customer is a public sector body (*see* 17.3.13 below).

17.3.6 Obtaining funding

If substantial investment in the services is required, it may be easier to obtain external finance if

4 *See* Chapter 1 for an explanation of the term "business outcome-based charging".

the assets and revenue stream are ring fenced in a separate company over which the funder can take security.

17.3.7 Transparency of charges

The joint venture approach can result in a more transparent arrangement between the parties. However, the question arises as to which party manages the financial systems and accounts of the joint venture.

17.3.8 Responsibility and conflicts of interest

Responsibility under a joint venture is more complicated. It may be more difficult for the customer to enforce its rights against a joint venture that it partly owns. For this reason it may be seen as a lower-risk approach from the supplier's perspective. It is advisable for the customer to keep its role as customer and its role as shareholder at arm's length as far as it is able, for example by ensuring the contract manager is not the same person as its nominated director or representative on the board of the joint venture vehicle.

17.3.9 Management time

Joint venture vehicles may be complicated to establish as a members agreement (either a shareholders agreement or a partnership agreement as applicable) will need to be negotiated and agreed. It is sometimes argued that this process can divert attention from agreeing the details of the services to be provided to the customer and other key issues. However, this can be taken into consideration when planning the procurement process and timetable. Again, whether a joint venture will represent value for money in the long term will depend upon the strength of its business plan, and providing proper management time and effort to getting this right is often overlooked by both parties in their eagerness to get a deal done.

17.3.10 Control

Joint ventures involve a more collaborative management style. However, one of the parties will usually own a controlling share. Public sector customers will often only take a minority share, limiting their input to significant decisions and not the day-to-day running of the business.

17.3.11 Staff

Staff may be reluctant to transfer or be seconded to a joint venture company if they are uncertain as to its future prospects.

17.3.12 Political considerations

A joint venture company may be politically more acceptable to the customer than disposing of the assets.

17.3.13 Additional considerations for public/private joint venture vehicles

Joint ventures between the public and private sector are becoming more commonplace as the government continues to encourage public bodies to find new ways to make the most of public assets and achieve efficiency saving targets.[5] Local government in particular has been exploiting its new powers to trade[6] and invest[7] in commercial activity for some time by taking equity investments in joint venture companies.[8]

Where one party to a joint venture of this kind is a public body, there are a number of additional considerations which must be taken into account by the parties:

(a) Procurement law: the establishment of a joint venture with a private company is not itself subject to the public procurement regulations;[9] however, the regulations will apply to the grant of the service contract to the joint venture and so a procurement which has been advertised in OJEU will be necessary.[10] The public body will not be able to guarantee any future contracts to the joint venture vehicle unless such work was envisaged by the original procurement.

(b) State aid: the terms of the joint venture must be structured to ensure that there is no element of subsidy or aid to the vehicle, but rather the agreement is on full arm's-length commercial terms in order to avoid state aid to the vehicle and the supplier partner.

(c) Powers: the public sector body must be clear upon the powers on which it will be relying to enter into the joint venture.

(d) Accounting implications: the parties will need to understand any regulatory and accounting requirements which may apply to the vehicle as a result of the public sector's involvement.[11]

17.3.14 Conclusion

The additional expense and effort involved in setting up and managing a joint venture mean that

---

5 *See* "Infrastructure procurement: delivering long-term value" in particular Section 2 "The Broadening Range of Procurement Approaches" at www.hm-treasury.gov.uk.

6 *See* Section 95 of the Local Government Act 2003.

7 *See* Section 12 of the Local Government Act 2003.

8 Non-departmental public bodies such as Regional Development Agencies and other "quangos" are governed by guidance from Treasury in respect of their joint venture activities. At the time of writing, the Treasury was in the process of updating this guidance.

9 *See* the Public Contracts Regulations 2006 and the Public Utilities Regulations 2006 as applicable.

10 *See* Commission Interpretative Communication on the Application of Community Law on Public Procurement and Concessions to Institutionalised Public Private Partnerships ("IPPP") 05.02.2008 C(2007)6661.

11 Consider the application of the Local Government and Housing Act 1989 where the public body is a local authority for the purposes of that Act and also the CIPFA Code of Practice on Local Authority Accounting. If the public body is a non-departmental public body, *see* relevant guidance from Treasury and the Office of National Statistics which will classify the vehicle as either public or private sector for the purposes of government accounting, depending upon the level of public sector control.

it should only be adopted where substantial benefits can be obtained as a result and those results cannot be achieved by alternative simpler means, for example by the supplier investing in shares in the customer organisation.

17.4 Shared services

The paragraphs above have dealt with the complications involved where the customer and supplier enter into a joint venture. Complications also arise where several customers, whether within the same company or organisation or not, set up a shared services centre to provide services and then decide to outsource the services provided by that centre. In this situation, the parties will need to take great care to consider the specific facts surrounding the arrangement, but in any event will need to consider the following issues:

(a) ARD – the implications of the ARD are likely to be particularly complicated in this situation and the customer should ensure that it take specialist employment and pensions advice early on in the process.

(b) Services: if the different customers require different services, then they will need to consider the best way to describe the services. It may be helpful to describe a catalogue of services which customers select.

(c) Governance: the parties should consider whether they will need additional governance structures, such as a shared services board, to discuss issues which affect more than one customer.

(d) Assets: the parties will need to agree and document the arrangements regarding ownership, licence and refresh of assets.

(e) Change: the parties will need to decide how changes will be approved and when changes will need the approval of more than one customer.

(f) Termination: the customers will need to decide what will happen if one or more of the customers decide to leave the arrangement before expiry of all of the agreements.

(g) Dispute resolution: the parties will need to decide which dispute resolution procedures will be appropriate – arbitration may not be helpful.

Part Five – Charging

Chapter 18

The Charging Regime

18.1 Outline

Chapter 17 describes the structure of the outsourcing arrangement which can have a fundamental impact upon the charging mechanism. This chapter deals with issues relating to charging. It describes common charging regimes for the services. There are various ways in which the charges under an outsourcing arrangement can be calculated, determined in part by the extent to which the supplier accepts responsibility for achievement of the customer's business objectives (business outcome risk profile), the provision of the services (service output risk profile) or the provision of resources (input risk profile).[1] This is a crucial area for customer and supplier, as, if they make mistakes, it can have a major impact upon the value that the arrangement has to them.

18.2 Risk/reward

18.2.1 Appropriate if supplier is responsible for business outcomes

If the supplier is responsible for business outcomes, then a risk/reward charging mechanism will be appropriate. In this situation, the payment mechanism will involve the supplier being paid charges that reflect the business benefit that the customer receives as a result of the outsourced services, for example, that the customer's bills go out (and hence are paid) earlier. The charging model must take into account the fact that the customer's business objectives will change during the term of the arrangement.

A business outcome-based charging regime is particularly appropriate for transformational outsourcing arrangements where the purpose of the outsourcing arrangement is to effect a change in the customer's organisation. The customer may favour the mechanism, if it considers that it will ensure that the supplier will only be paid if the customer receives the benefit it seeks. It may also be effective in encouraging a closer relationship between the supplier, with the supplier being seen as demonstrating confidence in its services and its commitment to the customer and its business objectives.

1 This distinction is described in Chapter 1.

18.2.2 Not appropriate if difficult to measure or demonstrate

The risk/reward charging mechanism will not be appropriate if it is difficult to measure or demonstrate achievement of the specific business objective that the customer is endeavouring to achieve.

18.2.3 Not appropriate if supplier lacks control over outcomes

The supplier may be reluctant to accept a risk/reward payment mechanism if it does not have full control over the manner in which the benefit is to be achieved, for example, if the customer is seeking improvements in its margin – various factors will influence this (e.g. the economic climate).

In practice, it will be rare that the supplier will have full control over the achievement of the customer's business benefit. Usually, external events will affect the achievement of the benefits. At the very least, the supplier and customer will usually need to cooperate to achieve the benefits, for example the supplier will make recommendations which the customer will need to implement. The supplier may suggest that it should receive the payment if its recommendations would have achieved the benefit but the customer decides not to implement them. This may be unsatisfactory from the customer's perspective if it pays for the services but does not receive the benefit it desires. It also begs the question as to why the customer decides not to implement the recommendations. The customer may want to limit the obligation to pay to circumstances in which it acts unreasonably in failing to implement the recommendations.

18.2.4 Not appropriate if payment too high

In practice, dissatisfaction may also be caused even if the customer achieves its desired benefit, if the payment to the supplier is seen as being unjustifiably high. The customer may, therefore, want to cap the potential benefits that the supplier may receive.

18.2.5 Not appropriate during final years

Lastly, the risk/reward payment mechanism may be impractical as a mechanism for ensuring that both parties contribute towards new capital expenditure during the final few years of the agreement if there is insufficient time left during which the supplier will be able to recover a return on its investment before expiry of the agreement. A similar issue arises if the agreement is terminated early. *See* Chapter 25 for a discussion of this issue.

18.2.6 Appropriate with other charging mechanisms

The risk/reward payment mechanism may be helpful if it is used with other payment mechanisms so that it acts as a bonus and incentivises the supplier to achieve the benefit but does not assume that the supplier has sole responsibility for achievement of the business benefit.

18.2.7 Share of profits on exploiting assets

Sometimes the charging mechanism provides for the customer to receive a share of profits generated by the supplier in exploiting assets or premises transferred to or made available by the customer for a nominal amount. This is properly regarded as part of the arrangement by which the customer makes the assets and premises available to the supplier rather than part of the charging regime for the services. Accordingly, this issue is dealt with in Chapter 16.

18.3 Fixed price

18.3.1 Appropriate for service output deals[2]

If the supplier is responsible for the provision of the outsourced service (service output risk profile) then a fixed-price charging mechanism is appropriate.

Calculating the charges on a fixed-price basis may be advantageous for the customer and the supplier. From the customer's perspective, this charging regime will mean that the charges it will pay will be predictable. From the supplier's perspective, it will receive a predictable revenue stream; it has control of its costs, it takes the risk that its cost base will increase and receives the benefit if it can reduce its cost base. Because the supplier takes the risk of increases in its cost base, the charges are likely to be more expensive than if they were calculated on a cost plus basis as the supplier will usually increase its charges by a premium to cover the risk of increases in its cost base.

The fixed-price charging regime is straightforward for the customer and supplier to administer for budgetary and other purposes.

The charging regime incentivises the supplier to reduce its costs so as to improve its margin. Therefore, in fixed-price charging arrangements it is important for the customer to ensure that its service description is reasonably complete – otherwise there is a risk that it will not receive the services it needs. From the supplier's perspective, in fixed-price charging arrangements, it is crucial that the boundaries of the services are defined clearly.

The customer does not have price transparency in fixed-price charging mechanisms and so it may want to agree a breakdown of the charges so that it can understand which elements of the services are most expensive and amend the services accordingly or an open book arrangement so that it can investigate what margin the supplier is making.

18.3.2 Fixed price linked to volume adjustments

From the customer's perspective, the disadvantage of this charging regime is that it may be tied in to paying the fixed price even if the volume of the services decreases in the future. Equally, from the supplier's perspective, it may be unable to increase the charges if the volume of the services increases.

2 "Service output" deals are described in greater details in Chapter 1.

Therefore, if it is likely that the volume of services will change, the charges should be calculated in one of two different ways:

(a) On a fixed-price basis *per transaction*, for example per claim processed, or alternative methods may be used to ensure that the customer pays for the volume of services that it uses. However, the customer should be aware of the behaviour this charging regime will encourage. Thus, it could be argued that any charging regime which involves the supplier being paid for the number of help-desk calls it deals with relating to problems with equipment or premises being maintained is likely to encourage the supplier to refrain from carrying out scheduled maintenance or problem management/root cause analysis to prevent problems from occurring.

(b) On the basis of an overall fixed charge linked to the provision of certain volumes of services. The parties may agree, in advance, pricing variations that will apply for certain changes in the volumes of the services, for example the number of users receiving the services or number of servers being maintained.[3] They may agree that no changes will occur in the charges until the volumes increase or decrease by more than a specific figure, for example 10 or 20 per cent.

18.3.3 Volume adjustment procedure

If volume adjustments are likely to occur on a regular basis, the parties may agree a procedure for adjusting the charges on a regular quarterly or annual basis. If the parties agree that the charges will be adjusted retrospectively, the customer may ask the supplier to provide regular reports showing the charges it is incurring, so that the customer can budget for the charges. Equally, it may be appropriate for the customer to give the supplier notice of future changes in volumes so that the supplier can plan for these.

From the customer's perspective, it is usually advantageous to agree charging variations for the possible changes in the volumes of services before the agreement is signed, as its bargaining power is usually greater at this stage. (*See* Chapter 22.)

18.4 Pay as you go

18.4.1 PFI payment mechanism

A related charging mechanism to the fixed-price charging regime is that employed in PFI contracts where the charges are also payable on a fixed-price basis. However, there are two differences.

18.4.1.1 Delayed commencement

The customer does not start paying for the services until the supplier starts to provide them. This means that (unless the supplier is delayed by the customer or other specifically agreed

3 If the charges are to be varied depending upon the number of servers maintained, the parties need to be clear as to whether they mean physical or virtual servers.

"compensation events") the supplier takes the risk that it is late in providing the services. If the agreement provides for a definite expiry date (rather than the contract expiring a specific period after the supplier starts to provide the services), then any delay by the supplier will reduce the total income received by the supplier.

18.4.1.2 Deductions in the charges

Also, after the supplier has started to provide the services, if it fails to provide them in part or totally in a particular month in accordance with the contract requirements, it will suffer deductions in the charges, which means that the supplier will not be paid in full and may not get paid anything that month. PFI contracts are covered in greater detail in Chapter 35.

18.4.2 Non-PFI pay as you go payment mechanisms

A similar pricing mechanism, which may be appropriate for certain types of services (e.g. where applications or computer capacity are made available to the customer as part of an application service provider ("ASP"), utility computing, software on demand, software as a service ("SAAS") or cloud computing model), allows customers to use services when they need them and to pay only for those services they use.

18.5 Cost or cost plus

If the supplier is responsible for inputs only, then a cost plus or resources-based charging mechanism will be appropriate. Cost plus is described here; resource-based charging is described in 18.6 below.

18.5.1 When appropriate

A cost plus charging regime means that the charges are calculated on the basis of the supplier's actual costs plus an agreed margin, calculated as a percentage of the costs. This may be a particularly useful charging mechanism if the costs of providing the services are likely to change so frequently that it will not be practical for the parties to commit to fixed prices, for example in a vehicle support outsourcing agreement.

In any event, the parties will need to define which costs will be reimbursed and which will not. For example, the customer will not want to pay additional costs which are incurred because the supplier did not follow agreed service management procedures. This is an important area, as if the costs are not clearly defined, this is likely to lead to disputes throughout the agreement.

The advantage of this charging regime from the customer's perspective is that the customer does not pay an excessive margin to the supplier.

The advantage from the supplier's perspective is that this charging mechanism is low risk for the supplier as the supplier is guaranteed to receive charges that cover its costs and its margin.

The disadvantage from the customer's perspective is that the customer may not get value for money, as the supplier has no incentive to reduce its costs. On the contrary, the supplier has an incentive to increase its costs if the margin is a percentage of the costs. This problem may be mitigated by the parties agreeing a capped margin or a fixed margin if this is acceptable to the supplier.

This charging mechanism does not incentivise good performance and so the customer will want to ensure that it includes a suitable service level and service credit regime.

Another disadvantage from the customer's perspective is that it does not have price certainty. To enable the customer to budget for the charges, the supplier may agree to warn the customer when certain spending limits are reached or the parties may agree a target budget and incentives for meeting the target and service credits for failure to meet the target.

The charging mechanism is also not ideal from the supplier's perspective as the supplier has little or no opportunity to maximise its margin.

18.5.2 Use with other charging mechanisms

Even where the cost plus mechanism is not attractive as a charging mechanism for the overall outsourcing agreement, it may be appropriate for certain elements. For example, the parties may agree that the supplier will manage certain third-party contracts on behalf of the customer. These may or may not be transferred to the supplier. In either case, the parties may agree that the fees paid under these contracts will be passed on to the customer. The agreement should state clearly whether the customer is required to reimburse the supplier for the fees or also to pay an administration fee or a margin in addition to the fees themselves. In this sort of arrangement, the customer takes the risk that the fees charged by the third-party supplier increase, but the customer will benefit if the fees are reduced.

18.6 Resource based[4]

An alternative approach for an outsourcing arrangement which has an input-based liability profile is for the charges to be calculated on a resource basis. For example:

(a) an IT outsourcing agreement may include the provision by the supplier of a basic number of man days of development services, which will be paid for at an agreed man-day rate, with additional man days of development services being charged at that or another agreed man-day rate;

(b) an offshore outsourcing agreement may include the provision of certain services, which the parties assume will require a certain number of full-time equivalents ("FTEs"). The charges will be calculated based on the number of FTEs multiplied by a rate card covering the relevant types of skills.

The parties may want to clarify how many hours or effective hours (i.e. hours at the desk) the relevant FTEs will be expected to work per annum.

4 If the supplier is going to provide the services in whole or in part from Spain or France, then *see* Chapter 42 or 43 before including resource-based charging mechanisms.

The basic number of man-days or FTEs may be fixed over the term of the agreement or notified to the supplier by the customer or agreed by the parties on a regular basis.

The customer should consider its requirements carefully to ensure that it is not tying itself in to receiving services which it does not use.

18.6.1 Flexibility to change resources provided

To preserve its flexibility, the customer may also want to consider whether it needs the right to increase or reduce the basic number of man days of services or FTEs provided.

The supplier may want to limit the customer's ability to reduce the requirement. This may be achieved by capping any proposed reduction to a specified percentage of the original requirement or by increasing the man-day or FTE rate if the reduction means that different volume-related discounts apply. The supplier may also require a specified period of notice before any change in the number of man days of services or FTEs.

18.6.2 Notice of requirement for resources

The supplier may want to ensure that the customer gives reasonable notice of its requirement for man days of services.

18.6.3 Use of resources over the relevant period

The supplier may want the customer to commit to using the man days of services evenly over the contract year, so that the supplier can assign specific consultants to provide those services.

The customer, on the other hand, may want to preserve its flexibility as much as possible so that, if the man days of services are divided up, leading to the customer having a specific number each month, quarter or year, it can carry forward unused man days to subsequent months, quarters or years.

18.6.4 Payment for resources not used

The customer will want to avoid paying for man days of services which it has not received. Thus, it may suggest that the charges are on a pay-as-you-use basis. The supplier may not agree to this if it is granting the customer the benefit of certain preferential rates for the services on the basis that the customer will request the minimum level of services. However, the supplier will usually agree that the customer will not be required to pay for services which it has requested but which the supplier has failed to provide.

18.7 Charging assumptions

The supplier may also want to state that the charges are calculated on the basis of specified pricing assumptions. Sometimes the supplier may want to link the charges to pricing assumptions because it has not been given a sufficient opportunity to carry out a due diligence exercise on the services it is to provide. This may arise because to carry out a due diligence exercise would be impractical bearing in mind the scale of the services, or would lead to disruption to the customer's business or undue delay in signing the agreement. This problem was discussed in Chapter 6. In this situation, the supplier will not want to take the risk that information it has been given relating to the services is incorrect or that assumptions that it has made about the type or scope of services it is to provide are inaccurate.

18.7.1 Uncertain charges – the problem for the customer

The inclusion of charging assumptions is a contentious issue. Usually, the customer's business objectives will relate in some form or other to the charges to be payable under the outsourcing agreement, with the result that the business case for entering into the outsourcing agreement will be undermined if the charges exceed a certain amount – this is particularly true where the charges are calculated on a fixed-price basis. Therefore, the customer will want to know with certainty before the agreement is signed the amount of the charges payable to the supplier. The customer will not want to enter into an agreement where the existence of pricing assumptions means that the supplier can vary the charges payable under the agreement after the contract has been signed. This is particularly so if the customer has enjoyed a good bargaining position before the agreement is signed (e.g. because there are competing suppliers interested in providing the services) which will be reduced on signature of the agreement. There may be a suspicion that the supplier is endeavouring to improve its margin after signature of the agreement.

If this is the case, then it is in the customer's interests to ensure that the supplier is given the opportunity to carry out as much due diligence as is practical and not to agree pricing assumptions which are designed to ensure that the customer bears the risk that the supplier's due diligence has been badly carried out.

18.7.2 When charging assumptions may be appropriate

This does not mean the customer should never agree to link the charges to pricing assumptions. If the supplier is dependent upon information provided by the customer and cannot verify that information independently, unless it can agree some form of relief with the customer then the supplier may be forced to include a risk premium in the pricing to cover the additional risk it is taking.

18.8 Risk premium

The discussion about charging assumptions raises the issue of the extent to which the supplier will find it necessary to increase its charges by a risk premium to cover any risk that it is taking, for example:

(a) the risk that its costs will increase as a result of inflation or otherwise (in circumstances where the charges are fixed price and there is no indexation clause);

(b) the risk that it will have to pay service credits or liquidated damages – it will assess the risk premium taking into the account its evaluation of the likelihood that it will be able to meet the necessary service levels or implementation deadline;

(c) the risk that it will be in breach of the agreement, for example because the customer will not agree a reasonable force majeure clause or reasonable limitations of liability – it will assess the risk premium taking into account its evaluation of the likelihood that it will be in breach of contract;

(d) other risks that it takes over in signing the agreement, for example the risk that it will have to pay redundancy costs in respect of transferring staff.

The supplier will usually calculate the risk pricing taking into account the financial impact of the risk and the likelihood of it occurring.

There are three points to make about risk premiums, from the customer's perspective:

(a) The important issue is for the customer to understand if the supplier is being forced to add a risk premium and to satisfy itself that it provides value for money. In some cases, it may result in the customer deciding that it does not present value for money and that it makes more sense for the customer to amend the service levels or other aspects of the agreement so that they are achievable.

(b) It highlights the importance of the customer organisation ensuring that its negotiation team operates as a team and not in silos; for example, it would be self-defeating if the procurement department were negotiating the outsourcing agreement with a view to achieving costs savings for the customer, but the operations department or the legal department agree unrealistic service levels or liability provisions so that the supplier is forced to increase the charges to include a risk premium.

(c) Whether the supplier includes a risk premium and the amount it includes will clearly depend upon whether it is in a competitive tender with other suppliers to provide the services. The supplier will usually endeavour to negotiate the service levels and the agreement so that they are reasonable, so that it does not need to add a risk premium to the charges, particularly if it is in a competitive tender.

18.9 Expenses

The parties should also agree whether the supplier can charge the customer for expenses incurred in providing the services. If the fees do involve an element for expenses, the customer may want to agree the type of expenses to be incurred and may want to give its approval before expenses are incurred. Before refunding expenses, it may want the supplier to produce receipts for actual expenditure.

Reimbursement of expenses is ordinarily a supply of services for VAT purposes, so that the person reimbursed would ordinarily charge VAT on the amount reimbursed. In practice, where supplier and/or customer are not in a position to recover the VAT in full, consideration may need to be given as to whether the customer should incur the expenses rather than the supplier, particularly if any "mark up" is or is treated as being charged by the supplier.

Even where VAT is not an issue, it may make sense for the customer to incur the expenses, for example where it can achieve greater discounts for hotels.

18.10 Inflation

The parties will need to agree how inflation will be dealt with. There are three possible approaches that can be taken.

18.10.1 Fixed-price charges

The customer can expect the supplier to include the risk of inflation in its charges. In this situation the supplier will usually build into its prices a figure for anticipated inflation. The supplier will take the risk that the actual inflation over the term of the agreement is more than that anticipated by the supplier. The customer will take the risk that inflation is less than the supplier anticipated.

18.10.2 Charges are indexed

Alternatively, the parties can agree that the charges will be indexed using an appropriate index. The parties may agree to break the charges down into the percentage of costs relating to, for example, salaries, and the percentage of costs relating to assets. They may then agree that the salaries costs will be linked to a salaries-based index and the assets linked to an assets-based index.

18.10.3 Compromise between the two

Lastly, the supplier can take the risk of a certain level of inflation, but retain the right to increase its charges if inflation is greater than a specified amount.

18.10.4 The relevant index

When considering which index to use, the parties should bear in mind that, in June 2003, the Bank of England decided that its inflation target is to be set by reference to the Consumer Price Index ("CPI"; previously the Harmonised Index of Consumer Prices) rather than the Retail Prices Index ("RPI") or RPI excluding mortgage interest ("RPIX"). The CPI measures inflation each month in the European Monetary area as a whole and individually measures and compares each Member State. CPI differs from RPI in several respects. For example, CPI excludes various items of housing costs (e.g. council tax, mortgage interest payments and buildings insurance), which are included in RPI. Therefore, the two indices may well produce different numbers in terms of inflation and accordingly result in different price changes under indexation provisions in contracts.

The Office for National Statistics will continue to publish the RPI. However, as official inflation will come to be measured by reference to CPI, the parties will need to decide which is more appropriate (or indeed whether another index may be more suitable).[5]

5 *See* the article in *The Times* on 21 October 2005, in which it is argued that the RPI has failed to adapt to modern spending habits.

18.11 Minimum charge

Paragraph 18.3 above mentioned the possibility that the charges may be reduced if the volume of services is reduced or that the charges may be calculated on the basis of the volume of services used. Paragraph 18.6 above mentioned that the customer may want to reduce the amount of man days of resources it has ordered from the supplier. Both of these situations mean that the supplier will bear the risk that its income stream will reduce if volumes fall. The supplier may be more willing to provide the customer with this level of flexibility if the customer commits to an overall minimum commitment of revenue.

Another factor that will influence the supplier's willingness to accept the risk that its income stream will reduce if volumes fall is whether it is given the exclusive right to provide the relevant services or resources. It will usually be unwilling to take the risk that the volumes will fall because the customer has ordered the services or resources from another supplier, particularly if it has had to invest in providing the services, for example by taking over staff or assets from the customer.

18.12 Breakdown of the charges

The customer may want the supplier to provide a detailed breakdown of the charges between the different service elements, so that it can reassure itself that the charges are reasonable. This will also be necessary if the customer wants to benchmark different service elements (*see* Chapter 20 for a description of benchmarking) or to terminate different service elements (*see* Chapter 23 for a discussion of termination in part). The customer may also want to see a breakdown of the charges to help it to understand how charges for changes in the services are calculated (*see* Chapter 22 for details of change management).

18.13 Payment profile

18.13.1 Profiling of the charges

Apart from delaying payment of the charges until the supplier starts to provide the services (as described in 18.4 above), there may be other reasons why the charges payable by the customer may not reflect the costs incurred by the supplier during the relevant period:

(a) It is not unusual for the supplier to incur set-up costs at the beginning of the arrangement in preparing for the provision of the services. These fees may be payable in a lump-sum transition, or development charge payable in advance or on completion of the transition or development. Sometimes, however, the making of the transition charge by the customer would result in the customer paying more for the outsourcing services in the first years than it had previously paid for its in-house services. This may be politically unacceptable for the customer organisation.

(b) Equally, during the term of the agreement, the supplier may need to make specific additional investment so that it can continue to provide the services, for example if it needs to replace obsolete equipment or to relocate from a particular site on expiry of the lease.

In both of these circumstances, the supplier may agree to profile its payments so that they are spread over the term of the agreement, with the customer paying a similar charge each year of the agreement. If this results in payments being delayed, then the supplier will usually also need to recover the cost of financing the investment. If it results in payments being made early, then the supplier will usually grant the customer a reduction to reflect the early payment.

18.13.2 Implication for termination or change

When the agreement is changed or terminated, the parties will need to bear in mind the profiling of the payments. Thus, for example, if the agreement is terminated midway through its term, after the supplier has made an investment in the services but before the customer has paid the charges due for that investment, then the supplier may want the customer to pay a termination charge covering the unrecovered investment costs.

There are two ways that the termination charge can be calculated: on the basis of demonstrable unrecovered investment costs or as a fixed termination charge. The advantage of the latter is that it is a certain amount. If, however, the termination charge is to be calculated on this basis, the customer will need to ensure, if the investment concerned investment in assets, that it does not pay for the assets twice. This would happen, for example, if the customer agrees to pay a fixed termination charge but also pays a separate amount to buy the assets from the supplier.

The customer may need the right to pay the termination charge, whether calculated as a fixed amount or otherwise, in instalments.

18.13.3 Payment of termination charge for supplier breach

In addition, the customer may want to consider the appropriateness of a termination charge if the agreement has been terminated for breach. Thus, if the agreement was terminated because the supplier provided the services with defective assets, then the customer will not want to be obliged to purchase the assets. *See* Chapter 25 for a discussion of termination charges.

18.14 Payment of the charges

In addition to agreeing the amount of the charges and the payment profile, the parties will also have to agree when the charges will be paid. Charges may be paid monthly, quarterly or annually in advance or in arrears. They may be paid on completion of specified services, for example the transition charges.

18.14.1 Payment in advance or arrears

If the charges are paid in advance, then the customer takes the risk that the supplier will become insolvent before it has provided the services. If the customer is paying in advance for development work to be carried out by the supplier, it may want to have the right to reclaim these amounts if the development is not ultimately successful and it may want the supplier to provide guarantees or bonds to safeguard any payments made in advance.

If the charges are paid in arrears, the supplier takes the risk that the customer will become insolvent before it has paid and it may want to consider requesting guarantees from the customer.

18.14.2 Payment period

The parties will need to specify how long the customer will have to pay invoices. The customer may want to reserve the right not to pay invoices if there is a dispute about the amount covered by the invoice. The supplier will want the customer to pay any undisputed amount covered by an invoice.

The supplier may also want the customer to pay an amount equal to the net VAT that the supplier will have to pay over to the tax authorities on the undisputed amount (or, if the supplier issues an invoice and so creates a "tax point" for VAT purposes, for the full disputed fee) pending resolution of the dispute, so that the supplier is not "out of pocket".

18.14.3 Reconciliation of charges

The charges may also need to be reconciled if they have been made in advance on the basis of estimates, for example estimated volumes or usage, and the actual volumes or usage vary from that estimated.

18.15 Remedies for non-payment

The supplier may be anxious to ensure that its cash flow does not suffer as a result of late or non-payment by the customer.

18.15.1 Interest

Usually the parties will agree that the customer will pay interest on late payments.[6]

18.15.2 Suspension

The supplier may also want to reserve the right to suspend provision of the services if the customer does not pay. This is an extremely powerful, and some would argue excessive, weapon in particular if the suspension may cause interference or disruption to its business. In any event,

6 If the agreement does not include a right to charge interest, then the supplier will be able to claim interest under the Late Payment of Commercial Debts (Interest) Act 1998. This Act provides a right to claim interest on late payment in commercial contracts for the supply of goods and services. It applies where all parties to the contracts are businesses or public authorities. In most cases, however, the parties will prefer to include an express right to charge interest in the agreement.

the customer will not want the supplier to exercise this remedy until it has given the customer notice of its intention and has given a reasonable time period within which to pay.

18.15.3 Termination

Ultimately, the supplier will usually want the right to terminate for breach if the customer fails to pay the charges. For more information on termination rights, *see* Chapter 23.

18.16 Value added tax

18.16.1 Payments include or exclude VAT

There may be various payments to be made under the agreement apart from the charges, such as service credits and payments for the purchase of assets. The parties will need to document in the agreement whether the payments are inclusive or exclusive of any VAT which is chargeable. In principle, if a supply of goods or services is liable to VAT, the consideration is deemed to include VAT unless stated to the contrary.

18.16.2 Supply taxable, exempt or outside the scope of VAT

Where there is uncertainty as to whether a supply is taxable, exempt or outside the scope of VAT, the parties will need to consider who takes this risk, which may affect the cash flow and profitability of the party taking the risk. Where necessary, the supplier may seek indemnities from the customer for risks that it agrees to take.

Many supplies of land are exempt from VAT unless an election to charge VAT has been made and notified to HM Revenue & Customs. A customer that is unable fully to recover VAT may want its supplier to agree not to elect to charge VAT on land transactions and, by agreeing to bear a slightly increased rent, compensate the supplier for any VAT that the supplier cannot recover in respect of the exempt lease.

18.16.3 Recoverability of VAT

Before progressing with the outsourcing procurement, the parties must also check carefully whether any VAT payable will be recoverable, and if there is a possibility that it will not be recoverable they should take expert taxation advice as soon as possible. It should be noted that, in certain circumstances, irrecoverable VAT may be taken into account in a party's corporation tax computations either as regards the extent to which it qualities for capital allowances or reduces its chargeable profits, although this in effect is only a 28 per cent offset not a full 100 per cent offset if the VAT on the supply had been offsettable or recoverable.

18.16.4 Requirement for VAT invoice

The parties will usually want to clarify that VAT will only be paid upon receipt of a valid VAT invoice. This is an important point, as the party paying VAT will ordinarily not be able to recover it unless it pays against a valid VAT invoice. In some agreements, the parties clarify the situation for the charges payable for the services but forget to state what happens with regard to other payments to be made under the agreement.

18.16.5 Timing of payment

There may be timing issues too. For example, the parties may agree that the VAT element of the consideration charged by a supplier will only be paid over to the supplier two days before it has to account for the VAT to HM Revenue & Customs. (There are detailed rules relating to "continuous supplies" of services which in some cases may mean that issue of a VAT invoice accelerates the date VAT is due.)

18.16.6 Reverse charging

With the increasing interest in offshore outsourcing, parties need to be aware of the reverse charge mechanism. Very broadly, this causes the customer to have to charge itself VAT on supplies actually received from overseas which would have been liable to VAT if they had been received from a UK person. If the customer is able to recover all of the VAT, there is no VAT cost. Indeed the customer may benefit from a cash-flow advantage compared to paying VAT to a UK supplier. But, if the customer is partly exempt, some of the VAT that the customer has charged itself will have to be paid to HM Revenue & Customs.

Chapter 19

Service Credits and Service Bonuses

19.1 Outline

Chapter 18 describes the various charging regimes and how they reflect the liability profile under the agreement. One element of the charging regime has not been discussed. This is the service credit/service bonus regime, which results in deductions from the charges being made if the service levels are not met and bonuses being paid if specified service levels are met or exceeded. As explained in Chapters 9 and 10, the service levels themselves can relate to the provision of the services or the management of the services. This chapter deals with service credits and service bonuses. It describes the different types of service credit or service deduction regimes, whether service credits should be the customer's exclusive remedy, how the customer may prevent evasion of the service credit regime and how service credits should be paid.

19.2 Types of service credit and service bonus regimes

There are various different ways that service credit and service bonus regimes can be drafted and each one will encourage a different type of behaviour in the supplier. *See* Table 32 for examples of different approaches.

Table 32 *Service credit regimes*

Incentive to rectify

The service credit regime could operate over a running three-monthly period. If the supplier fails to achieve the service level in the first month, a small service credit applies or no service credit applies. If the supplier fails to achieve the same service level in the second month, then a greater service credit applies and if the supplier fails to meet the service level after the second month then a substantial service credit applies. This service-level regime is appropriate where failures cannot be avoided and the supplier is incentivised to rectify the defect once it has occurred.

Deter unacceptable performance

The service credit regime could apply so that service credits increase at an exponential rate the greater the failure. This service-level regime is designed to ensure that the service does not reach a certain unacceptable level.

Highlight critical services or service elements

The service credit regime can apply so that service levels for different elements of the services are given a different weighting, so that the supplier can see which service elements are most important to the customer and prioritise its service delivery accordingly.

Transparent service performance

The customer may decide that it wants service levels for each service element (e.g. in an IT outsourcing agreement, the desktop service, the telecommunications service, the server service and the printing service) so that it can see the standard being achieved for the individual service elements, but that service credits will be calculated taking into account the end-to-end service for which the supplier is responsible (e.g. availability of the applications on the server at the desktop, or time taken for cheques printed out by the supplier to be delivered to the user).

This example illustrates that it is not necessary for service credits to apply to all service levels. The two regimes can be drafted to achieve different aims. They can also operate over different periods. For example, the supplier may be required to report on the service levels on a monthly basis but (to reduce the administrative effort involved) the service credits may be calculated on a quarterly basis.

Highlight critical periods

The customer may have a critical period. For example, if the customer is a retail organisation it may be essential that its call centre is open to take orders during the six weeks prior to Christmas. To give another example, if the customer is a body that marks school examination papers, the months of July and August may be critical. Lastly, if the customer is a water utility, it may need to send out most of its bills over a specific period in February to March. The service description may require greater levels of availability over this critical period, with substantial service credits for failure to achieve these. Service credits may not apply during the rest of the year, or may only apply for serious failures to meet the service levels.

Deter service deterioration in the final months

The customer may be concerned that the supplier will take less care in meeting the service levels over the last 12 months of the arrangement, particularly if the supplier knows that the customer is not intending to renew the arrangement. Therefore, it may suggest that the amount of the service credits increases over the final 12 months.

Incentivise business benefit achievement

The customer may pay a service bonus if the supplier achieves certain service levels or satisfies certain business objectives. In the latter situation, the approach is similar to having a risk/reward element in the charges. (*See* Chapter 18 for a more detailed discussion of risk/reward schemes.)

The customer (or indeed the supplier) may pay the supplier's service manager (and possibly other key staff) bonuses which are linked to achievement of certain business objectives or customer satisfaction levels.

As stated in Chapter 9, service levels and service credits should be drafted so that they support the business objectives of the customer. Ideally, each service level and service credit should be justified on the basis that it is achieving a specific business benefit, taking into account the cost to the customer of the supplier complying with the service level, monitoring and reporting upon its performance in meeting the service level.

19.3 Relationship with control

The customer will want to understand and draft the service credit regime taking into account whether achievement of the service levels is within the control of the supplier.

If the supplier is pressurised to sign up to service credits for service levels it cannot guarantee that it will achieve, then it will usually endeavour to increase the amount of its charges by the amount of the service credits, on the assumption that it may have to pay them every month. Thus, the service credit regime will act more like a service bonus regime. The supplier will have assumed that it will have to pay service credits. Therefore, when it is successful in meeting the service levels, it will receive a bonus, in addition to the charges which it expected to receive. Accordingly, the supplier will still be incentivised to take measures to meet the service levels.

In this situation, however, it is important for the customer to realise that this is what is happening so that:

(a) it can consider whether action needs to be taken to reduce any adverse impact resulting from failure to meet the service levels; and
(b) it can satisfy itself that it is getting value for money by paying the additional bonus.

19.4 Evasion of the service credit regime

19.4.1 Gaming

Another factor which needs to be taken into account in drafting service credit regimes is whether the supplier has any opportunities for gaming – that is, evading the service credits. A good example of gaming is where the supplier has an obligation to rectify defects within a specified period of them being recorded by the supplier's help desk and the supplier avoids the service-level failure by not recording all of the problems reported to it. Another example is where a supplier is obliged to refill the cash in cash machines before they are empty, but the supplier is not responsible for technical defects affecting the cash machine. The supplier avoids the service-level failure by ensuring that the last note in each cash machine is folded so that it creates a technical fault in the cash machine before it runs out of cash. A well-drafted service credit regime should prevent gaming.

19.4.2 Failure to report

Another way that a supplier can attempt to avoid service credits is to fail to report that it is not meeting service levels. Sometimes the supplier is the only party who can obtain accurate information about whether it is meeting the service levels. In this situation, there are two ways that this can be dealt with in the agreement:

(a) the customer can ensure that the reporting obligation forms part of the invoicing procedure so that the supplier will not get paid until it provides the necessary information;

(b) the agreement can provide that, if the supplier fails to submit a report, the customer can require it to produce the report within a specified period, for example 30 days. If the supplier fails to produce the report (other than as a result of a force majeure event or a failure by the customer) then the supplier will be regarded as having failed to meet the service levels.

19.5 Complexity of service credit regime

Penalising the supplier for failure to report on service credits is only fair where the supplier can reasonably be expected to report on them. For this reason, it is important that the amount of effort required to measure and report on service levels and service credits is not burdensome. Clearly, if service levels cannot be measured, then there is little point in including them. Equally, it is not helpful if the service level or service credit regime is so onerous or complex that the service managers from both parties decide not to implement it.

In practice, the right number of service credits should be included in the regime if a focused approach is taken, as described in that last section of 19.2 above, with each service credit supporting the customer's business objectives.

19.6 Exclusive remedy – supplier's perspective

Service credits or service deductions are amounts that are payable by the supplier without the customer having to prove that it has suffered any losses as a result of a failure by the supplier to meet the service levels.

If service credits are not the customer's sole financial remedy, then, if the customer suffers fewer losses than the value of the service credit, it can recover the service credit; if it suffers greater losses, it can recover the difference between the two. For this reason, suppliers usually argue that service credits are unfair if they are not in full and final satisfaction of the customer's remedies. Limiting the customer's remedies to the service credits also enables the supplier to limit its total liability for failure to meet the service levels.

19.7 Exclusive remedy – customer's perspective

Despite the supplier's argument that service credits should be the sole financial remedy of the customer for breaches of the service levels, in many cases the customer will not want to agree to this.[1]

1 If the parties agree that the service credits will not be the customer's exclusive remedy, the agreement will need to be drafted carefully to preserve the customer's rights. Thus it must be expressly stated that service credits are not the exclusive remedy and are not liquidated damages. In addition, the relationship between service credits and charges will need to be drafted so that it does not appear that the supplier has an option to provide a lesser level of service and receive a reduced charge.

19.7.1 Service credits may not reflect the customer's losses

The first problem with accepting the supplier's argument is that customers usually do not see service credits as liquidated damages but rather as a useful way of incentivising the suppliers to comply with the service levels. Therefore, customers do not usually investigate or quantify the losses they would suffer if the supplier did not meet the service levels and they do not draft the service credit regime to compensate them for losses, except where the losses are straightforward. For example, if the supplier is processing bills on behalf of the customer, it can be assumed that a delay of two days in sending the bills out will cause the creditor to pay the bill two days late and hence result in losses calculated by reference to the amount of the bill multiplied by the agreed daily interest rate multiplied by two.

19.7.2 Service credits capped

Suppliers usually endeavour to cap their exposure to service credits to a fixed amount. This amount varies greatly, depending on the type of outsourcing arrangement, from 5 per cent to 100 per cent of the annual charge. Fixing a cap (particularly if it is at the lower end of this scale) may mean that the amount of the service credits will be inadequate to cover the losses that the customer will suffer.

19.7.3 Service credits less than the investment required to correct the defect

The customer will be anxious to avoid the situation where, because of the cap on service credits, the service credits act not as an incentive but as a disincentive to rectify defects in the services because the service credits are lower than the amount of investment required to correct the defect.

19.7.4 Importance of keeping records

If the service credit regime does mean that substantial amounts may be payable, then the customer should keep records showing how the amount of the service levels was fixed and that they were not intended to operate as a penalty for breach of contract (as penalties are unenforceable at law[2]).

19.8 Exclusive remedy – possible compromises

In the absence of agreement by one of the parties to accept the other side's preferred position, there are various compromises which may be appropriate in different circumstances.

2 *See* for example the cases of *Dunlop Tyre Company Limited* v *New Garage and Motor Company Limited* (HL1915) AC 79, *Philips Hong King Limited* v *AG of Hong Kong* (1993) 61 blr 41 and the more recent cases of *Cine Bes Filmcilik Ve YapimClick* v *United International Pictures* [2005] EWCA Civ 1669, *Murray* v *Leisureplay plc* [2005] EWCA Civ 963, 28 July 2005 and *McAlpine* v *Tilebox Ltd* [2005] EWHC (TCC), 25 February 2005. *See* also *Steria LTD* v *Sigma Wireless Communications Ltd* [2007] EWHC 3454 (TCC), which stresses the point that if a liquidated damages clause is unenforceable as a penalty, the customer will still have an uncapped claim for damages.

19.8.1 Exclusive remedy except for termination

The parties can agree that the service credits will be the customer's sole remedy unless the customer terminates the agreement or has grounds for terminating the agreement.

19.8.2 Service credits apply to minor failures

Alternatively, the service credit regime can apply to minor failures to meet the service levels, with the customer reserving its right to claim damages under the common law if the service levels deteriorate further. The logic behind this regime is that, if the customer is suffering material losses, it should be possible for it to prove them and claim them under the common law.

19.9 Payment of service credits

The parties will need to agree the mechanism by which service credits will be paid.

19.9.1 Set off

Suppliers prefer to state that service credits may be set off against the charges payable by the customer for the period to which the service credits relate, or if they are not known at that time, by the following period.

If a customer is not able to recover VAT, it will usually prefer the service credits to be set off against the charges payable by the customer for other periods rather than recovering them as a debt.

19.9.2 Recover as a debt

This mechanism will not work during the final period of the agreement when, if charges are payable in advance, no further charges may be payable to the supplier. In this situation, the customer may want the right to recover them as a debt from the supplier. The customer may want to have this right throughout the term of the agreement.

19.9.3 Waiver

Another problem with setting the charges off against the next month's charges is that often, in practice, the supplier fails to achieve the service levels for several periods; the customer does not claim the service credits for the first period, but as it becomes clear that the supplier is not remedying the problem, the customer wants to claim service credits for the current period and retrospectively for the previous period or periods. If this is likely, the customer may want to clarify this right in the agreement so that it is not seen as waiving its rights to seek payment of the service credits for previous periods.

Chapter 20

Ensuring Competitive Charges

20.1 Outline

Chapter 19 deals with adjustments to the charges resulting from the application of a service credit regime. This chapter deals with other adjustments to the charges.

During the term of the arrangement, the customer may want to ensure that the charges continue to represent good value, particularly if the outsourcing arrangement is long term. This concern may be of particular importance where the customer's business objectives in entering into the outsourcing arrangement include the achievement of cost savings. The issue also has special significance in the public sector, where local authorities are subject to the "best value" regime. This means that they have a statutory duty to secure continuous improvement in the delivery of their services, focusing on economy, efficiency and effectiveness.[1]

There are various ways in which the customer can ensure that the charges remain good value, apart from relying upon the supplier's goodwill in wanting to satisfy the customer in order to encourage the customer to extend the current agreement and to give the supplier additional business. The following paragraphs deal with the most common mechanisms used, including benchmarking, maximum margin and the most favoured customer guarantee. Each mechanism provides a different type of protection, and the customer may want to rely upon a combination of the various protections.

20.2 Benchmarking[2]

Benchmarking involves comparing the supplier's charges against other charges available in the marketplace. The process can take up to four or five months to carry out (depending upon the services) and may be costly. Accordingly, the approach may not be useful in lower-value outsourcing arrangements.[3]

There are various different elements to a benchmarking regime.

---

1 Local Government Act 1999.

2 Local authorities must comply with the Local Government Act 1999, which provides that they must compare their performance with other local authorities and the private sector. They have a duty to ensure continuous improvement in delivery of the services, focusing on economy, efficiency and effectiveness. As a result, they will be obliged to benchmark the charges under the outsourcing agreement. They will be obliged to carry out fundamental performance reviews every five years. As a result, a number of benchmarking clubs have been established.

3 *See* Neil Barton's interesting article on benchmarking, "A benchmark for Benchmark Clauses" in *The Magazine of the Society for Computers and the Law*, Volume 18, Issue 1, April–May 2007.

20.2.1 Benchmarking methodology

There are two main types of benchmarking methodology: cost benchmarking and contract benchmarking.

Cost benchmarking involves the benchmarking agent analysing the resources which it anticipates a reasonable supplier would use in providing the services and then building a cost model showing the cost of these resources, taking into account relevant factors relating to the contract being benchmarked. This type of benchmarking is suitable where the benchmarking agent has sufficient information about the relevant costs in the market for it to be able to provide reliable cost information. The supplier may want to state that any cost information must be based on a representative sample of contracts, which may involve information from 10 or more agreements.

Contract benchmarking involves the benchmarking agent selecting a small number of agreements (usually between four and six) which are most similar to the agreement being benchmarked, adjusting them to make them resemble the customer's contract by taking into account relevant factors and making a professional judgment as to whether they are more or less expensive than market value.

Neither benchmarking methodology is a statistical process. Benchmarking does not rely on representative sampling in a statistical sense. This would imply that there is a homogeneous set of prices out there for the same commodity services, but the reality is that every single service contract is unique, not homogeneous.

The only way of obtaining comparative prices for the same arrangements would be to ask other suppliers to bid for providing similar services. This would usually be more expensive, resource hungry and potentially disruptive to the business than benchmarking. In addition, other suppliers are unlikely to take the invitation to bid seriously unless the current outsourcing agreement is due to expire or the customer is seriously considering terminating it for convenience.

Benchmarking involves an expert opinion of what would be a fair market price, based on the best available comparative data, adjusted to account for the differences.

20.2.2 Adjustments

So what factors should the supplier ensure are taken into account in adjusting the data to ensure that the benchmarking agent is making a like-for-like comparison?

The supplier will want to state that the benchmarking agent should take into account all relevant factors, such as, for example:

(a) the nature of the customer, where relevant;
(b) the specific services being provided, in particular any additional security or governance requirements;
(c) the quality of services being provided;
(d) the volume of services being provided;
(e) the geographic area in which the services are being provided;
(f) the costs and liabilities transferred to the supplier from the customer on commencement of the arrangement. The customer may argue that this should only apply for

a certain period and that the supplier should be expected to reduce the cost base over time, where practical. Whether this is reasonable depends upon the particular circumstances;

(g) whether the supplier is restricted from using certain assets for the provision of services to other customers;

(h) the terms and conditions under which the services are being provided and in particular the risk profile of the specific arrangement; and

(i) the size and capabilities of the suppliers.

It should be noted that some factors cannot be benchmarked but need to be considered and removed from the comparison with other contracts. Examples of this include transition charges which are amortised over the life of the contract, and financial engineering schedules of charges which distort the relationship between the cost of delivery and the charges levied (*see* 18.11 above). The benchmarking methodology will need to identify these factors and ensure that they do not skew comparisons with other contracts, so that the charges considered relate only to the services being delivered and profiled within the analysis.

The supplier may want the benchmarking agent to explain what adjustments it is making to take into account the relevant factors.

20.2.3 Benchmarking changes

The customer will want to be able to benchmark the charges proposed by the supplier for changes to the outsourcing arrangement.

20.2.4 Benchmarking part of the services

The customer will often also want to have the option of either benchmarking the charges for all of the services or individual service elements (e.g. in an IT outsourcing agreement, the customer may want to have the right to benchmark the desktop services separately from the telecommunications services).

In a multinational outsourcing project, particular care will need to be taken in deciding which parts of the services the customer may benchmark separately. For example, the customer may want to divide the services into parts depending upon:

(a) the branch or country of the customer who is outsourcing to the supplier;

(b) the country or region from which the services are being provided;

(c) the language in which the services are being provided.

For the customer to be able to benchmark the charges for individual service elements they will need to be priced separately. From the supplier's perspective, there is a crucial difference between the supplier providing the customer with some reassurance that the overall price of the services will remain competitive and the supplier providing reassurance that every service element will remain competitive. The supplier may be unwilling to provide this additional level of reassurance. The acceptability of benchmarking in part depends upon the sector and the type of services being benchmarked. It also depends upon the country in which the services are being provided. For example, apparently benchmarking in part for small elements of IT services is more widely accepted in Germany.

20.2.5 Benchmarking all of the services

There may be problems with restricting benchmarking to the services as a whole. In particular, the customer should consider whether it will be possible to benchmark all service elements. If it is not possible, then restricting the customer's ability to benchmark the services as a whole will prevent it from carrying out any benchmarking exercises. In addition, this approach may act as a severe disincentive for the customer to carry out benchmarking as, if the customer is concerned that one service element is overpriced, it will not want to be obliged to incur the cost of benchmarking all of the other service elements.

20.2.6 Honeymoon period before benchmarking applies

If the supplier was selected as a result of a competitive procurement process, then the customer may feel that it does not need the right to benchmark until after the first 12 or 24 months of the agreement.

In addition, the information required to carry out a benchmarking exercise may change during an initial transition or transformation period, making it difficult to establish an accurate representative month and so it may be impractical for a customer to carry out a benchmarking exercise until the completion of the transition or transformation.

20.2.7 Frequency of benchmarking

After the initial honeymoon period, the customer may agree not to carry out benchmarking exercises more than once every 12 or 24 months for example. Gartner Consulting recommends benchmarking the total charges every two or three years within the contract (post transition), or carrying out a programme of annual but partial benchmarking (e.g. desktop and help desk in the first year, networks the next year etc.).

The customer will need to ensure that any such restrictions do not apply to benchmarking charges for changes to the services.

20.2.8 Benchmarking agent

Benchmarking regimes often provide for the benchmarking to be carried out by an impartial third party. There are various benchmarking agents who have experience of benchmarking specific types of services, including, for IT services, for example, Gartner Consulting and Compass. Before the agreement is signed, the supplier and the customer may want to agree who will carry out the benchmarking exercise.

If the services are such that some of the benchmarking agents are competitors of the supplier, then the supplier may want the customer to engage benchmarking agents who are not competitors. The customer will need to consider whether this is practical.

To emphasise the impartiality of the benchmarking agent, it makes sense for the benchmarking agent to be appointed by the customer and supplier jointly, with all information provided to or by the benchmarking agent going to the customer and the supplier. The benchmarking agent should be required to show the customer and the supplier how it reaches its findings, giving as much detail as possible without breaching the confidentiality of the peer group companies. Each party should be given an opportunity to comment on the information provided by the benchmarking agent and on the final report. These measures help ensure that the process is fair and hence encourage mutual "buy in" to the process and methodology, and hence greater acceptance of the independent results and conclusions when they are delivered.

The parties will need to agree who will pay the costs of the benchmarking agent. Most contracts encapsulate joint funding, but some contracts insist that the supplier will pay the benchmarking agent's costs if the supplier's charges are found to be expensive and the customer will pay if the supplier's charges are found to be reasonable.

20.2.9 What findings will result in an adjustment to the supplier's charges?

The parties will need to decide when the benchmarking process will result in an adjustment to the supplier's charges. For example:

(a) Will it do so if the supplier's charges are more than the comparative prices?
(b) Will it do so if the supplier's charges are more than, for example, 10 per cent higher than the comparative charges (or for that matter if the supplier's charges are not 10 per cent lower than the comparative charges)?
(c) Will the supplier's charges be compared with those in the marketplace on the date of signature of the agreement to see how they relate to those and to ensure that they maintain a similar relationship with comparative charges?

The customer and supplier will need to decide upon the desired approach when they agree the benchmarking regime.

Some outsourcing contracts state that the supplier's charges must be within the top quartile of charges. Benchmarking agents do not recommend this approach if the benchmarking agent is to use a contract benchmarking approach, as this approach inevitably involves a small sample of contracts.

20.2.10 Adjustments imposed or agreed

The issue of whether price adjustments will be imposed or agreed is one of the most contentious aspects of the benchmarking regime.

20.2.10.1 Adjustments imposed

The customer will usually prefer a mechanism whereby the charges are automatically reduced within a specified period (e.g. a month from the date of the finding) to the market rate or no more than an agreed percentage above the market rate.

20.2.10.2 Adjustments agreed

The supplier will argue that the customer should not have the unilateral right to amend the supplier's charges. Agreeing such a change will fundamentally undermine the supplier's expectation that the outsourcing arrangement will provide the supplier with a certain level of guaranteed revenue. It may also undermine the supplier's margin and the supplier may suggest that no reduction should be made if it reduces that margin below a specified percentage or if it reduces the charges by more than a fixed percentage.

The supplier will argue, therefore, that it should have to justify its charges and the parties should then negotiate any change in the supplier's charges. This option allows the parties to negotiate other solutions to ensure that the customer receives value for money, such as changes in the service levels. The customer may be concerned that, even if the supplier's charges are too high, any such provision will constitute an agreement to agree.[4] It may be concerned that it will not have the bargaining power to negotiate an equitable adjustment to the supplier's charges.

20.2.11 Adjustment in the form of a credit

The parties may be able to agree a compromise whereby, instead of the customer receiving a reduction in the charges, it will receive a credit which can only be used to buy additional services from the supplier.

20.2.12 Remedies if adjustment not agreed

If the parties are unable to agree a satisfactory amendment to the agreement within a specified period (usually about a month) after the final benchmarking report, the customer may want the right to terminate the agreement. This is likely to be extremely contentious and the supplier may argue that the customer should pay the same compensation as that payable on termination for convenience (*see* Chapter 25 for a discussion of termination rights). The customer will be reluctant to pay compensation if this will undermine the cost benefit it will obtain by transferring to another supplier.

Different considerations may apply in relation to charges for additional services if the customer has an option to ask other suppliers to provide the new services.

20.2.13 Supplier's right to benchmark

The assumption so far has been that the customer will have the right to benchmark the services to ensure that they remain competitive in the marketplace throughout the term of the outsourcing arrangement. However, in certain outsourcing arrangements the supplier may argue that an indexation provision is insufficient and that it should also have the right to benchmark the services and to impose an increase in the charges if they are lower than market rate. In practice,

4 Agreements to agree are generally unenforceable at law – *see Walford* v *Miles* [1992] 2 AC 128. However, the case of *Petromec Inc Petro-Deep Societa Armamento Navi Appoggio SpA* v *Petroleo Brasileiro SA* [2005] EWCA Civ 891 includes some obiter comments regarding circumstances in which agreements to agree which are of a narrow scope will be enforceable.

customers are unlikely to agree to this, as it will usually be entering into the outsourcing arrangement on the basis that the charges will be a specific amount and it will not be able to increase its budget to cover any increased charges.

20.3 Open book

In certain sectors, particularly the public sector, it is becoming increasingly acceptable for suppliers to be required to disclose information to the customer relating to how its charges are broken down and the margin it is making. Some suppliers are unwilling in principle to do this.

20.3.1 Different levels of open book

In practice, much depends upon the level of open book required by the customer. The phrase "open book" can describe a wide variety of different arrangements ranging from one in which the supplier divides its charges into overheads and margin, staff costs, asset costs and other costs to, at the other extreme, one in which the supplier may be obliged to disclose information relating to the salaries of staff and the costs of individual subcontracts and supplier agreements.

20.3.2 Confidentiality problems

There may be various problems with the supplier providing information relating to individual supplier agreements.

(a) In providing the services to the customer, the supplier may be relying upon goods or services purchased from other suppliers under corporate arrangements, whereby the supplier receives preferential rates which it is prevented from disclosing to other parties such as the customer.

(b) Most contracts which the supplier enters into with its suppliers to provide the services to the customer will include confidentiality obligations restricting the supplier from disclosing any information about the arrangement.

(c) The supplier may also be relying upon goods or services provided from other members of its own group, where the internal charging mechanisms under which they are provided are highly confidential.

(d) Any information provided relating to staff will have to comply with the Data Protection Act 1998 (*see* Chapter 32).

20.3.3 Administrative effort

If the customer wants the supplier to disclose information about specific supply agreements, then this may involve substantial work by the supplier in approaching its suppliers and obtaining their consent to the disclosure of the information. Also, some suppliers may not be able to obtain information about costs relating to individual contracts from their accounting systems and may need to get the figures manually for the customer. The supplier may want to charge the customer for any additional administrative effort involved in complying with any open book requirements.

20.3.4 Open book for changes

The supplier may suggest a compromise, whereby information is provided on an open book basis for changes to the charges, as the customer may be particularly concerned about these.

20.3.5 Limitations on value of open book

Customers should also be aware that the supplier has a considerable amount of control over its cost base and over how costs and overheads are attributed to the customer's agreement rather than other arrangements. Therefore, open book arrangements may provide a limited amount of reassurance for the customer.

It is worth pointing out that an open book provision on its own will only enable the customer to receive information about the supplier's cost base and margin. It will not ensure that the customer receives value for money. For the open book provision to have any impact in reducing the charges, it will need to be linked to, for example, a provision restricting the supplier's margin, as described at 20.4 below.

On the contrary, the biggest drawback of open book arrangements, if not drafted and managed properly, is that, by incorporating the supplier's assumptions about its anticipated margin, the supplier may argue that its charges should be increased if it fails to make that margin and so open book often implies and encapsulates some sort of "guaranteed margin" for the supplier.

20.4 Maximum margin

A maximum margin provision involves the supplier accepting that it will not make more than a specified margin or accepting that, if it does make more than a specified margin, it will share the excess profits with the customer.

The supplier may feel that, as it is taking the risk that it will fail to achieve its margin, for example as a result of unanticipated costs, it should not be required to share any increase in its margin with the customer. It may therefore suggest that the provision only apply if the supplier makes "super-profits".

The supplier may also be concerned that the profitability of the transaction will vary from year to year and that it should not be required to share profits with the customer unless the overall margin earned by the supplier over the term of the agreement exceeds the specified amount. This would be achieved by ensuring that the regime applies to the cumulative profit at the end of each year, with payments of profit shared with the customer being clawed back if the following years are less profitable. Alternatively, the supplier may prefer the regime to operate at the end of the term, when the supplier's profit over the full term of the agreement can be assessed. Depending upon the length of the arrangement, the customer may be unwilling to wait until the end of the term to receive its share, and may be concerned that it will have little bargaining power to enforce the provision at that stage.

20.5 Most favoured customer

Some customers want more protection than that afforded by the maximum margin provision. They want the supplier to agree that the customer will be a favoured customer, in that the supplier will not agree to provide similar services to other customers at a cheaper price.

Although this may seem like a helpful provision from the customer's perspective, it is difficult to see how it is practical. If auditing the maximum margin provision involves the customer having access to the supplier's books relating to the individual contract with the customer, the most favoured customer provision would, in theory, allow the customer or its agent access to all of the supplier's agreements with all of its customers.

In addition, suppliers will usually be unwilling to agree to this clause because of the manner in which it restricts them from carrying out their business. Suppliers may want to reserve the right to decide what margin they charge on other outsourcing arrangements and may, for example, want to reserve the right to enter into other arrangements at or below cost where necessary to break into a new market or where it makes sense for other business reasons.

20.6 Ensuring value for money for transferred assets

If the customer is transferring its assets to the supplier, it will want to ensure that it obtains value for money from the transaction. This issue is dealt with in Chapter 16.

20.7 Overlap

If suppliers agree charging variations such as those specified in this chapter, it is essential that they consider the relationship between the different regimes. For example, an agreement for call-centre services could include provisions stating that the charges will be reduced in line with reductions in call volumes and that the customer will share any revenue generated as a result of the supplier using the call centre to provide services to other parties. The supplier will want to ensure that the two provisions do not apply at the same time. Thus, if there is a fall in the volume of calls to the call centre, and as a result the supplier is able to use the call centre to provide services to other clients, the customer should be obliged to choose between either receiving the benefit resulting from the reduction in call volumes or receiving a share of the revenue generated by using the spare capacity.

20.8 Multisourcing

The concern for the customer to ensure ongoing competitiveness in long-term outsourcing arrangements must also be seen in the context of the debate as to whether the customer's outsourcing strategy should be one based on a multisourcing or a unisourcing approach. This topic is dealt with in Chapter 17.

Part Six - Change

Chapter 21

Transformational and Developmental Outsourcing

21.1 Outline

Chapter 20 deals with mechanisms for ensuring the competitiveness of the supplier's charges in an outsourcing arrangement. A fundamental part of this involves the arrangement for dealing with charges for changes in the services. Chapters 21 and 22 deal with this and other aspects of change management. This chapter focuses on outsourcing arrangements whose purpose is to implement change.

21.2 Using outsourcing transactions to implement change

If the customer's internal resources are insufficient to implement change, using outsourcing arrangements rather than external consultants may make sense for two reasons:

(a) the outsourcing supplier may have a greater knowledge and understanding of the customer; and

(b) the supplier may have a greater commitment to the customer if the parties have entered into a reasonably long-term relationship.

Outsourcing arrangements designed to implement change can be divided into three categories, transformational outsourcing, developmental outsourcing and PFI projects. These types of outsourcing agreements are described in the following paragraphs.

21.2.1 Transformational outsourcing

Transformational outsourcing arrangements involve the provision of business process re-engineering services to suggest ways in which the customer's processes and procedures may be improved. For example, the customer may engage a supplier to carry out a Six Sigma audit. "Six Sigma" is based on the Greek letter "sigma" which is used in statistical analysis to mean standard deviation. The aim of Six Sigma is to reduce the amount of deviation from standard processes to reduce the variability of performance and hence improve performance.

The supplier will then usually provide the re-engineered services to the customer for a specific period.

21.2.2 Developmental outsourcing

Developmental outsourcing arrangements involve the development, for example, of new IT systems, their implementation, maintenance and management. Over the last years there has been a trend away from developing new software and towards the customisation and the configuration of existing software.

Some outsourcing arrangements may involve an element of developmental outsourcing (possibly ongoing) and an element of transformational outsourcing (also possibly ongoing). If the outsourcing arrangement involves transformational and developmental outsourcing for the same function, then generally it is more logical for the transformational outsourcing to take place first. This will avoid a situation where a system (e.g. an SAP system) is developed for the current business and then proves to be inappropriate for the re-engineered business.

If the outsourcing arrangement involves developmental outsourcing, then various issues will arise depending upon the development methodology used for the project. There are numerous different types of software development methodologies. Broadly speaking, the methodologies fall into two different types: waterfall methodologies and agile methodologies. These different types of methodology are discussed below. This is an extremely complex (and contentious) topic and, in practice, most customers use a hybrid of the two methodologies. The paragraphs below are designed to illustrate the point that software development methodologies differ considerably and that commercial and legal specialists advising customers on developmental outsourcing agreements will need to understand the specific software methodology being adopted for the particular project before they will be in a position to draft suitable commercial and legal provisions.

21.2.3 PFI

PFI agreements may involve the construction of a school, hospital or other facility, which is then maintained by the supplier and made available to the customer as a service. PFI arrangements are considered in Chapter 35.

21.3 Waterfall methodologies

21.3.1 Description of the methodologies

The waterfall model is a sequential development process, in which development is seen as flowing steadily downwards (like a waterfall) through the phases of conception, initiation, analysis, design (validation), construction, testing and maintenance. To follow the waterfall model, it is necessary to proceed from one phase to the next in a purely sequential manner.

If the software or system is to be developed using the waterfall methodology then, as part of the conception phase, the customer will prepare and agree with the supplier a functional specification describing the functionality that it requires. The functional specification may distinguish between mandatory and desirable requirements. (This will be separate from the service description because that will be a description of services and the specification will be a description of an asset and the functionality and operation of that asset.)

The supplier will then, as part of the design phase, prepare a technical specification showing how the functionality will be achieved from a technical perspective.

The parties will have to agree how the system will be developed or the services provided and in accordance with what timetable.

21.3.2 Advantages and disadvantages

There are various advantages and disadvantages of the waterfall methodology, including the following.

21.3.2.1 Preparation

The advantage of preparing detailed functional and technical specifications is that time spent early on in software production may lead to greater efficiency later on in the software life cycle.

21.3.2.2 Written communication

The waterfall methodology relies upon the agreement of detailed documentation. This can be particularly useful for large projects involving many developers. It can also be helpful if developers leave the project. However, the reliance on written communication can lead to misunderstandings between the parties.

21.3.2.3 Sequential

The methodology assumes that the customer will describe its requirements and that these will be fixed before the supplier develops the software. In practice, the customer may not be aware of exactly what requirements it wants before it sees a working prototype and can comment upon it. The initial specification may include functionality which is not essential or which will not be used in practice.

The methodology assumes that the design is fixed before the programmers start to implement the software. However, it may only become clear in the implementation phase that a particular area of program functionality is extraordinarily difficult to implement. If this is the case, it may be better to revise the design than to persist in using a design that was made based on faulty predictions and that does not account for the newly discovered problem areas.

Because of the problems with the sequential nature of the pure waterfall methodologies, modified versions of the methodology have been developed which provide for overlapping phases so that information on problem spots can be acted upon during phases that would typically, in the pure waterfall model, precede others.

21.3.2.4 Not collaborative

The methodology assumes that the client will describe its requirements and then the supplier will go away and develop software which satisfies that requirement. In practice, the customer may need to work with the supplier to clarify its requirements and the supplier may benefit from collaborating with the customer to ensure that its interpretation of what the customer wants is correct.

21.3.2.5 Inflexible

The methodology assumes that the parties will agree the customer's requirements at the beginning of the process and that any changes will be agreed by the parties through the change control procedure. This may not be a problem where the customer's requirements are stable and where it is possible and likely that designers will be able to fully predict problem areas of the system and produce a correct design before implementation is started.

However, this can be inflexible and unsuited to situations in which the customer's requirements will change during the development process leading to "scope creep" and possibly to disputes between the parties regarding the charging and timetable implications of the changes.

21.3.3 Legal and commercial considerations

21.3.3.1 Business outcome liability

Where software is developed using a waterfall methodology, the supplier will (subject to 21.3.3.2 below) be responsible for developing software which meets the customer's functional requirements and doing so within the agreed deadlines.

The supplier will therefore want to document any dependencies it has upon the customer.

21.3.3.2 Acceptance of the technical specification

The supplier will usually want the customer to accept the supplier's technical specification before the supplier starts developing the software. This will ensure that the supplier fully understands the customer's requirements before it starts to develop the system.

However, if the customer accepts the technical specification, it may take the risk that the supplier's technical solution will not satisfy the functional specification. This will mean that the arrangement will be more of a service output-based arrangement than a business outcome-based arrangement,[1] unless there are other provisions which, for example, state that the acceptance criteria (*see* below) or service levels will incorporate business outcome-based measures or the charges will be payable on a business outcome basis. Often the customer will be relying upon the supplier's expertise and will not have the technical knowledge to confirm whether the supplier's technical solution meets its functional specification. The customer and supplier need to decide whether the arrangement will be business outcome or service output based. The parties may need to carry out a certain amount of due diligence to ensure that the technical solution will satisfy the customer's business objective. This may involve feasibility studies or pilots.

In PFI contracts, the customer does not usually accept that the system or service satisfies the specification and the supplier retains the risk that the system or services will satisfy the functional specification throughout the term of the agreement.

21.3.3.3 Payment for development of technical specification

Developing the technical specification may require extensive work by the supplier, which the supplier will be reluctant to carry out unless it is paid for the work. In this situation, the customer may have to pay the supplier to carry out a scoping study to enable the parties to finalise the

1 *See* Chapter 1 for an explanation of the distinction between "business outcome", "service output" and "input" based arrangements.

specification. The advantage of this approach, from the customer's perspective, is that if the parties can prepare a clear, detailed specification, this may enable the supplier to agree a fixed price for the development.

21.3.3.4 Payment for development of software

The parties may not know whether the software or system works until the whole system is finally tested. This may take many months. The supplier will not want to fund the entire development without any payment by the customer. If the customer agrees to pay instalments before the delivery of the final system, the question arises as to whether the customer should be entitled to a refund if the system ultimately fails the acceptance tests.

21.3.3.5 Implementation timetable

If it is important to the customer that the development is completed by a specific date (e.g. that it is completed before a peak trading period) then the customer may want the supplier to send it reports showing progress made in meeting the deadline, so that problems can be resolved.

The customer will usually require remedies if the system or services do not pass the acceptance tests on time. These may include, for example, liquidated damages payable for each day of delay for the first month or two of delay until the acceptance tests are passed. Thereafter, the customer may want the right to claim damages.

21.3.3.6 Acceptance tests

The parties will usually agree acceptance tests that will be designed to ensure that the developed system or (where appropriate) business process outsourcing ("BPO") services satisfy the customer's requirements. Both parties will want to ensure that the criteria laid down for acceptance are objectively measurable.

The supplier will want to ensure that it has appropriate opportunities to rectify problems with the system or services. It will also want to ensure that the acceptance tests are not failed where there are minor problems with the system or services.

21.3.3.7 Remedies for failure to pass the acceptance tests

If the development and provision of services for the system or the BPO services constitute all of the services covered by the outsourcing arrangement services, then the customer may require the right to terminate the agreement and recover any investment made in the system.

If the system has been provided in phases, then the supplier may want the customer to pay for phases which have been successfully completed, even if later phases fail, and the customer may want the right to reject earlier phases if they fail the tests as a result of later developments.

If the system or services are one of several elements of the outsourced services, then the parties will need to decide whether the customer will have the right to terminate the entire agreement or only the element of the agreement relating to the development of the system or provision of the BPO services. If the development of the system or provision of the services is a key part of the outsourcing arrangement, then the customer may want to terminate the entire agreement. The supplier will be unwilling to allow the customer to receive a refund of any payments made for outsourcing services in respect of which the supplier is not in breach.

21.4 Agile methodology

21.4.1 Description of the methodologies

An alternative development approach is that involved in agile development methodologies, in which the parties develop software in small increments with minimal planning. Agile methods produce completely developed and tested features (but a very small subset of the whole) every few weeks. The emphasis is on obtaining the smallest workable piece of functionality to deliver business value early, and continually improving it and adding further functionality throughout the life of the project.

Using the agile methodology, the parties work in cycles which are time boxed, usually a month long. At the beginning of the process, the parties agree the number of cycles. At the beginning of each cycle, there is a planning meeting to agree the requirements and the goals. The customer also prioritises the requirements. At the end of the cycle, the parties demonstrate what has been built and fully test it. The idea is to quickly develop a product which the customer can use.

Under the agile methodology, the customer has far greater responsibility. The supplier's obligations are to provide resources – the outsourcing is an input-based development project. The parties agree the length and number of cycles and the supplier is obliged to provide agreed resources during the cycles.

The charges for the software developed using the agile methodology will usually be calculated on the fixed-price basis on the assumption that the supplier will work with the customer during a specific number of cycles, where the cycles are of a specific length. The variable factor will be the functionality which can be produced as part of this project, with the customer prioritising the changes it needs.

21.4.2 Advantages and disadvantages

There are various advantages and disadvantages of the agile methodology, including the following.

21.4.2.1 Unstructured

The lack of emphasis on planning may be unsuitable for a customer where the company culture is structured and prefers order. This can be remedied in part by the parties agreeing and documenting iteration goals at the beginning of each iteration and dates by which these goals must be achieved. The methodology is likely to be more successful where the software developers are senior. Also, the lack of planning may be inefficient. If the requirements for one area of code change through various iterations, the same programming may need to be done several times over, whereas if a plan had been agreed up front, the supplier would only have needed to write a single area of code. Lastly, it is arguable that the use of an agile methodology can increase the risk of scope creep due to the lack of detailed requirements documentation.

21.4.2.2 Oral communication

The agile methodology relies upon the running of a series of cross-functional workshops, with representatives from the customer and supplier, to clarify the customer's requirements. Agile methods emphasise face-to-face communication over written documents. Most agile teams are located in a single open office to facilitate such communication.

The disadvantage of this approach is that it may be more difficult for large software development projects or projects where members of the team are at different locations.

It can also be argued that the large number of meetings may result in the software development project being unduly expensive.

In an agile project, documentation and other project deliverables ("artefacts") all rank equally with working software. Stakeholders are encouraged to prioritise them with other deliverables based exclusively on business value perceived at the beginning of the iteration. This may mean that less documentation is produced as part of the project, creating problems when members of the team leave.

21.4.2.3 Collaboration

The methodology assumes that the customer and the supplier will collaborate in clarifying the customer's requirements and developing software which satisfies them.

This emphasis on collaboration prevents problems being hidden.

21.4.2.4 Iterative process

The methodology is more flexible than the waterfall methodology as the customer can change its requirements as it goes along, as the implications of different decisions become clear.

21.4.2.5 Incremental

As the system is produced in stages, the customer can use the releases as they are developed. The customer will pay for these releases.

21.4.2.6 Prioritisation

The customer prioritises requirements as the project proceeds.

21.4.3 Legal and commercial considerations

21.4.3.1 Input liability

Because of the lack of a detailed specification which the supplier signs up to, and the collaborative nature of the development process, the use of an agile methodology is likely to lead to the supplier having an obligation to provide resources for the software development project (input-based liability), without the supplier guaranteeing any particular end product.

In this situation, the customer may want to ensure that it has the right to terminate the project for convenience where it feels that it is not obtaining sufficient benefit from the project.

21.4.3.2 Staff capabilities

Because of the resource-based nature of the project, the customer will usually want some reassurance of the abilities and experience of the individual developers who will develop the software and will usually want key personnel clauses to apply to them.[2]

2 *See* Chapter 8.

21.4.3.3 Payment for development of technical specification

The customer can pay for the software at the end of each cycle or they can pay for each release.

21.5 Balance sheet treatment

If the outsourcing initiative envisages significant investment by the supplier, as part of a developmental arrangement, it may be important to the customer to ensure that the assets developed or acquired by the supplier do not appear on the customer's balance sheet. If this is the case, it is important that accountancy advice is taken early on in the procurement.

21.6 Ongoing change

If the outsourcing arrangement involves the development of several systems over the term of the agreement, then the parties will need to provide for the development of each system. If the parties are to use a waterfall methodology for developing the new system then the customer may be reluctant to commit to instructing the supplier to develop the systems before the parties have agreed suitable specifications, development obligations, implementation timetables and acceptance tests for each system. In this case, the customer may commit to procuring the first system only and leave it open for the parties to add the development of additional systems once specifications have been agreed.

A similar problem can arise in transformational outsourcing projects, where the customer may not know what services it will require until the business process re-engineering services have been completed. Once again, a possible solution is for the customer to agree individual work packages involving the re-engineering of specific functions. After signature of the agreement, the parties may agree further work packages for the supplier to carry out. These agreements are sometimes called "incremental partnering agreements" in the public sector.

21.7 Transition period

Even in outsourcing agreements whose purpose is not focused on implementing change, the supplier may need a transition period during which it will carry out various changes to improve the services or the assets used to provide the services. It may also need to set up its help desk and establish its service management function and any necessary communications links between its premises and those of the customer.

In situations where there are substantial transition requirements, the customer may require protections similar to those described for transformational and developmental outsourcing arrangements, for example a transition plan, acceptance tests and remedies for failure to pass the acceptance tests.

Chapter 22

Change Management

22.1 Outline

Chapter 21 describes outsourcing arrangements whose purpose is to implement change. This chapter describes other aspects of change management. It deals with how change can be anticipated or, where it cannot be anticipated, how changes to the arrangement can be agreed. It also deals with dispute resolution mechanisms which may be employed where the parties cannot agree changes to the arrangement.

Public authorities and utilities should be aware that they cannot rely on a widely drafted variation clause to bring about endless changes to a contract that was originally tendered in accordance with the public and utilities Procurement Directives. *See* Chapter 34 for further details of the implications of these Directives upon changes to the outsourcing arrangement.

22.2 Anticipating change

In all outsourcing arrangements, even those whose purpose is not to implement change, the parties should be proactive about anticipating change. The customer should consider whether its requirements or its business may change.

Before the agreement is signed, the parties should discuss the extent of the flexibility which the customer will have to change the services, so that the customer understands the implications of investments which the supplier will need to make in order to be able to provide the services.

The parties may want to agree the implications of any foreseeable changes. For example, it is often foreseeable that the volumes of services required will change and so (if the charges payable depend upon the volumes of services to be provided) the parties may want to agree in advance the effect of increases or reductions in volumes upon the charges. It may also be foreseeable that the customer will need the supplier to make resources available to it (e.g. man days of consultancy). In this situation, the parties may agree, before the agreement is signed, the man-day rates which will apply.

In most outsourcing transactions, the customer will not be able to predict all changes that will occur during the term of the arrangement and the parties will need to agree changes to the agreement.

22.3 Agreeing change – the change control procedure

The second element of flexibility in an outsourcing arrangement involves the inclusion of a change control procedure for agreeing changes to the services which have not been anticipated before the contract is signed. Where appropriate, the customer may want to document in the change control procedure that it is a fundamental requirement that the supplier acts flexibly and reasonably in agreeing changes to the services.

The change control procedure also needs to meet various requirements. These are described below.

22.4 Effect of the change upon the customer's business objectives

The change control procedure will need to remind the customer or (where relevant) the parties to consider the effect of the change upon the achievement of the customer's business objectives, so that they are not unintentionally undermined. The nature of this obligation and the party who will be required to comply with it will depend upon whether the supplier is responsible for the achievement of the customer's business objectives (business outcome risk profile), whether it is responsible for the provision of the service (service output risk profile) or whether it is only responsible for the provision of resources to be used by the customer as it wishes (input risk profile). *See* Chapter 1 for an explanation of the difference between business outcome, service output and input-based outsourcing arrangements.

22.5 Effect of the change upon the services

From both parties' perspective, the change control procedure should ensure that the supplier carries out an impact analysis to highlight the effect of the change upon the services and the achievement of the service levels. The impact analysis should also consider whether the change will affect the security risks relating to the outsourcing arrangement and whether the security requirements need to be updated. The supplier may want to specify circumstances in which it can charge for carrying out this work.

The parties will need to consider the best way to implement the change and whether any communications or training will be required to ensure that users are aware of and take advantage of the change.

The customer may also want to consider whether the change will have any effect upon the assistance that it will need the supplier to provide in a business continuity situation or on termination. In addition, it must consider whether it needs to change its software licences or maintenance agreements as a result of the change.

Lastly, the parties will need to document any resulting change in relevant documentation such as the service description, business continuity plan or the exit management plan. In an IT outsourcing context, this is part of what is known as "configuration management", which involves ensuring that all information relating to the IT infrastructure is reliable and up to date, including asset registers, software licences and maintenance agreements.[1] However, even in non-IT situations, it makes sense for the customer to ensure that documentation about its services is kept up to date.[2]

22.6 Effect of the change upon the terms of the agreement

The change control procedure should ensure that the parties consider whether any terms of the agreement will need to be amended as a result of the change in the services. It is not uncommon for serious problems to arise, affecting customers and suppliers, where the parties have incorporated changes into the services without taking legal advice and without considering whether the original terms of the agreement are appropriate for the changed services. The moral of the story is for the parties to take legal advice where they want to agree substantial changes to the services or changes in the nature of the services, for example use of the outsourcing agreement for the sale of goods.

22.7 Effect of the change upon the charges

From the customer's perspective, often the most worrying aspect of change management is the agreement of changes to the supplier's charges. In some cases, reducing the costs of the outsourced services over the term of the agreement is an important business objective of the customer in entering into the outsourcing transaction, so that this issue is particularly important. Usually, the customer will have entered into the agreement having budgeted for specific charges and may be anxious to avoid unreasonable and unexpected increases in the charges.

There is a perception that some outsourcing suppliers enter into outsourcing agreements expecting to increase their margin by making substantial charges for any changes requested by the customer. The customer may be particularly concerned about this if it has selected the supplier following a competitive process in which the supplier has been under some pressure to offer the outsourcing services at a particularly low margin.

There are four main ways that the customer can protect itself from unreasonable increases in the charges, apart from agreeing as many changes as possible during the competitive process where these can be anticipated. These ways are described in 22.8–22.11 below. Having said this, if changes are inevitable, then it makes sense for the customer to estimate the nature and cost of the changes in preparing its business case, and to include in its budget an allowance for the cost of these.

22.8 Clear definition of changes

It is essential that the parties have comprehensively defined the services to be provided by the supplier so that it is clear what services are included in the charges and which will be regarded

1 Configuration management is one of the elements of ITIL service management. *See* 7.2.3.
2 *See* 24.3 and 25.3.

as changes in the services, for the provision of which the supplier is entitled to make an additional charge. This is in both parties' interests and will avoid disputes later on. This issue is dealt with in greater detail in Chapters 7, 8 and 9.

22.9 Good bargaining power

Each party will be anxious to ensure that it has good bargaining power when negotiating changes to the services. In practice, any clauses that result in the party having power under the agreement are beneficial to it. For example, if the customer can include a right to terminate the agreement for convenience (assuming that this is cost effective), this may increase its bargaining power.

On a practical level, the customer may find that if it leaves it until the last minute to agree changes, it undermines any bargaining power it has, particularly if the customer has no alternative at that stage other than to ask the supplier to implement the change. (*See* Chapter 17 on multisourcing versus exclusive supplier arrangements.) Provision of sufficient notice to the supplier may also enable the supplier to implement the charge over a longer time period, using under-utilised staff and assets rather than having to mobilise additional staff or assets.

22.10 Control over additional expenditure

The change control procedure needs to ensure that the customer has control over additional expenditure.

22.10.1 Prior notice from supplier

This can involve ensuring that the supplier informs the customer before carrying out services for which it claims it can make an additional charge. The customer may want the supplier to inform it that it believes the services are out of scope and to provide the customer with a written statement explaining why it believes the services to be out of scope. It may then want the supplier to comply with the change control procedure before implementing the services, unless the customer requires the services urgently. Some agreements state that if the supplier implements the change before agreeing it through the change control procedure, then it will not be able to charge for the change.

22.10.2 Approval of additional expenditure

The customer may also want to ensure that any changes that result in additional charges being payable by the customer must be approved by specific authorised representatives of the parties. This may be particularly important where the company is a multinational and the agreement comprises a framework agreement with specific agreements or service-level agreements signed between the supplier and the individual members of the group. In this situation, the customer will need to decide the extent to which the members of the group will be entitled to vary the services they receive so that they differ from the framework agreement. In certain circumstances, the customer may want to set minimum levels of service which must be contracted for. The customer will then need to set out who within its organisation has the ability to change the local service-level agreements and who can change the framework agreement.

22.11 Reasonable changes to the charges

The procedure needs to ensure that any changes to the charges are reasonable. This has two elements.

22.11.1 Increase in the charges

Additional charges quoted by the supplier for changes that involve additional services must not be unreasonable. The customer may want the agreement to provide that, if the supplier proposes charging extra for any additional services, it must demonstrate that the cost is reasonable, possibly by making available information on an open-book basis or by allowing the customer to benchmark. (*See* Chapter 20 for a discussion of open book and benchmarking arrangement.) The customer may also want to reserve the right to market test the charges for the changes by asking other suppliers to quote for providing the additional services and to either instruct another supplier to provide the additional services, where practical, or to use the resulting information to renegotiate the supplier's charges. If the change is to be implemented by a subcontractor of the supplier, the customer may want to be able to require the supplier to obtain competitive quotes from other suitable subcontractors.

22.11.2 Reductions in the charges

On the other hand, the customer may want to ensure that the change control procedure clarifies that changes can result in reductions in the charges as well as additional charges. In particular, problems may arise where the customer wants to make a change that involves a reduction in the services to be provided to it, for example deleting a service that it no longer requires.

Some suppliers may argue that they have entered into the agreement assuming that they have been guaranteed certain revenue and so are not required to reduce the charges at all if the customer decides to reduce the services to be provided. To avoid this misunderstanding, the parties should clarify, in appropriate cases before the agreement is signed, whether the charges are guaranteed, whether there is a minimum commitment or whether the charges may be reduced if the scope of the services is reduced.

If the parties agree that the charges may be reduced in circumstances where the scope of the services is reduced, then the next question is, on what basis should the charges be reduced? The supplier may argue that the services should only be reduced by the amount of cost savings the supplier actually achieves as a result of the reduction in the scope of the services. Particularly where the supplier may not have a financial incentive to maximise the cost savings it achieves, the customer may want to ensure that the charges will be reduced by a reasonable amount, for example by specifying that the charges will be reduced by the amount of the cost savings which a professional supplier could reasonably be expected to achieve or that the supplier must use reasonable endeavours to reduce the costs.

22.11.3 Relationship between charges for increases and reductions

In ensuring that the charges for changes in the services are reasonable, it is essential that the customer considers the relationship between the regime for calculating increases in the charges and the regime for calculating reductions in the charges. Customers often fail to notice that there is a mismatch between the two. For example, the charges for additional services may be calculated on the basis of the supplier's additional costs plus a margin and the charges for reductions in the services may be calculated on the basis of cost reductions only. The effect of this arrangement, particularly over a long-term agreement, may be that the supplier's margin gradually increases. Depending upon the specific circumstances of the outsourcing arrangement, there are various ways that the customer may avoid this problem:

(a) Before the agreement is signed, the customer may agree that it will have the right to terminate individual service elements, in which case the charges will be reduced by the amount of the charges for that service element. In this situation the agreement will usually define the service elements and the period of notice required to terminate them and the charges will be broken down so that there is a separate charge for each element. This option will only be acceptable to the supplier if it has priced the service elements on the basis that they are severable.

(b) The customer can specify that if there are reductions in the services, then the charges will be reduced by the amount of the cost savings plus the margin. The supplier may be reluctant to agree to this unless the parties also agree a minimum charge or a minimum margin.

(c) The customer can specify that the supplier cannot charge a margin on additional services, although the supplier is likely to resist this approach.

(d) The effect of change can be fed into a financial model, prepared by the supplier and agreed with the customer at the outset, which preserves the supplier's overall margin.

(e) The customer may rely upon general protections such as the maximum margin, benchmarking procedures or open book provisions described in Chapter 20.

22.11.4 Taxation implications

The parties may need to consider the taxation implications of a proposed change in the services. From a VAT perspective, extending or decreasing the scope of the service may mean that the nature of the supplies changes so that they start to fall within a VAT exemption (e.g. group 5 of Schedule 9 VAT Act 1994 for financial services) or cease to satisfy an exemption. The significance of changes to the consumption of services from a VAT viewpoint is that, depending on whether the services are treated as a "composite supply" (so that the VAT liability is determined by the principal component) or a series of supplies with their individual VAT treatment, a change in the components could affect whether VAT is charged.

The parties should also consider the taxation implications of any investment to be made by the supplier. For example, additional expenditure may benefit from tax relief. In this situation, the customer may argue that it should only need to reimburse the supplier for the net cost.

22.12 Minor changes

The parties may want to ensure that minor or routine changes do not need to go through a formal change control procedure, to prevent the procedure becoming overloaded or bureaucratic. This would be helpful if the change does not result in a change in the customer's business objectives, does not impact upon other elements of the services and does not necessitate a revision to the charges.

ITIL[3] sets out an arrangement whereby changes which it calls "standard changes" are dealt with via a service request under incident management. Standard changes include, for example, requests to create new user IDs.

22.13 Operational change management procedure

When drafting the contractual change control procedure, the parties will need to ensure that it is consistent with the operational change management procedure which will be used in practice to deal with such matters as recording, prioritising, planning, approving, implementing, testing and evaluating changes. The operational change management procedure may also involve agreeing and testing (and possibly implementing) a back-out procedure for reversing a change which has been unsuccessful.

22.14 Timescales

The customer may also want to consider whether it needs the supplier to respond to change controls within a certain period and whether it is appropriate to see the supplier's role in dealing with change control requests as part of the services, with applicable service levels and service credits.

22.15 Mandatory changes

Paragraph 22.3 above explained that the change control procedure is a way in which the parties can agree changes to the services. In most cases this is correct and the supplier will not want the customer to have the right to unilaterally vary the agreement without the supplier's agreement.

There are a few instances, however, where the customer may not want the supplier to have the right to refuse to implement the change. The next three paragraphs deal with three such circumstances.

22.15.1 Changes in the law

The first example of such a situation is where changes are necessary to ensure that the services comply with changes in legislation or regulations. In this situation, the customer will need the

3 *See* 7.2.3.

supplier to commit to complying with the legislation. The supplier will want to ensure that it is protected from any adverse consequences upon the services that arise as a result of implementing the change in law.

The question arises as to when the supplier can make an additional charge for complying with changes in the law. The following paragraphs explain the three different approaches which can be taken to deal with this question.

22.15.1.1 Specific changes

In accordance with the principle described at 22.2 above, the parties should be proactive about anticipating change. Accordingly, they should endeavour to agree who will take the risk of specific changes in law, for example changes in taxation affecting the customer or supplier. One example of this is changes in taxation resulting from changes in environmental law such as in the rapidly developing field (under international, EU and national law) of climate change.

As the parties will usually be unable to foresee all changes in the law, they will also need to include some general fallback provisions which will apply for unforeseen changes.

22.15.1.2 Customer takes the risk

Some customers take a view that they do not want the supplier to increase their initial charges to compensate them for taking any risk relating to future changes in law. As a result, the customer takes all of the risk of changes in the law and the supplier is always entitled to make an additional charge for complying with changes in the law. This approach is common in facilities management outsourcing agreements influenced by practices in the construction industry.

22.15.1.3 Parties share the risk – non-PFI arrangements

An alternative approach, common in the IT industry, is for the customer to expect the supplier, at no additional charge, to comply with general legislation, compliance with which is seen by the customer as part of the supplier's costs of running its business. In this context, general changes in the law refer to changes which do not affect the customer's requirements, for example an increase in the minimum wage. They do not include changes which do affect the customer's specific requirements.

The customer may also expect the supplier to share some of the risk of there being changes in legislation which affect the services, for example by only being able to charge for a limited percentage of the costs incurred. The supplier will usually increase its charges to cover this risk. This approach may or may not represent good value to the customer depending upon whether, during the term of the outsourcing arrangement, there are actually more or less changes in legislation than the supplier anticipated when setting its charges.

This approach may, however, give the supplier an incentive to implement the necessary change efficiently, for example by anticipating changes in health and safety requirements for PCs before carrying out a technology refresh and hence ensuring that all new PCs comply with the change in law before it is introduced.

22.15.1.4 Parties share the risk – PFI arrangements

PFI agreements take a slightly different approach, distinguishing between discriminatory legislation, specific legislation and general legislation:

(a) discriminatory legislation is legislation that affects PFI contracts or the specific customer, but is not of general application;
(b) specific legislation is legislation that affects the customer's requirements or the particular services, but is not of general application; and
(c) general legislation is any legislation that is neither specific nor discriminatory.

Under a PFI agreement, the customer will generally be responsible for the implications of any specific or discriminatory changes in law, with the responsibility for general changes in law being shared between the customer and the supplier. The sharing of risk may be by reference to time (e.g. the supplier may be responsible for any general changes in law during the initial five years, such period being linked to the period of initial investment in the project, or for the periods between fixed market testing dates) or by reference to financial caps on any capital expenditure required by the change in law. Tax changes in law (excluding VAT rates) and general operating costs are normally a supplier risk.

22.15.2 Changes in customer's policies

The customer may want the supplier to agree to provide the services in accordance with changed corporate policies, for example its security policy. In this situation, the supplier will have several concerns:

(a) it will want to make sure that the policy is reasonable and that it can comply with it;
(b) it will want to ensure that it receives adequate notice of the change;
(c) it will want to be paid for any costs it incurs in complying with the changed policy; and
(d) as for a change in law, it will want to ensure that it is protected from any adverse consequences upon the services that arise as a result of implementing the change in the customer's policies.

22.15.3 Similar services

The third example of where the customer may want the right to insist that the supplier agrees certain services is where the customer requires additional services which cannot for commercial, technological or other reasons be provided by another supplier without great inconvenience to the customer.

The supplier may want to ensure that it will not be contractually obliged to provide services that it cannot in practice provide, for example by limiting the obligation to provide services already afforded by the supplier to other customers. The customer may want to extend this to cover services that the supplier could provide if it engaged a subcontractor. The supplier may prefer a general principle that changes to the services must be agreed, but that the supplier will not unreasonably refuse to provide services.

22.16 Resolving disputes about changes

Apart from anticipating change and including a change control procedure for agreeing changes which cannot be anticipated (as described in this chapter), the agreement should also include escalation and dispute resolution procedures for dealing with changes which cannot be agreed by the parties. These may be specifically tailored to suit the particular type of issue and may not be the same as the general dispute resolution provisions described in Chapter 11. For example, a pricing issue may be referred to an industry expert.

Part Seven – Termination

Chapter 23

Term and Termination Rights

23.1 Outline

Chapter 22 describes how the parties manage change in the outsourcing arrangement. This chapter outlines how the parties deal with the greatest change in the arrangement, its termination. It includes a discussion of the factors that the parties should take into account in fixing an appropriate term for an outsourcing arrangement. It also covers the circumstances in which the parties should be able to terminate the outsourcing transaction.

23.2 Determining an appropriate term

The parties should take into account various factors in determining an appropriate term for the outsourcing arrangement.

23.2.1 Fundamental changes in arrangement

The customer should consider over what period it can realistically anticipate its future needs. Even over a short period, the customer may find that it changes its requirements and has to negotiate changes to the outsourcing arrangement. This should not undermine the outsourcing arrangement. Chapter 22 explains how change can be managed in an outsourcing arrangement. However, the customer should decide the term of the agreement taking into account when it anticipates that it may need to re-examine the reasons for outsourcing, the current outsourcing solution or the justification for selecting the current outsourcing supplier.

As technology is continually changing, customers often find it more difficult to anticipate their technology requirements than, for example, their property needs.[1] This is particularly the case where the customer's technology requirements are affected by changes in the customer's business or operation. Therefore, it makes sense that, typically, IT outsourcing agreements are shorter than business process outsourcing deals, which, in turn, are shorter than property outsourcing agreements.

1 The change to virtualised servers and more recently virtualised desktop is a good example of how changes in technology can fundamentally affect the way the technology is used and hence the technology requirements of businesses.

23.2.2 Expected life of assets

The parties should determine the term of the arrangement in the light of the expected life of the assets used to provide the services. This is linked to the customer's anticipation of its future needs, as the customer may want to reassess its requirements when key assets need replacing.

23.2.3 Costs saving

The parties should take into account the financial implications of the length of the agreement.

23.2.3.1 Ongoing charges
Thus the outsourcing supplier may be able to provide the services more cheaply on an ongoing basis.

23.2.3.2 Transition charges
However, establishing the outsourcing arrangement will usually involve a financial investment. An investment may be required, for example, in implementing the initial transition from the provision of the services by the customer or its previous supplier to the outsourcing supplier. The parties will also need to establish service management structures and processes. If the arrangement is a developmental outsourcing transaction, then development costs may be incurred, which will often be spread over the term of the agreement.

23.2.3.3 Termination assistance costs
Lastly, additional costs may be incurred when the services are transferred back to the customer or the replacement supplier on termination of the arrangement.

23.2.3.4 Traditional outsourcing models
If the term of the outsourcing arrangement is too short, the investment needed to establish and dismantle the arrangement will outweigh the savings made during its term. The savings will generally be greater the longer the agreement, unless further investment would be required, for example because the assets will need replacing.

23.2.3.5 Non-traditional outsourcing models
Not all outsourcing models involve substantial transition and termination assistance costs. Non-traditional outsourcing models (including application service provider ("ASP"), utility computing, software on demand, software as a service ("SAAS"), cloud computing and business process utility ("BPU") models) under which IT or business process services are made available to the customer on a rental basis may involve a more straightforward transition and termination, as they involve the provision of a commoditised service by the supplier. Therefore, agreements for these types of outsourcing arrangements are usually shorter (two to three years) than traditional outsourcing agreements.

23.2.3.6 Extensions of the agreement
Whether the outsourcing arrangement is a traditional or a non-traditional model, the customer may want the option to extend the agreement on expiry if the arrangement is still satisfying its

business objectives. The supplier, for its part, may be anxious to retain the business and may therefore be happy to extend the arrangement. However, just as the customer may find it difficult to anticipate its requirements many years in advance, the supplier may find it difficult, when the original arrangement is entered into, to anticipate its cost base in advance and may be unable to commit to a fixed price for the extension. If the charges for the extension cannot be agreed before the original arrangement is entered into, the parties should endeavour to agree an appropriate mechanism for objectively determining the charges at the relevant date. Otherwise this undermines the value of the option to the customer, as in any event (subject to 23.2.4 below) the parties may agree to extend the arrangement, whether an option was included in the original agreement or not.

23.2.4 Public sector considerations

The term must be consistent with that stated in the OJEU notice and must not be extended otherwise than in accordance with the Services Regulations (*see* Chapter 34).

If the customer is a local authority, the term of the agreement must be fixed taking into account the authority's obligations to carry out a best-value review every five years.

If the outsourcing agreement is, or incorporates, a framework agreement (i.e. those agreements under which a public authority has one or more suppliers on a panel from which it can "call off" contracts for work or services on pre-agreed terms and price) then public sector customers are restricted by the Services Regulations from entering into framework agreements for longer than four years, although it should be noted that there is no restriction on the length of specific contracts "called off" under such agreements.

23.3 Termination grounds

In addition to fixing the term of the agreement, the parties should also decide in what circumstances each party may terminate the agreement before expiry.[2]

23.3.1 Importance of agreeing appropriate termination rights

Termination is an extremely important issue. If the customer has not negotiated the necessary rights to terminate, then it may find that it is locked into an agreement that is not satisfying its business objectives or that is causing damage to its operations.

If the supplier has conceded to the customer extensive rights to terminate, then it may find that it has invested in the services in circumstances where the customer can terminate the agreement before the supplier has been able to recover its investment. It may also find that the customer is

2 All discussions on termination rights within a contract must be linked to the consequences of termination and, crucially, the requirement for compensation payments to be made by either party. These are considered further in Chapter 25.

able to evade the payment of termination charges for example by exploiting widely drafted clauses enabling it to terminate for breach.

There are various grounds for termination which may be included in the outsourcing arrangement.

23.3.2 Insolvency

See Chapter 26 for a discussion of insolvency issues including termination rights.

23.3.3 Breach

Each party will usually want the right to terminate the agreement if it is breached by the other party. The parties may decide to distinguish between a breach that can be remedied and one that cannot. If the breach is remediable, then the party in breach may be given a period (e.g. 30 days) to remedy the breach. An example of a remediable breach is non-payment of an amount of money. An irremediable breach could be, for example, failure to carry out a task by year end when the year end has subsequently passed and the task cannot be carried out.

The parties may also want to specify that the right to terminate only applies to certain types of breach, for example material breaches.[3]

23.3.3.1 Supplier breach

The parties may want to define which breaches of the agreement by the supplier will be regarded as material breaches. For example, the right to terminate may be tied in to the key performance indicator regime, so that the customer will have the right to terminate if the supplier's performance falls below a certain level. The parties may also agree that the customer will have the right to terminate if the supplier fails certain acceptance tests or implementation tests relating to the transition of the services or the implementation of changes in the services.

The customer will usually want any list to be non-exhaustive so that it does not take the risk of having to anticipate all future breaches by the supplier. The supplier will usually want the certainty

3 Without going into too much detail, clauses in an agreement may be classified into conditions and other clauses, such as warranties or innominate clauses. Conditions are key clauses, the breach of which will constitute a material breach of the agreement. Innominate clauses are clauses which are not conditions or warranties and which may or may not be key, depending upon the circumstances. A "breach" of the agreement (as compared to a "material breach"), will include any failure by the supplier to comply with its obligations, whether the breach is of a condition or any other type of clause. However, to complicate matters, in the case of *Rice (T/A The Garden Guardian)* v *Great Yarmouth Borough Council*, *The Times* 26 July 2000, the customer tried to rely upon a express contractual right to terminate for any breach and the court held that, in a contract for the provision of outsourced garden maintenance services, where the supplier was required to make a substantial investment so that it could provide the services, the contract would be interpreted to mean that the customer could only terminate if there was a repudiatory breach by the supplier. This question will need to be carefully considered in the particular circumstances of each case. In *Alan Auld Associates Ltd v Rick Pollard Associates* [2008] EWCA 655, the Court of Appeal found that a persistent and cynical delay in making payments to a party providing consultancy advice amounted to a repudiation of the contract made with that party. *See Dalkia Utilities Services plc* v *Celtech International Ltd* [2006] EWHC 63 (Comm) for a summary of the leading authorities on "material breach".

of having an exhaustive list. In any event, the customer should bear in mind that it will usually want the right to terminate the agreement for reasons other than those relating to performance, for example a breach of the confidentiality or security obligations or failure to comply with relevant regulatory requirements.

If the parties do decide to limit the general right to terminate to material breaches of the agreement, then the customer may want an additional right to terminate for persistent non-material breaches. If the supplier agrees to this, then the parties may define persistent breach in the context of the particular agreement. Once again, the customer may want the definition to be non-exhaustive and the supplier may want it to be exhaustive.

23.3.3.2 Customer breach

The supplier may want to have the right to terminate for a breach of the agreement by the customer.

The customer may argue that its obligations are limited to paying the charges and enabling the supplier's provision of the services. Accordingly it may suggest that, if it fails to comply with obligations enabling the provision of the services, the supplier's remedies should be limited to being granted relief from failure to perform and being compensated for any additional expense incurred in carrying out the services. This is because:

(a) the customer will not want to deal with the disruption caused by the agreement being terminated; and
(b) the customer may consider that the supplier will be adequately compensated for situations in which the customer breaches service-related obligations if the supplier can claim relief due to failure to provide the services and can recover any additional expenses incurred as a result of the customer breach.

The supplier may want the additional right to terminate the agreement if these remedies are not sufficient, for example if the customer breaches confidentiality or security obligations which cause damage to the supplier's business or to its other customers.

The customer may want non-payment by it to be treated as a remediable breach which it will have a period of time to correct (e.g. 30 days), so that the supplier cannot terminate the agreement due to a single administrative error by the customer's accounts department. The supplier may be concerned to ensure that this does not result in the customer deciding to pay invoices late, hence undermining the supplier's cash flow. The agreement may provide the supplier with other remedies to deal with this concern, for example the payment of interest on late remittances.

23.3.4 Force majeure

See Chapter 30 for a description of force majeure events.

23.3.5 Corruption

The customer, in particular in the public sector, will usually reserve the right to terminate the agreement if the supplier or any employee or subcontractor of the supplier is guilty of bribery or corruption in connection with the grant of the contract. Sometimes the corruption clause is drafted quite widely, for example so that it applies if the customer believes that the supplier is guilty of corruption. The supplier may want to amend the clause. However, the supplier is advised to be extremely careful about negotiating any amendments to the corruption clause. It must avoid giving the customer the impression that it is negotiating the clause because it is worried that its employees may be guilty of corruption or because it has had a problem with corrupt employees in the past.

Sometimes the supplier feels that termination is too severe a remedy and that it should be allowed to resolve the situation by terminating the subcontract or the employment of the corrupt employee. The HM Treasury Guidance on the Standardisation of PFI Contracts[4] suggests that the authority's right to terminate the agreement should be restricted where the employee or subcontractor was acting independently of the supplier (i.e. they did not act under the authority of or with the knowledge of a director of the supplier) and the supplier terminates the subcontract or employee's employment within a specific period. This guidance applies to PFI and public private partnership ("PPP") contracts. However, even if the agreement is a public sector agreement which is not a PFI or PPP agreement, the supplier may argue that the guidance illustrates the type of approach which is acceptable in the public sector.

23.3.6 Fraud related to the provision of the services

If the nature of the outsourced services are such as to provide an opportunity for the supplier to commit a fraud (e.g. in payroll services, payment collections services or local authority revenues and benefits services) then the customer may want the right to terminate the agreement as a result of the fraud. The customer may also want the right to suspend provision of the services if there is a suspicion of fraud and this is necessary to prevent further acts of fraud. The supplier will usually want to ensure that it will be compensated if the customer's suspicions later prove to be unfounded.

23.3.7 Other fraud

The customer may want the right to terminate if the supplier is guilty of fraudulent reporting relating to its financial accounts, or if it fails to comply with relevant securities law and regulations in the countries in which it is established or if there is a regulatory enquiry into its running.

23.3.8 Change of control

If the customer has selected the supplier partly on the basis of the particular character or culture of that supplier, then it may want to have the right to terminate the agreement if there is a change of control in the supplier.

The supplier may be reluctant to agree to this, as it will undermine the value of the supplier's business in a subsequent merger or acquisition. The supplier will also stress that this ground for

4 HM Treasury Guidance – Standardisation of PFI Contracts, revised 2007, paragraph 21.4.3.

termination will only be relied upon where the supplier is providing the services in accordance with all of its contractual obligations, as otherwise the customer would be able to rely upon a right to terminate for breach of the agreement. Accordingly, the supplier may agree to the right of termination on the basis that it is regarded as a termination for convenience and the supplier is paid a reasonable termination charge if the supplier would otherwise not be compensated for its investment in the services.

An alternative approach would involve restricting the right to circumstances which the customer is particularly concerned about, for example where the change of control:

(a) could have a material effect upon the services;
(b) involves the supplier being taken over by a competitor of the customer; or
(c) results in a conflict such as where the customer has outsourced its finance function to the supplier and the supplier is taken over by the customer's auditors.

In public sector agreements, the customer may also want to cover the possibility that control of the supplier could pass to an organisation which is unacceptable for political or security reasons.

23.3.9 Change of organisation or management

Customers sometimes want the right to terminate the agreement not only if there is a change of control but also if there is a change of organisation or management in the supplier. The FSA suggests that customers consider including this right in their agreements. Suppliers may be reluctant to agree to this as it may undermine their ability to establish the best organisation or management for their business. The comments on termination for change of control apply equally to this situation.

The question arises as to whether the supplier should have the right to terminate the agreement if there is a change of control, organisation or management in the customer. If the parties have been able to define the boundaries of the services effectively, then any such change in the customer should not increase the burden to the supplier of providing the services and the parties should be able to agree appropriate changes to the services and charges in accordance with the agreed change control procedure. (*See* Chapter 22 for a discussion of the change control procedure.)

23.3.10 Loss of licence or approval

The customer (or indeed the supplier) may want to have the right to terminate the agreement if the supplier loses a licence that it requires in order to provide the services, for example a telecommunications licence or approvals from the FSA. The supplier may want to be given an opportunity to rectify the situation before the agreement is terminated.

23.3.11 Termination for convenience

The customer may want to have the right to terminate the arrangement for convenience, even in circumstances where there is no fault by the supplier. The right may be a general right, subject only to the giving of a certain period of notice, or it may apply in certain specified circumstances only.

If the customer wants to have the right to terminate for convenience after an initial period, for example five years, then the supplier may see the arrangement as a five-year agreement and calculate its charges accordingly. Thus the supplier would calculate its charges so that it recovers its set-up costs and fixed costs over the first five years of the agreement. This would mean that the customer would lose the advantage of being able to pay the costs over a longer period. An alternative approach may be to allow for a longer period (e.g. seven years) with the supplier spreading its fixed costs over the longer period. The customer could then have a right to terminate the agreement after the first five years provided it pays the supplier a termination charge that compensates the supplier for unrecovered costs. The supplier may argue that it should also be paid the margin that it should have been paid during the rest of the agreement.

23.3.12 Failure to agree

The customer (or the supplier) may sometimes want the right to terminate the agreement if the parties fail to agree to changes to it or fail to agree service descriptions, service levels or other details relating to the arrangement, which the parties were not able to resolve before the agreement was signed.

This approach may be helpful if the threat of termination has the effect of incentivising the parties to act reasonably and agree the issues in dispute.

From the customer's perspective, terminating the agreement is not the best way of dealing with such problems as it is a costly approach. (*See* 7.3 above for a discussion of problems in agreeing the service description and 9.5 above for a discussion of problems in agreeing service levels.) The customer may prefer to agree dispute resolution provisions which will apply in such circumstances.

From the supplier's perspective, termination will not be acceptable unless the supplier is compensated for any investment it has already made in the services but for which it has not yet been paid.

23.3.13 Termination under the common law

Paragraphs 23.3.2 to 23.3.12 cover possible grounds for termination that the parties may want to expressly include in their outsourcing agreements. In addition, depending upon the nature of the provision breached, the parties may have the right to terminate the agreement under the common law. The categorisation of contractual terms into conditions, warranties and innominate terms is explained below (in footnote 2). In general terms:

(a) the breach of a condition will give the innocent party the right to terminate the agreement;
(b) the breach of a warranty will not give the right to terminate; and
(c) breach of an innominate term (i.e. one that is not a condition or a warranty) may give rise to a right to terminate, depending upon whether the consequences of the breach are sufficiently serious to justify such action.

A misrepresentation which induces the entry of a contract may give rise to a right to rescind the contract. *See* 4.5.2.

PFI contracts will usually include a provision excluding any rights to terminate other than in accordance with the express provisions of the agreement. The parties in non-PFI contracts may want to consider doing likewise.

23.4 Other remedies

The customer may want remedies other than termination if the grounds mentioned in 23.3 above apply. The remedies could include:

(a) the right to require the supplier to disclose further information about the problem (e.g. regulatory investigation);
(b) the right to terminate the supplier's exclusive right to provide the services or the minimum revenue commitment; or
(c) the right to exercise step-in rights (*see* 8.6).

23.5 Time limits

Each of the parties may be anxious to ensure that the other party does not abuse its rights of termination. They may therefore agree, for example, that a party cannot rely upon a breach or change of control beyond a specified period after the event has occurred.

If parties agree such limitations, they must ensure that they do not lose legitimate rights to terminate as a result of affirmation of the contract or delay. If a party is considering termination, it must take legal advice as soon as possible so that its legal advisers can start investigating whether it has sufficient evidence to be able to prove that the ground for termination exists. This may take many months to investigate. The party is strongly advised not to terminate the agreement until its lawyers have confirmed that it has sufficient proof of its entitlement to do so. If it terminates in circumstances where it is not entitled to do so or cannot prove that it is entitled to do so, then the other party can rely upon the purported termination as an act of repudiation which it can then use to bring the agreement to an end and claim damages for wrongful termination from the innocent party.[5]

5 In *Golden Strait Corporation v Nippon Yusen Kubishka Kaisha* [2007] UKHL 12, the House of Lords had to consider where damages for an accepted repudiation of a contract are claimed, in what circumstances the party in breach can rely on subsequent events to show that the contractual rights which have been lost would have been rendered either less valuable or valueless. By a majority of three to two, the House of Lords found that the respondent charterers could rely on a subsequent event to show that the appellant ship owner's contractual rights had been rendered less valuable. The majority of their Lordships found that considerations of certainty and finality in commercial transactions had "to yield to the greater importance of achieving an accurate assessment of the damages based on the loss actually incurred". This case is of interest because the principles outlined by the House of Lords are of general application in assessing damages for repudiatory breach of contract and the issue has never been considered before.

23.6 Termination in part

One of the issues that the parties will need to decide is whether the services to be provided by the supplier are severable so that, when terminating for convenience, breach or as a result of force majeure, the customer can terminate one service element and not others.

23.6.1 Division of services into service elements

The services may be divided into various service elements which are different in nature from each other (e.g. in an IT outsourcing agreement, the services may include desktop services and telecommunications services).

The services may also be classified by:

(a) the branch or country of the customer who is outsourcing to the supplier;
(b) the country or region from which the services are being provided;
(c) the language in which the services are being provided.

These additional forms of classification are particularly relevant for multinational outsourcing agreements.

The customer may want the right to terminate the services in part in the above cases.

23.6.2 Severability of the services

From the customer's perspective, whether the services are severable will depend on the facts of the individual arrangement. The customer may decide that the failure of the supplier to provide certain service elements will not necessarily affect its faith in the ability of the supplier to provide other service elements. If it is practical for the customer to arrange for another supplier to provide the defective service elements on their own, then it may want the right to decide to terminate those individual elements of the services only. The parties will then need to look at the people and assets used to provide each service element to see if it is practical to terminate them individually.

23.6.3 Severability of the charges

The supplier will need to see if the charges can be calculated on the basis that the services are severable. The customer may prefer that the service elements are priced separately, so that the financial effect of terminating any particular element is clear. If the supplier has spread transition costs or other fixed costs relating to the terminated service element over the term of the agreement, it will want to ensure that these are recovered. The supplier will also need to see how service management costs will continue to be recovered. The supplier may not want to agree to termination in part if it does not want to provide the services in circumstances where the value of the contract is substantially reduced. On the other hand, the supplier may prefer not to lose the entire account if it is having difficulty with one service element only.

23.6.4 Avoiding abuse

If termination in part is agreed, the supplier will be anxious to ensure that the customer cannot abuse the right. Hence it will want to clarify that:

(a) in relation to the right to terminate for breach, the customer can only cease the specific service elements in which the supplier is in breach; or
(b) in relation to the right to terminate for force majeure, the customer can only cease those service elements affected by the force majeure.

23.6.5 Option to terminate all services

Usually the customer will want the option to decide whether it terminates all of the services or individual service elements only. If the service elements are severable, however, the supplier may argue that, if the supplier breaches the key performance indicators for a particular service element, or a force majeure event affects one service element only, then the customer should be entitled to terminate that service element only. The contractual provisions dealing with this topic need to be drafted very carefully so that both parties are aware of the precise circumstances in which termination of part may be exercised and the exact consequences.

23.7 Termination of multinational arrangements – right to terminate services to the group

A similar issue relating to the application of termination rights arises if the customer comprises a group of companies that have entered into outsourcing arrangements with the supplier. In this situation, the parties will need to decide whether, if the supplier defaults in providing the services to one particular member of the group, the customer should have the right to terminate all of the services being provided to the group as a whole.

If the parties fail to deal with the specific issue, the customer's right to terminate will depend upon whether the arrangement has been entered into as one agreement, with one company contracting on behalf of the group, or whether the customer and supplier have agreed a framework agreement with the individual companies entering into direct agreements with the supplier based on the framework agreement.

If the parties have signed a framework agreement then, unless the framework agreement provides for termination of all agreements in the event of a breach of one of the various subsidiary agreements (and either the subsidiary agreement contains appropriate provisions mirroring such rights or the terms of the framework agreement are incorporated by reference into the subsidiary agreements), the customer's right to terminate may be limited to termination of the particular subsidiary agreement in reliance either on some specific provision in that agreement or a common law right of termination (e.g. a material breach of the relationship). If the parties have entered into direct agreements, the customer will usually only have the right to terminate the specific agreement.

In both cases, the parties should decide from a business perspective what rights of termination are desirable. If they wish to agree the wider rights of termination referred to above they will need to think very carefully about the interrelationship between the framework and subsidiary agreements.

Chapter 24

The Termination Decision

24.1 Outline

Chapter 23 covers the circumstances in which each party will have the right to terminate the agreement. This chapter describes the information and documentation that the customer will need to decide whether to exercise its right to terminate the agreement with the supplier.

24.2 More due diligence

If the customer has been told by its legal advisers that it has the right to terminate its agreement with the supplier, whether for convenience or for cause, the process which it will go through in deciding whether to exercise that right or not will, in some ways, mirror the process described in Chapter 2, when the customer decided whether to enter into the outsourcing arrangement with the supplier. Thus the customer will need to decide what its business objective will be in terminating the agreement with the supplier and whether termination will support the customer's business objective. To describe the situation another way, the customer should not terminate the agreement until it understands the resulting business consequences.

However, a word of caution is needed about such an assessment. The party considering termination may lose the right to terminate if it demonstrates an intention to continue with the agreement. Prior to communicating a decision to terminate, the innocent party should do nothing which is inconsistent with that position, for example by placing an order for additional services or making an advance payment of charges due under the agreement.

24.3 Information and documentation

In order for the customer to understand the consequences of terminating the arrangement with the supplier, it will need certain information and documentation so that it can understand the costs involved in terminating and transferring the services either in-house or to a new supplier and so that it can evaluate how difficult it will be from a practical perspective to effect a transition of the services. The customer may require some or all of the information and documentation described in Table 33, depending upon the individual circumstances.

This information will also be required by the customer on expiry of the agreement, when the customer will need to decide whether to renew the existing outsourcing agreement, enter into a secondary outsourcing arrangement or bring the services back in-house.

Table 33 *Information and documentation required on possible termination*

Current services

What services are currently being provided?

How are the services being provided?

What service levels are being achieved?

What volume of services is being provided?

What trends are there regarding the volume of services?

Are there any specific problems or challenges that are currently being faced or which the customer or incoming supplier would need to deal with?

Is there a backlog where services have not been provided?

Assets or premises with regard to which the services are provided

Where relevant, what assets or premises are covered by the services? Is there an accurate list of these?

Employees

What staff and contractors currently provide the services?

Will employees transfer from the incumbent supplier to the customer or to the new supplier?[1]

How much of the time of the relevant employees is dedicated to providing the services to be outsourced?

How long have the staff been employed?

Have they been transferred recently?

Does the customer agree that the relevant staff will transfer under TUPE?

Are there any other employees who are assigned to the business but are on long-term absence or maternity leave and who would transfer under TUPE?

What are the relevant terms and conditions of employment of the transferring staff?

What are the salaries and other benefits received by the employees?

What are the other terms and conditions of the transferring employees (including pension arrangements, special redundancy entitlements, notice period, overtime payments, loans, company car arrangements or entitlement to parking spaces)?

Have any variations to the terms and conditions been agreed?

1 *See* Chapter 27 for an explanation of relevant staffing issues.

Is the supplier entitled to agree variations to the terms and conditions?

Do the employees belong to a trade union?

Is the supplier aware of any possible claims against it by staff?

Over the last 12 months what payments have been made in overtime payments?

What accrued holiday entitlements are owing?

What details are available of performance monitoring arrangements?

What are the staff sickness levels over the previous 12 months?

Are any of the staff subject to disciplinary proceedings?

At which sites are the employees based?

What are the employees' ages?

What is the normal retirement age under the employees' terms and conditions?

Are any of the employees approaching retirement age?

Staffing and contractors

Is the number and quality of the staff that would transfer to the customer or new supplier on termination sufficient to provide the services?

Are specific members of the supplier's staff or contractors key to the provision of the services?

Are the key staff transferring?

Are the key contractors willing to work for the customer or new supplier?

Is the supplier intending to transfer staff out of the business so that they will not transfer to the customer or new supplier?

Is the supplier aware of any staff intending to resign?

How difficult would it be to replace key staff or contractors in the time available?

What skills transfer will the customer or new supplier need and what training will need to be provided to staff or contractors who will supply the services?

Assets used to provide the services

What assets are used to provide the services, whether used exclusively for the provision of the outsourced services or not (identified by type, quantity and location)?

Are any of the assets owned or leased by the supplier?

Does the customer have the right to purchase the assets on termination? If so, at what cost?

If not, is the supplier willing to make these available to the customer or new supplier and if so, on what conditions (financial and otherwise)?

Has the customer or new supplier been able to check the condition of the assets or premises?

Would it be difficult to replace any of the assets in the time available (e.g. because they are specially configured)?

Software licences and other supply agreements

What software licences and other intellectual property rights are needed to provide the services?

Are any bespoke materials or software used by the supplier in providing the services? (This applies whether they were developed as part of the services or not and also relates to any modifications made to the customer's bespoke materials or software.)

How can the customer or new supplier obtain the necessary rights?

What maintenance agreements, support agreements and other supply agreements are used by the supplier to provide the services (identified by name of supplier, term of contract and charges payable under the contract)?

Are any supply agreements transferable from the supplier to the customer or new supplier?

Are the terms of the third-party contracts acceptable?

Would it be difficult to replace any of the software or supply agreements?

What is the cost of the customer or new supplier taking out new software licences or supply agreements?

Because the customer will require the above information and documentation before termination, in order that it can decide whether to terminate the agreement or not, it is essential that the supplier is obliged to maintain the documentation throughout the term of the agreement and make it available to the customer on request.

Chapter 25

Implications of Termination

25.1 Outline

Chapters 23 and 24 describe the circumstances in which each party will have the right to terminate the agreement and the process that the customer will have to go through to decide whether or not to exercise its right. This chapter covers the implications of termination. From the customer's perspective, this includes a discussion of the termination assistance which it will require, whether relating to information, documentation, data, assets, staff, premises or other assistance. From the supplier's perspective, this includes a discussion of termination charges.

25.2 Consideration of termination before signature of the contract

The customer will be concerned to ensure that, on termination of the agreement, it will not be locked into receiving services from the supplier and will be able to ensure a smooth transition to the provision of services by its in-house department or by the replacement supplier. The supplier will need to ensure that it recovers any investment it has made in the services. The rest of this chapter deals with these issues.

The important point to make, however, is that all of these issues will need to be considered before the agreement is signed. Thus, the customer should consider whether adopting a particular solution proposed by a supplier will tie it in to that supplier and hinder a transfer of the services on termination. For example, in an IT outsourcing project, adopting proprietary technology may make it difficult for the customer to move to another supplier.

25.3 Information and documentation

25.3.1 Information and documentation required

The customer will need certain information and documentation to bring the services back in-house or to arrange for a successor supplier to take over the services. This is particularly so for IT and business process outsourcing arrangements, where the documentation will usually be one of the most important things that the customer will require on termination to enable it to move the services away from the supplier. The customer may be particularly dependent upon documentation relating to the services where staff who used to provide the services are not going to transfer to the incoming supplier or the customer on termination, for example in an offshore outsourcing arrangement.[1]

Some of this documentation has already been described in Chapter 24. In addition, the customer may require copies of any documentation required to provide the services, including, for example, system design and configuration documents, capacity and performance reports, bandwidth report and network diagrams. If the documentation has been prepared by the supplier as part of the services, the customer may want to agree that it will own the copyright in this documentation or that it and its suppliers will have a perpetual licence to use it.

25.3.2 When required

It is not advisable for the customer to specify that the supplier must simply collate and produce the information on termination of the agreement because:

(a) it may be difficult to collect the information if it has not been maintained throughout the term of the agreement;
(b) if the supplier is to manage the service efficiently, it should in any event be keeping the specified documentation; and
(c) it is likely that the relationship between the parties may deteriorate in the run up to or on termination of the agreement and the customer will then find it more difficult to obtain the documentation than previously.

25.3.3 Who will need the information and documentation

The customer is not the only one who may need access to information about the services. Chapter 6 describes the due diligence activities which any supplier who is considering entering into an outsourcing arrangement will need to carry out. On termination of an initial outsourcing agreement, suppliers who may be interested in providing the services after termination of the agreement will need to carry out similar due diligence activities to those described in Chapter 6. At this stage, the required information will often be in the hands of the incumbent outsourcing supplier. The customer will need the supplier to retain this information and make it available to the customer and the prospective new suppliers.

25.3.4 Cooperation with due diligence

The customer may need the supplier to respond to any questions which it or the prospective new suppliers may have as part of their due diligence activities. The customer may also want the incumbent supplier to cooperate with any due diligence activities which it or the other prospective contractors may wish to carry out. For example, the supplier may be required to provide access to:

(a) locations from which the services are provided;
(b) assets used to provide the services; or
(c) the relevant staff or subcontractors.

1 *See* Chapter 38 for a more detailed discussion of offshore outsourcing.

25.3.5 Supplier's concerns

The incumbent supplier will be anxious to ensure that confidential information about its business and the manner in which it operates (e.g. proprietary methodologies) or its charges is not passed on to its competitors. It will want to ensure that its obligation to assist the customer in ensuring a smooth transition will not interfere with its ability to provide the services prior to termination. For these reasons it may refuse to allow competitors access to its premises.

If the supplier has been asked to submit a proposal for providing the services after expiry of the agreement, it may be anxious to retain any advantage it has as incumbent supplier.

The supplier will also want to ensure that, before it enters into the outsourcing arrangement, it understands what information must be provided so that it can include the cost of maintaining the information in its charges. If it is difficult to evaluate the amount of effort involved in providing information or cooperating with due diligence, it may want to place a limit on the number of man days of assistance it will provide or reserve the right to charge extra for providing such assistance.

25.4 Data

25.4.1 Ownership of the data

In IT and business process outsourcing arrangements, it may be crucial to the customer that, after termination, it has access to its data in a usable format. This means that the customer will want the supplier to agree that all data provided by the customer or produced by it as a result of the services will belong to the customer and that the supplier will hand them over to the customer on termination.

If the data is held in databases, then it is essential that the customer clarifies who will own copyright and the various database rights (including the structure of the database and changes in the structure) and ensures that after termination it will be able to use the database containing its data.

25.4.2 Licence for software holding the data

If the data includes archived data held on legacy software which the customer is not intending to run after termination then the customer will need to ensure that it has a licence to use the legacy software to gain access to the archived data.

25.4.3 Format of data

The customer should reserve the right to specify the format in which the data will be provided. If this involves the supplier changing the format of the data, then it may want to specify that the format must be reasonable and that it can charge for converting the data.

25.5 Assets

In order to ensure a smooth transition on termination, the customer will need to consider the particular nature of its services and the assets used to provide them and will need to ensure that it will have access to everything that it or the replacement supplier will require to provide the services after termination. Many of the customer's termination requirements will depend upon the exact details of the services and the particular assets used to provide them. Paragraphs 25.6 to 25.10 include a description of issues that the customer may need to take into account.

In deciding what the customer needs on termination, it should be particularly aware of the substitutability of particular assets. For example, it may need certain hardware to provide the services. However, if it can procure the hardware on the open market, then it may not be tied into procuring it from the supplier. The situation is more complex if the hardware needs to be configured for the customer's specific needs and procuring new hardware and configuring it will disrupt the provision of the services.

25.6 Assets belonging to the customer

On termination, the customer will want the supplier to return to it any assets (e.g. the customer's bespoke software), documentation or other property belonging to the customer which it has made available to the supplier so that it can provide the services (as described in Chapters 13 to 15). The customer may want to provide in the agreement that the supplier will not have a lien[2] over any of the customer's property.

The customer may want the right to come onto the supplier's premises to regain control of its property, including its assets and data.

25.7 Hardware and other equipment

25.7.1 Customer's dependency upon the equipment

The customer should consider whether it will need any equipment used by the supplier to provide the services. It may be able to buy replacement equipment easily on the open market. If, however, the equipment is legacy kit which is difficult to locate or has been specially configured for the customer, then it may be easier to ensure a smooth transition if the same equipment is procured from the supplier. The customer may therefore want to reserve in the contract the right to buy some or all of the equipment used by the supplier to provide the services.

2 A lien is a right to retain possession as security for payment of a debt.

25.7.2 Deciding which equipment will transfer - exclusive or non-exclusive equipment

Just as the customer may want to procure the equipment, the supplier may no longer require the equipment after termination if it is being used solely to provide services to the customer. Thus the supplier may want to transfer the equipment to the customer.

The situation is more complex where the supplier has been using the equipment to provide services to other customers. The equipment may be more than is necessary for the customer's service. The supplier may be unwilling to transfer the equipment to the customer if this will interfere with the provision by it of services to its other customers. For this reason, the customer should decide before the agreement is signed whether it will require certain equipment on termination. The customer may want to require that the specified equipment must be used exclusively for the provision of the services to it. If the equipment could have been used for the provision of services to other customers, then this restriction may result in an increase in the charges to it if the cost of the equipment has to be included in the charges for its services only rather than being shared between several customers.

In some circumstances, the parties may be able to reach a compromise in which the supplier grants the customer a licence to use the relevant equipment after termination until the customer can replace it. However, the customer may not want to rely on a licence from the supplier if it has had to terminate the agreement due to the supplier's breach or insolvency.

25.7.3 Defining the equipment to be transferred

The parties will need to decide how to define the relevant equipment which will transfer to the customer on termination. It will be helpful if the particular items of equipment can be identified when the agreement is signed. However, in many cases it will not be possible to identify them because equipment will be replaced during the terms of the agreement as it becomes obsolete or the services change.

In this situation it may still be possible to describe the equipment. For example, in an IT outsourcing agreement, the customer may want to purchase any equipment used for the provision of the services other than:

(a) the service management and reporting tools; and
(b) common infrastructure at the supplier's premises or help desk.

25.7.4 Sale price of the equipment owned by the supplier

If the equipment is owned by the supplier and is being sold to the customer, what price should the customer pay? The supplier may argue that the customer should pay a fair market-value price, as this is the amount that the customer will pay to procure similar equipment on the open market. However, the customer needs to understand the extent to which the equipment costs have already been included in the outsourcing service charges and paid for. This will usually depend upon two different factors. It will depend upon:

(a) whether the supplier procured the equipment exclusively to provide the services to the customer; and

(b) whether termination has occurred on expiry of the agreement or on earlier termination. If termination occurs before expiry and a termination charge is payable, the customer will need to understand the extent to which the termination charge includes the supplier's unrecovered equipment costs.

If the supplier has used the equipment exclusively to provide the services to the customer and termination occurs on expiry of the agreement, then the supplier may have included the full cost of acquiring it in its charges for the services and the customer may be able to specify that the supplier will transfer the equipment to it for a nominal fee. The parties may then decide that, if the agreement is terminated before expiry, the customer will pay the supplier's unrecovered costs relating to the equipment.

The parties should also take into account whether the clause will be enforceable upon the supplier's insolvency, as a clause providing that equipment transfers back automatically to the customer is likely to be unenforceable whether as a matter of public policy or resulting from a liquidator's right to disclaim onerous contracts.

25.7.5 Transfer of leased equipment

If the supplier has leased the equipment from a third-party lessor then it may be difficult for the supplier to agree with the lessor on termination that its rights and obligations under the lease will be transferred to the customer, as leases are usually non-transferable. In this situation, if the customer wants to acquire the equipment, it will usually have to require the supplier to terminate the lease. The parties will need to agree who will pay any termination charges incurred in terminating the lease.

The lessor is likely to be more amenable if the supplier requests the right to transfer the lease to the customer before the lease is signed. For this reason, the customer may insist that the supplier ensures, before it enters into any leases for the relevant equipment, that they are transferable to the customer. The customer may prefer the leases to be transferable to the replacement supplier, although the lessor may be reluctant to agree to the transfer of the lease to a company whose identity will be unknown when the agreement is signed.

25.7.6 Title in the equipment

The customer will want the supplier to provide appropriate warranties for the equipment, for example relating to the supplier's title in the equipment.

25.7.7 Condition of the equipment

The customer may be concerned to ensure that any equipment that it procures from the supplier is in good condition. It may want the supplier to warrant the condition of the equipment. The readiness of the supplier to grant such warranties may depend upon whether the customer was willing to grant warranties about assets transferred to the supplier on commencement of the outsourcing arrangement.

The customer may want the right to require the supplier to rectify defects in the equipment or, if the supplier fails to do so, it may want the right to rectify the defects itself, at the supplier's expense.

The customer may want to ensure that any equipment that it acquires from the supplier will be suitable for providing the services for a certain period after expiry of the agreement. Otherwise the supplier will be entitled to use equipment for the provision of the services which needs replacement in its entirety on expiry. The customer may want to avoid a situation in which it is faced with replacing all of the equipment at the same time as transferring the services to the replacement supplier. If the customer wants the supplier to commit to this, it may have charging implications, with the charges increasing to cover the cost of replacing any equipment that would not otherwise need replacing.

25.7.8 Option or obligation to purchase the equipment

The customer will usually want an option (rather than an obligation) to purchase the supplier's equipment. However, the supplier may be concerned to ensure that it recovers its investment in the equipment and therefore may insist that the customer purchases the equipment in such circumstances. The customer may want to reserve the right not to purchase the equipment if it terminates the agreement for breach by the supplier or if the supplier has failed to maintain the equipment.

If the customer has an option to purchase the equipment, then the parties will usually want to agree a period within which the customer must notify the supplier whether it intends to exercise the option. The period may be extended if the supplier fails to provide the customer with sufficient information about the equipment to enable the customer to decide whether it wants to exercise its option or not. An option to purchase on the part of the customer can have tax consequences.

25.8 Third-party software licences

25.8.1 Return of customer's licences

In the past, most software has been licensed on the basis of an up-front payment for a perpetual licence, with recurring annual payments of approximately 10 per cent to cover support. Microsoft has changed its pricing model so that the up-front payment is replaced by annual charges for annual licences. It is possible that other suppliers will follow this model in time. For the present, however, the traditional model means that customers must ensure that they do not need to take out new licences for software on termination, thus exposing themselves to the possibility of having to pay the up-front charge again.

If the customer intends to transfer its third-party software licences to the supplier on commencement of the outsourcing arrangement, it should ensure that the licensor agrees that the licences may be transferred back to the customer on termination. This issue will be more problematic if, in order to gain a better price for the customer, the supplier intends to merge the software licences with other corporate arrangements that it has with the software licensor. This may mean that it is not practical to carve out the software licences and transfer them to the customer on termination, or that it is possible, although the customer will not continue to benefit from the supplier's corporate discounts for the software.

25.8.2 New licences

If the supplier has taken out other software licences for the provision of the services, the customer may want the supplier to ensure that these can also be transferred to it on termination. The supplier will want to ensure that, if the agreement is terminated prior to expiry, the customer has an obligation to pay any unrecovered software licence costs. The customer will want to ensure that it will not be liable to pay the unrecovered software licence costs if it is terminating the agreement for breach by the supplier and does not want to take over the software licences.

25.9 Supplier's bespoke software

The customer should be particularly careful to ensure that it can use any bespoke software developed by the supplier if it is necessary for the provision of the services and there are no ready substitutes.

25.9.1 Software developed as part of the services

If the software is developed by the supplier as part of the services, then the customer may want to own the software or to have a perpetual licence so that it and replacement suppliers can use it. The supplier will usually want to own the software so that it can exploit it by licensing it to other customers.

Unless the customer has a reason for wanting to own the software (e.g. because it is a modification to the customer's bespoke software, or it wants to control the use of the software so that it is not licensed to competitors), a perpetual, royalty-free licence covering the customer and future outsourcing suppliers will usually be sufficient.

The customer may want to ensure that it has obtained some financial benefit in return for allowing the supplier to retain intellectual property rights in the bespoke software.

Some customers suggest that they should receive a share of the profit or revenue received by the supplier from licensing the software to other customers. This may appear to be an attractive idea in principle, but it is often extremely difficult to apply in practice. Thus any licence to other customers will usually form part of a general outsourcing agreement so that there is no specific charge for the licence. If there is a separate charge and the supplier is providing additional services to the other customers, the supplier will be in control of how the charges are allocated between the licence and the services. In any event, the other customers may want to keep details of the arrangement with the supplier confidential.

Therefore, unless substantial amounts of money are involved, it may be simpler for the parties to agree a reasonable reduction in the charges payable by the customer under the outsourcing agreement. (*See* 16.2.3 to 16.2.4 for a further discussion of these issues.)

Where substantial amounts of money are involved, the parties may decide to set up a joint venture company to exploit the software (*see* Chapter 17 for a more detailed discussion of joint ventures). This may be particularly appropriate where the software has been developed with the customer's expert knowledge of its particular sector or type of business and where the customer can contribute to the marketing of the software.

25.9.2 Other software

The customer may be concerned about the supplier using bespoke software other than that developed as part of the services. It may want to avoid a situation where the supplier has integrated its bespoke software into the customer's solution in such a way that the customer is locked in to the relationship with the supplier. Therefore, the customer should ensure that the supplier grants it and the replacement supplier a licence to use the bespoke software, so that the replacement supplier can provide the services after termination for a reasonable period until the software can be replaced. If the customer has not requested the supplier to integrate the software into the solution, then the customer may argue that it should not have to pay for the licence, unless agreed by the parties to the contrary. This may act as a warning to the supplier not to integrate its bespoke software into the solution without the customer's consent.

If the supplier develops software that would improve the solution, it could then be open to the supplier to explain the benefits of the software to the customer and agree with the customer a suitable charge. The disadvantage of this approach, from the supplier's perspective, is that there is a risk that its employees will forget to obtain the customer's consent before implementing the software.

25.9.3 Escrow

The customer may want the supplier to deposit the source code of any supplier bespoke software in escrow with a third party. This issue is discussed in Chapter 26.

25.10 Support, maintenance and other contracts

If the customer is procuring equipment and software from the supplier, it may want the supplier to transfer to it any equipment maintenance and software support agreements for the relevant equipment and software.

Whether the supplier will be able to agree to this provision will depend upon the particular terms which it has agreed with its suppliers. If the supplier has agreed volume discounts with suppliers based upon the maintenance and support of equipment and software used for the provision of services to various customers, then the customer will not be able to obtain the benefit of the volume discount after termination. The supplier may be able to carve out from the group-wide agreement with the supplier the maintenance and support of the specific customer equipment and software. However, the charges for the maintenance and support will usually reflect the market rate for such services.

The customer may also want to take over other supply agreements used for the provision of the services, in which case similar considerations will apply to those described above.

25.11 People issues

The people issues relating to termination are discussed in Chapter 27.

25.12 General assistance

The customer may find it difficult to anticipate all of the assistance that it will require on termination. Therefore, it should consider including a general provision, obliging the supplier to cooperate fully with the customer and the replacement supplier so that any transfer of the services on termination is achieved with the minimum of disruption, and to provide any other assistance that the customer may require at the time. This could cover, for example, training required by the customer on termination.

If the supplier is not able to estimate the amount of effort required to comply with this obligation, it will want to limit it to a certain number of man days of effort or specify that it can charge extra for providing the necessary cooperation. The customer may want the supplier to agree a man-day rate in accordance with which the supplier's charges will be calculated.

25.13 Termination management

The customer should consider how the transition of the services on termination can be effected with the maximum efficiency. This may involve the agreement by the parties of a detailed exit plan. The parties may agree a draft exit plan before signature of the agreement. Usually, however, priority is given to implementing a transition plan for the supplier to take over the services. As a result, preparation of an exit plan is often postponed for six or 12 months.

The parties may also agree to review the exit plan on a regular basis or when the parties change the services, to ensure that it is still applicable.

The parties may agree on the appointment by the supplier (or by both parties) of a termination manager who will be responsible for implementing the exit plan. The customer may want control over the choice of the termination manager (see Chapter 8).

The customer may want the right to extend the agreement in part for different service elements, where relevant, to ensure that it does not need to effect the transition of the services on termination all at the same time, in a "big bang". If the charges for the individual service elements are specified in the agreement, then the customer may want the right to extend the agreement, for a limited period, at the same charge or another specified charge. Otherwise, the parties will need to agree the charges to be payable by the customer under the change control procedure (see Chapter 22).

25.14 Termination charges

25.14.1 Supplier's costs

One of the most contentious aspects of termination concerns the payments which should be made by each party and when these payments should be made.

The supplier will need to consider how, in the event of early termination of the agreement under any of the grounds mentioned in 23.3 above, it will ensure that it recovers its investment in the services once it is no longer receiving revenue from the outsourcing arrangement. In some cases, the supplier will have invested in procuring, configuring or customising assets that can be sold to the customer or to the replacement supplier, so that it can provide the services after termination. In other cases, the investment will not have been in assets but in, for example, the training of staff.

The supplier may want the customer to pay a charge if the agreement is terminated early. However, the customer may not want to pay any termination charge or any other charges for termination assistance if the agreement is terminated for breach or insolvency of the supplier. In this situation, it is crucial for the supplier that the agreement includes reasonable provisions relating to termination for breach.

If the agreement is terminated by the customer for breach or insolvency, then the supplier may find itself in a situation where not only has it lost its investment, but it may also be liable to the customer for damages. Chapter 31 deals with ways in which the supplier may want to limit its liability in such circumstances.[3]

In circumstances where the supplier has terminated the agreement as a result of the customer's failure to pay or insolvency, the supplier may be reluctant to provide any termination assistance unless the customer pays for the assistance in advance.

25.14.2 Payment for termination assistance

The supplier will also be concerned to ensure that it is clear what services it must provide on termination, so that it can ensure that it has included the cost of compliance in its charges.

25.14.3 Agreement of termination charge in advance

Just as the supplier will want to ensure that it understands what services it must provide on termination, the customer may want to ensure that it understands what payments it will have to make on termination and may prefer for these to be agreed before the agreement is signed, except where the customer is unable to specify its requirements in advance.

---

3 The parties may want to clarify whether termination of the agreement for insolvency constitutes termination for breach. *See* the interesting case of *Balfour Beatty* v *Technical & General Guarantee Co. Ltd* [2000] CLC 252 in which Lord Justice Waller commented that liquidation is not a breach of contract in most instances.

An extreme approach to this issue is that adopted in PFI agreements where, before the agreement is signed, the parties agree complex provisions for determining the termination charge that the customer will make upon any early termination. The method of calculation will depend upon the grounds for termination. In the case of supplier breach, the termination payments will be based upon the market value of the PFI contract if it were sold to an alternative supplier. In the case of customer breach, compensation is designed to ensure that the supplier (and its funders) are fully compensated, so as to be no worse off than they would have been if the PFI contract had continued as expected. These payments are in full and final settlement of the supplier's liability and exclude the customer's rights under the common law.[4] Some other types of outsourcing arrangements have adopted this approach, for example some telecommunications or web hosting arrangements.

25.14.4 Retention of charges

The customer may be concerned that the supplier will not cooperate in the transfer of the services to a competitor or back to the customer. Therefore, the customer may want the right to make a specified retention from the charges until the supplier has fulfilled its obligations to provide termination assistance and executed the exit plan. However, the supplier will be concerned that the customer will never in fact pay the retention, even after the supplier has carried out all of its duties. It may be unwilling to agree to any retention unless the sums outstanding are held by a third party. It may also suggest that no retention should be made unless the supplier is in breach of the agreement or insolvent or that a reduced retention should be made in other circumstances.

25.14.5 Taxation treatment of termination payments

The taxation treatment of termination charges needs careful consideration. If termination payments replace income to which the supplier would have been entitled, then they may be liable to taxation as income. Otherwise they may potentially be liable to taxation as chargeable gains.[5] The customer may find that taxation relief which had previously been available in regard to payments of the service charges will not be available for termination payments. From a VAT viewpoint, agreed out-of-court settlement payments are not usually liable to VAT unless part or all of the payment relates to services over which there has been a dispute, in which case that part of any settlement which relates to the services will be taxed in the same way as the underlying services.

25.15 Termination in part and step in

The customer should consider the extent to which it will require the supplier to provide termination assistance, such as that specified in this chapter, in circumstances in which the agreement is terminated in part or in which the customer steps in to provide the services (see Chapter 8 for a description of step in).

4 HM Treasury Guidance – Standardisation of PFI Contracts, version 4 issued March 2007 Chapter 21.

5 PFI contracts will usually include "grossing-up" provisions for compensation payments made for customer default to put the supplier in a net position. The parties may want to consider doing the same.

Part Eight – Insolvency, People and Competition Issues

Chapter 26

Insolvency Issues

26.1 Outline

Chapter 25 describes the termination of the outsourcing arrangement whether for breach or insolvency or otherwise. This chapter deals with other issues relating to insolvency. Typically, the insolvency provisions of an outsourcing agreement are viewed at the negotiation stage as "standard boilerplating" to which the parties probably pay relatively little attention. However, in the current rocky economic climate, there is naturally an increased risk that the supplier or the customer to the outsourcing agreement may be in financial difficulty. Insolvency of a counterparty will always be a potential commercial hazard of doing business. However, adopting sensible precautions alongside a well-planned and drafted agreement will help to reduce the risk of counterparty insolvency and reduce the loss when insolvency does arise.

This chapter covers due diligence that each party should carry out before and after the agreement is signed and guarantees or protections that each side may want to request from the other side. It also discusses issues relating to restrictions upon the transfer of the agreement, and deals with the right to terminate on insolvency-related grounds.

26.2 Due diligence before the agreement is signed

Chapters 2 and 6 describe the due diligence that the customer and supplier must carry out before the agreement is signed. A key element of the due diligence to be carried out by either side relates to the financial standing of the other side. The customer should only be prepared to go forward with the transaction if satisfied that the supplier will be able to perform both operationally and financially.

Each party should consider whether it requires additional protection by way of third-party guarantees (typically from the other side's parent company) and/or performance bonds. Possible guarantees and protections are described at 26.2.1 and 26.2.2 below.

26.2.1 Parent company guarantee

Either party may request a guarantee from the parent company of the other party. There are two types of guarantee:

(a) A performance guarantee provides reassurance to the customer that if the supplier fails to provide the services then the parent company will provide them instead. This type of guarantee is appropriate where the parent company has the ability to provide the services.

(b) A financial guarantee is a guarantee under which the parent company agrees to indemnify the customer or supplier against sums of money owing to it.

26.2.2 Performance bond

Performance bonds are agreements by a bank to pay certain amounts of money to the customer if specific circumstances are satisfied. For example:

(a) if the bank receives a written notice from the customer and the supplier agreeing that an amount of damages is payable to the customer; or

(b) if the bank is presented with a certified copy of a judgment of a court having jurisdiction or of an award issued in arbitration proceedings under which damages are payable by the supplier to the customer with a statement by the customer showing the amount of the damages which remain unsatisfied as at the date of the claim.

26.2.3 Payment terms

In addition to considering whether guarantees are required, both supplier and customer should consider whether the charges should be payable in advance or in arrears. Clearly the customer is taking the insolvency risk if the charges are payable in advance and the supplier is taking the insolvency risk if the charges are payable in arrears.

26.2.4 Liens

The supplier and customer may also want to clarify that the other party will not have a lien[1] over their property.

26.2.5 Source code escrow

The customer should consider whether it needs the supplier to deposit the source code of any software necessary to provide the services in escrow. Software will usually be deposited with a recognised body, such as the National Computer Centre ("NCC"), who will agree to release it in certain circumstances, for example if the supplier becomes insolvent. It is important that the supplier agrees to deposit up-to-date versions of the relevant software. The customer should also check that it has any necessary rights it needs to modify or support the software after release.

1 A lien is a right to retain possession as security for payment of a debt. *See* Section 246 Insolvency Act 1986 regarding the unenforceability of certain liens.

26.3 Ongoing due diligence

Each party should ensure that it investigates the other party's financial standing throughout the term of the agreement. The party may want to include triggers that give rise to additional rights if the other party (or, if a parent company guarantee is given, the guarantor) suffers an adverse event.[2]

26.3.1 Trigger events

Table 34 shows possible trigger events.

Table 34 *Example trigger events*

Credit rating downgraded and the other side does not provide reassurances that it is able to comply with its obligations.
Adverse decline in the financial ratios below a specified level.
Cash flow deteriorates below specified level.
Late payment of a subcontractor or a material subcontractor by the supplier.
Material breach of covenants to its lenders.
Turnover declines below a certain level.
Profitability decreases to a certain level.
Share price reduces below specified price.
Reduction in tangible net worth below a specified threshold.
Commencement of any litigation with respect to any financial indebtedness.

26.3.2 Additional rights

The additional rights could involve:

(a) the right to require the other side (or its auditors) to provide additional information about its financial standing or evidence that it will be able to comply with its obligations, including, for example, regular updates on its financial position;

(b) the right to require the other side to provide a plan setting out how the other side will ensure the continuity of the provision of the services in the event that they become insolvent;

(c) the provision of additional financial guarantees or charges over assets. The innocent party must take specialist insolvency advice to check whether the additional guarantees will be enforceable if the other party subsequently becomes insolvent;

2 A similar approach has been adopted by the OGC in its model IT outsourcing contracts.

(d) the right to terminate if the other side fails to provide the necessary guarantees or reassurances;
(e) the right for the customer to pay charges due under the outsourcing arrangement into an escrow account that is used to pay key subcontractors; and
(f) the right to withhold payments of specified amounts from the sums held in escrow, to cover the cost of transferring the services to a replacement supplier if the supplier subsequently becomes insolvent.

26.4 Assignment or novation of the contract[3]

Before the outsourcing arrangement is agreed, each party will generally carry out a due diligence exercise relating to the specific financial standing and character of the other side. Therefore, neither party will usually be willing to allow the other party to transfer their rights or obligations under the agreement to another company without their consent.

The supplier and customer may want the ability to transfer the agreement to another company within the same group as part of a corporate reorganisation. The other side is more likely to agree to this where the parent company of the other side has provided a parent company guarantee and that guarantee will be transferred to cover the liabilities of the group company to whom the agreement will be transferred.

The ability of each party to transfer the agreement in other circumstances will usually be subject to the consent of the other party, although the parties may agree to act reasonably in giving or refusing approval.

26.5 Termination rights[4]

Contracts are not automatically terminated on the other party's insolvency. Each party needs to ensure that there are express terms within the agreement to terminate in the event of the other party's insolvency (unless the other party is a public sector body). The clause needs to be carefully drafted. Naturally the clause needs to give a right to terminate at the very outset of formal insolvency (i.e. liquidation, administration, receivership). However, to maximise the options available to the party, a party may want the right to terminate to be triggered by events that occur earlier in time and which indicate that formal insolvency may follow. Typical examples include the other side becoming "unable to pay its debts as they fall due" or its credit rating being downgraded.

The corporate insolvency provisions in the Enterprise Act 2002 came into force on 15 September 2003. One of the reforms introduced by the Act was that the administration

3 An assignment is a transfer of part or all of the benefit of a contract. The third party will still be able to enforce the contract against the customer. Novation extinguishes the contract between the customer and the third party and replaces it with a new contract between the supplier and the third party.

4 The parties may want to clarify whether termination of the agreement for insolvency constitutes termination for breach. *See* the interesting case of *Balfour Beatty* v *Technical & General Co Ltd* [2000] CLC 252 in which Lord Justice Walter commented that liquidation is not a breach of contract in most instances.

procedure was reformed and streamlined. Rights to terminate will need to reflect this legislation so that they refer to an application to the court for an administration order and to the giving of a notice of appointment or intention to appoint an administrator.

26.6 Direct agreement with subcontractors or funders

A supplier experiencing financial problems may fail to pay key subcontractors on time or it may fall behind with repayments to funders. In this situation, there is a risk that a subcontractor will terminate the subcontract or that a funder will terminate the funding arrangement and repossess the assets which it has funded. Either of these situations could cause serious problems for the customer (although in practice, if the funder knows that the assets funded have been specifically customised for the customer, it may seek to sell them to the customer).

Therefore, the customer may want a direct agreement with the subcontractor or funder under which they agree that they will not terminate their agreements with the supplier without notifying the customer and giving the customer a right to step in to the agreement in place of the supplier.

If the supplier has not finalised its funding arrangements by the date of signature of the agreement, then the customer may want the supplier to agree that it will not, without the customer's consent, enter into any funding arrangements or charge key assets used to provide the services. The customer may then make its consent conditional upon, for example, the funder entering into a direct agreement with the customer.

Similarly, in outsourcing agreements which are externally funded (and in particular PFI contracts) the funder will usually require a direct agreement with the customer to provide that the customer will not terminate the outsourcing arrangement without giving the funder notice, and giving the funder the right to preserve the contract by substituting an alternative supplier.[5]

26.7 Transactions which can be set aside

If the supplier does go into an insolvency regime, it is likely to go into either administration or liquidation. Administrators and liquidators ("office holders") have extensive powers to investigate the activities of the supplier in the run up to the insolvency. In certain prescribed circumstances, office holders can lawfully get court orders to claw back assets and set aside security over assets with a view to swelling the insolvent estate. Therefore, the customer should seek specialist insolvency advice to ensure the enforceability of particular rights that it will require to guarantee the continuity of its business if the supplier becomes insolvent. It is outside the scope of this Guide to describe this issue further or to cover other issues relating to general insolvency law.

5 In a PFI contract, where the supplier is generally a special purpose vehicle, which subcontracts all of its obligations to more substantial companies, the funder will also require the right to preserve the subcontracts by stepping in to the place of the supplier.

Chapter 27

People Issues

27.1 Outline

Chapters 23 to 26 deal with termination-related matters, including the grounds for termination, the termination decision and assistance, and the effect that the insolvency of either party has upon these.

This chapter deals with people-related matters, whether on termination of the outsourcing arrangement or on its commencement.

It describes the impact of the application of the Acquired Rights Directive (properly known as Council Directive 2001/23/EC regarding the safeguarding of employees' rights in the event of transfers of undertakings) ("ARD") to outsourcing.

It also assesses how employees of both the customer and the supplier can be affected by the outsourcing of services and it offers practical hints and tips on how each party can attempt to inject some control over the process and minimise its exposure to liability.

This chapter deals with legal and business issues. Where it deals with legal issues, it sets out the position under English law. Where an outsourcing agreement involves employees outside the UK, it is essential that the parties take advice on local employment law. Part 12 of this Guide deals with employment law issues in other key EU jurisdictions and Chapters 39 and 40 deal with the employment issues in India and China.

27.2 Mandatory provisions in ARD

The purpose of ARD is to "provide for the protection of employees in the event of a change of employer, to ensure that their rights are safeguarded".

Under ARD, there are a number of provisions which Member States must adopt in order to give effect to the Directive. Although some of the details may be subject to national law, the principles in Table 35 apply throughout the EU.

Table 35 *Mandatory provisions in ARD*

Application

ARD applies to any transfer of an undertaking, business or part of an undertaking or business to another employer as a result of a legal transfer or merger.

A transfer occurs where there is a transfer of an economic entity which retains its identity; an economic entity is an organised grouping of resources which has the object of pursuing an economic activity, whether that is central or ancillary, public or private, or profit-making or not.

Transfer of rights and obligations

ARD operates to transfer rights and obligations under the contract of employment from the transferor to the transferee.

Collective agreements

After a transfer, the transferee must honour the terms of any collective agreement.

Dismissal

The transfer of an undertaking must not itself constitute grounds for dismissal unless the dismissal is for an economic, technical or organisational reason entailing changes in the workforce; any termination of employment due to a substantial change in working conditions to the detriment of the employee shall be regarded as a dismissal by the employer.

Consultation

Any employees who are affected by a transfer are entitled to have representatives and the representatives must be given certain information about the transfer in good time before the transfer takes place and before the employees' conditions of work and employment are affected by the transfer; if measures are envisaged, the representatives must also be consulted in relation to the measures with a view to reaching an agreement.

If there are no employee representatives, the employees must be given the information directly.

27.3 Optional provisions in ARD

Under ARD, a number of provisions are either optional for Member States to adopt or can be limited to comply with national laws. Some examples of these provisions are described in Table 36.

Table 36 *Optional provisions in ARD*

Definitions

The definitions of "employee", "employee representatives" and "employment relationship" are matters for national law.

Joint and several liability

Member States can provide for joint and several liability (the UK has done this only in relation to liability for failure to inform and consult).

Transfer of information

Member States may adopt measures to provide for the transfer of information from the transferor to the transferee in relation to the employees.

Collective agreements

Collective agreements must transfer, but Member States can limit this to a year after the transfer.

Dismissal

Member States can limit the categories of employees who are protected from dismissal by virtue of the transfer.

Consultation

Member States may limit the information and consultation obligations to undertakings with a minimum number of employees.

27.4 Application of ARD and TUPE to outsourcing

27.4.1 Background

ARD was originally implemented in the UK by the Transfer of Undertakings (Protection of Employment) Regulations 1981 ("TUPE Regulations"). The impact of the TUPE Regulations was not felt immediately, but grew over time.

Through a series of cases in the UK courts and the ECJ, the importance of the TUPE Regulations gradually increased as decisions held that the scope of the TUPE Regulations extended, for example, to non-commercial undertakings and to intra-group transfers.

In addition, a substantial body of case law developed in the late 1980s and 1990s on the issue of whether the contracting out of services and the change of contractors fell within the TUPE Regulations, with the courts taking a "multi-factorial" approach, looking at a series of relevant factors in each case and reaching a finding based on those facts. This resulted in courts drawing a distinction between asset-intensive undertakings and labour-intensive undertakings.

27.4.2 New TUPE Regulations

In the UK, the new TUPE Regulations of 2006 ("New TUPE Regulations") have now rendered much of that case law irrelevant because they expressly apply where there is a "service provision change" (*see* below). It remains to be seen whether the definition of service provision change itself will result in a further body of case law.

However, other EU jurisdictions have not all embraced the definition of service provision change within their national laws and therefore the case law will continue to be relevant in determining whether ARD applies to outsourcing arrangements in those countries.

27.4.3 Effect of New TUPE Regulations

The New TUPE Regulations provide for two alternative applications of TUPE (which are not mutually exclusive) – where there is a transfer of an economic entity and where there is a change in the provision of a service.

This is an extremely complex subject and this section is intended to provide a short summary of some of the key relevant factors. Customers and suppliers must take expert advice on this area before entering into any outsourcing agreement.

27.4.3.1 Identifiable economic entity

TUPE applies where there is an identifiable economic entity which retains its identity before and after the transfer, for example the catering function at a factory. Economic entity is defined as "an organised grouping of resources which has the objective of pursuing an economic activity, whether or not that activity is central or ancillary".

TUPE will not apply if there is no identifiable entity, so if, for example, the cleaning in an office is done on an ad hoc basis by all of the office staff in addition to their other duties, the cleaning function will not be an economic entity and the appointment of a cleaning contractor to take over this function will not be a TUPE transfer.

27.4.3.2 Service provision change

Under the New TUPE Regulations, there is express reference to the application of TUPE to contracting out, contracting in and re-tendering, where there is an identifiable grouping of employees dedicated to meeting one client's needs. It does not apply to a single specific event or task of short-term duration, nor does it apply to contracts for the supply of goods.

TUPE will therefore apply in outsourcing situations, including:

(a) the initial outsourcing of a service to a supplier;
(b) where the services are taken in-house by the customer from the supplier; or
(c) where an existing outsourcing agreement with a supplier is terminated and the contract is granted to a new supplier.

27.4.3.3 The sale of shares

TUPE will not apply where the transaction is the sale of shares in a company (e.g. a subsidiary company of the customer which provides the service to the customer which is being outsourced to the supplier). If the supplier purchases the company, TUPE will not apply, but the people employed by that company will continue to be employed by that company. If they are to be dismissed, the normal unfair dismissal rules will apply.

27.4.3.4 Changes in application of TUPE

Paragraphs 27.4.3.1 to 27.4.3.3 show that TUPE applies extremely widely so that it will apply in most outsourcing arrangements. Parties should be aware, however, that the interpretation of TUPE can change as case law develops and if further amendments are made to the Regulations themselves. Therefore, specialist legal advice must be taken at the relevant time with regard to the individual outsourcing arrangement.

27.5 Legal effect of TUPE applying

There are various implications of TUPE applying to an individual outsourcing arrangement. Paragraphs 27.2 and 27.3 explain the implications in outline. This section describes the specific implications for outsourcing transactions.

27.5.1 Transfer of contracts of employment

TUPE is designed to preserve employees' terms and conditions of employment when a business or undertaking, or part of one, is transferred to a new employer. Therefore, if TUPE applies, it will operate to transfer the contracts of employment of those employees engaged in the undertaking from the customer to the new supplier.

27.5.2 Transfer rights, powers, duties and liabilities

TUPE will also transfer to the new supplier all rights, powers, duties and liabilities under those contracts of employment, including accrued liabilities (but excluding certain rights under occupational pension schemes (*see* Chapter 28). This has the practical effect of putting the new supplier into the shoes of the customer (or the old supplier, if the transfer involves a change of supplier). This means that the new employer takes over all liabilities, including, for example, arrears of pay or liability for unlawful acts of discrimination, unless the parties agree to apportion the liability differently by way of indemnities[1] (*see* 27.7 below).

27.5.3 Employees can object

Under TUPE, employees who are unhappy about the transfer can object to it, in which event their existing employment comes to an end at the point of transfer and does not transfer to the new supplier. In this situation, the individual generally has no remedy against either party.

27.5.4 Dismissals automatically unfair

Any dismissals by reason of a transfer are automatically unfair as are any dismissals in connection with a TUPE transfer unless they are for an "economic, technical or organisational reason entailing a change in the workforce" ("ETO reason") (Regulation 7(2) TUPE).

The ETO reason must relate to the employer which carries out the dismissals, which means a customer cannot dismiss in anticipation of the outsourcing and rely on the supplier's ETO reason.

Redundancy qualifies as an ETO reason, so any redundancies following a transfer will be fair, provided the procedure required for any redundancy dismissal is followed (the normal unfair dismissal rules will be used to assess the fairness of the dismissal). In the context of a transfer, it is particularly important that any selection is fair and it is not assumed that the existing

1 For a description of the legal effect of indemnities, *see* 28.12.

employees of the supplier will have preference over those employees who have transferred from the customer.

Provided that he has one year's service, any employee (who works in the part of the business or undertaking being transferred) who is dismissed either before or after the transfer for a reason connected with the transfer, will be able to claim unfair dismissal. The liability for such dismissal transfers under TUPE to the party to which the undertaking is transferred unless the parties agree otherwise.

In order to determine which party bears liability for TUPE-related dismissals, it is necessary to establish the nature and timing of the relevant dismissal:

(a) if an employee is dismissed by the customer or existing supplier before the change and that dismissal is connected with the change of supplier, liability will transfer to the new supplier; or

(b) if an employee is dismissed by the customer or existing supplier before the change and that dismissal is for a reason unconnected with the change of supplier (e.g. if the dismissal is conduct related) liability will remain with that customer or supplier and will not transfer to the new supplier.

In practice, however, it is often difficult to establish whether such a dismissal is or is not connected with the transfer. Therefore, properly drafted indemnities are essential. Indemnities are considered in greater detail in 27.7 below.

27.5.5 Constructive dismissal

Surprisingly, where an employee resigns from the customer or existing supplier and claims constructive dismissal on the grounds of an anticipated breach of contract by the new supplier after the transfer, for example if the new supplier proposes a variation to working conditions, liability remains with the old employer.

27.5.6 Union recognition agreements transfer

TUPE also deals with collective rights and provides that union recognition agreements transfer automatically.

27.6 Duty to consult

There is also an obligation to inform and/or consult on a collective basis with the trade union, if one is recognised, or elected employee representatives. Note that the obligation to consult under TUPE may be in addition to other general consultation obligations that the employer may be subject to.

27.6.1 Obligations of existing employer

If the New TUPE Regulations apply, the existing employer is placed under a duty to provide "Employee Liability Information", which is:

(a) information regarding the identity of the employees transferring and their ages;
(b) information contained in their statement of particulars of employment;
(c) information relating to any relevant collective agreements;
(d) details of any disciplinary action taken or grievances raised under the statutory procedures within the previous two years; and
(e) details of any legal action within the previous two years or any potential legal action in relation to any of the transferring employees.

The information must be given at least 14 days before the transfer and be in writing or in a readily accessible format and must be updated if it changes after being given to the transferee.

If the existing employer fails to provide the information, a tribunal can award compensation to the new employer of at least £500 per employee in most cases.

The existing employer is also obliged, if measures are envisaged by it, to carry out formal consultation with the employee representatives.

27.6.2 Obligations of new employer

The new supplier (or the customer if the service is being taken in-house) is placed under a corresponding duty to provide the existing employer with information about any "measures" which it intends to take in respect of the employees after the purported transfer. These measures include, for example, any proposal to make redundancies or relocate the workforce.

27.6.3 Timing

Consultation must be carried out properly with a view to seeking agreement to the measures and so information must be available or consultation should take place (if required) long enough before the transfer actually occurs to enable meaningful consultation to take place.

27.6.4 Remedies

If consultation does not take place or is carried out improperly or late, the affected employees or their representatives are entitled to complain to an employment tribunal, which can award a protective award of up to 13 weeks' gross pay for each employee depending on what a tribunal considers is just and equitable in the circumstances.

Under the old TUPE rules, liability for failure by the customer to inform and consult the transferring employees transfers to the incoming supplier unless the parties agree otherwise, but under new TUPE, the transferor and transferee are jointly and severally liable for this.

27.7 Transfer of staff from customer to supplier

Paragraphs 27.5 and 27.6 show that one of the effects of TUPE is to make one party responsible for the acts and failures of the other. For example, on commencement of the outsourcing arrangement, it makes the supplier responsible for the acts of the customer. It may be difficult for the supplier, without the cooperation of the customer, to defend a claim which arose before the transfer and which relates to the customer's actions.

On the basis that employees are not entitled to contract out of their rights under TUPE, there is no way for customers or suppliers to ensure that TUPE will not, as a matter of law, apply.

Therefore, customers and suppliers are always advised to include warranties and indemnities or other provisions to protect them.

27.7.1 Details of employees

A prudent supplier should ensure that the customer provides full warranties in relation to the due diligence information provided in respect of a specified list of transferring employees. A supplier may also ask the customer for warranties in relation to the Employee Liability Information, but the customer may resist this on the grounds that breach of this obligation carries its own remedy under new TUPE.

27.7.2 Indemnity for precommencement liabilities

The supplier should request full indemnity protection against liabilities connected to the transferring employees which arise from acts or omissions of the customer prior to the commencement of the outsourcing agreement and which will transfer to the supplier pursuant to TUPE (including liability for failure to comply with the information and consultation requirements). The customer may specify that the indemnity is subject to it having conduct of any litigation by transferring employees.

27.7.3 Indemnity for employees not listed

The supplier should also request full indemnity protection against claims by any employees of the customer (other than the listed employees) that they transfer to the supplier under TUPE as a result of the outsourcing arrangement. This can include a provision allowing the supplier a window of time to dismiss the individual and claim under the indemnity. After that period, the employee becomes the supplier's responsibility. If the parties consider that TUPE will not apply, the customer would, in effect, be providing the supplier with full indemnity protection in relation to a claim by any person that he transfers to the supplier under TUPE as a result of the outsourcing arrangement.

27.7.4 Indemnities for constructive dismissal

The customer should request full indemnity protection against claims for constructive dismissal where the employee is relying on the anticipated breach of contract by the supplier.

27.7.5 Failure to consult

Each party will want an indemnity from the other against failure to comply with their obligations to consult with the employees.

27.7.6 Mutual indemnities

In some cases, TUPE will effectively transfer staff from the customer to the supplier on the commencement, and from the supplier to the customer on termination of the outsourcing arrangement, so that the parties will be incentivised to agree broadly similar "mirror" provisions on commencement and termination.

27.7.7 Indemnities in favour of new supplier

In other cases, however, if the services are not brought back in-house on termination, TUPE will have the effect of transferring the employees and liabilities relating to them to the new supplier. Therefore, the customer will want any indemnities on termination to benefit the new supplier. Otherwise, if the indemnity is in the customer's favour only, it will not cover losses incurred by the new supplier, who will endeavour to pass these losses on to the customer in its charges. Paragraph 27.8 below examines this situation in greater detail.

27.8 Secondary TUPE

27.8.1 Effect of TUPE applying

If the services are to be provided by a new supplier rather than being outsourced for the first time, in the absence of any contractual provisions between the customer and the previous supplier dealing with this situation, TUPE will operate as follows:

(a) It will operate to transfer the relevant staff from the previous supplier to the new supplier. They will transfer on their existing terms and conditions, as explained above. In the absence of agreement to the contrary, the previous supplier can "cherry pick" the best staff and move them away prior to the transfer date, and deploy their weakest staff so that they are the employees who transfer at the transfer date. This practice, which is sometimes referred to as "dumping", can render the new supplier unable to perform the services properly on commencement of the outsourcing arrangement.

(b) Liabilities under the contracts of employment also transfer. This means the new supplier inherits the workforce with all attendant liabilities, and has no means of controlling this. Not only does the new supplier inherit all liabilities, the previous supplier can effectively control what liabilities its competitor will have to pick up. The previous supplier can fail to pay wages or can increase the salaries and benefits of the transferring staff so that the new supplier is burdened with the extra costs.

(c) There is an obligation on the previous supplier to consult or inform staff about the transfer, but liability for failing to do this can transfer to the new supplier, as the liability is joint and several.

27.8.2 Protections on termination

To avoid the problems mentioned in 27.8.1 above, during the last six months of the agreement or after notice of early termination has been given:

(a) The customer may want to prevent the previous supplier from cherry picking the best staff and therefore may restrict the previous supplier from moving staff into or out of the undertaking, unless the customer has consented to the move. The supplier may see this as an unwarranted interference with its control of how it provides the services and may suggest that consent is only required if the move would adversely affect the provision of the services.

(b) The customer may want to restrict the supplier from changing the employees' employment contracts unless the change is being made throughout the supplier's organisation.

(c) The customer may also be concerned that staff will be demotivated during the final stages of the agreement and may seek the supplier's cooperation in ensuring that staff remain with the supplier and transfer to the customer or new supplier.

27.8.3 Indemnities

If the services are to be provided by a new supplier rather than being outsourced for the first time, the new supplier will also need indemnities similar to those required on commencement (*see* 27.7 above) as described below.

27.8.4 Details of employees

The supplier will need the previous supplier to provide it with full details about the employees providing the service. Under new TUPE, there is the obligation to provide Employee Liability Information (*see* 27.7 above).

From a practical perspective, this type of information is invaluable to a new supplier. It renders negotiations in relation to the retendering far less problematic: the new supplier will have access to at least some due diligence in relation to those employees who will transfer under TUPE and can, therefore, assess costs and contingent liabilities more accurately. However, one drawback is that the information does not need to be given until at least 14 days before the transfer, which may be too late for the purposes of some negotiations.

It will need the previous supplier to warrant the accuracy of due diligence information provided in respect of a specified list of transferring employees.

27.8.5 Indemnity for pre-commencement liabilities

The supplier will need indemnities relating to liabilities connected to the transferring employees which arise from acts or omissions of the previous supplier (or subcontractor – *see* below) prior to the commencement of the outsourcing agreement and which will transfer to the new supplier pursuant to TUPE (including liability for failure to comply with the information and consultation requirements).

27.8.6 Indemnity for employees not listed

It will need indemnities relating to claims by any employees (other than the listed transferring employees) that they transfer under TUPE to the new supplier as a result of the outsourcing arrangement. This can include a provision by which the new supplier has a window of time to dismiss the individual and claim under the indemnity, after which the employee becomes the new supplier's responsibility.

27.8.7 Transfer from subcontractors

The new supplier will need the information and indemnities relating to employees whether they transfer from the previous supplier or from its subcontractors.

27.8.8 Failure to consult

Each party will want an indemnity from the other against failure to comply with their obligations to consult with the employees.

27.8.9 Grant of the indemnities

The supplier needs the indemnities listed in 27.8.4–27.8.8 above. The question arises as to how it will ensure that it is granted the requisite warranties:

(a) If the customer has agreed that the previous supplier will grant indemnities in favour of the new supplier, as mentioned in the last paragraph of 27.7.7 above, then the new supplier will be able to benefit from these.

(b) Can the new supplier agree indemnities directly with the previous supplier? In most situations, the transfer is taking place because the previous supplier has lost the customer's business and therefore may be uncooperative with the customer and with the new supplier, particularly where the new supplier is a direct competitor. However, if the customer has other ongoing commercial interests with the previous supplier or the previous supplier has assets that it wants to sell to the new supplier, there may be some scope for agreement. Also, the previous supplier may be willing to take a more pragmatic approach and provide some indemnities if it thinks that in the future it may win business from other customers of the new supplier and hence that staff may transfer from the new supplier to it.

If the supplier cannot agree indemnities with the incumbent supplier, then it will have to agree with the customer who will take the risks associated with TUPE applying. If the customer wants the supplier to accept the risks, then the supplier will usually increase its charges so that they include a risk premium.

27.9 "Soft" effects of TUPE

From a human perspective, the effect of TUPE can be extremely severe. Staff who have accepted employment with one company and in some cases worked loyally for that company for many years, find themselves being made redundant or working for another company. In the latter case, in some circumstances there may be significant differences between the culture in the customer and supplier organisations. For example, the customer may be a public sector body and the supplier may be a private sector body. For this reason, transferring staff may be worried and disturbed by the outsourcing process.

It is extremely important that these concerns are dealt with properly, as the transferring staff are key to the success of the outsourcing arrangement in several ways:

(a) The transferring staff will usually have information about the services previously being provided to the customer and how those services will need to change to reflect the business objectives of the customer. Chapter 2 stresses the criticality of this information and Chapter 7 highlights the importance of ensuring that the customer has a clear and detailed description of the services that it requires. The transferring staff may be unwilling to cooperate or they may feel a conflict of interest in advising the customer on suitable service-level regimes if they are ultimately going to be working for the supplier.

(b) The standard of the services provided by the supplier will depend in part upon the motivation of the staff employed to provide the services. Most suppliers realise this and are extremely adept at dealing sensitively with the concerns of any transferring staff.

27.10 Secondment

Because of the concerns that staff will not be happy about transferring from the customer to the supplier, in particular where the customer is in the public sector and the supplier is in the private sector, in some cases the parties agree that the staff previously employed in providing the services will be seconded to work for the supplier rather than transferred. This approach has been adopted by many NHS Trusts, in particular those who use the "Retention of Employment Model". In a recent case, the Employment Appeal Tribunal held that an employee who objected to the transfer but had worked for the transferee for a period on secondment had in fact transferred. This casts doubt on the effectiveness of this model. However, in most cases, applying the model suits all of the parties and is therefore unlikely to be challenged in the courts. The advantages and disadvantages of this approach are described in Table 37.

Table 37 *Secondment of staff*

Advantages

The staff remain employed in the public sector.

The staff are less likely to be hostile to the outsourcing arrangement if they perceive that they have been protected.

Disadvantages

The supplier may feel that it has less control over the staff and hence less control over the provision of the services.

There may be practical issues relating to day-to-day management and disciplinary control over the staff.

The supplier may have less control over the activities carried out by the employees. For example, the employees may be seconded to the supplier so that it may provide the services, in which case the supplier will not be able to employ the staff in providing services to other customers.

The VAT implications of transferring staff or seconding staff may differ, particularly if the services supplied are exempt from VAT. However, with effect from April 2009, the VAT exemption will be removed, which may result in this model being used less in sectors where the supplier is not VAT registered.

27.11 Competence of transferring staff

As part of its due diligence exercise (*see* Chapter 6), the supplier will need to reassure itself that it will be able to provide the services. Therefore, the due diligence exercise may involve the supplier effectively interviewing the staff to ensure that they are appropriately experienced and skilled for the jobs that they will need to carry out. Most suppliers are aware of the sensitivity required to handle this procedure well, and gain the cooperation of the relevant staff.

Any decision to enter into an outsourcing arrangement must be made taking into account the effects of TUPE. Thus, one effect of TUPE is to hinder the customer from improving the quality of its services simply by changing supplier. If a customer is dissatisfied with the quality of staff carrying out the work for the supplier, the customer should bear in mind that, if it appoints a new supplier, that supplier may end up with the same employees. However, in some circumstances the new supplier may be able to retrain the employees or redeploy them.

27.12 Adequacy of transferring staff

There are various reasons why staff who have previously provided the services to the customer may not transfer to the supplier:

(a) If there is no TUPE transfer, there will be no automatic transfer of employees.
(b) Even where there is a TUPE transfer, the staff of the customer who are not engaged in that part of the undertaking do not transfer. This would apply to staff who provide support to many aspects of the customer's business including the part transferring but who are not actually "assigned" to that part.
(c) Under TUPE, employees who are unhappy about the transfer can object to it, in which event their existing employment comes to an end at the point of transfer and their employment does not transfer to the new supplier. In this situation, the individual generally has no remedy against either party.

Where the staff who have previously provided the services do not transfer, the supplier will have to provide the services using its own resources. The supplier may be concerned if it is dependent upon the knowledge and skills of certain staff in order to provide the services and these staff do not transfer. The supplier will need to investigate this issue carefully when it carries out its due diligence (*see* Chapter 6). In appropriate circumstances, it may need to agree with the customer what will happen if the staff (or key staff) will not transfer. For example, the parties may decide that the supplier will have a transition period to carry out a skills transfer.

27.13 Managing transferring staff

Once the staff have transferred to the supplier, the supplier will be anxious to ensure that it can provide the services to the customer in the most efficient manner. However, the effect of TUPE is that the staff will transfer to the supplier on the same terms and conditions as those that they previously enjoyed. It also provides that any attempt to contract out of TUPE is void.

27.13.1 Varying terms and conditions on transfer

An agreement to vary terms and conditions on transfer is void and the employees do not have legal capacity to consent to a change unless the change is for an ETO reason (*see* 27.5.4 above). This means that even consensual changes will be ineffective if there is no ETO reason.

The main problem with the definition of an ETO reason is the requirement that the reason "entails a change in the workforce". This means that a change (even if consensual), such as a variation to benefits, which does not result in changes to employee numbers or functions will not qualify as an ETO reason.

There are less stringent provisions which apply in certain insolvency situations which allow changes to terms and conditions in order to safeguard employment opportunities by ensuring the survival of the undertaking.

27.13.2 Varying changes unrelated to transfer

The other way changes to terms can be introduced effectively with the consent of the employees is if it can be established that such changes do not relate to the transfer itself.

What is needed essentially is an event that can be said to break the link between the transfer and the change or the passage of time. A lengthy gap between the transfer and the change will increase the possibility of the changes being seen as not relating to the transfer itself, but instead to the changing circumstances of the business. The employment tribunal will carry out a factual assessment of the circumstances surrounding the change.

However, the new supplier will almost certainly be in a stronger position to enforce changes to terms and conditions of employment if it can demonstrate effectively that they have been introduced:

(a) in respect of the entire workforce (and not specifically in relation to the staff who have transferred);
(b) as part of a wider restructuring of the business as a whole; and
(c) at a time distant from the date of the transfer.

27.13.3 Dismissal of employees who refuse to agree changes

If consent to the changes cannot be obtained and the new supplier dismisses an employee who refuses to accept the changes, there is a strong argument that the dismissal was for a reason connected with the transfer and there will, therefore, be the possibility of a claim for automatic unfair dismissal.

27.13.4 Unilateral variation of the changes

Alternatively, if the supplier pursues a strategy of unilaterally enforcing the changes on the staff after the transfer, not only is the variation unlikely to be legally binding, but also the affected individuals may claim that the new supplier has fundamentally breached the terms of the original contract of employment and as a result they have been constructively dismissed (i.e. dismissed by virtue of the employer's conduct rather than expressly dismissed). In the event that this is successfully established, the employees will have a claim for wrongful dismissal and unfair dismissal.

27.13.5 "Two-tier" workforce

Where public services are contracted out, there is a possibility that any new recruits will be employed on less favourable terms than the former public sector employees, thus creating a two-tier workforce. Trade Unions are pressing for legislation to require employers to offer similar terms to new employees, while employers' organisations are proposing a voluntary code to deal with this issue. New TUPE does not resolve this and it is likely to remain a political issue.

27.14 Termination of the outsourcing agreement

On termination, the process described on commencement is reversed. Staff of the supplier or its subcontractors may transfer to the customer, the successor supplier or the successor supplier's subcontractors.

27.14.1 Transfer to the customer

In the first example, staff who are transferring back to the customer may include some of those who transferred from the customer to the supplier on the commencement of the outsourcing arrangement. These staff may have been persuaded by the outsourcing supplier that their career prospects would improve after they moved to the supplier. Therefore, it may be difficult for them to come to terms with the fact that they are transferring back to the customer. They may even feel that the customer betrayed them by transferring them to the supplier.

27.14.2 Transfer to incoming supplier

Staff who transfer to other suppliers may feel ambivalent about a situation in which they are now working for competitors of their previous employer. Whether staff transfer to the customer or to an incoming supplier, the party to whom the employees are transferring will need to deal sensitively with their concerns.

27.14.3 Indemnities

In addition, the new supplier will need to ensure that it has indemnities similar to those described in 27.7 above.

27.14.4 Effect of the economic climate on termination

Customers should bear in mind that the impact of TUPE depends upon the economic climate or financial position of the supplier when the agreement is terminated. Thus the application of TUPE depends on how the services are provided, a factor that will usually be within the control of the supplier depending, for example, upon whether dedicated staff are used on the contract or if the services are provided by a pool of employees who also work on other contracts. When there is a skills shortage, the supplier may be anxious to retain skilled staff. In contrast, if there is a recession and work is scarce, then the supplier may be anxious to reduce its head count. In a recession, staff who previously worked on services provided to several customers may find that they are working for only one customer if the supplier has lost the contracts for the other customers.

27.14.5 Changes in the law of TUPE

Parties should also be aware that the interpretation of TUPE could change as case law develops and if amendments are made to the Regulations themselves. Therefore, the effect of TUPE at the time of termination may be different from that anticipated when the agreement was drafted.

27.15 Redundancies

If the employer's requirement for employees of a particular kind in the place where they are engaged ceases or diminishes (or is expected to do so), there will be a redundancy situation.

27.15.1 When redundancies may occur

Redundancies can occur in the following situations:

(a) In some cases the customer and the supplier may decide that staff who would otherwise have transferred to the supplier will be made redundant if the outsourcing project goes ahead.

(b) The customer may have to make redundancies where an outsourced activity is discontinued altogether. For example, a business may decide to stop offering a canteen service to its staff, so the employees providing the catering services will be redundant unless they can be redeployed by the supplier on another contract.

(c) The customer may have to make redundancies among staff who do not transfer if, for example, their workload reduces as a result of the outsourcing. This might include central support staff, part of whose function was to support the business function being outsourced.

27.15.2 Legal background on redundancies

Redundancy is a potentially fair reason for dismissal, but the employer must follow a fair procedure in order to avoid liability for unfair dismissal. This involves consultation with the employee, fair selection and consideration for alternative employment as well as compliance with statutory dismissal procedures. Employees with more than two years' service will be entitled to a statutory redundancy payment if dismissed as a result of redundancy.

27.15.3 Redundancy costs

Where the parties anticipate that redundancies may occur, they can cater for the redundancy costs, whether within the charging framework or by use of a retention fund, out of which the redundancy costs, if any, are paid. If the parties do not expressly deal with the redundancy costs, then the supplier may include them in its charges irrespective of whether redundancies are actually made. The parties may also deal with the costs of redundancy when the contract terminates, although in the absence of any agreement, it will be the liability of the supplier (unless the redundancy is in connection with a TUPE transfer, in which case the liability will transfer to the customer or new supplier).

Chapter 28

Pension Issues

28.1 Outline

28.1.1 What this chapter deals with

Chapter 27 describes the effect of the application of TUPE to outsourcing. This chapter deals with a specific but related issue, the subject of the pension rights of employees transferring from the customer to the supplier (or a first-generation supplier to a second-generation supplier) under TUPE. This can be a particularly tricky issue and one which customers and suppliers ignore at their peril. It is not unheard of for outsourcing agreements to be primarily motivated by a desire to reduce the customer's headcount and resulting pensions liabilities. Pensions issues will vary substantially from country to country, depending upon the types of pensions which are popular and any relevant local legislation. This chapter describes the situation in the UK.

28.1.2 Pensions outside of the UK – a case-by-case approach

Not only can occupational pension schemes in the UK be individual to a specific employer or a group of employers but, throughout Europe and the rest of the world, pension arrangements that predominate in one jurisdiction can vary significantly to those that are the norm in another.

Therefore, as far as Europe is concerned, it is hardly surprising that the original Acquired Rights directive ("ARD") in 1977 and the later two directives have fairly wide exclusions from the automatic transfer provisions for occupational pension rights.

The original 1997 directive carved out employees' rights to old age, invalidity and survivors' benefits under occupational pension schemes that are outside of the statutory social security scheme in the Member State from automatically transferring on the transfer of an undertaking.

Each Member State can decide on the level of pension protection and how it is to be achieved. They can implement their own approach under their own national legislation including, if they choose to, providing that benefits do transfer.

Consequently since, first, pension provision itself differs throughout Europe; and, second, Member States can implement their own version of pension protection on the transfer of an undertaking, the result is that there is no "one fits all" approach.

Pension provisions on a multi-jurisdictional outsourcing arrangement (whether in Europe or elsewhere) must therefore be approached on a case-by-case basis.

28.2 Transfer of pension rights under TUPE

28.2.1 No automatic transfer – occupational pension schemes

There is an important exception to the provision in TUPE that automatically transfers employment contract rights and liabilities. That exception applies to occupational pension schemes. Specifically, the automatic transfer provisions do not apply to an employment contract, and the liabilities under that contract, to the extent to which they relate to old age, invalidity and survivors' benefits under an occupational pension scheme. Company final salary and money purchase pension schemes (also known as defined benefit and defined contribution schemes) are occupational pension schemes.

28.2.2 Automatic transfer – personal and stakeholder pension schemes

Personal pension schemes and stakeholder pension schemes are not occupational pension schemes, so obligations on the part of an employer to contribute to a personal or stakeholder pension scheme of the transferring employees (including obligations under a group personal pension scheme) do automatically transfer.

28.3 The Pensions Act 2004 and the Transfer of Employment (Pension Protection) Regulations 2005

28.3.1 Implications of the legislation

The Pensions Act 2004 and the Transfer of Employment (Pension Protection) Regulations 2005 ("2005 Regulations") do not amend the situation described above (i.e. that rights under occupational pension schemes do not automatically transfer). However, they do require the new employer, following a TUPE transfer, to offer pension arrangements meeting minimum standards ("Minimum Pension Protection"), if the transferring employees had access to an occupational pension scheme with their old employer.

28.3.2 Description of Minimum Pension Protection

The new employer must offer:

(a) a defined contribution ("DC") arrangement in which the employer matches employees' contributions to a maximum of six per cent of basic pay (i.e. excluding bonus, overtime etc.); the arrangement has to be an occupational DC scheme or a stakeholder scheme and cannot be a group personal pension scheme – presumably so that transferring employees avoid the higher charges often found in group personal pensions; or

(b) a defined benefit scheme that meets the requirements of the so-called "reference scheme test" (the minimum standard required by law to allow a scheme to contract out of the State Second Pension); or

(c) a scheme providing benefits with a value equal to members' contributions plus six per cent of pensionable pay (however defined in the scheme rules); for example a "cash balance" plan (one in which the employer takes the investment risk by promising a defined pot of money at retirement – leaving the individual member to buy the pension and take the annuity cost/longevity risk).

28.3.3 Changing Minimum Pension Protection arrangements

The Pensions Act 2004 expressly allows the new employer and the transferring employees to agree, at any time after the transfer, to contract out of the effect of these new provisions.

28.4 Beckmann/Martin liabilities

Following two recent decisions of the European Court of Justice ("ECJ"), there is uncertainty about whether early retirement benefits that are not ill-health early retirement benefits under an occupational pension scheme are covered by the exception in TUPE for old age benefits.

28.4.1 The *Beckmann* case

Under the *Beckmann* case,[1] a former NHS employee whose employment was transferred to Dynamco under TUPE was subsequently dismissed on redundancy grounds. She claimed entitlement to an early retirement pension and other benefits, on the basis that these had transferred under the ARD (which an earlier version of TUPE was supposed to implement). The ECJ decided that only benefits paid from the time when an employee reaches the end of his normal working life as laid down by the general structure of the pension scheme can be classified as old age benefits. As a result, the right to an early retirement pension on redundancy was held to transfer.

28.4.2 The *Martin* case

In the *Martin* case,[2] Martin and others transferred into a different pension arrangement following the transfer of their employment from the NHS to South Bank University. The claimants subsequently opted to take early retirement on leaving service in circumstances which the Employment Tribunal found to be "in the interests of efficiency of the service". They claimed that they were entitled to an early retirement redundancy pension payable with the agreement of their employers. It was held that the rights that transfer under TUPE include those rights contingent upon either dismissal or early retirement by agreement with the employer.

1 *Beckmann v Dynamco Wicheloe Macfarlane Ltd* (ECJ Case C 164/000) [2002] IRLR 578.
2 *Martin v South Bank University* (ECJ Case C-4/01) [2004] IRLR 74.

28.4.3 Implications of *Beckmann/Martin* cases

It appears, therefore, that benefits payable under an occupational pension scheme on dismissal in the interests of efficiency of the service or redundancy will transfer under TUPE. However, it is arguable that other benefits payable before normal retirement date may also transfer, such as a simple early retirement pension (particularly if it is not actuarially reduced to take account of early receipt).

The problem with the *Beckmann/Martin* cases is that the exact scope of the application of the ECJ's judgment is not known. To the extent that these types of benefits transfer under TUPE, the supplier will have to provide a defined benefit early retirement pension (or appropriate compensation for such). The supplier may only have intended and budgeted to provide simple money purchase benefits.

Accordingly, on an outsourcing transaction involving a TUPE transfer, it is important for the supplier to examine the pension terms which are currently offered by the customer and, in particular, to identify any special pension terms which apply on redundancy or in similar situations. The cost to the supplier of replicating these benefits may be substantial.

28.4.4 Hidden Beckmann/Martin liabilities

There is also the possibility of a "hidden" Beckmann/Martin liability in the following circumstances. If transferring employees have previously been transferred to the customer pursuant to a TUPE transfer, then it is possible that Beckmann rights may also have transferred. If they transferred to the customer, then they will similarly transfer on to the supplier. The customer may have no information about previous pension benefits of transferring employees whom it currently employs as a result of a series of TUPE transfers.

28.4.5 Risk of Beckmann/Martin liabilities

Where the customer's pension scheme is a money purchase occupational pension scheme and there are no "hidden" Beckmann/Martin liabilities, the treatment of pension benefits is unlikely to be problematic. Beckmann/Martin type benefits are almost exclusively found in defined benefit arrangements.

Beckmann/Martin liabilities can be a consideration even when pension benefits are provided on a defined benefit basis both pre and post transfer. However, they are most likely to create a greater degree of commercial exposure when pension provision changes from a generous defined benefit pension scheme pre transfer to a substantially less generous defined contribution pension scheme post transfer.

28.4.6 Ill-health retirement benefits

Ill-health early retirement benefits will not transfer automatically under TUPE and do not need to be replicated. They continue to fall under the exception in TUPE for invalidity benefits.

28.5 Commercial outsourcing - contractual agreement to continue to provide defined contribution benefits post transfer

When the customer's existing pension arrangements are defined contribution, the customer and the supplier may agree to continue to provide the same type of benefits with the same level of contributions post transfer despite the fact that this is more than the supplier has to do to provide Minimum Pension Protection.

This seldom gives rise to any significant issues. There is certainty around the cost of providing these benefits. This makes contractual agreement easier to achieve.

28.6 Commercial outsourcing - contractual agreement to continue to provide defined benefits post transfer

In some commercial outsourcing contracts, when the customer has a defined benefit pension scheme, the customer and the supplier may agree that the supplier will continue to provide a defined benefit pension scheme post transfer. The commercial agreement will usually (but not always) be that the supplier's pension scheme provides defined benefits that are broadly comparable to the benefits provided by the customer's pension scheme.

28.6.1 Agreement regarding future benefits for service

The agreement might only relate to future benefits for service with the supplier. Transferring employees will retain their deferred benefits for service with the customer in the customer's pension scheme. The cost of providing defined benefits for future service with the supplier throughout the contract term is more difficult to price for than for money purchase benefits, but less difficult to price than when past service benefits are also involved.

28.6.2 Agreement regarding past and future benefits for service

When the supplier undertakes contractually to provide a defined benefit pension scheme for both past and future service, the transferring employees will usually be given an option to transfer the value of the benefits they have already accrued in the customer's pension scheme from the customer's pension scheme to the supplier's pension scheme.

Depending on the commercial agreement, the supplier might undertake to procure that its scheme provides a service credit based on the value of the amount of assets transferred from the customer's pension scheme in respect of the transferring employees' past service benefits in the customer's pension scheme ("Transfer Value").

On other occasions, the commercial agreement might be that the supplier's scheme will provide a day-for-day service credit (or actuarially equivalent) in return for the Transfer Value.

In both cases (and in particular when a day-for-day service credit (or equivalent) is being provided) pricing for past and future pension benefits is complex. The Transfer Value that comes across from the customer's pension scheme to fund the assumed liabilities in the supplier's scheme is crucial. Unless there are very few transferring employees and potential exposure is not material in the overall context of the transaction, this whole process requires actuarial input.

28.7 Commercial outsourcing – contractual agreement to change pension benefits from defined benefit to defined contribution

When the commercial agreement is to change from a defined benefit pension scheme to a defined contribution pension scheme post transfer, that agreement may go beyond what is required for Minimum Pension Protection.

That in itself is seldom an issue, since the money purchase benefits that the supplier undertakes to provide can be accurately priced for. However, Beckmann/Martin liabilities (and the costs associated with them) can potentially add to cost/risk.

In order to manage Beckmann/Martin-type liabilities there are a number of strategies that can be deployed. These include some or all of the following depending on the nature of the risk:

(a) effective due diligence to properly identify (and in some cases eliminate) risk;
(b) actuarial due diligence to determine the financial cost associated with risk;
(c) commercial agreement as to who bears what level/cost of risk.

28.8 The unintended charge

It may appear to employers that new pension legislation is usually designed to impose more onerous and prescriptive obligations on them. However, recent changes to the Occupational Pension Schemes (Employer Debt) Regulations 2005 (the "Employer Debt Regulations") might actually be helpful to employers who are engaged in outsourcing.

28.8.1 Section 75 debt

An ever-present pensions exposure in outsourcing is what is sometimes referred to as the "unintended charge". If the customer is one of a number of participating employers in a defined benefit occupational pension scheme ("Group Scheme") and both the customer and other participating employers employ active scheme members, Section 75 of the Pensions Act 1995 will trigger a debt which the customer will be liable for if it ceases to have an active Group Scheme member ("Section 75 debt"). This can happen if all of the customer's active Group Scheme members transfer to the supplier under TUPE. The customer may not intend to trigger the debt. It can be unaware that it has done so until after the event.

The Section 75 debt can be substantial. It is calculated on a buyout basis (which is more expensive than ongoing funding). It is not solely based on the customer's liabilities. It includes "orphan liabilities". These are liabilities that relate to the Group Scheme's employers that are no longer around/not liable/cannot pay them. All of this means that the customer can be faced with having to make a large capital payment to the Group Scheme.

This can cause difficulties on outsourcing at the beginning and end of the contract and during the contract term.

28.8.2 Problems at the beginning of the contract

At the beginning of the contract, it can create a problem for the customer if the pension fund ceases to have an active Group Scheme member because all of the customer's active Group Scheme members transfer to the incoming supplier under TUPE.

28.8.3 Problems at the end of the contract

At the end of the contract, the outgoing supplier could face the Section 75 debt if it has undertaken to continue to provide a defined benefit pension scheme and the pension fund ceases to have an active Group Scheme member because all of the customer's active Group Scheme members transfer to the customer or the successor supplier under TUPE.

28.8.4 Problems during the term

It is a natural process for transferred staff to leave employment with the supplier and be replaced by new employees during the contract term. New employees are not necessarily given the same pension benefits in the same pension scheme. Over time, the last transferred active scheme member can simply leave employment with the supplier or retire. At that point a Section 75 debt can be triggered.

28.8.5 Options offered by Employer Debt Regulations

Up until recently, although there were some options, they were practically difficult. Unless action was taken before the debt was triggered the opportunity was lost. Recent changes to the Employer Debt Regulations offer a number of different possibilities for managing the Section 75 debt, even after it has been triggered. The changes that are likely to be the most helpful in outsourcing situations are discussed below. They refer throughout to the customer, but could equally apply to the supplier.

28.8.5.1 Period of grace

This applies when the customer's last active member is leaving/has left service but the customer intends to employ at least one active member within 12 months of that event. The customer may, by giving appropriate notice to the Group Scheme trustees, make use of the "period of grace" provision. If it does actually employ an active member within the 12-month period, effectively the Section 75 debt is deemed not to have been triggered. The customer will not have to pay the amount of the debt to the Group Scheme.

28.8.5.2 Scheme apportionment arrangement

This allows the customer not to pay any of, or to pay only part of, its Section 75 debt. The liability/remainder of the liability is apportioned to one or more of the other participating employers. The Group Scheme trustees must agree to the apportionment.

28.8.5.3 Withdrawal arrangement

This also allows the customer to pay less than its Section 75 debt (subject to a minimum level of payment). Here someone else (possibly but not necessarily one or more of the other participating employers) provides a guarantee in relation to the remainder of the Section 75 debt.

28.8.5.4 Approved withdrawal arrangement

This is similar to a withdrawal arrangement but here the customer proposes to pay less of the Section 75 debt than it would have to do under a withdrawal arrangement. This type of arrangement must be approved by the Pensions Regulator, who can impose additional conditions and can call in the guarantee early.

28.8.5.5 Summary

All of the above options have been described only very briefly and very generally. Many detailed conditions are attached to them. Legal and actuarial advice is needed in order to consider using any of these in practice.

28.9 The situation in the public sector

Although TUPE applies in the same way to both commercial outsourcing and public sector outsourcing, additional protections are afforded to public sector employees' pension benefits when services are being outsourced from a public authority to a private sector supplier.

Public sector employers operate under guidelines which require them to procure pension protection for public sector employees who are transferring to a private sector supplier.

Different public sector bodies can use different pension models to achieve the pension protection required for their transferring employees. Pension models that are commonly used in public sector outsourcing are discussed below.

28.10 The guidelines for pension protection in the public sector

28.10.1 Fair Deal

For public sector outsourcing contracts that were entered into for the first time from 1999 onwards (with the possible exception of contracts that were in the process of being negotiated at that time), guidelines have existed which in practice require suppliers to provide broadly comparable pension benefits post transfer for transferring public sector employees on both first generation and second generation transfers. The guidelines are known as "Fair Deal".

28.10.2 The additional considerations

In addition to Fair Deal, there are further considerations when best-value authorities ("BVAs") are concerned. BVAs include local authorities, the police authority, the fire authority and various other bodies. These are discussed below.

28.10.3 First generation and second generation transfers

First generation transfers occur when public sector employees transfer their employment to a private sector supplier for the first time. Second (and subsequent) generation transfers occur when the same ex-public sector employees subsequently transfer their employment from the outgoing contractor to the incoming contractor on a contract re-let.

28.10.4 The pension models that are used to deliver the pension protection

In order to deliver the required level of pension protection, three different pension models are commonly used in public sector outsourcing. Which one applies in a particular contract depends on:

(a) which public sector pension scheme is involved;
(b) supplier's choice; and
(c) the basis on which the public sector body in question decides to contract.

The three commonly used pension arrangements are:

(a) *A GAD-approved Scheme*: the supplier provides pension benefits for both past and future service through a pension scheme that the government actuary's department ("GAD") has judged to be broadly comparable to the public sector pension scheme in question. This can be achieved by GAD providing a passport for the supplier's scheme or by GAD providing a certificate of broad comparability. GAD certificates relate specifically to one particular transfer. GAD passports are used by private sector suppliers who are engaged in a lot of outsourcing activities. They apply for a fixed period (usually two years) which means the pubic sector supplier's scheme can be used for a number of outsources without having to revert to GAD each time there is a transfer.
(b) *Admission Body*: when the transferring public sector or ex-public sector employees are members of the Local Government Pension Scheme ("LGPS") the supplier can become an Admitted Body in LGPS. This allows the new private sector employer to participate in the appropriate LGPS Fund. The public sector transferring employees can continue to be members of LGPS for as long as they continue to be employed in providing the services. In order to become an Admitted Body, the supplier has to enter into an Admission Agreement with the relevant LGPS Fund. It will usually also be required to provide a bond or indemnity which acts as a guarantee to protect the LGPS Fund in the event of supplier insolvency.
(c) *Retention of Employment*: in some outsourcing arrangements from the National Health Service ("NHS"), a retention of employment model is used to retain employees in NHS employment. This allows them to continue to be members of the NHS Pension

Scheme. The retained NHS employees are then seconded to the supplier for the period of the contract.

28.11 What is Fair Deal all about?

28.11.1 The "Fair Deal" ethos and where it comes from

For central government outsourcing, the Cabinet Office Statement of Practice ("COSOP") was issued in 2000. This has a document called "Fair Deal for Staff Pensions" appended to it ("Fair Deal 1999"). A revised edition of Fair Deal was issued in 2004 ("Fair Deal 2004") (together "Fair Deal"). Fair Deal 2004 sought to remedy some of the problems that had emerged in practice since Fair Deal 1999.

28.11.2 Application of Fair Deal

Fair Deal is essentially guidance for central government departments. It does not directly apply to local government outsourcing. The Local Government Act 1999 requires BVAs to follow directions issued by the government. In 2003 and again in 2007, the government issued directions to BVAs that relate to the treatment of pension benefits in public sector outsourcing ("2003 Direction" and "2007 Direction"). The 2003 Direction required BVAs to follow Fair Deal. The 2007 Direction builds on the 2003 Direction. Therefore, in practice, Fair Deal will apply to both central government and BVA outsourcing, with additional requirements in the 2007 Direction applying only to BVA outsourcing.

Fair Deal is not directly binding on suppliers. However, because central and local government departments must operate within its guidelines, the pension protection that Fair Deal seeks to achieve is imposed as obligations on the supplier in the outsourcing contract.

28.11.3 Description of Fair Deal

The thrust of Fair Deal is to ensure that public sector employees/ex-public sector employees who transfer their employment to a supplier when the services they perform are outsourced are provided with (at least) broadly comparable pension benefits for future service.

In addition, if they choose to transfer the value of their pension benefits from their public sector pension scheme to the supplier's pension scheme, they must also be provided with broadly comparable pension benefits for past service on a continuous service basis (or actuarial equivalent). This is the case on first generation and second generation transfers.

Fair Deal 2004 recognised that there was a problem with protecting past service on second generation transfers that Fair Deal 1999 had not really addressed. The outgoing supplier is not a party to the re-let contract. Consequently, the public sector contracting authority has no direct control over the Transfer Value that the outgoing supplier's pension scheme offered to fund the past service liabilities that were being transferred to the incoming supplier's scheme. More often than not, the Transfer Value was insufficient to fund the assumed liabilities. The effect of this was that the incoming supplier was often at a commercial disadvantage as compared with the incumbent supplier when bidding on a contract re-let.

Fair Deal 2004 attempted to tackle this by requiring exit provisions to be put into outsourcing contracts. Consequently, most public sector contracts will now require the outgoing supplier to procure that the trustees of its pension scheme provide a Transfer Value on a basis that is no less generous than those that applied in its contract on entry.

Despite the application of Fair Deal 2004, agreeing transfer values from outgoing suppliers to incoming suppliers continues to be problematic in public sector outsourcing contracts.

Fair Deal is not retrospective. It does not apply to ex-public sector employees who were the subject of a first generation transfer before 1999.

28.11.4 Description of the 2007 Directive

In BVA outsourcing, the 2007 Direction applies to outsourcing contracts entered into since 1 October 2007. It builds on Fair Deal. It has three significant effects:

(a) it provides a statutory framework for pension protection, but only in relation to future service with the supplier;

(b) it requires contracting BVAs to ensure that their contract with the supplier gives the relevant transferring employees a direct right to enforce the pension protection directly against the supplier; and

(c) it provides pension protection to ex-public sector transferring employees who were not covered by Fair Deal on their first generation transfer and who are now the subject of a second (or subsequent) generation transfer. The pension protection is by reference to broad comparability with the outgoing supplier's pension scheme and is only for future service with their new supplier. There is no requirement to protect their past service either with their original public sector employer or with the outgoing supplier.

28.12 Beckmann/Martin liabilities in the public sector

Public sector defined benefit pension schemes generally have generous benefit structures. Beckmann/Martin-type benefits often form part of the benefit structure in public sector pension schemes.

Public sector pension schemes can be funded or unfunded arrangements. However, even when the public sector scheme is a funded scheme, enhanced pension benefits on redundancy are not usually funded within the scheme on an ongoing basis. When they arise, the employer in question makes a capital payment to the scheme to fund the additional cost of providing the benefits.

Other early retirement benefits may be funded on an ongoing basis, but, because the funding is based on assumptions that may not match experience, there can be a funding shortfall.

Transfer values from public sector schemes will not normally be calculated on a basis that includes any element of funding for enhanced pension benefits on redundancy. They will be based on assumptions as to early retirement. It is therefore as important to assess the impact of Beckmann/Martin-type considerations in public sector outsourcing as it is in private sector outsourcing since they can give rise to a significant funding requirement.

28.13 The Two-Tier Workforce Code

There are also guidelines in the public sector relating to the level of pension benefits that new employees who are engaged by the supplier to provide the services during the contract terms should receive. This is commonly referred to as the Two-Tier Workforce Code.

The requirements under the Two-Tier Workforce Code fall short of requiring the supplier to provide the same level of pension benefits to new employees as those that apply to the ex-public sector employees that they work alongside.

New employees can be given either:

(a) membership of a good quality occupational pension scheme (which can be defined benefit or defined contribution with matching employer/employee contributions of up to six per cent); or
(b) membership of a stakeholder scheme (with matching employer/employee contributions of up to six per cent).

28.14 Special protections

Some pension scheme members benefit from specific statutory protections for their pension benefits. Commonly these occur in industry sectors that were previously nationalised industries with the protections being linked to denationalisation. Examples include the Electricity Supply Pension Scheme and the Railways Pension Scheme, but there are others.

The degree of protection varies depending on the legislation that it is derived from. These need to be considered on a case-by-case basis. They can impact significantly on the treatment of pension benefits.

Chapter 29

Competition Issues

29.1 Outline

Outsourcing arrangements can give rise to competition issues, including merger control, exchanges of information, and the enforceability of exclusivity and non-compete provisions. This chapter considers these issues and provides some practical tips on dealing with competition issues in outsourcing arrangements.

29.2 Merger control

Outsourcing arrangements may constitute a merger which is subject to UK or EU merger control.

An example is the *Exel/NHS Logistics Authority/NHS Purchasing and Supply Agency* decision[1] of the Office of Fair Trading ("OFT") in July 2006, where the facts were as follows:

(a) Exel Europe Limited was a UK subsidiary of Deutsche Post AG, whose core activities in the UK were contract logistics (including warehousing and distribution) and freight forwarding.
(b) Exel agreed to take over the provision of certain procurement and logistics services for consumable products to the Department of Health.
(c) The services had previously been provided (respectively) by the NHS Purchasing and Supply Agency and NHS Logistics who provided the services as in-house "shared services" centres.
(d) The agreement included the transfer from the NHS Purchasing and Supply Agency and NHS Logistics to Exel of up to 1,600 employees and the transfer of certain assets (including information technology and office equipment) and the grant to Exel of the right to use certain NHS intellectual property rights.
(e) The agreement also included the transfer of outsourcing agreements entered into by the shared services centres with the Department of Health and third parties (although the agreements with third parties were low value).

The OFT held that it was possible to attribute an open market value to the services provided by the shared services centres, and this market value exceeded the £70 million turnover threshold under UK merger control (*see* 29.3.2 below). Accordingly, the OFT held that the transaction was subject to UK merger control.

1 www.oft.gov.uk/advice_and_resources/resource_base/Mergers_home/decisions/2006/exel.

29.2.1 EU merger control

A major outsourcing arrangement will be subject to EU merger control if it involves a "concentration" with a "Community dimension".[2]

29.2.1.1 "Concentration"

A "concentration" includes the acquisition of direct or indirect control over all or part of an enterprise or "undertaking".[3]

The Commission's Consolidated Jurisdictional Notice (the "Jurisdictional Notice")[4] provides details of the Commission's approach to deciding whether outsourcing constitutes a concentration for EU merger control purposes.

If an outsourcing supplier, in addition to taking over a previously internal activity, acquires associated assets which "constitute a business with a market presence, to which a market turnover can be clearly attributed",[5] the arrangement will constitute a concentration. So would a deal involving the transfer of a discrete section of a business, which had provided services to third parties before the transfer.[6] In some circumstances, the transfer of a client base[7] or an exclusive licence for intangible assets can constitute a "concentration" if this in itself generates turnover (i.e. revenue).

However, there will not be a concentration if no assets or employees are transferred to the supplier, or if the supplier acquires only a right to direct the customers' assets and employees which will be used exclusively to service the customer.[8] Where activities are outsourced to a new subsidiary within the same corporate group, there is no "concentration" if the new subsidiary entity continues to be solely controlled by the ultimate parent of the group.

For an outsourcing arrangement to constitute a concentration, the assets previously dedicated to the in-house activities of the customer must enable the supplier to provide services not only to the customer, but also to third parties, either immediately or "within a short period after the transfer" (normally not exceeding three years, but depending on the specific conditions of the market in question).[9] This will be the case if the transfer relates to a subsidiary which already provides services to third parties.

However, some commentators argue that the transfer of the assets or personnel in an outsourcing agreement will only qualify as a "concentration" under the Merger Regulation if the transferred

---

2 For example decisions in Case M.4981 – *AT&T/IBM*,14 December 2007, Case M.3171 *Computer Sciences Corporation/Royal Mail Business Systems* (2003/C187/09) and M.560 *EDS/Lufthansa*, 11 May 1995.

3 Article 3(1)(b) of Regulation 139/2004, OJ L24, 29.1.2004, p1.

4 Commission Consolidated Jurisdictional Notice, available at http://eur-lex.europa.eu/LexUriServ/LexUriServ.do?uri=OJ:C:2008:095:0001:0048:EN:PDF. *See* OJ 2008 C95/1, 16 April 2008.

5 Commission Consolidated Jurisdictional Notice, paragraph 24, available at http://eur-lex.europa.eu/LexUriServ/LexUriServ.do?uri=OJ:C:2008:095:0001:0048:EN:PDF. *See* OJ 2008 C95/1, 16 April 2008. *See* also Case M.3867 – *Vattenhall/Elsam and Energi E2 assets*.

6 Case M.3571 *IBM/Maerskdata/DMData* (2005/C28/02).

7 COMP/M.4981 *AT&T/IBM*,14 December 2007.

8 Commission Consolidated Jurisdictional Notice, at paragraph 25.

9 Commission's Consolidated Jurisdictional Notice (*see* footnote 4 above), at paragraphs 26, 97 and 100.

assets or personnel appreciably strengthen the market position of the supplier. On this basis, an outsourcing agreement exclusively involving the transfer of employees and related office equipment previously engaged in in-house activities such as IT cannot be regarded as an acquisition of a business with a market presence and therefore does not represent a concentration under the EC Merger Regulation.[10]

Some outsourcing agreements prevent the service provider from using relevant assets for third parties. If such "sole use" restrictions apply, it is not clear from the Jurisdictional Notice whether this in itself means that "control" has not been acquired by the supplier, so there will not be a concentration, though this would appear to be the position.

To be a concentration, the assets transferred have to include at least those core elements that would allow an independent market presence. Many transfers of in-house facilities to an outsourced supplier will not meet these criteria. In the case of manufacturing businesses, if third parties are not yet supplied, there will not be a concentration unless assets transferred contain production facilities, relevant know-how and the means for the purchaser to develop market access within a short period (e.g. including existing contracts or brands). In the case of services businesses, there will not be a concentration unless the assets transferred include the required know-how (e.g. relevant personnel and IP) and facilities which allow market access (e.g. marketing facilities).[11]

The level of control necessary to establish a concentration may arise contractually, but the contract must confer control of the administration and assets, which is comparable with that arising on an acquisition of assets or shares.[12] The contract must be of "a very long duration" to result in a structural change, and must generally be without the possibility of early termination for the party granting the contractual rights – presumably the customer. Some commentators have suggested that this probably means the contract must be for a minimum of at least 8–10 years. It is not clear whether or how the typical break clauses in such contracts would affect the Commission's view of control, especially as termination is not always realistic in practice.

The European Commission applied the above principles in its *Flextronics/Nortel* decision in October 2004,[13] the facts of which were as follows:

(a) Flextronics International Ltd provided electronics manufacturing services ("EMS") to original equipment manufacturers ("OEMs") in the telecommunications, networking, consumer electronics, computer and medical device industries. EMS entail manufacturing various types of electronic products on an outsourced procurement basis.

---

10 *See* Jan Lohrberg and Matti Huhtamaki, *Outsourcing Transactions and Merger Control*, European Competition Law Review 2008, 29(6), 349–55, at p352. *See* also '*You can't outsource compliance: the relevance of competition law to outsourcing transactions*,' by James Killick and Ashley Winton, Competition Law Insight, 7 April 2009. In cases where the Commission has considered the requirements of a "concentration" to have been met, there was in addition to the transfer of personnel, also the transfer of material assets allowing access to the market: Case M.2629 *Flextronics/Xerox*; Case M.1841 *Celestica/IBM (EMS)*; Case M.1968 *Solectron/Nortel*; Case M.1849 *Solectron/Ericsson*; Case M.286 *Zurich/MMI*.

11 Commission's Consolidated Jurisdictional Notice, at paragraph 26.

12 Commission's Consolidated Jurisdictional Notice, at paragraph 18.

13 Case M.3583 *Flextronics/Nortel*, 28 October 2004.

(b) Nortel Networks Limited was a supplier of products and services that supported the internet and other public and private data, voice and multimedia communication networks.
(c) Flextronics acquired some of Nortel's manufacturing assets, employees and related supply chain activities.

The Commission decided that the transaction implied the acquisition by Flextronics of control of parts of Nortel and as such amounted to a "concentration".

29.2.1.2 "Concentrations" and joint ventures

Outsourcing agreements will constitute a concentration if they involve the creation of a "full-function" joint venture on a "lasting basis",[14] meaning that the joint venture operates independently on the market, its activities go beyond one specific function for its parents, and its sales and purchases do not rely on its parents.[15] To be a "full function" joint venture, the joint venture must be economically autonomous from an operational viewpoint,[16] dealing with the outsourcing parent at arm's length on the basis of normal commercial conditions and supplying its goods or services to third parties in a revenue-maximising manner.[17] However, an outsourcing joint venture can rely almost entirely on its parents during its start-up period whilst being a "full-function" joint venture, if it can build up sufficient market presence in a reasonable time.[18,19]

The supplier may be able to provide services to the customer and to third parties, within the required timescale, without necessarily becoming a "concentration". This would be the case if the transfer related to an internal business unit, without the transfer of associated assets or personnel, and any third-party revenues are likely to remain "ancillary" to the joint venture's main activities for the outsourcing customer.[20]

29.2.1.3 "Community dimension"

An outsourcing arrangement which constitutes a "concentration" will only be subject to EU merger control if it has a "Community dimension", that is, if the turnover of the relevant

14 For example, in *British Gas Trading/Group 4 Utilities* the two parties assumed joint control of a venture providing meter-reading services to the gas industry. Case M.791 *British Gas Trading/Group 4 Utility Services* [1996] 5 CMLR 526; Case M.2122 *BAT/CAP Gemini/* Ciberion, 11 September 2000.

15 Article 3(4) of Regulation 139/2004, OJ L24, 29.1.2004, p1 and paragraph 100 of the Commission's Consolidated Jurisdictional Notice (*see* footnote 35 above). *See*, for example, the European Commission's decisions in Cases M.2478 *IBM Italia/Business Solutions/JV*, 29/6/2001 and M.560 *EDS/Lufthansa*, 11/5/1995.

16 Case T-282/02 *Cementbouw Handel & Industrie BV* v *Commission* [2006] ECR II-319.

17 Case M.556 *Zeneca/Vanderhave*, 9 April 1996.

18 Case M.560 *EDS/Lufthansa*, 11 May 1995.

19 For example, Fiat combined two business units that had provided in-house IT services to the Fiat group with five IBM businesses which had previously been active in the wider market. The resulting joint venture was held to be subject to EU merger control. The Commission stressed the importance of the fact that Fiat wanted both to achieve cuts to its IT spending through outsourcing, and make successful entry into new markets. Case M.2478 *IBM Italia/Business Solutions/JV*, 29/6/2001 (2001/C/278/05).

20 Commission's Consolidated Jurisdictional Notice (*see* footnote 35 above), at paragraph 100. *See* also paragraphs 25 to 27.

parties satisfies certain turnover thresholds. Satisfying these thresholds requires in particular that:

(a) the combined worldwide turnover of the relevant parties exceeds €2.5 billion;
(b) each of them has EU turnover exceeding €100 million; and
(c) neither of them achieves more than two-thirds of their EU turnover in one and the same EU Member State, for example the UK.

In relation to outsourcing transactions, turnover of the "relevant parties" means the turnover in the preceding financial year of the whole of the supplier's group and the part of the customer's business that is being outsourced.

Turnover is usually calculated from the most recent financial year's audited accounts. However, the Jurisdictional Notice referred to above states that where an outsourcing transaction involves a business unit which only had internal revenues in the past, "the turnover should normally be calculated on the basis of the previously internal turnover or of publicly quoted prices, where such prices exist". Where this does not appear to correspond to a market valuation or the expected future turnover, "the forecast revenues to be received on the basis of an agreement with the former parent may be a suitable proxy".[21]

Most outsourcing transactions will not meet the above turnover thresholds.

29.2.1.4 Implications of EU merger control

Subject to limited exceptions, the European Commission has exclusive jurisdiction over concentrations with a Community dimension. Notification of such transactions to the European Commission is mandatory and the parties cannot complete the transaction before EU merger clearance has been obtained. It is therefore vital to establish whether EU merger control will apply to a proposed outsourcing transaction – especially transactions involving larger service providers or consortiums, where turnover thresholds are more likely to be met.

Where EU merger control applies, the European Commission must consider whether the arrangement in question "significantly impedes effective competition, in the Common Market or in a substantial part thereof, in particular as a result of the creation or strengthening of a dominant position". If the European Commission does consider that the transaction significantly impedes effective competition, it may make approval conditional on certain conditions, such as divesting a particular business, or it may even prohibit the transaction.

Where EU merger control applies, UK merger control (*see* below) will usually not apply.

29.2.1.5 EU merger control decisions

To date, there have only been a few EU merger control decisions regarding outsourcing, and those decisions offer little guidance in relation to other transactions. The *Computer Sciences Corporation (CSC)/Royal Mail Business Systems (RMBS)* decision held that the provision of services by CSC to Royal Mail was a notifiable concentration, despite the lack of any market

21 Commission's Consolidated Jurisdictional Notice, at paragraph 163.

presence before the transfer.[22] The deal involved the acquisition of all the shares in a wholly owned subsidiary of Royal Mail, so was more clearly a "merger" than many outsourcing transactions. However, the decision suggests that the transfer of an entity previously operating entirely in a captive market, with no wider market presence, may still attract EU merger control.

To date, no outsourcing transaction has been blocked under EU merger control.

29.2.2 UK merger control

UK merger control applies to outsourcing transactions which cause two or more "enterprises" to cease to be distinct, if EU merger control does not apply and one of the two jurisdictional tests considered at 29.2.2.3 below is satisfied.

29.2.2.1 Definition of an "enterprise"

An "enterprise" means "the activities or part of the activities of a business" including, typically, the assets and records needed to carry on the business, together with the benefit of existing contracts and/or goodwill. The transfer of customer records is likely to be important in assessing whether an enterprise has been transferred.

29.2.2.2 Definition of enterprises "ceasing to be distinct"

Two cases are helpful in illustrating the OFT's approach to defining when enterprises cease to be distinct.

In the first case, *Exel/NHS Logistics Authority/NHS Purchasing and Supply Agency*,[23] the facts of which are set out at 29.2 above, the OFT concluded that the transaction did involve "enterprises ceasing to be distinct".

The outcome was different in the second case, an OFT decision of October 2006 involving an award of a management contract at University College London Hospital NHS Foundation Trust to HCA International Limited.[24] The facts of the case were as follows:

(a) The transaction concerned the commercial leasing by University College London Hospital Trust ("UCLH") to HCA International Limited ("HCA") of premises, which were previously vacant (except for very limited outpatient visits), for an initial period of five years for use as a private patient unit.
(b) UCLH agreed that HCA could access and use a linear accelerator and MRI scanner, but the equipment was not in working order and no title to this equipment was to pass from UCLH to HCA.
(c) UCLH agreed to allow HCA to use certain UCLH facilities (including two bunkers and a scanner room) and support services relating to the operation and administration of a

22 Case M.3171*Computer Sciences Corporation/Royal Mail Business Systems* (2003/C187/09).
23 www.oft.gov.uk/advice_and_resources/resource_base/Mergers_home/decisions/2006/exel.
24 www.oft.gov.uk/advice_and_resources/resource_base/Mergers_home/decisions/2006/university.

private patient unit (e.g. pathology, facilities management, information technology and telecommunication services) for an initial period of five years.

(d) While UCLH was to second some support staff to the private patient unit, no employees would be transferred to HCA. They would remain employees of UCLH. No medical staff would be transferred to HCA.

(e) No goodwill, customer details or other business assets were transferred to HCA.

(f) No liabilities were transferred.

Here, the OFT held that the relevant outsourcing transaction did not involve "enterprises ceasing to be distinct". The OFT stated that "no current business activity [was] being carried on in the premises being transferred to HCA; no physical assets [were] passing; no UCLH employees [were] being transferred to HCA; and no customer details or contracts [were] passing".

29.2.2.3 Jurisdictional tests

UK merger control will only apply if one of two tests is satisfied.

The first is a "turnover test". This is satisfied in relation to outsourcing arrangements if the UK turnover of the part of the customer's business being outsourced exceeds £70 million.

The second is the "share of supply test". This is satisfied in relation to outsourcing arrangements if, as a result of the transaction, the supplier and the part of the customer's business that is being outsourced together supply 25 per cent or more of all the goods or services of a particular description supplied in the UK or in a substantial part of it. The share of supply test is much less clear cut than the turnover test and narrow descriptions of services and/or local markets can make it fairly easy to satisfy.

Whether there is a substantive merger control issue will therefore depend on the position of the parties in the relevant product or service and geographic markets.

29.2.2.4 Implications of UK merger control

Subject to limited exceptions, the OFT has a duty to refer mergers which satisfy either of the above jurisdictional tests to the Competition Commission ("CC") for further investigation where the relevant merger has resulted (or may be expected to result) in a "substantial lessening of competition within any market(s) for goods or services in the UK". The CC can block the merger, clear it or clear it subject to conditions, for example divestment.

It is not compulsory to notify a qualifying merger to the OFT, but it is risky to complete a transaction which qualifies for UK merger control without obtaining merger clearance from the OFT. The buyer could be forced by the authorities at a later stage to sell all or part of the business acquired. The authorities may also impose severe restrictions on the buyer's ability to deal with the acquired business while a competition investigation is carried out. In an outsourcing transaction, the authorities could prevent the transfer of relevant people and assets to the supplier and frustrate both parties' commercial objectives by preventing the supplier from performing its obligations to the customer.

29.2.2.5 UK merger control decisions

Merger decisions in outsourcing cases have to date not required the authorities to reach a conclusive view on the relevant market, as the transactions investigated did not give rise to competition concerns, regardless of the way the relevant market was defined.[25] This may change over time if relevant markets become more concentrated. However, several of these merger decisions concern (and include useful guidance on) market definition in IT service markets, a major outsourcing market.[26]

The OFT is considering the treatment of outsourcing transactions following its consultation on its new "Jurisdictional and Procedural Guidance" between March and June 2008. The OFT is due to publish the final version of this new guidance in 2009.

29.3 Prohibited anti-competitive agreements

Article 81(1) of the EC Treaty and Chapter I of the Competition Act 1998 prohibit agreements that have the object or effect of preventing, restricting or distorting competition and which may affect trade between EU Member States or within the UK, respectively (the "Prohibitions"). Breaches of those Prohibitions are punishable with heavy fines (up to 10 per cent of turnover); infringing agreements are unenforceable and the parties to them may be sued for damages. Under the Enterprise Act 2002, individuals who are involved in a breach of competition law may be disqualified as directors for up to 15 years and, in the case of serious infringements (involving price fixing, market sharing and bid-rigging), may be subject to unlimited fines and up to five years' imprisonment.

29.3.1 Exclusivity and non-compete clauses

Outsourcing arrangements commonly contain exclusivity and non-compete provisions. These may restrict competition and must therefore be considered in the light of the Prohibitions (*see* above).

29.3.1.1 Ancillary restraints

The competition law analysis of the above provisions depends on whether the transaction is a "concentration" for competition law purposes, as to which *see* above.

Obligations that are "directly related and necessary to the implementation of a concentration" (or "ancillary restraints") are deemed not to fall within the scope of the Prohibitions. They will be automatically covered by any European Commission merger clearance decision authorising a transaction. It is up to the parties to assess whether a restriction is "directly related and necessary".

---

25 *See*, for example, OFT decision *Exel/NHS Logistics Authority/NHS Purchasing and Supply Agency* (July 2006) www.oft.gov.uk/advice_and_resources/resource_base/Mergers_home/decisions/2006/exel; OFT Decision *Vertex/Marlborough Sterling* (May 2005), www.oft.gov.uk/advice_and_resources/resource_base/Mergers_home/decisions/2005/vertex; OFT decision *Northgate/Systems Solutions* (May 2005), www.oft.gov.uk/advice_and_resources/resource_base/Mergers_home/decisions/2005/northgate.

26 *See*, for example, Commission decisions M.3555 *Hewlett Packard/Synstar*, 9 September 2004; and M.2478 *IBM Italia/Business Solutions/JV*, 29 June 2001.

A European Commission Notice (the "Ancillary Restraints Notice") sets out the Commission's practice in relation to ancillary restraints.[27] Where a merger does not meet the turnover thresholds in relation to European merger control, strictly speaking the European Commission's Ancillary Restraints Notice will not apply. It would, however, remain relevant as other EU Member States may apply a similar approach to that notice under their national merger control rules. Such an approach may find that the ancillary restrictions relating to the merger are justified, or may benefit from an individual exemption from the rules on anti-competitive agreements (see below 29.3.1.3 *Individual Exemptions*). In the UK, the OFT's approach follows the Ancillary Restraints Notice (whether or not the merger is notified to the OFT).[28]

Covenants by the vendor not to compete with the business being sold or transferred (or in an outsourcing context, for example, covenants by the customer not to provide the services in-house) are generally permissible, provided they are limited both in scope (as to the product and geographic area covered) and in duration.

The Ancillary Restraints Notice states that, when the transfer includes both goodwill and know-how, a vendor non-compete covenant for up to three years is permissible. When only goodwill is included (i.e. no know-how is transferred), a vendor non-compete covenant can only be justified for up to two years. If the transfer is limited to physical assets (e.g. land, buildings or machinery) or to exclusive intellectual property rights, a vendor non-compete covenant will not be permissible as an ancillary restraint.

Purchase or supply obligations (and service agreements) between vendor and purchaser, which are aimed at guaranteeing the quantities previously supplied, can be justified for up to five years. Obligations providing for fixed quantities, possibly with a variation clause, are permissible as ancillary restraints, but obligations providing for unlimited quantities, exclusivity or conferring preferred-supplier or preferred-purchaser status are not treated as ancillary restraints. They therefore have to be considered separately (see below).

Arrangements which are not concentrations and which contain exclusivity or non-compete provisions may infringe the Prohibitions, which, as mentioned above, will affect the enforceability of the arrangements and have other potentially serious consequences. It is therefore necessary to consider whether those agreements have an appreciable effect on competition and/or are exempted from the Prohibitions.

29.3.1.2 Agreements of minor importance

Arrangements are only prohibited under competition law if they have an "appreciable" impact on competition. The European Commission's Notice on Agreements of Minor Importance (the "De Minimis Notice") provides that agreements will generally not appreciably restrict competition if:

(a) the parties' aggregate market share on any relevant "affected market" does not exceed 10 per cent in the case of actual or potential competitors, or 15 per cent in the case of non-competitors; and

27 European Commission Notice on restrictions directly related and necessary to concentrations, 2005/C56/03, OJ C56, 5.3.2005, p24.

28 OFT guidance *Mergers: Substantive Assessment Guidance*, May 2003, paragraph 11.13.

(b) the agreement does not contain any "hardcore" restrictions (e.g. price-fixing or market-sharing arrangements, or those allocating markets or customers).[29]

Many outsourcing arrangements will therefore be treated as of "minor importance" for competition law purposes and therefore not infringe the Prohibitions. However, market definition is crucial to this. A supplier operating in a narrowly defined service market may have a market share of more than 15 per cent; exclusive agreements entered into by it with its customers may therefore have an appreciable effect on competition, in which case further competition law analysis may be required to determine whether the provisions are enforceable.

Arrangements that are not covered by the De Minimis Notice, but contain restrictions on competition, may still be exempted from the Prohibitions by virtue of an individual or block exemption.

Where the parties' market shares are too high for the De Minimis Notice to apply, an exclusivity obligation lasting over five years may be prohibited under Article 81(1). EU case law shows that if the duration is "manifestly excessive" in relation to the average duration of contracts concluded in the relevant market, the Article 81(1) prohibition will apply.[30] Within the UK, the common law principle of restraint of trade may also apply, for instance where the duration or geographic scope of a restriction goes further than necessary to protect the legitimate interests of the parties and/or if the restriction is contrary to the public interest.[31]

29.3.1.3 Individual exemptions

To benefit from an individual exemption, an arrangement must satisfy several conditions, set out in Article 81(3) of the EC Treaty, designed to ensure that the economic benefits provided by the arrangement outweigh its negative effects on competition. These require that the agreement in question:

(a) contributes to improving production or distribution, or to promoting technical or economic progress, while allowing consumers a fair share of the resulting benefit; and
(b) does not impose restrictions which are "not indispensable" to the attainment of those objectives, or give the parties the possibility of eliminating competition in respect of a substantial part of the products or services in question.

29.3.1.4 Vertical Agreements Block Exemption

Where an arrangement is covered by a block exemption, the above conditions are presumed to be met. An outsourcing agreement will fall within the scope of the European Commission's Vertical Agreements Block Exemption ("VABE")[32] where the supplier's share of the relevant

29 In determining whether an agreement has an appreciable effect on competition, the OFT will have regard to the European Commission's approach as set out in the Notice on Agreements of Minor Importance. *See* OFT Guidance *Agreements and concerted practice*, December 2004, paragraph 2.18.

30 *See*, for example, Case C-234/89 *Delimitis/Henninger Bräu*, Judgment of 28/02/1991, (Rec.1991, pI-935), at paragraph 26; Case C-214/99 *Neste*, Judgment of 07/12/2000, (Rec.2000,p. I-11121) at paragraphs 27 and 32; and Commission Decision IV/29.021 *BP Kemi*, OJ L 286, 14/11/1979, at paragraph 68.

31 *See*, for example, *Esso Petroleum* v *Harper's Garage*, House of Lords [1967] 2 WLR 871; *Panayiotou* (aka George Michael) v *Sony Music*, High Court [1994] EMLR 229.

32 Commission Regulation of 22 December 1999 on the application of Article 81(3) of the Treaty to categories of vertical agreements and concerted practices (2790/99/EC).

market does not exceed 30 per cent and the arrangement does not contain certain specified "hardcore restrictions".

The VABE does not normally apply to vertical agreements between competitors, but it can apply where the buyer does not provide services competing with those it purchases from the supplier – for example because the buyer has outsourced all of those services to the supplier.

For the purposes of the VABE, a non-compete obligation in an outsourcing arrangement means any obligation on the customer not to compete with the contract services, or any obligation on the customer to purchase from the supplier more than 80 per cent of the customer's total purchases of the contract services (or substitutes for them). An obligation on the customer to buy specified services only from the supplier – that is, an exclusive purchasing obligation – will therefore be a "non-compete" provision. Such a non-compete provision will only benefit from the VABE if its duration does not exceed five years. An indefinite obligation – such as one which will be renewed automatically after five years – will not benefit from the VABE.

The VABE is due to expire on 31 May 2010, and at the time of writing it was being reviewed by the European Commission.

29.3.1.5 Notice on subcontracting agreements

Where the outsourced supplier needs to use the customer's technology or equipment to provide services to that customer, certain provisions in the agreement may benefit from the European Commission's Notice on subcontracting agreements.[33] This applies where a contractor (customer) entrusts a subcontractor (supplier) with the supply of services, manufacture of goods, or performance of work under the contractor's instructions, to be provided to the contractor. The Notice states that the Prohibitions do not apply to clauses whereby technology or equipment provided by the contractor may not be used except for the purposes of the subcontracting agreement, or may not be made available to third parties, or whereby services resulting from the use of that equipment or technology may be supplied only to the contractor. In each case, this applies only where the technology or equipment is necessary to enable the subcontractor to supply the services, not when the subcontractor already has them at its disposal or could obtain access to them under reasonable conditions. However, many outsourced suppliers will be selected precisely because of their technology or equipment.

29.3.1.6 Specialisation Block Exemption

Exclusive purchasing and/or supply obligations can be valid for more than five years under the European Commission's Specialisation Block Exemption,[34] which is due to expire at the end of 2010.[35] In an outsourcing context, this can apply to "unilateral specialisation agreements", when

33 Commission Notice of 18 December 1978 concerning its assessment of certain subcontracting agreements (79/C1/01) (OJ C1, 3.1.1979, p2).

34 Commission Regulation of 29 November 2000 on the application of Article 81(3) of the Treaty to categories of specialisation agreements (2658/2000/EC); (OJL304, 5.12.2000, p3).

35 At the time of writing, the European Commission had launched a public consultation (to run until 30 January 2009) on the functioning of the current regime for the assessment of horizontal cooperation agreements under EU competition law, including the Specialisation Block Exemption. The review evaluated how these rules worked in practice, to consider what rules should apply from 2011.

two competitors agree that one will stop producing (or not produce) certain products or services and will buy them from the other. It can also apply to "reciprocal specialisation agreements", when two competitors agree that each will stop producing (or not produce) different products or services and will buy them from one another. In each case, the block exemption applies only if the parties' combined market share does not exceed 20 per cent and the arrangement does not contain any hardcore restrictions on competition.

29.3.1.7 Notice on Horizontal Cooperation Agreements

Where an outsourcing arrangement involves one competitor outsourcing to another, the Commission's Notice on Horizontal Cooperation Agreements (the "Horizontals Notice") may well be relevant,[36] provided the arrangement may generate efficiency gains which adequately benefit consumers. Outsourcing the production of goods or services is considered in detail in the Horizontals Notice, for instance as "unilateral" specialisation agreements, where one party agrees to purchase the relevant products from the other, while the other party is obliged to produce and supply those products.[37]

The Horizontals Notice allows the parties to an outsourced production agreement to agree on the "output directly concerned by the production agreement" (such as the agreed amount of outsourced products) despite the normal prohibition on agreements which limit output or share markets or customer groups.[38]

The Horizontals Notice states that, where the outsourced element represents only a small proportion of the parties' total costs, or only a small proportion of the costs of the final product, it is unlikely to lead to coordination of their competitive behaviour or to infringe the Prohibitions, though the position of the parties in the markets concerned is an important issue. Market concentration and market shares are relevant factors.

29.3.2 Information exchange

Competition law requires businesses to act independently and not to coordinate their behaviour with their competitors. Exchanges of information between actual or potential competitors may therefore breach the Prohibitions where the object or effect of the information exchange is to influence competitors' competitive conduct, or to disclose a competitor's plans or intentions, thereby making that market artificially transparent.

This will be particularly relevant where a customer outsources services to a competitor, or on a transfer of outsourced services from a supplier to a competing successor supplier. In the former case, the customer and its prospective supplier or suppliers will be discussing many details of the customer's business, including its required services, service levels and costs, which would not normally be disclosed by one competitor to another. In the latter case, negotiations leading to

36 Guidelines on the applicability of Article 81 of the EC Treaty to horizontal cooperation agreements (2001/C3/02) (OJ:C3, 6.1.2001, p2).

37 *See* paragraph 79, Guidelines on the applicability of Article 81 of the EC Treaty to horizontal cooperation agreements (2001/C3/02) (OJ:C3, 6.1.2001, p2).

38 Ibid., paragraph 90.

the transfer of services from the incumbent supplier to the successor supplier (who are likely to be competitors), will involve a degree of information exchange (perhaps via the customer) concerning the outsourced business, although clearly the incumbent supplier will be anxious in these circumstances to ensure that it is not obliged to disclose any proprietary information to its competitor.

It is not always easy to distinguish legitimate from prohibited exchanges of information. The analysis should be carried out on a case-by-case basis, taking into account the nature and type of the information exchanged, the level and aggregation of the information, the period to which the information relates and the structural characteristics of the market on which the exchange takes place. In the context of outsourcing, various tips are set out in Table 38. In general, however:

(a) commercially sensitive information that may influence the competitive conduct of actual or potential competitors (such as information regarding pricing policies, investment plans or capacity), or that discloses a competitor's unpublished competitive intentions, should not be exchanged; while

(b) information which is historical, anonymous, aggregated, independently compiled and publicly available may be exchanged.[39]

29.4 Practical tips on competition in outsourcing

Table 38 provides some practical tips for dealing with competition issues when outsourcing.

Table 38 *Practical tips for dealing with competition issues in outsourcing*

Consider the structure of the arrangement and whether it would constitute a "concentration" or merger.
Consider the potential application of merger control as early as possible.
Carefully consider the allocation of regulatory risks, including whether the transaction is to be conditional on merger clearance.
If merger control is relevant, allow time to resolve jurisdictional issues, gather market information and for pre-notification contacts with the competition authorities.
Check the legitimacy of the relevant transaction under competition law before any information exchange takes place relating to it, especially when outsourcing to a competitor.
Agreements by the customer not to compete with a business transferred to the supplier are justifiable for up to three years if know-how is transferred, or two years if goodwill alone is transferred, if the transfer amounts to a "concentration".

39 For further guidance, *see* paragraphs 38 to 59 in the European Commission's "Guidelines on the application of Article 81 of the EC Treaty to maritime transport services" at http://eur-lex.europa.eu/LexUriServ/LexUriServ.do?uri=CELEX:52008XC0926(01):EN:NOT.

Exclusive purchasing obligations on the customer may benefit from the Vertical Agreements Block Exemption where they do not last for more than five years and the supplier's market share is not over 30 per cent.

Exclusive purchasing and supply obligations may be imposed for more than five years under the Specialisation Block Exemption if the parties' combined market share is not over 20 per cent – but if market shares are higher and the duration is excessive compared with the market average, exclusivity may infringe competition law.

Outsourcing arrangements may be "of minor importance" for competition law purposes if the parties' market shares are low enough and no "hardcore" restrictions are included.

Information exchanged between competitors should be kept to the minimum required to negotiate, conclude or give effect to the relevant transaction, with appropriate information barriers established to restrict information to those who need to know it for those purposes.

Where information has to be exchanged to enable a successor supplier to take over from an incumbent supplier, ensure this happens via the customer (or with the customer's express knowledge and consent) and that the exchange of information is confined to what is necessary to serve that customer.

Part Nine – Liability

Chapter 30

Liability and Risk

30.1 Outline

Chapter 27 considers the people issues relating to outsourcing transactions and the parties' respective liabilities under TUPE. This chapter considers other issues relating to the legal liability of the parties to the outsourcing arrangement.

These may sound like dry legal issues best left to the lawyers, but in fact they are crucial business matters. There is no standard way of dealing with these issues and the choice of approach will affect the profitability of the deal from the supplier's perspective or the cost savings made by the customer in entering into the outsourcing arrangements.

30.1.1 Different approaches to legal liability

The various different ways of dealing with legal liability under an outsourcing agreement include:

(a) the supplier is liable for breach of contract except where its failure is due to a force majeure event (commercial contracts);
(b) the supplier is liable for breach of contract subject to provisions on relief events and force majeure (PFI regime in the public sector);
(c) the supplier is liable for breach of contract subject to provisions on compensation events (construction industry and facilities management outsourcing agreements); or
(d) the supplier is liable for negligence only (custody and fund administration agreements in the financial services sector).

These different approaches are described below.

30.1.2 Customer retains business risk

Before describing the approaches to legal liability, it is necessary to emphasise that any discussion of liability must recognise the fact that the customer cannot pass on to the supplier the risk (if the supplier is unable to provide the services) of the customer's brand being affected or ultimately of the customer being unable to operate its business. The customer may be entitled to terminate the agreement and claim damages from the supplier up to the agreed limitation of liability. However, this may not compensate the customer in circumstances where, for example, the customer's business has become insolvent because of the damage suffered as a result of the supplier's failure. Therefore, it is crucial that the customer considers how it will deal with a failure by the supplier on an operational level. This will involve the customer ensuring that it has satisfactory business contingency arrangements, supported by business interruption insurance cover, where appropriate.

30.2 Liability of supplier for failure – force majeure

Chapter 7 explains how the agreement must specify the services to be provided by the supplier. Chapter 12 mentions the importance of documenting the actions which the customer must carry out to enable the supplier to provide the services.

The parties must also agree in what circumstances the supplier will not be responsible for failure to comply with its obligations. It is usual in commercial contracts to state that the supplier will not be responsible for failure to the extent to which it is caused by an event of "force majeure" and this approach has been adopted in many IT and BPO agreements.

Negotiation of a force majeure provision is about the allocation of risk. This legal approach therefore is based on an assumption that, if risks are allocated to the party who has the most control over them, then they will be incentivised to take action to reduce the risk of them occurring, to both parties' benefit.[1]

30.3 Definition of force majeure

Force majeure does not have a strict meaning in English law and so must be defined by the parties. It may be defined in different ways. There are two approaches that can be taken in defining force majeure, both based upon the principle that the supplier should not be responsible for events outside its control.

30.3.1 Specific definition

The first approach involves listing (exhaustively) the events treated as outside the supplier's control, for example terrorist attack or floods. The advantage of this approach is that the definition is clear.

The disadvantage of this approach, from the supplier's perspective, is that the definition may fail to cover an event which is actually outside the supplier's control. The approach puts the onus upon the supplier to predict all events from which it wants relief, which could be inappropriate if the nature of the events is unpredictable.

30.3.2 General definition

The second approach, favoured by suppliers, is to define force majeure in general terms as any event beyond the control of the supplier. The definition may include a non-exhaustive list of

1 This approach is different from the common law doctrine of frustration, which applies in restricted circumstances only and which provides that a party is relieved from performance of a contract where performance has become impossible.

possible events with a statement at the end that it will include any other event beyond the control of the supplier.

Suppliers sometimes want to list specific circumstances in which they will not be responsible for failure to meet the service levels. It is usually better for the supplier to include these circumstances in the list of force majeure events so that they apply generally to failure by the supplier to provide the services.

30.4 Conditions that the supplier must satisfy

The supplier will usually have to satisfy certain conditions relating to the force majeure event. Examples of possible conditions are listed in Table 39.

Table 39 *Examples of conditions which the supplier must satisfy*

Service continuity

It must have taken all reasonable steps to prevent and avoid the force majeure event.

It must carry out its duties to the best level reasonably achievable in the circumstances of the force majeure event.

It must take all reasonable steps to overcome and mitigate the effects of the force majeure event.

It must comply with an agreed disaster recovery or service continuity plan (where relevant).

Notification requirements

It must notify the customer of the force majeure event – sometimes within a specific time period.

It must provide reasonable evidence of the force majeure event.

It must notify the customer when the event of force majeure has stopped.

The customer may want the supplier's right to rely upon the force majeure event to be conditional upon the supplier satisfying all of the specified conditions. The supplier may see the notification requirements as mere procedural requirements. Therefore, it may not want to lose its substantive right to rely upon force majeure as a result of a failure to comply with the notification requirements and may accept the procedural requirements but not want its right to relief to be conditional on satisfying them. The supplier may also want to ensure that the notification requirements need to be satisfied within a reasonable period rather than immediately or within a specified inflexible period. This will take into account the fact that the supplier may feel that its first priority should be to concentrate on remedying the force majeure event.

However, the customer may need notification of the force majeure event so that it can take steps to ensure that its business does not suffer as a consequence. Therefore, it may see the notification requirements as essential and not as a mere bureaucratic requirement. Much will depend upon the individual nature of the services.

30.5 Effect upon the charges

The parties will need to decide if the supplier will be paid if it is unable to provide the services as a result of a force majeure event. There are various possible approaches.

30.5.1 No payment

The customer may argue that it should not be obliged to pay for a service which it is not receiving. This approach involves a sharing of risk resulting from the occurrence of a force majeure event. The supplier will not have to pay the customer damages for failure to provide the services. However, the supplier will not receive the charges.

30.5.2 Payment of all of the charges

The supplier may argue that, as it has not been at fault, it should be paid all of its charges. It may argue that it will in fact be incurring additional costs in overcoming the force majeure event. The supplier may point out that, despite the fact that the service is not being provided, it will still be incurring costs, for example the salaries of the employees engaged to provide the services and equipment lease costs payable under equipment leases transferred to the supplier as part of the outsourcing arrangement. The supplier may stress that, if the services were still being provided in-house, then the customer would have had to pay these costs despite the fact that the services could not be provided.

30.5.3 Part payment

If the supplier will incur fewer costs if it is not providing the services, then the parties may agree a compromise whereby the customer pays a specified percentage of the charges, perhaps reflecting the supplier's fixed costs.

30.5.4 Payment or non-payment depending upon the force majeure event

The parties may also decide that whether the customer pays the supplier will depend upon the nature of the force majeure event, for example whether it affects the customer's site or the supplier's site. The logic behind this is that the customer should bear a greater responsibility if its site is affected than if the supplier's site is affected. This is similar to liability for compensation events (*see* 30.10).

30.6 Termination rights

The parties will also need to decide whether either party will have the right to terminate the agreement as a result of a force majeure event.

30.6.1 Customer's right to terminate

The customer may want the right to terminate the agreement if a force majeure event prevents the supplier from providing the services for a specific period of time. Normally, force majeure clauses do not distinguish between the types of force majeure events that may entitle the customer to terminate the agreement. The supplier may want to ensure that it receives adequate compensation on termination to cover the investment it has made in the services (*see* 18.11 and Chapter 25 for a discussion of termination charges).

30.6.2 Supplier's right to terminate

If the supplier is being paid in full despite the fact that it has been prevented by an event of force majeure from providing the services, then it may not need a right to terminate the agreement in this situation. Otherwise it may require such a right.

30.7 Force majeure and service continuity

30.7.1 Importance of service continuity

The discussion of liability for events of force majeure should also tie in with the customer's risk assessment process described in Chapter 2. This process may highlight the risks that could affect the services, their likelihood and what actions should be taken by the customer and the supplier to manage the risks. The process will usually result in the supplier accepting obligations to provide disaster recovery or service continuity arrangements. The obligations will be specific to the individual contract and will reflect the level of disaster recovery or service continuity which it is cost effective for the supplier to provide and which the customer wishes to pay for in the particular circumstances. The following paragraphs describe the different types of disaster recovery services.

30.7.2 Exclusive disaster recovery services

The disaster recovery service may be an exclusive service, in which facilities are developed exclusively for the customer and the customer bears the entire cost.

30.7.3 Shared disaster recovery services

Alternatively, the disaster recovery services may be a shared service in which facilities are shared between several customers and made available on a "first come first served" basis. In the shared service, the costs of the disaster recovery service will be shared between the various customers.

In this situation, the customer may want to find out (or control) how many sites belonging to the various customers are sharing the facilities and whether they are likely to be affected by incidents affecting the customer (e.g. if they are all financial institutions near each other in the City of London).

30.7.4 Reliance upon force majeure

As stated in Table 39, if the services include a disaster recovery service, the supplier should not be able to rely upon the force majeure event if it has not provided that disaster recovery service, (i.e. it should not be able to claim relief) unless an event of force majeure affects both the main site and the disaster recovery site, or the supplier is otherwise unable to provide the disaster recovery service (e.g., because the service is a shared service and another customer has invoked it first).

30.8 Liability for subcontractors and third-party suppliers

Whichever approach to force majeure is adopted, the parties should ensure that the supplier's liability is clear. A common area of confusion concerns the supplier's responsibility for subcontractors and third-party suppliers.

30.8.1 Supplier's third-party suppliers

The customer will usually want the supplier to be responsible for third-party suppliers that the supplier selects and with whom it enters into subcontracts.

30.8.2 Customer's third-party suppliers – before novation to the supplier

But what about third-party contracts entered into by the customer which are to be novated to the supplier? Who will be responsible for the actions of the third-party supplier before the contract is novated? The supplier may be unwilling to accept responsibility for the actions of the third-party supplier until it has a contractual relationship with the third-party supplier. If the supplier is responsible for managing the third-party supplier in the interim, then it will usually accept responsibility for its failure to manage the third party.

30.8.3 Customer's third-party suppliers – after novation to the supplier

Should the supplier be responsible for the actions of the third-party supplier once the contract has been novated to it? If the supplier has not managed to carry out adequate due diligence in respect of the third-party supplier's performance, or if the customer has selected the third-party supplier, the supplier may want a honeymoon period during which it will not be responsible for the actions of the third-party supplier. The honeymoon period should ideally (from the supplier's perspective) give the supplier sufficient time to carry out due diligence on the third-party supplier and (if necessary) arrange for a replacement third-party supplier (taking into account the period of time needed to give notice terminating the agreement with the third-party supplier).

If the customer wants the supplier to accept responsibility for the quality of the service before the supplier has had time to terminate the agreement with the unsatisfactory third-party supplier, then the supplier may have to arrange for another third-party supplier to provide the services, whilst still paying the unsatisfactory third-party supplier. In this situation, the customer will pay twice for the third-party service, until the agreement with the unsatisfactory third-party supplier expires.

30.9 Liability of supplier for failure – PFI approach

30.9.1 Principle behind PFI contracts[2]

The approach taken in limiting the liability of the supplier for events of force majeure is based upon the principle that the supplier should not be responsible for events outside its control. The logic behind the principle is that the overall risk under the contract will be reduced if each party is responsible for factors within its control.

A different approach is taken in PFI contracts, where one of the purposes of the contract is to transfer to the supplier risks which are more appropriately managed by the private sector. This may mean the supplier accepting risks that it cannot control but which the parties agree are best managed by the supplier. The supplier will usually add a risk premium to its charges to cover the additional risks that it is accepting.

The PFI approach is described in greater detail in 30.9.2 to 30.9.4 below. This is an extremely complex subject and this Guide only provides a short summary of some of the key issues.

30.9.2 Definition of force majeure

PFI contracts adopt the first approach described in 30.3.1 above, where there are specific definitions of events. Confusingly for those used to commercial, non-PFI contracts, there are two separate definitions, one called "relief events" and one "force majeure".

(a) Relief events include some of the types of events that would be defined as a force majeure event in a non-PFI contract. For example, they include natural events (such as fire, lightning, storm, tempest and flood); riots and civil commotion; failure by a public body or utility to carry out works or to provide services; accidental damage; failure or shortage of power, fuel or transport; blockades or embargoes or strikes generally affecting the supplier's industry, unless these have been caused by a wilful act or omission of the supplier.[3]

(b) Force majeure events are very narrowly defined and include, for example, war, terrorism, and nuclear and chemical contamination. They are generally viewed as catastrophic

2 *See* HM Treasury Guidance on Standardisation of PFI Contracts version 4 – March 2007.

3 The intention is that relief events should cover events that are outside either party's control, but the impact of which the supplier is better placed to manage.

events which are unlikely to occur. Some of the risks may be uninsurable.[4] The intention is that force majeure events should cover events which are outside either party's control and which are of such an extreme nature that neither party is in a better position than the other to manage the effects of the risk.

30.9.3 Conditions that the supplier must satisfy

30.9.3.1 Relief event

The supplier cannot claim relief from a relief event unless it can demonstrate that it could not have avoided the event or mitigated its effect without incurring material expenditure and can demonstrate that it is using reasonable endeavours to perform its obligations under the contract. The supplier must also satisfy specific procedural requirements before it can claim relief.

30.9.3.2 Force majeure event

In the event of a force majeure event, both parties must use reasonable endeavours to prevent and mitigate the effects of any delay and the supplier must take all steps in accordance with good industry practice to overcome or minimise the consequences of the event, and to agree appropriate terms upon which the services can continue to be supplied to the customer.

30.9.4 Implications of relief and force majeure events

30.9.4.1 Relief events

The supplier bears all of the financial consequences of relief events. If the relief event results in poor or no service being supplied, the customer will be entitled to make appropriate deductions from the charges payable to the supplier on an indefinite basis. This is similar to the "no payment" option referred to in 30.5.1. The supplier is expected to take out loss of profit or business interruption insurance against relief events, where available. The only "relief" which the supplier is in fact entitled to is relief against termination for failure to provide the full service.

30.9.4.2 Force majeure event

Similarly, if a force majeure event results in limited service being supplied, the customer will be entitled to make appropriate deductions. However, the supplier does not bear all of the financial consequences of a force majeure event on an indefinite basis, since (given the severity of the definition of force majeure events) the effects are likely to last for a long time. Therefore, if the force majeure event continues to prevent full performance for a specified period, either the supplier or the customer may be entitled to terminate the agreement.

4 There are conventional property insurance exclusions for nuclear, chemical, biological and radiation ("NCBR") risks. Those and war risks are generally uninsurable. Terrorism risk is generally insurable with regard to business interruption risks affecting commercial property as a result of *Pool Re*.

30.9.5 Termination rights

30.9.5.1 Relief event

Neither party will be entitled to terminate the agreement as a result of poor performance or failure to achieve milestones if the poor performance arises as a result of a relief event, provided that the supplier is attempting to mitigate the effect of such event and satisfying the other related technical requirements. The customer will continue indefinitely to receive less than full services, and the supplier will continue indefinitely to receive less than full payment. This is seen as appropriate since, in practice, relief events are less severe than force majeure events and, in all probability, the supplier will be able to respond in an appropriate manner so as to resume full service.

30.9.5.2 Force majeure event

In the event of a force majeure event, which prevents full performance for a protracted period (often six months), if the parties cannot agree a suitable course of action whereby the contract can be preserved by amending the terms in some way, either party will be entitled to serve notice to terminate the agreement. If the notice is served by the supplier, the customer will be entitled to prevent termination of the agreement by electing to pay the supplier in full, as if the performance failure arising from the force majeure event was not continuing. Otherwise, the agreement will terminate, and the supplier will be paid a substantial compensation payment.[5]

30.10 Liability of supplier for failure – facilities management approach

In the construction industry, as in the PFI industry which grew out of it, it is common for liability to be apportioned to the party best able to manage and insure against risks. Some facilities management agreements adopt this approach by stating that the supplier will be responsible for the services except where it is prevented from providing the services by a “compensation event”.

30.10.1 Definition of compensation event

A compensation event is defined as including breach of agreement by the customer, changes proposed by the customer as well as external events such as the following, provided that they affect the premises the subject of the facilities management services:

(a) a third party carrying out unanticipated work on the premises;
(b) unexpected defects in the physical condition of the premises; and
(c) loss of or damage to any part of the premises due to war, civil war, rebellion, revolution, insurrection, military or usurped power, strikes, riots and civil commotion not confined to the supplier’s employees, radioactive contamination, fire, lightning, explosion, storm,

5 The compensation payment will not put the supplier in the same position as it would have been in if the contract had continued until its natural expiry, as would be the case if the contract terminated for customer default. The supplier will bear some of the pain, by agreeing to a reduced payment.

flood, escape of water from any water tank, apparatus or pipes, earthquake, aircraft and other aerial devices or articles dropped from them.

The definition thus makes a distinction between external events which affect the customer's premises and which the customer can insure against and those which affect the supplier's premises.

The types of events which comprise compensation events could theoretically be drafted in general or specific terms (as for force majeure events). In practice, however, they tend to be specifically listed. The customer will need to ensure that they do not apply in circumstances where the supplier is responsible, as part of the facilities management services, for preventing the relevant event, for example a flood caused by a boiler which has not been maintained when the supplier is responsible for maintaining it.

30.10.2 Conditions that the supplier must satisfy

The supplier will usually have to satisfy certain conditions relating to the compensation event before it can claim relief. The customer should consider whether the conditions listed in Table 39 are appropriate.

30.10.3 Effect upon the charges

In facilities management agreements which rely upon the compensation event concept, the customer bears the full financial consequences of the event.

30.10.4 Termination rights

Neither party is granted the right to terminate as a result of the occurrence of a compensation event.

30.10.5 Application of the concept outside facilities management

Customers may like to consider whether it is helpful in their outsourcing arrangements to deal with force majeure issues in the context of which risks are best managed by each party. For example, in a call-centre service where part of the services are provided on site (e.g. the one-stop shop attending to the public) and part are provided from the supplier's premises (e.g. the call-centre services dealing with telephone queries) the customer may decide to take responsibility for fire or flood affecting its premises and the supplier may take responsibility for fire or flood affecting its premises. This will incentivise the supplier to provide (and charge for) a very high level of disaster recovery and service continuity support.

30.11 Liability of supplier for failure – custody and fund administration approach

30.11.1 Liability in custody agreements

All of the above approaches to liability are based on the supplier being responsible for breach of contract. Custody agreements in the financial services sector take a radically different approach.

In these contracts the custodian sees itself as the directed agent of the customer. The custodian's fundamental obligation is to take reasonable care of the customer's assets and it is not unusual for the parties to feel that they do not need to document the custodian's obligations in a service description. Accordingly, the custodian excludes all liability for breach of contract and accepts liability only if it is negligent. In return, it accepts unlimited liability for the value of the assets in its custody. The customer usually has the ability to terminate the custody agreement on short notice (usually 30 days) at any time, so that the customer can terminate if it is dissatisfied with the services provided by the custodian. Custody services are commodity services and so moving the services to another custodian is not as substantial a task as in some outsourcing agreements, so termination may provide an effective remedy for the customer.

30.11.2 Liability in fund administration agreements

Over the last few years, some custodians have endeavoured to extend their service offerings to include other services, including fund administration or management services. In this situation, they assume that liability will be based on a negligence basis, partly because that is what they are accustomed to seeing in custody agreements.

30.11.3 Problems with the approach

There are various problems with this approach, and the result is that the negotiation of the liability clauses is often the most difficult part of the negotiation of such agreements.

The first problem is that fund administration agreements are not commodity agreements like custody agreements, cannot usually be terminated on short notice, and transferring the services on termination may involve substantial risk and expense.

The second problem is a cultural one as, on the one hand, customers who negotiate fund administration agreements are often used to negotiating other commercial IT or BPO agreements and hence are entirely unfamiliar with the idea of contracting on the basis of negligence. They see the restriction of liability to negligence as undermining the supplier's liability under the agreement and in particular the usefulness of the detailed service descriptions and service level agreements they negotiate with the supplier.

The supplier, on the other hand, may be unfamiliar with accepting liability on a breach-of-contract basis and see the customer's approach as an attempt to force it to accept far higher liability than it has been used to or is comfortable with accepting. The supplier may not have negotiated the service level agreement with a view to accepting liability for breach. The supplier's concerns can be addressed to a certain extent by agreeing service levels which the supplier can achieve in practice, and thus making it clear that the supplier is not expected to meet all of the service levels 100 per cent of the time.

The problem of liability in fund administration agreements is a serious one. In the end, the problem is usually determined by the party with the most powerful bargaining power prevailing.

30.12 Liability of the customer for failure

So far, this chapter has considered the circumstances in which the supplier should be responsible for failure to provide the services. Paragraph 30.2 explained that one approach taken is for the *supplier* to be granted relief from failures arising as a result of force majeure events. The question arises as to whether the *customer* should also be protected from force majeure events.

30.12.1 Relief from delaying payment

Sometimes suppliers want to specify that the force majeure clause does not apply to the customer's obligation to pay the charges. In the past, customers may have agreed to this provision because they thought that a force majeure event was unlikely to prevent them paying the charges. Since the terrorist incidents on 11 September 2001 and the recent credit crunch, some customers have been more reluctant to agree to this clause, as it is not inconceivable that they will be prevented from paying the charges as a result of a banking failure caused by a terrorist attack or otherwise.

30.12.2 Customer's other obligations

The question is more complicated in relation to the extent to which it relates to the customer's obligations other than those relating to payment, for example the customer's obligation to make certain facilities available or to provide data or information so that the supplier can provide the services. The supplier will not expect to be liable for failure to provide the services as a result of the customer failing to comply with its obligations, whether the customer's failure has been caused by a force majeure event or not.

Equally, the customer will not expect to be in breach of the agreement if it fails to comply with its obligations as a result of a force majeure event.

30.12.3 Payment of compensation by customer

If the supplier incurs additional expenditure as a result of the customer failing to comply with its obligations, then the supplier will usually expect to be compensated for this (*see* Chapter 12).

Should the customer have to pay compensation if it fails to comply with its obligations as a result of a force majeure event? If the approach is taken that parties should not be responsible for events outside their control, then it may be argued that the financial consequences of the services not being provided in these circumstances should be the same as if the services are not provided as a result of a force majeure event affecting the supplier, namely the consequences described in 30.5 above.

An alternative approach is to argue that the customer is in the best position to manage risks affecting its actions and that therefore the financial consequences of the customer failing to comply with its obligations should be the same whatever the reason for the failure – namely that the customer will pay compensation, as described in Chapter 12. Note that in a PFI agreement the customer will not receive relief if it is unable to fulfil its obligations as a result of a "relief event". It will only be able to claim relief for events of "force majeure". (*See* 30.9.2 above for a definition of relief events and force majeure in PFI contracts.)

30.13 Supplier's liability for damages

If the supplier fails to comply with its obligations and is unable to claim protection under force majeure provisions, then it may be liable to the customer for damages. Paragraphs 30.13.1 to 30.13.6 describe the supplier's liability for damages. This is an extremely complex subject and this chapter provides a short summary of the key relevant issues only. The paragraphs are not intended to summarise the law of damages and the reader must take legal advice on the application of the law to the particular facts of the case.

30.13.1 Measure of loss

The aim of an award of damages is to compensate the innocent party for the loss it has suffered as a result of the other party's breach of contract. The innocent party will be expected to take reasonable steps to minimise its loss to the extent that this is possible.

30.13.2 Expectation damages

The general rule is that the compensation paid by the party in breach should, as far as possible, restore the innocent party to the position it would have been in had the contract been fully performed. This is referred to as the expectation measure of damages (the contract creates an expectation of performance). For example, *see* the case of *Pegler* v *Wang*.[6] Wang entered into a contract with Pegler, a manufacturer of brassware, to provide computer hardware, software and related services designed to improve Pegler's business efficiency. The total price agreed was £1,198,130 plus £235,000 annually for three years for maintenance. Wang's performance was poor and it ultimately abandoned the contract. Pegler served formal notice of breach and required Wang to remedy its various breaches. Wang took no steps to comply. Pegler treated Wang's failure to do so as a repudiation of the contract which it relied on to bring the contract to an end. In tandem it exercised a contractual right of termination. Pegler used third parties to provide the services it needed and issued proceedings against Wang claiming damages of nearly £23 million.

Wang eventually admitted liability and the trial of the claim was principally concerned with examination of the damages claimed. Pegler was ultimately awarded £9 million – far in excess of the original contract price. Heads of loss included the following:

(a) lost sales;
(b) lost opportunity to increase margins;
(c) lost opportunity to make staff cost savings;
(d) cost of replacement systems and consultancy services;

6 *Pegler* v *Wang* [2000] BLR 218.

(e) lost opportunity to reduce finished stock held;
(f) lost ability to negotiate improved purchasing terms; and
(g) wasted management time.

In addition to looking at damages that have already been incurred, this approach to assessment may also involve looking into the future to assess the value of benefits that it had been expected would be delivered; for example, in circumstances where a lucrative contract that was intended to run for several years has been prematurely terminated.

The general rule was that such losses should be valued at the date of the breach of contract (in the example given this would be the date of wrongful termination). If parties cannot agree on the appropriate level of compensation then a court will do the best it can, on the basis of expert evidence, to assess such matters as expected profit margins and costs etc. However, a recent House of Lords case[7] has caused a debate amongst lawyers by suggesting that a court may also take into account events which occur after the date of the breach but prior to the court's assessment of the loss and which would have had an impact upon actual losses incurred had the contract been allowed to run its course. While it is acknowledged that such an approach may result in a more just assessment of loss, this is achieved at the expense of certainty and there has been speculation as to whether the defaulting party may try to delay assessment of damages to see if circumstances arise which may improve its position on damages.

30.13.3 Reliance damages

There is an alternative basis of assessment to expectation damages, sometimes looked at following early termination for breach, which an innocent party may elect to adopt in appropriate cases. This is referred to as reliance damages, where the intention is to put the innocent party into the position it would have been in if it had not entered into the contract at all. In very broad terms this will comprise the wasted expenditure incurred in connection with the contract. This is not limited to expenditure incurred *after* the contract was concluded. The innocent party can also claim expenditure incurred *before* the contract was entered into provided it was within the

7 *Golden Strait Corporation* v *Nippon Yusen Kubishka Kaisha* [2007] UKHL 12. The case concerned the premature termination of a time charter by charterers. The shipowners claimed damages linked to the amount of hire that they would have received from the charterers during the remaining four years of the contract. The contract had a term that said the charterers could terminate the contract in the event of war breaking out between a number of countries including the US, the UK and Iraq. After termination of the contract but before the assessment of damages took place the Gulf war broke out. The court found that the shipowners were only entitled to loss of hire for the period up to the outbreak of war because the charterers would have terminated on that date and the shipowners would not therefore have received any hire beyond that date had the contract still been in place. In applying this approach to other circumstances it should be remembered that the contract in this particular case made express reference to the particular event (the outbreak of war) which was later relied upon by the charterers. *See* also the later case of *Seatbooker Sales Limited* v *Southend United Football Club Limited* [2008] EWHC 157 in which the Judge said: "In my judgment, in the light of the speeches in *Golden Strait Corp* v *Nippon Yusen Kubishika Kaisha* from which I have quoted, the current state of the law is that damages for breach of contract fall to be assessed as at the date of the breach, but that in making that assessment it is appropriate to take into account matters which have occurred and which impact upon the question how valuable the contractual rights lost or broken would have proved to be, but for the breach of contract complained of".

reasonable contemplation of the parties that it would be likely to be wasted as a result of the other party's breach.[8]

An example of this type of claim was made in the case of *The Salvage Association* v *CAP Financial Services Ltd.*[9] The case concerned a contract for the development of new accounting software by the supplier for its customer. When it became clear that the supplier would fail to sort out serious problems in the system in time to meet an extended deadline agreed for completion of the project, the customer exercised a right of termination and engaged another company to design a replacement system from scratch. It succeeded in recovering from the supplier as damages:

(a) £291,388 paid under the two (development and implementation) contracts entered into with the supplier;
(b) £231,866 wasted expenditure (including payments made to a bureau facility, on which the system was installed, for use of terminal time), wasted computer stationery, and payments to consultants and to an independent third party in connection with testing; and
(c) £139,672 wasted management time that could have been put to productive use in connection with other activities.

In a major outsourcing project, reliance expenditure may be substantial. However, it is important to distinguish between costs incurred in connection with the project which may have been entirely wasted and costs that have provided some value or relate to steps that will not need to be undertaken again, for example if the contract is put out to tender a second time.

30.13.4 Which measure of loss to claim

Naturally enough, the innocent party is in most cases only going to be interested in pursuing the "reliance" measure of loss where it exceeds "expectation" damages, although a further possibility may be a case where it is difficult in practice to prove what the expectation losses would have been.[10] In certain cases, it may be appropriate to carry out an assessment of loss under both heads before deciding on the best approach.

8 *See* comments of Lord Denning in *Anglia Television Ltd* v *Reed* [1972] 1 QB 60, a case in which an actor failed to honour his contract with a TV company to appear in a film. The company was unable to find a substitute and the film was never made. The TV company could not say what its profits on the project would have been and chose instead to make a wasted-expenditure claim. The Judge found that the TV company was entitled to recover wasted expenditure on fees paid to the director, designer and stage manager both *before* and after the contract had been entered into on the basis that the actor must have known perfectly well that such expenditure was likely to be incurred and would be wasted if he broke his contract.

9 *The Salvage Association* v *CAP Financial Services Ltd* [1995] FSR 654. *See* also *South West Water Services Limited* v *ICL* [1999] ITVLR 439 in which the Judge permitted recovery (on the basis of a restitutionary claim) of money paid for a package of hardware and software because SWWS had received nothing of value in circumstances where ICL had delivered compliant hardware which could not be used without appropriate bespoke software that ICL (in breach of contract) was unable to supply.

10 For example, the case of *McRae* v *Commonwealth Disposals Commission* [1951] 84 CLR 377 in which one party agreed to sell to the other the wreck of a tanker said to contain oil and lying on the Jourmand Reef. The claimant embarked on an expedition to salvage the wreck which was found not to exist. It was impossible for the claimant to show what loss it had suffered as a result of the wreck not existing and its claim was assessed by reference to its expenses incurred in connection with the expedition and its prepayment to the other party. (*See* also *Anglia Television* v *Reed* [1972] 1 QB 60).

30.13.5 Limitations of recovery – remoteness of loss

Loss that is too remote cannot be recovered. The thinking underlying this restriction on recovery is that it would be unfair to expect the defaulting party to be liable to compensate for all losses however unusual or unforeseeable. The general test is broken down into two parts. To recover the particular loss claimed, such loss must fall within one of two heads:

(a) a loss that occurs "naturally" or in the "usual course of events" after a breach of contract. There are many ways of expressing this, for example "a serious possibility" or "a real danger" or that it must have been "not unlikely" that the loss would occur;[11] or

(b) the loss must have been within the reasonable contemplation of the parties at the time the contract was made.

One way to ensure that the loss is within the contemplation of the other party is to notify it during negotiations for the contract of any "special" losses that might be suffered as a result of breach.

The case of *Victoria Laundry (Window) Ltd* v *Newman Industries Limited*[12] is often used to illustrate the distinction between losses that flow naturally from the breach and those which must be categorised as "special" losses. In that case the defaulting party, an engineering company, had agreed to the immediate delivery of a boiler to the claimant, a laundry business. The defendant did not know that the boiler was needed to extend the business. The boiler was delivered five months late and the claimant sued for loss of profits.

The court found that the claimant was entitled to compensation for loss of normal profits (it being an entirely natural consequence of late delivery that the claimant's business should suffer), but that it was not entitled to recover losses under especially lucrative contracts that it had just entered into with the Government which the claimant could not perform without the new boiler. The defendant did not know about these contracts and the loss was not within the reasonable contemplation of the parties.[13]

This approach has been affirmed by the House of Lords in *Transfield Shipping Inc.* v *Mercator Shipping Inc.*,[14] a case in which the late return of a chartered ship led to the ship owner having to agree a reduced price with its next charterer. The court found that it would be contrary to the principle stated in the *Victoria Laundry* case to suppose that the parties were contracting on the basis that the original charterer would be liable for any loss, however large, occasioned by a delay in redelivery in circumstances where it had no knowledge or control over the new fixture entered into by the ship owner.

---

11 *See Koufos* v *C. Czrnikow* [1969] 1 AC 350 (judgment of Lord Pearce at pages 414–415).

12 *Victoria Laundry (Window) Ltd* v *Newman Industries Limited* [1949] All ER 997.

13 It has been suggested, however, that the law should not ignore the extent of the loss if it is to achieve reasonable restrictions on recovery. In a commercial contract the *kind* of loss will nearly always be within the contemplation of the parties (e.g., in the *Victoria Laundry* case (above) the loss under the normal contracts and under the lucrative contracts was the same in nature – it was only the amount of profit under the lucrative contracts that was exceptional) and it is legitimate to distinguish between ordinary and exceptional losses in relation to both direct and consequential losses. *See* Professor Ewan McKendrick, *Contract, Tort and Restitution Statutes 2003/04*, Sweet & Maxwell, 2003, p429.

14 [2008] UKHL 48.

30.13.6 Liability for damages in PFI contracts

An important point to note about PFI contracts is that the supplier in such a contract is not generally liable for damages. The extent of its liability for failure to provide the services will be the agreed basis upon which deductions may be made from the charges payable by the customer and, in the case of breaches leading to termination, the agreed basis upon which the termination payments to be made by the customer will be calculated. The parties may want to consider whether the certainty afforded by this approach is one that they would like to adopt in their outsourcing arrangement.

30.14 Liability under indemnities

30.14.1 Legal effect of indemnities

The supplier's liability will be different from that described in 30.13 above if it has accepted indemnity obligations. An indemnity is an express contractual obligation to reimburse the other party for some defined loss or damage, provided that the particular conditions set out in the indemnity are satisfied.[15] As a result:

(a) the company benefiting from the indemnity will not need to establish a cause of action;
(b) as an indemnity claim is an action for a debt, there is no duty to mitigate one's losses;[16] and
(c) an indemnity may effectively sidestep the test for remoteness by providing a guaranteed remedy in circumstances which may not necessarily give rise to a claim in damages. Suppliers should therefore ensure all indemnities are narrowly drafted, for example referring to "direct losses" rather than "all losses" and subject to appropriate controls.[17]

Indemnities are often used in outsourcing agreements to cover situations in which one of the parties agrees to compensate the other party against liability it incurs to a third party, as these claims go beyond what the party would be able to claim for breach of contract.

Whether the supplier's liability under indemnities is unlimited or not will depend upon the terms of the agreement. The parties should ensure that the issue is dealt with clearly in the outsourcing agreement.

15 The conditions may include, for example, that the customer will notify the supplier promptly in writing of any claim of which it is aware, that it will permit the supplier, at the supplier's expense, to conduct any litigation and negotiations for a settlement of the claim, giving the supplier reasonable assistance at the supplier's expense and that the customer will not make any admission or take any other action which might be prejudicial without the express consent of the supplier.

16 *See Roy Scott Commercial Leasing* v *Is Mail* (Court of Appeal), 29 April 1993.

17 Staughton LJ stated in *Total Transport Corporation* v *Arcadia Petroleum Limited (the "Eurus")* (1998) (CA) that an indemnity covers "all loss suffered which is attributable to a specified cause, whether or not it was in the reasonable contemplation of the parties". However, he tempered this wide interpretation by confirming that there was no authority for the proposition that remoteness is always irrelevant to an indemnity obligation.

30.14.2 IPR indemnity from the supplier

The customer may want to be indemnified against any liability it incurs as a result of being in breach of third-party intellectual property rights. The supplier will usually provide an IPR indemnity for breaches of IPR resulting from use of assets it has made available for the provision of the outsourcing services. This may involve it accepting liability, as prime contractor, for software it has licensed from third-party licensors, even if the licensors of the software are unwilling to grant the supplier IPR indemnities on similar terms to those set out in the outsourcing contract. An extreme example of this arises if the supplier is using open source software. If the customer has requested solutions using open source software, then the supplier may take the view that it should not take the risk that the open source software breaches third-party IPR.

30.14.3 IPR indemnity from the customer

The supplier will not want to grant the IPR indemnity for assets provided by the customer and may want the customer to provide a mutual indemnity for these assets. The customer may be willing to grant an IPR indemnity either mirroring that given by the supplier or reflecting that granted to it by its third-party suppliers.

30.14.4 Other indemnities

There may be circumstances in which the supplier may want an indemnity from the customer covering claims by other companies or individuals. For example, if a customer outsources its call-centre services, including the provision of advice to members of the public. In this situation, the supplier will usually deal with the queries from the public in accordance with scripts written by the customer. If the scripts are incorrect, then the members of the public may argue that they have a claim in negligence against the supplier. The supplier may want an indemnity from the customer covering this liability.

In some situations, the customer may request general indemnities from the supplier which do not relate to third-party liabilities, for example indemnities for breaches of key clauses of the agreement. In that case, the supplier may decide either to accept or reject the indemnity or to modify the effect of the indemnity, for example by stating that the customer must mitigate its losses before it can claim under the indemnity.

30.15 Liability to third parties

Some complex outsourcing arrangements may involve third parties and the customer may want the supplier to accept liability to such parties.

30.15.1 Members of the customer's group

The customer may be contracting on behalf of other members of its group of companies. The customer may want to be able to claim on behalf of other members of the group for losses suffered by them or may want them to have the ability to claim against the supplier. The supplier may prefer all claims to go through the customer.

In this situation, the supplier may want the customer to accept liability for compliance by other members of its group with relevant provisions in the outsourcing arrangement (e.g. confidentiality and licensing terms). The customer may need to enter into back-to-back agreements with the other members of its group.

30.15.2 Incoming contractor

Chapter 27 has already explained the importance of any incoming contractor being able to enforce TUPE indemnities on termination of the original outsourcing agreement (or the customer being able to claim for losses suffered by the incoming contractor).

30.15.3 Employees

In some circumstances, the customer may agree enhanced protections for transferring employees (e.g. that the supplier will not make any of the transferring employees redundant within a specified number of years) and may want the transferring employees to be able to rely upon these promises by the supplier.

30.15.4 Customer's clients

If the outsourcing service is key to the provision by the customer of services to its clients, the customer may want the supplier to accept responsibility for claims by those clients. Whether this is acceptable to the supplier or not will depend upon the particular circumstances and whether the supplier can evaluate and control this liability.

30.15.5 Contracts (Rights of Third Parties) Act 1999

The Contracts (Rights of Third Parties) Act 1999, which came into force in 2000, provides a facility for a person who is not a party to a contract to enforce in its own right a term of the contract if the contract expressly provides for this. If this facility is to be used, then it is important to express this clearly in the contract. The third party who is intended to have a right to enforce the contract must be expressly identified in the contract for this purpose. The third party can be identified either by name or generically and need not be in existence at the time the contract is entered into.

This Act also states that a party to the contract can rely against third parties on the limitations of liability in the outsourcing agreement. It is possible to exclude the application of the Act. Therefore, to avoid disputes, in circumstances where third parties are intended to have rights under the outsourcing arrangement, it is important to clarify the third parties' specific or generic identities and the precise circumstances in which (or conditions upon which) the entitlement to enforce arises.

Chapter 31

Limitations of Liability

31.1 Outline

Chapter 30 explains the supplier's liability under the outsourcing agreement. This chapter describes how the supplier's liability may be limited and the enforceability of such limitations of liability. It also discusses whether the customer's liability should be limited.

31.2 Financial caps

The supplier will usually want to limit its liability for damages by agreeing a financial cap. This will usually be acceptable to the customer except in certain sectors where it is industry practice not to limit liability, for example in some defence contracts or in some types of business process outsourcing agreements in the financial services sector.

31.3 Relevant factors in deciding the cap

From the customer's perspective, the supplier's liability should be negotiated taking into account the types of breaches that are likely to occur, the likelihood of the breaches occurring and the type and amount of damages that the customer will suffer if the breaches occur.

From the supplier's perspective, its liability and hence its risk should reflect the benefit that it is receiving under the agreement, namely the receipt of the charges. It may not want the limitation of liability to take into account capital expenditure it is making so as to be able to provide the services.

The limit of liability should always be drafted in the light of the insurance coverage the parties can arrange and whether it is easier for one party rather than the other to take out insurance. The courts will usually take these factors into account in assessing the reasonableness of any cap.

31.4 Structure of the cap

Chapter 19 has already mentioned that the supplier will look to cap its exposure to service credits. There are various ways in which the supplier's total liability may be limited.

31.4.1 One limit

The supplier's liability may be limited to one overall figure or one annual figure.

31.4.2 Several limits

The limitation of liability clause may distinguish between different types of liability:

(a) The supplier may fix a limit for damages caused by loss of or damage to physical property. As these losses will usually be covered by insurance, the supplier may be willing to accept a higher limitation of liability for them. The limitation will be determined in the light of the supplier's insurance cover but will not necessarily reflect the full extent of the insurance cover as the insurance policy will usually be required to cover other risks of the supplier's business.

(b) The parties may agree to fix a separate, lower cap for specific types of liability, for example consequential loss (if it is not excluded; *see* 30.6 below).

(c) The supplier may fix a separate liability limit for "other losses" (which may not be covered by insurance[1]). The limit may be a fixed amount or a percentage of the charges payable under the agreement. The customer may want to fix the limitation by reference to the greater of a fixed amount and a specified percentage of the charges so that the limitation increases as the amount of the charges increases (for example, because the customer orders additional services from the supplier). In circumstances where it may want to terminate the agreement early on where the customer has not yet started to pay for the services or has paid little for the services, the customer should avoid fixing the limitation of liability solely as a percentage of the charges paid by it over the previous 12 months.

There are benefits to the supplier in drafting the cap in "layers". If a court strikes out a provision on the grounds that the provision seeks to exclude liability which it is not reasonable to exclude, the courts will not re-write the provision so that it only covers liabilities which it is reasonable to exclude. Therefore, drafting the cap as a number of sub-clauses may mean that the elements which are reasonable will still stand. It is also helpful to include a "severability" clause allowing part of a provision to be severed without affecting the remaining text.

31.4.3 Unlimited

The parties will not at law be able to limit their liability when it arises from:

(a) death or injury to persons resulting from their negligence;[2]

(b) fraud;

(c) breach of the implied obligations as to title;[3] or

(d) breach of the implied term as to quiet possession.[4]

---

1 It is more difficult to procure insurance cover for pure economic loss. Many policies contain exclusions for penalties or liquidated damages clauses.

2 Section 2 UCTA 1977.

3 Section 12 Sale of Goods Act 1979.

4 Section 25 Sale of Goods Act 1979.

The customer may want to extend the supplier's unlimited liability to cover other circumstances, including, for example, the supplier's intellectual property rights indemnity or the confidentiality obligation (or to agree a higher cap for these types of liability).

There are various other circumstances in which the customer may want the supplier to accept unlimited liability. For example, the customer may want to avoid a situation where the supplier abandons or repudiates the contract because it realises that the customer has already suffered losses equal to the supplier's limitation of liability and hence the supplier is not concerned about the customer suffering further losses. Even without such an exception, the supplier is advised against abandoning the contract once it believes that the customer has already suffered losses equal to the supplier's limitation of liability, because of the risk that the limitation of liability provision will be unenforceable for the reasons outlined in paragraph 31.5 below.[5]

Suppliers are usually reluctant to accept any unlimited liability except where they cannot at law limit their liability. Ultimately, however, the details of any limitation of liability will be agreed by the parties and will depend upon the bargaining power of the supplier and customer.

31.4.4 PFI approach

A different approach is taken in a PFI contract where the supplier's liability for most breaches of contract will be the amount that the payment mechanism permits the customer to deduct from the charges payable to the supplier for the services from time to time and, ultimately, the deductions which the customer is entitled to make from termination payments to reflect the impact of the breach. The customer will waive its rights to claim damages from the supplier in the usual way, other than for breaches of contract which are not covered by the payment mechanism.

31.5 Enforceability of caps

The supplier's limitation of liability is fundamental to an assessment of the risk it accepts in entering into the outsourcing arrangement and so the supplier will be anxious to ensure that its limitation of liability is enforceable at law. The following paragraphs describe the factors affecting the enforceability of the supplier's limitation of liability under English law.

5 *See* also the case of *Internet Broadcasting Corporation Ltd (t/a NETTV) and NETTV Hedge Funds Ltd (formerly MARHedge TV Ltd) v MAR LLC (t/a MARHedge)* [2009] EWHC 844, in which the High Court held that there is a rebuttable presumption that an exclusion clause should not apply to a deliberate personal repudiatory breach of contract. A deliberate repudiation by a party, especially a personal repudiation, was either uninsurable, or very unlikely to be insurable, and as such the innocent party would be unable to protect himself against the risk of such a breach. Very clear and strong drafting would be required to persuade a court that the parties intended an exclusion clause to cover a deliberate personal repudiatory breach of contract: pointing to the literal meaning of the words was not enough. Where a party is a corporate body, a repudiation will be personal if it is taken by the "controlling mind" of the body.

31.5.1 UCTA 1977

The Unfair Contract Terms Act 1977 ("UCTA 1977")[6] provides that a party cannot rely on a contractual term unless the contract term is *reasonable* if the term limits liability:

(a) for negligence causing loss (other than death or personal injury);
(b) for breach of the implied conditions of conformity; or
(c) under a contract in which a party is *dealing* on the other party's *standard* written terms.

There are a number of key phrases wrapped up in this provision.

31.5.1.1 "Deals"

The requirement to deal on standard terms does not mean that there may be no negotiations on the terms, provided the terms ultimately agreed are in fact standard terms.[7]

31.5.1.2 "Standard"

To determine what constitutes standard terms, the courts take a clause-by-clause as opposed to a "whole contract" approach. This means that if the liability provisions are not materially amended, they will be standard terms covered by Section 3, even if there are many other changes to the contract.[8]

For terms to be a party's standard terms they should be regarded as such by that party, who should also contract on those terms on a regular basis.[9]

Where a standard form contract is the subject of meaningful negotiation between parties of equal bargaining power, the terms may cease to be standard within the meaning of Section 3.[10]

---

6 Subsection 3(2)(a).

7 *See* the judgment of Nourse LJ in *St Albans* v *ICL* [1996] 4 All ER 481 at 490.

8 In the case of *Pegler* v *Wang* (*see* above), the contract included some of Pegler's standard terms and some of Wang's standard terms. The court held that Pegler had been dealing with Wang on Wang's standard terms: Wang had insisted on using its standard exclusion clauses which, apart from one small and inconsequential exception, were not negotiable.

9 *Chester Grosvenor Hotel Co. Ltd* v *Alfred McAlpine Management* [1991] 56 BLR 122 (Judge Stannard at pages 131–133). That case concerned a contract between the plaintiff and McAlpine, the latter having been appointed as contract manager in relation to some building work to be carried out at the plaintiff's premises. It was established that of 17 contracts that McAlpine had entered into over a period of nearly three years, some seven contracts (in addition to the two entered into with the plaintiff) were in similar form being based on terms put forward by McAlpine but modified in each case to take account of particular features. It was accepted by the court that the terms were clearly regarded by McAlpine as being its standard terms of business and were found to be standard terms for the purposes of UCTA 1977. The Judge stated: "it does not follow that because terms are not employed invariably, or without material variation, they cannot be standard terms ... In my judgment the question is one of fact and degree. What are alleged to be standard terms may be used so infrequently in comparison with other terms that they cannot realistically be regarded as standard, or on any particular occasion may be so added to or mutilated that they must be regarded as having lost their essential identity. What is required for terms to be standard is that they should be regarded by the party which advances them as its standard terms."

10 *The Salvage Association v CAP Financial Services Ltd* 1995 FSR 654 (at 672) in which the court indicated that the following factors may be relevant – the degree to which the "standard terms" are consid-

It may not be easy to persuade a court that an exclusion/limitation clause is not a standard term, so if an agreement has been heavily negotiated it is advisable to keep the drafts.

31.5.1.3 "Reasonable"

Section 11(1) of UCTA 1977 provides the following definition of reasonableness:

> "in relation to a contract term, the requirement of reasonableness ... is that the term shall have been a fair and reasonable one to have been included having regard to the circumstances which were, or ought reasonably to have been known to or in the contemplation of the parties when the contract was made."

It is for the party relying on the exclusion or limitation clause to show that it is reasonable.[11] Also, reasonableness is to be assessed at the date of the contract, not the date of breach.

Generally speaking, the courts are more likely to give effect to a limitation clause than to an exclusion clause.

Reasonableness is assessed against the list of factors set out in Schedule 2 of UCTA 1977 which (if relevant) should be taken into account in assessing whether the reasonableness requirement is met. Although Section 11(2) of UCTA 1977 states that these factors should be taken into account in assessing the reasonableness requirement as regards Sections 6 and 7 (exclusion of liability for breach of statutory implied terms), the courts have also looked at the factors in assessing the reasonableness requirement for other purposes.

The Schedule 2 factors are:

(a) strength of bargaining position of the parties;[12]
(b) whether the customer received an inducement to agree to the term, or could have entered into a similar contract with someone else without the term;
(c) whether the customer knew or ought reasonably to have known about the term;
(d) where the term excludes or restricts liability if a condition is not complied with, whether it was reasonable to expect compliance with that condition;
(e) whether the contract goods were provided to the special order of the customer.

A further (and important) factor that the courts will take into account in assessing reasonableness is the availability of insurance. Where a party seeks by a contract term to limit its liability to a financial cap, in assessing the reasonableness requirement, regard should be had to:

(a) the resources available to that party to meet the liability, should it arise; and
(b) how far it was open to that party to cover itself by insurance.[13]

---

ered by the other party as part of the process of agreeing the terms of the contract, the degree to which the "standard terms" are imposed on the other party by the party putting them forward, the degree to which the party putting them forward is prepared to negotiate the terms, the extent and nature of any amendments agreed and the extent and duration of the negotiations.

11 Section 11(5) of UCTA 1977.

12 *Watford Electronics Ltd* v *Sanderson CFL Ltd* 2001 1 All ER (Comm) 696. This concerned a contract for supply of a bespoke integrated software system which included an exclusion of liability clause re indirect or consequential loss in which the court found that the parties were of equal bargaining power and well understood and agreed the allocation of risk reflected in the exclusion clause adopted.

13 Section 11(4) UCTA 1977.

It is the *availability* of insurance which is the key factor, not the actual cover. The position in respect of insurance – one of the most commonly overlooked aspects in drafting such clauses – should always be considered, as the courts will take this into account in assessing reasonableness.

The following paragraphs explain how courts have applied the above principles in specific cases.

31.5.2 *St Albans City and District Council* v *ICL*[14]

This was a case where the issue of reasonableness was considered. ICL entered into a contract with St Albans to supply a computer system to be used in administering its collection of community charge. Due to an error in the system, the population figure against which the community charge was calculated was overstated – the end result being that the council's total receipts were £484,000 less than they ought to have been. The council sued ICL for damages for breach of contract claiming the amount of under-collection together with an additional £685,000 by way of increased precept payments to the county council. The court (having established that the council had dealt on ICL's standard terms of business for the purposes of Section 3(1) UCTA 1977) held that a limitation of liability clause in the contract, capping damages recoverable by the council to £100,000, was unreasonable in the circumstances of the case. Two of the principal factors taken into account were that:

(a) ICL had very substantial resources and insurance cover; and
(b) ICL was one of a small number of companies who were able to supply what the council had been looking for and because of this, and the tight timescale to which the council was working, ICL had a better bargaining position than the council.

31.5.3 *Watford Electronics* v *Sanderson*[15]

In this case, the court held that an exclusion of consequential loss and cap on contractual liability linked to the price paid were reasonable. Chadwick LJ in the Court of Appeal explained:

> "Where experienced businessmen representing substantial companies of equal bargaining power negotiate an agreement, they may be taken to have had regard to the matters known to them. They should, in my view be taken to be the best judge of the commercial fairness of the agreement which they have; including the fairness of each of the terms in that agreement. They should be taken to be the best judge on the question whether the terms of the agreement are reasonable. The court should not assume that either is likely to commit his company to an agreement which he thinks is unfair, or which he thinks includes unreasonable terms. *Unless satisfied that one party has, in effect taken unfair advantage of the other – or that a term is so unreasonable that it cannot properly have been understood or considered – the court should not interfere.*"

14 *St Albans City and District Council* v *ICL* [1995] FSR 686.
15 [2001] EWCA Civ 317.

31.5.4 *Horace Holman Group* v *Sherwood International*[16]

In this case, the court held that the exclusion of statutory implied terms, an exclusion of consequential loss and a cap on contractual liability to reflect the price paid were all unreasonable.

The court felt that the evidence of the availability of insurance was a key factor in the decision. The court found that it would have been easier and cheaper for the supplier to insure against its software not performing, than for the customer to insure against its losses if the software did not perform. This case led advisers to suppliers to warn them that the odds were heavily against a limitation clause linked to the price paid surviving scrutiny by the court.

31.5.5 *SAM Business Systems Ltd* v *Hedley & Co*[17]

The dispute arose in connection with the supply of a computer system by SAM Business Systems Ltd ("SAM") to Hedley and Company ("Hedley"). It was accepted that the licence and maintenance contracts entered into by the parties were both on SAM's standard terms. Problems arose on implementation and the project was never completed. SAM sued Hedley for non-payment. Hedley counterclaimed for damages in connection with delivery of the defective system.

The licence agreement contained an exclusion of liability provision upon which SAM relied. The provision fell within UCTA and the Judge therefore had to consider whether the clause was reasonable. In finding that it was reasonable, the Judge took into account the existence of an acceptance criteria procedure laid down in the agreement which, in the event of a defective system being delivered by SAM and going unremedied within the prescribed time, would have permitted Hedley to terminate the agreement and claim back all sums paid to SAM. This provision reflected negotiations and representations made by SAM in terms that it offered "a standard money back guarantee licence" and against this background the exclusion provisions were considered reasonable.

31.5.6 *Frans Maas* v *Samsung*[18]

In this case, the court held that a cap on contractual liability of £25,000 in a contract worth £2.2 million was reasonable.

The court considered whether the limitation provisions contained in the BIFA terms satisfied the requirement of reasonableness under UCTA. In determining that clause 27(A) of the BIFA terms (which provided the mechanism for a cap of £25,000) was reasonable, the court considered the following circumstances:

(a) the parties were of equal bargaining power;
(b) the limit in clause 27(A) was calculated in terms of weight, not value of the goods;

---

16 [2000] All ER(D) 83 (Nov) (the subsequent CA hearing is [2002] EWCA Civ 170).
17 *SAM Business Systems Ltd* v *Hedley & Co.* [2003] QBD (T&CC), 19 December 2002, 1 All ER (Comm)
18 [2005] 2 All ER (Comm) 783.

(c) SEUK could have contracted under clause 27(D) of the BIFA terms "by special arrangement" for a higher limit had it wished to do so;
(d) clauses such as clause 27(A) are commonly used by freight forwarders; and
(e) SEUK could have obtained insurance cover in respect of the goods.

On UCTA, the court cited the remarks of Tuckey LJ in the CA decision of *Granville Oil & Chemical Ltd* v *Davis Turner & Co Ltd* with approval:

> "The 1977 Act obviously plays a very important role in protecting vulnerable consumers from the effect of draconian contract terms. But I am less enthusiastic about its intrusion into contracts between commercial parties of equal bargaining strength, who should generally be considered capable of being able to make contracts of their choosing and expect to be bound by their terms."

31.5.7 *Regus (UK) Ltd* v *Epcot Solutions Ltd*[19]

The significance of the availability of insurance was highlighted once again in this case, which concerned the provision of serviced office accommodation by Regus to Epcot. The contract between the parties excluded any liability on the part of Regus for loss of business, loss of profits and consequential loss. Following a forced transfer to alternative accommodation, Epcot made a claim for relocation expenses. Having found that there was no inequality of bargaining power between the parties, the Judge found that it was entirely reasonable for Regus to restrict damages for loss of profits and consequential losses. He found that Regus had advised its customers to protect themselves by insurance for business losses and that it was generally more economical for the person by whom the loss would be sustained to take out insurance. In these circumstances the clause was found to meet the requirements of reasonableness.

The cases indicate that arbitrary financial caps which do not properly reflect the accepted allocation of risk and/or opportunity to manage risk as between the parties may be vulnerable to attack under the reasonableness requirement.

31.5.8 Changes in the law

It must be borne in mind that this important area of law is under review and suppliers and customers are advised to look out for future changes which come into effect. In 2001, the Department of Trade and Industry asked the Law Commission to rewrite the law of unfair contract terms in clearer and more accessible language and in a way that embraced both the provisions of domestic legislation (in the form of UCTA 1977) and the EU regulation applicable to consumer contracts (The Unfair Contract Terms in Consumer Contracts Regulations 1999). In February 2005, the Law Commission published a final report and draft Bill. The recommendations made by the Law Commission have been accepted by the government and, subject to completion of a regulatory impact assessment and the availability of Parliamentary time, new legislation is expected. The draft Bill produced by the Law Commission maintains the effect of

19 *Regus (UK)* v *Epcot Solutions Ltd* [2008] EWCA Civ 361.

the current law relating to commercial agreements (although it does introduce some additional protections for small businesses). Application of the "fair and reasonable" test is preserved (clause 14 of the draft Bill) although the facts to be applied in determining whether a term is fair and reasonable are now stated to be:

(a) the extent to which the terms are transparent; and
(b) the substance and effect of the term and all of the circumstances existing at the time it was agreed.

Schedule 2 of the draft Bill lists various factors to be considered under (b) above. These include express reference to the balance of the parties' interests, the risks to the party adversely affected by the term, the possibility and probability of insurance and other ways in which the interests of the party adversely affected by the term might have been protected.

31.5.9 Documenting the limitation of liability

The supplier is advised to keep documentary evidence which will help it to argue that its limitation of liability is reasonable, for example evidence showing that the customer has a reasonable bargaining power and that the customer negotiated the agreement extensively. It will be helpful if it documents the circumstances that led the limitation of liability to be agreed (taking into account the factors listed in 31.5.1.3 above). The supplier may want to include a short preamble or recital at the beginning of a limitation of liability clause in order to explain the reasons for or background to its insertion.

31.6 Exclusion by the supplier of consequential loss and other specified losses

31.6.1 Exclusion of consequential loss

In addition to agreeing a financial cap to its liability under the agreement, the supplier may want to exclude certain liabilities in their entirety. In particular, the supplier will usually want to exclude liability for consequential loss.

A number of recent cases have established (or confirmed) that, in this context, "consequential loss" refers to those losses which would be recoverable only under the "second limb" of the test for remoteness laid down in *Hadley* v *Baxendale*.[20]

---

20 (1854) 9 Ex. 341. The innocent party may only recover damages for loss suffered as a result of the breach provided it is not too remote. The principles of remoteness are given in *Hadley* v *Baxendale* ([1854] 9 Exch. 341) and provide that the following losses are recoverable: (a) all loss which flows naturally from the breach; and (b) all loss which was in the contemplation of the parties at the time the contract was made as a probable result of the breach. If the loss does not fall within the above categories, then it will be too remote and will not be recoverable. The rule in *Hadley* v *Baxendale* has been interpreted to mean that only loss which is within the reasonable contemplation of the parties may be recovered (*The Heron II* [1969] 1 AC 350). *See* also the case of *Ferryways NV* v *Associated British Ports* [2008] EWHC 225 (Comm) in which the court reviewed a number of cases in which the meaning of this

Losses which fall within the first limb are those which arise in the "ordinary course of things", that is, they are the sort of losses which any reasonable person in the position of the defendant would have expected at the time of the contract.

Losses which fall within the second limb are those which should have been reasonably contemplated by the defendant at the date of the contract because of special circumstances going beyond the "ordinary course of things" which were known to the defendant.

This is not always an easy distinction to draw and in *BHP Petroleum Ltd* v *British Steel plc*[21] Rix J referred to it as "conceptually difficult". The particular conceptual difficulty he had in mind is this: a loss is usually said to fall into the second limb so as to explain that it cannot be recovered at all, that is, it is too remote because the special circumstances were *not* known to the defendant at the time of the contract. If they were known to the defendant, then it could be said they would also have been known to a reasonable person in the position of the defendant and they are therefore recoverable because they fall within the first limb. It appears that it is necessary to first decide whether a loss is recoverable at all and then attribute it to one limb or the other for the purpose of the relevant exclusion clause – no easy matter, as Rix J points out.

To clarify the issue, the parties may want to document in the agreement what they regard as consequential loss.

31.6.2 Definition of consequential loss

The supplier may want to define in greater detail losses for which it will not be responsible, for example:

(a) indirect or consequential loss;
(b) loss of profits or indirect loss of profits;[22]
(c) loss of business or loss of revenue;
(d) loss of goodwill;
(e) loss of data; and
(f) loss of anticipated savings arising out of or in connection with the agreement.

---

phrase had been judicially considered and concluded that it now had a well-recognised meaning as embracing losses that did not arise directly and naturally from the breach. In that case, it had been argued that the contract contained a definition of 'indirect and consequential' that was wider than the recognised meaning, and that the adopted definition had the effect of excluding a particular kind of loss (liability to third parties) that would otherwise have been accepted as being a direct and natural consequence of the breach. The court found that such loss was not excluded by the particular wording used and suggested that the parties could not have intended to exclude such loss under the umbrella of " indirect or consequential loss" however widely defined.

21 [1999] 2 Lloyd's Rep 583 (affd. in part, [2000] 2 Lloyd's Rep 277).

22 The cases make it clear that loss of "ordinary profits" will often fall within the first limb of *Hadley* v *Baxendale* and will not fall within the meaning of "consequential loss". *See British Sugar* v *NEI Power Projects Ltd* [1998] 87 BLR 42 (claim for increased production costs and loss of profits caused by defective electrical equipment fell within the first limb and did not amount to "consequential loss") and *Deepak* v *ICI* [1999] 1 Lloyds's Rep 387 (claim for wasted overheads and loss of profits caused when chemical plant was destroyed by defective design technology fell within the first limb and did not amount to "consequential loss").

31.6.3 Clarification of losses claimable

On the other hand, the customer may want to clarify that certain losses (including the losses it is most likely to suffer) will not be excluded by the exclusion of liability for consequential loss. The customer will have to determine these losses in the light of the specific services it has outsourced and the specific damage it will suffer. It will also need to ensure that the exclusion of liability for consequential losses and any carve out from the exclusion reflect the risk that the parties have agreed will be transferred to the supplier. For example, if the parties have agreed that the supplier will accept business outcome-related risk for the achievement by the customer of a certain level of improvement in its profits, the customer should ensure that the agreement does not incorporate standard liability clauses which exclude liability for loss of profits.

Table 40 provides some examples of losses which the customer may want to state will not be excluded.

31.7 Limitation of liability by the customer

The customer should consider whether it should limit its liability under the agreement, for example if one of its employees damages the premises of the supplier when carrying out an audit inspection. The customer may also consider that it may be easier to agree a reasonable limitation of the supplier's liability if the clause is mutual.

The customer may also suggest that the supplier's exclusion of liability for consequential loss is mutual. In this situation, the supplier should consider whether the exclusion of liability for loss of profit should be mutual, bearing in mind the importance of this claim to the supplier.

31.8 Insurance

The customer may want the supplier to take out certain insurance to cover its liability under the agreement. The parties should remember in particular to ensure that it is clear who is responsible for insuring the various assets and premises used to provide the services. The customer may also want the supplier to take out public/product liability insurance and professional indemnity insurance. In certain cases, where the services give the supplier's employees an opportunity to commit fraud, the customer may want the supplier to take out fidelity insurance (including computer crime risks).

The customer will usually want to see evidence that the supplier has taken out the requisite insurance policies and may reserve the right to take out insurance at the supplier's cost if the supplier has failed to do so.

Most suppliers will want to take out general group-wide insurance policies and the customer should bear in mind that, if it requests the supplier to take out additional insurance for the specific project, there will be a cost implication.

Table 40 *Examples of carve outs for consequential loss exclusion*
Costs of selecting and negotiating with a contractor or contractors to replace the supplier.
The difference in cost between what the customer would have paid to the supplier for the services that the supplier should have delivered under the agreement and what the customer reasonably contracts to pay a replacement contractor to provide services that are materially similar to the services.
The cost of taking emergency measures, including changing over to other computer systems.
Operational and administrative costs and expenses.[23]
Costs of internal and external staff including costs of staff providing or re-providing the services which should have been provided by the supplier.
The cost of idle time of staff, goods and facilities of the customer and any third parties engaged by the customer.
Costs associated with reconstruction of lost or corrupted data. (This will be particularly contentious from the supplier perspective.)
Any fines or payments imposed by a regulatory authority as a result of the supplier's failure to provide the services. Losses suffered by other parts of the customer's group or its customers.
Losses resulting from breach of third-party intellectual property rights.
Losses covered by liquidated damages provisions.
Direct loss of profit.[24]

23 *See Bridge UK Com Ltd* v *Abbey Pynford plc*, [2007] EWHC 728 (TCC) in which Ramsey J awarded the claimant damages for wasted management time where this was caused by the defendant's negligent installation of a printing press.

24 *See Bridge UK Com Ltd* v *Abbey Pynford plc*, [2007] EWHC 728 (TCC) in which Ramsey J awarded the claimant damages for loss of profits where these were caused by the defendant's negligent installation of a printing press. Damages for breach of contract may be recovered on the basis of loss of profits or wasted expenditure. Where damages are awarded for lost profits, the sum awarded will be net of any expenses which the claimant would have had to incur in order to earn the profits in question. In that sense, the claimant may not recover for both lost profits and wasted expenditure (*see Cullinane* v *British Rema Manufacturing Co Ltd* [1954] 1 QB 292).

Chapter 32

Confidentiality, Data Protection and Security

32.1 Outline

Chapters 30 and 31 deal with general issues of liability and limitations of liability. This chapter deals with specific issues of liability for complying with data protection, confidentiality and security requirements. Confidentiality and security are both extremely topical issues at the moment[1] with companies in the private and public sectors struggling to cope with the challenges raised by technological developments which have resulted on the one hand in greater access by the customer's own staff and outsourcing suppliers to increasing quantities of confidential data and on the other hand the growth in the use of portable devices such as memory sticks and laptops, which present security risks of their own. Cloud computing will present additional security and data protection issues.[2] At the time of writing this Guide, at least one outsourcing supplier had a major contract with its customer terminated as a result of the loss of data on an unencrypted memory stick.

32.2 Data protection

The customer and the supplier will need to ensure that they comply with their respective obligations under relevant data protection legislation.

32.2.1 Background to the Data Protection Directive (95/46/EC)

The privacy and protection of personal data in the European Union ("EU") is governed by the Data Protection Directive (95/46/EC) (the "Data Protection Directive"). The Data Protection Directive was designed to protect individuals with regard to the processing, using and exchanging of personal data. The Directive is based on principles set out in the European Convention on Human Rights.

---

1 *See* for example the Burton Review into the loss of personal data by the MOD and the Poynter Review into security at HM Revenue and Customs.

2 *See* Bridget Treacy, Hunton and Williams' article on "Learning to Trust Cloud Computing", published by the Society for Computers & the Law, 16 February 2009.

32.2.2 Content of the Data Protection Directive

32.2.2.1 Personal data

The Data Protection Directive is concerned with "personal data", which is information which relates to an identified or identifiable person (the "data subject"). Identification may be direct or indirect, but in particular it can be by reference to one or more factors specific to a person's physical, physiological, mental, economic, cultural or social identity. Data is considered to be "personal" when it enables a person's identity to be disclosed.

32.2.2.2 Processing

The Data Protection Directive covers the "processing" of such personal data, for example where a set of operations are performed on personal data, whether or not by automatic means, such as collection, storage, use or destruction.

The rules about how to treat personal data, which are set out in the Data Protection Directive, apply where those who control data ("data controllers") do so within the EU. Therefore, even if a data controller operates outside of the EU, where it processes personal data within the EU, the Data Protection Directive (as applied by each Member State) will apply.

32.2.2.3 Data controller

The data controller will determine the purpose for which and the manner in which personal data are to be processed.

In most outsourcing arrangements, the data controller will be the customer, as the supplier will be processing personal data solely as part of the services, in accordance with the instructions of the customer, and therefore will not be exploiting the data for its own purposes.

32.2.2.4 Data processor

The supplier will usually be the "data processor" – the person who processes personal data for a data controller.[3]

32.2.2.5 Processing of personal data

The Data Protection Directive lays down guidelines determining when the processing of personal data is lawful. The guidelines are summarised in Table 41 below.

Table 41 *The Data Protection Directive – data protection guidelines*

Quality of data: personal data must be processed fairly and lawfully, and collected for specified, explicit and legitimate purposes. It must also be accurate and, where necessary, kept up to date.

3 This is not always so. *See* for example the interesting opinion – Opinion 10/2006 on the processing of personal data by the Society for Worldwide Interbank Financial Telecommunication ("SWIFT"), 01935/06/EN WP128 – in which it was decided that both SWIFT and the instructing financial institutions shared joint responsibility for the processing of personal data as "data controllers" within the meaning of Article 2(d) of the Directive.

Legitimacy of data processing: personal data may be processed only if the data subject has unambiguously given his/her consent *or* processing is necessary:

(a) for the performance of a contract to which the data subject is party;
(b) for compliance with a legal obligation to which the controller is subject;
(c) in order to protect the vital interests of the data subject;
(d) for the performance of a task carried out in the public interest; or
(e) for the purposes of the legitimate interests pursued by the controller.

Special categories of processing: it is forbidden to process personal data revealing racial or ethnic origin, political opinions, religious or philosophical beliefs, trade union membership, and data concerning health or sex life. This provision comes with certain qualifications concerning, for example, cases where processing is necessary to protect the vital interests of the data subject or for the purposes of preventive medicine and medical diagnosis.

Data subject's right to information: the controller must provide the data subject from whom data is collected with certain information relating to himself/herself (the identity of the controller, the purposes of the processing, recipients of the data etc.).

Data subject's right of access: every data subject should have the right to obtain from the controller:

(a) confirmation as to whether or not data relating to him/her is being processed and communication of the data undergoing processing;
(b) the rectification, erasure or blocking of data the processing of which does not comply with the provisions of this Directive in particular, either because of the incomplete or inaccurate nature of the data, and the notification of these changes to third parties to whom the data have been disclosed.

Exemptions and restrictions: the scope of the principles relating to the quality of the data, information to be given to the data subject, right of access and the publicising of processing may be restricted in order to safeguard aspects such as national security, defence, public security, the prosecution of criminal offences, an important economic or financial interest of a Member State or of the EU or the protection of the data subject.

Data subject's right to object to processing: the data subject should have the right to object, on legitimate grounds, to the processing of data relating to him/her. He/she should also have the right to object, on request and free of charge, to the processing of personal data that the controller anticipates being processed for the purposes of direct marketing. He/she should finally be informed before personal data is disclosed to third parties for the purposes of direct marketing, and be expressly offered the right to object to such disclosures.

Confidentiality and security of processing: any person acting under the authority of the controller or of the processor, including the processor himself, who has access to personal data must not process it except on the instructions of the controller. In addition, the controller must implement appropriate measures to protect personal data against accidental or unlawful destruction or accidental loss, alteration, unauthorised disclosure or access.

Notification of processing to a supervisory authority: the controller must notify the national supervisory authority before carrying out any processing operation. The supervisory authority will carry out prior checks to determine specific risks to the rights and freedoms of data subjects following receipt of the notification. Measures are to be taken to ensure that processing operations are publicised and the supervisory authorities must keep a register of the processing operations notified.

32.2.3 Transfer of data

32.2.3.1 Transfers within the EU

One of the objectives of the Data Protection Directive was to enable the free movement of data between the Member States, once Member States of the EU had equivalent protections for data.

32.2.3.2 Transfers outside the EU

Transfers outside of the European Union are not prohibited by the Data Protection Directive, but the eighth data protection principle states that transfers must be to a country which provides an adequate level of protection, unless one or more specific exceptions are satisfied or, alternatively, the data controller can adopt one of the approaches set out in 32.2.3.4–32.2.3.6 below to legitimise the data transfers. This restriction creates a situation that effectively imposes EU data protection standards in jurisdictions outside Europe.

32.2.3.3 Specific exceptions to the restriction

There are exceptions to the restriction in the eighth data protection principle in that the Act allows data transfers if:

(a) the transfer is necessary for the performance of the contract (e.g. if a bank's customer wishes to send money to a relative living abroad, it will be necessary for the bank to pass the customer's details to the beneficiary's bank to fulfil the contract with the customer); or

(b) the transfer is a necessary part of precontractual steps taken by the customer at the request of the individual; or

(c) the individual provides an unambiguous consent to the transfer of his/her personal data to a country which does not have adequate data protection laws.

These exceptions are narrowly construed and this is confirmed by the opinion of the influential EU Article 29 Working Party, which states that the exceptions should only be relied on as a last resort, since they do not provide protection for the data once it has been transferred to the entity based outside the EEA.[4] It is therefore preferable for the customer to rely on one of the contractual protections set out below which impose stringent requirements on the supplier in relation to its processing of the customer's personal data.

4 *See* option 2093/05 EN adopted on 25 November 2005.

32.2.3.4 Countries deemed adequate by the European Commission

The Council and European Parliament gave the European Commission the power to determine which countries have adequate protection. Accordingly, the European Commission has deemed that Norway, Liechtenstein, Iceland, Switzerland, Canada, Argentina, Guernsey and the Isle of Man provide adequate protection.

The European Commission has also decided that the US Department of Commerce's Safe Harbour Privacy Principles and the Transfer of Air Passenger Name Records to the United State's Bureau of Customs and Border provide adequate protection.

32.2.3.5 Assessment of adequacy for other countries

Where the European Commission has not deemed that a country provides adequate protection, a customer will need to make the assessment, taking into account the following factors:

(a) the nature of the personal data being transferred;
(b) the country to which the data is being transferred;
(c) the purposes for which the data will be processed;
(d) the law in force in the country and the relevant enforceable rules and code of conduct;
(e) the security measures taken in respect of data in that country.

32.2.3.6 Contractual protections

If the supplier's country has not been recognised as providing sufficient protection for data, then the parties will have to seek alternative ways of protecting the data. There are two ways that the data can be protected. These are described below.

Model contractual clauses

The data can be protected by making sure that the outsourcing agreement contains specific contractual provisions ensuring that the supplier provides sufficient protection for data. The European Commission has approved standard "model" contractual clauses which can be used in outsourcing agreements to provide adequate protection for the data transferred.

Where a UK-based customer decides to rely on these EU model clauses to circumvent the data exports restriction, it does not need to take any further steps to legitimise the data transfers such as lodging a copy of the contract with the UK Information Commissioner. Note that other national data protection authorities in EU Member States may require an organisation transferring personal data from that jurisdiction to notify the authority and/or lodge a copy of the data protection provisions in the outsourcing agreement.

The technical and organisational security measures the supplier will adopt will need to be specified in the annexes to the EC Model Contract Clauses, and it is therefore necessary for the parties to assess what the supplier will actually be doing with the data, and what the security measures should be. It is not appropriate to adopt a blanket approach to the security measures to be taken, as the data controller remains liable for security failures by the service provider.

Binding corporate rules

The second way in which the data can be protected is by the supplier agreeing to adopt and follow an internal set of rules and policies drafted by the customer that provide adequate protection for individuals' personal data, with the parties agreeing legally enforceable penalties for non-compliance. These rules are known as Binding Corporate Rules ("BCR").[5] BCR are primarily designed to legitimise transfers of personal data within a multinational corporation, rather than to an external supplier. However, there is nothing in principle which would prevent a UK-based customer from securing adequate protection via BCR in the context of an outsourcing, by including in the outsourcing contract a contractual obligation requiring the supplier to adopt the rules within its organisation.

BCR must be submitted to the Information Commissioner for approval before they can be relied on to export data lawfully to the supplier. Once the Commissioner has approved the BCR (by confirming that they provide adequate protection for individuals' personal data), the Commissioner will liaise with all the other relevant national data protection authorities within the EU to obtain their approval for the BCR.

A downside of BCR is that this approval process can be both complex and time consuming and at present not all of the EU national data protection authorities recognise BCR as a solution to the data exports restriction. The advantages of BCR are that they provide a tailored global solution for the customer to the data exports restriction, whereas the EU model clauses are rigid and cannot be adapted in any way. BCR also generate a high level of awareness within the organisation, which is especially useful given that privacy laws are proliferating.

32.2.4 Implementation of the Data Protection Directive in the EU

Each Member State has enacted its own data protection legislation to implement the Data Protection Directive into its local law. In outsourcing transactions, it is therefore important to consider the Data Protection Directive and how it has been applied in the relevant Member State in which personal data is being processed. This is particularly important, as different Member States have implemented the Data Protection Directive in different ways. *See* part twelve of this Guide for specific information about how the Data Protection Directive has been implemented in some of the key EU jurisdictions.

32.2.5 Implementation of the Data Protection Directive in the UK

In the UK the Data Protection Directive was implemented in the Data Protection Act 1998 (the DPA 1998) and UK data controllers therefore need to ensure that they comply with their respective obligations under the DPA 1998.

The obligations imposed upon data controllers by the DPA 1998 include the obligation to notify the Information Commissioner's Office of the purposes for which the data controller processes information, and to be compliant with the eight data protection principles listed in Table 42.

5 For an explanation of how this would work, *see* the document published on 3 June 2003 by the independent body of EU data protection authorities known as the Article 29 Working Party.

Table 42 *Data protection principles – The Data Protection Act 1998*

1 Personal data shall be processed fairly and lawfully and shall not be processed unless one of the conditions set out in Schedule 2 to the DPA 1998 or, for sensitive personal data, Schedule 3 to the DPA 1998, is also met.

2 Personal data shall be obtained only for one or more specified and lawful purposes, and shall not be further processed in any manner incompatible with that purpose or those purposes.

3 Personal data shall be adequate, relevant and not excessive in relation to the purpose or purposes for which it is processed.

4 Personal data shall be accurate and, where necessary, kept up to date.

5 Personal data processed for any purpose or purposes shall not be kept for longer than is necessary for that purpose or those purposes.

6 Personal data shall be processed in accordance with the rights of data subjects under the DPA.

7 Personal data shall be kept secure and appropriate technical and organisational measures shall be taken against unauthorised or unlawful processing of personal data and against accidental loss or destruction of, or damage to, personal data.

8 Personal data shall not be transferred to a country or territory outside the European Economic Area unless that country or territory ensures an adequate level of protection for the rights and freedoms of data subjects in relation to the processing of personal data.

32.2.6 The Information Commissioner

The Data Protection Directive states that each Member State must provide one or more public authorities responsible for monitoring its application within the Member State. In the UK the supervisory authority is the Information Commissioner. The Information Commissioner's Office ("ICO") is an independent public body set up to promote access to official information and to protect personal information.

The Information Commissioner's Office in the UK issues guidance relating to the practical implementation of the data protection obligations, for example on the notification of data security breaches to the Information Commissioner,[6] how to design systems which comply with the DPA

6 The guidance states:

> "Although there is no legal obligation on data controllers to report breaches of security which result in loss, release or corruption of personal data, the Information Commissioner believes serious breaches should be brought to the attention of his Office. The nature of the breach or loss can then be considered together with whether the data controller is properly meeting his responsibilities under the DPA."

1998 and how to deal with data sharing between different departments within a local authority. The Information Commissioner's Office has also published guidance which sets out a number of basic good practice recommendations for organisations that outsource the processing of personal information. The recommendations give some practical guidance on how to comply with the legal obligations set out in the DPA 1998, such as selecting a reputable supplier and ensuring that the supplier has adopted appropriate data security measures. The guidance reminds businesses that, in the context of outsourcing, it is the customer who retains liability under the DPA 1998 for the security and accuracy of the personal information processed by its supplier.

32.2.7 Implications of the data protection legislation for outsourcing

In accordance with the seventh data protection principle, the customer must:

(a) choose a supplier who provides sufficient guarantees that appropriate technical and organisational measures will be taken against unauthorised or unlawful processing of personal data and against accidental loss or destruction of or damage to personal data;
(b) take reasonable steps to ensure compliance with those measures;
(c) ensure that the processing is carried out under a contract which is made or evidenced in writing under which the supplier is to act only on instructions from the customer; and
(d) ensure that the contract requires the supplier to comply with obligations equivalent to those imposed on the customer by the seventh principle, that is, to take appropriate technical and organisational measures against unauthorised or unlawful processing of personal data and against accidental loss or destruction of or damage to personal data. (This may include a commitment to satisfy security standards, such as BS 7799 or ISO 27001.)

For additional obligations relevant for international or offshore outsourcing, *see* 32.2.3 above.

32.2.8 Criticism of the DPA 1998 in the UK

Following some highly publicised breaches of security within the United Kingdom, there have been various criticisms of the DPA 1998. This had led to numerous reports[7] particularly in the public sector[8] and the financial services sector[9] and calls for amendments to the DPA 1998 and increased powers for the Information Commissioner.[10]

---

7 The House of Lords Science and Technology Committee has recommended that bodies who lose personal data should be required to notify members of the public who are placed at risk. *See* also House of Lords Justice Committee, first report of session 2007–08 on Protection of Private Data HC154, January 2008 and review of data protection and data sharing, commissioned by the Prime Minister in 2008 and carried out by Professor Mark Walport and the Information Commissioner Richard Thomas.

8 *See* Chapter 36.

9 *See* Chapter 33.

10 *See* the Information Commissioner's report on "Data Protection Powers and Penalties – the case for amending the Data Protection Act 1998" which can be found on the Information Commissioner's website.

As a result, the Criminal Justice and Immigration Act 2008 (which received Royal Assent on 8 May 2008) has been introduced, which will greatly strengthen the powers of the Information Commissioner by enabling him to levy fines against those who are guilty of serious breaches of the Act. Furthermore, as a result of concerns about the increase in the illegal trading of personal data, the existing financial sanctions for unlawfully obtaining or disclosing personal data in breach of Section 55 of the Act will be extended to include custodial sentences of up to two years.

The Information Commissioner's new powers will be brought into force by way of secondary legislation. This will include details about the maximum penalty and the circumstances in which a fine will be levied.

32.3 Supplier's security and confidentiality obligations[11]

Security concerns include those relating to:

(a) confidentiality;
(b) integrity; and
(c) availability.

Security concerns must be considered at every stage of the outsourcing arrangement.

32.3.1 During the procurement stage

Chapter 3 explains the importance of the customer considering its confidentiality and security concerns and the supplier considering its potential security obligations during the procurement stage.

32.3.2 Prior to signature of the agreement – security requirements

The security requirements of the customer (and indeed of the supplier) will vary profoundly from one outsourcing arrangement to another depending upon the nature of the customer's business, the nature of the personal data being processed, the type of services being outsourced and the security measures achieved by the customer in its business. Customers in some sectors will have to comply with sector-specific guidance or regulation.[12]

The outsourcing contract will need to specify in detail the customer's specific confidentiality and security requirements. If the security requirements are stated in the form of a security policy, the customer should ensure that this has been specifically drafted for the outsourcing arrangements and that it is drafted in terms of obligations. The customer should also ensure that the

11 For additional information on security requirements in an outsourcing arrangement, *see The Intellect Data Security and Data Protection Guidelines for Offshoring and Outsourcing*, published in April 2008.

12 *See* Chapters 33 and 36 for details of specific requirements affecting the financial services and public sectors.

information disclosed to the supplier in the security policy will not endanger the security of the customer's business.

The supplier's security obligations may include a commitment to satisfy security standards, such as BS 7799 or ISO 27001 or business continuity standards, such as BS 25999 or ISO/PAS 22399:2007. The Information Commissioner has confirmed that the recommendations in BS 7799 may deal with security risks. The supplier may also need to comply with the Payment Card Industry (PCI) standard, if the services include the processing of credit card transactions.

The customer may require the supplier to take some of the actions listed in Table 43.

Table 43 *Security*[13]

Confidentiality

Keeping a register of confidential information identified by the customer.

Taking specified measures to ensure that the information is protected.

Restricting the taking of certain documents off site.

Restricting the printing of certain documents.

Ensuring printed documents with confidential or sensitive data are disposed of securely in accordance with an agreed policy.

Providing guidance on the destruction of confidential or sensitive data including specific guidance for staff travelling or working at home.

Data security

Identifying sensitive and critical data affected by the outsourcing arrangement.

Classifying different levels of sensitive or critical data.

Determining which networks and systems generate or process sensitive or critical data.

Keeping the customer's data segregated from other customers of the supplier.

Ensuring that data is not corrupted by other companies' data.

Installing anti-spyware and firewalls of an appropriate level and keeping them up to date.

Installing and regularly updating virus detection software.

Restricting access to data to validated and authorised employees.

Ensuring appropriate levels of authorised access with audit trails of all access being provided.

13 *See* Chapter 34 for a description of the FSA's April 2008 report on "Data Security in Financial Services", which includes a long list of what the FSA regards as good and bad security practice.

Providing access rights standards.

Ensuring that users need passwords to gain access to particular systems.

Ensuring that passwords comply with good industry practice.

Taking all reasonable steps to ensure that employees cannot and do not copy data or take data off the supplier's premises.

Having detailed written procedures for data handling, data retention and destruction.

Ensuring that data is held in valid secure storage on appropriately licensed software.

Ensuring that hard drives and portable media are destroyed or wiped prior to disposal or sale.

Staff security

Carrying out appropriate role-based security checking for all authorised personnel including contractors' and subcontractors' staff before they are granted access to confidential or sensitive data.

Providing the customer with details of relevant staff who will be involved in the processing of the customer's personal data.[14]

Only using validated contract staff to maintain physical or technical security and access.

Developing an acceptable use policy.

Reviewing and updating the policy where necessary.

Ensuring that staff are aware of the policy and agree to comply with it.[15]

Implementing role-based user access profiles.

Having a procedure for staff leaving the supplier's employment or ceasing to work on the provision of the services to the customer, so that relevant access rights are disabled or deleted promptly and any customer data is returned by the employee.

Monitoring and reporting on users' access to different systems.

Using software to detect suspicious behaviour by staff with access to confidential or sensitive data.

Periodically checking that authorised personnel are following designated procedures.

Ensuring that new staff are appropriately trained and made aware of all procedures.

Carrying out regular training to stress the importance of security measures.

---

14 The supplier should ensure that it complies with the Information Commissioner's Employment Practices Code in disclosing any information about its staff to the customer. *See* www.ico.gov.uk/upload/documents/library/data_protection/detailed_specialist_guides/employment_practices_code.pdf.

15 The Department of Trade and Industry's Security breaches Survey 2006, conducted by PwC, found that only 31 per cent of employees were aware of their firm's policy.

Imposing restrictions on staff installing their own software.

Ensuring that the approval of two members of staff is required for relevant actions.

Ensuring that staff who have access to particularly confidential information relating to the customer are restricted from working for its competitors.

Server and hardware security

Ensuring that all servers are maintained in an appropriate secure location.

Ensuring that access to servers is restricted to the minimum number of approved personnel.

Ensuring appropriate access control and intruder monitoring regarding servers.

Keeping the location of the servers secret.

Ensuring that any fire protection measures take into account the possibility of damage to the servers.

Providing a validated hardware list to the customer.

Allowing the customer to inspect and query the hardware used.

Conforming to any legislative or procedural requirement for physical hardware maintenance.

Ensuring that data are removed in a secure manner from redundant, broken or otherwise damaged hardware.

Providing a log of the procedures for removing data from hardware.

Providing a log of all hardware disposed of.

Laptop security

Ensuring all data on laptops is encrypted.

Reviewing levels of encryption and complying with any sector-specific and regulatory requirements regarding encryption.

Only issuing laptops to staff who need them to do their job.

Keeping an accurate register of laptops and any security tokens used to enable the laptop to connect to the customer's systems over the public network.

Imposing appropriate restrictions upon the holding of data on laptops.

Portable media (including USB and CDs) security

Ensuring all data on portable media is encrypted.

Reviewing levels of encryption.

Only issuing portable media to staff who need them to do their job.

Using software to restrict use of personal portable media.

Keeping an accurate register of portable media.

Checking copying to portable media.

Imposing appropriate restrictions upon the holding of data on portable media.

Ensuring that equipment is swept before it leaves the supplier's premises.

Physical security

Ensuring that building signage takes into account any security requirements.

Ensuring that the supplier's premises have appropriate locks and alarm system on entry to the building and on entry to the specific area where the staff providing the services work.

Ensuring that entry to areas with sensitive data is restricted to staff who need it to perform their functions.

Checking swipe-card records for suspicious behaviour.

Ensuring that the doors on data racks have appropriate locks and alarms.

Installing intruder detection systems.

Complying with procedures for logging in all visitors and ensuring that they are adequately supervised.

Enforcing a "clear desk" policy.

Ensuring sensitive records are kept in locked filing cabinets.

Backups and service continuity

Keeping all data appropriately backed up.

Ensuring that data on backups is encrypted.

Ensuring that backups are maintained off site (or as allowed by the nature of the data) in fireproof cabinets.

Ensuring that correct power, UPSs (uninterruptible power supply), air conditioning and fire prevention are available for hardware.

Ensuring the appointment of an incident management team.

Implementing and testing a major incident process.

Implementing an escalation process for reporting emergencies.

Considering specific service continuity risks and taking action to deal with them, for example by ensuring residence of the network and key servers and by ensuring that hot drinks are not allowed in the data room.

Having appropriate service continuity plans and procedures in place.

Ensuring relevant staff are aware of the service continuity plans and procedures.

Periodically testing all service continuity plans.

Notifying the customer of the results of the service continuity tests and any actions which will be taken to remedy problems revealed as a result of the test.

Documenting service continuity procedures and ensuring that valid recovery contracts are in place.

Security management

Appointing security staff with specific roles for ensuring compliance by the supplier with its security obligations.

Security tests

Carrying out regular and adequate stress testing and penetration testing.

Security documentation and reporting

Providing to the customer physical and technical access logs.

Providing reports to the customer on any security breach together with remedial action taken.

Ensuring that security breaches by staff are quickly investigated and penalised so that the security procedures do not lose credibility with staff.

Liaising with the customer representative responsible for reporting to regulatory and other bodies, for example the Information Commissioner and the FSA.

Documenting how customers of the customer will be notified of breaches of security, where relevant.

In the public sector, documenting the process to be followed by the supplier if it receives a freedom of information ("FOI") request.

Documenting all security procedures.

Insurance

Ensuring that relevant general liability policies have data protection and privacy extensions or taking out tailor-made insurance policies for these risks.

The supplier will usually accept responsibility for compliance with confidentiality and security obligations by its subcontractors and will ensure that they commit to back-to-back arrangements, mirroring the supplier's obligations under the main agreement.

32.3.3 Prior to signature of the agreement – remedies for breach of security requirements

As well as specifying the security requirements in the agreement, the customer may also want to include specific remedies for breaches of security or loss of data.

If the customer's data is lost, it will need to be restored from backups. Which party is better suited to restore the data will depend upon the facts of the case. If the supplier is responsible for taking backups and providing technical support for the customer's IT systems, then it may be appropriate for the supplier to be responsible for restoring the data. This applies irrespective of who caused the loss of data, as in any event the customer will need its data. However, if the loss has not been caused by the supplier, then the supplier may expect to be able to charge for restoring the data. The customer may want to have the right to restore the data if the supplier fails to do so within a certain period.

The customer may require the supplier to indemnify it against breaches by the supplier of its security obligations and want the supplier to accept a higher limit of liability or unlimited liability for damages caused by security breaches. The customer may also want an express right to terminate the agreement for breaches of security.

32.3.4 During the term

The customer will need to monitor the supplier's compliance with its security obligations. This may involve the supplier self-certifying that it is complying with the relevant obligations. The customer may require the supplier to notify it of security breaches. The customer may want to audit the supplier to ensure that it is complying with the agreed security measures – this may involve carrying out spot checks to see if security measures are being complied with.[16]

The parties will need to review the security requirements on an ongoing basis (particularly when the services or the security risks or threats change) and agree appropriate changes to these requirements.

32.3.5 On termination

The supplier may have specific security obligations which apply on termination, such as that all confidential information and customer data be returned to it or be destroyed.

32.4 Customer's confidentiality and security obligations

32.4.1 During the procurement stage

Chapter 3 discusses the supplier's confidentiality concerns during the procurement stage.

32.4.2 During the term

The supplier will want to document what information it regards as its confidential information and include in the contract an obligation for the customer to keep the information confidential. This should not be contentious.

16 *See* Section 10.14 for a detailed discussion of audit rights.

In the public sector, the supplier may want the customer to agree a list of commercially sensitive information which the supplier does not wish the customer to disclose under the Freedom of Information Act 2000. The customer may want to negotiate the list and confirm that the agreement of any list is without prejudice to its obligation to comply with the Freedom of Information Act 2000 itself.

The situation is slightly more complicated if the supplier wishes the customer to take responsibility for the actions of third parties. In local authority situations, the customer will have to disclose details relating to the proposed arrangement to its elected members but will not want to take responsibility for the actions of the elected members, as it has no control over them.

All public sector bodies will have to ensure that confidentiality provisions enable them to disclose information to their auditors and to other regulators who may investigate them. Suppliers who work for public sector customers need to understand and cooperate with public sector audit requirements.

The supplier may also want the customer to commit to maintaining specified security measures to protect the supplier's assets and data, including some measures similar to those specified in section 32.2.2 above.

32.4.3 On termination

Confidentiality issues are more likely to be contentious on termination. The customer will be anxious to make sure that it will have access to the information that it requires to ensure that the services can be provided by the customer itself or by a successor supplier. However, the supplier will want to ensure that its proprietary procedures and information, which it regards as giving it competitive advantage over other suppliers, will not be disclosed. Usually, these issues are resolved in the context of the specific circumstances of the outsourcing arrangement, before the agreement is signed.

32.5 Publicity

In private sector outsourcing arrangements, it is common for the customer and supplier to agree that neither party will publicise the outsourcing arrangement without the approval of the other side. Suppliers may want to be able to refer to the customer's agreement in their marketing material but be particularly anxious to ensure that customers do not publicise security breaches by the supplier.

In the public sector, the situation is more complex, in that a public sector body may want to reserve the right to publicise the agreement in accordance with any legal obligation and to comment on issues relating to the contract when it is deemed appropriate politically. However, the supplier may be extremely reluctant to allow the customer a right to comment on the outsourcing arrangement in circumstances where the supplier has no right to respond.

32.6 Security and data protection issues in the financial services sector and the public sector

This chapter has described general data protection and security regulations and issues. Firms in the financial services sector are subject to additional regulation in the form of EU directives and FSA regulations, some of which relate to security issues. They are also subject to the supervision of the FSA, which has enforcement powers far in excess of those of the Information Commissioner.[17] These aspects of FSA regulation and others are described in the following chapter.

Security issues relating to the public sector are described in Chapter 36.

17 For example, in December 2007, the FSA fined a company £1.26 million for exposing its customers to fraud.

Part Ten – Regulations

Chapter 33

Financial Services Sector

33.1 Outline

Chapters 33 to 37 describe regulations that will be relevant for specific sectors (the financial services sector, the public sector and the utilities sector), highlighting in addition any lessons that organisations which are not subject to such regulations can learn from the approach taken in the regulations.

This chapter deals with the growing amount of regulation of the financial services sector, including:

(a) EU regulation of banks and fund managers (i.e. the Capital Requirements Directive ("CRD") and the Markets in Financial Instruments Directive ("MiFID"));
(b) general FSA regulation;
(c) application of general FSA regulation to security;
(d) specific FSA regulation for insurance companies (i.e. CP142); and
(e) international and sector-specific regulation.

The EU directives and the international regulation referred to above will be relevant throughout the EU, although this chapter also explains how the relevant directives have been implemented within the UK. The other FSA regulations mentioned in this chapter will apply to the UK only. Part twelve of this book describes how the above EU directives have been implemented in key EU countries and other relevant regulation in the financial services sector in that country.

In its 2009 Financial Risk Outlook, published in February 2009, the FSA in the UK outlined the main risks facing firms, consumers and the regulatory system in the economic downturn. It stressed (*inter alia*) the risks of outsourcing:

> "The risk involved in outsourcing functions to third-party service providers is another risk that is exacerbated by the continued volatility in market conditions. In these challenging times it is of great importance that effective oversight and risk management of third-party service providers continues to be exercised. It is also important that firms are aware of the risks posed by the concentrated exposure to a small number of vendors providing critical services (e.g. of pre/post-trade compliance systems), and to ensure that firms have contingency plans in place to deal with interruption of service."[1]

Firms in the financial services sector who enter into outsourcing arrangements should note that, since 2006, the FSA has changed its strategy in dealing with breaches of FSA regulation. Prior

1 Insolvency issues are dealt with in Chapter 26.

to 2006, it was rare for the FSA to pursue enforcement action against individual approved persons,[2] preferring instead to discipline the authorised firms themselves. Since 2006, whenever a firm is suspected of breaching its regulatory requirements the FSA will take a close look to see whether the relevant approved person has fulfilled his duties. If he has not, then the FSA can pursue disciplinary action against the relevant individual, leading to an unlimited fine and possible prohibition from acting as an approved person in the future. Individuals must pay fines from their own pockets as authorised firms are not permitted to indemnify their approved persons against fines and insurance cannot be purchased to cover fines. This means that it is particularly critical for approved persons to ensure that their authorised firms comply with relevant FSA regulation (including the regulations described in this chapter as applying to outsourcing).

33.2 Key themes

It should be borne in mind that the regulations and guidance affecting outsourcing are several hundred pages in length. This chapter summarises the key issues covered by the relevant regulations. It cannot be comprehensive. In particular, this chapter focuses on the following key themes in the outsourcing regulations:

(a) outsourcing policies;
(b) processes and systems;
(c) notification to the FSA;
(d) due diligence;
(e) written agreement between service provider and firm;
(f) control over service provider's employees and subcontractors;
(g) service management;
(h) change management;
(i) disclosure and audit;
(j) confidential information, intellectual property rights ("IPR") and security;
(k) business continuity;
(l) rights of termination;
(m) termination assistance; and
(n) offshore outsourcing.

It does not deal with specific issues such as those relating to the outsourcing of a controlled function, outsourcing of a firm's internal audit function, use of third-party processors in home finance and insurance or use of a rating system or data.

The full text of the FSA regulations can be found on the FSA's website (www.fsa.gov.uk).

2 Under the approved persons regime in the UK, any person conducting "controlled functions" within the firm is required to obtain individual permission from the FSA to do so. If the FSA is not satisfied that the individual is "fit and proper" to conduct those functions then it will refuse the application to become an approved person.

33.3 Definition of outsourcing

Outsourcing is defined (in accordance with the MiFID Implementing Directive[3]) as:

> "an arrangement of any form between a firm and a service provider by which that service provider performs a process, a service or an activity which would otherwise be taken by the firm itself."[4]

33.4 Outsourcing by banks and investment firms - MiFID

33.4.1 Background to MiFID

MiFID replaced the Investment Services Directive. It is part of the EU's Financial Services Action Plan, which is intended to create an integrated market for financial services throughout the EU, in which investors are effectively protected and the efficiency and integrity of the overall market are safeguarded.

33.4.2 Application

33.4.2.1 Application to firms

Outsourcing by retail banks, investment banks, venture capital firms, stockbrokers, investment managers, proprietary trading firms, corporate finance firms, wholesale market brokers and the providers of custody services that provide investment services or which undertake investment activities will be governed by MiFID.

33.4.2.2 Definition of investment services and activities

Investment services are covered by MiFID. Investment services and activities include (Annex 1 Section A of MiFID):

- (a) reception and transmission of orders in relation to one or more financial instruments;
- (b) execution of orders on behalf of clients;
- (c) dealing on own account;
- (d) portfolio management;
- (e) investment advice;
- (f) underwriting of financial instruments and/or placing of financial instruments on a firm commitment basis;
- (g) placing of financial instruments without a firm commitment basis; and
- (h) operation of multilateral trading facilities.

33.4.2.3 Ancillary services

Some of the ancillary services are not regulated activities under the Regulated Activities

3 Commission Directive No. 2006/73/EC Implementing Directive 2004/39/EC of the European Parliament and of the Council as regards organisational requirements and operating conditions for investment firms and defined terms for the purposes of that Directive ("MiFID Implementing Directive").

4 Article 2(6) of the MiFID Implementing Directive.

Order ("RAO"). Other ancillary services are covered by MiFID. Where ancillary services are covered by MiFID, an investment firm can apply for passporting[5] rights that include ancillary services, but only if these are carried on together with one or more investment services and activities.

Ancillary services include (Annex 1 Section B of MiFID):

(a) safekeeping and administration of financial instruments for the account of clients, including custodianship and related services such as cash/collateral management;
(b) granting credits or loans to an investor to allow them to carry out a transaction in one or more financial instruments, where the firm granting the credit or loan is involved in the transaction;
(c) advice to undertakings on capital structure, industrial strategy and related matters and advice and services relating to mergers and the purchase of undertakings;
(d) foreign exchange services where these are connected to the provision of investment services;
(e) investment research and financial analysis or other forms of general recommendation relating to transactions in financial instruments;
(f) services related to underwriting; and
(g) investment services and activities as well as ancillary services of the type included under Section A or B of Annex 1 related to the underlying of the derivatives included under Section C – 5, 6, 7 and 10 – where these are connected to the provision of investment or ancillary services.

33.4.3 Exemptions

There are various exemptions from the application of MiFID, for example:

(a) Article 2 MiFID contains various exemptions relevant to a wide range of persons, services and activities including insurers, group treasurers, members of professions providing incidental investment services, professional investors who invest only for themselves, company pension schemes, collective investment undertakings and their operators, commodity producers, commodity traders and locals; and
(b) Article 3 MiFID creates an optional exemption for certain receivers, transmitters and advisers who do not hold client money or securities and comply with other prescribed conditions.

A key point to note here is that this does not relate to outsourcing by the fund itself, assuming the fund to be outside the MiFID jurisdiction (e.g. the Cayman Islands). Only the firm itself is caught to the extent that its critical functions are outsourced.

33.4.4 Levels of legislation

MiFID is a so-called "Lamfalussy Directive". This is a type of legislation that follows a process to allow the Council of Ministers and Parliament to focus on key political decisions. The technical implementing details are worked through afterwards. This is why the Directive is split into two levels.

5 Passporting permits a firm which has the right to perform a particular function in one EU country to perform the same function in another EU country (a "third country").

The level 1 Directive is intended to set out broad, general "framework" principles.

The level 2 Directive contains "technical implementing measures". The intention is that level 2 implementing measures should be used more frequently, to ensure that the technical provisions can be kept up to date with market and supervisory developments. Regulators are expected to issue interpretative guidance on provisions in the level 2 Directive to clarify the practical application of the requirements in the Directive. The Commission and the Committee of European Securities Regulators ("CESR") may also issue guidance on the Directive. CESR has the mandate under MiFID to provide level 2 technical advice. Its advice will be transcribed into legislation and from there it will flow into the implementation procedures adopted by the regulator in each EU Member State. CESR consists of a number of members. The UK representative on level 2 consultations is the FSA. The FSA has a role both in providing advice on outsourcing issues under MiFID and then in the subsequent implementation. The technical advice committees of CESR are made up of industry representatives from various Member States. They, in turn, bring with them familiarity with the local regulatory positions.

The level 1 Directive came into force on 30 April 2004. The level 2 Directive came into force on 1 November 2007. However, both Directives apply retrospectively to agreements signed before these dates.

33.4.5 Key elements of the level 1 Directive relating to outsourcing

Table 44 summarises some of the key elements of the level 1 legislation.

Table 44 *MiFID level 1 Directive*

Article 13(5) – Critical outsourcing – obligation to avoid undue additional operational risk

A firm must take reasonable steps to avoid undue additional operational risk arising from the outsourcing of critical operational functions.

Critical operational functions are defined as those operational functions which are critical for the provision of continuous and satisfactory service to clients and the performance of investment activities on a continuous and satisfactory basis.

A firm must ensure that outsourcing of "important" operational functions is not carried out in a way which materially impairs the quality of a firm's internal controls or the regulator's ability to monitor the firm's compliance with its obligations.

Article 13(2) – Outsourcing of investment services – obligation to have adequate policies and procedures

The firm must establish adequate policies and procedures sufficient to ensure compliance of the firm including its managers and employees and tied agents with its obligations under the Directive, as well as appropriate rules governing personal transactions by such persons.

33.4.6 Other relevant requirements

The Directive contains other general organisational requirements which are of general application but which will also be relevant to a firm considering an outsourcing project. These are described in Table 45.

Table 45 *Other relevant requirements*

Business continuity

The firm must take reasonable steps to ensure continuity and regularity in the performance of investment services and activities (Article 13(4)).

General requirements

The firm must have sound administrative and accounting procedures, internal control mechanisms, effective procedures for risk assessment and effective control and safeguard arrangements for information processing systems (Article 13(5)).

33.4.7 Key elements of the level 2 Directive

The following paragraphs summarise some of the key provisions in the level 2 Directive.

33.4.7.1 When outsourcing is permitted

The MiFID Implementing Directive specifies that regulators should not make the authorisation to provide investment services or activities subject to a general prohibition on the outsourcing of one or more critical or important functions or investment services or activities. Investment firms should be allowed to outsource such activities if the outsourcing arrangements established by the firm comply with certain conditions (*see* 33.4.7.5 below).

However, if the outsourcing of critical or important operational functions or investment services or activities would lead to a delegation of functions to such an extent that the firm becomes a "letter-box entity" then this should be considered to undermine the firm's authorisation conditions. (Article 5 MiFID)

33.4.7.2 Notification

The outsourcing of investment services or activities of critical and important functions is capable of constituting a material change of the conditions for the authorisation of the investment firm, as referred to in Article 16(2) of Directive 2004/39/EC. If such outsourcing arrangements are to be put in place after the firm has obtained an authorisation, the outsourcing arrangements should be notified to the competent authority where required by Article 16(2) of Directive 2004/39/EC.

33.4.7.3 Risk management policy

The preamble to the MiFID Implementing Directive makes it clear that outsourcing is of such concern that it is necessary to "specify concrete organisational requirements and procedures for investment firms involved in outsourcing".

This takes the form of a requirement for a firm to establish, implement and maintain an adequate risk management policy that should cover risks associated with the outsourcing of critical or important functions or of investment services or activities. Such risks should include those associated with the firm's relationship with the service provider and the potential risks posed where the outsourced activities of multiple investment firms or other regulated entities are concentrated within a limited number of suppliers.

33.4.7.4 Meaning of critical and important operational functions

An operational function shall be regarded as critical or important if a defect or failure in its performance would materially impair the continuing compliance of an investment firm with the conditions and obligations of its authorisation or its other obligations under Directive 2004/39/ EC, or its financial performance, or the soundness or the continuity of its investment services and activities.

The following functions shall not be considered as critical or important:

(a) the provision to the firm of advisory services, and other services which do not form part of the investment business of the firm, including the provision of legal advice to the firm, the training of personnel of the firm, billing services and the security of the firm's premises and personnel; and
(b) the purchase of standardised services, including market information services and the provision of price feeds. (Article 13)

33.4.7.5 Role of the firm

The firm must remain fully responsible for discharging all of its regulatory obligations and comply, in particular, with the following conditions:

(a) the outsourcing must not result in the delegation by senior management of its responsibility;
(b) the relationship and obligations of the firm towards its clients under the terms of MiFID must not be altered;
(c) the conditions with which the firm must comply in order to be authorised in accordance with Article 5 of MIFID, and to remain so, must not be undermined; and
(d) none of the other conditions subject to which the firm's authorisation was granted must be removed or modified. (Article 14)

33.4.7.6 Managing the outsourcing relationship under MiFID

Firms must exercise due skill, care and diligence when entering into, managing or terminating any arrangement for the outsourcing to a service provider of critical or important operational functions or of any investment services or activities (SYSC 8.1.7). The firm must retain the necessary expertise to supervise the outsourced functions effectively and manage the risks associated with the outsourcing and must supervise those functions and manage those risks.

In particular, the firm must comply with the management requirements in Table 46.

Table 46 *Managing the outsourcing arrangement under MiFID*

Due diligence

The firm must ensure the service provider has the ability, capacity and any authorisation required by law to perform the outsourced functions, services or activities reliably and professionally. (Article 14.2(a), implemented in SYSC 8.1.8R(1))

Service management – standard of performance

The service provider must carry out the outsourced services effectively, and, to this end, the firm must establish methods for assessing the standard of performance of the service provider. (Article 14.2(b), implemented in SYSC 8.1.8R(2))

Service management – supervision

The firm must properly supervise the carrying out of the outsourced functions, and adequately manage the risks associated with the outsourcing. (Article 14.2(c), implemented in SYSC 8.1.8R(3))

Service management – appropriate action

In managing the outsourcing arrangement, the firm should take the appropriate action if it appears that the service provider may not be carrying out the functions effectively and in compliance with applicable laws and regulatory requirements. (Article 14.2(d), implemented in SYSC 8.1.8R(4))

Disclosure

The service provider must disclose to the investment firm any development that may have a material impact on its ability to carry out the outsourced functions effectively and in compliance with applicable laws and regulatory requirements. (Article 14.2(f), implemented in SYSC 8.1.8R(6))

Audit

The service provider must cooperate with the competent authorities of the investment firm in connection with the outsourced activities. (Article 14.2(h), implemented in SYSC 8.1.8R(8))

The investment firm, its auditors and the relevant competent authorities must have effective access to data related to the outsourced activities, as well as to the business premises of the service provider, and the competent authorities must be able to exercise those rights of access. (Article 14.2(i), implemented in SYSC 8.1.8R(9))

The service provider must make available on request to the regulator all information necessary to enable the authority to supervise the compliance of the performance of the outsourced activities with the requirements of the MiFID Implementing Directive. (Article 14.5, implemented in SYSC 8.1.11R)

Maintenance of records of personal transactions

The investment firm must ensure that the firm to which an activity is outsourced maintains a record of personal transactions entered into by any relevant person and provides that information to the investment firm promptly on request (Article 12 (2), implemented in COBS 11.7.4R(2)B)

Confidential information

The service provider must protect any confidential information relating to the investment firm and its clients. (Article 14.2(j), implemented in SYSC 8.1.8R(10))

Business continuity

The investment firm and the service provider must establish, implement and maintain a contingency plan for disaster recovery and periodic testing of backup facilities, where that is necessary having regard to the function, service or activity that has been outsourced. (Article 14.2(k), implemented in SYSC 8.1.8R(11))

Termination

The firm must be able to terminate the arrangement for outsourcing where necessary without detriment to the continuity and quality of its provision of services to clients. (Article 14.2(g), implemented in SYSC 8.1.8R(7))

Written agreement

The respective rights and obligations of the investment firms and of the service provider must be clearly allocated and set out in a written agreement. (Article 14.3, implemented in SYSC 8.1.9R)

33.4.7.7 Intra-group outsourcing

MiFID applies to intra-group outsourcing arrangements. However, if the investment firm and the service provider are members of the same group, the investment firm may take into account the extent to which the firm controls the service provider or has the ability to influence its actions when considering the application of the conditions to the outsourcing arrangements. (Article 14.4, implemented in SYSC 8.1.10R)

33.4.7.8 Retail client portfolio management

When an investment firm outsources the investment service of portfolio management provided to retail clients to a service provider located in a third country, that investment firm must ensure that the following conditions are satisfied (Article 15(1), implemented in SYSC 8.2.1R):

(a) the service provider must be authorised or registered in its home country to provide that service and must be subject to prudential supervision; and
(b) there must be an appropriate cooperation agreement between the competent authority of the investment firm and the supervisory authority of the service provider.

If these conditions are not satisfied, a firm must give prior notification to its regulator about the outsourcing arrangement. The notification must include:

(a) details about which of the conditions is not met;

(b) if applicable, details and evidence of the supplier's authorisation or regulation, including the regulator's contact details;
(c) the firm's proposals for meeting its obligations under SYSC on an ongoing basis;
(d) why the firm wishes to outsource to the supplier;
(e) a draft of the outsourcing agreement between the supplier and the firm;
(f) the proposed start date of the outsourcing arrangement; and
(g) confirmation that the firm has had regard to the guidance in Table 47 below, or if it has not, why not.

Table 47 *Retail client portfolio management – FSA guidance*

Subcontracting

If the outsourcing allows the supplier to subcontract any of the services to be provided under the outsourcing, any such subcontracting shall not affect the supplier's responsibilities under the outsourcing agreement. (SYSC 8.3.4G)

Termination

The firm should be entitled to terminate the outsourcing if the supplier undergoes a change of control or becomes insolvent, goes into liquidation or receivership (or equivalent in its home state) or is in persistent material default under the agreement. (SYSC 8.3.5G)

The following should be taken into account where the supplier is not authorised or registered in its home country and/or not subject to prudential supervision.

Voluntary regulation

The firm should examine, and be able to demonstrate, to what extent the supplier may be subject to any form of voluntary regulation, including self-regulation in its home state. (SYSC 8.3.6(1)G)

Sufficient, competent resources

The supplier must be obliged to devote sufficient, competent resources to providing the service. (SYSC 8.3.6(2)G)

Disclosure

In addition to the requirement to ensure that a supplier discloses any developments that may have a material impact on its ability to carry out the outsourcing (SYSC 8.1.8R(6)), where the conditions are not met, the developments to be disclosed should include, without limitation (SYSC 8.3.6(3)G):

(a) any adverse effect that any laws or regulations introduced in the supplier's home country may have on its carrying on the outsourced activity; and
(b) any changes to its capital reserve levels or its prudential risks.

Ability to meet liabilities

The firm should satisfy itself that the supplier is able to meet its liabilities as they fall due and that it has positive net assets.

Annual reports and accounts

The firm should require that the supplier prepares annual reports and accounts which:

(a) are in accordance with the supplier's national law which, in all material respects, is the same as or equivalent to the international accounting standards; and
(b) have been independently audited and reported on in accordance with the supplier's national law which is the same as or equivalent to international auditing standards.

Audited annual report and accounts

The firm should receive copies of each set of the audited annual report and accounts of the supplier. If the supplier expects or knows its auditor will qualify his report on the audited report and accounts, or add an explanatory paragraph, the supplier should be required to notify the firm without delay. (SYSC 8.3.6(6)G)

Confidential information

The firm should satisfy itself, and be able to demonstrate, that it has in place appropriate procedures to ensure that it is fully aware of the supplier's controls for protecting confidential information. (SYSC 8.3.6(7)G)

In addition to the requirement at SYSC 8.1.8R(10) that the supplier must protect any confidential information relating to the firm or its clients, the outsourcing agreement should require the supplier to notify the firm immediately if there is a breach of confidentiality. (SYSC 8.3.6(8)G)

Governing law

The outsourcing agreement should be governed by the law and subject to the jurisdiction of an EEA state. (SYSC 8.3.6(9)G)

The following should be taken into account by a firm where there is no cooperation agreement between the FSA and the supervisory authority of the supplier or there is no supervisory authority of the supplier.

Provision of Information

The outsourcing agreement should ensure the firm can provide the FSA with any information relating to the outsourced activity that the FSA may require in order to carry out effective supervision. The firm should therefore assess the extent to which the supplier's regulator and/or local laws and regulations may restrict access to information about the outsourced activity. Any such restriction should be described in the notification to be sent to the FSA. (SYSC 8.3.7(1)G)

The outsourcing agreement should require the supplier to provide the firm's offices in the UK with all requested information required to meet the firm's regulatory obligations. The FSA should be given an enforceable right to obtain such information from the firm and to require the supplier to provide the information directly. (SYSC 8.3.7(1)G)

The guidance applies whether a firm outsources portfolio management directly or indirectly via a third party. The firm must only notify the FSA of the arrangement once it has carried out due diligence regarding the supplier and has taken into account the FSA guidance in Table 46.

If a firm can demonstrate that it has taken the guidance in Table 46 into account and has satisfactorily concluded that it would be able to continue to satisfy the common platform outsourcing rules and provide adequate protection for consumers despite not satisfying the conditions, the FSA is unlikely to object to the outsourcing arrangement. (SYSC 8.3.3G)

The regulator is not expected to authorise or otherwise approve any such arrangement or its terms. The purpose of the notification, rather, is to ensure that the competent authority has the reasonable time to intervene in appropriate cases. It is the responsibility of the investment firm to negotiate the terms of any outsourcing arrangement, and to ensure that those terms are consistent with the obligations of the firm, without the formal intervention of the competent authority.

The firm's notice must include adequate details of the outsourcing arrangement. The FSA may seek further information about the outsourcing proposal.

The firm may enter into the outsourcing arrangement if it has not received notice of objection or a request for further information from the FSA within one month. (SYSC 8.2.4G)

Where the FSA has not objected to the outsourcing agreement, the firm should notify the FSA of any matters which could affect the firm's ability to provide adequate services to its customers or could result in serious detriment to its customers or where there has been material change in the information previously provided to the FSA in relation to the outsourcing. (SYSC 8.2.9G)

33.4.7.9 Other relevant requirements

The level 2 Directive contains other organisational requirements which are of general application, but which will also be relevant to outsourcing arrangements. These are described in Table 48.

Table 48 *Level 2 Directive – other relevant requirements*

General organisational requirements

Taking into account the nature, scale and complexity of the business of the firm, and the nature and range of the investment services and activities undertaken in the course of that business, a firm must (Article 5(1) final paragraph, implemented in SYSC 4.1.4R):

(a) establish, implement and maintain adequate internal control mechanisms designed to secure compliance with decisions and procedures at all levels of the firm (Article 5(1)(c)); and
(b) establish, implement and maintain effective internal reporting and communication of information at all relevant levels of the firm (Article 5(1)(e)).

Business continuity

A firm must establish, implement and maintain an adequate contingency and business continuity policy aimed at ensuring, in the case of an interruption to its systems and procedures, the preservation of essential data and functions, and the maintenance of investment services and activities, or, where that is not possible, the timely recovery of such data and functions and the timely resumption of its investment services and activities. (Article 5(3), implemented in SYSC 4.1.7R)

Regular monitoring

A firm must monitor and, on a regular basis, evaluate the adequacy and effectiveness of its systems, internal control mechanisms and arrangements established and take appropriate measures to address any deficiencies. (Article 5(5), implemented in SYSC 4.1.10R)

General

The systems, internal control mechanisms and arrangements established by a firm must take into account the nature, scale and complexity of its business and the nature and range of investment services and activities undertaken in the course of that business. (Article 5(1) final paragraph, implemented in SYSC 5.1.13R)

A firm must monitor and, on a regular basis, evaluate the adequacy and effectiveness of its systems, internal control mechanisms and arrangements established in accordance with this chapter, and take appropriate measures to address any deficiencies. (Article 5(5), implemented in SYSC 5.1.14R)

33.5 Outsourcing by banks and investment firms - Capital Requirements Directive ("CRD")

33.5.1 Introduction to the CRD

The CRD consists of the recast Capital Adequacy Directive ("recast CAD") and the recast Banking Consolidation Directive ("recast BCD").

33.5.2 Application

Broadly, the CRD applies to credit institutions and investment firms to which MiFID applies. Most banks and fund managers will therefore need to comply with the CRD, unless an exemption applies.

The FSA proposes certain exemptions. For example, broadly speaking, a UCITS management firm will be regarded as a limited licence firm and will therefore be exempt from the requirement to hold capital to cover operational risk.

33.5.3 Robust governance arrangements

Article 22 of the recast BCD requires that credit institutions have robust governance arrangements with a clear organisational structure, well-defined, transparent and consistent lines of responsibility and adequate internal control mechanisms.

These requirements also apply to all outsourcing arrangements, including non-MiFID business whether of critical or important functions or not.

33.5.4 Business continuity

BCD Annex V, paragraph 13 states that a firm must have a contingency and business continuity policy in place aimed at ensuring its ability to operate on an ongoing basis and limiting losses in the event of severe business disruption.

33.5.5 Outsourcing fees as part of the relevant indicator

The full implications of CRD are not discussed in this Guide. However, it is important for reporting requirements to note that the fee relating to outsourcing can be deducted from the relevant indicator when the outsourcing is to a third party which is:

(a) a parent or subsidiary of the firm whose process, service or activity is being outsourced, or a subsidiary of the parent which is also the parent of the firm; or
(b) subject to supervision under, or equivalent to, the CRD.

Otherwise, fees paid for outsourcing shall be included in operating expenses (and so not deducted from the relevant indicator).

If a firm falls within the scope of the CRD, the proposals set out above represent an opportunity for firms to reduce their regulatory capital as a result of the outsourcing of services, provided the services are either outsourced to a group company or a service provider that is subject to supervision under the CRD or equivalent prudential capital regulation. For service providers to firms, the FSA is obviously concerned that there is no outflow of regulatory capital from banking and financial services systems and so service providers that are subject to the CRD (or equivalent) will need to calculate their indicator, taking into account the services they are providing, in the usual way.

It is assumed that, in determining whether a service provider is subject to supervision under, or equivalent to, the CRD, this means that the service provider must be subject to supervision in respect of the activities outsourced. This may be problematic, for example, where functions such as transfer agency are outsourced to jurisdictions such as the US.

33.5.6 Timetable

From 1 January 2007, CRD firms had to comply with the CRD provisions for systems and controls (SYSC Chapter 3) and continue to apply the existing SYSC provisions until they moved to the common platform. The common platform provisions applied to all CRD firms from 1 November 2007 but firms had the option to adopt them earlier in 2007 if they wished to do so for practical reasons.

33.6 Implementation of MiFID in the UK

33.6.1 Impact of MiFID

From an outsourcing perspective, MiFID did not introduce a substantially different position, as insurers, banks and building societies had previously been regulated by the outsourcing provisions in the Interim Prudential Sourcebook for Insurers, Interim Prudential Sourcebook for Banks and the Interim Prudential Sourcebook for Building Societies (respectively). Investment services had not previously been regulated but many fund managers had in practice implemented similar protections as they regarded that the regulations represented good practice.

33.6.2 General approach – no super-equivalence

The FSA's general approach to implementing CRD and MiFID was that rules were based on copied-out Directive text, to avoid the FSA placing any unintended additional obligations on firms. For this reason, Table 44, which describes the MiFID Directives, also lists the sections in the FSA Handbook in which the relevant provisions in the Directives were implemented.

33.6.3 Exception to no super-equivalence – common platform

Despite its intention to limit "super-equivalence", the FSA chose to create a unified set of requirements applying to common platform firms[6] implementing MiFID and CRD as:

(a) both MiFID and CRD cover management oversight, internal governance and systems and controls requirements;
(b) although both MiFID and CRD have independently set requirements for management oversight, internal governance and systems and controls, they share a common approach and their requirements are broadly compatible, even if they are formulated differently;
(c) most firms which are subject to CRD will also be subject to MiFID; and
(d) a unified set of requirements will be simpler and more cohesive.

33.6.4 Exception to no super-equivalence – extension to non-insurers

In December 2007, the FSA proposed (in Chapter 6 of CP07/23) to extend the outsourcing provisions in SYSC 8 to non-scope firms other than insurance companies. The FSA proposed to apply the provisions as guidance except for the key provision, on retaining regulatory responsibility, which would become a rule. The FSA consulted on CP07/23 until 19 March 2008 and

6 Broadly speaking, the following will be subject to the common platform:

(a) investment firms to which MiFID applies;
(b) banks and building societies.

An investment firm for MiFID purposes is any legal person whose regular occupation or business is:

(a) the provision of one or more investment services to third parties; and/or
(b) the performance of one or more investment activities on a professional basis.

responded to the feedback in Policy Statement 08/09. The most important development to arise out of Policy Statement 08/09 was that the FSA decided to exempt non-scope firms' existing material outsourcing arrangements. Non-scope firms need only take the SYSC 8 provisions into account from 1 April 2009 when entering into new material outsourcing arrangements or when existing material outsourcing arrangements are renegotiated.

33.6.5 Exception to no super-equivalence - extension to insurers

The FSA intends to propose extending the common platform to insurers in 2010, subject to the outcome of the Solvency 2 Directive requirements currently under negotiation.

The FSA's proposals to extend the common platform to insurers are a means of standardising provisions in this area.

33.6.6 Exception to no super-equivalence - application of guidance

The FSA decided that the unified standard for outsourcing would apply to common platform firms' outsourcing of critical or important functions relating to:

(a) a firm's MiFID business;
(b) non-MiFID regulated activities;
(c) listed activities under the BCD; and
(d) ancillary services under MiFID.

This goes beyond the MiFID minimum, which is limited to regulating outsourcing of critical or important operational functions related to a firm's MiFID business but is only super-equivalent to the extent that it goes beyond CRD requirements.

33.6.7 Exception to no super-equivalence - extension to non-material outsourcing

The FSA decided that compliance with the general principle in the recast BCD Article 22 (that a firm has robust governance arrangements and adequate internal control mechanisms for example) should cover all outsourcing arrangements (both material and non-material) in relation to the whole of a firm's business. Failure by a firm to have adequate arrangements regarding its outsourcing would be a failure to have robust governance arrangements or internal control mechanisms under Article 22.

The FSA has stated that firms should take the other material outsourcing rules into account, as appropriate and proportionate, for its non-material outsourcing (SYSC 8.1.3).

33.7 MiFID Connect guidelines on outsourcing (May 2007)

33.7.1 MiFID Connect

MiFID Connect is a joint project set up by 11 trade associations to support their members in implementing the Directive. MiFID Connect has published guidelines on implementing MiFID and, in particular, guidelines on applying MiFID to particular circumstances, as described below.

33.7.2 Which activities constitute outsourcing?

The MiFID Connect guidelines suggest that firms should consider the following in deciding whether an activity constitutes outsourcing:

(a) If the firm provides investment services part of which are contracted to a third party, does the client have a direct contract with the third party? If the answer is yes, this should fall outside the definition of outsourcing.
(b) If the firm provides investment services part of which are contracted to a third party, does the client have a direct contract with the third party? If the answer is no, this may fall within the definition of outsourcing.
(c) Is the service by a third party the provision of a particular process, service or activity that is not within the service offered by the firm? If yes, this is not likely to be outsourcing.

The guidelines give the example of a global custodian putting in place a sub-custodian arrangement. This would not be outsourcing. However, if a global custodian delegates its central custody functions by appointing a global custodian, then this would be outsourcing.

33.7.3 Which functions are critical and important?

The MiFID Connect guidelines stress that what is critical or important will be a subjective test and will depend upon the nature and circumstances of a particular firm. However, the guidelines classify the following as likely to be outsourcing and likely to be critical and important:

(a) provision of regular or constant compliance, internal audit, accounting or risk management support;
(b) provision of credit risk control and credit risk analysis;
(c) portfolio administration or portfolio management by a third party;
(d) provision of data storage (physical and electronic);
(e) provision of ongoing, day-to-day systems maintenance/support; and
(f) provision of ongoing, day-to-day software/systems management (e.g. where third party carries out day-to-day functionality and/or runs software or processes on its own systems).

The guidelines classify the following as unlikely to be outsourcing or, if they are outsourcing, unlikely to be critical and important functions:

(a) appointment of sub-custodians;
(b) participation in securities settlement systems and payment systems;
(c) provision of one-off, expert assistance with compliance, internal audit, accounting or risk management issues;
(d) provision of logistical support, for example cleaning, catering and procurement of basic services/products;
(e) provision of human resources support, for example sourcing of temporary employees and processing of payroll;
(f) buying standard software "off the shelf" or engaging a software designer to develop bespoke software; and
(g) reliance on software providers for ad hoc operational assistance in relation to off-the-shelf systems.

33.7.4 Subcontracting

The MiFID Connect guidelines suggest that subcontracting by an outsourcing service provider should require the prior consent of the firm to the possibility and circumstances of any sub-outsourcing and that the firm should ensure that any terms agreed between the service provider and any third party do not contradict the terms of the agreement between the firm and the service provider. SYSC 8.1.9R is used as the basis for this interpretation.

33.7.5 Supervision of services

The MiFID Connect guidelines suggest that a firm can use a number of tools to assess the standard of services including:

(a) agreeing and documenting quantitative and qualitative service level standards/performance targets for the performance of the outsourced functions so as to ensure that the outsourced functions meet the performance and quality standard that would apply if the firm were to perform the relevant activities itself;
(b) putting in place procedures to continuously monitor and assess the performance of the service provider (e.g. scheduling regular update meetings with the service provider, assessing the appropriate frequency and carrying out on-site inspections);
(c) adopting measures to identify and report instances of unsatisfactory performance or non-compliance, such as service delivery reports, self-certification or independent review by auditors; and
(d) imposing regular reporting obligations on the service provider and scheduling update meetings with the service provider to monitor compliance with obligations.

33.7.6 Actions to be taken if services are not provided to an adequate standard

Whether a particular action is "appropriate" will depend on the nature of the breach and the terms of the agreement between the parties. The MiFID Connect guidelines suggest that steps that firms might take in complying with this requirement include:

(a) implementing a service credit regime for non-compliance with performance targets in order to address minor breaches; and
(b) warning the service provider, activating step-in rights or terminating the agreement where a significant or persistent breach is identified.

The requirement for "step-in" rights is frequently referred to as a regulatory obligation. This is not the case – step in is not expressly mentioned in the FSA Handbook. However, the requirement to ensure business continuity may mean that firms need the step-in right in appropriate cases, if it is a practical remedy in practice.

33.7.7 Status of guidance

The MiFID Connect guidelines are not mandatory and are not FSA guidance. In May 2007, however, the FSA confirmed that its supervision of outsourcing by firms will in future take account of the guidance which has been issued by MiFID Connect. This is the first industry-developed guidance recognised by the FSA since publishing its Discussion Paper "FSA confirmation of Industry Guidance" in November 2006.

33.8 Outsourcing by insurance companies - SYSC 13

33.8.1 Application

Outsourcing of services by insurance companies in the UK is subject to guidance in SYSC 13. This will change if the FSA extends the common platform to insurers in 2010, subject to the outcome of the Solvency 2 Directive[7] requirements currently under negotiation as explained in 33.6.3 above. Note that the FSA's view is that SYSC 13.9 on outsourcing covers broadly the same ground as SYSC 8.[8]

33.8.2 Background

33.8.2.1 Application
SYSC 13 covers all outsourcing, including:

(a) non-material outsourcing (although particular care should be taken to manage material outsourcing agreements); and
(b) intra-group outsourcing.

It will be relevant to some extent to other forms of third-party "dependencies" (SYSC 13.9.1G).

SYSC 13 applies to new arrangements and retrospectively to existing contracts (which may have to be renegotiated if they do not satisfy the Policy Statement).

33.8.2.2 Guidance
Operational risk can have a different application for different firms. Therefore, SYSC 13 is drafted in the form of guidance. A firm must assess the appropriateness of the guidance in the light of the scale, nature and complexity of its activities. (SYSC 13.2.2G)

However, the status of a service provider as either a regulated firm or intra-group should not, in itself, necessarily imply a reduced operational risk. (SYSC 13.9.3G)

Table 49 summarises some of the key elements of SYSC 13.

7 Solvency II will involve a number of changes to the way in which insurance firms calculate their regulatory capital and demonstrate operation of their risk management activities, as well as change the way in which they are supervised. Solvency II imposes a requirement that firms remain fully responsible for outsourced activities. UK firms will be required to notify the FSA "prior to the outsourcing of important activities".

8 *See* Policy Statement 08/09.

Table 49 *Key elements of SYSC 13*

Business strategy

The FSA states that, before it enters into an outsourcing contract, the firm should consider the extent to which the outsourcing arrangements support its business strategy. The FSA also adds that the firm should continue to check its business strategy on an ongoing basis throughout the term of the agreement. (SYSC 13.9.4G(1))

Processes and systems

SYSC 13.7.1G states that a firm should ensure that its service provider establishes and maintains appropriate systems and controls for the management of operational risks that can arise from inadequacies or failures in processes and systems. This process might include, but is not limited to, consideration of:

(a) the importance and complexity of the processes and systems used in the end-to-end operating cycle for a firm's products and activities (e.g. whether systems are sufficiently integrated, in particular, for high-volume business);
(b) the controls that will help a firm to prevent system and process failures or identify them to permit prompt rectification (e.g. pre-approval or reconciliation processes);
(c) whether the design and use of a firm's processes and systems allow it to comply adequately with regulatory and other requirements;
(d) a firm's arrangements for the continuity of its operations in the event that a significant process or system becomes unavailable or is destroyed; and
(e) the importance of monitoring indicators of process or system risk (such as reconciliation exceptions, compensation payments, and documentation errors) and experience of operational losses and exposures.

Notification

The FSA reminds firms of their obligations under SUP 15.3.8G(1)(e) to notify the FSA when it intends to enter into a material outsourcing arrangement.

Due diligence of service provider

The FSA highlights the need for firms to carry out appropriate due diligence relating to the service provider's financial stability and expertise. (SYSC 13.9.4G(3))

Risk management

The FSA stresses the importance of firms analysing, before entering into the outsourcing agreement and on an ongoing basis, how the proposed outsourcing will affect their overall risk profile and their ability to meet their regulatory obligations. (SYSC 13.9.4G(1))

The FSA suggests that firms consider whether the arrangements will allow them to monitor and control their exposure to operational risks from outsourcing. (SYSC 13.9.4G(2))

Transition

The FSA states that firms must consider how they will ensure a smooth transition of their operations from their current arrangements to a new or changed outsourcing arrangement. (SYSC 13.9.4G(4))

Service management – control over the outsourced service providers

The FSA reminds firms that, under SYSC 3.2.4G, they cannot contract out of their regulatory obligations and must take reasonable care to supervise the discharge of outsourced functions by the service provider.

In SYSC 13.6.2G, the FSA suggests that firms consider:

(a) the service provider's operational risk culture and variations in risk culture and HR management practices across its operations;
(b) whether the way the service provider's employees are remunerated exposes the firm to the risk that it will not be able to meet its regulatory obligations;
(c) (if the outsourcing involves client-facing processes) the extent to which inadequate or appropriate training exposes clients to the risk of loss or unfair treatment, including by not enabling effective communication with the firm;
(d) compliance with applicable regulatory and statutory requirements relating to the welfare and conduct of the service provider's employees;
(e) the service provider's arrangements for the continuity of operations in the event of unavailability or loss of its employees; and
(f) the relationship between indicators of people loss (such as sickness and turnover rates) and exposure to operational losses.

The guidance stresses this point by adding that, to the extent that it is necessary, a firm should review and consider the adequacy of the staffing arrangements and policies of a service provider. (SYSC 13.6.2G)

Service management

The FSA states that firms should consider the inclusion of reporting and notification requirements, in particular so that the firm can monitor and control its exposure to operational risks. (SYSC 13.9.5G(1))

It states that, in implementing a relationship framework and drafting service level agreements, a firm should consider the need for (SYSC 13.9.6G):

(a) the identification of qualitative and quantitative performance targets to assess the adequacy of service performance;
(b) the evaluation of the service provider's performance through service delivery reports, periodic self-certification or independent review by internal or external auditors; and
(c) remedial action and escalation processes for dealing with inadequate performance.

Service provider's resources

The FSA suggests that firms consider the extent to which exclusivity arrangements are needed to protect access to the service provider's resources. (SYSC 13.9.5G(6))

Change management

The FSA suggests that the firm consider the processes for making changes to the outsourcing arrangement including changes in processing volumes, activities and other contractual terms. (SYSC 13.9.5G(8))

The FSA suggests that the firm consider the conditions under which the firm or service provider can choose to change the outsourcing arrangement, such as:

(a) a change of ownership or control of the service provider or firm;
(b) insolvency or receivership of the service provider or firm, significant change in the business operations of the service provider or firm (including subcontracting); and
(c) inadequate provision of the services may lead to the firm being unable to meet its regulatory obligation. (SYSC 13.9.5G(8))

Audit

The FSA suggests that the firm should consider whether sufficient access to the firm's "books, accounts and vouchers" will be made available to internal auditors, external auditors, actuaries and the FSA under Section 341 FSMA 2000.

In particular, the FSA reminds firms of their obligations under SUP 2.3.5R (access to premises) and SUP 2.3.7R (service providers under material outsourcing arrangements). (SYSC 13.9.5G(2))

The FSA points out that, in certain circumstances, it may be of benefit to seek comfort as to the adequacy and effectiveness of systems and controls in place at the service provider, through the use of externally validated reports commissioned by the service provider itself. However, the use of these reports should not imply that a firm is absolved of the responsibility to maintain any other oversight. In addition, the firm should not normally have to forfeit the right for itself or its agents to gain access to the premises of the service provider. (SYSC 13.9.7G)

Confidentiality and IPR

The FSA suggests that firms consider the need for information ownership rights, confidentiality agreements and Chinese walls to protect client and other information (including on termination). (SYSC 13.9.5G(3))

Security

The FSA points out that failures in the processing of information or the security of the systems on which it is maintained can lead to significant operational exposure, with not only financial but also regulatory, other legal and reputational implications. (SYSC 13.7.7G)

The FSA stresses that a firm should establish and maintain appropriate systems and controls for the management of its information security risks. This might include, but is not limited to, consideration of:

(a) confidentiality: ensuring that information is accessible only to an authorised person or system (this may require firewalls within a system, as well as entry restrictions);
(b) integrity: safeguarding the accuracy and completeness of the information and its processing;
(c) availability: ensuring that an authorised person or system has access to the information when required;
(d) authentication: ensuring that the identity of the person or system processing the information is verified; and
(e) non-repudiation and accountability: ensuring that the person or system that processed the information cannot deny their action. (SYSC 13.7.7G)

The FSA recommends that a firm should consider the adequacy of the systems and controls used to protect the processing and security of its information and may wish to have regard to established security standards such as ISO 17799 (Information Security Management). (SYSC 13.7.8G)

Firm's policies and procedures

The FSA suggests that firms consider the extent to which the service provider must comply with the firm's policies and procedures (e.g. information security). (SYSC 13.9.5G(5))

Business continuity

The FSA clarifies that the high-level requirement in SYSC 3.1.1R for appropriate systems and controls applies at all times, including following the invocation of a business continuity plan (although GEN 1.3 (Emergency) sets out conditions for relief from complying with this rule). (SYSC 13.8.4G)

The FSA stresses that a firm should implement appropriate arrangements to maintain the continuity of its operations. This might include, but is not limited to, the use of:

(a) activities to reduce the likelihood of a disruption, such as succession planning, systems resilience and dual processing; and
(b) activities to reduce the impact of a disruption, such as contingency arrangements and insurance. (SYSC 13.8.6G)

The FSA highlights the need for firms to document appropriate business continuity arrangements. (SYSC 13.8.7G)

In particular, it stresses the need for the firm to ensure that it has appropriate contingency arrangements to allow business continuity in the event of a significant loss of services from the service provider, such as:

(a) a significant loss of resources at the service provider;
(b) financial failure of the service provider; and
(c) unexpected termination of the outsourcing arrangement. (SYSC 13.9.8G)

It points out that firms should consider the extent to which the service provider will provide business continuity for outsourced operations. (SYSC 13.9.5G(6))

It includes a useful suggestion (often overlooked by firms) that where firms are outsourcing the business continuity services themselves, as part of a shared disaster recovery service, they should evaluate the likelihood and impact of multiple calls on shared resources. (SYSC 13.8.8G)

The guidance also points out that firms should consider the concentration risk implications of using a particular service provider, such as the business continuity implications where a single service provider is used by several firms. (SYSC 13.9.4G(5)) Some firms feel that this conflicts with the requirement that firms use experienced service providers, as the most experienced firms are likely to have a higher proportion of the market. In addition, leading service providers may be concerned that this comment could discourage firms from using them.

Lastly, the guidance stresses the need to ensure continued availability of software. (SYSC 13.9.5G(7))

Rights of termination

The FSA reminds firms to consider including in their outsourcing agreements the usual rights for either party to terminate the agreement for insolvency or receivership. (SYSC 13.9.5G(8)(a))

The FSA suggests that firms consider other termination issues, including whether they should have a specific right to terminate the agreement if the inadequate provision of services might lead to the firm being unable to meet its regulatory obligations. (SYSC 13.9.5G(8)(c))

Comment – It is assumed that this is intended to be in addition to the right of the firm to terminate for breach.

The guidance also suggests that firms consider a right of termination for change of ownership or control. (SYSC 13.9.5G(8)(a))

Comment – Although this is not an unusual requirement, it is a contentious issue with service providers as it undermines the value of their business.

Lastly, it suggests that firms consider a right to terminate if there are significant changes in the business operations of the service provider including subcontracting. (SYSC 13.9.5G(8)(b))

Comment – This is also likely to be an extremely contentious issue with service providers.

The FSA also suggests that firms consider whether service providers should have the right to terminate the agreement if there is a change of control or significant change in the business operations at the firm. (SYSC 13.9.5G(8))

Comment – The FSA has included these provisions to cover the situation where the service provider is also an authorised firm or is subject to further regulatory controls for example under competition law. In other situations, it may not be in the customer's interests to include this provision, as any termination of the outsourcing arrangement by the service provider is likely to increase the customer's operational risk.

Comment – Before taking action to terminate under any of the above rights to terminate, the firm will clearly need to consider whether it will be able to ensure a smooth transition on termination.

Termination assistance

The FSA states that firms must consider how they will ensure a smooth transition of their operations on termination of an outsourcing arrangement. The FSA reminds firms that this needs to be considered before entering into the outsourcing arrangement – it is too late to consider termination assistance issues when the agreement is about to expire or be terminated. The guidance stresses the importance of firms reconsidering termination assistance requirements whenever they are about to change the outsourcing arrangements significantly – a point which is often overlooked. (SYSC 13.9.4G(4))

Guarantees and indemnities

The FSA suggests that firms consider the adequacy of any guarantees or indemnities. (SYSC 13.9.5G(4))

Comment – The FSA does not suggest what types of guarantees or indemnities might be regarded as adequate.

Offshore outsourcing

The FSA has specific guidance for offshore outsourcing projects (SYSC 13.7.9G) and reminds firms that they should consider:

(a) the business operating environment of each country, for example the likelihood and impact of political disruptions or cultural differences;
(b) relevant local regulatory and other requirements regarding data protection and transfer;
(c) the extent to which local legal and regulatory requirements may restrict a firm's ability to meet its regulatory requirements in the UK; and
(d) the timeliness of information flows to and from its headquarters and the levels of delegated authority and risk management structures.

33.9 General UK provisions

33.9.1 Introduction

In addition to the EU regulation, there are various general principles and regulations in the FSA Handbook which need to be borne in mind in any UK outsourcing arrangement, although they are of wider application than outsourcing projects. Some of these principles and regulations are of general application and others apply either to common platform firms or insurers. These include provisions in:

(a) the FSA's Principles for Businesses ("PRIN"), which describe firms' fundamental obligations under the regulatory system, including in particular, Principle 3;

(b) the High Level Standards set out in Chapter 4, 8 and 13 the Senior Management Arrangements, Systems and Controls ("SYSC"), which are designed to amplify Principle 3; and
(c) the Supervision Sourcebook ("SUP"), which contains supervisory provisions.

Similar references to outsourcing obligations in IPRU – Banks and IPRU – Building Societies were deleted in January 2007.

33.9.2 High level Principle 3 - organisation of affairs and risk management

Principle 3 sets out the high level principle which requires a firm to take reasonable care to organise and control its affairs responsibly and effectively, with adequate risk management systems (PRIN 2.1). In practice, breach of the other guidance on outsourcing in the FSA Handbook will be seen as breach of Principle 3.

33.9.3 Reputational risk

BIPRU 2.2.62G requires an asset management firm, when assessing reputational risk to consider issues such as how poor customer services can affect its financial position. For example, a firm which has outsourced the management of customer accounts may want to consider the impact on its own reputation of the service provider failing to deliver the service.

33.9.4 Systems and controls

SYSC 3.1.1R requires a firm to take reasonable care to establish and maintain appropriate systems and controls. In an outsourcing context, this means that a firm must obtain sufficient information from the service providers to assess the impact of outsourcing on its systems and controls.[9]

SYSC 3.2 provides guidance on issues which a firm is expected to consider in complying with SYSC 3.1.1R. It includes various guidance on delegation within the firm, which it states is also relevant to external delegation or outsourcing. This guidance includes the following:

> "SYSC 3.2.3G
>
> A firm's governing body is likely to delegate many functions and tasks for the purpose of carrying out its business. When functions or tasks are delegated, either to employees or to appointed representatives, appropriate safeguards should be put in place.
>
> When there is delegation, a firm should assess whether the recipient is suitable to carry out the delegated function or task, taking into account the degree of responsibility involved.
>
> The extent and limits of any delegation should be made clear to those concerned.
>
> There should be arrangements to supervise delegation, and to monitor the discharge of delegates' functions or tasks.

9 FSA CP142/02 discussed the actions a firm should consider.

If cause for concern arises through supervision and monitoring or otherwise, there should be appropriate follow-up action at an appropriate level of seniority within the firm."

SYSC 3.2.6R states that a firm must take reasonable care to establish and maintain effective systems and controls for compliance with applicable requirements and standards under the regulatory system. This includes prevention of financial crime and money laundering.

33.9.5 Internal controls

33.9.5.1 Non-insurers

SYSC 4.1.1R states a common platform firm must have robust governance arrangements, which include a clear organisational structure. The structure should:

(a) be well defined with transparent and consistent lines of responsibility;
(b) have effective processes to identify, manage, monitor and report the risks it is or might be exposed to; and
(c) contain internal control mechanisms, including sound administrative and accounting procedures and effective control and safeguard arrangements for information processing systems.

There are similar provisions applicable to BIPRU firms. BIPRU firms must also ensure that their internal control mechanisms and administrative and accounting procedures permit the verification of compliance with rules adopted in accordance with the Capital Adequacy Directive at all times. (SYSC 4.1.3R)

33.9.5.2 Insurers

SYSC 14.1.27R states that a firm must take reasonable steps to establish and maintain adequate internal controls. The outsourcing of control functions to third parties creates a particular risk and firms should consider the consequences of such actions especially if it would compromise the objectives as set out in SYSC 14.1.28G of:

(a) safeguarding both the assets of the firm and its customers, as well as identifying and managing liabilities;
(b) maintaining the efficiency and effectiveness of its operations;
(c) ensuring the reliability and completeness of all accounting, financial and management information; and
(d) ensuring compliance with its internal policies and procedures as well as all applicable laws and regulations.

33.9.6 Responsibility for regulatory obligations

The FSA is particularly concerned that firms which outsource their activities may suffer some loss of control over them.

SYSC 3.2.4G(1) stresses that a firm cannot contract out of its regulatory obligations. So, for example, under Principle 3, a firm should take reasonable care to supervise the discharge of outsourced functions by its service provider.

SYSC 3.2.4G(2) adds that a firm should take steps to obtain sufficient information from its service provider to enable it to assess the impact of outsourcing on its systems and controls.

33.9.7 Business continuity

SYSC 3.2.19G stresses that a firm should have in place appropriate arrangements, having regard to the nature, scale and complexity of its business, to ensure that it can continue to function and meet its regulatory obligations in the event of an unforeseen interruption. These arrangements should be regularly updated and tested to ensure their effectiveness.

33.9.8 Record keeping

33.9.8.1 Records to be retained

SYSC 3.2.20R requires a firm to take reasonable care to make and retain adequate records. These records must be capable of being reproduced on paper and in the English language unless the records relate to business carried on from an establishment in a country or territory outside the UK. In the latter situation, the records can be in the official language of that country instead of English.

The FSA Handbook includes various detailed record-keeping requirements, which are summarised in Schedule 1 to the Handbook. (SYSC 3.2.22G)

For insurers there are similar provisions in SYSC 14.1.51 to 14.1.64 (*see* below).

33.9.8.2 Retention periods

A firm should have appropriate systems and controls in place to fulfil the firm's regulatory and statutory obligations with respect to adequacy, access, periods of retention and security of records. The general principle is that records should be retained for as long as is relevant for the purposes for which they are made. (SYSC 3.2.21G)

The FSA Handbook contains extensive provisions relating to the retention and treatment of records, each being linked to the type of record or transaction. These general provisions are not covered in this chapter.

33.9.8.3 Security of records

Insurers

In accordance with SYSC 3.2.21G, a firm should have adequate systems and controls for maintaining the security of its records so that they are reasonably safeguarded against loss, unauthorised access, alteration or destruction. (SYSC 14.1.64G)

33.9.8.4 Where records should be retained

Insurers

A firm must keep the records required in SYSC 14.1.53R in the UK, except where they relate to business carried on from an establishment in a country or territory that is outside the UK and they are kept in that country or territory. (SYSC 14.1.60R)

When a firm keeps the records required in SYSC 14.1.53R outside the UK, it must periodically send an adequate summary of those records to the UK. (SYSC 14.1.61R)

33.9.8.5 Storage of records

Insurers

When a firm outsources the storage of some or all of its records to a third-party service provider, it should ensure that these records are readily accessible and can be reproduced within a reasonable time period. The firm should also ensure that these records are stored in compliance with the rules and guidance on record keeping in GENPRU, INSPRU or SYSC. (SYSC 14.1.62G)

A firm may rely on records that have been produced by a third party (e.g. another group company or an external agent, such as an outsourcing service provider). However, where the firm does so, it should ensure that these records are readily accessible and can be reproduced within a reasonable time period. The firm should also ensure that these records comply with the rules and guidance on record keeping in GENPRU, INSPRU or SYSC. (SYSC 14.1.63G)

33.9.9 Notification

Principle 11 of PRIN 2.1 requires a firm to deal with its regulators in an open and cooperative way and to disclose to the FSA appropriately anything relating to the firm of which the FSA would reasonably expect notice.

SUP 15.3.8G clarifies that compliance with Principle 11 includes, but is not limited to, giving the FSA notice of any proposed restructuring, reorganisation or business expansion which could have a significant impact on the firm's risk profile or resources, including, but not limited to entering into, or significantly changing, a material outsourcing arrangement.

In the FSA Handbook, outsourcing is defined (except in SYSC 8) as:

> "the use of a person to provide customised services to a firm other than:
> a member of the firm's governing body acting in his capacity as such; or
> an individual employed by a firm under a contract of service."

A material outsourcing arrangement is defined as:

> "outsourcing services of such importance that weakness, or failure, of the services would cast serious doubt upon a firm's continuing satisfaction of the threshold conditions or compliance with the Principles".

33.9.10 Audit arrangements

The FSA imposes upon firms that enter into material outsourcing agreements an obligation to take reasonable steps to ensure that the service provider:

(a) provides access, with or without notice, during reasonable business hours to any of its business premises (SUP 2.3.5R);

(b) deals in an open and cooperative way with the FSA (SUP 2.3.7R);

(c) makes itself readily available for meetings with the FSA if reasonably requested (SUP 2.3.3G);
(d) gives the FSA reasonable access to any records, files, tapes or computer systems, which are within the service provider's possession or control, and provides any facilities which the FSA reasonably requests (SUP 2.3.3G);
(e) produces to the FSA specified documents, files, tapes, computer data or other material in the service provider's possession or control as reasonably requested (SUP 2.3.3G);
(f) prints information in the service provider's possession or control which is held on computer or on microfilm or otherwise converts it into a readily legible document or any other record which the FSA reasonably requests (SUP 2.3.3G);
(g) permits the FSA to copy documents or other material on the premises of the service provider and to remove copies and hold them elsewhere, or provides any copies, as reasonably requested (SUP 2.3.3G); and
(h) answers truthfully, fully and promptly all questions which are reasonably put to it by representatives or appointees of the FSA (SUP 2.3.3G).

The FSA Handbook acknowledges that, in some circumstances, a firm may find it beneficial to use externally validated reports commissioned by the service provider, to seek comfort as to the adequacy and effectiveness of its systems and controls. The type of report is not specified but could include ISA, SAS[10] and other similar audit standard reports. However, it is stressed that the use of such reports does not absolve the firm of responsibility to maintain any other oversight. In addition, the firm should not normally have to forfeit the right for it or its agents to gain access to the service provider's premises. (SYSC 13.9.7G)

33.9.11 Outsourcing of a controlled function

If the outsourcing services involve the provision of a controlled function, then the outsourcing arrangement falls within the "approved persons" regime. This means that the regulated firm will need to obtain approval from the FSA for any person who performs the controlled function. It is outside the scope of this chapter to describe the approved persons regime in greater detail.

33.9.12 Segregation of duties

Common platform firm

A common platform firm must ensure that the performance of multiple functions by its relevant persons does not and is not likely to prevent those persons from discharging any particular functions soundly, honestly and professionally.[11] (SYSC 5.1.6R)

10 SAS 70 Statement of Accounting Standards, Service Organisations. A SAS 70 statement is an auditing statement which assesses the internal controls of a service provider. There are two types of reports. A Type I report includes the auditor's opinion on the fairness of the presentation of the service organisation's description of controls that had been placed in operation and the suitability of the design of the controls to achieve the specified control objectives. A Type II report includes the information contained in a Type I report and also includes the auditor's opinion on whether the specific controls were operating effectively during the period under review.

11 Article 5(1)g of the MiFID Implementing Directive.

The senior personnel of a common platform firm must define arrangements concerning the segregation of duties within the firm and the prevention of conflicts of interest.[12] (SYSC 5.1.7R)

Insurers

When determining the adequacy of its internal controls, a firm should consider both the potential risks that might hinder the achievement of the objectives listed in SYSC 14.1.28G, and the extent to which it needs to control these risks. More specifically, this should normally include consideration of the need for adequate segregation of duties (*see* SYSC 3.2.5G and SYSC 14.1.30G to SYSC 14.1.33G). (SYSC 14.1.29G)

33.10 Application of general FSA provisions to data security

33.10.1 Background to FSA report

Confidentiality and security are both extremely topical issues at the moment.[13] The FSA has taken a particular interest in this topic. In April 2008, it published a report on "Data Security in Financial Services" following an FSA review of current data security standards.

The report concludes that poor data security is currently a serious, widespread and high-impact risk to the FSA's objective to reduce financial crime. Recent incidents of data loss have brought many firms to consider data security for the first time. Some progress has been made, in that firms are beginning to understand more about this risk and are becoming more assertive in their efforts to contain it. However, there exists a very wide variation between the good practice demonstrated by firms committed to ensuring data security, and the weaknesses seen in firms that are not taking adequate steps to treat fairly the customers whose data they hold. Overall, the report found that data security in financial services firms needs to be improved significantly. Many firms, particularly small firms, still need to make substantial progress to protect their customers from the risk of identity fraud and other financial crime. As a result of the FSA's findings, one firm was referred to the FSA's enforcement division.

33.10.2 Contents of report

The report:

(a) stresses the importance of implementing adequate security measures to ensure compliance with relevant FSA and data protection regulation; and
(b) identifies good practice to share with the industry and highlights areas where improvement is required.

If firms fail to take account of the report and continue to demonstrate poor data security practice, the FSA may refer them to enforcement. The FSA has also declared that it will issue further guidance to supervisors to ensure that data security is reviewed as part of normal supervision.

12 Annex 1 paragraph V of the Banking Consolidation Directive.
13 *See* Chapter 32 for a description of general data protection and security issues.

Although the report is not directed specifically at outsourcing, clearly data security is an extremely important issue in outsourcing agreements[14] and so the following paragraphs summarise the key points made in the report.

33.10.3 FSA and data protection regulations

The report stresses the importance of safekeeping customer data to ensure compliance by the firm with the regulatory obligations described below.

33.10.3.1 FSA Principles for Businesses

The FSA "Principles for Businesses", Principle 2 requires that "a firm must conduct its business with due skill, care and diligence" and Principle 3 states that "a firm must take reasonable care to organise and control its affairs responsibly and effectively, with adequate risk management systems".

33.10.3.2 FSA Rule SYSC 3.2.6R

FSA Rule SYSC 3.2.6R states that:

> "a firm must take reasonable care to establish and maintain effective systems and controls for compliance with applicable requirements and standards under the regulatory system and for countering the risk that the firm might be used to further financial crime".

33.10.3.3 FSA Rule SYSC 3.2.6A

Firms have a responsibility to assess the risks of data loss and take reasonable steps to prevent that risk occurring. SYSC 3.2.6A states that firms' relevant systems and controls must be "comprehensive and proportionate to the nature, scale and complexity of their operations". In essence, firms should put in place systems and controls to minimise the risk that their operations and information assets may be exploited by thieves and fraudsters.

33.10.3.4 "Treating Customers Fairly"

The report highlights that the secure handling of customer data is also part of the "Treating Customers Fairly" standard that all firms must adhere to. Financial services firms, particularly banks, are often the first to be told when a customer becomes the victim of fraud. Indeed, the principal response to financial fraud in the UK is action by firms, mainly through anti-fraud systems and controls that must constantly evolve to counter the threat.

It is good practice for firms to have procedures in place to investigate fraud and help the customer where appropriate. For example, firms can place blocks or anti-fraud flags on an account, change details and passwords and provide advice to the consumer on how they can protect themselves from further fraud.

14 *See* in particular the speech published by Philip Robinson, FSA Director Financial Crime & Intelligence Division, on 26 November 2008, on financial crime, in which he said "Increasing numbers of data loss incidents involve outsourcing".

33.10.3.5 Legal Responsibilities under the Data Protection Act 1998

The Data Protection Act 1998 (DPA 1998) gives legal rights to individuals in respect of personal data processed about them by others. The legal responsibilities of firms in relation to these rights are referred to in Chapter 32. Firms should note that the FSA supports the Information Commissioner's position that it is not appropriate for customer data to be taken off site on laptops or other portable devices which are not encrypted. The FSA may take enforcement action if firms fail to encrypt customer data taken off site.

33.10.4 Examples of Good and Poor Data Security Practice

The report identifies examples of good and poor practice to share with the industry. These examples are listed in Table 50.

Table 50 *Examples of good and poor practice from the FSA Report "Data Security in Financial Services" (April 2008)*

Governance

Good practice

Identification of data security as a key specific risk, subject to its own governance, policies and procedures, and risk assessment.

A senior manager with overall responsibility for data security, specifically mandated to manage data security risk assessment and communication between the key stakeholders within the firm such as: senior management, information security, human resources, financial crime, security, IT, compliance and internal audit.

A specific committee with representation from relevant business areas to assess, monitor and control data security risk, which reports to the firm's board. As well as ensuring coordinated risk management, this structure sends a clear message to all staff about the importance of data security.

Written data security policies and procedures that are proportionate, accurate and relevant to staff's day-to-day work.

An open and honest culture of communication with predetermined reporting mechanisms which make it easy for all staff and third parties to report data security concerns and data loss without fear of blame or recrimination.

Firms seeking external assistance if they feel they do not have the necessary expertise to complete a data security risk assessment themselves.

Firms liaising with peers and others to increase their awareness of data security risk and the implementation of good systems and controls.

Detailed plans for reacting to a data loss including when and how to communicate with affected customers.

Firms writing to affected customers promptly after a data loss, telling them what has been lost and how it was lost.

Firms offering advice on protective measures against identity fraud to consumers affected by data loss and, where appropriate, paying for such services to be put in place.

Poor practice

Treating data security as an IT issue and failing to involve other key staff from across the business in the risk assessment process.

No written policies and procedures on data security.

Firms do not understand the need for knowledge sharing on data security.

Failing to take opportunities to share information with, and learn from, peers and others about data security risk and not recognising the need to do so.

A "blame culture" that discourages staff from reporting data security concerns and data losses.

Failure to notify customers affected by data loss in case the details are picked up by the media.

Training and awareness

Good practice

Simple, memorable and easily digestible guidance for staff on good data security practice.

Testing of staff understanding of data security policies on induction and once a year after that.

Competitions, posters, screensavers and group discussion to raise interest in the subject.

Poor practice

Reliance on staff signing an annual declaration stating that they have read policy documents without any further testing.

Staff being given no incentive to learn about data security.

Staff recruitment and vetting

Good practice

Vetting staff on a risk-based approach, taking into account data security and other fraud risk.

Enhanced vetting – including checks of credit records, criminal records, financial sanctions lists and the CIFAS Staff Fraud Database – for staff in roles with access to large amounts of customer data.

Liaison between HR and financial crime to ensure that financial crime risk indicators are considered during the vetting process.

A good understanding of vetting conducted by employment agencies for temporary and contract staff.

Formalised procedures to assess regularly whether staff in higher-risk positions are becoming vulnerable to committing fraud or being coerced by criminals.

Poor practice

Allowing new recruits to access customer data before vetting has been completed.

Temporary staff receiving less-rigorous vetting than permanently employed colleagues carrying out similar roles.

Failing to consider continually whether staff in higher-risk positions are becoming vulnerable to committing fraud or being coerced by criminals.

Controls – access rights

Good practice

Specific IT access profiles for each role in the firm, which set out exactly what level of IT access is required for an individual to do their job.

If a staff member changes roles or responsibilities, all IT access rights are deleted from the system and the user is set up using the same process as if they were a new joiner at the firm. The complexity of this process is significantly reduced if role-based IT access profiles are in place – the old one can simply be replaced with the new.

A clearly defined process to notify IT of forthcoming staff departures in order that IT accesses can be permanently disabled or deleted on a timely and accurate basis.

A regular reconciliation of HR and IT user records to act as a failsafe in the event of a failure in the firm's leavers process.

Regular reviews of staff IT access rights to ensure that there are no anomalies.

Least privilege access to call recordings and copies of scanned documents obtained for "know your customer" purposes.

Authentication of customers' identities using, for example, touch-tone telephone before a conversation with a call centre adviser takes place. This limits the amount of personal information and/or passwords contained in call recordings.

Masking credit card, bank account details and other sensitive data like customer passwords where this would not affect employees' ability to do their job.

Poor practice

Staff having access to customer data that they do not require to do their job.

User access rights set up on a case-by-case basis with no independent check that they are appropriate.

Redundant access rights being allowed to remain in force when a member of staff changes roles.

User accounts being left "live" or only suspended (i.e. not permanently disabled) when a staff member leaves.

A lack of independent checking of changes effected at any stage in the joiners, movers and leavers process.

Controls – passwords and user accounts

Good practice

Individual user accounts – requiring passwords – in place for all systems containing customer data.

Password standards at least equivalent to those recommended by Get Safe Online – a government-backed campaign group. At present, their recommended standard for passwords is a combination of letters, numbers and keyboard symbols at least seven characters in length and changed regularly.

Measures to ensure passwords are robust. These might include controls to ensure that passwords can only be set in accordance with policy and the use of password-cracking software on a risk-based approach.

"Straight-through processing", but only if complemented by accurate role-based access profiles and strong passwords.

Poor practice

The same user account and password used by multiple users to access particular systems.

Names and dictionary words used as passwords.

Systems that allow passwords to be set which do not comply with password policy.

Password sharing of any kind.

Controls – monitoring access to customer data

Good practice

Risk-based, proactive monitoring of staff's access to customer data to ensure it is being accessed and/or updated for a genuine business reason.

The use of software designed to spot suspicious activity by employees with access to customer data. Such software may not be useful in its "off-the-shelf" format so it is good practice for firms to ensure that it is tailored to their business profile.

Strict controls over super-users' access to customer data and independent checks of their work to ensure they have not accessed, manipulated or extracted data that was not required for a particular task.

Poor practice

Assuming that vetted staff with appropriate access rights will always act appropriately. Staff can breach procedures, for example by looking at account information relating to celebrities, be tempted to commit fraud themselves or be bribed or threatened to give customer data to criminals.

Failure to make regular use of management information about access to customer data.

Failing to monitor super-users or other employees with access to large amounts of customer data.

Controls – data backup

Good practice

Firms conducting a proper risk assessment of threats to data security arising from the data backup process – from the point that backup tapes are produced, through the transit process to the ultimate place of storage.

Firms encrypting backed up data that is held off site, including while in transit.

Regular reviews of the level of encryption to ensure it remains appropriate to the current risk environment.

Backup data being transferred by secure internet links.

Due diligence on third parties that handle backed-up customer data so the firm has a good understanding of how it is secured, exactly who has access to it and how staff with access to it are vetted.

Staff with responsibility for holding backed-up data off site being given assistance to do so securely. For example, firms could offer to pay for a safe to be installed at the staff member's home.

Firms conducting spot checks to ensure that data held off site is done so in accordance with accepted policies and procedures.

Poor practice

Firms failing to consider data security risk arising from the backing up of customer data.

A lack of clear and consistent procedures for backing up data, resulting in data being backed up in several different ways at different times. This makes it difficult for firms to keep track of copies of their data.

Unrestricted access to backup tapes for large numbers of staff at third-party firms.

Backup tapes being held insecurely by firms' employees; for example, being left in their cars or at home on the kitchen table.

Controls – access to the internet and email

Good practice

Giving internet and email access only to staff with a genuine business need.

Considering the risk of data compromise when monitoring external email traffic, for example by looking for strings of numbers that might be credit card details.

Where proportionate, using specialist IT software to detect data leakage via email.

Completely blocking access to all internet content which allows web-based communication. This content includes web-based email, messaging facilities on social networking sites, external instant messaging and peer-to-peer file-sharing software.

Firms that provide cyber cafés for staff to use during breaks ensuring that web-based communications are blocked or that data cannot be transferred into the cyber café, either in electronic or paper format.

Poor practice

Allowing staff who handle customer data to have access to the internet and email if there is no business reason for this.

Allowing access to web-based communication internet sites. This content includes web-based email, messaging facilities on social networking sites, external instant messaging and peer-to-peer file-sharing software.

Controls – key-logging devices

Good practice

Regular sweeping for key-logging devices in parts of the firm where employees have access to large amounts of, or sensitive, customer data. (Firms will also wish to conduct sweeps in other sensitive areas, for example, where money can be transferred.)

Use of software to determine whether unusual or prohibited types of hardware have been attached to employees' computers.

Awareness raising of the risk of key-logging devices. The vigilance of staff is a useful method of defence.

Anti-spyware software and firewalls etc. in place and kept up to date.

Controls – laptops

Good practice

The encryption of laptops and other portable devices containing customer data.

Controls that mitigate the risk of employees failing to follow policies and procedures.

Maintaining an accurate register of laptops issued to staff.

Regular audits of the contents of laptops to ensure that only staff who are authorised to hold customer data on their laptops are doing so and that this is for genuine business reasons.

The wiping of shared laptops' hard drives between uses.

Poor practice

Unencrypted customer data on laptops.

A poor understanding of which employees have been issued or are using laptops to hold customer data.

Shared laptops used by staff without being signed out or wiped between uses.

Controls – portable media including USB devices and CDs

Good practice

Ensuring that only staff with a genuine business need can download customer data to portable media such as USB devices and CDs.

Ensuring that staff authorised to hold customer data on portable media can only do so if it is encrypted.

Maintaining an accurate register of staff allowed to use USB devices and staff who have been issued with USB devices.

The use of software to prevent and/or detect individuals using personal USB devices.

Firms reviewing regularly and on a risk-based approach the copying of customer data to portable media to ensure there is a genuine business reason for it.

The automatic encryption of portable media attached to firms' computers.

Providing lockers for higher-risk staff such as call centre staff and super-users and restricting them from taking personal effects to their desks.

Poor practice

Allowing staff with access to bulk customer data – for example, super-users – to download to unencrypted portable media.

Failing to review regularly threats posed by increasingly sophisticated and quickly evolving personal technology such as mobile phones.

Physical security

Good practice

Appropriately restricted access to areas where large amounts of customer data is accessible, such as server rooms, call centres and filing areas.

Using robust intruder deterrents such as keypad entry doors, alarm systems, grilles or barred windows, and closed circuit television ("CCTV").

Robust procedures for logging visitors and ensuring adequate supervision of them while on site.

Training and awareness programmes for staff to ensure they are fully aware of more-basic risks to customer data arising from poor physical security.

Employing security guards, cleaners etc. directly to ensure an appropriate level of vetting and reduce risks that can arise through third-party suppliers accessing customer data.

Using electronic swipe card records to spot unusual behaviour or access to high-risk areas.

Keeping filing cabinets locked during the day and leaving the key with a trusted member of staff.

An enforced clear-desk policy.

Poor practice

Allowing staff or other persons with no genuine business need to access areas where customer data is held.

Failure to check electronic records showing who has accessed sensitive areas of the office.

Failure to lock away customer records and files when the office is left unattended.

Disposal of customer data

Good practice

Procedures that result in the production of as little paper-based customer data as possible.

Treating all paper as "confidential waste" to eliminate confusion among employees about which type of bin to use.

All customer data disposed of by employees securely, for example by using shredders (preferably cross-cut rather than straight-line shredders) or confidential waste bins. Checking general waste bins for the accidental disposal of customer data.

Using a third-party supplier, preferably one with BSIA accreditation which provides a certificate of secure destruction, to shred or incinerate paper-based customer data. It is important for firms to have a good understanding of the supplier's process for destroying customer data and their employee vetting standards.

Providing guidance for travelling or home-based staff on the secure disposal of customer data.

Computer hard drives and portable media being properly wiped (using specialist software) or destroyed as soon as they become obsolete.

Poor practice

Poor awareness among staff about how to dispose of customer data securely.

Slack procedures that present opportunities for fraudsters, for instance when confidential waste is left unguarded on the premises before it is destroyed.

Staff working remotely failing to dispose of customer data securely.

Firms failing to provide guidance or assistance to remote workers who need to dispose of an obsolete home computer.

Firms stockpiling obsolete computers and other portable media for too long and in insecure environments.

Firms relying on others to erase or destroy their hard drives and other portable media securely without evidence that this has been done competently.

Managing third-party suppliers

Good practice

Conducting due diligence of data security standards at third-party suppliers before contracts are agreed.

Regular reviews of third-party suppliers' data security systems and controls, with the frequency of review dependent on data security risks identified.

Ensuring third-party suppliers' vetting standards are adequate by testing the checks performed on a sample of staff with access to customer data.

Only allowing third-party IT suppliers access to customer databases for specific tasks on a case-by-case basis.

Poor practice

Allowing third-party suppliers to access customer data when no due diligence of data security arrangements has been performed.

Firms not knowing exactly which third-party staff have access to their customer data.

Firms not knowing how third-party suppliers' staff have been vetted.

Allowing third-party staff unsupervised access to areas where customer data is held when they have not been vetted to the same standards as employees.

Allowing IT suppliers unrestricted or unmonitored access to customer data. A lack of awareness of when/how third-party suppliers can access customer data and failure to monitor such access. Unencrypted customer data being sent to third parties using unregistered post.

Internal audit and compliance monitoring

Good practice

Firms seeking external assistance where they do not have the necessary in-house expertise or resources.

Compliance and internal audit conducting specific reviews of data security which cover all relevant areas of the business including IT, security, HR, training and awareness, governance and third-party suppliers.

Firms using expertise from across the business to help with the more technical aspects of data security audits and compliance monitoring.

Poor practice

Compliance focusing only on compliance with data protection legislation and failing to consider adherence to data security policies and procedures.

Compliance consultants adopting a "one size fits all" approach to different clients' businesses.

33.11 International and sector-specific guidance

33.11.1 Outline

33.11.1.1 International guidance

Outsourcing has attracted considerable international regulatory interest in recent years. In addition to the EU regulations described above:

(a) The Joint Forum established a set of high level, voluntary principles designed to provide a minimum standard against which firms in the banking, securities and insurance sectors can evaluate their approach to outsourcing. It also sets out broad guidance for regulators in dealing with outsourcing. The Joint Forum has also released a paper on High Level Principles of Business Continuity.[15] The Joint Forum was established in 1996 under the aegis of the Basel Committee on Banking Supervision, IOSCO and the IAIS to deal with issues common to the banking, securities and insurance sectors. The UK representative is the FSA.

(b) IOSCO, an international association of securities regulators, produced a set of principles on outsourcing, aimed at securities companies, which are designed to be complementary to the Joint Forum's set of principles. The member agencies currently assembled together in the International Organisation of Securities Commissions have resolved, through its permanent structures to co-operate to promote high standards of regulation in order to maintain just, efficient and sound markets, to exchange information on their respective experiences in order to promote the development of domestic markets, to unite their efforts to establish standards and an effective surveillance of international securities transactions and to provide mutual assistance to promote the integrity of the markets by a rigorous application of the standards and by effective enforcement against offences. The UK member is the FSA. The US member is the Securities and Exchange Commission ("SEC").

33.11.1.2 Sector-specific guidance

Sector-specific guidance on outsourcing includes the following:

(a) On 14 December 2006, the Committee of European Banking Supervisors ("CEBS")[16] published Guidelines on Outsourcing aimed at credit institutions' business activities. The Guidelines take into account international initiatives, such as the work by the Joint Forum, and EU initiatives, such as MiFID. CEBS has also issued a "mapping" document to ensure that their standards are compatible with MiFID.

(b) The Basel Committee's e-banking Group is carrying out a review of IT outsourcing practices among its members. The Committee's members come from Belgium,

---

15 *See* www.iosco.org/library/pubdocs/pdf/IOSCOPD224.pdf.

16 CEBS (Committee of European Banking Supervisors) is comprised of high level representatives from the banking supervisory authorities and central banks of the European Union. Its role is to advise the EU Commission, either at the Commission's request, within a time limit which the Commission may lay down according to the urgency of the matter, or on the Committee's own initiative, in particular as regards the preparation of draft implementing measures in the field of banking activities. The FSA is the UK's representative.

Canada, France, Germany, Italy, Japan, Luxembourg, the Netherlands, Spain, Sweden, Switzerland, the UK and the US. The FSA is the UK's representative on the Joint Forum that published the outsourcing principles.

(c) In January 2008 the Hedge Funds Working Group (the "HFWG") published its Final Report intended to assist hedge fund managers by setting out revised best practice standards (the "Standards") based on the results of consultation it carried out in October 2007.

33.11.1.3 Relationship between the different guidance

There is considerable overlap and cross-fertilisation between the various regulatory groups. For example, the FSA participates as a member or as a technical adviser in CESR, Bank of International Settlements – Basel Committee, CEBS, IOSCO and the Joint Forum.

Regulators and central banks from other jurisdictions participate in a similar way. These organisations either have direct influence upon developing legislation, for example CESR has the mandate under MiFID on level 2 technical advice, or can influence industry standard (e.g. the Basel Committee).

33.11.2 Joint Forum principles

A summary of the Joint Forum principles is set out in Table 51.

Table 51 *Joint Forum principles*

Outsourcing policy

I. A regulated entity seeking to outsource activities should have in place a comprehensive policy to guide the assessment of whether and how those activities can be appropriately outsourced. The board of directors or equivalent body retains responsibility for the outsourcing policy and related overall responsibility for activities undertaken under that policy.

Risk management

II. The regulated entity should establish a comprehensive outsourcing risk management programme to address the outsourced activities and the relationship with the service provider.

Obligations and supervision

III. The regulated entity should ensure that outsourcing arrangements neither diminish its ability to fulfil its obligations to customers and regulators, nor impede effective supervision by regulators.

Due diligence

IV. The regulated entity should conduct appropriate due diligence in selecting third-party service providers.

Written contracts

V. Outsourcing relationships should be governed by written contracts that clearly describe all material aspects of the outsourcing arrangement, including the rights, responsibilities and expectations of all parties.

Business continuity

VI. The regulated entity and its service providers should establish and maintain contingency plans, including a plan for disaster recovery and periodic testing of backup facilities.

Confidentiality

VII. The regulated entity should take appropriate steps to require that service providers protect confidential information of both the regulated entity and its clients from intentional or inadvertent disclosure to unauthorised persons.

Regulatory supervision

VIII. Regulators should take into account outsourcing activities as an integral part of their ongoing assessment of the regulated entity. Regulators should assure themselves by appropriate means that any outsourcing arrangements do not hamper the ability of a regulated entity to meet its regulatory requirements.

Risks of outsourcing

IX. Regulators should be aware of the potential risks posed where the outsourced activities of multiple regulated entities are concentrated within a limited number of service providers.

33.11.3 IOSCO principles

The key IOSCO principles are set out in Table 52.[17]

Table 52 *IOSCO principles*

Topic 1: Due diligence in selection and monitoring of service provider and service provider's performance

Principle: An outsourcing firm should conduct suitable due diligence processes in selecting an appropriate third-party service provider and in monitoring its ongoing performance.

Topic 2: The contract with a service provider

Principle: There should be a legally binding written contract between the outsourcing firm and each third-party service provider, the nature and detail of which should be

17 IOSCO has also issued a consultation paper on regulatory standards for funds of hedge funds which will cover the specific circumstance where hedge funds wish to outsource any aspect of its due diligence. The deadline for responses was 5 January 2009.

appropriate to the materiality of the outsourced activity to the ongoing business of the outsourcing firm.

Topic 3: Information technology security and business continuity at the outsourcing firm

Principle: The outsourcing firm should take appropriate measures to determine that procedures are in place to protect the outsourcing firm's proprietary and customer-related information and software; and its service providers establish and maintain emergency procedures and a plan for disaster recovery, with periodic testing of backup facilities.

Topic 4: Client confidentiality issues

Principle: The outsourcing firm should take appropriate steps to require that service providers protect confidential information regarding the outsourcing firm's proprietary and other information, as well as the outsourcing firm's clients, from intentional or inadvertent disclosure to unauthorised individuals.

Topic 5: Concentration of outsourcing functions

Principle: Regulators should be cognisant of the risks posed where one service provider provides outsourcing services to multiple regulated entities. *See* comments in Table 49 about concentration risk.

Topic 6: Termination procedures

Principle: Outsourcing with third-party service providers should include contractual provisions relating to termination of the contract and appropriate exit strategies.

Topic 7: Regulator's and intermediary's access to books and records, including rights of inspection

Principle: The regulator, the firm, and its auditors should have access to the books and records of service providers relating to the outsourced activities and the regulator should be able to obtain promptly, upon request, information concerning activities that are relevant to regulatory oversight.

33.11.4 Committee of European Banking Supervisors Guidelines

The Committee of European Banking Supervisors Guidelines are set out in Table 53. The Guidelines on Outsourcing can be found at www.c-ebs.org.

Table 53 *Committee of European Banking Supervisors Guidelines*

Guideline 2 – responsibility

The ultimate responsibility for the proper management of the risks associated with outsourcing or the outsourced activities lies with an outsourcing institution's senior management.

Guideline 3 - no delegation

Outsourcing arrangements can never result in the delegation of senior management's responsibility.

Guideline 4 - restrictions on outsourcing

4.1 An authorised entity may not outsource services and activities concerning the acceptance of deposits or to lending requiring a licence from the supervisory authority according to the applicable national banking law unless the service provider either: (i) has an authorisation that is equivalent to the authorisation of the outsourcing institution; or (ii) is otherwise allowed to carry out those activities in accordance with the relevant national legal framework.

4.2 Any area of activity of an outsourcing institution other than those identified in Guideline 2 and 3 may be outsourced provided that such outsourcing does not impair:

(a) the orderliness of the conduct of the outsourcing institution's business or of the financial services provided;
(b) the senior management's ability to manage and monitor the authorised entity's business and its authorised activities;
(c) the ability of other internal governance bodies, such as the board of directors or the audit committee, to fulfil their oversight tasks in relation to the senior management; and
(d) the supervisory authority's ability to fulfil its supervisory tasks.

4.3 An outsourcing institution should take particular care when outsourcing material activities. The outsourcing institution should adequately inform its supervisory authority about this type of outsourcing.

Guideline 5 - no other restrictions on non-material outsourcing

There should be no restrictions on the outsourcing of non-material activities of an outsourcing institution.

Guideline 6 - outsourcing policy

6.1 The outsourcing institution should have a policy on its approach to outsourcing, including contingency plans and exit strategies.

6.2 An outsourcing institution should conduct its business in a controlled and sound manner at all times.

Guideline 7 - risk management

An outsourcing institution should manage the risks associated with its outsourcing arrangements.

Guideline 8 - written contract

All outsourcing arrangements should be subject to a formal and comprehensive contract. The outsourcing contract should oblige the service provider to protect confidential information.

Guideline 9 - service management

In managing its relationship with an outsourcing service provider an outsourcing institution should ensure that a written agreement is put in place. This should include definitions of the responsibilities of the parties and quality descriptions. The agreement should contain a mixture of quantitative and qualitative performance targets.

Guideline 10 - chain outsourcing

10.1 The outsourcing institution should take account of the risks associated with "chain" outsourcing.

10.2 The outsourcing institution should agree to chain outsourcing only if the subcontractor will also fully comply with the obligations existing between the outsourcing institution and the service provider, including obligations incurred in favour of the supervisory authority.

10.3 The outsourcing institution should take appropriate steps to address the risk of any weakness or failure in the provision of the subcontracted activities having a significant effect on the service provider's ability to meet its responsibilities under the outsourcing agreement and SLA.

Part 3: Guidelines on outsourcing addressed to supervisory authorities

Guideline 11 - audit

Supervisory authorities should require that the outsourcing institution has established supervisory authority access to relevant data held by the service provider and, where provided for by the national law, the right for the supervisory authority to conduct onsite inspections at a service provider's premises.

Guideline 12 - concentration risk

Supervisory authorities should take account of concentration risk.

33.11.5 Hedge Funds Working Group

Standards 19 and 20 of the Hedge Funds Working Group (the "HFWG") Final Report are summarised in Table 54.

Table 54 *Hedge Fund Standards 19 and 20*

Governance Standards Guidance (19)

A hedge fund manager should ensure that careful due diligence on third-party service providers is conducted before recommending them to the fund governing body.

This could include using Due Diligence Questionnaires or evaluating "reports on controls" from an independent reporting accountant issued by the respective third-party service provider.

A hedge fund manager should do what it reasonably can to enable and encourage the fund governing body to review third-party service providers properly and regularly.

Valuation and administration

A hedge fund manager should, where appropriate, do what it reasonably can to enable and encourage the fund to put a service level agreement ("SLA") in place with relevant service providers (commonly, this will be attached as a schedule to the agreement between the fund and the relevant service provider).

An SLA would normally be expected to:

- *set out in precise detail the services to be provided by the relevant service provider along with deadlines for completion of the services;*
- *make clear accountability and responsibility for the orderly operation of all administration or other functions performed by the relevant service provider on behalf of investors; and*
- *include "Key Performance Indicators" to provide hedge fund managers and fund governing bodies with a means of measuring whether the objectives set out in the SLA are met by the relevant service provider.*

Further examples of the contents of SLAs are provided in Appendix J [of the Hedge Funds Standards: Final Report] (Examples of functions often covered by service level agreements).

A hedge fund manager should do what it reasonably can to enable and encourage the fund governing body to review the services provided by the relevant service provider against contractual or other agreed standards.

Prime brokers

A hedge fund manager of a large hedge fund should carefully consider whether it is appropriate for the hedge fund to appoint more than one prime broker (taking into account in particular the potential advantages of diversification of funding and other services) and do what it reasonably can to enable and encourage the fund governing body to act accordingly.

HFSB is aware that there is a spectrum of criteria to consider when choosing a prime broker, including efficiency and operational risk considerations.

In carrying out due diligence on a prime broker, a hedge fund manager should consider the potential prime broker's credit rating, policy on re-hypothecation and general ability to fulfil all process functions accurately and efficiently.

Auditors

A hedge fund manager should do what it reasonably can to enable and encourage the fund governing body to appoint reputable auditors.

In addition to the Standards set out in this report, AIMA provides further guidance in its Guide to Sound Practices for European Hedge Fund Managers, (2007) (chapter 3.8).

Disclosure Standards and Guidance (20)

A hedge fund manager should disclose the names of its principal third-party service providers in its due diligence documents or upon request.

A hedge fund manager should, to the extent it is able or permitted to do so, provide information on the fund's committed funding or financing arrangements with prime brokers/lenders to investors in its due diligence documents or upon request.

A hedge fund manager should disclose the nature of any special commercial terms with its third-party service providers which result in potential conflicts of interest (e.g. in-house brokerage or rebates).

A hedge fund manager to the extent applicable should disclose the monitoring procedures in relation to its third-party service providers in its due diligence documents or upon request.

In addition to the Standards set out in this report, AIMA provides further guidance in its Guide to Sound Practices for European Hedge Fund Managers, (2007) (chapter 3.8).

33.12 Conclusion

33.12.1 Consistency

This chapter demonstrates that the outsourcing regulations in MiFID (excluding the specific principles relating to portfolio management outsourcing), CRD, SYSC 8, SYSC 13, the Joint Forum principles, the IOSCO principles and the CEBS Guidelines are broadly consistent.

33.12.2 Best practice

The FSA's view is that the regulations in the FSA Handbook reflect best practice in outsourcing and this is no doubt correct in many cases.

33.12.3 Contentious

Some provisions in the guidance are particularly contentious with service providers, in particular the audit provisions, the provisions regarding control over the service provider's employees and subcontractors and the termination provisions.

Both service providers and firms have raised issues with the provisions relating to concentration risk, the issue being that the firm has a duty to use service providers with the appropriate expertise. A service provider with the appropriate expertise is likely to be used by other firms and this increases the concentration risk.

33.12.4 Not exhaustive

It should be stressed that, as the regulations include a non-exhaustive list of issues mainly concerned with controlling operational risk, there are numerous other key issues which firms will need to consider to ensure that their outsourcing arrangements are successful, for example issues of liability, limitations of liability, TUPE, preparation of the service description, charging and service credit issues and protections against service provider insolvency.

33.13 Lessons for customers not regulated by the FSA

Can customers who are not regulated by the FSA learn any lessons from the guidance? The FSA guidance is interesting because of its emphasis upon the need for flexibility as a result of the great variety of outsourcing arrangements. This is a point which this Guide has also taken care to stress. However, the concern to ensure flexibility has meant that much of the FSA guidance is extremely high level.

There are a few instances of specific advice. In particular, customers outside the financial services sector may like to take into account the suggestions that, if they outsource business continuity services, they should evaluate the likelihood and impact of multiple calls on shared resources. They may also find the FSA's report on Data Security in Financial Services interesting, in particular the list of good and bad security practices.

The FSA's approach of analysing the effect of the outsourcing agreement upon the customer's operational risk is also an interesting approach, which may be helpful for other sectors.

Lastly, the FSA's insistence that firms may need to retain certain controls over the supplier supports the argument raised in Chapter 7 that there may be circumstances when the customer will need control over the manner in which the services are provided.

33.14 Shar'ia compliant outsourcing

Where the outsourcing agreement is carried out with regard to customers offering Shar'ia compliant products, specific concerns will arise, including those relating to the payment of interest, liquidated damages, service credits, additional governance regimes and specific approval of the agreement.[18]

18 *See* the article by John Buyers "Shar'ia compliant outsourcing: the basics", *Finance and Credit Law*, October 2008 for a description of the relevant issues.

Chapter 34

Public Procurement

34.1 Outline

Chapter 33 deals with outsourcing by financial services firms regulated by the FSA. This chapter concerns regulation in the public sector. It includes a short description of the directives affecting public sector procurement.

A study by DeAnne Julius, an economist and former member of the Bank of England's monetary policy committee in 2008, demonstrated the importance of public sector outsourcing in the UK. The report found that a third of all public services – far more than previously thought – are now delivered by the private and voluntary sectors. The study shows the public service industry has doubled in little more than a decade and now embraces everything from health to waste management, IT, welfare-to-work, training, construction and legal services. It also shows that the UK is at the forefront of the outsourcing trend. Although the US spends more cash on outsourced services, the UK spends a larger share of its gross domestic product than the US or any other Organisation for Economic Co-operation and Development country except Sweden and Australia.

34.2 Public Procurement Directives

Public procurement within the European Union ("EU") is governed by EU legislation in the form of separate directives covering the procurement of services, works and supplies by the public sector and procurement of the same by utilities.[1] The directives are designed to regulate the award of public contracts above specified financial thresholds by providing transparent award procedures and promoting the equality of treatment of all undertakings in Member States of the EU.

The World Trade Organization ("WTO") agreement on government procurement ("GPA") governs public procurement relations between EU Member States and a number of non-EU states that have chosen to accede to that agreement. The GPA governs the procurement of works, services and supplies and supersedes the old General Agreement on Tariffs and Trade ("GATT"), as well as a number of other related WTO agreements.

1 This chapter focuses on the directive applicable to public sector procurement (as opposed to utilities sector procurement which is dealt with in Chapter 37).

34.2.1 Application of the directives – countries

(a) Suppliers within the EU are protected. As a result of the expansion of the EU, suppliers in offshore outsourcing countries such as Hungary, the Czech Republic and Poland will be protected by the procurement directives. It will be interesting to see whether this will result in an increase in offshore outsourcing by the public sector to these countries, as suppliers within these countries become more organised.

(b) The GPA is an optional agreement for WTO members and only undertakings in those states that have acceded to the GPA can benefit from it. The EU has acceded to the GPA on behalf of all of its Member States and some of the non-EU states that have acceded to the GPA are as follows: US, Canada, Japan, Switzerland, Israel, Korea, Norway, Liechtenstein and Iceland. Public bodies in states that have acceded to the GPA must comply with its requirements when conducting procurements over specified thresholds. The provisions are similar to the procurement directives, and, in the EU, compliance with the procurement directives constitutes compliance with the GPA.

(c) India is not a signatory to the GPA and so Indian suppliers are not protected by the procurement directives.

See Chapter 38 for a discussion of offshore outsourcing.

34.2.2 Main changes in the directive

The Consolidated Public Procurement Directive (referred to in this chapter as the "Public Procurement Directive")[2] consolidated three pre-existing directives relating to public works contracts, public services contracts and public supplies contracts. It also updated the legislation to reflect more recent case law, sought to clarify certain points over which questions were raised in the previous directives and introduced a number of innovations.

The main innovations are the regulation of framework agreements for the first time in the public sector, the introduction of a new procurement procedure known as the competitive dialogue and the introduction of electronic procurement systems.

34.3 When does the Public Procurement Directive apply?

For a proposed outsourcing to be subject to the Public Procurement Directive, a number of requirements must first be met. These requirements are as follows:

(a) the entity putting the contract out to tender must be a "contracting authority";

(b) the contract in question must be a "public service contract", "public works contract" or "public supply contract";

(c) the estimated value of the contract must equal or exceed the relevant financial threshold; and

(d) the contract must not fall within one of the exemptions contained in the Public Procurement Directive.

2 Directive 2004/18/EC.

These issues are described in Table 55. All four of the requirements in Table 55 must be met in order for the Public Procurement Directive to apply. Therefore, even if only one of these requirements is not met, the Public Procurement Directive will not apply. If the Public Procurement Directive does not apply, the entity in question may establish its own rules of competition, following private sector tender principles.

However, it should be noted that "contracting authorities" are bound not only by the Public Procurement Directive but also by the general EC Treaty principles of equal treatment, non-discrimination, transparency and proportionality. As a result, even if the Public Procurement Directive itself does not apply or does not apply in full, the general EC Treaty principles may still apply. This is relevant in two particular instances:

(a) for a particular type of "public service contract" known as an "Annex II B" service contract; and
(b) for contracts with an estimated value that falls below the relevant financial threshold.

These two particular instances (Annex II B service contracts and below threshold contracts) are also discussed in Table 55 and an explanation of the impact of the general EC Treaty principles in these instances is also provided.

Table 55 *When does the Public Procurement Directive apply?*

Contracting authorities

The concept of a "contracting authority" is defined in Article 1.9 of the Public Procurement Directive. The definition is broad and covers essentially public sector bodies, including the state, regional and local authorities, bodies governed by public law, and associations formed by regional or local authorities. It is generally clear whether an entity is a public sector body falling within the definition of a "contracting authority", although this determination can be more complicated in the case of mixed public/private partnerships or companies.

Public contracts

"Public service contracts", "public works contracts" and "public supply contracts" are defined in Article 1.2 of the Public Procurement Directive. Most outsourcing contracts are likely to fall within the definition of "public service contracts": "contracts for pecuniary interest concluded in writing between one or more economic operators and one or more contracting authorities having as their object the provision of services ..."

Annex II A and Annex II B services

Annex II to the Public Procurement Directive classifies services as either "Annex II A" or "Annex II B" and this classification determines the level of regulation that will apply to the procurement of a service.

Annex II A services

Annex II A services are subject to the full application of the Public Procurement Directive. Annex II A services include, for example, maintenance and repair, certain financial and insurance services, computer and related services, architectural services and refuse collection.

Annex II B services

Annex II B services include educational services, health services and legal services. These services are only partially covered by the Public Procurement Directive. In the case of Annex II B services, contracting authorities:

(a) must comply with the requirements as to technical specifications; and
(b) must publish a contract award notice in the Official Journal of the European Union.

There is therefore no obligation under the Public Procurement Directive to advertise Annex II B service contracts at an EU level. Nevertheless, case law has established that Annex II B service contracts are subject to the general EC Treaty principles (highlighted above). This means that, where an Annex II B contract may be of certain cross-border interest (e.g. due to its nature or value), the obligation of transparency will require some form of advertisement and open competition. Therefore, the letter of the Public Procurement Directive need not be followed, although the Directive may serve as a guide. In many cases, advertisement on the contracting authority's web portal or buyer profile[3] may suffice for an Annex II B service contract, although this should be assessed on a case-by-case basis. In any event, it is always open to a contracting authority to advertise an Annex II B contract free of charge at EU level in the Official Journal of the European Union.

Financial thresholds

The Public Procurement Directive will only apply to contracts worth more than a specified threshold. The thresholds were most recently revised on 1 January 2008 and are €133,000 in relation to public services contracts[4] for central government bodies and €206,000 for other public sector bodies.[5]

In the case of below threshold contracts, the application of the general EC Treaty principles must still be considered. Their application is broadly the same as set out above in respect of Annex II B service contracts, meaning that generally some form of advertisement and open competition will be necessitated. Advertisement and competition may not be required, however, if the contract value is very modest (i.e. significantly below

3 The buyer profile is one of the new innovations introduced by the latest Public Procurement Directive. It is effectively a page on an authority's website which displays, for the benefit of interested providers, information on the authority's past, ongoing and future tender processes, as well as general information on and contact details for the authority.

4 With the exception of certain services, which have a threshold of €206,000. These include Annex II B (residual) services, Research & Development Services (Category 8), certain types of telecommunications services in Category 5 (including CPC 7524 – Television and radio broadcast services, CPC 7525 – Interconnection services, CPC 7526 – Integrated telecommunications services) and subsidised services contracts under Article 8 of the Public Procurement Directive.

5 The thresholds are revised every two years, so the next time they are due to be revised is 1 January 2010.

the relevant financial threshold), such that it is unlikely to generate cross-border interest. For very small contracts, therefore, it may be possible for a contracting authority to make a direct award of contract (although this is subject to any other national laws or policies that may be relevant).

Exemptions to the Public Procurement Directive

Article 16 of the Public Procurement Directive contains various specific exemptions covering, for example, contracts for the acquisition of land and buildings and contracts for certain R&D services.[6] Exempted contracts fall fully outside the scope of the Public Procurement Directive and, as such, may be entered into directly by a contracting authority and its preferred provider.

34.4 The award procedures

If a proposed outsourcing is subject to the Public Procurement Directive, the contracting authority has to decide which award procedures it will use.

34.4.1 Open procedure

Under the open award procedure all interested parties may tender for a contract. There is no scope for negotiation pre or post submission of tenders. Post tender submission, any discussions between the contracting authority and bidders must be limited to clarifications. A contracting authority is bound to make its choice solely on the basis of the written tender, subject to such clarifications. There is also no opportunity for the contracting authority to limit the number of tenders it has to consider.

As a result, this procedure is not used for the procurement of complex contracts. It is most applicable for the procurement of goods, where there is a clear and comprehensive specification, and price is likely to be the key determinant.

34.4.2 Restricted procedure

In the restricted procedure, the contracting authority invites expressions of interest and only those organisations short-listed by the contracting authority may submit tenders. The contracting authority must invite a minimum of five bidders to tender, provided there are five suitably qualified candidates.

Similarly to the open procedure, there is no scope for negotiation pre or post submission of tenders (post tender discussions are limited to clarifications on the information provided or the content of the tenders) and the contracting authority is bound to make its choice solely on the

6 The exemption covers R&D services for the general public's benefit, as well as R&D services for the sole benefit of the authority where those services are partly or wholly funded by the private sector.

basis of the written tenders, subject to these clarifications. Again, this procedure is seen as inappropriate for complex projects.

If the proposed outsourcing project is not complex, however, the restricted procedure is a relatively quick and straightforward procedure to use. In addition, it is helpful to note that the "accelerated" restricted procedure (a quicker version of the normal restricted procedure) will be automatically available to public authorities during 2009 and 2010. This "accelerated" procedure is normally only available in cases of "urgency" and its use must be justified by public authorities. However, at the end of 2008, the European Commission announced that the current economic climate justifies the use of this quicker procedure to procure major projects (which could include outsourcing projects). In practical terms, the "accelerated" restricted procedure permits a contract to be awarded within one month, compared to the three-month timescale under the normal restricted procedure.

34.4.3 Competitive dialogue procedure

The competitive dialogue procedure may only be used for the procurement of "particularly complex contracts". A contract will satisfy this requirement where it is not objectively possible for the contracting authority to define the technical means capable of satisfying its needs or to specify either the legal or financial make-up of a project.

Under the competitive dialogue procedure, contracting authorities may select a shortlist of bidders with whom to conduct a dialogue. The shortlist must contain a minimum of three bidders, provided there are three suitably qualified bidders.

The dialogue may cover all elements of the contract and the aim should be to identify the means best suited to satisfying the contacting authority's needs. Once the contracting authority is able to identify this, it must invite all of the bidders to submit final tenders and select the winning bidder using its pre-stated award criteria (which must go to determining the most economically advantageous tender, rather than the lowest-priced tender).

Discussions post tender are confined to clarification, specification and fine tuning (the scope of such discussions is essentially limited in the same way as post tender discussions under the open or restricted procedures). Once the preferred bidder is appointed, the contracting authority may ask it to clarify aspects of its tender or confirm commitments, provided this does not have the effect of altering substantial aspects of the tender (e.g. risk, price) or call for competition and does not lead to a distortion of competition or cause discrimination. Changes to the preferred bidder's tender may be accommodated where they are necessitated by external circumstances that could have affected the preferred bidder, regardless of the preferred bidder's identity. Changes should not in any event affect the status of the preferred bidder as the most economically advantageous tender.

34.4.4 Negotiated procedure

The negotiated procedure may only be used in exceptional circumstances where the conditions required for its use are fulfilled. Under the negotiated procedure, the contracting authority consults suppliers of its choice and negotiates the terms of the contract with one or more of them.[7]

There are two types of negotiated procedure: a competitive version which is pre-advertised in the Official Journal of the European Union and a non-competitive version which does not have to be advertised.

34.4.5 Competitive negotiated procedure[8]

The competitive negotiated procedure can only be used exceptionally, for example when the nature of the services to be provided, or the risks involved, do not allow prior overall pricing, or where, because of the nature of the services, the specifications cannot be established with sufficient precision to permit a contract award using the open or restricted procedures.

34.4.6 Non-competitive negotiated procedure[9]

The use of the non-competitive negotiated procedure is very exceptional and can only be used under certain conditions which have been construed narrowly by the courts, and the burden of proving that these conditions have been met rests with the contracting authority. The conditions include, for example:

(a) where a restricted or open procedure has failed (e.g. all bids were unacceptable, being irrelevant to or totally incapable of meeting the contracting authority's requirements);
(b) where there is only one possible provider (where due to technical or artistic reasons or reasons connected with the protection of exclusive rights[10] the services can be provided by only one provider); or
(c) where additional services are required from an existing provider and the services were unforeseen at the time of the original advertisement, provided that there are technical or economic reasons why the new services could not be separated from those already provided without great inconvenience to the authority; or the new services are strictly necessary for the completion of the contract. The additional services must be worth less than 50 per cent of the original contract value.

34.5 The procurement process

Once it has been established that a proposed outsourcing project is subject to the Public Procurement Directive and the contracting authority has chosen an appropriate award procedure, the next step is to embark upon the actual procurement process.

7 In practice, pre 2006, most PFI contracts within the UK were procured using the negotiated procedure. Now most PFI contracts are awarded under the competitive dialogue, according to guidance from the European Commission and Office of Government Commerce.

8 Article 30 Public Procurement Directive.

9 Article 31 Public Procurement Directive.

10 Exclusive rights does not extend, however, to situations where the exclusive right is licensed or can be reasonably obtained on licence.

34.5.1 Advertising the project – the OJEU notice

The choice of award procedure will determine the advertising obligations that a contracting authority will be subject to. The OJEU notice (also referred to as the contract notice) is basically a short advert for the contract prepared by the contracting authority, using an OJEU notice template, which must be published in the Official Journal of the European Union; hence the name OJEU.

The OJEU notice is an essential document for the tender process and great care must be taken in drafting the notice as it sets the parameters for the entire project. If the contract notice is incomplete or poorly drafted it may be open for interested parties to claim subsequently that all or part of the project has not been advertised properly.

There is a prescribed form of OJEU notice that must be used[11] and if the correct information is not included it can become necessary to re-advertise the award procedure. Since the adoption of the Public Procurement Directive, there has been an increased requirement for transparency and information about the selection and award criteria should now be included where possible in the OJEU notice.

The Public Procurement Directive sets out various time limits for the dispatch of the OJEU notice and time limits for interested parties to respond to the contract notice. These periods normally begin to run from the date on which the notice is sent to the OJEU.

34.5.2 Pre-qualification

Pre-qualification is essentially the initial shortlisting of the respondents to the OJEU notice. The Public Procurement Directive sets out prescriptive rules for this shortlisting,[12] including eligibility, financial and economic standing and technical or professional ability. There are also now grounds on which economic operators must be excluded, where directors or other decision-makers in a company have been convicted of criminal offences, including corruption and money laundering.

34.5.3 Tender stage

The tender stage follows pre-qualification. Here the pre-qualified bidders will be issued with the tender documents which they will use to prepare their tenders.

Article 53 of the Public Procurement Directive provides that a contract must be awarded on the basis of either the most economically advantageous tender ("MEAT") or the lowest price.[13]

The contracting authority is required to specify clearly in advance, in either the OJEU notice or the invitation to tender/participate in dialogue, the criteria by which it will select its preferred bidder. The contracting authority must, if possible, state the weighting which it gives to each of the criteria chosen.

---

11 Standard form OJEU notices are available on the SIMAP website: www.simap.europa.int

12 Articles 45–52 Public Procurement Directive.

13 Most outsourcing contracts would be awarded on the basis of the most economically advantageous tender, as otherwise the customer is prevented from assessing tenders on a qualitative basis.

Once bids have been evaluated in accordance with the evaluation criteria the contract will be awarded.

34.5.4 Framework agreements

The Public Procurement Directive legislates for the use of framework agreements for the procurement of works, services and supplies for the first time in the public sector. Framework agreements have been used for a number of years across various Member States and in many respects the Public Procurement Directive provides for what has become best practice.

Framework agreements are agreements between one or more contracting authorities and one or more economic operators establishing the terms under which future contracts may be awarded.

The procedures relating to the award of a framework agreement are identical to those for all other public sector contracts.

Where multiple economic operators are appointed under a framework agreement, it may be necessary to hold a mini-competition prior to awarding any contract under the framework agreement. Where only a single economic operator is appointed under a framework agreement, contracts may be awarded directly to that economic operator without further competition.

The existence of a framework agreement can limit competition in relation to the award of future contracts. Accordingly, they are generally only permitted to last a maximum of four years. A contracting authority may set up a framework agreement for longer than four years if it can justify that there are exceptional circumstances for doing so. One such exceptional circumstance might be where the framework agreement must be longer, for example six years, to allow the supplier appointed under it to recoup its investment and make a reasonable profit too. However, the contracts that are awarded under the framework agreement may last for more than four years.

34.5.5 Electronic procurement

The Public Procurement Directive provides for the use of email and electronic procurement systems for the first time. They allow the use of an e-auction phase under the open, restricted or negotiated procedures, as well as when competition is re-opened among parties to a framework agreement. Only those elements of tenders that are quantifiable may be subject to an e-auction as these systems are not suitable for subjective evaluation.

34.5.6 Alcatel notice and mandatory standstill period

Many Member States have by now amended their national procurement laws to incorporate the effects of recent case law, including the *Alcatel* case, that introduced a requirement for a standstill period between the decision on contract award and the contract being entered into. The standstill period is intended to avoid any "race to signature" that might deprive unsuccessful bidders of effective remedies, including a review of the contract award decision, with the possibility that it could be set aside if found to be in breach of the Public Procurement Directive.

By 20 December 2009, all Member States are required to bring their national laws into line with the provisions on the standstill period laid down in the new Remedies Directive.[14] This new directive requires the standstill period to be a minimum of 10 calendar days (if bidders are notified of the start of this period by email or fax) or 15 calendar days (if notification is by post). When contracting authorities notify bidders of the start of the standstill period, they must provide bidders with a summary of the reasons why they have been unsuccessful, as well as a summary of the characteristics and relative advantages of the successful tender, together with the name of the successful tenderer. Until the new Remedies Directive is implemented into Member States' national laws, contracting authorities should continue to comply with their national laws on the standstill period.

34.5.7 Contract award

Following contract award, Article 35.4 of the Public Procurement Directive requires a contracting authority to send a contract award notice to the OJEU within 48 days. This notice must be prepared using a specific template.[15]

34.6 Remedies for breach of Public Procurement Directive

34.6.1 Current remedies regime

The Public Sector Remedies Directive[16] establishes a system of safeguards to protect bidders' rights when tendering for public contracts. It provides that unsuccessful bidders may apply to the relevant national court or body[17] for remedies in certain circumstances if they consider that the contracting authority has breached the Public Procurement Directive.

Remedies available include:

(a) interim measures (e.g. an interim injunction to suspend a tender procedure or prevent a contracting authority from proceeding to sign a contract with the winning bidder);
(b) final set aside of a contracting authority's decision or a requirement to amend discriminatory aspects of tender documents; and
(c) damages.

In many Member States, including the UK, remedies are limited to damages once a contract with the successful bidder has been entered into. However, this may not be the case with framework agreements, as was seen in the UK in 2008.[18] In two cases, the UK courts concluded that

14 Directive 2007/66/EC.

15 Also available on the SIMAP website, referred to in footnote 11 above.

16 Directive 89/665/EC.

17 In the UK (England, Wales and Northern Ireland), the relevant forum for public procurement actions is the High Court. In Scotland, actions should be brought in the Sheriff Court or Court of Session.

18 *McLaughlin & Harvey Ltd* v *Department of Finance & Personnel* [2008] NIQB 122; and *Henry Brothers (Magherafelt) Ltd and others* v *Department of Education for Northern Ireland* [2008] NIQB 153.

framework agreements could be set aside where they do not establish all the terms in respect of subsequent call-off contracts (so-called framework agreements *stricto sensu*).[19] Such framework agreements are to be distinguished from framework *contracts* that lay down all of the terms that will apply to subsequent purchase orders in a manner binding on the parties to the framework contract. However, according to the UK courts such framework contracts could not be set aside.

34.6.2 New Remedies Directive

Once the new Remedies Directive is implemented by Member States on or before 20 December 2009, a further remedy of "ineffectiveness" will become available to bidders. This will provide for the possibility of concluded contracts to be set aside. The precise meaning of "ineffectiveness" (and the associated consequences) will be for each Member State to determine. The Directive provides that "ineffectiveness" could mean retroactive cancellation of all contractual obligations or cancellation of only future contractual obligations, yet to be performed. Member States could also leave the decision of which type of "ineffectiveness" to apply in each case to the discretion of the national court or review body. Should the national court or review body consider that there are overriding reasons concerning the general interest why a particular contract should not be set aside, the court or body will retain the discretion to award alternative penalties (e.g. imposition of fines or shortening of contract).

Certain limits are placed on the availability of this remedy of ineffectiveness. First, it will be available to bidders only in respect of fundamental breaches of the Public Procurement Directive. This will include where the contracting authority has failed to advertise a contract that should have been advertised. It will also include where the contracting authority has not complied with the standstill period, thus depriving an unsuccessful bidder of the opportunity of bringing an action that it would otherwise have brought for interim or final measures (i.e. pre-contract) in respect of a breach of the Public Procurement Directive. Secondly, its availability will be limited in time, possibly for a period of six months after the contract has been entered into.

As noted above, the impact of the new Remedies Directive will be for each Member State to determine. However the directive is implemented in the UK, its introduction is likely to bring about a number of changes in practice. Increasingly, it will be in the interests of both the public authority and the successful bidder to ensure that the tender process leading up to contract award has been in line with the public procurement rules. A contract could stand to be rendered "ineffective" whether or not the successful service provider is aware of the alleged breach. Unsurprisingly, service providers are likely to want an indemnity from the public authority (as might the funders in question). Whether government policy will permit this has yet to be determined. Guidance is likely to be forthcoming from the government, including the Office of Government Commerce, in due course. Any protection for the supplier will have to be carefully structured (e.g. as a separate side letter). Whether retrospective or prospective ineffectiveness is

19 This distinction was also drawn in the European Commission's Explanatory Note on Framework Agreements issued in January 2006.

applied, any clause which attempted to pre-agree how termination should be managed could be void.

34.6.3 Conditions for claiming remedies

In any case, before a bidder can secure any remedies (whether under the current Public Sector Remedies Directive or new Remedies Directive), the bidder must fulfil certain requirements:

(a) it must write to the contracting authority informing it of the breach identified and of the intention to bring an action in respect of the breach;

(b) it must have the necessary standing to bring the action (having bid for the contract or would have bid for the contract had it been put out to tender); and

(c) it must bring the action within the relevant national timescale for doing so (if one is provided for).[20]

34.6.4 Complaints to the EC

While a remedies regime is provided for in the Public Sector Remedies Directive, bidders may decide as an alternative to make a complaint to the European Commission. This is a less direct course of action for a bidder – the complaint is made against the Member State, not the contracting authority in question and the bidder itself is not entitled to any remedies. The Commission will seek to negotiate a solution with the Member State and, if necessary, take action before the European Court of Justice. However, bidders may find this a cost-effective route – once a complaint is lodged with the Commission, the Commission takes forward the case. There is also no time limit on such a complaint.

There are pros and cons to both remedies routes; a bidder will have to decide on a case-by-case basis which one is most suited to its particular situation and priorities.

34.7 Procurement implications of change control procedures

Public authorities and utilities should be aware that the public and utilities procurement directives are still relevant even after a contract has been entered into. They cannot rely on a widely drafted variation clause to bring about endless changes to a contract that was originally tendered in accordance with these directives. Instead, public authorities and utilities alike must take care that variations to an existing contract are not "material", giving rise in effect to a new contract. This is an important consideration – if a new contract arises, this will require the advertisement of a new contract (or OJEU) notice. If this is not done, the essential requirement for the EU-wide advertisement of contracts will not have been met in respect of the new contract.

20 In the UK, for example, proceedings must be brought promptly and in any event within three months from the date of the grounds for bringing the proceedings arising (although this period may be extended at the discretion of the court if it considers there is good reason to do so).

There are three alternative tests for how a "material" change might arise:[21]

(a) Is the change such that, had it been incorporated in the original contract (or OJEU) notice and tender documents, the outcome of the pre-qualification or bid evaluation process would have been different?
(b) Does the change considerably expand the scope of the original contract?
(c) Does the change swing the economic balance of the contract in favour of the contractor?

If one of these tests is satisfied, the change may constitute a "material" one. At this stage, a public authority or utility has a number of options:

(a) do not proceed with the change for fear of breaching the directives;
(b) scale back the change so it is not "material";
(c) proceed with the "material" change having first weighed up the potential risk of challenge to the public authority or utility for doing so.

One way to minimise the possibility of this issue arising in the first instance is for the public authority or utility to anticipate as many of the potential changes as possible up front in its tender documents and accompanying draft contract. In this way, the potential changes may be said to form part of the original tender process and not to give rise to a new contract.

34.8 Public procurement in the UK

The UK has implemented the Public Procurement Directive in the UK through the Public Contracts Regulations 2006. These Regulations came into force in the UK on 31 January 2006 and apply to all contracts awarded on or after that date.

The Public Contracts Regulations 2006 give effect to all of the provisions of the Public Procurement Directive described above, including framework agreements, competitive dialogue and electronic auctions. In addition, the Regulations provide for a standstill period at Regulation 32. To a great extent, the provisions on the standstill period are already in line with the new Remedies Directive. The only real differences are:

(a) the emphasis in the Regulations on the need to send the standstill notification to bidders as soon as possible once the decision on contract award has been taken; and
(b) the requirement for an unsuccessful bidder to actively seek a fuller debrief from the contracting authority (under the new Remedies Directive, much of this information should be contained in the initial notification of the start of the standstill period).[22]

21 These alternative tests are derived from the European Court of Justice case of *Pressetext* (Case C-454/06).

22 To secure a full debrief during the standstill period, an unsuccessful bidder must submit a request in writing to the contracting authority by midnight at the end of the second working day of the standstill period. If the unsuccessful bidder does so, it is entitled to receive the full debrief and to have at least three working days to consider it, before the standstill period comes to an end.

Armed with such information, before the contract is entered into, an unsuccessful bidder may be better placed to determine whether to seek a review of the contract award decision before the courts.

Much guidance has been published by the OGC since the Regulations took effect and covers a range of areas, such as framework agreements, competitive dialogue, mandatory exclusion of tenderers and the standstill period.[23]

23 This guidance is available on the OGC's website: www.ogc.gov.uk.

Chapter 35

Private Finance Initiative

35.1 Outline

The last chapter described the Public Procurement Directives. This chapter continues the public sector theme by describing a particular form of outsourcing, the Private Finance Initiative ("PFI").

35.2 Introduction to PFI

35.2.1 History

The concept behind the launch of PFI in 1992 by the Conservative Government was to procure public sector projects through a mechanism which allocates risk to the party best able to manage it and hence achieve better value for money for the public sector. The emphasis was to look at the whole-life cost of a project being the construction or provision of the asset and its ongoing upkeep including renewal or replacement. The structures developed also enabled the assets created to be off-balance sheet to the public sector customer. However, in the Budget of 2008 the government announced that it will move to using the International Financial Reporting Standards ("IFRS") from 2009–10, which may mean that such projects are shown on the balance sheet in the future.

Although PFI was introduced by the Conservative Government, it has been used extensively by the Labour Government since 1997 and there are now over 510 PFI projects operational in the UK, with an aggregate capital value of £45.1 billion.

PFI has attracted criticisms as well as strong supporters. The principal concerns raised have tended to be linked to a perceived lack of transparency and objections to the involvement of the private sector in the provision of public services. The recently announced moved to IFRS should ensure that PFI projects are more clearly visible. However, the nature of PFI arrangements as long-term partnerships means they are likely to remain more complex than "traditional" procurement models, which is seen by some to restrict transparency. The guidance and standardised contracts provided by central government together with the increased use of PFI help to provide clarity and understanding on most aspects of PFI projects.

The UK government has clearly stated that it will only procure infrastructure under PFI where it represents value for money to do so. The value-for-money analysis entails looking at the whole-life cost of the project and PFI projects are subject to a relatively high level of scrutiny. Various reports have highlighted the successes of PFI, including a 2008 National Audit Office Report, "Making changes in operational PFI projects". In particular, this report found that 96 per cent of projects were performing at least satisfactorily; 97 per cent of project managers stated that the relationship between the public and private sector partners was satisfactory or better; and 90 per cent of project managers were satisfied or very satisfied with the quality of work done to implement changes.

35.2.2 Guidance

The development of PFI has been assisted by guidance and best practice notes being issued by the public sector. The first edition of the standardisation of PFI contracts was published in July 1999. This has been updated on a number of occasions and the current edition of the standardisation of PFI contracts is version 4 issued in April 2007 and commonly referred to as "SoPC4". Standard contracts have also been published for transactions in a variety of sectors including health, schools and street lighting.

35.3 Contract structure

Typically in a PFI contract, the supplier will incorporate a special purpose vehicle ("SPV") which is a limited company with the major subcontractors and any third-party equity providers being the shareholders. The SPV enters into the project agreement or concession with the customer, whilst at the same time entering into back-to-back arrangements with subcontractors and financing documentation in order to fund the capital costs of providing the assets.[1]

The customer will be required to enter into a direct agreement with the funders, primarily to enable the funders to exercise rights of step in (that is, the takeover of the supplier's rights and obligations under the project agreement) if the supplier defaults. The customer will have the benefit of direct warranties from the subcontractors, although these will only be enforceable in very limited circumstances.

Figure 1 sets out a typical structure.

Figure 1 *Typical contract structure*

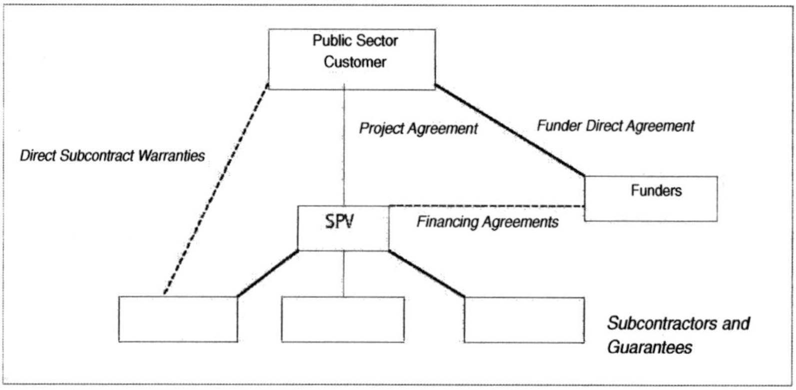

1 The structure is, in effect, a particular type of prime contractor relationship – *see* 17.2 above.

35.4 Finance

PFI transactions are financed with a mixture of debt and equity. The ratio varies from project to project; however, the typical ratio has been approximately 90 per cent senior debt to 10 per cent equity. Project finance techniques are used to finance PFI transactions with the senior debt being raised either through bank financing or via the capital markets, most usually by way of wrapped index-linked or fixed bonds. The financing depends largely on the customer being a public sector body, and therefore having an extremely strong covenant. Accordingly, there are tight controls (e.g. limited assignment rights) to ensure the public sector status is preserved for the life of the project.

35.5 Service description

As with many outsourcing agreements, the public sector customer under a PFI contract specifies its requirement in terms of outputs. The outputs are intended to describe what the customer requires the supplier to supply and the standards of performance required.[2] The supplier is afforded the flexibility to determine how the specified outputs are to be met. The customer must resist being prescriptive as to the methodology for service delivery as, by doing so, design or performance risk may be retained rather than being passed to the supplier.

35.6 Commencement of payment

A fundamental part of PFI contracts is that the customer pays for a service rather than for the construction or procurement of an asset. The doctrine is "no service – no fee". Accordingly, no payments are made until service provision commences. By way of example, in a PFI contract for the provision of accommodation services, the customer makes no payments to the supplier until the construction of the building required to provide the services is complete and it can move into the accommodation. The supplier therefore takes the risk of cost overruns or delays.

35.7 Financial deductions

Once service provision has commenced, the customer pays a unitary payment or service fee for the services it receives, subject to those services being provided to the standards specified in the contract. If the services are not provided to the required standards, the customer is entitled to operate the payment mechanism so as to make financial deductions for poor performance.[3]

The primary remedy in a PFI contract for poor performance is the application of the payment mechanism deduction regime. This is often expressed as a "sole remedy", thereby preventing the customer from suing the supplier for breach of contract for failure to deliver the required

2 PFI contracts will generally be either "business outcome" or "service output" based – *see* 1.7 above.
3 This type of payment arrangement is discussed more fully in 18.4 above.

services. However, the customer will also typically reserve to itself other contractual remedies if service delivery is below standard, including rights of self-help and the right to require the supplier to change its subcontractor.

35.8 Relief events and compensation events

Whilst the supplier accepts the risk of non-payment where services are not delivered even in no-fault situations, for example insured events, the supplier is given an element of relief against certain no-fault events, known as "relief events" or "force majeure events". These are described in greater detail in 30.9 above.

35.9 Adjustments to the charges

Typically, the unitary payment is indexed annually by reference to the RPI or other indexes. The supplier is generally not able to adjust its prices during the term of the project unless the customer changes the services required, in which case a prescribed change procedure will be followed (*see* Chapter 22). The project agreement may also provide for the adjustment of the unitary payment by the application of benchmarking or market testing of the services.

35.10 Term

Chapter 23 deals in detail with issues relating to the term of an outsourcing agreement and the basis for termination, although a few issues need to be considered in the context of PFI transactions. Generally, PFI contracts have a longer term than pure outsourcing agreements. This is particularly the case where significant capital expenditure has to be made by the supplier; the ability to cover this expenditure over, typically, 20 to 30 years assists the customer with affordability issues.

The length of the contract will cover any construction or procurement phase as well as the operational phase, during which the assets are made available to the customer. The duration is generally fixed, and a delay in service commencement will not entitle the supplier to an extended contract term. This further underpins the transfer of risk to the supplier.

35.11 Termination

The grounds for termination referred to in Chapter 23 apply to PFI agreements, although specific provisions apply in relation to force majeure and relief events (*see 30*.5 above).

35.12 Termination compensation

On termination of a PFI contract (other than for supplier default) the customer pays compensation to the supplier. SoPC4 sets out how that compensation should be calculated in a typical PFI.

It ranges from extensive compensation for the supplier, its subcontractors and funders if the authority defaults or voluntarily terminates, to a requirement to compensate only senior funders fully, with more limited compensation to the supplier and its subcontractors on a termination following force majeure.

On termination or expiry, usually the asset transfers or reverts to the customer. Exceptionally, where the supplier accepts the residual value risk of the asset, the customer "walks away" leaving the asset with the supplier.

35.13 Change in law

The approach to changes in law relating to outsourcing agreements is covered in 22.14.2 above.

35.14 Insurance

Historically, the public sector has not taken out commercial insurance, but has, in effect, self-insured. Under PFI contracts, the private sector supplier mitigates the impact of risks it has accepted by a matrix of insurances. For instance, if a building operated under a PFI agreement is damaged by a fire and the customer is unable to occupy it, the customer will not be required to make any service payment to the supplier. Therefore, the supplier will look to insurance cover to meet not only the cost of reinstating the building, but also its loss of income.

35.15 "PFI: Meeting the Investment Challenge"

The report "PFI: Meeting the Investment Challenge" was issued by the Treasury in May 2003. It covers PFI projects only and not other PPPs and relates to England. It does not apply in Scotland, Wales and Northern Ireland as policy on PFI is devolved in these regions.

The report states that the government will only use PFI where it is appropriate and where it will deliver value for money. The report concludes that PFI is appropriate where:

(a) there are major and complex capital projects with significant ongoing maintenance requirements;
(b) the structure of the services allows the public sector to define its needs appropriately as service outputs; and
(c) the nature of the assets to be procured allows them to benefit significantly from whole-of-life costing.

It concluded the PFI is appropriate for projects such as the provision of schools and hospitals. The report concluded that PFI was no longer appropriate for IT projects for the following reasons:

(a) **Fast pace of change**: the fast pace of change in the sector and the close links with the organisations' operational needs makes it difficult for the public sector to establish requirements in the long term. The service requirement in an IT project is likely to change frequently during the course of the contract.

(b) **Integration**: higher levels of integration with public sector business systems make it difficult to clearly delineate areas of responsibility to the client and the supplier and so make an appropriate sharing of risk more difficult to discern and enforce. IT projects are intricate and may involve the integration of proprietary technologies so that it is sometimes impossible to substitute in a timely manner a second IT service provider if the supplier fails to meet its obligations under the contract. This means that, if an adequate service is not delivered, the authority is often at a disadvantage in negotiating with its existing supplier.

(c) **Third-party finance**: there is little or no market for third-party finance. This imposes constraints on the ability of the supplier to finance long, upfront development costs and often requires these costs to be met from corporate borrowing. This has limited the number of suppliers bidding for PFI projects and weakened competition. It also removes a valuable source of due diligence which could ensure appropriate and effective risk allocation in a project.

(d) **Duration**: the duration and phasing of investment, where IT projects have a short life and include significant asset refresh, makes defining and enforcing long-term service needs more problematic.

(e) **Capital investment**: the fact that the costs of IT projects are dominated not by large up-front investment but by running costs.

35.16 "PFI: strengthening long-term partnerships"

The report "PFI: strengthening long-term partnerships" was issued by the Treasury in March 2006. The report confirms that PFI will continue to play a small but important role in the government's overall objective of delivering modernised public services. It states that PFI has and is expected to continue to make up 10–15 per cent of public sector investment.

It states that value for money will continue to be the predominant determinant as to whether to use PFI, but that there will be an increasing emphasis on employees' terms and conditions.

35.17 "Infrastructure procurement: delivering long-term value"

The report "Infrastructure procurement: delivering long-term value" was issued by the Treasury in March 2008. It sets out the government's policy for securing value for money in its procurement of significant assets, infrastructure and long-term service provision and builds, to a significant extent, on its experience of PFI. It states that the government expects procuring authorities and the private sector to consider the lessons from PFI.

The report reaffirms the government's support of the benefits that PFI can bring to the public sector and that PFI will continue to play a "small but important" part in its investment plans, repeating its statements in "PFI: strengthening long-term partnerships". It also states that the government will seek to embed these benefits within other approaches.

It confirms that it will continue to use SoPC4 as the standard form of contract. It also highlights a number of areas where further government guidance is being made available including use of the competitive dialogue procedure, project maturity, joint ventures and a range of specific PFI financing issues.

The report reaffirms that value for money should continue to be the test to determine whether to use conventional procurement, PFI or an alternative PPP approach. Value for money can be defined as being the optimum combination of whole-life cost and fitness for purpose to meet the user's requirement. The report also sets out the key principles driving value for money in procurements, building on the guidance developed for PFI. These include asking procuring authorities to:

(a) be clear in their objectives;
(b) focus on whole-life costs;
(c) use an output specification approach;
(d) optimise the allocation of risks;
(e) ensure there is a competitive market;
(f) structure the procurement process appropriately;
(g) leave sufficient flexibility;
(h) ensure there are sufficient incentives; and
(i) allow for robust competition.

One key aspect of the report is its emphasis on a risk-based approach to project structures, with risk being borne by the party best able to manage it, and also to project scrutiny. It stresses that appropriate risk allocation and associated contractual incentives are essential for cost-effective delivery.

Chapter 36

Other Public Sector Guidance

36.1 Outline

Chapter 34 described the EU public procurement directives and Chapter 35 described PFI projects. This chapter describes UK government guidance on public sector projects which are not PFI projects, including:

(a) Office of Government Commerce ("OGC") guidance for ICT procurement;
(b) OGC model ICT Contract;
(c) Intellect's best practice guidance; and
(d) other laws and guidance.

36.2 Guidance for IT procurement

Following the government's decision that PFI is no longer appropriate for IT projects, the OGC first issued draft guidance relating to IT on 28 November 2003[1] and the guidance and Model ICT Contract were most recently updated in May 2008.[2] The guidance covers the following key topics:

(a) Guidance Note 1 (Key Commercial Principles). This deals with both a principal supplier (Section 1) and multi-supplier arrangements (Section 2);
(b) Guidance Note 2 (Payment, Affordability and Asset Ownership). This guidance note deals with developing the right payment mechanism including the structure of the payment model, the basis of payment, legal title to assets and balance sheet treatment;
(c) Guidance Note 3 (Ownership and Licensing of Intellectual Property). This guidance note deals with the pros and cons of full ownership, licensing and joint ownership of intellectual property. It also discusses ownership of IP created during the contract and the consequences of expiry.

36.3 Model ICT Contract

In December 2004, the OGC published a series of model IT terms and conditions. Following their extensive use by the market and further OGC consultation since these first terms and

1 The guidance can be found on the OGC's website at www.ogc.gov.uk.
2 The guidance and model contract can be found on the Partnerships UK website at www.partnershipsuk.org.uk/ictguidance

conditions were produced, the OGC has now developed a full model ICT contract, together with schedules.

The schedules now include proposed drafting covering the full range of contractual matters including: service levels; continuous improvement; insurance requirements; licence terms; escrow terms; implementation plans and testing procedures etc.

The Model ICT Contract is now at version 2.2 and published on the Partnerships UK website. The latest revisions follow on from a consultation process with Intellect (the trade association for the UK technology industry) and input from professional advisers and others, include changes relating to due diligence, supply chain rights, freedom of information, limits of liability, step-in rights, termination rights and benchmarking. Further topics, such as financial distress, are scheduled for review by the OGC and Partnerships UK in the future.[3]

36.4 Mandatory OGC Data Security Drafting

In July 2008, the OGC published its mandatory requirements for the adoption of the OGC ICT Model Contract clauses and provisions relating to security and information assurance.[4] Also *see* the OGC's further information note dated 26 November 2008.[5]

The requirements apply to all new contracts entered into by government bodies post 1 July 2008. The basic mandatory requirement is for there to be contractual clauses in all agreements with suppliers which deal with the following issues in all contracts where personal or other confidential information will be used, disseminated or otherwise handled by a Procuring Authority and any other third party associated with the contract (i.e. not just applicable to ICT contracts):

(a) contractor personnel – staffing security;
(b) authority data;
(c) protection of personal data;
(d) freedom of information;
(e) confidentiality;
(f) security requirements;
(g) warranties.

There should also be a security requirements document and a security plan. The recommended drafting is that included in the Model ICT Contract.

3 *See* ICT Guidance, Version 2.2: Revisions from Version 2.1.

4 This followed a report reviewing the government's data handling procedures called "Data Handling Procedures in Government: Final Report" June 2008 *see* www.cabinetoffice.gov.uk/media/65948/dhr080625.pdf. The report sets out how government is improving its arrangements around information and data security, by putting in place core protective measures, getting the working culture right, improving accountability and scrutiny of performance.

5 Procurement Policy Note: Data Handling Review – Information note 13/08./ *see* www.ogc.gov.uk/documents/PPN13_08_Data_Handling.pdf.

36.5 Intellect's contracting best practice guidance

Intellect is the ICT industry body. In April 2006, it launched its "Contracting best practice guidance for suppliers" in response to the OGC's model terms and conditions. Intellect key comments are as follows:

(a) it is concerned that the public sector will take a "one size fits all" approach to public sector agreements, thus inhibiting flexibility;
(b) it recognises that competition is a necessary part of public sector procurement whilst stating that this should not be used as a means to impose onerous terms and conditions, lowest price and maximum perceived risk transfer to the supplier without addressing the real, longer term needs of the customer;
(c) it highlights that the customer's expectations and assumptions need to be clearly communicated to avoid misunderstanding;
(d) it feels that there is insufficient recognition within the public sector of the customer's necessary role in contributing towards successful IT projects;
(e) it suggests that agreements should provide for phased delivery without the customer having the right to claw back payments previously made if delivery is not completed.

36.6 "Sustainable Procurement"

If there was a prize for the most overused phrase in the public sector this decade it would be "sustainable procurement". "Sustainable procurement" is a generic term used to refer to "green" or "ethical" procurement. There is a growing impetus among public sector procurers to evaluate their supply chain on factors connected to their environmental impact (e.g. How much do they recycle? What is their carbon footprint?). An example of this is recent guidance published by IDEA, the Improvement and Development Agency.[6]

However, the government views "sustainable procurement" as a broader concept. The OGC defines it as "policy-through-procurement", that is, where public procurement is seen as a lever to achieve wider policy objectives. These include:

(a) environmental or "green" issues but also the creation of jobs and wealth in regeneration areas;
(b) opportunities for Small and Medium Enterprises ("SMEs") and Ethnic Minority Businesses ("EMBs");
(c) fair trade and the inclusion of developing countries;
(d) adult basic skills;
(e) disability, race and gender equality;
(f) innovation; and
(g) the promotion of ongoing and contestable supplier markets.

6 *See* "Sustainable Procurement – Making it Happen".

The compatibility between these factors and those permitted to be used to evaluate tenders under the procurement regulations has been questioned by some commentators, but for more information on how public bodies are encouraged to include such factors in procurement *see* www.ogc.gov.uk/documents/Efficiency_Sustainable_Procurement_Statement.pdf.

36.7 Other laws and guidance

There are numerous other laws and guidance relating to public sector outsourcing. Here are a few examples:

(a) OGC PFI Policy Statements, Technical Notes, Gateway Reviews and other releases;[7]
(b) Local Government Act 1999 in respect of the "Best Value" regime;
(c) Local Government Acts 2000 and 2003;
(d) Freedom of Information Act 2000;
(e) Human Rights Act 1998;
(f) OGC Best Practice Guides;[8]
(g) Strategic Partnering Taskforce reports;[9]
(h) various guidance on ownership of IPR;[10]
(i) various guidance on why IT projects fail;[11]
(j) dispute resolution guidance, recommending the use of alternative dispute resolution procedures;[12]
(k) government policy on better IT-enabled change;[13]
(l) guidance and reports on e-government projects, which includes guidance on everything from call centres to IT standards.[14]

7 *See* www.ogc.gov.uk and www.partnershipuk.org.uk.
8 *See* www.ogc.gov.uk.
9 *See* odpm.gov.uk. The final report of the Strategic Partnering Taskforce came out in March 2004.
10 *See* OGC Ownership of IPR – Guidance to Departments, which can be found at www.ogc.gov.uk.
11 *See*, for example, the Bateman Report 1999 and the McCartney Report 2000.
12 *See* the OGC Dispute Resolution Guidance, which can be found at www.ogc.gov.uk.
13 *See* EGUs Transformational Government Plan published in November 2005.
14 See, for example, the Cabinet Office's second progress report for the Transformational Government strategy: Transformational Government – our progress in 2007. The document contains reports from a broad range of public sector service providers, and highlights progress made in shared services, customer satisfaction, and making services more citizen-centric.

Chapter 37

Utilities Sector

37.1 Outline

Chapters 34 and 36 deal with outsourcing by public sector bodies. This chapter concerns regulation in utilities including procurement directives, which are in some ways similar to the public procurement directives. It also includes a short description of some of the other issues of particular relevance to utilities.

Outsourcing in the utility sector is a really fascinating topic with some utilities having embraced a model which involves wholesale outsourcing, some having entered into substantial offshore outsourcing agreements and yet others preferring to retain services in-house wherever possible.

37.2 Introduction

The Utilities Directive[1] is designed to regulate the award by utility bodies of works, services and supplies contracts above specified financial thresholds by providing transparent award procedures and promoting the equality of treatment of all suppliers.

37.3 When does the Utilities Directive apply?

In deciding whether the Utilities Directive will govern a proposed outsourcing, a utility must consider the issues described in Table 56.

Table 56 *When does the Utilities Directive apply?*

Contracts for works, supplies or services

For a proposed outsourcing to be subject to the Utilities Directive, the contract must come within the definition of "service contracts", "works contracts" or "supply contracts" as set out in Article 1 of the Utilities Directive. Most outsourcing contracts are likely to fall within the definition of "service contracts": "contracts for pecuniary interest concluded in writing between one or more [of the] contracting entities [...] and one or more contractors, suppliers, or service providers".

1 Directive 2004/17/EC which replaces the previous Utilities Directive 93/38/EEC.

Utilities

The Utilities Directive applies to a utility that seeks offers in relation to a proposed supply contract, works contract or service contract. The Utilities Directive refers to utilities as "contracting entities". Contracting entities are defined in Article 2(2) of the Utilities Directive and include public bodies, public undertakings and private undertakings, provided those private undertakings operate on the basis of "special or exclusive rights" (*see* further below). Moreover, each of these bodies and undertakings must undertake one of the relevant utility activities referred to in Articles 3 to 7 of the Directive in order to fall within the definition of a "contracting entity". (For ease of reference, this chapter will continue to refer to "contracting entities" as "utilities".) The relevant utility activities are activities in the gas, electricity, water, transport and postal sectors (e.g. operation of a fixed electricity network or supply of electricity into that network).

Special or exclusive rights

The Utilities Directive only applies to private sector undertakings where they carry out one of the relevant utility activities, where the contract is awarded in pursuit of that activity and they carry on that activity on the basis of special or exclusive rights. This test has been tightened up under the Utilities Directive and it seems likely that, as a result, private sector undertakings will be regulated less frequently than was the case prior to the introduction of the current Utilities Directive (Directive 2004/17/EC). Under the old Directive (93/38/EEC) a private undertaking could possess special or exclusive rights merely if it had been granted special rights (e.g. a licence) by a relevant Member State authority, allowing it to undertake the relevant utility activity. However, under the current Directive a private undertaking must possess similar special rights and it must also be the case that the effect of the grant of those special rights is to limit the exercise of the activity to one or more entities, thereby substantially affecting the ability of other entities to carry out such activity.

Financial thresholds

The Utilities Directive will only apply to contracts worth more than a specified threshold. The thresholds were most recently revised on 1 January 2008; the threshold is €412,000 in respect of services contracts.[2]

Annex XVII A and Annex XVII B services

Annex XVII of the Utilities Directive classifies services as either "Annex XVII A" or "Annex XVII B" and this classification determines the level of regulation that will apply to the procurement of a service.

Annex XVII A services are subject to the full application of the Utilities Directive and include, for example maintenance and repair services, financial services, insurance services, computer and related services, architectural services and refuse collection.

In relation to Annex XVII B services, utilities are required to ensure a certain degree of transparency in relation to their procurement process insofar as they must comply with

2 The thresholds are revised every two years, so the next time they are due to be revised is 1 January 2010.

the requirements concerning technical specifications and publish a contract award notice in the Official Journal of the European Union. It is not absolutely clear at present whether the implications of the case law for Annex II B public services contracts (i.e. the requirement to advertise these contracts and hold a fair competition where such contracts may be of certain cross-border interest) applies to Annex XVII B utilities services contracts. This will depend on the status of the utility in question. For example, if a utility is wholly or majority state owned, the case law is more likely to be relevant.

Exemptions to the Utilities Directive

Articles 19–26 of the Utilities Directive contain various specific exemptions covering, for example, contracts for the acquisition of land and buildings and certain contracts for research and development services.

However, the key exemption for many utilities is the "affiliated undertaking" exemption contained in Article 23 of the Utilities Directive. This exemption permits utilities to award contracts (for works, services or supplies) directly to "affiliated undertakings" as defined in the Directive (i.e. subsidiaries or fellow subsidiaries) provided the essence of the affiliated undertaking is to provide such works, services or supplies to the utility or other undertakings within the group of companies. A test is laid down in the Directive to determine whether that in fact is the case. Should a utility wish to rely on this exemption, it must consider in each case whether the affiliated undertaking acquired at least 80 per cent of its average turnover from the provision of such works, services or supplies to the utility or other undertaking with the group of companies. If this cannot be said to be the case, the exemption will not be available to the utility. In the case of start-up businesses, business projections may be used to establish the credibility of this test being met in future.

In a similar vein, there is an exemption for the award of contracts between members of a joint venture established exclusively by utilities.

Special exemption mechanism

The current Utilities Directive introduced a special exemption mechanism whereby Member States or utilities themselves can apply to the European Commission to have certain sectors exempted from the scope of the Utilities Directive. An exemption will be granted only if evidence can be adduced to show that the utility activity in question is directly exposed to competition and access to the market is not restricted (e.g. because steps have been taken in line with relevant Community law to liberalise the market). Examples of some sectors excluded on this basis include electricity and/or gas supply in England, Scotland and Wales,[3] the supply of certain courier and parcel services in Denmark,[4] the supply of certain postal services in Finland[5] and the production and sale of electricity in Sweden.[6]

3 Commission decision 2007/141/EC of 26 February 2007.
4 Commission decision 2007/169/EC of 16 March 2007.
5 Commission decision 2007/564/EC of 6 August 2007.
6 Commission decision 2007/706/EC of 29 October 2007.

37.4 The award procedures

If a proposed outsourcing is subject to the Utilities Directive, the utility may freely decide which award procedure it will use. The procedures it may choose from are set out below. It is worth noting that the competitive dialogue procedure which is available under the Public Procurement Directive is not provided for in the Utilities Directive.

37.4.1 Open procedure

Under the open procedure, all interested parties may tender for a contract. There is no scope for negotiation pre or post submission of tenders. Post tender, discussions between the utility and bidders must be limited to clarifications. A utility is bound to make its choice solely on the basis of the written tender, subject to clarifications. There is also no opportunity for the utility to limit the number of tenders it has to consider – tenders from all suitably qualified candidates must be evaluated.

As a result, this procedure is not used for the procurement of complex contracts. It is most applicable for the procurement of goods, where there is a clear and comprehensive specification, and price is likely to be the key determinant.

37.4.2 Restricted procedure

In the restricted procedure, the utility invites expressions of interest and only those organisations shortlisted by the utility may submit tenders. The number of organisations shortlisted must be sufficient to ensure genuine competition. At least three organisations would generally ensure sufficient competition, although this should be assessed on a case-by-case basis.

Similarly to the open procedure, there is no scope for negotiation pre or post submission of tenders (post-tender discussions are limited to clarifications on the information provided or the content of the tenders) and the utility is bound to make its choice solely on the basis of the written tenders, subject to those clarifications. Again, this procedure is seen as inappropriate for complex projects.

37.4.3 Negotiated procedure

Under the negotiated procedure, the utility consults suppliers of its choice and negotiates the terms of the contract with one or more of them.

There are two types of negotiated procedure: a competitive version which is pre-advertised in the Official Journal of the European Union and a non-competitive version which does not have to be advertised.

37.4.4 Competitive negotiated procedure

Under the competitive negotiated procedure, the utility negotiates the terms of the contract with one or more organisations shortlisted by it. Like the restricted procedure, the number of organisations shortlisted must be sufficient to ensure genuine competition (i.e. at least three).

37.4.5 Non-competitive negotiated procedure

The use of the non-competitive negotiated procedure is very exceptional and can only be used under certain conditions which have been construed narrowly by the courts, and the burden of proving if these conditions have been met rests with the utility. The conditions include, for example:

(a) where a previous procedure has failed (e.g. no bids were received or the bids received do not address the utility's requirements);
(b) where there is only one possible provider (where due to technical or artistic reasons or reasons connected with the protection of exclusive rights[7] the services can be provided by only one provider); or
(c) where additional services are required from an existing provider and the services were unforeseen at the time of the original advertisement, provided: (i) there are technical and economic reasons why the additional services could not be separated from those already provided without great inconvenience to the utility; or (ii) the additional services are strictly necessary for the completion of the contract. In contrast to the Public Procurement Directive, there is no threshold on the value of the additional services. However, it may be prudent to apply some form of threshold and the 50 per cent threshold in the Public Procurement Directive may be a suitable guide.

37.5 The procurement process

Once it has been established that a proposed outsourcing project is subject to the Utilities Directive and the utility has chosen an appropriate award procedure, the next step is to embark upon the actual procurement process.

37.5.1 Advertising the project

Where a utility is undertaking a competitive award procedure it must advertise the project. It can do this in one of three ways:

(a) place a contract (or "OJEU") notice in the Official Journal of the European Union;
(b) place a periodic indicative notice (or "PIN") in the Official Journal; or
(c) place a notice on the existence of a qualification system in the Official Journal.

These notices, which are essentially standard forms, are available on the SIMAP website.[8] Utilities commonly use qualification systems, as they are convenient. Qualification systems enable utilities to establish a list of qualified suppliers from which it can select suppliers to tender for a particular contract without having to go back out to the market each time. Moreover, a qualification system can be set up to run for up to three years without any further or refresher notice having to be published. A qualification system may be used in conjunction with the restricted or negotiated procedures only. (*See* also 37.5.4 below.)

7 However, exclusive rights does not extend to situations where the exclusive right is licensed or can be reasonably obtained on licence.
8 *See* SIMAP website at: www.simap.europa.int.

With all of these notices, it is important to take great care when drafting them as they set the parameters for the entire project or projects. If the notice is incomplete or poorly drafted it may be open for interested parties to claim subsequently that all or part of the project has not been advertised properly.

The Utilities Directive set out various time limits for the dispatch of the various notices and time limits for interested parties to respond to the notices. These periods normally begin to run from the date on which the notice is sent to the OJEU.

37.5.2 Pre-qualification

Pre-qualification is essentially the initial shortlisting of the respondents to the notice. The Utilities Directive require utilities to use objective criteria for shortlisting. This may include financial and technical capacity, although the Utilities Directive is not as prescriptive on this point as the Public Procurement Directive. There are also now grounds on which public sector utilities must exclude certain economic operators, such as those convicted of corruption or money laundering. Private sector utilities may exclude economic operators on this basis, but they do not have to.

37.5.3 Tender stage

The tender stage follows pre-qualification. Here the pre-qualified bidders will be issued with the tender documents which they will use to prepare their tenders.

Article 55(1) of the Utilities Directive provides that a contract must be awarded on the basis of either the most economically advantageous tender ("MEAT") or the lowest price.[9]

The utility is required to specify clearly in advance, in either the OJEU notice or the contract documents, the criteria by which it will select its preferred bidder. The utility must, if possible, state the weighting which it gives to each of the criteria chosen.

Once bids have been evaluated in accordance with the evaluation criteria the contract will be awarded.

37.5.4 Framework agreements and qualification systems

The Utilities Directive provides for the use of framework agreements and qualification systems.

The requirements for awarding a framework agreement are the same as for other contracts covered by the Utilities Directive. Where a utility awards a framework agreement in accordance with the Utilities Directive, it may call off contracts under that framework agreement without being required to advertise the contract by way of a separate notice. It is worth noting that the rules on framework agreements are more flexible for utilities than for contracting authorities under the Public Procurement Directive. For example, utilities are not subject to a specified time limit on such agreements, whereas framework agreements in the public sector cannot usually exceed four years.

9 Most outsourcing contracts would be awarded on the basis of the most economically advantageous tender, as otherwise the customer is prevented from assessing tenders on a qualitative basis.

The Utilities Directive requires, nevertheless, that framework agreements must not be used to hinder, limit or distort competition. This means that, for example, framework agreements should not be so long that they prevent new organisations from entering the marketplace.

Qualification systems are akin in certain ways to framework agreements. As noted above, they enable utilities to establish a list of qualified suppliers. However, the key difference with qualification systems is that they are an open list of qualified suppliers; a utility must allow economic operators to apply for qualification at any time during its operation. Framework agreements are closed lists; a supplier that fails to apply to qualify by the stated time limit may not be allowed to join the framework agreement at a later date.

37.5.5 Electronic procurement

The Utilities Directive provides for the use of email and electronic procurement systems for the first time. It allows the use of an e-auction phase under the open, restricted or negotiated procedures. Only those elements of tenders that are quantifiable may be subject to an e-auction as these systems are not suitable for subjective evaluation.

37.5.6 Alcatel notice and standstill period

The *Alcatel* case and the new Remedies Directive (*see* 34.5.6) also apply to utilities contracts. To recap, *Alcatel* imposes a standstill period between the decision on contract award and the contract being entered into. The new Remedies Directive (the provisions of which must be implemented in all Member States by 20 December 2009) states that the standstill period must last at least 10 calendar days (if all bidders are notified of the utility's decision at the beginning of this period by email or fax) or 15 days (if notification is by post). Utilities must notify bidders with a summary of the reasons as to why they have been unsuccessful, the name of the successful tenderer and the reasons why that tenderer was successful. Again, until the new Remedies Directive is implemented into Member States' national laws, utilities should continue to comply with their national laws on the standstill period.

37.5.7 Contract award

Following contract award, Article 43 of the Utilities Directive requires a utility to send a contract award notice to the OJEU within two months. This notice must be prepared using a specific template.

37.6 Remedies for breach of the Utilities Directive

There is a specific Utilities Remedies Directive[10] which sets out the remedies available to bidders participating in tender processes run by utilities under the Utilities Directive. The remedies and the requirements for obtaining them before the relevant national court or review body are the same as set out in the Public Sector Remedies Directive (*see* 34.6 above). They are due to be

10 Directive 92/13/EEC.

revised largely in the same way as the Public Sector Remedies Directive on or before 20 December 2009 (again, *see* 34.6 above).

An unsuccessful supplier also has a right to make a complaint to the European Commission where it suspects the Utilities Directive has been breached. However, this may be a less fruitful route if the utility is not in some way controlled or influenced by the State. In practice, most complaints to the Commission are in relation to public sector bodies.

37.7 Implementation of the Utilities Directive in the UK

The Utilities Procurement Directive has been implemented in the UK by the Utilities Contracts Regulations 2006 ("Utilities Regulations"). These Regulations came into force in the UK on 31 January 2006 and apply to all contracts awarded on or after that date. They include a mandatory standstill period as already referred to at 34.8 above.

37.8 Other issues relating to outsourcing by utilities

37.8.1 Criminal liability

Utilities will be reluctant to outsource operations where they have criminal liability for problems. For example, in the water industry there is a requirement that water supplied to any premises must be fit for human consumption. Breach of that requirement is a criminal offence. The duty is a statutory duty which cannot be delegated so as to avoid the criminal liability resulting from its breach. Therefore, water companies may prefer not to outsource operational activities which could lead to water being unfit for human consumption.

37.8.2 Price regulation

Regulated utilities may also be subject to additional restrictions when entering into transactions with associated companies. Typically, these will require the utility to undertake some form of market testing process to ensure that the contract terms are "arm's length" and that there is no cross-subsidy by the regulated business. In many cases, the utility will be required to report details of such transactions to the relevant regulator, who will have powers to investigate where cross-subsidy is suspected.

37.8.3 Unbundling requirements

The government is currently considering what to do about extending competition in the water industry. It commissioned Martin Cave to report on this, and at the time of writing he had just published his interim findings. The final report will come out in the spring of 2009. He has recommended that legislation be introduced to permit much wider competition than there is at the moment.

In the meantime, there is some preparation for expected competition in the future which is not dependent on legislation, namely the separation of the various parts of water and sewerage companies' businesses. This separation will be done on an accounting basis initially so that as and when any unbundling of the whole system is authorised, that part of the exercise will have been done. Longer term, if the break-up of the industry is sanctioned, it will be interesting to see whether this leads to an increase in outsourcing, as companies adjust to the new framework and consider how best to react to the competition forces that will come to bear on what they do.

37.8.4 Audit arrangement

See 10.13.

Part Eleven – Offshore Outsourcing

Chapter 38

Offshore and Near-shore Outsourcing

38.1 Outline

Chapters 33 to 37 deal with issues affecting different sectors.

This chapter covers the general commercial and legal issues relating to offshore and near-shore outsourcing, including: the additional due diligence which must be carried out; additional factors relating to structuring the offshore and near-shore outsourcing arrangement; special tips for preparing service descriptions, service levels and charging regimes for offshore and near-shore arrangements; termination grounds; the FSA guidance on offshore and near-shore arrangements; data protection issues and the relevance of TUPE.

Chapters 39, 40, 42 and 48 deal with specific issues relating to outsourcing to India, China, Spain and Ireland.

38.2 Services offshored and offshore destinations

38.2.1 Services offshored

Services commonly outsourced to offshore locations include software development, call-centre services, and some types of business process outsourcing services. There is a growing trend in the UK for customers to opt to retain their customer-facing operations in the UK and offshore their back-office processes.

38.2.2 Offshore destinations[1]

Services are outsourced to various different countries, depending upon the country from which the services are being outsourced and hence the language spoken by the customer. In Germany,

---

1 *See* also the Gartner Group's report on "Top 30 Countries for Offshore Services", published in December 2008. Gartner's top 30 locations for offshore services, by region, were:

(a) Americas: Argentina, Brazil, Canada, Chile, Costa Rica, Mexico and Panama.
(b) Asia Pacific: Australia, China, India, Malaysia, New Zealand, Pakistan, the Philippines, Singapore, Thailand and Vietnam.
(c) Europe, the Middle East and Africa ("EMEA"): the Czech Republic, Egypt, Hungary, Ireland, Israel, Morocco, Poland, Romania, Russia, Slovakia, South Africa, Spain and Ukraine.

the most common offshore outsourcing destinations are Africa and Eastern Europe (in particular Poland and the Czech Republic). In France they are North Africa and in Spain, they are South and Central America.[2]

In the UK, the most common destination has been India. Outsourcing of services to India became more common as technological advances made geographical location less critical to the provision of services. India was regarded as a good cultural fit with Britain, and English companies were impressed by the number of IT-trained workers graduating each year. Indian services used to be cheap, although, as at the date of writing this Guide, recent fluctuations in sterling and the rupee had undermined some of the financial benefits for UK customers, although the rupee has weakened about 20 per cent in 2008 against the dollar, making it cheaper for Indian companies to provide services to their global clients. Some commentators suggested that the terrorist attacks on Mumbai and the scandal involving Satyam would adversely affect outsourcing to India, although it is difficult to see that these factors will have a material long-term effect.

38.3 Political implications of offshore outsourcing

Offshore outsourcing arrangements are often highly political, high profile and extremely unpopular.[3] Although there is some evidence that offshoring does not lead to an overall reduction in job opportunities.[4] There is also research which indicates that there is a maximum number of jobs which can be outsourced to offshore locations.

38.3.1 US and UK policy

President Barack Obama has said that, while the US cannot "shy away" from globalisation, he will take measures to ensure that jobs are not shipped offshore. During his tenure as Senator, he co-sponsored the Patriot Employer Act (H.R. 5907, S. 1945) which would have amended the

2 *See* part twelve of this Guide for further information about outsourcing in key EU countries.

3 *See* for example the research by KPMG in 2005 which found that two-thirds of bank customers surveyed would be concerned if they knew that their personal banking details would be held in a customer service centre outside the UK.

4 *See* the statistics produced by the Office of National Statistics, which show that employment in the call centre and IT sectors increased by 8.8 per cent, almost three times as fast as the national average (which was 3.2 per cent) in the four years prior to September 2005, despite the growth of offshore outsourcing. *See* also the study by the US IT industry body the Association for Computing Machinery ("ACM"), which found that, while the annual job loss rate attributable to offshore outsourcing is around 2–3 per cent of the IT workforce in the US, there is a higher level of job creation. *See* the McKinsey study in 2005, which found that for every $1 spent by US companies in India on offshoring services, the US economy as a whole gained $1.14 to $1.17. The benefits resulted from cost savings made by US companies being passed onto customers and investors, profits in US offshoring centres being repatriated and US workers being re-employed in new jobs. US companies also increased their share of sales of IT products to India. It is interesting that the study found that the French economy gained only 86 cents from every €1 invested in offshoring centres, partly because the inflexibility of the French labour market meant that unemployed workers found it harder to find new jobs.

existing tax laws and provided a tax credit to employers who increase the number of full-time workers in the US relative to those outside the US.

Obama's online manifesto states:

> "[We] believe that companies should not get billions of dollars in tax deductions for moving their operations overseas,"
>
> "[We] will reward companies that create good jobs with good benefits for American workers, and provide a tax credit to companies that maintain or increase the number of full-time workers in America relative to those outside the US."

In the UK, the Prime Minister, Gordon Brown has spoken out in favour of free trade.

38.3.2 Effect of the current recession

The period of uncertainty in the latter part of 2008 led to a reduction in offshore outsourcing to India. *The Economist* reported on 13 December 2008: "Since Lehman Brothers went bust in September and financial markets froze, India's outsourcing firms have struggled to clinch deals."

S. Gopalakrishnan, the chief executive officer of Infosys Technologies, said in an interview that in his more than three decades in the domestic outsourcing industry, this was the worst slowdown he had witnessed.

The credit crunch has had other effects upon the offshore market. Most big firms hired fewer people in 2008. For example, Tata Consultancy Services ("TCS") recruited 3,000, a huge number, but down from 35,000 in the previous year. Partly because of falling demand, the average rise in IT wages halved, to around 10 per cent a year. Attrition rates fell by a similar amount.[5]

Now that it is clear that the UK is in a recession, outsourcing is forecast to increase (*see* Chapter 49). This raises the question of whether offshore outsourcing will increase (and if so whether near-shore or offshore locations other than India will become popular) or whether the economic problems will result in increasing protectionist approaches by governments.

A study by consultants KPMG (reported in the *Financial Times* on 20 February 2009) stated that the recession is expected to prompt a fresh "rush" of employers seeking to outsource services to new locations such as Belfast, Sofia and Cairo rather than to traditional centres such as Bangalore and Chennai. The report names 31 "locations to watch", which it says will "swallow up a large proportion of the new outsourcing work" as more traditional locations "rapidly approach saturation point". The locations range from well-known cities in developed countries such as Winnipeg, Belfast, Buenos Aires and Brisbane to lesser-known places in emerging markets such as Queretaro in Mexico, Davao City in the Philippines and Cluj-Napoca in Romania.

---

5 *See The Economist*, 13 December 2008.

38.4 Preparation by the customer

Chapters 2 and 4 emphasised the importance of the customer carrying out sufficient due diligence to ensure that its business objectives will be satisfied by the outsourcing arrangement. Customers considering offshore outsourcing arrangements will need to consider all of the issues raised in those chapters. They will also need to consider additional factors such as those mentioned in Table 57.[6]

Table 57 *Additional factors to be considered in due diligence*

Customer's business objective

Will offshore outsourcing satisfy the customer's short-term business objectives?

Will it continue to satisfy future business objectives (e.g. if the economy changes and the customer's business objective changes from cutting costs to expansion)?

Knowledge of the customer's business

How important is it that the staff providing the services understand the customer's business, operating practices and culture?

Will the staff of an offshore supplier have the necessary understanding?

How will any lack of understanding of such factors affect the services provided by the supplier?

How can any lack of understanding be addressed?

Time difference

What is the time difference between the customer's location and the supplier's location?

Is this an advantage (e.g. by enabling the development of software or the provision of call-centre services 24 hours a day, seven days a week)?

Is it a disadvantage (e.g. by making communication between the parties difficult)?

Will the customer need to select a supplier with a presence within the UK to liaise with the offshore service delivery unit?

If the customer has previously outsourced its IT and now outsourced its business processes, will it need to amend its agreement with its IT outsourcing supplier, for example to extend the services hours during which IT systems are available?

6 In September 2005, PwC examined experiences and best practice in offshoring by financial institutions, following a survey of 156 senior executives in financial institutions. In the resulting report "Offshoring in the financial services industry: risks and rewards", PwC stated that many firms felt that they would have benefited from investing more in planning and shaping the deal.

Termination

How would the customer bring the services back in house or transfer them to another supplier on termination of the offshore agreement? Should the customer adopt a multi-sourcing approach to ensure continuity on termination?

Will offshoring result in a loss of technical expertise or business knowledge? How will the customer ensure that it will have the information to transfer the services to another supplier or to bring the services back in house on termination?

Stability and security issues

How stable is the business and political climate?

What is the risk of natural disasters affecting the location from which the services will be provided?

Is the offshore country involved in a political conflict that may affect the safety and security of the location from which the services will be provided?

Are there any problems with data security and corruption?

Reputation

If the offshore element is unpopular, how will this affect the customer's brand or sales of the customer's products?

Government and laws

How supportive to offshore outsourcing is the government in the offshore location?

What is the legal system in the offshore location?

Are there any regulatory obligations which must be satisfied in the UK (e.g. FSA requirements) or in the offshore location?[7]

How difficult would it be to enforce a judgment against the outsourcing supplier in the foreign court?

Should the customer deal with any enforcement difficulties by agreeing that disputes will be resolved by alternative dispute resolution procedures or by requiring the supplier to provide a performance bond?

What protection is provided in the offshore legal system for the customer's IPR, for example is the offshore location a signatory of the WTO's TRIPS agreement and/or other international instruments?[8]

7 For a description of data protection issues, *see* Chapter 32.

8 TRIPS stands for Trade-Related Aspects of Intellectual Property Rights, which is part of the World Trade Organization ("WTO") agreement on international trade. Signatories to TRIPS are obliged to provide certain minimal standards of intellectual property protection. Customers entering into agreements with Indian suppliers must take specialist advice on IPR issues. The customer may want the supplier to hold seminars for its employees explaining about the protection of IPR.

Is confidential information protected by the relevant legal system?

Are there any exchange controls?

If the arrangement will involve a transfer of technology, will export controls apply?

Are there any restrictions on the customer owning companies in the offshore jurisdiction?

Are there any restrictions on software exports?

Will the relevant foreign court enforce a clause stating that the agreement will be governed by English law and that the English courts will have the exclusive jurisdiction to determine disputes?

Does the local law imply any provisions into the outsourcing agreement?

Are there any relevant employment laws which will affect the provision of the services?

Will the law in the offshore location limit the enforceability of certain provisions in the outsourcing agreement, for example limitations of liability, termination rights or dispute resolution provisions?

Costs and charges

How much cheaper will the services be if they are provided offshore?

For how long are they likely to remain at this price? For how long will the supplier guarantee the same prices?

How will fluctuations in exchange rates affect costs and who will bear the risk of these?

Are there any hidden costs of offshore outsourcing?

What increased costs will be incurred in the training of and knowledge transfer to offshore staff before they can provide the services being outsourced?

What increased costs will be incurred in training onshore staff?

What increased costs will be incurred in managing the transition to the offshore outsourcing supplier?

Will the customer need to amend its existing software licences to ensure that they cover a supplier in the offshore location and, if so, how much will this cost?

What increased costs will be incurred in managing the services after transition?

What increased costs will be incurred during the term of the arrangement?

What travel costs will be incurred in travelling to the offshore location?

Will there be additional telecommunications costs? Who will be responsible for these?

Taxation

Will the offshoring be regarded as a permanent establishment for taxation purposes?

Are there any transfer pricing issues?

Will withholding tax apply?

Are there any taxation incentives or lower tax rates? When will the taxation incentives expire?

Will outsourcing the service result in a reduction in revenue for the customer (e.g. if the services comprise the provision of a call centre taking orders for the customer's products)?

Labour pool characteristics

What is the quality of the staff who will provide the services?

Are there independent standards which can be used to assess the quality of the services to be provided by the staff?

Are the staff graduates?

What is the turnover rate for staff in the offshore location and how does it compare with the turnover rate at the customer's business?

Is this likely to change over time?

What are the language skills of the staff who will provide the services?

Do they need to be improved, for example by accent training?

What is the work ethic of the staff?

Geographical location

How far away is the supplier?

Where is the nearest airport and how difficult is it to get to the supplier's premises for the purpose of service management or audit visits?

Infrastructure

What is the quality of the communications, power and utility infrastructure at the offshore location?

How reliable is the internet bandwidth (where relevant)?

How reliable is the electricity network?

How reliable is the telecommunications network?

Culture and training

How different is the supplier's culture from that of the customer (and where relevant, the customer's users or the customer's clients)?

What training will be required to ensure that the supplier can provide the services?

Customer's skills

Does the customer have the skills necessary to run the procurement and then manage the service?

If not, what external advice or training would be necessary?

38.5 Structuring the arrangement

If the customer comes to the conclusion that there is a business case for transferring a service or business function to an offshore location, there are various ways in which it can do this, as described in Table 58.

Table 58 *Types of offshore structures*

Offshore insourcing

As an alternative to outsourcing, the customer may decide to set up its own subsidiary (or "captive") in an offshore location and not to outsource the services or function.

Offshore/onshore supplier

The customer may contract with a local subsidiary of the offshore supplier, which has been established to market the services of the offshore company or to assist in managing the arrangement with the customer, on a day-to-day basis.

Onshore/offshore supplier

The customer can contract with an established UK supplier with an offshore subsidiary.

Offshore supplier

The customer may enter into an agreement with an offshore supplier.

Joint venture

The customer may enter into a joint venture with an offshore supplier. *See* Chapter 15 for a discussion of the implications of the parties entering into a joint venture arrangement. As most offshore outsourcing arrangements are motivated by the customer's desire to achieve cost savings, joint ventures may be inappropriate, unless there are particular taxation incentives. If the customer does decide upon this approach, as well as the additional costs described in Chapter 15, it may have to relocate staff to the offshore location.

BOT (build, operate and transfer) deals

A variation on the joint venture approach is a BOT arrangement. This involves the customer entering into an agreement with an offshore supplier whereby the supplier builds and operates the offshore facilities for the customer for a fixed period of time. At the end of this period, the customer has the option of purchasing the offshore entity or terminating the arrangement and leaving the supplier with the offshore facilities, which the supplier can then use to provide services to other customers.

The factors to be taken into account by the customer in deciding between the various structures described in Table 58 are listed in Table 59.

Table 59 *Relevant factors*

Control

Clearly the customer will have more control over the quality of the offshore operation if it sets up a captive.

Dependence

If the customer sets up a captive, it will avoid becoming dependent upon a third-party supplier.

Cost

Entering into an agreement with a third supplier (whether an established UK company or an offshore company) may avoid some of the set up costs of creating a captive, although once the captive has been established, all of the cost efficiencies will be passed on to the customer.

Adopting a BOT approach may reduce the costs involved if the customer decides against setting up a captive after an initial trial period.

Entering into an agreement with an established UK company with an offshore subsidiary will usually be more expensive than entering into an agreement with an offshore company, as the UK company will charge for providing service management services.

Before the customer selects an appropriate offshore approach, it must take specialist taxation advice and consider the taxation implications of the different options, in particular if the offshore facility is going to be income generating, for example an offshore call centre taking orders for the customer's products.

Management

Contracting with a supplier with an onshore presence:

(a) may improve the management of the services if the onshore supplier acts as a link between the customer and the offshore supplier, ensuring that the offshore supplier understands the customer's requirements and culture;
(b) may undermine the quality of the services if it means that there is a distance between the customer and the offshore supplier who is actually providing the services to the customer; and
(c) may mean that the customer does not gain a real understanding of the risks and benefits of offshore outsourcing, if it is isolated from the offshore provider.

Financial standing

If the customer enters into an agreement with an established UK company then it will enjoy the benefit of entering into an agreement with a substantial company.

If it enters into an agreement with the onshore subsidiary of an offshore company, it should check the financial standing of the onshore company. Chapters 4 and 26 stress the importance of the customer investigating the financial standing of the supplier and ensuring that it has sufficient financial guarantees. If the onshore subsidiary is merely a marketing company then the customer may want to consider obtaining a parent company guarantee from the offshore company, entering into an agreement directly with the offshore company and ensuring that the onshore company takes out all appropriate insurance covering its liabilities under the agreement.

Enforcement

If the onshore company has substantial assets, enforcing a judgment against it will be easier than having to enforce a judgment against an offshore company.

Political implications

Contracting with an established UK supplier may make it less apparent that the customer has entered into an offshore outsourcing arrangement, particularly if the services being outsourced are not front-line services such as call centres.

In practice, the first phase of offshoring involved customers setting up their own captive or entering into agreements with established UK suppliers with an offshore subsidiary. In early 2006, a second phase of offshoring took off, in which customers, having become more confident about offshoring, entered into agreements directly with offshore suppliers. Some customers found that their smaller captives were expensive to run and that it was difficult to recruit staff for them. The recent recession has seen some financial services institutions selling off their captive to reduce costs.

38.6 The services

Chapter 7 describes how the customer should prepare its service description, to communicate to the supplier what its exact requirements are. Everything that has been explained in the chapter applies equally to offshore outsourcing arrangements. In fact, in offshore arrangements, the customer usually finds that it needs to describe the services in greater detail, first, because the differences of culture and experience mean that the supplier will not have the same shared assumptions as the customer and second, because the staff previously providing the services will not usually transfer to the supplier. The issue of describing the services and ensuring an adequate knowledge transfer relating to the performance of the processes being outsourced may be particularly key in business process outsourcing arrangements, where essential information relating to the processes may be lost when the current staff cease to provide the services. This information will be vital to the customer on termination of the offshoring arrangement.

In some cases, the service documentation may need to be translated into the language of the offshore supplier.

38.7 How the services are provided

Chapter 8 describes ways in which the customer should control the manner in which the services are provided. This chapter is equally appropriate for offshore arrangements. However, in offshore arrangements, the customer often expects to have substantially more control over how the services are provided than would be usual in other outsourcing arrangements, in particular the staff used to provide the services. This is because:

(a) the services are being provided from a site remote from the customer; and
(b) most offshore arrangements are input-based agreements for the provision of resources and the customer wants reassurance about the quality of the resources.

38.7.1 Staff used to provide the services

In offshore outsourcing arrangements, the staff who previously provided the services (whether they transfer to the supplier under the Acquired Rights Directive by law or not) will not usually be employed to provide the services. Therefore the customer will usually want to specify in detail the qualifications which the relevant staff must have and the training they must complete.

In the past some customers were concerned that offshore suppliers would find it difficult to find suitably qualified staff to provide the services, as the popularity of offshore outsourcing increased. Staff attrition was a serious problem in India for call centre staff. It was less likely to be a problem for more skilled jobs such as those involved in knowledge process outsourcing. Staff attrition has become less of a problem during the current recession although it may be a problem in the future.

The customer may want to agree a level of "buffer" staff who will have been suitably trained and will be available to provide the services to deal with problems of attrition.

The customer may also want to monitor the staff turnover rate at the supplier and have additional remedies if the staff turnover rate at the supplier increases. The parties need to consider how staff attrition will be measured, whether in total, by country, by location or by type of work. The supplier may want to exclude staff attrition relating to, for example:

(a) staff who leave within six months of joining the supplier;
(b) staff who are dismissed by the supplier for performance-related failings; or
(c) staff who are promoted within the supplier by agreement between the parties.

In addition, offshore outsourcing arrangements are often "resource-based" rather than "service-based" agreements. As a result, some customers include clauses which penalise the supplier if key management or other positions remain vacant.

Lastly, the customer may want the supplier to notify it of any changes which might have an adverse effect upon the supplier's performance.

38.7.2 Premises used to provide the services

Some customers feel the need to control not only the location from which the services will be provided but also the facilities which will be made available to staff providing services for them at that location. This may include a floor plan with details of the desks and other equipment to be made available to staff. The customer may also want to consider the branding of the location.

38.8 Service levels and service credits

Chapters 9 and 19 describe how the customer should draft suitable service levels and service credits. Once again, everything that has been explained in these chapters applies equally to offshore outsourcing arrangements. Indeed, if it is more difficult to enforce an outsourcing arrangement, service levels and service credits may be particularly important in explaining to the supplier the priorities between the different service elements and encouraging the supplier to meet the customer's requirements, although the customer should obtain local advice on whether the service credits will be enforceable or not.

38.9 Service management

Chapter 10 describes the service management issues that the customer and supplier will need to consider. These are as relevant for offshore arrangements as for onshore arrangements, although the transition may be more complex than for an onshore arrangement. In the transition phase, the question arises as to who should bear the cost if the parties move the services to the offshore location, the supplier is unable to provide them and they need to be moved back to the onshore location and the transition undertaken a second time.

Also, it may be more difficult for the customer to manage the relationship with a supplier who is geographically remote from it. If the supplier does not have a presence in the UK, the customer may need to establish a local presence in the offshore location, send out inspectors to the offshore location or appoint a local manager who will monitor the performance of the supplier on an ongoing basis. The customer may also want the supplier to demonstrate that it can carry out self-audits.

Lastly, some customers are concerned that problems with staff attrition and the shortage of staff in key offshore countries will undermine the supplier's ability to manage the services it provides and hence insist upon service levels and service credits applying to the failure to comply with key service management obligations such as the provision of key staff and the production of reports.

38.10 Charges

Chapter 18 describes various charging regimes appropriate for outsourcing arrangements. Everything described in Chapter 18 is applicable to offshore outsourcing, although resource-based charging structures are more common in offshore arrangements (e.g. based on the number of full-time equivalent staff ("FTEs") used to provide the services) than onshore outsourcing arrangements.

In addition, the customer may find that there are cultural differences which impact upon the charging arrangements. For example, the Indian culture does not favour the granting of credit and so the customer may find it more difficult to agree arrangements whereby payments are delayed or amortised over the term of the agreement.

If the customer is entering into an arrangement with a UK supplier with an offshore subsidiary, where only part of the work is being provided by the offshore company, the parties will need to clarify what work will benefit from the lower charges applicable to the offshore services. In addition, some customers, because they are nervous of offshore outsourcing arrangements, initially enter into short-term contracts. The customer should consider whether it can negotiate an option to extend the agreement at an agreed price. This could protect the customer if the popularity of the offshore services results in salary increases.

The parties will need to ensure that they document and agree any charging assumptions, for example who pays for telephone calls or video conferencing facilities. They will also need to document clearly who takes the risk of taxation changes which impact on the customer or supplier.

In addition, the customer may want to consider incorporating mechanisms whereby it shares in any future efficiency gains achieved by the supplier. The gainshare can be expressed as a sharing of any actual reductions in FTEs engaged in providing the services or as a reduced price per headcount which comes into effect at a certain point. In the latter case, both parties need to ensure that this point is defined clearly and is fair. If, for example, it is defined by reference to the end of the transition period, are there events which can delay the formal end of the transition period so that the customer is not technically entitled to the reduced rates?

Lastly, the parties will have to decide in what currency the services will be paid for and hence who will bear the risk of currency fluctuations.

38.11 Termination

In an offshore outsourcing arrangement, the customer will usually want the right to terminate the agreement in the general circumstances described in Chapter 23. The customer may want to consider whether it needs the right to terminate the agreement in specific circumstances relevant to the particular transaction, for example if the offshore location becomes involved in a war or other conflict or if the supplier is guilty of some form of corruption.

It may also need to amend the force majeure clause to allow a right to terminate if the supplier is affected by a natural disaster, whether or not the force majeure has continued for a specific period of time.

If the customer wants the right to terminate for insolvency-related grounds, it will need to take local advice on how insolvency is dealt with by local law.

38.12 FSA regulations

Firms regulated by the FSA will have to comply with the FSA's guidance on outsourcing. Chapter 33 describes the general FSA guidance. The FSA Handbook also includes specific guidance on offshore outsourcing for insurance companies in SYSC 13 – *see* 33.8.

The customer should also bear in mind the FSA's specific reminder to implement and document appropriate business continuity arrangements. The FSA includes a useful suggestion (often overlooked by firms) that, where firms are outsourcing the business continuity services themselves, as part of a shared disaster recovery service, they should evaluate the likelihood and impact of multiple calls on shared resources. The guidance also points out that firms should consider the concentration risk implications of using a particular supplier, such as the business continuity implications where a single supplier is used by several firms.

Lastly, firms should ensure that they include adequate FSA audit provisions in offshore outsourcing agreements (as described in Chapter 33) and should not assume that the FSA will not want to audit offshore locations.

38.13 FSA – offshore operations – industry feedback

38.13.1 Background to the report

In April 2005, the FSA decided to carry out a review of offshore operations in India. It visited 10 offshore operations (some captive and some external suppliers) in Mumbai and Bangalore providing services for major financial institutions, including banks and insurers. Most provide operations for UK banks and insurance companies. In addition, it had input from another five firms, which returned questionnaires with information on their operations.

Paragraphs 38.13.2 to 38.13.6 set out some of the key findings of the review. The full text of the report can be found at www.fsa.gov.uk/pubs/other/offshore_ops.pdf.

38.13.2 Staff attrition rate

The FSA raised questions about the high level of staff attrition at Indian companies. It found the attrition rate of staff providing back-office services was about 10 per cent, whilst those dealing with front-office services was about 30 per cent, as staff left to pursue higher education or to get married. It found that there was no shortage of suitable recruits in India. However, it stated that all companies covered by the review were aware of the risk and had strategies to deal with it.

38.13.3 Business continuity

The FSA also pointed out that, because of the high cost of office space, the Indian companies were less likely to have contingency sites in the event of a serious problem. Therefore firms had to find another solution. Most companies planned to repatriate work to the UK in the event of a problem.

38.13.4 Security

It concluded that (despite a few highly publicised security breaches involving Indian companies) there was no evidence to suggest that consumer data is at greater risk in India than in the UK. The FSA said that it had observed a high level of security in India. Most companies had swipe entry clearance in their premises. One had an airport-style detector.

38.13.5 Conclusion of the report

The FSA stated that offshoring can contribute a material risk to the FSA's objective of maintaining market confidence, reduction of financial crime and consumer protection.

The main risk is the complexity of achieving suitable management supervision from a distance. However, appropriate governance frameworks, risk management systems and controls can identify and mitigate operational risk. The main companies offshoring work were aware of the risks and were taking appropriate measures to mitigate them. The FSA stressed that it is important that, as offshoring becomes more common, the risks remain under scrutiny.

38.14 Data protection

The data protection issues described in Chapter 32, particularly those relating to transfers of data within or outside the EU, are particularly relevant for offshore outsourcing agreements.

38.15 TUPE

Customers often assume that if they enter into an offshore outsourcing arrangement TUPE will not apply. However, this is incorrect. As long as the legal requirements for its application are satisfied, namely that there is a transfer of a business situated in the UK immediately before the transfer, then TUPE will apply. Chapter 27 explains the application and effect of TUPE. The important point for the offshore outsourcing supplier to note is that, if TUPE applies:

(a) the customer will have an obligation to inform or consult with the trade union or elected employees' representatives;

(b) TUPE will operate to transfer to the outsourcing supplier the contracts of employment and the liabilities of the employer (which may include liability for failure to consult) under those contracts.

Therefore, it is imperative for any offshore outsourcing supplier to obtain specialist legal advice on the application of TUPE to the particular facts of the case and to seek full TUPE indemnities from the customer.

The situation on termination is that TUPE will not apply as the transferor will not be situated in the UK immediately before the transfer.

38.16 Publicity

As a result of the unpopularity of offshore outsourcing in some sections of the press in the UK, the customer may want to restrict the supplier from publicising the outsourcing transaction. The supplier will usually be eager to publicise its success in procuring the new business.

Chapter 39

India

Sajai Singh
Partner
J. Sagar Associates

39.1 Outline

Since the late 1990s, India has become a favoured offshore outsourcing destination, gaining a head start on competitors as a result of low labour costs and the availability of a large pool of highly skilled English-speaking workers. This chapter describes the specific considerations that need to be taken into account when outsourcing to India, including regulatory, contract, data protection, employee, IP and jurisdiction issues.

39.2 Background

39.2.1 Historical background

India's increasing significance in the globalised outsourcing market is based on the foundation laid by India's information technology ("IT") sector in the early 1980s. What began with the growth in IT businesses at a national level was followed by the emergence of the offshore outsourcing of medical transcription services in the mid-1990s and finally Y2K. These events served to expose the world to the capabilities of Indian human capital for the first time. In less than five years the IT industry branched out to provide a wide array of services including business process outsourcing ("BPO"), data processing, medical billing and customer support. This started a wave of information technology-enabled services ("ITES") industries. Whether captive offshore centres run by multinational companies ("MNCs"), build-operate-transfer ("BOT") operations or third-party offshore outsourcing, the ITES industry in India was here to stay.

39.2.2 Government support for outsourcing

The Indian government is aware of the importance and impact of the outsourcing industry on the economy and as a result has declared IT one of its five priorities. The government has also instituted a wide range of measures to support the outsourcing sector in order to ensure its growth.

Among these were the steps taken to boost liberalisation with the privatisation of the state-owned telecoms units in 1994. This was followed by the "New Telecom Policy" in 1999, resulting in the end of the state monopoly on international calling facilities. India now has a strong and highly competitive telecommunications market that allows inexpensive international calls, benefiting the IT sector.

In addition to liberalisation, the government has set up establishments and institutions to attract foreign investors who might be willing to outsource to India. These include "software technology parks" ("STPs") and "special economic zones" ("SEZs"). The Indian government has also granted tax holidays to increase the attractiveness of India to potential foreign investors.

Another measure taken has been to ensure that the Foreign Investment Implementation Authority ("FIIA") facilitates quick delivery of foreign direct investment ("FDI") approvals by helping foreign investors to access the necessary paperwork, sort out operational issues and find solutions to their routine and unique problems. The FIIA, with the help of the Fast Track Committee ("FTC"), operates in about 30 government ministries, monitoring and solving problems that affect sector-specific projects.

39.2.3 NASSCOM

Another institution, the National Association of Software and Service Companies ("NASSCOM"),[1] has created platforms for the dissemination of knowledge and research in the industry through the medium of surveys and conferences. NASSCOM acts as an adviser, consultant and coordinating body for the process outsourcing and ITES industries and liaises between the federal and state governments and industry.

39.2.4 Types of services outsourced to India

The Indian ITES industry already includes services like customer care, call centres, medical transcription, billing services, database marketing, web sales and marketing, accounting, tax processing, transaction document management, telesales and telemarketing, engineering services, financial services, creative services, web analysis services, healthcare services, digital image editing services, software services, research and analysis services.

39.2.5 Anticipated growth

In spite of the impending economic growth and security concerns, one of NASSCOM's recent studies (Indian IT-BPO Industry Factsheet), estimates that India's IT-BPO is on track to reach $60 billion in exports and $73–75 billion in overall software and service revenues by 2010. This forecast is strengthened by the fact that India's process-outsourcing industry demonstrated a compound annual growth rate of around 37 per cent over the last few years. Between 2004 and 2008 it grew from $3.1 billion to $11 billion and presently accounts for 37 per cent of the global business process offshoring pie.

1 www.nasscom.org.

39.3 Legal system

39.3.1 India's constitution

India has one of the oldest legal systems in the world and the country's commitment to the rule of law is enshrined in its Constitution. India's diversity in terms of religions, cultures, habits, nationalities, languages and written scripts is recognised within the Indian legal system. This can be explained to some degree by the sheer size of the country (in terms of geographic size, India is the seventh-largest country in the world and the second largest in terms of population).

India is governed by a federal system, with a central federal Parliament, state governments, an independent judiciary, guaranteed fundamental rights and the Directive of Principles of State Policy, which contains the governing principles of the nation. Both the federal and state governments are granted power to legislate by the Constitution.

39.3.2 India's judicial system

A special feature of the Indian Constitution is its judicial system. There is a single integrated network of courts that administer federal as well as state laws. The highest body in the judicial system is the Supreme Court based in New Delhi. Beneath the Supreme Court are the State High Courts and then a hierarchy of subordinate courts. Unlike the decisions of the Supreme Court, which are binding on all other Indian courts, the decisions of a High Court are binding only on courts within the same state. However, High Court decisions can be used persuasively to lend support in cases in other states.

The highest judicial role in the country is the position of the Chief Justice of India. The President of India appoints the Chief Justice and all the other judges in the Supreme Court. The scope of the Supreme Court's functions includes providing original and appellate hearings and advisory services. The jurisdiction of the Supreme Court encompasses the enforcement of fundamental rights and dealing with any legal dispute between the states *inter se* and between the states and the Government of India.

Arbitration is recognised by the government and by Indian businesses as being an alternative mechanism for dispute resolution. India's Arbitration and Conciliation Act, 1996 is based on the UNCITRAL model. Mediation is slowly gaining popularity in some courts as a dispute resolution mechanism. Conciliation and negotiation, prior to any legal process, are often adopted by courts and businesses, as methods of alternate dispute resolution, by court reference or under contract.

39.4 People issues

39.4.1 Sources of employment law

Indian employment law is comprehensive and well developed. Traditionally, an employer has been considered to be in a stronger leveraged position in comparison to its employee and therefore employment laws tend to strengthen employees' rights.

Based on federal and state regulations, employees in India are granted rights and benefits such as: the right to a minimum wage, a limit on working hours, a minimum number of days off, compensation in the event of redundancy, and statutory benefits in the shape of a gratuity, provident fund etc.

The following paragraphs cover federal and state employment legislation which may be relevant to outsourcing transactions.

39.4.2 Shops and Establishments Act, 1953

The Shops and Establishments Act, 1953 is state-made legislation and has been applied in almost all the states and union territories. The aim of the Act, as applicable in a state, is to regulate employment conditions in any and all shops and other establishments in that state. The term "establishment" as defined means a shop or a commercial establishment. This definition is exhaustive and includes within its purview businesses carrying out outsourcing activities.[2] The main provisions of the Act cover working hours, rest intervals, overtime, holidays, leave, termination of service and the maintenance of shops and establishments.

39.4.3 Employees' Provident Fund and Miscellaneous Provisions Act, 1952

This Act provides for the compulsory institution of contributory provident funds, pension funds and deposit-linked insurance funds for employees. It endeavours to secure the future of employees after retirement. Under the Act and the related schemes, both the employer and the employee contribute towards the employee's provident fund on a monthly basis. The statutory rate for the contribution is currently set at 12 per cent of an employee's basic pay.

39.4.4 Equal Remuneration Act, 1976

This is a gender anti-discrimination law. It guarantees equal pay for men and women performing the same or similar work. It prohibits discrimination against women during the recruitment or promotion processes, as well as during training or on any transfer. The provisions of the Act apply regardless of whether the employer has sufficient money to pay the male and female employees equally.

39.4.5 Payment of Gratuity Act, 1972

The Act applies to every business that has 10 or more employees. Owners of such businesses are obliged to pay a lump sum to an employee on retirement or on any other occasion when an employee's job is terminated. To be entitled to receive the payment, an employee must have worked at the business for at least five consecutive years. The level of payment is calculated at the rate of 15 days' wages multiplied by the number of completed years of service or part thereof

2 The term "establishment" will hereinafter, for ease of reference, be referred to as "business", with specific emphasis to outsourcing businesses.

in excess of six months. The current maximum amount payable is INR350,000. In order to ensure that an employer is capable of paying the sum due, it is compulsory for all employers, to whom the Act is applicable, to obtain insurance to cover the potential liabilities.

39.4.6 The Payment of Bonus Act, 1965

The aim of this Act is to allow the payment of bonuses which are linked to profit of the organisation or productivity of the workforce. The Act dictates either a minimum bonus of 8.33 per cent of the salary earned by an employee during a financial year or a lump sum of INR100, whichever is higher, whether or not the employer has any allocable surplus in that year. The Act also prescribes a maximum bonus to be paid by an employer to its employees at a rate of 20 per cent of the salary earned in that year, when the allocable surplus in that year exceeds the amount of the minimum bonus payable. However, the statute only applies to employees earning up to INR10,000 per month. Employees earning more than this would only be eligible to earn a bonus if their employment agreements provided for this. The Act applies to every factory and to every business where 20 or more workers are employed on any given day during an accounting year.

39.4.7 Payment of Wages Act, 1936

This Act regulates the payment of wages, imposition of fines, deductions from wages and the elimination of all malpractice by setting out wage periods and the timing and means for paying wages. The Act fixes an interval for the payment of wages, which should not exceed a month. Consequently, it is the duty of every employer to ensure that wages are paid to employees without unauthorised deductions and that the necessary registers are maintained and the required notices are displayed at the premises. This Act is not applicable to people whose wages exceed or are equal to INR1,600 per month.

39.4.8 The Employees' State Insurance Act, 1948

This Act covers factories and establishments with 10 or more employees. It provides for employees and their families to be given comprehensive medical care as well as cash benefits during sickness and maternity leave with monthly payments in the event of death or disablement. The benefits provided under the Act apply to employees who earn up to INR10,000 per month. Where an employee is covered under an Employee State Insurance Scheme, no compensation may be claimed from an employer under the Workmen's Compensation Act, 1923 in respect of any injury sustained by the employee in the course of their employment.

39.4.9 The Workmen's Compensation Act, 1923

This Act requires the payment of compensation to a worker or his family in the event of accidents arising out of or in the course of employment that cause either death or permanent or temporary, partial or non-partial, incapacity. The amount of compensation payable depends on the age of the worker, the degree of injury suffered and the average monthly wage paid to that individual. There are fixed limits to the maximum amount of compensation available (e.g. INR80,000 if the accident results in death).

39.4.10 The Employment Exchanges (Compulsory Notification of Vacancies) Act, 1959

This Act requires both public and private enterprises to publicise any vacancies before filling them.

39.4.11 The Trade Unions Act, 1926

This Act provides for the registration of trade unions in order to enable collective bargaining by workers. Under the Act, seven or more people may form a union and apply to have the union registered. Indian trade unions are given the same status as companies so that they enjoy perpetual succession and have a common seal. Like companies, they can also sue and be sued in their name.

39.4.12 The Maternity Benefit Act, 1961

The aim of this Act is to protect the health and life of any pregnant woman and her baby, especially in the six weeks before and after delivery. The Act states that, within this timeframe, a woman is entitled to be absent from work while claiming maternity benefit for up to a maximum of 12 weeks. The 12-week window includes a period of six weeks beginning the day after delivery, miscarriage or medical termination, when an employer is prohibited from employing that woman. If a woman does not avail herself of the six-week leave prior to the expected delivery date, that woman may not be required to do any arduous work or work which involves long hours of standing or which is likely to interfere with her health and her pregnancy.

39.4.13 Child Labour (Prohibition and Regulation) Act, 1986

This Act has five main goals:

(a) to ban the use of children under the age of 14 in specified occupations and processes;
(b) to decide modifications to the schedule of banned occupations and processes;
(c) to regulate the working conditions of children in jobs where they are not prohibited from working;
(d) to lay down enhanced penalties for the employment of children in jobs where they are prohibited from working; and
(e) to obtain uniformity in the definition of "a child" in related laws.

The Act applies, with a few exceptions, to all businesses and workshops where any industrial process is carried on.

39.4.14 Foreign workers

India has several restrictions and requirements relating to the employment of foreigners to work in India. The most important thing a foreigner needs to do when he is planning to work in India is to apply for an Indian work permit or visa at the Indian Embassy or High Commission in his country of residence. Alternatively, the employer offering the position may initiate the visa application process in India on behalf of the prospective employee. Applicants seeking an employment visa are required to submit proof of employment by the relevant company or organisation. Applicants who are nationals of countries such as Sri Lanka and the Philippines need to produce a letter from their employer justifying the appointment of a foreigner for that position.

Where the visa is valid for more than six months, foreign employees, including those of Indian origin, must register with the Foreigners Registration Office ("FRO") or Foreigners Regional Registration Office ("FRRO") within 14 days of arrival in India.

Under the "Foreign Exchange Management (Foreign Currency Accounts by a Person Resident in India) Regulations", a foreigner employed by a business that is either the office, branch, subsidiary or joint venture of a foreign company in India, is allowed to receive payment of up to 75 per cent of his salary directly into a foreign account from the Indian business. For the purposes of India's double-taxation agreements, employee salaries that a foreign company (and not its permanent establishment in India) pays for services rendered in India are taxable in India if the employee works for more than 182 days during any tax year.

39.5 Data protection

With the growth of the outsourcing sector in India, a number of data protection offences involving employees of BPO suppliers have come to light. Although there is no particular law that deals specifically with data protection in India, there are various legislative and non-legislative protections which are relevant for data protection.

39.5.1 Legislative safeguards

39.5.1.1 Constitution of India

Article 21 of the Constitution contains various relevant fundamental rights, including the right to life and personal liberty and the right to freedom of speech and expression, which includes the right to impart and receive information. The Supreme Court has recognised the right to privacy as being part of this right to life and personal liberty.

39.5.1.2 Information Technology Act, 2000 ("IT Act, 2000")

The Information Technology Act was enacted in 2000 with a view to providing legal recognition for transactions carried out electronically and to facilitate the emergence of electronic commerce in India. With the rapid increase in the use of computer systems and the internet in India, the government found itself unable to effectively deal with cyber crimes and issues of data protection. Therefore, the Act was amended in 2008 to deal with these issues.

The IT Act, 2000 as amended in 2008 is in consonance with all the mandatory regulations of the Model Law on Electronic Signatures as adopted by UNCITRAL.

Definition of Data

"Data", as understood under the IT Act, 2000, means a representation of information, knowledge, facts, concepts or instructions which are being prepared or have been prepared in a formalised manner, and is intended to be processed, is being processed or has been processed in a computer system or computer network, and may be in any form (including computer print-outs, magnetic or optical storage media, punched cards and punched tapes) or stored internally in the memory of the computer. Due to the fact that the definition was drafted in the widest possible terms, it covers all types of data in electronic form.

The main purpose of the IT Act, 2000 is to address privacy issues relating to computer systems. In addition to this, the Act contains provisions which provide protection for stored data, which are described below.

Prohibition on causing damage to computer, data and computer systems

Sections 43 and 66 state that if a person accesses, downloads or copies any data, introduces viruses, causes denial of access or destroys or alters any information stored on a computer without the permission of the person in charge of that computer system then, on proof that they acted dishonestly or fraudulently, they will be punishable either with imprisonment for up to three years or with a fine up to INR500,000 or both.

Section 43(i) also makes any person who steals, conceals, destroys or alters any computer source code liable to the punishments prescribed above.

Section 43A provides that if any body corporate which owns, operates or handles sensitive personal data or information in a computer resource is found to have been negligent in implementing and maintaining reasonable security practices and procedures, it will be liable to pay damages by way of compensation not exceeding INR50,000,000 to the person so affected. Reasonable security includes such security practices and procedures, as appropriate to the nature of the information, to protect that information from unauthorised access, damage, use, modification, disclosure or impairment as specified either by agreement between the parties or as may be prescribed by the government, in consultation with the self-regulatory bodies of the industry.

Protected systems

Under Section 70, if the federal or state government perceives that the incapacitation or destruction of a computer system will have a debilitating impact on national security, the economy, public health or safety then the appropriate government may declare such computer resource to be a protected system affecting the facility of "Critical Information Infrastructure" and only permit authorised persons to access the system.

Disclosure of information

Section 72 addresses issues regarding disclosure of information by any person who has gained access to such information in pursuance of a power granted under the IT Act, 2000 (including the controller and every person authorised through him). If a person who has secured access to any electronic record, book, register, correspondence, information, document or other material discloses any of these to any other person, he will be punished with imprisonment for a term of up to two years, or with a fine up to INR100,000 or both. Section 72A punishes any person who, while providing services under contract, discloses any material containing the personal information about another person without his consent or in breach of a lawful contract with imprisonment for a term that may extend to three years or with fine up to INR500,000 or both.

Enforcement
The provisions of the IT Act, 2000 are enforced through an adjudicating officer and the form of the enquiry follows the framework laid down by the government. The decisions of the adjudicator are open to appeal to the Cyber Appellate Tribunal and the findings of the Cyber Appellate Tribunal may, in turn, be appealed to the High Court of the relevant state.

Enforcement is also undertaken by the Cyber Crime Investigation Cell ("CCIC"), set up by the Central Bureau of Investigation ("CBI") with a mandate to investigate offences under the IT Act, 2000 and all other high-technology crimes. The CCIC operates by establishing cells across India based on need, and the organisation is a member of the Interpol Working Party on Information Technology Crime for South East Asia and Australia.

39.5.2 Other legislation

In addition to the above legislation, some of the general legislation mentioned in 39.8 below may be relevant to data protection.

39.5.3 Possible reform of data protection law

The government is aware that the lack of legislation regarding data protection is to some degree deterring companies from outsourcing to India. In the mid-1990s, India began to develop detailed personal data protection legislation which has yet to be implemented. Currently there is a review of the IT Act, 2000 aimed at inserting clauses to meet the requirements specified by the EU.

39.5.4 Non-legislative safeguards

39.5.4.1 Guidelines
In addition to the cluster of laws which may be used to some extent for data protection, non-governmental organisations are cooperating with the outsourcing industry in an attempt to create alternatives to meet customers' data protection concerns. For instance, NASSCOM has issued guidelines on privacy and confidentiality, but these guidelines are not binding.

39.5.4.2 Contractual provisions
Because the outsourcing industry is not willing to wait for the government to implement data protection laws, many suppliers are unilaterally making efforts to meet customers' data protection expectations by agreeing to specific data protection provisions in contracts with their customers. To make up for the lack of data protection laws in India, contracts customarily contain clauses covering confidentiality, privacy and related compliance processes and obligations.

When defining data protection terms, suppliers often find it useful to commit to meeting international data protection standards. Commonly used standards include the ISO Certificate or the BS 7799, a global standard that covers all security domains. In order to support these efforts, the Ministry of Information Technology has set up the Standardization, Testing and Quality Certification ("STQC") Directorate. The STQC functions as an independent third-party certification scheme as per BS 7799 Part 2 and provides services such as testing hardware and software products and product certification, and it also trains personnel in quality and security standards and processes.

Another measure taken by Indian suppliers aiming to convince their customers of their data protection capability is to allow their customers to conduct periodic inspections of their facilities, processes and compliance levels.

39.6 Intellectual property protection

Protecting intellectual property ("IP") is a major concern for outsourcing customers. As a consequence, India has established IP laws to ensure adequate protection is available.

IP protection in India takes two forms. On the one hand, there is IP protection based on statutes, such as the Copyright Act, 1957 or the Patents Act, 1970. On the other, there is protection based on international agreements, including the agreement on Trade Related Aspects of Intellectual Property Rights ("TRIPS").

39.6.1 Copyright

The Copyright Act, 1957, as amended in 1999, contains provisions stating that the Act applies to works first published outside India. The Act is also TRIPS compliant.

An author owns any copyright in the first instance. However, where the copyright arises out of work done by an employee in the course of his employment, an employer owns the copyright if there is no specific agreement to the contrary. The same general rule applies between an outsourcing customer and a supplier, so it is important to have provisions dealing with the ownership rights to any new IP that is developed in the course of a relationship. The "work for hire" concept does not exist in India as it does in the US, and so a clear contractual agreement is critical to control the ownership of any copyright (and other IP).

The author, publisher, owner or any other person with an interest in the copyright of a work may make an application to the Registrar for the particulars of that work to be recorded in the Register of Copyrights.

Copyright subsists in any literary, dramatic, musical or artistic work (other than a photograph) published within the lifetime of an author and lasts for 60 years beginning with the calendar year following that in which the author died.

The owner of the copyright in an existing work or the prospective owner of the copyright in a future work may assign the copyright, either wholly or partially, either generally or subject to limitations and either for the whole term of the copyright or any part thereof to any person.

Copyright is deemed to be infringed:

(a) When any person, without a licence granted by the owner of the copyright or the Registrar of Copyrights under the Act or in contravention of the conditions of a licence so granted or of any conditions imposed by a competent authority under the Act:

(i) does anything, the exclusive right to do which is conferred upon the owner of the copyright by the Act; or
(ii) permits any place to be used for the communication of the work to the public for profit where such a communication constitutes an infringement of the copyright in the work, unless he was not aware and had no reasonable ground for believing that such a communication to the public would be an infringement of the copyright; or

(b) When any person:
(i) makes for sale or hire, or sells or lets for hire, or by way of trade displays or offers for sale or hire; or
(ii) distributes either for the purposes of trade or to such an extent as to prejudicially affect the owner of the copyright; or
(iii) by way of trade exhibits in public; or
(iv) imports into India, any infringing copies of the work.

(c) Where any offence under this Act has been committed by a company, every person who at the time the offence was committed, was in charge of, or was responsible for the conduct of the business of the company, is deemed to be guilty of an offence and is liable to face prosecution.

39.6.2 Patents rights

The Patent Act, 1970, has been amended three times so that it is in tune with changing economic conditions. Since 2005, the Act has conformed with all the mandatory regulations of the TRIPS Agreement.

Some key provisions of the Act are as follows:

(a) The creator is the first owner of the patent, and not the company he works for.
(b) An application for a patent may be made to any of the Patent Offices located in Kolkata (Head office), Delhi, Chennai or Mumbai.
(c) Patent protection lasts for 20 years.
(d) The burden of proof is on the accused to show there has not been an infringement.

The Act protects biodiversity and provides safeguards and measures for protecting traditional knowledge. The right to apply for a patent should be made the subject of an agreement between an employer and employee or a customer and a supplier as in the first instance the owner is the creator. A common practice is for an employer to include a general assignment in the employment documentation, with a commitment to execute future documents to perfect the assignment and transfer of title as necessary. When a patentable work is identifiable, a specific assignment is executed between the employer and employee assigning the rights to the employer.

39.6.3 Trademarks

Under the Trademarks Act, 1999, a trademark is defined as:

> "a mark capable of being represented graphically and which is capable of distinguishing the goods or services of one person from those of others and may include the shape of goods, their packaging and a combination of colours".

Some key provisions of the Act are as follows:

(a) Trademarks may be registered in the Trademark Register with detailed information such as the name of the owner. The Register classifies goods and services in accordance with international classification standards for the registration of trademarks.
(b) Registration may be refused if registration of the trademark would create confusion among a part of the public.
(c) Opposition to registration of a trademark must be made within three months.
(d) Registration lasts for 10 years and may be renewed.
(e) It is an infringement of a trademark owner's rights for:
    (i) an unregistered trademark which is identical or similar to a registered trademark to be used in the course of business,
    (ii) for an unregistered trademark to be used in relation to goods or services which are not comparable to those for which an identical or similar trademark is registered and
    (iii) for any unauthorised use of a registered trademark.
(f) Infringement is punishable with imprisonment or a fine or both.

The Trademarks Amendment Bill (in the process of being passed at the time of writing) proposes to prescribe a period of 18 months for the registration of a trademark in order to align the Trademarks Act, 1999 with the provisions of the Madrid Protocol. Efforts are also currently being made to simplify the law relating to the transfer of ownership of trademarks.

39.7 Protection of confidentiality

Customers face pressure from their domestic authorities in the EU and US to ensure they comply with data protection regulations while outsourcing to India. There is no specific law on confidentiality in India and so there are barely any civil remedies to protect confidentiality. As a result, in outsourcing contracts, it is essential that the supplier and the customer include appropriate provisions relating to the confidentiality of data processed and collected during the performance of the services by the supplier. Such provisions usually stipulate the consequences in the event of a failure by the supplier to ensure the security of confidential information. Thus protection is achieved by contractual means until there is adequate legislation on the point.

39.8 Other relevant legislation

The following legislation may also be relevant for outsourcing projects in India:

39.8.1 Indian Contract Act, 1872

In the event that parties intend that the master/main outsourcing contract or any relevant contract be governed by Indian Law, then in such circumstances, the Indian Contract Act, 1872 will be the substantive law governing the contract. Care needs to be taken while drafting certain provisions as the Contract Act, 1872 discourages agreements in restraint of trade and agreements in restraint of legal proceedings. The Indian Contract Act, 1872 will not, in general, permit a contractual provision that imposes a post employment restraint on an employee to carry on employment and such a restraint will be considered to be void. Similarly, an agreement in restraint of initiation of legal proceedings by either of the parties is void. However, this provision is subject to any provisions in agreements in which the parties have agreed to arbitration as a dispute resolution mechanism.

39.8.2 Specific Relief Act, 1963

The Specific Relief Act, 1963 is complementary to the provisions of the Indian Contract Act, 1872 and states that a party, in the event of breach, can sue for specific performance of the Contract.

39.8.3 The Indian Penal Code

The Indian Penal Code punishes, amongst other things, fraud, misrepresentation, forgery and the making of false documents.

39.8.4 The Department of Telecommunication ("DOT") Regulations

In accordance with the New Telecom Policy ("NTP") 1999, other service providers ("OSPs") are allowed to operate by using infrastructure provided by various access providers for non-telecom services. In May 1999, the Telecom Commission accorded in principle approval for registration of call centres, both international and domestic, in the country under the above category. In accordance with the notification issued on 2 November 2005, the BPOs have been included under OSPs and the provisions applicable to such OSPs are also applicable to call centres.

A call centre is allowed to use internet telephony to the extent it is permitted by the ISPs. The call centre operator may or may not use internet telephony depending on their business model.

39.8.5 Reserve Bank of India Act, 1934

A BPO company undertaking support of banking and financial services overseas will need to ensure that its operations in India are not considered to be a non-banking financial institution under the RBI Act, 1934. If so deemed, it would have to fulfil obligations cast upon it by the RBI Act.

39.8.6 Indian Evidence Act, 1872

By virtue of the Information Technology Act, 2000, computer-generated documents are admitted as evidence under the provisions of the Indian Evidence Act, 1872. There are three types of computer-generated documentary evidence:

(a) computer-generated calculations and analyses obtained through software operations and information received;
(b) computer-generated documents and records that are copies of information obtained from humans;

(c) a combination of both computer-generated calculations and analyses and computer-generated documents based on information from human beings.

39.8.7 Tort law

The law of tort in India is derived from the English law of tort and has evolved from English common law principles. However, Indian courts depart from common-law rules if they are unsuitable for Indian conditions. The Code of Civil Procedure, which enables the civil courts to try all suits of a civil nature, impliedly confers jurisdiction on such courts to apply the law of torts as principles of justice, equity and good conscience. These include principles of negligence and vicarious liability.

39.8.8 Securities Exchange Board of India ("SEBI")

Outsourcing service providers need to take care that they are not construed as "brokers" while providing security market analysis and inputs on performance of scripts.

39.9 Enforceability of jurisdiction clauses

Indian companies consistently incorporate the laws of foreign jurisdictions into contracts, either in whole or in part. Such terms are generally accepted by the courts provided both the contracting parties are in agreement. Where there are no governing law provisions within the contract, the jurisdiction most appropriate to the transaction will be applied.

If a contract is valid under the law of its governing jurisdiction clause but its enforcement by the Indian courts would be contrary to public policy or law in India, then such contract may not be enforced by an Indian court.

In any event, issues regarding the transfer of IP, real estate, criminal acts, labour law or the enforcement of a foreign judgment or award will usually be subject to Indian law and not to the law which was agreed to within the terms of the contract.

39.10 Enforcement of judgments

India's approach to the enforcement of judgments made by foreign courts, is to adapt the judgments in terms of the "res judicata" This approach has been expressed by a jurist to mean that:

> "We (India) are not so provincial as to say that every solution to a problem is wrong because we deal with it otherwise at home and we shall not brush aside foreign judicial process unless doing so would violate some fundamental principle of justice, some prevalent conception of good morals, some deep-rooted tradition of the common wealth."

In practice, this approach leads to two categories of judgments.

39.10.1 Judgments from courts of reciprocating countries

Any judgment of a court of a reciprocating country can be directly enforced by filing an execution petition before an Indian court. The definition of a reciprocating country is shown in Section 44A of the Code of Civil Procedure 1908; a reciprocating country is a country or territory outside India which the central government has declared as such. Examples include the UK, Australia, Singapore or Hong Kong, but the US is not a reciprocating country for Indian purposes.

39.10.2 Judgments from courts of non-reciprocating countries

The judgment of a court in a non-reciprocating country may be enforced by filing an application for a judgment in an Indian court based on the foreign award. The suit must be filed within three years of the date of the foreign judgment.

Regardless of how enforcement is pursued, a foreign judgment will not be considered as conclusive if the judgment:

(a) has been given by a court lacking competent jurisdiction;
(b) has not been given based on the merits of the case;
(c) is not founded on a correct view of international law;
(d) followed proceedings in breach of the principles of natural justice;
(e) has been obtained by fraud; or
(f) breaches any law in force in India.

39.10.3 Enforcement of national and international arbitration awards

UNCITRAL Model Law based Indian Arbitration and Conciliation Act, 1996, states that an arbitration settlement shall be binding on all the claimants. Section 36 of the Act states that if after three months from the date of the award no application has been made for setting aside the award or if such an application has been made and rejected, then the settlement shall be enforceable as a decree of the court.

The following agreements will apply to any settlement regardless of whether it was awarded inside or outside India:

(a) the Geneva Protocol on Arbitration Clauses of 1923;
(b) the Geneva Convention on the Execution of Foreign Arbitral Awards, 1927; and
(c) the New York Convention of 1958 on the Recognition and Enforcement of Foreign Arbitral Awards.

Arbitration clauses are commonly used in most outsourcing contracts. As mentioned above, India is a signatory to the New York Convention so awards made in other signatory countries are enforceable in India.

39.11 Enforceability of other clauses

39.11.1 Non-compete provisions

Non-compete provisions are incorporated into some outsourcing agreements. Sometimes these apply to service providers and at times these may be in the context of an individual working on a particularly sensitive assignment. Whether they are enforceable or not in India depends upon the application of Section 27 of the Indian Contract Act, 1872. This Section states that no person may be restricted from carrying on a lawful profession, trade or business unless the purpose of such a restriction on an individual is to ensure the reasonable protection of a party's proprietary or commercial interest following the acquisition of a business with goodwill. A restriction will be reasonable if it is limited in duration, geographical scope or in some other way. Generally, the courts will enforce restrictive covenants that operate "during terms of employment or service" and not those that operate "after terms of employment", unless adequate consideration has passed and the restriction is deemed reasonable.

39.11.2 Provisions limiting liability

Parties to a contract are generally liable for all damages stemming from any breach unless that damage is remote or indirect. When assessing liability for breach, the courts tend to use the two basic principles of mitigation and restitution. The principle of mitigation requires a party suffering a loss as a result of a breach of contract to try to mitigate that loss. The principle of restitution seeks to put the party suffering a loss in the same position it would have been in had the breach not occurred. If the parties have agreed to liquidated damages the courts will generally accept those figures.

The courts are likely to accept the validity of outsourcing contracts which include terms limiting the liabilities of the contracting parties, provided the terms are reasonable. Notwithstanding this approach, terms limiting the liability of the parties in the event of death, personal injury, fraud or gross negligence are unenforceable under Indian law.

39.11.3 Termination provisions

The Indian Contract Act, 1872 gives contracting parties the freedom to agree termination clauses. However, the courts may look at the overall fairness of a contract when enforcing terms and it is not unusual to find damages being awarded in the event of termination of the contract.

39.12 Regulatory restrictions

39.12.1 Restrictions on software exports

There are limited restrictions on software exports, as explained below. Software exporters and exporters of specified services are required to register with the Electronics and Software Export Promotion Council.

39.12.2 Exchange regulation

Foreign exchange transactions are regulated by the Foreign Exchange Management Act, 2000 ("FEMA, 2000"). FEMA, 2000 provides that capital and current account transactions are fully convertible for non-residents. Generally foreign currencies may be purchased for trade and account purposes at market value, except for certain specific transactions which might require prior approval of RBI.

There are no such restrictions for the outsourcing sector. A customer who may be considering starting a business in India has multiple options, including the following.

39.12.2.1 Subsidiary company

The customer may set up a subsidiary company which must be incorporated in compliance with the requirements of the Indian Companies Act, 1957. It may be funded via equity, debt and internal accruals. The company will be treated as a domestic company for tax purposes. This option allows maximum flexibility for conducting business in India.

39.12.2.2 Branch offices

Instead of establishing a subsidiary company in India, the customer may set up a branch office. This will require specific approval from the RBI, which will limit the scope of any activities undertaken in India by such office. The branch will then be treated as an extension of the foreign company for tax purposes. In pure administrative terms, it is simpler to operate and close branch offices as opposed to setting up a subsidiary company in India.

39.12.2.3 Liaison offices

Alternatively, the customer could establish a liaison office. This will also require specific approval from the RBI, which will limit the activities that the office may undertake in India. It will not be able to undertake any business or revenue-generating activity in India.

39.12.2.4 Project offices

Lastly, the customer has an option to set up a project office. Permission for a project office is linked to execution of a project in India. The foreign company must report to the relevant regional RBI office. For tax purposes, the project office will be treated as an extension of the foreign company in India.

39.12.3 Export regulation

In general, goods and services may be exported unconditionally, although there are regulations covering certain items listed on the Special Chemicals, Organisms, Materials, Equipment and Technologies list ("SCOMET").

Section 2.50 of FEMA, 2000 details those items which are included in the SCOMET list. Export of SCOMET items is only permitted where an export licence has been issued and a licence may be denied if certain criteria are not met. Technological products on the SCOMET list include:

(a) Category 0 (nuclear materials, nuclear-related materials, equipment and technology);
(b) Category 3 (materials, material processing equipment and related technologies);

(c) Category 4 (nuclear-related equipment and technology not controlled under Category 0);
(d) Category 5 (aerospace systems and equipment, including production and test equipment, and related technology);
(e) Category 6 (defence products as listed in Annex VI to Appendix D of the Defence Procurement Policy of 2008); and
(f) Category 7 (electronics, computers and information technology including information security).

In order to export any of these items, an export licence must be secured from the Directorate-General of Foreign Trade ("DGFT").

39.13 General taxation issues

India's tax legislation has two branches. Direct taxes like personal income tax or corporate taxes and indirect taxes like central sales tax and service tax are levied by the federal government. Professional and similar taxes and state sales taxes are levied by the state governments.

The Indian fiscal year starts on 1 April and ends on 31 March the following year. Every company which has any Indian taxable income needs to register with the correct authority and file its annual tax return by October 31.

To attract investors, the Indian government has created a number of incentives, including duty-free import of capital goods and a system of tax holidays which benefit much of the outsourcing industry. Free Trade Zones ("FTZs"), Electronic Hardware Technology Parks ("EHTPs") and Software Technology Parks ("STPs") have additional tax benefits for companies located there, such as 100 per cent tax exemption for the first five business years followed by five years of 50 per cent tax exemption. The current STP tax incentives are due to end on 31 March 2010.

India has entered into tax treaties with a number of countries including the UK, Germany, Mauritius and the US in order to avoid double taxation.

39.14 Other considerations

39.14.1 Specific call-centre regulation

In order to set up a call centre there is a requirement for the centre to be registered under the category "other service provider" with the Department of Telecommunications. Depending on the kind of services the centre will provide, it may also have to obtain other specific approvals.

39.14.2 Environmental regulations

Apart from the Constitution in which India's commitment to a clean environment is mandated, the Environmental (Protection) Act, 1986 is the source of India's environmental legislation. The Act authorises the federal government to protect and improve environmental quality and to control and reduce pollution from all sources and to prohibit or restrict the setting-up and/or operation of any industrial facility on environmental grounds. Under the Forest Conservation Act, 1980 an approval is required for every project which it is proposed will take place in forestland.

39.14.3 Other local laws

In addition to complying with the legislation and regulations above, outsourcing suppliers have to ensure they comply with local laws. The applicability of a specific local state or municipality's laws will be decided based upon the location of the company's facilities as well as the location of the principal customer company of the outsourcing supplier.

Chapter 40

China

Dominic Hui
Partner
Vivien Chan & Co

40.1 Outline

Chapter 37 describes general matters for consideration when entering into offshore outsourcing deals. This chapter deals with the specific considerations which customers will need to take into account when outsourcing to the People's Republic of China ("China"). These can be conveniently categorised into:

(a) differences in legal system and legal concepts;
(b) people issues;
(c) trade protection issues;
(d) intellectual property rights issues; and
(e) dispute resolution issues.

Due to differences in the legal system and culture, foreign companies often find it difficult to understand and deal with local Chinese suppliers. Mastering contract negotiations in China is an art in itself. However, in any event, certain contractual provisions have become a prerequisite in any offshore outsourcing contract. These contractual provisions, as well as the issues listed above, are discussed in this chapter.

40.2 Background

40.2.1 General

Both low-end labour-intensive outsourcing and high-end technology outsourcing services are common in China. Suppliers can either provide the services through a corporate vehicle or individually (in the case of small projects).

First-tier cities with well-known universities such as Beijing and Shanghai remain popular choices for foreign customers regarding services requiring comparatively advanced technology. However, due to the escalating demand and costs in these cities, the outsourcing sector in northern and inland cities such as Suzhou, Chengdu and Shenyang have experienced rapid growth. This growth is also partly due to support from respective local governments provided in the form of financial incentives and various preferential treatment provided to outsourcing suppliers.

40.2.2 National investment in the technology sector

There has been substantial investment in the technology sector in China. Apart from the coastal regions, which are the traditional industrial belts, cutting-edge technology research projects can be seen in Sichuan and the north-east provinces, which have been hubs of scientific research since the 1960s and 1970s.

40.2.3 Expertise

The leading outsourcing companies normally have expertise to provide research, consulting and IT outsourcing services, and have experience in adopting international standards of performance such as ITIL. However, the level of sophistication of suppliers varies substantially depending on the relevant experience of the key personnel in charge of the project. Customers are recommended to carry out due diligence with regard to the relevant key personnel and the track record of the supplier so that they can obtain a more reliable and accurate assessment of the supplier's expertise.

40.2.4 Language

The language fluency of Chinese staff was once a major concern for foreign customers as English is not widely spoken in the community. Recently, there has been significant improvement in this area, and the senior and mid-management level staff of many suppliers are now generally capable of conducting business with foreign customers in English. Since a considerable number of Chinese nationals studied abroad as China grew into an economic power, local staff with foreign-language capabilities other than English, such as German, French or Japanese, can now be much more readily recruited.

40.3 Legal system

40.3.1 Law

40.3.1.1 Civil law influence

China is a civil law jurisdiction and, since the open-door policy in the late 1970s, has been reconstructing its economic and business laws. European influence can be easily identified in various areas, such as intellectual property law and company law.

40.3.1.2 Levels of law

There are different levels of statutory laws. At the top of the hierarchy are the national laws passed by the People's Congress. In the second tier, laws include regulations or implementation rules passed by the State Council. However, at times, the national laws may provide that the State Council regulations prevail in the event of a conflict. At the same time, although court decisions are not treated as having legal authority (as in the common law jurisdictions), the Supreme Court in Beijing issues judicial interpretations on particular issues, and they must be given sufficient weight. Finally, there are local rules, which can deviate from certain principles covered by the national law or other regulations at higher levels[1] to take into account local practices. Therefore, the national laws, regulations and judicial interpretations may not always provide a comprehensive answer to an issue, and the local practices may have to be considered from time to time.

40.3.1.3 Courts

There is also a hierarchical system of courts in China. Most cases involving foreign parties are first handled by either the city intermediate courts or the high courts. A civil case normally takes around 9–12 months to reach the judgment stage, but cases involving foreign parties can take more time. With no case law tradition, there are inconsistencies in judicial decisions. Advocacy is crucial in commercial cases, especially in explaining commercial practices to judges who have not practised law before the judicial appointment, although in theory judges should take an inquisitorial role in the proceedings.

40.4 Contract law

40.4.1 General principles

Most foreign parties insist on foreign law being the governing law in outsourcing contracts. However, it is necessary to briefly mention the local Contract Law. The current version of the Contract Law was introduced in 1999. Chinese Contract Law generally accepts the principle of freedom of contract. Apart from general sections of the Law which apply to all contracts, there are two specific sections of the Law that cover the outsourcing industry, namely those applying to subcontracting contracts and technology contracts.[2] However, the provisions contained in the relevant section of the Law are relatively simple and some modern contractual concepts are not defined or mentioned.

40.4.2 Fairness and reasonableness

A challenging feature of the Chinese Contract Law is the requirement of fairness and reasonableness, which states that a contract or particular provisions of a contract can be declared void if it is held by the court to be either unfair or unreasonable. Currently, there are no specific guidelines accepted throughout China as to what constitutes fairness or reasonableness.

The common way to minimise the effect of this issue is to include a provision in the contract saying that the parties entered into agreement after amicable negotiations and both parties further declare that the terms in the contract are fair and reasonable, taking onto account their respective economic interests.

1 There are a number of occasions in which coastal cities have departed from the national laws in drafting local rules, causing the central government to reiterate the position subsequently. In theory, local rules contradicting the national laws are invalid, but local courts or administrative bodies tend to apply local law until the issue is clarified by the central government or the Supreme Court.

2 Chapter 15 and Chapter 18 respectively of the Contract Law.

40.4.3 Good faith

Some Continental European regimes impose a duty of good faith in the course of contractual dealings. There are similar provisions in the Chinese Contract Law, but the duty of good faith is not clearly defined or explained in judicial decisions or interpretations. The courts have tended to focus on the issue of fraud[3] in investigating a claim of bad faith.

However, in the section in the Chinese Contract Law on subcontracts there is a provision requiring the subcontractor (who is in a similar position to a supplier in an outsourcing arrangement) to inform the customer if the customer's technical requirements are unreasonable. The subcontractor is given a right to damages if the customer does not reply with further instructions on a timely basis.[4] Therefore it is preferable to define carefully the extent of each party's responsibilities, especially the supplier's duty to identify potential problems with the contract instead of relying on the general duty of good faith, although it is arguable that a relatively vague duty of good faith may give certain advantages in providing customers with flexibility in the event of a dispute.

40.4.4 Damages and limitation of liability

In a subcontracting arrangement, if the subcontractor fails to meet the standard prescribed in the contract, generally it can be required to compensate the customer for its losses and damages.[5] Normally actual loss is the only recognised basis for the calculation of damages. However, the rules on damages are relatively general and undeveloped, and do not include details of how damages are to be assessed or calculated. There are occasions in which the common law concepts such as account of profits are accepted in some local courts. There is no prohibition of penalties under the Contract Law, although penalties will be subject to the general law on fairness and reasonableness described above.

Limitation of liability provisions is another issue frequently raised during the course of contract negotiations. Except for the fair and reasonable requirement described above, there are no specific further restrictions on limitations of liability which would be relevant for outsourcing agreements. Usually, the Chinese courts tend to recognise limitation of liability provisions in business transactions where the parties have been given a sufficient opportunity to negotiate the relevant provisions.

40.4.5 Lien

Under the section on subcontracts in the Contract Law, it is stipulated that unless otherwise agreed, the subcontractor may exercise a lien over the works until the customer has paid the service or contract fees.[6]

3 Article 6 of Contract Law.
4 Article 257 of Contract Law.
5 Article 262 of Contract Law.
6 Article 264 of Contract Law.

40.4.6 Remedies

Another issue to note is that some common law reliefs are not available under the Chinese legal system. For example, specific performance is not available as a remedy. Injunctions are normally only granted for infringements of intellectual property rights and not for pure breaches of contract disputes. When considering the potential remedies available, a claim for damages is therefore usually the only practical remedy in relation to outsourcing contracts with local Chinese parties.

40.4.7 Use of third party in providing services

Under the section on subcontracts in the Contract Law, there is a stipulation prohibiting the use of third parties by the supplier in providing the subcontracted services unless otherwise agreed.[7] Since outsourcing is a subcontracting relationship, the supplier should expressly provide for it to be able to use third parties where relevant.

40.4.8 Converting common law-style contracts for local use

The Chinese Contract Law does not distinguish between conditions, warranties and representations, and the rules on damages are relatively undeveloped. Therefore, to avoid uncertainty, contracts using Chinese law as the applicable law should contain more detailed provisions on the consequences of any breach. Equally, certain established concepts existing in common law such as time being of the essence should be clearly defined in order to be enforceable. A careful review should be made before converting a common law-style contract for local use.

40.5 People issues

40.5.1 Outsourcing and employment law

It is generally considered that the Chinese employment law regime has been tightening in favour of employees since 2007. Local and foreign enterprises have been using different methods to take advantage of the new legislation and policies.

In the main, Chinese courts are hostile towards structures set up to circumvent the employment laws. Customers sometimes set up outsourcing contractual structures to avoid their liability as employers. It is rare, other than in respect of contract processing arrangements in the past, for a customer to be responsible for all of the employment costs of an outsourcing operation in China, and this is an obvious sign of circumvention. However, specific provisions, such as a customer having control over the hiring and firing of the supplier's employees as well as the compulsory periodic change of the supplier's employees, are not uncommon despite the fact that they run the risk of being interpreted as attempts to avoid the obligation to enter into an open-term contract (which can only be terminated on statutory grounds). Recently, a number of labour-intensive outsourcing arrangements entered into by multinationals with these sorts of provisions

7 Article 253 of Contract Law.

have been disregarded by the Chinese courts as they were considered artificial. The relevant "ultimate employers" are then responsible for employment remuneration under the Labour Contract Law, which may defeat the original intention of the arrangement.[8]

However, there are no well-defined rules as to how an outsourcing arrangement should be structured and the courts will look at what is in the contract as well as the actual facts of the case. It may be helpful for the parties to expressly state in the contract that the relationship between the customer and the supplier's employees will not be one of employer/employee.

40.5.2 Highlights of prominent employment law issues under the Labour Contract Law

Although it is not strictly relevant to mention the Chinese Labour Contract Law, as customers in a typical outsourcing agreement should not be responsible for bearing the financial and contractual obligations of the suppliers' employees, the following may help a customer to understand why sometimes certain peculiar requests are made of them. In fact, some of following points may explain why outsourcing has been growing in China over the recent years.

40.5.2.1 Open-ended contract

Any employee whose contract has been renewed twice (provided that the renewals took place after 1 January 2008), or who has worked for the same employer for more than 10 years, has the right to require the employer to enter into an open-term contract, which can only be terminated on statutory grounds.

40.5.2.2 Statutory grounds for termination

There is no termination by notice under the Labour Contract Law, subject to special exceptions such as a material change in circumstances. Generally, all employment contracts can be terminated in the following situations:

(a) upon expiration of the term;[9]
(b) as a result of the employees' gross negligence or serious violation of corporate policy;[10]
(c) upon the completion of economic layoff procedures;[11]
(d) dissolution of the employer company; or
(e) other specific statutory grounds such as the employee being convicted of a criminal offence.

---

8 Article 62(2) and (3) of Labour Contract Law. The court will normally decide that the outsourcing supplier is actually an employment agent, and that the outsourcing relationship will be subject to the relevant provisions of Chinese Labour Contract Law.

9 Article 44(1) of Labour Contract Law.

10 Article 39(2) of Labour Contract Law.

11 Article 41 of the Labour Contract Law, and Enterprise Economic Layoff Regulations issued by the Labour and Social Security Department issued in 1994. Note, however, that the 1994 Regulations have been named as one of the existing regulations which are inconsistent with the Labour Contract Law and should therefore be amended. However, local employment bureaus maintain the view that the Regulations remain valid in the meantime.

40.5.2.3 Confidentiality and economic compensation
See 40.7 below.

40.5.3 Individual as supplier

It is not uncommon for customers to enter into outsourcing contracts with suppliers who are individuals. This can raise the risk of there being a deemed creation of an employment relationship, where the Labour Bureau takes the view that the outsourcing contract is intended to circumvent employment law. Therefore, the contract should clearly define the relationship, and the customer should preferably request the individual supplier to obtain and produce a "Getihu" (a concept similar to sole proprietorship) business licence before entering into the contract.

40.6 Data protection

There is no data privacy or data protection law in China except for the Contract Law[12] and the Anti-Unfair Competition Law,[13] in which there are few provisions protecting trade secrets.

40.7 Protection of IPR

40.7.1 Law and practice

China is a signatory to the WTO, TRIPS and a number of international treaties on intellectual property rights. Trademark, patents, copyright and industrial designs protection is available.

Both administrative and court proceedings are common routes for enforcing rights, although there are some differences in the remedies available.

40.7.1.1 Administrative procedures
One reason for the popularity of using administrative procedures in China is because the Administration of Industry and Commerce, which supervises all business activities and issues the Business Licence (a permit for operating a business) has the necessary authority to conduct administrative raids against infringers of trademarks and to impose penalties.

The patent office seldom conducts administrative raids as staff at local branches of the patent office often lack the necessary technical experience to conduct a proper examination of the alleged infringement.

40.7.1.2 Court proceedings
Although immediate relief is not available, normally there should be no specific problem in bringing actions for breach of copyright and industrial design in local courts. If local jurisdiction issues

12 Article 43 of Contract Law.
13 Article 10 of Anti-Unfair Competition Law.

can be resolved, suits enforcing patents should be brought in the first-tier coastal cities, where there are specialised judges with a technical background who will be able to understand technical issues.

40.7.2 IPR in outsourcing

In the context of outsourcing arrangements, a common issue is the potential for dispute over the ownership of the intellectual property rights developed during the course of or resulting from the outsourcing relationship, as there is not automatic transfer of ownership of these intellectual property rights to the customer under the Patent Law.[14] Therefore it is essential that the outsourcing contract includes clear provisions stipulating the rights and obligations of the parties involved with regard to intellectual property rights.

In addition, parties to an outsourcing agreement should note that, under the new Patent Law,[15] an employee who invents or creates intellectual property rights is entitled to financial compensation. The outsourcing agreement should set out who will be responsible for making this payment (usually it is the supplier).

40.8 Protection of confidentiality

40.8.1 General law

The Anti-Unfair Competition Law and the relevant regulations include provisions relating to the protection of trade secrets.

In addition, in the context of a subcontracting relationship, there is a provision in the Contract Law protecting confidential technical information and prohibiting the unauthorised retention of that information.[16]

The parties should define in the outsourcing contract exactly what information and documentation will be regarded as confidential information.

In practice, the customer will need to be reassured that the supplier has appropriate systems and processes in place to protect the confidentiality of information. A common pitfall for a foreign party working with a local party is the lack of any control over the local party's systems and processes for transferring and using confidential business and technical information. It is important for the foreign party to agree in the contract the specific systems and processes which the local party will implement and maintain.

40.8.2 Local practice on non-competition

A point to note is that in certain cities and local areas, specific rules on trade secrets apply. For instance, Shenzhen city and Zhuhai city each have their own rules on trade secrets.

14 Article 8 of Patent Law.
15 Article 16 of Patent Law.
16 Article 266 of Contract Law.

Although these rules operate in the context of an employment relationship, a foreign party should consider whether these local rules will have an impact on the proposed outsourcing relationship. For example, in Zhuhai, there are specific rules on the minimum amount of compensation which must be offered to a departing employee in return for him validating the post-employment non-competition clause, which is designed to protect confidential information obtained by such employee during the course of employment.

In such a case, it is necessary to consider whether there should be provisions in the outsourcing contract stipulating that the supplier must include non-competition provisions in its employment contracts with its staff. Also, if there is a local requirement for payment of economic compensation in order to validate the restrictive covenant, the customer may want to state in the outsourcing agreement that it can make such payment if the supplier fails to do so, and then recover the amount paid from the supplier.

40.9 Enforceability of jurisdiction clauses

Local suppliers are averse to foreign law being adopted as the applicable law for outsourcing contracts, but in practice they will accept foreign law it if is necessary to win the business. English laws and the laws of other leading common law jurisdictions such as the US and Hong Kong are common options.

The Chinese courts generally give effect to foreign jurisdiction clauses and will refuse to accept a case (at the acceptance of case stage) if there is a foreign jurisdiction clause in the relevant contract. However, the Civil Procedures Law does not prevent the Chinese courts from assuming jurisdiction notwithstanding there being a foreign jurisdiction clause. As long as the performance of the contract is in China, the Chinese courts can assume jurisdiction, but if parallel proceedings have already been commenced in another jurisdiction, the courts will consider the forum *non conveniens* principles in deciding whether the complaint should be accepted.[17]

40.10 Enforcement of judgments

40.10.1 Court proceedings

The effectiveness of enforcing foreign judgments in China depends on whether there is a reciprocal enforcement arrangement with the jurisdiction handling the dispute. The UK, most of the EU states, and the US do not have reciprocal enforcement arrangements with China. At the same time, in China there is no equivalent to the common law concept of enforcement of foreign judgments. A foreign law clause and a foreign dispute resolution clause may therefore ultimately disadvantage the foreign party, as if it breaches the agreement the Chinese party will

17 The factors considered by the court can be found in Paragraph 11 of Part 1 of the Minutes of Second National Working Meeting regarding cases involving foreign parties and admiralty cases issued by the Supreme People's Court on 26 December 2005.

be able to enforce the judgment against it, but if the Chinese party breaches the agreement and the foreign party obtains a judgment against it, the foreign judgment will not be enforceable in China.

Some foreign parties agree that the outsourcing agreement will be subject to Hong Kong laws and the jurisdiction of the Hong Kong courts as, subject to compliance with certain conditions, a Hong Kong judgment can be enforced in China.[18]

40.10.2 Arbitration

China is a signatory to the New York Convention, so arbitration is the preferred mode of dispute resolution for foreign parties with contracts with Chinese parties. It is usual for arbitration to be handled by the local arbitration commission, or in jurisdictions with reciprocal enforcement arrangements for arbitral awards, like Hong Kong.[19]

Parties sometimes elect to have two-level dispute resolution provisions, in which:

(a) for matters relating to the contractual terms and the validity of the contract, the parties must submit the dispute to arbitration;

(b) for confidentiality and intellectual property-related matters, the parties are at liberty to enforce their respective rights by administrative proceedings if they are available.

40.11 Government support and regulatory restrictions

40.11.1 Government support

The Chinese government provides considerable support for outsourcing, particularly in the high-technology sector. The support normally goes directly to the suppliers in the form of low land prices, loans and preferential policies on local tax and duties. Therefore, such high-technology suppliers are normally in a better position to compete both in terms of pricing and performance.

40.11.2 Software for export

There are registration and approval requirements for software export contracts, and the obligation to satisfy these requirements is on the local supplier. Consequently, it is necessary to include a provision in the outsourcing contract that the supplier should register the relevant contract and produce evidence of registration upon request.

---

18 Arrangement on Reciprocal Recognition and Enforcement of Judgments in Civil and Commercial Matters by the Courts of the Mainland and of the Hong Kong Special Administrative Region Pursuant to Choice of Court Agreements between Parties Concerned dated 14 July 2006.

19 The enforcement of Hong Kong arbitral awards is not done under the New York Convention. There is a separate reciprocal enforcement arrangement between Mainland China and Hong Kong.

The rules[20] state that the agreement must specify the method by which the software is to be exported, and the agreed mode should be used when the software is then exported. There are two options under the current rules:

(a) export through customs; or
(b) electronic transmission.

There are prohibitions on exporting software and data management services from China, but these restrictions only apply to the exporting of software connected to national security.[21]

40.11.3 Technology imports and exports

There are restrictions on importing and exporting technology in China.[22] Contracts for technology imports and exports are subject to registration and approval requirements, except where these are exempt pursuant to the relevant regulations.

40.11.4 Foreign exchange control

China controls the flow of foreign exchange and both inbound and outbound remittances are subject to an approval process overseen by the State Administration of Foreign Exchange or its local branch.

In general, control of inbound remittances is relatively lax, although recently the government indicated that speculating in renminbi was not to be encouraged because some foreign companies were acquiring renminbi as the currency appreciated.

For outbound remittances, evidence should be submitted together with the duly registered contract (such as in the case of software export and technology import/export contracts). Failure to produce evidence of registration will lead to delays in the approval process. It is common to have provisions covering registration, and customers may consider having a clause granting themselves authority to register the contracts on behalf of the supplier, if the latter fails to do so, although it is up to the local administrative authority whether such authority will be accepted.

Customers considering imposing a penalty on a supplier or charging certain fees for non-compliance with contractual terms, or requiring a performance bond or guarantee, should note that China has foreign exchange controls, which mean that all foreign exchange remittances will need to be approved by the relevant local branch of the State Administration of Foreign Exchange. The approvals are only granted when there is documentary proof of such payment obligations. Contracts and invoices are the normal documents provided for this purpose.

---

20 Article 5 of Measures for the Management and Statistics of Export Software.

21 Regulations of Management of Export of Restricted Technology and Regulations of Export Examination of National Secret.

22 Regulations on Management of Import and Export of Technology.

40.12 General taxation issues

Generally, the categories of tax appropriate to outsourcing relationships are Corporate Income Tax (including withholding tax), VAT and Business Tax. There are no tax implications for a foreign customer engaging a Chinese supplier unless there are goods or services provided by the customer or the customer has an establishment in China. However, it is always advisable to stipulate in the contract that the local supplier will bear all of the taxes and other governmental dues owing.

Tax can be imposed on the supplier in those cases where payments are made from China. If it is a royalty payment, it will be subject to withholding tax within the corporate income tax regime. In this case, the local supplier will be the withholding agent liable for the tax, which should be paid directly to the tax authority. If the money payable to the customer is a service fee, business tax will be payable provided that there is evidence to prove that the services are performed outside China (e.g. invoices showing that the location of the performance of the services is outside China).

40.13 Other considerations

40.13.1 Internet bandwidth

The internet or external bandwidth of China is limited. Therefore, if the outsourcing service is intended to provide real-time information to the customer, it is prudent for the customer to enquire if the local telecommunications service provider and authority can arrange a direct line or reserved internet capacity for the connection. It may be necessary to obtain a specific licence for the operation.

40.13.2 Scope of business

Chinese entities can only carry on the type of business prescribed in their respective Business Licence. Entering into contracts beyond the business scope may cause issues with the validity of the contract and the performance of the contractual obligations. As part of the due diligence process, it is important for the customer to require the supplier to provide a copy of the Business Licence so that the customer can verify the scope of business that the supplier is authorised to provide. The customer should also carry out a search of the public records.

Part Twelve – Other Key EU Jurisdictions

Chapter 41

Germany

Dr Stephan Witteler
Partner
Beiten Burkhardt

in cooperation with Dr Fabian Schäfer, Stefan Breider, Jörg Walzer, Dr Marcus Schwab, Martin Obermüller and Doreen Methfessel

41.1 Trends in outsourcing in Germany

41.1.1 Types of outsourcing

In the past, the German outsourcing market has seen slower growth and a smaller overall volume of deals than the UK. Germany's outsourcing market developed first in the general infrastructure and facility management sectors rather than the ICT sector or other, more complex service areas. In the ICT sector, outsourcing in Germany first appeared in the computing and desktop services area. In more recent years outsourcing has expanded into business process outsourcing and systems integration.[1]

Almost one-third of German companies have entered into outsourcing arrangements. Currently, large corporations are in the lead (39 per cent have made use of external suppliers) followed by medium-sized companies (of which 31 per cent have already resorted to outsourcing). Within the public sector the focus of outsourcing is on ICT. The statistics show that 50 per cent of public bodies in Germany have outsourced some or all of their ICT services, while 59 per cent have outsourced online or website services.

41.1.2 Motives for outsourcing

Customers who outsource in Germany are mostly motivated by a desire to achieve cost reductions, a strategic advantage resulting from enhanced access to specialised resources and competencies, and increased business flexibility allowing customers to focus on their respective core

---

1 Survey performed in medium and large businesses for Adecco Manpower Services LLP (Personaldienstleistungen GmbH) by TNS Infratest in the period January to February 2008; Survey performed by Accenture in cooperation with the Frauenhofer-Institut "Outsourcing in the public sector" ("Outsourcing im öffentlichen Bereich").

business.[2] In 2008 about 33 per cent of the companies stated quality improvement as their main reason for outsourcing, followed by access to subject matter expertise (20 per cent) and the desire to cut costs (18 per cent).

A considerable number of German corporations have reported negative experiences with outsourcing. In-sourcing became a noticeable trend in some industries, particularly the financial services and public sector. Customers saw the main disadvantages of outsourcing as a dependency on external suppliers, reduced flexibility, unsatisfied expectations regarding innovation, and the failure to meet quality and cost expectations. Further risks involved the threat of losing knowledge, data security and privacy concerns. A significant number of companies reject outsourcing, keeping their ICT services in-house or establishing ICT service subsidiaries.

Contrary to expectations, Germany's economic slowdown after the "burst of the bubble" in 2001 did not trigger a wave of financially driven outsourcing projects by companies eager to improve their balance sheets. It is still too early to forecast whether the global economic slowdown started by the sub-prime crisis in September 2008 will result in an increasing momentum of financial rather than strategic oriented outsourcing projects in Germany.

41.1.3 Multisourcing

Most customers have adopted a multisourcing approach. Only 15 per cent of all outsourcing contracts involve comprehensive end-to-end ICT services. According to a market analysis, 30 per cent of all German corporate outsourcing deals in 2006/07 showed a total contractual value ("TCV") of €10–20 million. On average, there are only three or four mega deals of more than €500 million per year.

41.1.4 Suppliers

Until recently, Germany's ICT outsourcing market was dominated by German, US and European outsourcing suppliers. These major players continued to acquire the large deals, especially in the banking, securities and retail sectors in 2006/07. Offshoring is not new for the German ICT sector and many of the large multinational customers headquartered in Germany offshore or near-shore to India, Asia or South America. However, privacy is a very important issue for Germany and German customers are reluctant to enter into offshoring transactions which involve the processing of personal data outside the EU. It will be interesting to observe the impact of the entry of Eastern European suppliers upon the German market, as they offer attractive pricing with specific German language and business process skills.

2 Survey performed in medium and large businesses for Adecco Manpower Services LLP by TNS Infratest in the period January to February 2008.

41.2 People issues - Acquired Rights Directive

41.2.1 Background

The Acquired Rights Directive ("ARD") has been implemented in Germany by the transfer of undertakings provisions in Section 613a of the German Civil Code ("BGB"). The purpose of the provisions is to protect employees' jobs. Section 613a BGB is particularly applicable to the acquisition of companies. However, it can also apply to outsourcing, as described in 27.4.2 of this Guide, provided that the prerequisites for a transfer of an undertaking are fulfilled.

41.2.2 Application of Section 613a BGB

41.2.2.1 Business or part of a business
Section 613a BGB applies if an initial outsourcing or secondary outsourcing arrangement involves a business or a part of a business within the meaning of Section 613a BGB. The case law of the German Federal Labour Court (in accordance with the European case law) defines a business or part of a business as a "long-term economic unit". The term "unit" is discussed in 27.4.3.1. A part of a business within the meaning of Section 613a BGB is an organisational subdivision of an overall business enterprise.

41.2.2.2 Transfer of a business or part of a business
Whether a transfer will be considered a transfer of a business unit will depend upon the following factors, as interpreted by the courts:[3]

(a) the type of business or company involved;
(b) whether the transfer involves a transfer of tangible assets;
(c) whether the transfer involves a transfer of intangible assets (e.g. customer list, know-how etc.);
(d) whether the transfer involves a transfer of employees or part of the employees (key employees);
(e) whether the transfer involves a transfer of customers and customer relationships;
(f) the similarity of activities carried out by the business unit before and after the transfer; and
(g) the duration of any interruption of activity.

This is a complex area and customers and suppliers are advised to take specialist legal advice.

41.2.3 Effect of Section 613a BGB

41.2.3.1 Information requirements vis-à-vis affected employees
Both transferor and transferee are obliged to inform employees affected by the transfer of undertakings of that transfer in writing (Section 613a, subsection 5, BGB). The notification must include:

3 For example, decisions of the European Court of justice in Case C-24/85 Spijkers, 18 March 1986; Case C-392/92 Christel Schmidt, 14 April 1994; Case C-13/95 Ayse Süzen, 11 March 1997; Case C-232,233/04 Güney-Görres/Demir, 15 December 2005; Case C-340/01 Carlito Abler/Sodecho MM Catering LLP, 20 November 2003.

(a) information regarding the transferee (e.g. legal (business) name, address etc.);
(b) the date or planned date of the transfer of undertakings;
(c) the reasons for the transfer of undertakings (legal basis, such as the outsourcing agreement) and the related motives of the transferor;
(d) the legal, economic and social consequences of the transfer of undertakings for the employees concerned; and
(e) the measures to be taken with respect to employees.

41.2.3.2 Transfer of contracts of employment

Where Section 613a BGB applies, the legal consequence is an automatic transfer of all employment contracts in the transferred business from the transferor to the transferee.

However, Section 613a BGB does not apply to managing directors of limited liability companies ("GmbH"), management board members of stock corporations ("AG"), or to former employees or pensioners who still have claims under a company pension plan.

In addition, employees concerned are entitled to object to the transfer of their employment relationships according to Section 613a, subsection 6, BGB. Employees have to exercise their right to object by written notice within one month of being informed of the transfer. They may exercise their right by notifying the transferor or the transferee. The time period of one month only starts to run once the employees have been completely and correctly informed about the transfer of the undertaking (as described in 41.2.3.1). If the transferor or the transferee fails to inform the employees, or fails to do so in a manner in line with the law, the employees will have an unlimited right to object to the transfer. Once an employee exercises his right to object, effectively his employment relationship will remain with the transferor even if the objection was exercised after the transfer of business has taken place. In such circumstances, the customer may be in a position to dismiss the objecting employee on operational grounds. However, the dismissal will have to comply with the requirements of the German Protection Against Unfair Dismissal Act.

41.2.3.3 Transfer of rights and duties

According to Section 613a BGB, the transferee must fulfil all of the obligations arising from the transferred employment relationship as if it were the original contracting party. The liability of the transferee extends, without any limitation, to all outstanding claims resulting from the existing employment relationships, regardless of how and when they arose.

The statutory law provides for a limited continued liability of the transferor, in addition to that of the transferee. Both parties are jointly and severally liable under Section 613a, subsection 2, BGB for obligations that arose prior to the transfer date and that are payable within one year of the date of transfer. This joint and several liability covers, for example, special payments such as Christmas bonuses which generally mature for payment at the end of a calendar year.

The liability provided by Section 613a BGB is mandatory law and cannot be restricted or excluded effectively vis-à-vis the employees concerned. Therefore, risks resulting from the mandatory liability provisions of Section 613a BGB should be covered by explicit clauses in the outsourcing agreement, allocating the risks between the customer and the supplier.

41.2.3.4 *Pensions liabilities*

All obligations relating to the employment relationship with the transferring staff pass on to the transferee without limitation. There are no special provisions providing for a different treatment of pension claims. Contracting parties should, therefore, insert clauses within the outsourcing agreement to deal specifically with the allocation of risks resulting from pension claims by transferring employees.

41.2.3.5 *Continued application of collective agreements*

Section 613a, subsection 1, sentences 1 to 4 of the BGB set out the legal consequences of a transfer of undertakings to existing collective agreements (works agreements and collective bargaining agreements) applicable in the customer's business. Depending upon the exact circumstances:

(a) The collective agreements applicable in the customer's business may remain entirely in force – this will apply if there is an existing collective agreement at the time of the transfer but no collective agreements applicable in the supplier's business. In this situation, the supplier may not change the collective agreements to the detriment of the employee before the end of one year after the date of transfer.

(b) The collective agreements applicable in the customer's business may be replaced by collective agreements with identical parameters applicable in the supplier's business – this will apply if there are collective agreements with identical parameters applicable in the supplier's business. In this circumstance, the supplier will be able to adjust the working conditions of the acquired business to the agreements prevailing in its own organisation.

(c) The collective agreements applicable in the customer's business may be transformed into individual contractual provisions for each employee with the consequence that they will have the same legal character as provisions in an employment agreement – collective agreements that no longer apply to a collective continue to apply in individual contractual provisions, binding for the employer and to the benefit of the employee.

Where collective agreements are transformed into individual contractual provisions (*see* point (c) above), the transferee will not be able to modify the provisions to the employee's detriment until at least one year has elapsed since the transfer of the undertaking. Any modifications within the one-year period will be void, irrespective of whether they have been carried out by the employer unilaterally or are based on mutual agreement with the employee.

41.2.3.6 *Ineffectiveness of dismissals*

Section 613a, subsection 4, BGB includes a prohibition against dismissals. A dismissal will be void if it is "due to the transfer of a business". According to the case law, a dismissal will be "due to the transfer of the business" if the transfer was the motive for the dismissal. However, dismissals on other grounds, for example relating to the employee's conduct or for operational reasons, are acceptable.

41.3 People issues – participation and consultation rights of elected employee representative bodies

The employees' representative bodies in companies in Germany are the works councils. A pure transfer of the whole business will have no impact on the employee representative bodies, and the works council will continue to exist unchanged. Thus, the works council of the transferor will have neither participation rights nor consultation rights prior to the transfer.

However, if the transfer of a business is accompanied by an operational change (such as a split of the plant or merger of premises on the transferee's side), the works councils may have participation rights under Section 111 et seq. of the German Works Constitution Act, in particular the right to negotiate a conciliation of interests and a social plan.

The transfer of part of a business will usually be considered a split of the business and thus will be an operational change, giving rise to participation rights.

If the transferor's business is to be divided on the transfer of business (e.g. split of the business) the works council will have a transitional mandate pursuant to Section 21a of the Works Constitution Act. The works council of the divided business unit will generally remain in office. It will continue to manage the affairs of the parts of the business unit created by the division on a transitional basis for up to, but no longer than, six months. This mandate will end as soon as a new works council has been elected in the divided part of the business unit and the results of the election have been announced.

The transferor's trade union is not entitled to participation or consultation rights unless expressly agreed, for example, in collective bargaining agreements. However, based on the case law of the Federal Labour Court, the trade union is entitled to call a strike in order to enforce negotiations about a tariff social plan. The works council's right to negotiate a social plan, as mentioned above, remains unaffected. If the transferor faces the risk of a strike, it may be able to take tactical measures in order to minimise the trade union's influence.

41.4 Contract law

41.4.1 Contract types

German contract law sets out different implied warranties and liability provisions depending upon the basic type of contract. For this purpose, contracts are categorised depending upon the type of services or deliverables to be provided under them.

The BGB, the central codification of German contract law, was created more than a century ago and has not changed substantially since its inception. The codex provides sections for, *inter alia*, lease contracts, loan contracts, purchase contracts, contracts for works and materials, contracts for services or service contracts.

Considering its age, the BGB understandably does not include specific provisions for more "modern", hybrid types of agreement like outsourcing contracts. Therefore, it is necessary to assess, for each outsourcing contract, which basic types of contract are involved and which statutory provisions are applicable.

Outsourcing contracts usually comprise elements of various basic contract types. Typically, they are a combination of an asset or share purchase agreement, and a services agreement. The asset or share purchase agreement would be considered a purchase agreement within the meaning of

Section 433 BGB. The services agreement, depending on the specific facts, could either be a contract to produce a work in the sense of Section 631 BGB (i.e. a contract in which a supplier is obligated to produce a work for a customer for remuneration), a contract for work and materials in the sense of Section 651 BGB, or a service contract in the sense of Section 611 BGB (i.e. a contract in which one party promises services to another for remuneration). Different provisions apply to each type of contract.

41.4.1.1 Purchase agreement

The buyer will have a statutory warranty against material and legal defects under Section 437 BGB. For correctable defects, the buyer must first claim for cure under Section 439 BGB. For other defects, the buyer can withdraw from the agreement[4] or reduce the purchase price,[5] and claim for damages[6] or a reimbursement of futile expenditure.[7]

41.4.1.2 Contract to produce a work

Warranty regulations for contracts to produce a work are based both on general rules of the law of obligations and sales of goods law. According to Section 643 BGB, the customer will have different options in the case of defects. Again, with correctable defects, it must first seek a cure.[8] Otherwise, it will be entitled to withdraw from the contract, repair the faults manually and claim for reimbursement of expenditure,[9] reduce the purchase price[10] and claim damages or a reimbursement of expenditure.[11]

41.4.1.3 Contract for work and materials

A contract for work and materials combines aspects of sale of goods law and the law on service contracts. The supplier binds itself to produce a thing using specific materials. According to Section 651 BGB, these contracts will be regulated by sales of goods law, with the exception of contracts over non-fungible things, for which provisions on service contracts apply.

41.4.1.4 Service contract

The service contract rules do not contain specific warranty regulations regarding mis-performance. In cases of non-performance or mis-performance, the general provisions of sections 280 et seq. BGB may be considered as a basis for a claim in damages (*see* below).

41.4.1.5 Framework contract

From a structural perspective, outsourcing agreements often consist of a framework contract, generally containing the following elements: start date and duration of service provision, entry into force, duration, termination, default, warranty and liability.

4 *See* Section 437, no. 2, BGB in conjunction with Sections 440, 323 and 326 subsection 5 BGB.
5 Section 437, no. 2, BGB in conjunction with Section 441 BGB.
6 Section 437, no. 3, BGB in conjunction with Sections 440, 280, 281, 283, and 311a BGB.
7 Section 437, no. 3, BGB in conjunction with 284 BGB.
8 Section 643, no. 1, BGB in conjunction with Section 635 BGB.
9 Section 643, no. 2, BGB in conjunction with Sections 626, 323, 326 subsection 5 BGB.
10 Section 643, no. 3, BGB in conjunction with Sections 636, 280, 281, 283, 311a BGB.
11 Section 643, no. 4, BGB in conjunction with Section 284 BGB.

In addition to the framework contract, the customer and the supplier usually include specific legal provisions covering the transfer of assets or shares, service level agreements, the rent or lease of premises, the use of infrastructure and the transfer of personnel.

41.4.2 Impossible or frustrated performance[12]

41.4.2.1 Performance impossible or requires disproportionate effort or expense
Where special circumstances render it impossible for an obligor to fulfil its contractual obligations, under Section 275 BGB, it will not be required to perform.[13]

The obligor will also have the right to refuse performance according to Section 275, subsection 2, BGB to the extent that the performance requires expense and effort which, taking into account the subject matter of the obligation and the requirements of good faith, is grossly disproportionate to the interest in performance of the obligee. In determining the reasonableness of the effort, the responsibility of the obligor for the obstacle to performance will be taken into account.

The obligor's inability to fulfil his contractual obligations will not affect the validity of the contract but will be deemed to be a breach of duty. As a result, the obligee will have a right to claim damages for harm caused if the obligor is responsible for the breach.[14] According to Section 276 BGB, the obligor will be responsible for intentional or negligent breaches unless the parties have agreed a higher or lower level of liability, for example, in a guarantee. The obligor will also have strict liability for any breaches of duty caused by the intentional or negligent acts of its legal representatives or persons whom it uses to perform its obligations.

If the obstacle to performance existed at the time when the contract was signed, the contract will remain valid. The obligee will have the right to demand damages if the obligor was aware of the obstacle to performance when entering into the contract or should have been aware of the obstacle.

If a party has included an exclusion of liability for failure to perform as a result of a force majeure, the provision will not automatically cover industrial action within that party's company unless expressly agreed.

---

12 German law has both the doctrine of frustration of contract and the doctrine of impossibility. If performance is impossible in the sense of Section 275 BGB, Section 313 BGB is not applicable. Unlike impossibility, the doctrine of frustration of contract usually leads to the modification of the contract.

13 The code excludes claims for performance to the extent that performance is impossible for the obligor or for any other person under Section 275, subsection 1, BGB. This applies even if the obligor caused the circumstances from which the impossibility ensued. The code assumes that it is pointless to give the obligee a claim, which the obligor is factually unable to fulfil and which could not be fulfilled by means of execution of judgment.

14 Under German law there is a distinction between primary and secondary obligations. Primary obligations are those the obligor needs to fulfil according to the terms of an agreement or the law. Secondary obligations arise where there is an interference or cessation of the primary obligations. Therefore, in the case of impossibility where the primary obligations cease, the obligee can still claim a secondary obligation, for example damages, if the impossibility was caused by the obligor.

41.4.2.2 Frustration of contract

The doctrine of frustration of contract in Section 313 BGB is a codified regulation which deals with situations which are commonly covered by provisions of force majeure. It will apply where the continuation of the contract would be seen as an abuse of rights contrary to the duty to act in good faith, for example where performance will be impossible or in less serious circumstances. Where the doctrine of frustration applies, the effect is that the contract will be modified to fit the changed circumstances or, in extreme circumstances, the contract will be terminated. This effect cannot be influenced by any contractual provision as far as the respective contract does not explicitly address a certain risk and the frustration is caused by the realisation of this risk.

41.4.3 Liability and exclusions of liability

41.4.3.1 Standard of fault

Under the BGB, each party will be liable for breaches of duty caused by its intentional actions or negligence. This will apply unless a higher or lower level of liability is explicit or can be inferred from the subject matter of the obligation, including but not limited to the giving of a guarantee or the assumption of a procurement risk by one of the parties (Section 276 BGB).

The principle of liability for intent or negligence is modified by numerous exemptions in statutory law. For example, Section 278 BGB provides for a higher degree of liability, namely a strict liability for the acts of legal representatives and agents.

The principle of liability for intent or negligence may also be modified by agreement by the parties. Parties are permitted to agree higher degrees of liability insofar as this does not contradict public policy.

The obligee carries the burden of proof that the obligor has objectively breached its duty, and must prove the causal connection between the breach of duty and the damages (exceptions are e.g. Sections 280, subsection 1, sentence 2, 345, 363, 932 BGB). The obligor must then prove that it is not responsible for the breach of duty.

41.4.3.2 Liability for damages

Under Section 280, paragraph 1, BGB, breach of duty caused by a party's intentional actions or negligence triggers liability for damages.

41.4.3.3 Specific limitations of liability

The parties are free to negotiate limitations upon liability subject to certain exceptions, which are explained below. The parties can agree express provisions in the agreement which change the statutory standard of fault, or change or exclude the liability of the party for damages. It is also common practice to agree financial limitations on liability for damages.

41.4.3.4 Enforceability of limitations of liability – standard business terms

Whether exclusions of liability or warranties are enforceable depends first upon whether the outsourcing terms constitute standard business terms (as defined in Section 305 BGB) or individual agreements.

Standard business terms are contract terms, preformulated by one party with the intent to use the terms for more than two transactions. It is irrelevant whether the provisions form a separate part of a contract or are integrated within the contractual document itself. The usage of standard contract templates does not automatically mean that the resulting contract is based on standard business terms. The important point is whether the standard template clauses are subsequently negotiated in detail by the parties.

The following are impermissible in standard business terms:

(a) exclusion of liability for a breach of material contractual obligations;
(b) exclusion of liability for damage resulting from injury to life, body and health;
(c) exclusion of liability for intentional and grossly negligent breaches of duty by the obligor, his legal representatives and vicarious agents.

Where standard business terms infringe the above provisions of statutory law they are void and replaced by the statutory scheme. As such, standard business terms which exclude the statutory warranties set out in 41.5.2 will not be valid. Hence, if parties wish to contract for warranties and liabilities which deviate from the statutory framework, it is essential that they negotiate such clauses in depth to ensure that they are not construed as standard business terms.

41.4.3.5 Other unenforceable limitations of liability

Under German law, the parties may not exclude (whether in contracts drafted for multiple use or as an individual arranged and negotiated agreement) liability for:

(a) exclusion of material contractual obligations;[15]
(b) intentional breaches of duty;
(c) damage to body, life or health caused intentionally or negligently;[16]
(d) responsibility pursuant to Product Liability Act (Produkthaftungsgesetz, "ProdHaftG") for personal injury up to the statutory limit of €85 million (Section 10 ProdHaftG).

There are also specific provisions applicable in particular businesses like financial services, pharmaceutical production or telecommunications. Section 7, subsection 2 of the German Telecommunications Act (Telekommunikationsgesetz, "TKG"), for instance, requires the supplier to grant a statutory liability of €12,500 per customer for financial losses arising from a significant damage to property and a limit of up to €10 million per event for all claimants for unintentional damage. Under Section 1, subsection 2, TKG, the supplier can not exclude this liability.

41.4.3.6 Types of damages

German law distinguishes between direct and indirect damages. The decision of whether damage is direct or indirect is made on a case-by-case basis, as there is no standard definition for the concept of indirect damage in German law. German law does not usually allow for the award of punitive damages.

15 It is not possible to contract out of obligations which are required to duly execute the contract.
16 *See* Section 307, subsection 7A, BGB.

Provisions excluding liability for indirect damages are enforceable if the indirect damages are caused by slight negligence.

The parties cannot exclude liability for direct damages caused by intentional or grossly negligent acts or omissions.

41.4.4 Termination

Almost all outsourcing contracts include express provisions for the termination of the contract.

In the absence of express provisions, parties may terminate pursuant to Section 314, subsection 1, BGB, which allows for termination without notice with good cause. There are also specific termination rules that allow for termination without notice with good cause, for example Sections 543 and 626 BGB, which regulate the termination of leases and service relationships respectively.

41.5 Data protection

41.5.1 Data Protection Acts

The EU Data Protection Directive, described in Chapter 32 of this Guide, aims to create a common data protection level within the EU. The EU Data Protection Directive was implemented into German law by the Federal Data Protection Act (Bundesdatenschutzgesetz, "BDSG"), as amended in 2001.

German data protection laws differentiate between non-personal data and personal data. Non-personal data is, for example, technical and company data. The rules of the BDSG apply to personal data.

Where external suppliers are commissioned to process personal data, this can be classed as either commissioned data processing or the transfer of a function, depending upon whether the supplier has a discretion to make decisions regarding the processing of the data. The processing will be classified as commissioned data processing if the supplier does not have a discretion to make decisions regarding the processing of the data. The processing will be classified as the transfer of a function if the supplier carries out the transferred tasks independently as opposed to under instruction – in this case the supplier will also assume responsibility for compliance with the requirements of the Federal Data Protection Act and other legislation with regard to the collection, processing and use of personal data.

An outsourcing agreement may comprise a hybrid arrangement, with some parts of the services comprising commissioned data processing and others the transfer of a function.

The Federal Data Protection Act is subject to overriding laws, for example specific regulations for the public sector.

41.5.2 Data processing abroad

The cross-border transfer of personal data is regulated by the privacy laws of the receiving country. Since the privacy laws are largely harmonised in the EU through the European directives, transfers within the community are generally not problematic.

The export of data to non-EU and non-EEA countries is expressly referred to in the Federal Data Protection Act. Section 4c BDSG restricts the export of data to third countries with "adequate" privacy regulations unless certain conditions are met, namely:

(a) the data subject has given his consent;
(b) the transfer is necessary for the performance of a contract between the data subject and the controller or the implementation of precontractual measures taken in response to the data subject's request;
(c) the transfer is necessary for the conclusion or performance of a contract which has been or is to be entered into in the interest of the data subject between the controller and a third party;
(d) the transfer is necessary on important public interest grounds, or for the establishment, exercise or defence of legal claims;
(e) the transfer is necessary in order to protect the vital interests of the data subject;
(f) the transfer is made from a register which is intended to provide information to the public and which is open to consultation either by the public in general or by any person who can demonstrate a legitimate interest, to the extent that the statutory conditions are fulfilled in the particular case.

41.5.3 Duties of the parties

The data protection obligations of the parties of an outsourcing contract are as follows.

41.5.3.1 Duties of the principal

The principal has the following duties under the Federal Data Protection Act:

(a) it must comply with the Federal Data Protection Act and other privacy legislation with regard to the collection, processing and use of personal data;
(b) it must choose a suitable supplier (Section 11, paragraph 2, sentence 1, BDSG);
(c) it must give instructions to the supplier for collecting, processing or use of data and these instructions must be precise and transparent;
(d) it must ensure that employees preserve the secrecy of data (Section 5 BDSG);
(e) it must comply with privacy controls (Section 11, subsection 1, sentence 1, BDSG, appendix to Section 9 No. 6 BDSG);
(f) it must monitor the supplier's compliance with the agreed technical and organisational measures (Section 11, paragraph 2, sentence 4, BDSG).

41.5.3.2 Responsibilities of the supplier

The supplier has the following duties under the Federal Data Protection Act:

(a) it must collect, process or use data in accordance with the customer's instructions (Section 11, subsection 3, sentence 1, BDSG);
(b) it must ensure data secrecy (Section 11, paragraph 3, sentence 2, BDSG);
(c) if it thinks that an instruction of the principal infringes the Federal Data Protection Act or other data protection provisions, it must point this out to the customer without delay (Section 11, subsection 3, sentence 2, BDSG); and
(d) it must back up data (Section 11, paragraph 4 and Section 9 BDSG).

41.6 Insolvency issues

41.6.1 Insolvency law

German insolvency law is found predominantly in the Insolvency Act (Insolvenzordnung, "InsO"). Insolvency policy is aimed at satisfying creditors either through the distribution and sale of the debtor's assets or by the preservation of the company which is in danger of insolvency.

Once the bankruptcy proceedings have been opened, the Insolvenzverwalter (administrator) has administrative authority and power to dispose of the debtor's assets. During this period, any disposals of assets made by the debtor will have no effect pursuant to Section 81, subsection 1, sentence 1, InsO.

41.6.2 Effect of insolvency proceedings on the outsourcing contract

Where a supplier is the subject of bankruptcy proceedings, under Section 103 InsO, the administrator can opt to terminate the outsourcing contract or to leave it in force if none of the parties have fulfilled the contract.

The result is different where the customer is bankrupt. Typically, an outsourcing contract is a business management contract. Accordingly, the customer's bankruptcy will be subject to Sections 115, 116 InsO. Under these provisions, the opening of bankruptcy procedures on the principal's (here, the customer's) assets will cause the termination of the outsourcing contract and extinction of outstanding obligations for services and remuneration. Where Sections 115, 116 InsO are applicable, the administrator's voting right will be excluded pursuant to Section 103, para. 1, InsO.

41.6.3 Bankruptcy avoidance

In accordance with the principles in Section 129, subsection 1, InsO, transactions executed by the debtor before the commencement of bankruptcy proceedings, and which adversely affect the creditors, may be challenged. Property which has been alienated, disposed of or abandoned through a successfully challenged transaction must be restored to the bankrupt's estate pursuant to Section 143 InsO.

The decision whether the conclusion and execution of an outsourcing contract adversely affects a creditor within the meaning of Section 129 BGB depends on the terms of the individual outsourcing arrangement. Parties must take particular care when negotiating contracts which outsource parts of a business and transfer assets to prevent these being construed as bankruptcy avoidance transactions under Section 129 BGB.

In addition to Section 129 InsO, Sections 130 InsO et seq. contain specific prerequisites for the avoidance of bankruptcy. Without going into detail, the requirements for an avoidance of bankruptcy transaction are usually (except under Section 133 InsO) not fulfilled when the bankrupt receives instantaneous, equivalent counter-performance. The adequacy of the exchanged performance, the asset, the purchase price and the time frame are all-important.

The aforementioned provisions apply to transactions which the bankrupt has executed within 10 years of the application for insolvency, or subsequent to such application if they were made with the intent to disadvantage its creditors.

41.7 Financial services regulation

41.7.1 Financial services law

The German outsourcing regime allows credit institutions and financial services institutions to optimise business functions and processes by outsourcing operational areas to external suppliers.

In the financial services sector, outsourcing is defined as the assignment of an external company to carry out activities or processes related to the execution of banking transactions, financial services or other typical services which would otherwise be performed by the institution internally.

The relevant legal requirements for outsourcing arrangements can be found in Section 25a subsection 2 of the Banking Act (Kreditwesengesetz, "KWG"), which was adapted in conjunction with the implementation of the Markets in Financial Instruments Directive (MiFID) by the Finanzmarktrichtlinie-Umsetzungsgesetz ("FRUG"). In addition to this regulation, there are various principles contained in the Minimum Requirements for Risk Management (MaRisk) released by the Federal Financial Supervisory Office (BaFin) which must be observed.

41.7.2 Compliance and risk management

Section 25a (2) KWG states that a financial institution must take measures to avoid excessive risk when outsourcing activities and processes for the execution of banking transactions, financial services or other typical services. The appropriateness of these measures depends on the type, the extent and the concentration risk of the outsourcing.

The outsourcing must not impair the proper organisation of the institution's business. There should be an effective risk management procedure in place which details the outsourced activities and processes.

The institution retains responsibility for the outsourced activities and processes, and is fully responsible to the BaFin. As such, it must ensure that the BaFin, the internal and external auditors can access and examine the outsourced activities and processes. BaFin's rights to information and inspection must be guaranteed in the outsourcing agreement even if the supplier is based in a Member State of the European Economic Area or a third country. The outsourcing agreement must also contain a provision which stipulates the rights of the institution, for example to give directives and to terminate the agreement, and the corresponding obligations of the supplier on termination.

Since the implementation of MiFID in Germany, it is no longer necessary to notify the BaFin of planned outsourcing agreements. The BaFin only has a right to information according to Section 25a (2), sentence 6, KWG.

41.7.3 Minimum requirements for risk management

The regulatory requirements with respect to outsourcing set forth in Section 25a, para. 2, KWG are also implemented in Section AT 9 of the MaRisk (Minimum Requirements for Risk Management). This is discussed in 41.7.3.1 below.

41.7.3.1 Outsourcing within the scope of Section AT 9 of the MaRisk

Section AT 9 Nr. 1 describes outsourcing as the appointment of a supplier to carry out activities or processes related to the execution of banking transactions, financial services or other services that would otherwise typically be performed by an institution internally.

The reference to other services typical of the institution takes account of Article 13(5), sentence 1, MiFID. Examples of these services are found in Annex I, Section B, MiFID.

External procurement of services which do not fall under the MaRisk definition of outsourcing are, for example, one-off or occasional procurement of goods and services (e.g. consulting services), and procured services which the institution cannot normally perform either de facto or due to legal requirements (e.g. the use of clearing houses when settling payments and securities).

41.7.3.2 Material outsourcing ("wesentliche Auslagerung")

If outsourcing is within the scope of Section AT 9 of the MaRisk, it must be determined whether it is a material or non-material outsourcing taking into account all relevant aspects, including the type, scope, complexity of and the risk involved in the activities and processes to be outsourced.

Only material outsourcings have to comply with Section 25a, para. 2, KWG (*see* below). Outsourcings which are non-material must comply with the general requirements on proper organisation pursuant to Section 25a, para. 1, KWG (*see* Section AT 9 Nr. 3 of the MaRisk).

With an intra-group outsourcing, the implementation of a risk management system at group level and the right to take direct action can be taken into account in determining whether the outsourcing agreement is material or non-material.

41.7.3.3 Outsourcing restrictions

Within the post-MiFID outsourcing regime, any activities and processes can be outsourced as long as this does not impair proper business organisation pursuant to Section 25a, para. 1, KWG (Section AT 9 Nr. 4 MaRisk). However, outsourcing must not lead to a delegation of responsibility. This means that management duties (Leitungsaufgaben) such as corporate planning, coordination, controlling and managerial appointments may not be outsourced. The same applies to statutory duties of management (e.g. decisions regarding large exposures and credit risk pursuant to Sections 13 to 13b KWG).

However, there is an exception to the rule where the management uses functions and organisational units (Organisationseinheiten) to exercise its duties. An example is in the area of loan servicing, where the supplier must sometimes make decisions. Under the German regime, the risk and responsibility for decisions on the approval, modification or waiver of the loan agreement or the interpretation of the intention of the loan agreement must always remain with the bank.

41.7.3.4 Outsourcing contract terms

The MaRisk states that the following terms must be included in material outsourcing agreements (*see* Section AT 9 Nr. 6 MaRisk):

(a) a service description setting out the services to be performed by the supplier;
(b) the customer's right to obtain certain information and carry out internal and external audit rights of the supplier's performance;
(c) BaFins's right to obtain information and examine and control the supplier;
(d) the right of the customer to give instructions to the supplier, if necessary;
(e) the obligation of the supplier to comply with data protection provisions;
(f) the notice which is required to terminate the agreement and any termination assistance to be provided;
(g) provisions setting out when the supplier can subcontract its obligations and that any subcontractors must be subject to banking supervisory requirements;
(h) the obligation of the supplier to inform the customer of any developments that may impair the proper performance of the outsourced activities and processes.

41.7.3.5 Outsourcing of the internal audit

The internal audit function can be outsourced fully (*see* Section AT 9 Nr. 8 MaRisk). In this case, the management board must appoint an audit officer to ensure that the audit is functioning properly. The function of the audit officer cannot be outsourced.

The duties of the audit officer may be carried out by an organisational unit, an employee or a management board member, depending on the type, scope, complexity and risk content of the business activities of the institution.

41.7.3.6 Other requirements

As the customer continues to be responsible for the outsourced activities, it is vital that it retains a degree of control over the supplier. In addition to the requirements listed above, the customer must manage the risks associated with the outsourcing effectively. It must ensure that the supplier has the professional qualifications, capacity, licences etc. stipulated by law to execute the outsourced duties, services or activities properly. It must then monitor the performance of the supplier (*see* Section AT 9 Nr. 7 MaRisk).

If the customer intends to terminate an outsourcing contract, it shall take measures to ensure continuity of its services after termination of the contract (*see* Section AT 9 Nr. 5 MaRisk).

The above requirements must also be complied with when outsourced activities and processes are sub-outsourced by the supplier (*see* Section AT 9 Nr. 9 MaRisk).

41.8 Public procurement and utilities

Public procurement law deals with the purchase of goods and services by public authorities. It can be divided into two parts: the law implementing the European Directives, to which thresholds apply, and the law which applies below the thresholds.

41.8.1 Applicable law above thresholds

The European directives as implemented in German law are only applicable to public procurement agreements above a certain threshold. Different thresholds apply for different types of contract, for example those for supply and service contracts differ from those for construction contracts. In some circumstances, the identity of the supplier is relevant in determining the threshold.

The general regulations, including the regulations governing judicial remedies, can be found in the fourth part of the German Act Against Restraints on Competition (Gesetz gegen Wettbewerbsbeschränkungen, "GWB") and the Regulations for Awarding Contracts (Verordnung über die Vergabe öffentlicher Aufträge – Vergabeverordnung, "VgV"). Building contracts are governed by the Vergabe- und Vertragsordnung für Bauleistungen ("VOB"), service and supply contracts by the Verdingungsordnung für Leistungen ("VOL") and consultancy contracts (provided for instance by financial or legal advisers) by the Verdingungsordnung für freiberufliche Leistungen ("VOF").

In accordance with European Law, German public procurement law provides for different award procedures (open procedure, restricted procedure, negotiated procedure and competitive dialogue) with varying formal requirements.

German public procurement law also provides for a 14-day standstill period as contracts, once awarded, cannot be set aside or terminated due to infringements of the public procurement legislation. The standstill period begins at the point the unsuccessful tenderers receive notice of the successful bid and the reasons ("prior information duty"). An unsuccessful tenderer may initiate an award review procedure if it believes that the intended contract would be in breach of the public procurement rules.

41.8.2 Applicable law below thresholds

Procurement agreements which fall below the European thresholds are not subject to the fourth part of the GWB and the VgV. Below the thresholds, the contracting regulations for building contracts ("VOB"), service and supply contracts ("VOL") and consultancy contracts ("VOF") apply to the extent that the public contract authority is bound by the budgetary law. Bidders have less legal protection than bidders above the thresholds although the procurement procedures are almost identical.

41.8.3 Modernisation of public procurement law

On 21 May 2008, the federal government introduced a bill to modernise public procurement law. The bill aims to simplify and add greater transparency to the award of public contracts and to help midsize companies to win contracts with public sector bodies. The bill also strengthens the judicial review procedure and provides for penalties where contracts are awarded in breach of public procurement law.

The bill implements the European Public Procurement and Utilities Directives 2004/17/EC and 2004/18/EC and the Legal Remedies Directive 2007/66/EC into German public procurement law. Since 2006, these have only been partially implemented via amendments to the VgV, VOB, VOL and VOF. At the time of writing, the bill was being discussed in parliament and it was not clear whether it would become law. Whether or not the bill is passed, the European public procurement and utilities directives 2004/17/EC and 2004/18/EC will continue to have direct application to public procurement projects which meet or exceed the thresholds.

Note: there are model IT terms and conditions published in Germany with regard to IT procurement called EVBIT. These are new in the market and do not explicitly cover outsourcing agreements, although they may be relevant in part. The provisions have been criticised by IT suppliers as they provide a comparably strong position for the customer in the public sector.

PFI/PPP projects exist in Germany but are not as prevalent as in the UK. There are guidelines for public authorities with respect to PFI/PPP projects.

It is worth noting that, in January 2009, Germany started to implement a €50 billion federal investment to counter the effects of the global economical slowdown on German industries and businesses. The government plans to suspend parts of the public procurement provisions to accelerate the implementation of projects under this plan.

41.9 VAT issues

From a tax perspective, PPPs in Germany may be at a disadvantage compared with those in other EU Member States. This is because Germany does not have a general Value Added Tax privilege or a similar refund system for VAT on services obtained from suppliers. As such, the customer in a PPP is generally charged German VAT of 19 per cent unless the activity can be attributed to a business establishment ("Betrieb gewerblicher Art") of the state (Section 15, para.1 and Section 2, para. 3, VAT Act).

The activity will only be attributed to a business establishment of the state to the extent that the state's activity can actually be considered an economic activity clearly distinguishable from the state's sovereign functions (Section 4 Corporate Income Tax Act). Otherwise the state will not be entitled to input VAT ("Vorsteuerabzug").

The German government has been slowly amending these tax restrictions. Since 2005, the transfer of real estate within a PPP has been exempt from German Real Estate Transfer Tax, Section 4, No. 9 German Real Estate Transfer Tax Act. At the time of writing, the subject of how the additional VAT burdens might be removed (e.g. by establishing a VAT refund system) was being discussed. However, it remains to be seen whether any action will be taken.

41.10 Competition law

41.10.1 Merger control

Outsourcing deals which involve companies with high turnover may be subject to merger control regulations. In Germany, the Federal Cartel Office is responsible for merger control pursuant to Section 35 et seq. GWB.

If the companies had total global revenues of more than €500 million in the last fiscal year, and at least one of the companies had revenues of more than €25 million in Germany, it may be necessary to notify the Federal Cartel Office prior to concluding the agreement.

The German merger control regulations ("GWB") apply to:

(a) acquisitions by one company of the assets of another in whole or in substantial part;
(b) acquisition of direct or indirect control by one or more companies over the whole or parts of one or more other companies;
(c) acquisitions by one company of shares in another company, if the shares alone or together with other shares the company already owns reach 25 per cent of the shares in capital or voting rights of the other company or reach 50 per cent of the capital or the voting rights of the other company or any other connection of companies that allows one or more companies to be able to exert significant influence over another company according to competition law.

In cases of "community-wide importance", the EU Commission and not the German Federal Cartel Office is responsible. "Community-wide importance" is implied when the parties have a worldwide turnover of more than €5 billion and at least two of the contracting companies have a community-wide turnover of more than €250 million.

The EU Commission set out its position in 2007 with the adoption of the Consolidated Jurisdictional Notice on the Control of Concentrations Between Undertakings on the notification requirement. The EU Commission has determined that notification will be required if assets such as hardware and software, personnel and/or contractual relationships are transferred to the supplier, in circumstances where a business unit with its own market presence is simultaneously transferred to the supplier.

41.10.2 Exclusivity agreements

In order to prevent the transfer of know-how and business secrets of the customer to competing companies within outsourcing projects, parties often conclude exclusivity agreements which bind the supplier to work exclusively for the customer and not for its competitors.

Pursuant to Section 16 GWB, the German Federal Cartel Office may declare commercial services agreements invalid if they prevent the supplier from providing services to third parties.

The validity of exclusivity commitments must also be reviewed under competition and antitrust law (Article 81 EC).

41.11 Other relevant laws

In addition to the statutory provisions, there are numerous schemes which can or must be used for German outsourcing projects. These include, for example:

(a) Circular 18/2005, which covers the minimum requirements for risk management (MiFID);
(b) The Corporate Governance Codex, which covers Germany's corporate governance rules and leads to transparency for both national and international investors;

(c) Corporate Sector Supervision and Transparency Act, which increases the responsibilities of the board, supervisory board and auditors in the company for outsourced services. It also requires company management to introduce a corporate-wide risk management programme;

(d) Act on Limited Liability Companies ("GmbHG") as well as German Stock Corporation Act ("AktG"), which state in Section 43 GmbHG and/or Section 93 AktG that the duty of the managing director in limited liability companies and/or the managing board in stock corporations require the diligence of a prudent businessman in all affairs of the company.

41.12 Summary

It is foreseeable that changes in corporate management, the globalisation of businesses and the constantly changing technological environment will be decisive factors in the development of the outsourcing market in Germany. The shift of world economic emphasis to Asia, the international interdependence of producers, customers and suppliers will necessarily result in an adjustment to the new world economic conditions.

The current financial crisis is likely to increase the popularity of IT outsourcing. The outsourcing industry will need to adapt to the new situation and the new requirements. The industry expects particular growth in 2009 and 2010.

German law provides a solid if complex basis for outsourcing transactions. Foreign professional advisers in this field frequently consider the legal environment (in particular German labour law) inconvenient for outsourcing transactions particularly for the supplier. Yet, considering the practical experiences gained from small to multi-billion euro projects in Germany, from the customer or the supplier perspective there are no particular legal impediments that make outsourcing less advantageous than in the UK. In fact, all concerns, whether technical or commercial, can be covered under German law.

Chapter 42

Spain

José Ramón Morales
Partner
Garrigues

42.1 Background to outsourcing in Spain

42.1.1 Introduction

According to recent published research, the Spanish outsourcing market (measured in terms of the revenues of the suppliers operating in this market) accounted for a figure somewhere in the region of between €3,000 and €4,000 million in 2007. Outsourcing has seen significant growth in recent years, and the published forecasts indicate ongoing growth.

The most important recent research providing figures and statistics on the Spanish outsourcing market include:

(a) "La Consultoría en España 2007" (Consultancy in Spain 2007), a report published by Asociación Española de Consultoría – AEC, the Spanish Association of Consultancy Firms.[1]

(b) "Informe Especial Outsourcing Informático – Abril 2008" (Report on IT Outsourcing, April 2008) (7th edition), published by DBK, S.A.

(c) "Outsourcing en España y Europa el sector público y privado" (Public and private sector outsourcing in Spain and Europe), published by Steria, June 2005.[2]

42.1.2 Outsourcing suppliers in Spain

The suppliers of outsourcing services operating in Spain include many global players with local presence (such as Accenture, Atos Origin, Capgemini, EDS, Fujitsu, Hewlett Packard, IBM, Siemens, T-Systems), as well as a good number of major industry players having their head office in Spain (including Indra, Everis, Gesfor, Ibermática, Informática El Corte Inglés, IT Deusto, Satec, Tecnocom, Telefónica).

---

1 This document can be accessed in Spanish at http://consultoras.c2csoluciones.com/frontend/aec/La-AEC-Presenta-El-Informe-%93La-Consultoria-En-Espana-En-2007%94-vn8009-vst85.

2 This document can be accessed in Spanish at: www.socinfo.info/contenidos/pdf16/p46-50steria.pdf.

42.1.3 Outsourcing customers in Spain

Although the phenomenon of outsourcing has existed in the Spanish market for over a decade, at the outset the pivotal customers were major companies from particular industries (financial, telecom or utilities companies), and the practice of outsourcing was considerably less widespread in other industries and fields.

42.1.4 Factors which discourage outsourcing

The factors that may traditionally have served to discourage the use of outsourcing can be summed up as follows:

(a) a certain delay in the adoption and implementation on a large scale of IT systems in some industries, which may have caused the Spanish outsourcing market to mature at a slower rate;

(b) the reluctance of the trade unions to accept outsourcing processes for certain operations within companies, and the existence of an employment law framework that requires certain precautionary measures and restrictions to be in place to protect workers, which may make the outsourcing process less flexible.

42.1.5 Factors which encourage outsourcing

The growth of the Spanish economy in recent years, the strengthening of Spain-based multinationals which have gained an increasingly firm foothold abroad (and find themselves obliged to integrate standardised information systems and complex organisations), and the example set by significant outsourcing deals in certain industries (banking and insurance, telecoms, utilities etc.) have helped to speed up the development of the outsourcing market, which has experienced considerable growth on a sustained basis.

42.1.6 The attitude of the Spanish government to outsourcing

Until recently, the Spanish government had not adopted a clear stance (favourable or otherwise) with respect to outsourcing. However, it did display a certain concern about the subcontracting of services by outsourcing suppliers, particularly in situations which presented the following risks:

(a) the risk that the subcontracting arrangements may adversely affect workers' rights (due to the fragmentation of the workforce, the unlawful supply of workers and the failure of the supplier to comply with occupational risk prevention legislation); or

(b) the risk that chains of subcontracts may have an adverse impact on safety checks in the performance of certain tasks regarding the maintenance or security of hazardous industrial facilities.

42.1.7 Promotion of Spain as a near-shore destination

The Spanish government has launched an initiative in order to promote Spain's outsourcing model. This initiative ("Valueshore") aims to promote Spain as a home for technology outsourcing for

European companies (near-shoring), which can benefit from their geographical and cultural proximity when supplied by Spanish companies in the sector and capitalise on the advantages yielded by industry specialisation and skilled human resources. Valueshore was presented on October 2008 jointly by the Spanish Association of Consultancy Firms ("AEC") and "Invest in Spain", the Government Agency for the Promotion and Attraction of Foreign Investment.

Valueshore has the dual aim of attracting foreign investment to Spain in order to develop the country's supply of technology outsourcing services, while also furthering reinvestment in, and the strengthening of, foreign companies with technology development units in Spain, thereby enhancing such companies.

42.1.8 Influences upon outsourcing practices in Spain

The presence of a multitude of international outsourcing service suppliers in the Spanish market, some of which hail from Anglo-Saxon countries, combined with the increasing international business of Spain-based customers, has meant that outsourcing practices in Spain have been influenced in certain key areas by outsourcing trends in the UK and the US.

In particular, a marked influence can be seen in the way that outsourcing deals are approached in areas such as pricing structures or tools for measuring performance (service-level methodology), and even in terms of the standard agreements and clauses used. Recent years have also seen an increasing influence from Anglo-Saxon countries with the adoption of best practice as regards supplier selection and evaluation procedures, the use of benchmarking and remedies which will apply in situations in which suppliers fail to meet their obligations.

Nevertheless, it is increasingly the case that it is the Spanish customer (particularly in the case of major companies or groups) that provides the initial draft of the agreement, to which the potential suppliers competing in the selection process then propose amendments, which then form part of the items to be considered in the selection process itself. In any event, all agreements with Spanish customers must be brought into line with Spanish legislation in a range of areas, for example, with regard to contractual liability, to observe the civil law provisions in force in Spain, as well as the specific employment law and privacy/data protection rules and regulations, to name but a few (as described later in this chapter).

42.1.9 Growth in outsourcing

The 1990s saw the first noteworthy outsourcing deals in Spain, the most significant of which came about with the outsourcing of IT services, above all in the field of financial services, before spreading to other industries (telecoms, the public sector, utilities and an array of other industries).

Practically all of the reports analysing the outsourcing market in Spain point to a trend towards growth in recent years, and forecast continued growth in the years to come. The 2007 report of the Spanish Association of Consultancy Firms ("2007 AEC Report") states that the consultancy industry experienced average growth of 11.4 per cent in the period from 2004 through 2007, particularly in 2007, when revenues increased by 13.7 per cent, to reach a total turnover of €8,561 million. It also reveals that the industry has gained a more prominent position in the Spanish economy, with the increase in revenues of companies in the consultancy industry (11.4

per cent) outperforming the growth in national GDP during the same period (7.7 per cent). Of these figures, the portion relating to outsourcing services amounted to 36 per cent of the revenues of Spanish consultancy firms (accounting for some €3,081 million), compared to 44 per cent from development and integration services and 20 per cent from consultancy services. The average annual growth rate in outsourcing revenues was 17 per cent between 2004 and 2007, and its contribution to the growth in the industry accounted for 49 per cent.

Elsewhere, the data published by DBK shows that the free market in IT outsourcing services has confirmed its position as the fastest-growing area of consultancy and IT services firms, posting a 14.4 per cent rise in 2006 and a 16.3 per cent increase in 2007, to reach revenues of €3,800 million (free market).

The research carried out into the Spanish market forecasts ongoing growth in 2008 (ranging from 11 per cent to 14 per cent, depending on the source), although it remains to be seen whether the actual figures will reflect any impact from the major change in the economic environment that has taken place over recent months.

42.1.10 Types of outsourcing

The various studies carried out arrive at the same conclusion, namely that the largest share of the Spanish outsourcing market is taken by infrastructure management services (47 per cent of the market in 2007, according to DBK data, and 43 per cent of outsourcing revenues at consultancy firms according to the 2007 AEC Report); followed by a marked increase in applications management services (41 per cent in 2007); with business process outsourcing in third place (12 per cent of the market in 2007 according to DBK, accounting for 16 per cent of outsourcing revenues at consultancy firms according to the 2007 AEC Report).

The leading and fastest-growing business sectors in the Spanish market in contracts for consultancy services in general, and outsourcing services in particular, are:

(a) the financial services industry (accounting for 27 per cent of the revenues from consultancy services and 30 per cent of the revenues from outsourcing services in 2007);
(b) the public sector (17 per cent of the revenues from consultancy services and 14.6 per cent of the revenues from outsourcing services in 2007);
(c) the industry and energy sector (22.4 per cent of the revenues from outsourcing services in 2007); and
(d) the telecommunications industry (16.4 per cent of the revenues from outsourcing services in 2007).

42.1.11 Offshore destinations

One of the most notable and specific features of the Spanish market has to do with the geographic location of the outsourcing services hired by Spanish companies. In particular, for linguistic reasons, offshore outsourcing contracts to companies located in Latin American countries tend to predominate (call centres, as well as software development in countries such as Argentina) as well as to those located in areas such as North Africa (business process outsourcing ("BPO"), particularly call centre services).

However, the restrictions laid down by Spanish legislation (in line with EU directives) on personal data processing outside the EU or those countries deemed by the EU to have an appropriate level of protection (*see* 42.5 below) pose an obstacle to offshore outsourcing in the field of IT and business process outsourcing to the countries more commonly used in the international markets (India, for example).

42.2 People issues - ARD

42.2.1 The employment law framework governing outsourcing in Spain

In Spanish law, there are no specific regulations defining the concept of outsourcing from the standpoint of employment law. In addition, there are no specific regulations (as there are in other jurisdictions such as the UK) governing a "service provision change". Although certain industries (e.g. cleaning, hospitality and telemarketing) have clauses in their collective employment agreement specifically dealing with changes in service provision and stating the employment law effects resulting from such changes.

Outsourcing will therefore be covered by the general regulations on business succession, in article 44 of the Workers' Statute. This provision derives from Council Directive 2001/23/EC, of 12 March 2001, on the approximation of the laws of the Member States relating to the safeguarding of employees' rights in the event of transfers of undertakings, businesses or parts of undertakings or businesses (ARD). Article 44 is described in more detail in this section below.

Once a succession or transfer has taken place on the terms set forth in article 44 of the Workers' Statute, the customer and supplier will enter into a contract for services subject to the rules in article 42 of the Workers' Statute, which are described in 42.3 below.

42.2.2 Business successions in the context of subcontracts or outsourcing

42.2.2.1 Definition of a business succession

According to article 44, a business succession will be considered to occur where the transfer affects an economic unit that retains its identity, as a set of resources organised so as to pursue an essential or ancillary economic activity. It will be necessary to analyse the structure of each outsourcing deal individually to assess whether it will be classified as a "business succession" on the terms of article 44 of the Workers' Statute given that, if it is, the application of this regime is compulsory.

42.2.2.2 Requirement for a business succession

The Spanish Supreme Court (Supreme Court Judgment of 27 October 1986, among others) has held that two essential requirements must be met for a business succession to exist:

(a) *owner requirement*, consisting of a change of ownership: a direct transfer or a chain of title comprising any type of transfer; and
(b) *subject-matter requirement*, consisting of the actual delivery of all of the essential elements enabling the business to continue. In other words, the assets transferred must

form a production unit that can be operated on an independent basis and is capable of supplying goods and services to the market.

Nevertheless, in light of the case law precedents handed down by the European Court of Justice,[3] this second requirement has generally been restrictively interpreted to mean that:

> "where the business activity essentially lies in the hands of the workforce, the identity may be retained following the transfer where the new employer does not restrict itself to continuing the activity in question, but rather also takes on an essential part, in terms of number and skills, of the personnel specifically assigned by its predecessor to that task".

With this in mind, the Spanish Supreme Court announced (with certain reservations) in judgments on 20 and 27 October 2004, that:

> "succession applies not only where there is a transfer of assets, but also in any other circumstances in which the transferee of an activity takes on, in significant qualitative and numerical terms, part of the personnel of the transferor".

This has come to be referred to as "workforce succession".

42.2.2.3 Employment law consequences of business succession

Principle of continuity

The consequences of the occurrence of a business succession under article 44 of the Workers' Statute are as follows:

(a) the employment contracts of the employees assigned to the performance of the relevant tasks will be transferred to the supplier;
(b) the employees at the customer company will become part of the workforce of the supplier of the service, without the need for employees' consent;
(c) the employees at the customer company will be able to claim in court for their status as workers at the supplier company.

Thus, the legislation on business succession imposes the principle of continuity of the employment relationships with the new supplier of the service.

Liability for employment obligations

Social security legislation notwithstanding, the customer and the new supplier will be jointly and severally liable for three years following the transfer in respect of any employment obligations that arose before the transfer and which have not been satisfied.

The customer and the supplier will also be jointly and severally liable in respect of any obligations that arise after the transfer, where the transfer is held to be in breach of the law or illegal (i.e. with the purpose of depriving employees of their rights).

3 *See* Süzen, dated 11 March 1997; Hernández Vidal, dated 10 December 1998; Sánchez Hidalgo, dated 2 December 1999; Allen, dated 14 September 2000; Collino, dated 26 September 2000; Mayeur, dated 25 January2001; Liikenn, dated 15 January 2002; Temco, dated 24 January 2002; and Sodexho, dated 20 November 2003.

Pensions

The comments made above also apply in relation to pensions: pursuant to article 44 of the Workers' Statute, where the outsourcing process entails the transfer of employees as part of the transfer of an undertaking, of a workplace or of an independent production unit, the employment relationship is not extinguished, and the rights and obligations of the former business owner are transferred to the new business owner, including the pension obligations and, generally speaking, any and all supplementary welfare obligations that the former employer may have acquired.

Collective agreements

Unless agreed otherwise, after the succession, the employment relationships of the workers affected by the succession will continue to be governed by the collective employment agreement which, at the time of the transfer, was in force at the company, workplace or independent production unit transferred. This agreement will remain in force until the expiration date of the original collective employment agreement or until the entry into force of another new collective employment agreement that is applicable to the transferred business unit.

Workers' legal representatives

Where the transferred business, workplace or production unit preserves its independence, the change of business owner will not per se extinguish the mandate of the workers' legal representatives, who will continue to perform their functions on the same terms and subject to the same conditions as those previously in force.

Notification

The customer and the supplier must inform the legal representatives of the workers affected by the change of ownership of the following particulars:

(a) scheduled date for the transfer;
(b) grounds for the transfer;
(c) legal, economic and welfare consequences for the workers of the transfer; and
(d) planned measures with respect to the workers.

If the workers have no legal representatives, the customer and the supplier must supply the information mentioned above to the workers who may be affected by the transfer.

The customer will be required to provide the information mentioned above with sufficient notice before the transfer is performed. The supplier will be required to notify the workers of these details with sufficient notice and, in all cases, before the workers have their employment and working conditions affected by the transfer.

Consultation

Any customer or supplier who intends to adopt, by reason of the transfer, employment measures in relation to their workers, will be required to commence a consultation period with the workers' legal representatives on the planned measures and their consequences for the workers. This consultation period will have to be held with sufficient notice, before the measures are brought into effect. In the consultation period, the parties must negotiate in good faith, to secure an agreement. Where the planned measures consist of collective transfers or substantial modifications of working conditions on a collective basis, the procedure for the consultation period must conform to the provisions in the Workers' Statute for making such modifications to contracts.

The information and consultation obligations provided for in this chapter will be applied regardless of whether the decision relating to the transfer has been adopted by the customer or supplier business owners or by companies exerting control over them. Any justification by them based on the fact that the company that took the decision did not provide them with the necessary information is irrelevant.

42.3 People issues – other employment issues – outsourcing arrangements and subcontracts for services under article 42 of the Workers' Statute

If the new supplier is not to take on the employees of the customer company (or the supplier is to take on part of those employees and therefore they must be considered on an individual basis), the applicable legislation is article 42 of the Workers' Statute governing subcontracts for projects and services, as amended by Law 43/2006 of 29 December 2006.

The use by a company of contracts with external parties to decentralise the production process is considered to be a lawful procedure based on the constitutional principle of freedom of enterprise. However, a series of protection mechanisms has been established to avoid the fraudulent use of outsourcing to disguise an unlawful supply of workers, which is prohibited in article 43 of the Workers' Statute.

42.3.1 Definition of unlawful supply of workers

According to article 43 of the Workers' Statute, an unlawful supply of workers occurs where either:

(a) the subject matter of the services agreements between the companies is confined to the supply of the workers of the supplier company to the recipient company; or

(b) the supplier company has no activity or does not have its own stable organisation, does not have the resources needed to perform its activity, or does not carry out the functions inherent to a business owner.

42.3.2 Implications of unlawful supply

The consequences of a breach of the above provisions are that the supplier and recipient will be liable jointly and severally for the salary and social security obligations relating to the workers. The workers supplied unlawfully will have the right to become part of the permanent staff, at either the supplier or recipient, at their choice; their rights and obligations will be the same as those of a worker of an equivalent category or position; and they will have the length of service they had when the unlawful supply commenced.

42.3.3 Exception – temporary employment agencies

The only exception to the above prohibition relates to temporary employment agencies which, through supply contracts, create a triangular relationship between the temporary employment agency, the worker and the user company.

42.3.4 Application to outsourcing

There is no general treatment in employment law of outsourcing arrangements or subcontracts. Therefore, the characteristics of each individual case must be examined. Thus, a contract for services will be lawful where the supplier meets the following requirements:

(a) it carries out its own business activity and has stable assets, instruments and machinery and a stable organisation assigned to that activity;
(b) it is allocated actual contractual obligations, it manages the performance of the contract for services and assumes the risk of non-performance of the services;
(c) it retains the right to control its workers and preserves with respect to them the rights, obligations, risks and liabilities inherent to its status as employer.

42.3.5 Recommendations to avoid an unlawful supply of workers

The following are recommendations to avoid the consequences of having a contract for services between customer and supplier classed as an unlawful supply of workers:

(a) ensure that the powers of control and discipline of the supplier's staff are exerted directly by the supplier and not by the customer;
(b) ensure that the supplier's employees receive their instructions from the supplier's manager and that the supplier organises what work is to be carried out by which employee;
(c) avoid any type of participation by the customer's personnel in the selection of the personnel of the supplier;
(d) ensure that the working hours and shifts of the employees of the customer and supplier are different;[4]
(e) avoid charging for work performed by the hour, or by the person, but rather by the project or service;
(f) ensure that the supplier provides its own tools, work equipment and maintenance items for that equipment, and (where necessary) has, at the customer's facilities, areas used exclusively by its workers;
(g) ensure that the employment regime for the supplier's workers is its own regime based on its applicable collective employment agreement.

4 Note that, as stated in 42.2 above, in this case transfer legislation would not apply. Thus, outsourcing will fall under the scope of article 42 of the Workers' Statute governing subcontracts for projects and services where the continuity of employment relationships (and related rights) does not apply.

42.3.6 Implications of a contract for services

The employment law effects of a contract for services that involves an outsourcing process are provided for in article 42 of the Workers' Statute, which states as follows.

42.3.6.1 Salary and social security obligations

Any business owners who enter into contracts or subcontracts with others to perform services relating to their own business activity must ascertain that the suppliers of those services are up to date with payment of their social security contributions. To do this, they must obtain in writing, specifying the name of the company concerned, a certificate verifying that the supplier pays the corresponding social security contributions. Social security authorities must issue the certificate within a non-extendable period of 30 days following the request and on the terms determined in the legislation. At the end of this period, the applicant company will be released from any liability vis-à-vis social security contributions.

Unless the 30-day period mentioned above has expired, for a year following the end of the services contract, the customer will be jointly and severally liable for the salaries of the supplier's (and subcontractors') workers and for their social security contributions.

42.3.6.2 Notification

The workers of the supplier and subcontractors must be informed in writing by the business owner of the name of the principal for which they will be performing work at any given time. This information must be supplied before the respective services start to be provided and must include the name or business name of the customer business owner, its registered office and taxpayer identification number. The supplier or subcontractors must also notify the Spanish social security authorities of the name of the customer company on the terms determined in the legislation.

In addition to the information to be provided to the workers' representatives under the provisions on subcontracts in the Workers' Statute, where the company enters into an agreement for a project or service with a supplier or subcontractor company, it must inform the legal representatives of its workers of the following:

(a) the name or business name, address and taxpayer identification number of the supplier or subcontractor company;
(b) the subject matter and term of the services or outsourcing agreement;
(c) the place of performance of the agreement;
(d) if applicable, the number of workers that will be put to work by the supplier or subcontractor at the customer's workplace; and
(e) the measures envisaged for the coordination of functions from the standpoint of the prevention of occupational risks.

Where the customer, supplier or subcontractor share the same workplace on an ongoing basis, the customer must have a book in which it records the above information in relation to all of those companies. That book must be available to the workers' legal representatives.

The supplier or subcontractor must also inform the workers' legal representatives before the contract for services starts to be performed of the particulars described in the first paragraph of 42.3.6.2 and points (b)–(e) above.

42.3.6.3 *Queries by workers*

Where the workers of the supplier or subcontractor companies do not have legal representatives, they will be entitled to submit queries to the representatives of the workers of the customer on the conditions for the performance of their activity of employment while they share the workplace and have no representatives. This will not apply to any claims by the workers with respect to the company they are accountable to.

42.3.6.4 *Workers' representatives*

Where the workers' representatives at the customer and at the supplier or subcontractor share a workplace on an ongoing basis, they may hold meetings to coordinate with each other in relation to the conditions of employment on the terms provided in the Workers' Statute.

The representative capacity and scope of the functions of the workers' representatives, and their paid time for union duties will be determined by the current legislation and by the applicable collective employment agreements, if any.

42.3.6.5 *Liability*

The liability regime applicable to contracts for services pursuant to article 42 of the Workers' Statute is as follows:

(a) Salaries: the customer and supplier will be jointly and severally liable during the term of the outsourcing arrangement and up to one year later.

(b) Social security obligations:

   (i) obligations before the term of the contract for services: the customer will have secondary liability unless the customer does not apply for a certificate of no deficiency in payment to the social security authorities, or applies for a certificate but no certificate is granted, in which case it will have joint and several liability;

   (ii) obligations during the term of the services agreement and one year later: the customer and supplier will be jointly and severally liable;

   (iii) obligations after expiry of the contract for services: from the second to the fourth year following its termination date, liability is secondary.

(c) Occupational risk prevention: in addition to the liabilities acquired respectively by each business owner (principal contractor and supplier) in this respect, the supplier acquires the obligation to coordinate its occupation risk prevention activity with the customer company.

42.4 Contract law

42.4.1 Introduction

42.4.1.1 *Principle of freedom of contract*

Outsourcing contracts are not specifically regulated in Spanish Civil law. As in other systems based on Civil Law, however, Spanish law is based on the principle of freedom of contract (article 1,255 of the Civil Code), which gives the contracting parties the right to establish the covenants, clauses and conditions they see fit, except those against the law, morality and public policy. Obligations arising from outsourcing contracts between private parties will be enforceable (articles 1,091 and 1,258 of the Civil Code). Where the two parties to an outsourcing contract are business owners, in principle they can include in the contract any conditions that they may freely agree upon, with some exceptions based on compulsory rules, some of which are mentioned in this section. Where the customer is a public authority, the specific provisions on public contracts must be taken into account (*see* 42.8 and 42.9 below).

42.4.1.2 Outsourcing agreements as service or project agreements

The acknowledgment of the outsourcing of services in Spanish case law is relatively recent. It has been discussed whether in Spanish law the outsourcing contract may be treated as a services agreement (and accordingly the supplier would perform its obligation by providing the resources, and it would be the customer who must prove the breach and also fault on the part of the supplier); or project work (which would compel the supplier to obtain a result, and accordingly if the result is not obtained, the supplier could only be released from blame by proving the existence of a fortuitous event or force majeure). There is a court judgment[5] that states that, although in simple projects a contract could be concluded in which the outsourcing arrangement could be formulated as project work, in which the result sought by the user is perfectly defined, for legal commentators outsourcing has more in common, in principle, with the concept of a services agreement. This is the case above all in large projects where it is difficult at the pre-contract stage to define the actual needs of the customer, specify the conditions on which the project must be delivered, or give an exact estimate of the total cost of the project and in which quality and efficiency in the work performed has priority over the cost of the work.

42.4.1.3 Outsourcing agreements as adhesion agreements

There is also a judgment[6] that expressly states that the outsourcing contract could also be an adhesion contract, in which case it would be subject to the provisions in Law 7/1998 of 13 April 1998 on Standard Business Terms (Ley de Condiciones Generales de la Contratación) that refer to contracts between business owners. The main purpose of these provisions is to ensure that both parties have an adequate opportunity, before entering into the contract, to acknowledge and accept the contents of the standard business terms.

42.4.2 Contractual obligations

42.4.2.1 Basic obligation

The parties to an outsourcing contract are required to meet the agreed terms (article 1,091 of the Civil Code). In particular, the supplier is required to perform its agreed obligations in accordance with the agreed terms and conditions (article 1,098 of the Civil Code).

42.4.2.2 Practical hints

In the above circumstances, in view of the complexity of outsourcing projects, when drafting the contract the customer is advised to:

5 Madrid Provincial Appellate Court judgment dated 7 June 2004.
6 Navarra Provincial Appellate Court judgment dated 1 October 2003.

(a) State clearly and categorically the obligations that the supplier is required to perform, stating in as much detail as possible the important features that define the obligation, including a description of the services, service levels and methods for measuring them, terms, duties of the supplier to cooperate with the customer, and any other significant obligations. What is advisable is to identify as far as possible the circumstances that would determine whether the supplier is complying with or breaching its obligations.

(b) Provide information in the contract that could help to identify the standard of care required of the supplier, including by referring to the standards of the industry in which it operates, the professional qualification of the supplier, the type of services to be provided, the specific risks associated with the customer's business activities, or other similar standards.

(c) Determine what level of breach of the agreed obligations is considered sufficiently serious to entitle the customer to terminate the contract. Contractual mechanisms can be established to provide a solution to minor breaches (e.g. penalties for breach of certain level of service parameters).

42.4.3 Force majeure events

42.4.3.1 Statutory force majeure provisions

Under Spanish law, the supplier will not be required to provide compensation where the breach of its obligations was caused by events that could not be foreseen or, if they could be foreseen, were unavoidable (force majeure), unless the law or the contract provides that it must be liable in such cases (article 1,105 of the Civil Code).

42.4.3.2 Contractual force majeure provisions

It is common practice for the parties to include express clauses in outsourcing contracts releasing the supplier from liability in force majeure events. Force majeure events are sometimes defined in the contract in general terms (e.g. events that could not be foreseen or, if they could be foreseen, were unavoidable, in line with article 1,105 of the Civil Code) and sometimes they are defined in a list of specific events.

It must be borne in mind that the Spanish courts interpret force majeure clauses restrictively. In particular, the supplier cannot be released from liability for a breach if it has clearly acted with negligence, either in its supervision (culpa in vigilando), or in its choice of agents (culpa in eligendo).

42.4.3.3 Practical hints

In any event, in drafting the outsourcing contract, the customer is advised to:

(a) Ensure that the supplier is not entitled to rely upon the force majeure regime (article 1,105 of the Civil Code) in the case of certain unforeseeable or unavoidable events that the parties have expressly agreed to cover (e.g. in respect of obligations relating to business continuity and contingency plans in the case of natural disasters).

(b) Expressly provide certain rules on the conduct of the parties in the case of force majeure events that prevent the supplier from providing the services, to ensure, as far as possible:

(i) basic continuity of the services (e.g. a right for the customer to obtain the services from other suppliers on a transitional basis, with the supplier having a duty to cooperate with these suppliers);
(ii) rapid resumption of the services (e.g. an obligation on the supplier to act with the greatest standard of care to recover them);
(iii) a definitive change of supplier if the force majeure event continues beyond a certain length of time (e.g. a right for the customer or of any of the parties to request termination of the contract); and
(iv) notification of the events so that the parties, in good faith, can do everything possible to fulfil their obligations.

42.4.4 Remedies for breach – performance or termination

In the event of a breach of contract by the supplier, Spanish law gives the customer the right to choose between two alternatives (article 1,124 of the Civil Code):

(a) Require performance of the obligation. To give effect to this right, the judge may order the supplier to carry out its obligation at its own cost (article 1,098 of the Civil Code).
(b) Require termination of the agreement.

42.4.5 Remedies for breach – damages

42.4.5.1 Liability for damages
In both of the cases mentioned in 42.4.4 above, the customer will be entitled to claim compensation from the supplier for damage caused by the breach (article 1,124 of the Civil Code) but only if there has been wilful misconduct or negligence by the supplier (article 1,101 of the Civil Code). The supplier will not be required to pay compensation if it can be proved that the breach was due to an event of force majeure. In determining whether there has been negligence, the standard of care will be that required according to the nature of the obligation and, if no measure of the standard of care is mentioned, the standard of care of a good *pater familias* will be required (article 1,104 of the Civil Code).

42.4.5.2 Quantum of damages
Spanish law establishes that the obligation to provide compensation is to cover not only the value of the loss that has taken place or "*damnum emergens*" but also the gains that the customer failed to make or "loss of profit" (article 1,106 of the Civil Code). Compensable damage and losses are those that were foreseeable, or could have been foreseen, when the obligation was created and are a necessary result of the breach of that obligation.

However, where the breach is due to wilful misconduct, the debtor must be liable for all of the damage and losses that are known to result from a breach of the obligation (article 1,107 of the Civil Code).

42.4.5.3 Limitations on liability

Under the principle of freedom of contract (article 1,255 of the Civil Code) it is lawful for business owners[7] who are parties to an outsourcing contract to agree in the contract to exclusions from, and limitations of, liability, subject to the conditions described below:

(a) It is expressly prohibited to exempt from liability, or limit the liability of, any party who breaches an obligation as a result of wilful misconduct. This is a compulsory rule, and therefore a contractual clause of this type would be considered null and void as a matter of law (article 1,102 of the Civil Code).

(b) Nor is it allowed for the contract to contain an exclusion from, or limitation of, liability for breach if there is serious or very serious negligence, although in these cases the liability could be moderated by the courts (article 1,103 of the Civil Code).

These legal limits on the ability of the parties to agree on exclusions from, or limitations of, liability will apply regardless of the contractual mechanisms that are agreed upon to de-limit liability (e.g. maximum amount of compensation, exclusion of certain types or compensable items).

42.5 Data protection

42.5.1 Relevant statutory provisions

In Spain, the right to personal data protection is included in the Constitution as a basic right (article 18.4).

This right is also implemented in the law in Organic Law 15/1999, of 13 December 1999, on the protection of personal data ("LOPD"), which implemented in Spain the provisions of Directive 95/46/EC of the European Parliament and of the Council of 24 October 1995 on the protection of individuals with regard to the processing of personal data and on the free movement of such data. The LOPD provisions were recently implemented by Royal Decree 1720/2007, of 21 December 2007, approving the LOPD Regulations ("Royal Decree 1720/2007"), which entered into force on 20 April 2008.

42.5.2 Obligations of the data controller

The basic aim of the LOPD and of Royal Decree 1720/2007 is to secure and protect, as regards personal data, the public freedoms and basic rights of individuals, and in particular their rights to their honour, personal privacy and the privacy of their family. To do this, it sets out a series of obligations that must be performed by the data controllers for data files containing personal data.

The LOPD defines "data file" as "a structured set of personal data, regardless of the form or way in which it is created, stored, organised and accessed".

These obligations are described below.

7 Where one of the parties is a consumer, the specific rules on the protection of consumers and users must be taken into account, which allows less room for freedom of contract to provide the appropriate protection for the weaker party in the contractual relationship.

42.5.3 Registration with the AEPD

The data controller has a formal duty to register the data files with the Registrar of the Spanish Data Protection Agency ("AEPD") before they are created.

42.5.4 Quality of data and the duty of secrecy

The data controller is responsible for ensuring the quality of the data. This requirement is linked to the principle of proportion of the data, and requires data kept to be appropriate, relevant and not excessive in relation to the scope of and purposes for their collection. Moreover, the law obliges a data controller to ensure that personal data is accurate and up to date, so it gives a true reflection of the current situation of the data subject.

42.5.5 Duty to provide information

One of the main principles of the LOPD and its implementing legislation is that the data subject must be informed before his personal data is obtained. The minimum of information that must be conveyed to the interested party includes the name and address of the data controller, the purpose behind collecting the data and the interested party's option to exercise rights of access, rectification, cancellation and objection to the data processing.

42.5.6 Consent for the processing and disclosure of data

As a general rule, the inclusion of personal data in a data file will involve processing personal data, which will generally require the consent of the data subject. The LOPD provides for both express and implicit consent according to the type of data to be processed, and states that in all cases consent must be freely given, specific, informed, and unequivocal.

42.5.7 International data transfers

Under the LOPD, international data transfers made from Spain will generally require prior authorisation from the AEPD.

Article 34 of the LOPD provides certain exceptions to the principle of prior authorisation, notably the prior consent of the data subject, or where the transfer is to a Member State of the European Union, the European Economic Area, or a state which the European Commission has declared guarantees an appropriate level of protection (currently, Switzerland, Canada, Argentina, Guernsey, Isle of Man, Jersey, and the US but only in relation to those US companies that adhere to the Safe Harbour Principles developed by the Department of Commerce in coordination with the European Commission[8]).

The rules on authorisation or prior consent have a direct effect and are critical in relation to outsourcing contracts where the provision of services involves the supplier processing personal

8 To obtain more information on the "Safe Harbour" framework, *see* www.export.gov/safeharbor/SH_Overview.asp.

data and where the service is provided outside the EU or countries that are held to have appropriate levels of protection.

42.5.8 Allowing citizens to exercise their rights

As a general rule, the data controller must comply with its duty to allow individuals to exercise their rights of access, rectification, cancellation and objection. If those rights are denied, the data subject can apply for the protection of the AEPD.

42.5.9 Implementation of security measures

Article 9 of the LOPD applies the principle of security to personal data and imposes on the data controller the obligation to adopt the technical and organisational measures needed to ensure the security of the personal data and to prevent data from being altered, lost, processed or accessed without authorisation. The obligation extends to cover both automated and hard-copy data files. These security measures were implemented by Royal Decree 1720/2007, which allocated security levels: basic, medium and high, according to the type and sensitivity of the data. The appropriate security level must be described in the relevant security document.

42.5.10 Inspection and enforcement activities of the AEPD

The AEPD is a public legal entity, with its own legal personality and full authority to act vis-à-vis citizens, companies, other private entities and public authorities. The main functions of the AEPD include:

(a) overseeing compliance with data protection legislation and controlling its application, particularly in relation to the rights of information, access, rectification, objection and cancellation regarding personal data;
(b) dealing with the claims and petitions of citizens;
(c) promoting public information initiatives on the LOPD and implementing legislation;
(d) issuing instructions and recommendations for bringing processing into line with the LOPD;
(e) securing the rights and protection of subscribers and users in the area of electronic communications, including the delivery of unsolicited commercial communications by email or equivalent electronic communications media; and
(f) exercising enforcement power.

In relation to the last activity on this list, the LOPD establishes penalties of up to €600,000 for each infringement relating to a data subject whose rights to personal data protection have been infringed. To date, the AEPD has been particularly active in its inspection and enforcement functions. It publishes the relevant decisions of its director on its website.

42.5.11 Implications of the data protection legislation in relation to outsourcing

Under article 12 LOPD, any outsourcing services that imply access by the supplier to personal data included in the data files controlled by the customer must be set forth in a contract that is required, *inter alia*, to provide for the following:

(a) Processing: obligations on the data processor (i.e. the supplier), to process data only according to the instructions it receives from the data controller (the customer) and not apply or use them for any purpose other than that stated in that contract.
(b) Disclosure: prohibition on the data processor (i.e. the supplier) from disclosing the data, not even for storage, to other persons.
(c) Security measures: description of the security measures that the data processor (i.e. the supplier) is required to implement, according to the type of processing and the type of personal data to which it will have access during the provision of the services.
(d) Destruction or return: it must state that, once the contractual obligation has been performed, the personal data (in addition to any media or documents containing any of the processed personal data) must be destroyed or returned to the data processor (i.e. the customer) or to any controller that the processor may have appointed. Royal Decree 1720/2007 clarifies this principle and establishes that:
    (i) the data will not have to be destroyed where there is a legal provision requiring it to be stored, in which case it must be returned and the controller must ensure that it is stored; and
    (ii) the data processor shall store the data, duly blocked, whilst any liability may arise from its relationship with the data controller.
(e) International data transfers: in the case of international data transfers, it is necessary:
    (i) to obtain the authorisation of the Director of the AEPD or the consent of the data subjects to the data transfer (these requirements are not necessary where the European Commission has held that the destination country for the international data transfer affords an appropriate level of protection); and
    (ii) that the data processor can comply at all times with the security measures that are applicable to the processed data.

These rules are particularly important in cases of offshore outsourcing, especially where the supplier is based and is going to provide its services from places that have not been acknowledged by the European Commission to be countries with appropriate levels of data protection. This means that the frequent cases where services are provided from India or from the US (in this latter case, except for the companies that have adhered to the special Safe Harbour system for the protection of data) are required to comply with the *ad casum* authorisation regime.

42.6 Insolvency issues

In Spain, insolvency is regulated by the Insolvency Law ("Ley 22/2003, de 9 de julio, Concursal"), in force since 1 September 2004, which brought about a sweeping change to the legislation previously in force.[9]

9 Since this new legislation has only been in effect for a short period, there are still issues on which Spanish courts have not yet had the opportunity to establish case law to determine a preferred interpretation of the new law.

As a general rule, an insolvency order does not in itself interrupt the debtor's activity (controlled or replaced by insolvency managers), although it may have an effect on the debtor's power over his assets.

The aim of this section is to outline:

(a) the general principles of Spanish insolvency law regarding the effects of the insolvency order in relation to creditors; and
(b) the steps available under Spanish law, to protect the position of a creditor in the event of insolvency.

42.6.1 General principles

The general principles in the Spanish insolvency law covering the effects of an insolvency order on any creditors are the following:

(a) there is a ban on individual action by creditors against the debtor's property or enforcement of security interests (i.e. a mortgage);
(b) there is a ban or prohibition on offsetting once the insolvency order has been made;
(c) the accrual of interest stops;
(d) contractual clauses that establish termination of a contract as the consequence of an insolvency order become null and void;
(e) contracts do not mature automatically or early upon the insolvency order;
(f) contracts with reciprocal obligations remain in effect, without prejudice to the right to terminate them in certain cases, either in the interests of the insolvency proceeding or due to a breach of the acquired obligations;
(g) hire purchase contracts may be reinstated;
(h) recovery action may be brought, that is, action may be brought to render invalid any acts that may be detrimental to the assets available to creditors carried out by the debtor within a two-year period prior to the insolvency order;
(i) liability arises for the directors of a company subject to an insolvency order; and
(j) Spanish insolvency law establishes a classification of the insolvency claims against the assets available to creditors.

42.6.2 Steps to be taken by creditors

Once a creditor becomes aware of an insolvency order on any of its debtors (assuming that this creditor had not initiated the insolvency proceeding), the first step it must take is to assert its rights to appear in the insolvency proceeding, and notify the insolvency managers of its claim.[10]

A claim regarding obligations which fell due before or after the insolvency order, in principle, will be recognised as an ordinary claim and will be paid according to the terms and conditions

10 The insolvency order must be published either in the Spanish Official Gazette ("BOE") or in a widely read newspaper in the place where the debtor's domicile is located. Before this publication, the Commercial Courts inform of insolvency proceedings (if initiated) regarding debtors whose domicile is located in the area where the court has jurisdiction.

established in the creditors' agreement. If the insolvency order leads to liquidation, these claims will be paid after claims against assets available to creditors and preferred claims. If a claim is secured (with a mortgage or pledge, for example) it will be considered a special preferred claim and will be paid against the assigned assets, with preference over the debtor's other creditors.

If a creditor wishes to continue working with the debtor (or providing additional financing during the insolvency proceeding), the expenses arising for the debtor after the insolvency order from its normal business or from obligations acquired during the insolvency proceeding (by the insolvency managers or by the debtor with the approval of the managers) will be treated as claims against assets available to creditors and must be paid when they fall due.

42.6.3 Protecting the creditor

On the basis of the comments outlined above, the ways to protect the position of a creditor, prior to the insolvency order, and reduce risks in the event of a possible insolvency order affecting its debtors are described below.

Whenever a creditor suspects that any of its customers may be experiencing financial hardship which may lead to an insolvency order, the parties, by mutual consent, may renegotiate the terms of payment established in the contract in order to eliminate deferred payment or shorten the payment period.

Another solution to protect any creditor's position in the event of the risk of insolvency of its customers would be to request that the transaction be guaranteed by a third party (company shareholder, bank etc.) or by the debtor (with a mortgage or pledge of his assets). In all of these cases, in the following two years, the insolvency managers or other creditors can bring action to render these guarantees invalid if they are detrimental to the other creditors (recovery or claw-back actions).

In the case of refinancing, if the debtor is later held to be insolvent, the provider of the financing will be a creditor for the amount of the principal and interest, and any sums that accrued before the insolvency order will qualify as a subordinated claim. If financing is provided by a parent company, this claim will be classified as a subordinated claim. Under Spanish law, loan acceleration is valid if there is a default in payment by the debtor. However, the insolvency managers for the company may request the re-establishment of loans, credit facilities and other financing agreements, if any of those agreements were "accelerated and fell due" in the three months prior to the insolvency order, provided that the creditor did not initiate enforcement of its claim prior to the insolvency order, subject to certain conditions.

If a debtor breaches the contract, and the creditor has a commercial interest in the assets forming the subject matter of the contract, it is important to file an action to request enforcement of the contract or termination of the contract due to a breach, plus damages if appropriate.[11] After

11 In the case of contracts in which a creditor makes instalment sales of moveable property with a retention of title clause executed pursuant to Law 28/1998 of 13 July 1998 on instalment sales of moveable property, if those assets are subject to or assigned to a business activity it would be advisable, in the event of default in payment of two instalments or the last instalment, to bring action immediately in order to recover the asset.

the insolvency order, only the creditor bound to the insolvent debtor by a contract with reciprocal obligations is able to request termination of the contract on the grounds of a breach of the contract carried out by the debtor after the insolvency order.

42.7 Financial services regulation

Recent Spanish regulations implementing MiFID and the Capital Requirements Directive principles provide specific rules for outsourcing by certain financial firms. These regulations are in addition to the general rules described above relating to outsourcing agreements (e.g. employment law and data protection regulations).

42.7.1 Outsourcing of the activities of credit institutions

Outsourcing by banks and other credit institutions is regulated by article 71 of Royal Decree 216/2008, dated 15 February 2008 ("RD 216/2008"), which was implemented in a Circular of the Bank of Spain (Circular number 3/2008), dated 22 May 2008, which covered the determination and control of own funds/equity ("Circular 3/2008"). Article 72 of RD 216/2008 states that any credit institution performing investment services will also be subject to article 70.ter.2.d of Law 24/1988 (Securities Market Law, Ley del Mercado de Valores), in accordance with the provisions of RD 216/2008.

These regulations have implemented most of the Joint Forum's high-level principles for outsourcing in financial entities (affecting the outsourcing of critical and non-critical functions), as well as the MiFID rules for the outsourcing of critical operational functions, in terms similar to those described in Chapter 33 of this Guide. Nevertheless, some of these principles and rules have been implemented by the Spanish regulations with a number of particular features:

(a) There are certain rules on the scope of the services that can be outsourced (the outsourcing arrangement must not leave the entity "devoid of content" in its general activity; and the outsourced services or functions cannot involve the delegation of any of the functions which are reserved to credit institutions, except for the delegation of certain tasks to an agent for credit institutions).

(b) The written contract for the formalisation of the delegation agreement must contain certain provisions, among others, those intended to preserve the supervisory powers of the Bank of Spain and to give the Bank of Spain the right to confirm the suitability of all systems, tools and applications used to perform the outsourced services or functions.

(c) Due diligence duties of the credit institution when selecting the supplier and negotiating the agreement expressly refer to assessing the quality, experience and stability of the potential suppliers, the degree of dependence they may cause, and the level of control they may have over the agreement (the credit institution should have a right to terminate the agreement when considered appropriate, at a reasonable cost).

(d) As regards business continuity, credit institutions are required to ensure that the contingency plans they have in place include or make appropriate provision for the outsourced services or functions, in particular those considered critical functions.

(e) Outsourcing of critical functions (*servicios o funciones esenciales*): Spanish rules incorporate a definition of "critical functions"[12] and regulate the specific duties and conditions applicable to the outsourcing of such functions. These specific duties and conditions (which are additional to those generally applicable to the outsourcing of any kind of services) are in line with some of the Joint Forum's high-level principles: duty of the credit institution to establish a comprehensive policy for the management of its outsourcing of functions; retention of responsibility by the senior management of the credit institution; the outsourcing arrangement must not undermine the conditions with which the credit institution must comply in order to remain authorised to operate, alter the relationships and obligations of the credit institution towards its clients, or diminish internal control mechanisms.

Finally, it should be noted that the Bank of Spain retains the power to establish further limitations on the delegation of functions at each credit institution, by reference to the type and critical nature of the functions or their effects on the internal governance of the institution.

42.7.2 Outsourcing of investment firms' functions

The outsourcing of investment firms' critical operational functions is regulated in article 70.ter.2.d of Law 24/1988 (Securities Market Law, Ley del Mercado de Valores), as implemented by article 36 and article 37 of Royal Decree 217/2008 dated 15 February 2008 (RD 217/2008). Article 38 of RD 217/2008 regulates the delegation of portfolio management services to outsourcing suppliers based in any third country.

In addition, as noted before, article 72 of RD 216/2008 states that any credit institutions performing investment services will also be subject to article 70.ter.2.d of Law 24/1988 but in accordance with the provisions of RD 216/2008.

The conditions established by the Spanish regulations for the outsourcing of critical services or functions of investment firms are those necessary to implement and develop key elements and other relevant requirements set forth in the MiFID regulations and in the Joint Forum's high-level principles, in terms similar to those described in Chapter 33 of this Guide, with a number of particular features that are detailed in articles 36 and 37 of RD 217/2008.

The term "critical functions" has been defined, in the field of investment services (article 70 ter.2.d of Law 24/1988), consistently with the definition stated for credit institutions (*see* point (e) of 42.7.1 above), although a non-exhaustive list of activities that shall not be considered critical functions has been added, namely advisory services outside the company's investment activities (including legal advice, employee training, invoicing services and surveillance and security services for the company's premises and personnel) and the purchase of standardised services (including information services regarding markets and prices).

12 Critical functions are those in which any deficiency or anomaly in their performance may have a material effect on the capacity of the credit institution to fulfil on an ongoing basis the conditions and obligations resulting from its authorisation to operate as such and from its legal regime, or may have an effect on the financial performance or the soundness or continuity of its activity (article 71.5 RD 216/2008).

42.8 Public Procurement Directives

42.8.1 Regulations based on EU Directives

Since Spain joined the European Community in 1986, the Public Procurement Directives have been implemented by Spanish public procurement legislation.

The first Spanish legislation to result from the implementation of European Community directives was Law 13/1995, dated 18 May 1995 on public authority contracts, which incorporated into Spanish law the provisions of Directives 92/50/EEC, 93/36/EEC and 93/37/EEC, among others. This legislation marked a turning point in Spanish public procurement provisions.

A new law on public procurement, which implemented Directive 2004/18/EC, has been in force since 1 May 2008: Law 30/2007, dated 30 October 2007, on public sector contracts ("LCSP").

Spanish law requires compliance with all European Community public procurement principles: equal access to procurement processes, advertising and transparent procedures, non-discrimination and equal treatment for tendering parties. It was chosen to apply European law to the greatest extent on many occasions.

42.8.2 Reform of Spanish law

The Public Sector Contracts Law did not merely implement Directive 2004/18/EC, since the opportunity was also taken to reform the law applicable to public procurement contracts. Spanish public procurement legislation is one of the most extensive and complex that exists, especially when compared to the legislation of Spain's closest neighbours.

Broadly speaking, the Public Sector Contracts Law has a very complex systematic structure, it is difficult to read and gives rise to doubts as to its interpretation.

42.8.2.1 Application of the Public Sector Contracts Law

The Spanish regulation on public sector contracts and the above-mentioned principles are applicable to the procurement processes run by what the EC legislation calls "contracting authorities", and applies more widely than merely to those institutions which, according to the law, may be deemed to be public authorities.

42.8.2.2 Relevance for outsourcing

The Public Sector Contracts Law governs public authority contracts for works, public works concessions, management of public services, supplies, services and cooperation between the public and private sectors. Contracts for outsourcing services or activities in which the customer is a Spanish public authority will be subject to the Public Sector Contracts Law, specifically, within those considered as contracts for services, defined by the law as "having in their subject matter affirmative covenants consisting of the performance of an activity or the achievement of a result other than a work or works project or a supply".

The provisions on contracts for services in Spain contain certain specific features that stem from traditional Spanish law rather than the EC Directives.

42.8.2.3 Effects and termination of contracts

The Public Sector Contracts Law deals with the effect, performance and termination of the above-mentioned contracts for outsourcing services. These specific features include:

(a) a limit on their term to four years with extensions up to a total term of six years (this limit would not be applied, for example, if the contract for services complements another for a longer term);
(b) the supplier's liability, to third parties and the public authorities, for the technical quality of the services provided and for the consequences of the errors made in performing the contract; and
(c) the wide powers of the public authorities when it comes to amending, interpreting and unilaterally terminating the contract.

42.8.2.4 Exercising public authority

In relation to contracts for services, it must be taken into account that, under Spanish law, public bodies cannot enter into outsourcing agreements which imply that the supplier will be exercising the authority inherent to public powers.

42.8.2.5 Waiver of rights

As regards exclusions from and limitations to the supplier's liability, under the principles of public procurement and case law, public authorities cannot, by entering into agreements, waive the rights and powers conferred on them by the law, which include claiming liability from the contractors for the poor technical quality of their work or the errors made in performing the contract.

42.9 Utilities Directive

42.9.1 Implementation of the EU Directive

Directive 2004/17/EC of the European Parliament and of the Council dated 31 March 2004 coordinating the procurement procedures of entities operating in the water, energy, transport and postal services sectors ("Utilities Directive") was implemented in Spanish law in Law 31/2007, dated 30 October, on procurement procedures in special sectors. This Law replaces the provisions in Law 48/1998 (with the exception of the provisions relating to the Spanish Public Airports and Aviation Agency), and came into force, generally, on 1 May 2008 (although for postal services the law came into force on 1 January 2009).

42.9.2 Application of the EU Directive

In principle, Law 31/2007 applies to contracting entities that are public law agencies or public companies, and contracting entities which, without being public law agencies or public companies, have special or exclusive rights, provided that they carry out any of the functions listed in article 7 to article 12. The Law considers "entities with special or exclusive rights" to be those entities which, without being contracting authorities or public companies, carry on, among their functions, any of those envisaged in article 7 to article 12 of the Law or more than one of those functions and have special or exclusive rights conferred by a competent body of a public authority, of a public law agency or of a business public company.

The Law will therefore apply to certain water, gas, heating, electricity, transport, postal, oil and coal companies.

42.9.3 Minimum threshold

Law 31/2007 will only be applicable to contracts for services, supplies and works that exceed the minimum thresholds for the various types of contract envisaged, in this case, in article 16. That is:

(a) €412,000 in contracts for supplies and services; and
(b) €5,150,000 in works contracts.

42.9.4 Exceptions

Law 31/2007 will be applicable unless any of the exceptions provided in article 18 of the Law applies, in line with the terms provided in the Utilities Directive. Special attention must be paid to the exceptions in sub-articles 4, 5 and 6 of the same article 18, which state that the Law will not be applicable to:

(a) contracts awarded by a contracting entity to an affiliate, meaning a company which, under article 42 of the Commercial Code, files consolidated financial statements with the contracting entity;
(b) contracts awarded by a joint venture, set up exclusively by several contracting entities to carry out the functions envisaged in article 7 to article 12, to an affiliate of one of the contracting entities

These last two exceptions will be applied to contracts for services, where at least 80 per cent of the average volume of business that the affiliate has had in the past three years in relation to services comes from the provision of these services to affiliate companies.

Lastly, article 18.6 states that the Law will not apply to contracts awarded:

(a) by a joint venture, set up exclusively by several contracting entities to carry out the functions envisaged in article 7 to article 12, to any of those contracting entities;
(b) by a contracting entity to a joint venture of which it is part, where the joint venture was set up to carry out the activity concerned for at least three years, and that the instrument in which the joint venture is created stipulates that the contracting entities that created it will be part of it at least in the same period.

42.9.5 Effect of application

As regards the principles of procurement, capacity and classification of the business operators, contract techniques and procedures for awarding contracts, Spanish law has substantially the same terms as the Utilities Directive.

42.10 Competition law

The implications of Spanish competition law on outsourcing arrangements are similar in most respects to those contained in Chapter 29 of this Guide: merger control, exchanges of information and the enforceability of exclusivity and non-compete provisions. The aim of this section is to address those specific rules in Spanish competition legislation that may affect outsourcing deals in the Spanish market.

42.10.1 EU merger control

The contents on "EU merger control" in 29.2.1 of this Guide apply in full to those outsourcing deals involving Spanish parties that can be classed as a "concentration" with a "Community dimension".

42.10.2 Spain merger control

Spanish merger control applies to outsourcing deals that constitute mergers on the conditions described below.

42.10.2.1 Legal framework

Under Spanish Competition Law 15/2007 dated 3 July 2007 (the "Competition Law"), concentrations above certain thresholds (as described in 42.10.2.3 below) must be notified to the Spanish competition authorities (Comisión Nacional de la Competencia, or "CNC"). Notification in Spain is mandatory in such cases and the transaction cannot be carried out until it is cleared either expressly or implicitly by the CNC. The CNC has the power to impose fines for failure to notify (including daily penalties until notification is filed), for providing incorrect or misleading information, and/or for any failure to abide by the final decision.

Proceedings are governed by the Competition Law and by Royal Decree 261/2008, dated 22 February 2008 (the "Competition Provisions").

42.10.2.2 Outsourcing deals subject to merger control

Outsourcing arrangements may constitute a merger which is subject to Spanish merger control where they meet the requirements to qualify as a concentration.

Although there are no decisions from the Spanish authorities relating to IT or business process outsourcing transactions, there are specific cases involving the outsourcing of industrial activities in which the CNC held that the transaction was subject to Spanish merger control.[13]

42.10.2.3 Thresholds

Given that article 7 of the Competition Law largely borrows the definition of concentration from the EU Merger Regulation, notification is compulsory in Spain where a transaction does not fall within the exclusive jurisdiction of the European Commission under the EU Merger Regulation and at least one of the two following circumstances occurs:

---

13 Decision of the Council of the CNC dated 7 February 2008 in case C-0043/08, Fuertes/Carrefour.

(a) as a consequence of the concentration, a share equal to or greater than 30 per cent of the relevant product or service market at a national level or in a geographical market defined within that same market, is acquired or increased;
(b) the combined aggregate turnover in Spain of the undertakings concerned in the last accounting year exceeds the amount of €240 million, providing that at least two of the undertakings concerned achieve an individual turnover in Spain exceeding €60 million.

42.10.2.4 Proceedings

Pre-notification phase
Prior to formal notification, the undertakings concerned may submit a draft of the notice to the CNC in order to clarify either issues of form or substance relating to the concentration.

Phase one
Following notification, and assuming that the transaction does not raise competition concerns, the concentration may be approved implicitly (i.e. without an express decision) if no objection is received within one month of notification. The Council of the CNC usually clears the transaction with a formal decision, issued within a month of notification, and includes the report from the Investigation Directorate of the CNC on the concentration.

If the Council of the CNC (usually following the recommendation contained in the Investigation Directorate's report) has doubts about the transaction, because it may hinder the maintenance of effective competition in the Spanish market, the Council may request that the parties propose commitments in return for clearing the transaction in phase one. In such a case, the term of phase one will be extended for a further 10 days.

Where there are serious doubts over a transaction, the CNC will decide to initiate phase two.

Phase two
If the concentration has not been cleared in phase one, the Investigation Directorate of the CNC will draft a statement of objections which will be given to the interested parties so that they can file any pleadings within 10 days. At the request of the notifying parties, a hearing will be held before the Council of the CNC. The Council of the CNC will have two months to adopt the final resolution.

When obstacles for the maintenance of effective competition may result from the concentration, the Council of the CNC may request that the parties propose commitments in return for clearing the transaction. In such a case, the term of phase two will be extended for a further 15 days.

Notice of the final decision will be given simultaneously to the interested parties and to the Minister of Economy and Finance. In cases where a concentration is prohibited or subject to commitments, the Minister of Economy and Finance may decide to refer the concentration to the Spanish government for reasons of general interest within 15 days. In such a case, the final decision on the concentration lies with the Spanish government who will have one month to decide whether to confirm the decision issued by the Council of the CNC or to authorise the concentration with or without conditions.

The parties may appeal decisions issued by the Council of the CNC to the Administrative Chamber of the National Appellate Court. The Spanish government's decision can be contested at the Spanish Supreme Court.

42.10.3 Prohibited anti-competitive agreements

In addition to the prohibition contained in article 81(1) of the EC Treaty for anti-competitive agreements which may affect trade between EU Member States (*see* Chapter 29 of this Guide), Spanish Competition Law (article 1) prohibits agreements that have the object or effect of preventing, restricting or distorting competition and which may affect trade within Spain (the "Prohibition"). Breaches of the Prohibition attract heavy fines (up to 10 per cent of turnover); infringing agreements are unenforceable and the parties to them may be sued for damages. In addition, when the offender is a legal entity, fines of up to €60,000 may be imposed on each of its legal representatives or on the persons on the managing bodies that have participated in the agreement or decision involving a breach of competition law.

42.10.3.1 Exclusivity and non-compete clauses

Exclusivity and non-compete provisions contained in outsourcing arrangements may restrict competition and must be considered in light of the Prohibition in article 1 of the Spanish Competition Law and article 81(1) of the EC Treaty. For these reasons, the general considerations in 29.3.1 of this Guide will apply.

42.10.3.2 Information exchange

Anti-competitive agreements that may arise from certain outsourcing agreements (where a customer outsources services to a competitor, or in a transfer of outsourced services from a supplier to a competitor) as a result of information exchanged between actual or potential competitors, should be analysed in the light of the general considerations in 29.3.2 of this Guide.

42.11 Other relevant laws and best practice

42.11.1 Best practice in the Spanish market

Recently the AEC, an association of the main consultancy firms established in Spain, has published two important documents which attempt to describe best practice in the industry:

(a) Código de la Actividad de Consultoría para las Administraciones Públicas[14] (Code of Conduct for Consultancy Services Provided to Public Authorities). This code contains the basic rules of conduct for consultants who are members of the AEC in projects for providing services to their customers, including public authorities. The rules are classified under the headings of Professional Conduct, Services Agreement, Mutual Trust, Objectivity and Impartiality, Incompatibility, Quality and Confidentiality.

14 This document can be accessed in Spanish at http://consultoras.c2csoluciones.com/frontend/aec/LA-MODERNIZACION--DE-LOS-SERVICIOS-PUBLICOS--EN-LAS-ECONOMIAS-AVANZADAS-vn184-vst16.

(b) White paper of good practices in the consultancy market.[15] The intention behind the paper, submitted in 2008, was to propose practices that could contribute to improving market relationships between customers and suppliers of consultancy services. It is the result of research performed by the AEC and leading companies in the industry, in which large organisations in the public and private sector, that use consultancy services, took part. It contains a catalogue of good practices classified according to each of the phases of a project: presale and needs identification; specifications; selection of suppliers; negotiation and the contract; provision of the service; continuity or close of the project.

42.11.2 Some tax implications of outsourcing

42.11.2.1 VAT on outsourcing services

Spanish law generally requires 16 per cent VAT to be charged on the provision of outsourcing services. This will in principle be neutral in financial terms, that is, it will not create a tax cost since the company receiving the outsourced services can deduct all of the input VAT it has paid with the charge for the services.

However, this neutrality will not be possible for customers of outsourcing services (who are required therefore to bear the VAT charged on the services they receive) who perform VAT-exempt activities and therefore cannot deduct all of the input VAT paid (e.g. financial, educational, healthcare or welfare institutions). In these cases, the receipt of services under an outsourcing arrangement may entail a higher tax cost than if the services had been performed internally by the company's own personnel (on which VAT would not be charged).

Outsourced services in the financial industry can be VAT exempt if their effect is to provide the essential and specific activities of an exempt financial service. Since 2008, a special regime for groups of companies for VAT purposes has been in force which allows this negative effect to be reduced or eliminated where the outsourcing supplier belongs to the same group as the customer company.

42.11.2.2 Potential liability for the customer in respect of certain of the supplier's tax debts

Article 43.1f of the General Taxation Law 58/2003, dated 17 December 2003, includes a case of secondary liability for individuals or entities that enter into a contract or subcontract to perform projects or services relating to their main business activity. According to these provisions, the customer in an outsourcing contract could be held secondarily liable for tax obligations relating to taxes that the supplier must charge or to tax that must be withheld from workers, professionals or other business owners, in the portion relating to the project or services under the contract or subcontract.

The liability would include VAT chargeable by the supplier, in addition to the corporate income tax, personal income tax or non-resident income tax that the supplier must withhold. However,

15 This document can be accessed in Spanish at http://consultoras.c2csoluciones.com/frontend/aec/La-AEC-Potencia-El-Esquema-%91ganador-ganador%92-En-Las-Relaciones-Entre-Clientes-Y-Proveedores-Con-La-C-vn7999-vst272.

the customer would have a right to be reimbursed by the supplier on the terms provided in civil law (article 41.6 of the General Taxation Law).

The liability under article 43.1f of Law 58/2003 cannot be claimed where the supplier provides a specific certificate issued by the tax authorities evidencing that it is up to date with its tax obligations. This certificate must be issued within 12 months before the payment of each invoice relating to the contract or subcontract. The tax authorities have to issue these certificates within three days of a request by the supplier or subcontractor, and they must provide copies upon request.

In practice, in outsourcing contracts it is advisable:

(a) to include as a contractual obligation for the supplier the duty to evidence to the customer that the supplier is up to date with its payment and compliance with its tax obligations by delivering on a periodic basis valid certificates issued by the Spanish Tax Agency; and
(b) to establish an obligation for the supplier to protect the customer from and against potential claims from the tax authorities in respect of the supplier's debts, to avoid being forced to pay for these items (without prejudice to the right to be reimbursed, which is recognised in the law).

42.12 Summary

The Spanish outsourcing market has not yet fully matured, and there is much room for growth, which could take place as and when the following trends are confirmed:

(a) The perception of outsourcing as a strategic option for the management of IT systems and business processes needs to become more firmly established among the Spanish business community.
(b) Those business sectors that to date have remained outside the market need to become more familiar with outsourcing.
(c) The customers need to make more widespread use of competitive processes for the selection of, and contracts with, suppliers.

In any event, there are some opportunities that could contribute to the significant growth of outsourcing in the Spanish market in the short to medium term:

(a) There is a potential for growth in outsourcing contracts by public authorities and private companies in various sectors as a result of the need to comply with their new legal obligations under the laws recently published in Spain (as a part of the Spanish government's "Plan Avanza" for the expansion and use of information and communications technologies):
    (i) Law 11/2007, on electronic access by citizens to public services, approving the principles of e-Government in Spain and recognising the right of citizens to communicate with the public authorities electronically;
    (ii) Law 56/2007, of December 2007, approving certain measures to promote the information society. Among other measures, the obligation of suppliers to

provide certain key services to consumers (electronic communications, financial services, utilities, and travel agencies), to provide customers with electronic channels of communication for a number of procedures (i.e. electronic contracts, filing of complaints, incidents and suggestions, or fulfilment of data protection rights).

(b) Many companies will have to reduce and rationalise production costs in order to adapt themselves to the current economic climate, which may mean:

(i) a rise in the number of automated processes, requiring modernisation of information systems and business processes, and in many cases the use of outsourcing arrangements with specialised suppliers;

(ii) in particular, customers may decide to enter into business process outsourcing agreements to increase their productivity and improve their flexibility.

Chapter 43

France

Thierry Bernard
Partner

Mary-Daphné Fishelson
Partner
Lefèvre Pelletier & associés, Avocats

43.1 Background to outsourcing in France

Outsourcing has been practised in France for around 15 years and is steadily developing. According to a 2008 study,[1] 63 per cent of French companies with revenues in excess of €100 million outsource at least one company activity (compared with a European average of 70 per cent).

The most commonly outsourced activities are office services, distribution/logistics and IT and telecommunications. In France, companies outsource five activities on average, which is high compared with the European average (three activities).

In France, outsourcing is primarily valued for the improvements it can bring in the flexibility of management (labour legislation is highly restrictive compared with the UK, for instance), service quality and strategic organisation.

In France, 22 per cent of the companies questioned stated they would implement new outsourcing projects in the coming two years – 2009 to 2010, a percentage that is in line with the European average, compared with a rate of 12 per cent in the UK (undoubtedly the most mature market in Europe).

43.2 People issues – ARD

43.2.1 Application of ARD to outsourcing in France

ARD was not transposed into French law, which already provided similar rules. The applicable French rules stem mainly from article L.1224-1 of the Labour Code and relating case law.

---

1 Baromètre Outsourcing Europe 2008, Ernst & Young/TNS Sofres.

43.2.1.1 Article L.1224-1 of the Labour Code

Article L.1224-1 (formerly L. 122-12) of the Labour Code states:

> "If the employer's legal status changes, particularly by way of succession, sale, merger, conversion of the business, or incorporation of the company, all contracts in progress on the day of the change subsist between the new employer and the company's personnel."

This rule is supplemented by article L. 1224-2 of the Labour Code, which states that liability for outstanding wages will be transferred to the new employer in accordance with the European Directive of 14 February 1977.

43.2.1.2 Case law of the French Cour de Cassation (Court of Cassation – Supreme Court)

Many decisions have been reached in this area, some of which deal with questions unresolved by the legislators. French and European courts have not always seen eye to eye in the past, particularly concerning the notion of "economic entity" and the necessity for a legal link between successive employers. However, this is no longer the case and decisions of both courts concur with and complement each other. The Court of Cassation often refers to article L. 1224-1 of the Labour Code in the light of ARD.

43.2.1.3 Application of ARD to outsourcing

The outsourcing of an activity, whether it constitutes the first outsourcing of the service or a secondary outsourcing, will not automatically result in the application of ARD.

ARD will only apply if the outsourcing entails:

(a) the transfer of an economic entity that retains its identity; and
(b) the activity previously carried out by the economic entity is continued or taken over.

The activity must enjoy real autonomy, both with regard to its human resources as well as its organisation and operating resources.

The existence of personnel specially dedicated to operating the transferred entity is a prerequisite. This condition is satisfied in particular if the relevant employees require a special qualification.

The existence of an economic entity also requires tangible or intangible assets. The transfer does not necessarily imply transfer of the ownership of assets. It is sufficient if the new operator of the transferred entity ("the supplier") is loaned the assets needed to run the activity.

Judges assess the conditions for the application of article L. 1224-1 on a case-by-case basis, very often putting employees' interests first. The transfer of employees also depends in practice on the results of the negotiations between the employer and the works council according to whether the works council considers that it is in employees' interest to be transferred (particularly depending on the advantages provided or not provided by the new employer).

43.2.1.4 Refusal of the employees to transfer

If article L. 1224-1 of the Labour Code applies, the employee cannot refuse the transfer of his employment contract. His refusal constitutes a breach of his employment contract. Thus, for instance, if the employee does not show up for work after the transfer, the supplier, who is now the employer, may dismiss him for serious misconduct.

43.2.1.5 Modification of the employment contract simultaneously with/after the transfer
Outsourcing may result in a modification of the employment contract of the employee whose employment contract is transferred. It may entail a change in the location of the workplace. If the place of work is specified in the employment contract, or if the new place of work is very far from the old one (in a different geographical sector) and the employee's contract has no mobility clause, the employee will be entitled to refuse the change of his employment contract. Since, in theory, the employment contract is transferred on the day of the transfer, it is, in principle, up to the supplier to dismiss the employee.

Following the transfer, the supplier may propose amendments to the transferred employees' employment contracts, in accordance with the usual rules:

(a) if a simple change in working conditions is concerned, the supplier is free to modify them unilaterally (e.g. change of working hours or of task);
(b) if a modification of the employment contract is concerned (i.e. change of essential elements such as compensation, place of work or working time), the supplier must obtain the express consent of the employee; in the absence of the employee's consent and if the supplier cannot forgo the modification, he may dismiss the employee for economic reasons if he can prove that real and serious economic grounds exist.

However, there is a limit in the case of fraud as defined in article L. 1224-1. The purpose of the modification must not be to avoid the effect of the transfer. In practice, if the employment contract is modified after the transfer, the following conditions should be met to avoid the risk of fraud as defined in article L. 1224-1:

(a) the employment contract must have been in effect with the supplier for some time (evaluated on a case-by-case basis);
(b) the modification must be for economic reasons; and
(c) the dismissal must not be pronounced until after applying the dismissal order criteria and only if there is no possibility of redeployment.

43.2.1.6 Outstanding wages
Under article L. 1224-2 of the Labour Code, the supplier is liable to the transferred employees for:

(a) all sums owed to the employees for the period following the outsourcing; and
(b) all sums owed and not paid by the previous supplier/former employer for the prior period.

However, the supplier may claim against the previous employer in respect of the sums that he pays to employees that relate to the period prior to the date of transfer, unless:

(a) the previous employer is involved in receivership or winding-up proceedings;
(b) there is no agreement between the successive employers (for example, if there is a succession of suppliers).

43.2.1.7 Transfer of part of a contract of employment
Article L.1224-1 will apply to employees assigned to the transferred activity on a full-time basis. It will also apply for those employees who, before the outsourcing, were assigned partly to the

transferred activity and partly to the retained activity. In this case, their employment contracts will be transferred on the same partial basis. This will result in the employees working part time for the new supplier and part time for their former employer.

However, this mechanism, which will modify the employees' employment contracts in that they will be transformed into part-time employment contracts, will require the consent of the employees. Moreover, it is particularly difficult to apply in practice.

After the automatic transfer of the contracts of employment, the former employer, the supplier and each employee concerned may conclude a tripartite agreement where the employee agrees to work full time for either his former employer or the supplier instead of part time for each of them.

43.2.1.8 Transfer of protected employees

Protected employees are staff representatives, that is, member of a work council, union delegate, member of the Committee for Health and Safety at Work, etc.

The transfer of an entire economic entity according to article L. 1224-1 of the Labour code involves the automatic transfer of the protected employees' employment contracts.

In the case of a partial transfer of the company (such as in an outsourcing arrangement), the transfer of protected employees' employment contracts is subject to the prior authorisation of the labour inspector, whose job it is to ensure that there is no discrimination against protected employees and that the transfer is not an excuse to "get rid" of them. Consequently, the former employer will have to obtain authorisation for the transfer of the protected employees from the labour inspector before the transfer. Authorisation must be requested 15 days prior to the planned date of the transfer.

The protected employees will be transferred on the date of the labour inspector's authorisation.

If the inspector rejects the transfer, then the situation will be complicated since the employees' previous jobs will in fact have ceased to exist, so maintaining their employment with their previous employer will require a modification of their employment contracts, which will need their formal approval.

If protected employees are transferred without the labour inspector's authorisation, they will be entitled to request reinstatement with their previous employer.

43.2.1.9 Mandates of staff representatives

Concerning the mandates of staff representatives, two situations may apply.

(a) If article L. 1224-1 of the Labour Code applies, because an autonomous economic entity is transferred, then the mandates of staff representatives will be transferred to the new supplier as well, provided that the transferred entity remains legally autonomous. Consequently, the protected employees who are transferred will keep their mandates as staff representatives and will have the right to exercise their duties within the supplier until the expiry of their initial mandate. However, the length of their mandate can be extended or reduced in order to correspond to the date of election of staff representatives at the new supplier by way of a collective agreement concluded between the new employer and the union delegates.

(b) Otherwise, the mandates of the staff representatives will be terminated automatically on the effective date of the outsourcing. However, they will be protected from any dismissal for a period of six months for staff representatives and 12 months for union delegates, unless the prior authorisation of the labour inspector is obtained.

43.2.1.10 Collective benefits

In addition to the advantages provided for in their employment contracts, employees may enjoy collective benefits which apply to all employees or certain employee categories, pursuant to a collective bargaining agreement or an in-house collective agreement[2] applicable to the company or pursuant to custom etc., for example a bonus, or a thirteenth-month salary.

Collective bargaining agreements

Pursuant to article L. 1224-1, there are four different situations:

(a) Where a different collective bargaining agreement is applied by the former employer and by the supplier. The transferred employees will be entitled, for a maximum period of 15 months, to claim the most favourable provision in either collective bargaining agreement. After 15 months, only the collective bargaining agreement in force within the supplier will apply to the transferred employees in addition with the transferred employees' personal vested rights ("*avantages individuels acquis*"), unless a specific agreement ("*accord d'adaptation*") is concluded with the supplier's trade unions.
(b) Where the former employer and the supplier apply the same collective bargaining agreement. This collective bargaining agreement will remain applicable.
(c) Where the former employer has no collective bargaining agreement but the supplier has one. The transferred employees will be entitled as from the transfer of their employment contract to benefit from the collective bargaining agreement of their new employer.
(d) Where the former employer has a collective bargaining agreement and the supplier does not. The transferred employees will be entitled, for a maximum period of 15 months, to claim the application of the collective bargaining agreement of their former employer. After 15 months, only the transferred employees' personal vested rights will apply to the transferred employees, unless a specific agreement is concluded with the supplier's trade unions.

In-house collective agreements

Different types of in-house collective agreements may exist.

(a) Health plans: pursuant to article L. 1224-1, there are various different situations. If the transferred employees did not benefit from a health plan whilst they were employed by

2 There is a difference in France between:

(a) collective bargaining agreements ("*conventions collectives nationales*") negotiated and signed at a national level between the big employers' trade unions and employees' trade unions; and
(b) in-house collective agreements ("*accords collectifs d'entreprise*") negotiated and signed between the trade unions of the company and the employer.

the previous employer, then they will be immediately entitled to the supplier's health plan as from the date of the transfer if one is applied by the supplier.

Otherwise, the effect of the outsourcing arrangement will depend upon how the previous employer's health plan was set up:

(i) if the health plan was incorporated into the employees' employment contracts, the health plan will be transferred with the employment contracts if article L. 1224-1 of the Labour Code applies;

(ii) if the health plan was incorporated into a company-wide agreement, the applicable rules relating to the collective bargaining agreements will apply (*see* 43.2.1.10);

(iii) if the health plan was incorporated into an in-house agreement concluded by referendum/unilateral commitment of the former employer/customer, it will still apply after the transfer of the employees until the supplier terminates it according to the applicable procedure set out in the relevant agreement.

(b) Profit-sharing agreements: according to articles L. 3313-4 and L. 3323-8 of the Labour Code, in the event of the transfer of an activity with its employees to a new company, the following will happen to any mandatory profit-sharing agreement and any optional profit-sharing agreement in force with the previous employer:

(i) if the former employer had profit-sharing agreements but the supplier does not, the employees will no longer be entitled to the benefit of the profit-sharing agreements. If, after the transfer, there are more than 50 employees employed by the supplier, the supplier will have to start to negotiate in order to enter into a mandatory profit-sharing agreement and an optional profit-sharing agreement that would be appropriate for the supplier's business, within six months of the outsourcing;

(ii) if both the former employer and the supplier have profit-sharing agreements, the agreements with the former employer will no longer be applicable from the date of the transfer. The transferred employees will have the benefit of the agreements in force with the supplier as from this date.

Companies should pay particular attention to the drafting of profit-sharing agreements and consider how they will apply in the event of the company deciding to outsource any of its services.

43.3 People issues – other employment issues

43.3.1 Unlawful types of outsourcing agreements

The outsourcing contract must not consist of a service entailing the supply of employees to the customer's site or supply of employees to the supplier's site by a subcontractor, at the risk of it being considered:

(a) the unlawful leasing of a work force ("any operation for profit whose exclusive purpose is the leasing of labour") – this will be punishable by one year of imprisonment and a fine of €30,000 for the company's executive if he is an individual and a fine of €150,000 if it is a legal entity (article L. 8243-1 of the Labour Code); or

(b) improper subcontracting ("any operation for profit entailing the supply of manpower which has the effect of causing prejudice to the employee concerned or eluding the application of legal provisions or the stipulations of an agreement or of a collective bargaining agreement") – this will also be punishable by one year of imprisonment and a fine of €30,000 for the company's executive if he is an individual and a fine of €150,000 if it is a legal entity (article L. 8234-1 and 8 of the Labour Code).

To avoid these risks, the following rules should be followed:

(a) the parties should precisely define in the contract the services to be rendered and the supplier's special know-how in the performance of the services;
(b) exclusive supervisory control over and responsibility for staff of the supplier should be left with the supplier as the sole employer;
(c) the charges should be calculated on the basis of a lump-sum payment and not on the basis of the number of employees assigned to the service provision or their qualifications;
(d) the parties should ensure that supplier/subcontractor performs its services using its own materials and resources and remains independent.

43.3.2 Duty to consult

French law does not contain an obligation to inform employees of the proposed outsourcing arrangement in the absence of staff representative. In practice, it is highly recommended that they be informed individually prior to their transfer.

The works councils of the supplier and its customer must be informed and consulted in respect of the planned outsourcing arrangement (article L. 2323-6 of the Labour Code). The works council must be asked to give its opinion on the outsourcing plan sufficiently in advance so that its opinion can be taken into account by the company before any contract is signed with the supplier. However, the outsourcing project must be sufficiently advanced so that the management of the company can provide the works council with comprehensive information. If the works council is not in favour of the outsourcing arrangement, this does not prevent the outsourcing arrangement from being pursued, but if the works council refuses to give its opinion, the employer cannot proceed with the transfer, and must obtain an interim order requiring the works council to give an opinion.

Failure to comply with the obligation to inform or consult with the works council constitutes an offence, the maximum penalty for which is imprisonment of one year and a fine of €3,750 for the company's executive if he is an individual and a fine of €18,750 if it is a legal entity (article L. 2328-1 of the Labour Code).

43.3.3 Transfer under a collective bargaining agreement

In some sectors, collective bargaining agreements provide for the transfer of employment contracts in the event of outsourcing, even if there is no transfer of an autonomous economic entity. The sectors concerned are in particular the restaurant, cleaning, security, railway handling and connected work, cleaning and handling of the airports, road transport companies and waste companies.

The collective bargaining agreements will usually set out the scope (i.e. the transfer may be limited to some specific category of employees) and the conditions of transfer. They may also impose specific obligations on the former employer or the supplier.

43.3.3.1 Employees' refusal to transfer

Unlike the situation where employees transfer under article L. 1224-1,[3] where employees transfer under a collective agreement, they are entitled to refuse the transfer of their employment contract and their refusal is not a ground for dismissal. If the employer intends to terminate such an employee, it will have to consider another reason (generally an economic reason).

43.3.3.2 Protected employees

The transfer of protected employees under a collective agreement (similar to a transfer under article L. 1224-1) is subject to the prior authorisation of the labour inspector (*see* 43.2.1.8).

Like other employees, protected employees are entitled to refuse the transfer of their employment contracts. If they object, the employer can only notify them of their dismissal after obtaining the opinion of the works council, if any, and obtaining the authorisation of the labour inspector.

For protected employees who accept their transfer, there are two situations:

(a) Where there is no provision regarding their mandate as staff representatives in the collective bargaining agreement, their mandates will not be maintained. They will be terminated at the date of transfer of the employment contracts. The protected employees only benefit from their protection against dismissal for a period of six months after the termination of their mandates.
(b) Where the collective bargaining agreement provides for the transfer of their mandates as staff representatives, their mandates will be maintained with the supplier until their date of termination.

43.3.3.3 Consequences for collective benefits

The transfer will be limited to the employment contracts and the collective benefits will not be transferred to the supplier. As a consequence, the collective benefits provided by custom, in a collective bargaining agreement or in in-house agreements will no longer be enforceable from the date of the outsourcing. The sole exception is when benefits have been integrated into the employment contract. In such a case, they will remain in force.

43.3.4 Voluntary transfer

The supplier may still need the employees who previously worked on the outsourced activity even if no collective bargaining agreement provides for the transfer of the employment contracts and article L. 1224-1 of the Labour Code does not apply to the outsourcing arrangement, for example because:

3 *See* 43.2.1.4.

(a) the employees may have worked only occasionally on the outsourced activity;
(b) the outsourced activity does not have any tangible or intangible assets;
(c) the outsourced activity may have been an autonomous economic entity with the former employer, but it will be reorganised by the supplier after which it will cease to be an autonomous economic entity.

In such cases, the former employer, the supplier and the employees will need to agree a voluntary transfer of the employment contracts.

43.3.4.1 Form of the agreement

The transfer of the employment contracts constitutes a modification of these contracts, which will require the prior express consent of the employees affected. The employee's approval must be in writing. The voluntary transfer can be effected by one of the following methods:

(a) amicable termination, or "*rupture conventionnelle*" since the new law dated 25 June 2008, of the former employment contract and conclusion of a new contract with the new supplier: this method should be used very carefully in order to avoid any claim from the employee for wrongful dismissal with the resulting liability for severance pay;
(b) resignation by the employee and signing of a new contract with the supplier: employees are usually reluctant to resign, they may lose the benefit of unemployment allowances should they be terminated by their new employer in the months following the signing of a new contract;
(c) a tripartite agreement: this is the easiest and the most secure method. It is concluded between the former employer, the new supplier and the employee. It should set out the conditions for the transfer (date of effect, seniority, applicable collective bargaining agreement etc.); it is neither considered as a resignation nor as a dismissal.

43.3.4.2 Outstanding wages

The parties will agree in the voluntary agreement upon each party's liabilities. Despite the terms of the agreement, the transferred employees will still be able to claim from their former employer for any liabilities due prior to the transfer of the employment contracts and from their new employer for any liabilities arising after the transfer outsourcing, even if they relate to the period before the transfer – in this case, the new employer will be entitled to claim a reimbursement from the former employer.

43.3.4.3 Consequences for collective benefits

The consequences with regard to collective benefits will be the same as those with regard to the transfer under a collective bargaining agreement (*see* 43.3.3.3).

43.4 Pensions issues

In principle, outsourcing, if it entails the application of article L. 1224-1, will not affect the employees' entitlement to basic old-age insurance benefits, which are paid by the French social security system. However, it may affect the employees' rights to benefits granted under collective bargaining agreements, the content of which will vary from company to company.

43.4.1 Supplementary pensions

Every employee in France must be affiliated to a supplementary pension scheme. There are two mandatory regimes:

(a) the "Arrco" regime: for employees and executives but only for a part of their remuneration ("A bracket");
(b) the "Agirc" regime: for B and C brackets of executives' remuneration.

Levels of annual gross remuneration are divided into three brackets:

(a) Remuneration A bracket involves the part of remuneration below the ceiling provided by the social security every year, that is, €34,308 for 2009;
(b) Remuneration B bracket involves the part of the remuneration between the above ceiling and four times that amount, that is, between €34,308 and €137,232;
(c) Remuneration C bracket involves the part of the remuneration B bracket and eight times the above ceiling, that is, between €137,232 and €274,464.

Agirc and Arrco pension schemes are provided by several institutions depending upon the location of the company and the nature of the company's activity. Every company created after 1 January 2002 must be affiliated to an Agirc institution and an Arrco institution from the same group of insurance coverage. A company's adherence to a supplementary pension institution (Agirc/Arrco) is, in principle, definitive. That is, the company may change the institution only in limited circumstances, such as in a merger, franchise etc.

It may happen that the pensions schemes provided by the former employer and the supplier or the two successive suppliers belong to different pensions institutions. However, outsourcing does not belong to the limited cases, where the change of institution is possible. If the supplier, after the transfer of employees, wants to move to the pension schemes with institutions from the same group, it can still make a request to the Agirc and Arrco, which will be approved under certain conditions (circular 2007-9-DRE).

43.4.2 Pension schemes

If the employee benefited from a collective pension fund (a "Perco") with his initial employer, two situations are possible:

(a) if the new supplier has set up a Perco, the employee may request the transfer of his entitlements to the Perco of his new employer;
(b) if the new supplier does not have a Perco, the employee may continue to pay into the Perco of his previous employer, but he will no longer benefit from the employer's contribution and will have to pay the related management costs (article R. 3332-13 of the Labour Code).

43.4.3 Savings schemes

Concerning savings schemes:

(a) if the new supplier has implemented a savings scheme the employee may request the transfer of his entitlements to the savings scheme of his new employer;

(b) if the new supplier does not have any savings scheme the employee's savings will be maintained in the scheme of his previous employer until the end of the inalienability period.

43.4.4 Self-funded pension scheme

What happens to self-funded pension schemes will depend upon how they were set up by the previous employer:

(a) if they were part of the employment contract, the scheme will be transferred with the employment contract if article L. 1224-1 of the Labour Code applies;
(b) if they were set up under a company-wide agreement or collective bargaining agreement, the rules above will apply relating to the collective status (*see* 43.2.1.10);
(c) if the agreement was concluded by referendum/unilateral commitment of the former employer/customer, it will still apply after the transfer to the employees concerned until the new supplier terminates it according to the applicable procedure set out under case law.

43.5 Contract law

43.5.1 Formation of contract under French law

According to article 1108 of the French Civil Code ("FCC"), there are four requirements essential for a valid agreement:

(a) the consent of the party who binds himself;
(b) capacity to contract;
(c) a definite object which forms the subject matter of the undertaking; and
(d) a lawful cause in the obligation.

43.5.1.1 Consent

A party's consent can be provided orally or in writing. Some contracts must be formalised in writing to be valid, such as sale contracts for real-estate properties.

According to article 1109 of the FCC, there is no valid consent, where the consent was given by error, or where it was extorted under duress or by deception. An agreement entered into by error, duress or deception is not voided by operation of law. Instead it gives rise to an action for annulment or rescission in accordance with article 1117 of the FCC.

43.5.1.2 Object

According to article 1126 of the FCC, a contract must have as its object a thing which one party binds himself to transfer, or which one party binds himself to do or not to do.

The thing must be determined at least as to its nature. The quantity of the thing may be uncertain, provided it can be determined (article 1129 FCC).

For sale contracts (for instance, within the framework of an outsourcing agreement, the sale of IT hardware by the client to the supplier), the price must be determined and stated by the parties, or it may be left to the determination of a third person (articles 1591 and 1592 of the FCC).

If the provisions of articles 1591 and 1592 of the FCC are not followed, other than where specifically excepted, the contract becomes automatically void by operation of law.

43.5.1.3 Cause

Article 1129 of the FCC provides that an obligation without cause or with a false cause, or with an unlawful cause, may not have any effect. A cause is unlawful where it is prohibited by law or where it is contrary to public morals or to public policy.

43.5.2 Effects of binding agreements under French law – remedies

According to article 1134 of the FCC, agreements lawfully entered into are considered like a law between the parties who have made them and oblige them to respect their terms and conditions. They may be revoked only by mutual consent or on grounds authorised by the law. They must be performed in good faith.

Article 1142 of the FCC provides that if a party to any agreement fails to comply with a contractual obligation to do or not to do something then the other party will be entitled to receive damages. The other party may also have the obligation performed itself, at the expense of the defaulting party (article 1144 of the FCC).

43.5.3 Interpretation of agreements

The FCC (articles 1156 to 1164) regulates the interpretation of agreements with the following rules:

(a) in agreements, one must endeavour to ascertain the common intention of the contracting parties, rather than paying attention to the literal meaning of the words in the agreement;
(b) where a clause has two meanings, the meaning shall be favoured that gives the clause effect over that which produces none;
(c) where a term has two possible meanings, the meaning which best suits the subject matter of the contract shall prevail;
(d) any ambiguity shall be interpreted with reference to the meanings in use in the region where the contract was made;
(e) in case of doubt, an agreement shall be construed against the beneficiary of the obligation and in the favour of the obligor.

43.5.4 Time-limitation/prescription rules

It should be noted that a new law dated 17 June 2008 has fundamentally modified the rules that apply to prescription issues.

Before 17 June 2008, all claims, *in rem* as well as *in personam*, were limited to a standard 30-year period which applied unless specific statutory exclusions stated otherwise.

Now, article 2224 of the FCC provides that all claims, *in rem* as well as *in personam*, are limited to a five-year period.

There are some exceptions:

(a) claims *in rem* regarding real-estate matters are still limited to the 30-year period (article 2227 of the FCC);
(b) claims for tort liability are barred after 10 years from the date of the damage or of its causation. Where the injury is caused by torture and acts of cruelty, assault or sexual aggression committed against a minor, the action in tort is barred after 20 years.
(c) the limitation period for real estate is 10 years when the purchaser has a valid title and acts in good faith and 30 years in all other cases.

Prescription may not be excluded in advance but a prescription that has accrued may be (article 2250 of the FCC).

According to the new provision in article 2254 of the FCC, parties can agree to either shorten or extend the prescription duration within the respective limit of one year and 10 years, except for payment claims regarding yearly or shorter instalment.

43.5.5 Types of contracts

Under French law, the outsourcing contract as described in Chapter 1 is classified as a contract for services or work (articles 1779 and following of the FCC).

A work contract is defined as a "contract relating to work, requested by one person of another without the latter being at the former's service, and most frequently for a fee"[4] or a contract in which "a person (the contractor) undertakes for a fee to independently carry out work to the benefit of another (the client), without acting as the latter's representative".[5]

A work contract differs from an employment contract because of the independence of the parties and the lack of subordination of the supplier to the client.

Although, in principle, the work contract places general obligations of due care on the supplier, in practice the parties are advised to include in the outsourcing contract detailed provisions setting out the supplier's performance obligations, including a definition of deliverables, deadlines, definition of performance indicators in the service level agreement, etc. as described in Chapters 1 to 10 of this Guide.

43.5.6 Liability and force majeure

43.5.6.1 Liability

In accordance with statutory contract law (article 1147 of the FCC) and in the absence of provisions to the contrary, the supplier will be liable for any damages resulting from the non-performance of all or a part of its contractual obligations.

4 J. Huet, *Les principaux contrats spéciaux*, L.G.D.J. 2e édition. N° 32102.
5 Malaurie, Aynès et Gautier, *Les contrats spéciaux*, Edition CUJAS, 14e édition, n° 708 s.

The damages will, as a rule, cover the loss which the other party has suffered and the profit of which it has been deprived, subject to force majeure.

Before the customer can file a liability claim against the supplier, the following conditions must be met:

(a) the loss must be a consequence of the breach of contract by the supplier;
(b) the customer must establish that it suffered a loss which is recoverable at law such as loss of earnings because of the delay in performance;
(c) the supplier must not be able to cite facts that justify the loss (such as that the breach of contract was caused by force majeure or by an act of the customer); and
(d) in the absence of facts that constitute justification, the customer must prove that the loss is caused by the supplier and that there is a causal link between the supplier's fault and the loss incurred.

In order to be recoverable, the loss must be (article 1151 of the FCC):

(a) certain (actual and not simply potential);
(b) direct (the loss must result directly from the fault); and
(c) personal (only the person that sustained the loss may seek reparation).

In principle, compensation is only available for a foreseeable loss (article 1150 of the FCC). Whether a loss is foreseeable is evaluated as on the day the contract was signed. Under French law it is possible to provide contractually for compensation for unforeseeable losses. Moreover, compensation for unforeseeable damage is available if the party committed the damage intentionally or as a result of gross misconduct.

43.5.6.2 Force majeure

A debtor is not required to compensate the other party for a loss arising as a result of an event of force majeure (article 1147 of the FCC).

Case law defines a force majeure event as one which was unforeseeable when the contract was signed and one which makes it impossible to perform the service in question. It is irrelevant whether or not this event is beyond the debtor's control. However, the parties are free to define the scope of force majeure in the contract.

A debtor who proves that non-performance resulted from force majeure will not need to make good the corresponding loss. If the force majeure event renders the performance of the contract impossible, the contract will automatically terminate.

The debtor will also be exonerated from having to offer compensation if the loss is ascribable to a fault of the creditor or the unforeseeable and unavoidable actions of a third party.

43.6 Limitations of liability

The principle of contractual freedom allows the parties to stipulate certain clauses that limit the liability of one or both of the parties in the case of non-performance of the contract, within the limits of good faith and provided that limitation clauses must not:

(a) exonerate the debtor in the case of non-performance owing to intentional breach[6] (fraud perpetrated against the other party) or gross misconduct;
(b) exclude liability for bodily injury suffered by the other party;
(c) exclude the essential obligation of the contract and exonerate the debtor in advance from liability for breach of its obligation;[7] or
(d) limit possible compensation to an absurdly low amount.

In general, the parties limit their liability by agreeing to a compensation ceiling and/or by limiting themselves to compensating "direct" damage only. It is essential that this notion of direct or indirect damage (loss of custom, damage to image, etc.) is defined in the contract.

43.7 Confidentiality, data protection

43.7.1 Confidentiality

There are no specific provisions under French law relating to the duty to safeguard confidential information.

The confidentiality obligation must be for a specific period. As a general rule, it is impossible to contract for a "perpetual" obligation. A perpetual obligation is null and void. Consequently, if there is a confidentiality obligation expressed to survive the outsourcing contract, the term of this obligation must be defined. A term of 5–10 years following the end of the contract is customary.

43.7.2 Data protection

The protection of personal data has been regulated in France since the Data Protection Act 78-17 of 6 January 1978 was passed. The Act was amended by Act 2004-801 of 6 August 2004 on the protection of natural persons with regard to the processing of personal data, in order to transpose Directive 95-46 of 24 October 1995.

Data Protection Act 78-17 of 6 January 1978 already contained the main principles of the Directive 95-46 of 24 October 1995. Consequently, the Act 2004-801 of 6 August 2004 consists mainly of amendments to the pre-existing French provisions on personal data protection, such as: a simplification of the declarative formalities (the preliminary control of the French Data Protection Authority – Commission Nationale Informatique et Libertés ("CNIL") – being henceforth limited to treatments presenting particular risks of infringement of rights and liberties), a consequent increase of the powers of intervention of the CNIL, and the strengthening of the rights of the data subject to their data.

The CNIL is the administrative authority in France responsible for implementing and controlling the application of obligations relating to personal data protection. It has powers to carry out

6 Article 1150 C.civ. "A debtor is liable only for damages which were foreseen or which could have been foreseen at the time of the contract, where it is not through his own intentional breach that the obligation is not fulfilled".
7 Cass. 1re civ., 28 avr. 1987 : D. 1988, jurispr. p1, note Ph. Delebecque.

investigations into all companies at any time or following a complaint by any person concerned. It may also impose sanctions, pursuant the Data Protection Act (no. 78-17 of 6 January 1978, as amended by the Act 2004-801 of 6 August 2004). The CNIL exercises *a priori* and *a posteriori* control of the automatic processing of personal data.

Its powers to carry out on-site inspections, inspect documents and take measures have been increased and precisely defined. It may order the blocking, erasure or destruction of data at risk.

Depending on the seriousness of the breaches committed, the CNIL may issue warnings likely to be made public, formal notices or injunctions to discontinue the treatment in question and it may impose fines of up to €300,000 for serious breaches of statutory data processing obligations. Since 2004, the CNIL has imposed penalties on several occasions. To date, the highest fine imposed by the CNIL is €40,000 (decision of 11 December 2007 CNIL/SIG).

43.7.3 Data protection issues in offshore outsourcing

Data protection is a particularly sensitive topic in the context of offshore outsourcing, where activities are often outsourced to countries that are not yet recognised as offering adequate protection within the meaning of the Data Protection Directive.

It should be noted that, under pressure from European supervisory authorities, these countries seem to be more and more aware of the need to conform to European data protection regulations. Morocco, for instance, recently passed a law that almost exactly reproduces the French regulations in this area.

43.8 Insolvency issues

43.8.1 General

Bankruptcy and winding-up proceedings in France were governed by the Commercial Code and the Decree of 27 December 1985 until 2006. Law no. 2005-845 of 26 July 2005 (effective as of 1 January 2006) and implementing decree no. 2005-1677 of 28 December 2005 have significantly modified this area, with the aim of simplifying and adapting existing procedures while improving the tools available to prevent French businesses from being wound up. A new procedure, called the safeguard procedure (*procédure de sauvegarde*), has been embodied in the Commercial Code and was inspired, to a certain degree, by the US Chapter 11 proceedings.

The order 2008-1345 of 18 December 2008 (effective as of 15 February 2009) has modified the rules to improve the mechanism of the safeguard procedure and to improve the procedure of judicial winding up.

Cross-border aspects of bankruptcy in France should be reviewed taking into account EC Regulation no. 1346/2000 of 29 May 2000 on insolvency proceedings and the French principles applicable to international private law and case law.

French law provides for voluntary arrangements with creditors, generally before the bankruptcy stage is reached, such as the *mandat ad hoc* (counselling proceedings) or the conciliation (mediation proceedings). A certain overlap exists between the bankruptcy prevention mechanisms and the judicial procedures.

The main objectives of bankruptcy proceedings under French law are, in order of priority:

(a) to preserve the activities of distressed companies and to enhance prospects for recovery;
(b) to save jobs; and
(c) to pay creditors.

From a foreign investment perspective, the importance given in France to the preservation of jobs (and consequently, the unavoidable costs of preserving them) is considered particularly disadvantageous to possible rescue plans.

The traditional bankruptcy proceedings under French law are receivership (*redressement judiciaire*) and judicial winding up (*liquidation judiciaire*).

43.8.2 Commencement of proceedings

When a French company reaches the stage where it is unable to meet its liabilities with available (cash or cash equivalent) assets (known as *cessation de paiements*), its representative must file a petition with the local Commercial Court within 45 days of the *cessation de paiements* (if it has not first opted for the conciliation proceedings). The court must then decide either:

(a) to place the distressed company in receivership (*redressement judiciaire*) (for example, if the company has reached the stage of *cessation de paiements* while under the conciliation scheme); or
(b) to liquidate it immediately (*liquidation judiciaire*) if there is no possibility of recovery or if it has ceased its activities.

The court may also seize the assets of all related companies at any moment, should it be proven that the defaulting company was created to defraud creditors or that the assets of the companies within a group (including those of the distressed French company) are intermingled.

43.8.3 Professional bodies

Upon commencement of proceedings, the court appoints the following persons.

In the event of receivership:

(a) A receiver who will be responsible for:
    (i) temporarily assisting the management of the company while the debtor remains in possession and continues to manage the company in person; and
    (ii) preparing a recovery plan.
(b) A creditors' representative who will represent the creditors and record and verify their claims.

In the event of a winding up:

(a) a liquidator, generally the same person as the receiver;
(b) the creditors' representative, who will be vested with the power to sell the assets and apportion the funds between creditors; and
(c) a Judge to handle the proceedings (the Judge Commissaire).

43.8.4 Creditors

Secured and unsecured creditors whose claims existed before the company was placed in receivership or liquidation proceedings by the court ("pre-bankruptcy creditors") must file their claims with the creditors' representative within two months of publication of the court's opening judgment in a legal gazette known as the "BODACC".

43.8.5 Insolvency solutions

43.8.5.1 Recovery plan

Since 1 January 2006, the aim of receivership has been solely the continuity of the business through a recovery plan (*plan de continuation*) with its current management. Creditors may be required under the plan to defer payment of their claims for a maximum period of 10 years.

43.8.5.2 Liquidation

Since 1 January 2006, the total or partial sale of the business is one of the objectives of the judicial winding-up proceedings in cases where the debtor himself is no longer capable of managing the business towards recovery (*see* also Part III, Acquisition of a Bankrupt Company).

43.8.6 Termination rights

In practice, to protect a party from the insolvency of the other party, formal clauses are generally inserted into the contract. Such clauses stipulate that if insolvency proceedings are initiated against one party, the other party may terminate the contract. They may even provide for the automatic cancellation of the contract.

However, from a legal point of view, both of these types of clause are null and void on the grounds that they are against public policy.[8]

Therefore, the customer may want to insert an automatic termination clause in the outsourcing agreement which comes into effect on the occurrence of an insolvency event (such as non-performance) prior to the commencement of the collective proceedings, as this clause will not be void as being in breach of public policy.

In the absence of a valid automatic termination clause in the outsourcing agreement, a party to a contract is obliged to maintain contractual relations with the other party even if non-performance occurs before insolvency proceedings are commenced.

8 CA Paris, 21 mars 1997, D. Aff. 1997, p702.

If the contract is in progress, the party who has entered into a contract with the party involved in insolvency proceedings may formally ask the receiver to make a pronouncement on the continuation of the contract. In that case the receiver has one month (in some cases the judge in charge of the procedure may grant him an extra month) in which to make his decision. If no reply is given after that time, the contract is considered terminated.

If the receiver decides to continue with the contract, the principle of contract enforceability applies: the contract is continued with the same terms, conditions and sanctions. The receiver must ensure that the company in receivership complies with its obligations, as promised.

43.9 Financial services regulation

Directives 2004/39/EC and 2006/73/EC on markets in financial instruments were transposed into French law by order 2007-544 of 12 April 2007, Conseil d'Etat decree 2007-901 of 15 May 2007, decree 2007-304 of 15 May 2007 and the decision of 15 May 2007 approving the modification of the general regulations of the financial markets authority (*Autorité des Marchés Financiers* ("AMF")).

The French government and the AMF have tried to remain as faithful as possible to the Directives when transposing them, avoiding the addition of specific domestic rules. Whenever possible, the same terminology as in the Directives was used.

The first paragraph of article 13.5 of Directive 2004/39 was transposed to article L. 533-10-4 and 5 of the Monetary and Financial Code. However, the rest of article 13.5 and all of the provisions of the Directives concerning outsourcing were transposed to subsection 5 of the AMF General Regulations, whose articles almost exactly reproduce the wording of the articles of Directives 2004/39/EC and 2006/73/EC.

The AMF General Regulations only apply to asset management companies. In the case of investment suppliers that are not asset management companies, outsourcing terms and conditions are set out in Chapter II of Regulation 97-02 of the *Comité de la réglementation bancaire et financière* ("CRBF"), the wording of which is very close to that of the AMF General Regulations.

43.10 Public Procurement Directives

Decree 2006-975 of 10 August 2005 established the new Public Procurement Contracts Code, which adopted into French law Directive 2004/18/EC on the coordination of procedures for the award of public works contracts, public supply contracts and public service contracts. The procedure for the award of public procurement contracts defined in Directive 2004/18/EC was reproduced in the Public Procurement Contracts Code.

The Public Procurement Contracts Code applies to contracts concluded with all public entities with the exception of state commercial or industrial public institutions.

The provisions of Directive 2004/18/EC have led to modifications in other codes. Order 2005-645 of 6 June 2005 amended the Local and Regional Collectivity Code in order to harmonise the latter with the provisions of Directive 2004/18/EC.

Directive 2004/18/EC also led to the publication of order 2005-649 of 6 June 2005 on contracts concluded with certain private or public persons not subject to the Public Procurement Contracts Code.

Order 2004-559 of 17 June 2004 introduced "*contrats de partenariat*" (the French equivalent of PFI projects) which it defines as:

> "an administrative contract by which the State or a public institution of the State confers on a third party, for a period determined in accordance with the investment amortisation term or the chosen financing terms and conditions, a global mission the purpose of which is the financing, construction or conversion, maintenance, servicing, operation or management of works, equipment, or intangible assets necessary for the public service."

The *contrat de partenariat* is not a public contract within the meaning of the Public Procurement Contracts Code. The provisions of the Public Procurement Contracts Code (*see* public procurement contracts governed by Directive 2004/18/EC) do not apply to it. However, in order to reinforce the legal security of this type of contract, order 2004-559 of 17 June 2004 stipulates that all of the EU rules on the award of public contracts apply to these contracts.

43.11 Utilities Directive

Directive 2004/17/EC was transposed into French law by order 2005-649 of 6 June 2005 and decree 2005-1308 of 20 October 2005 to form the second part of the Public Procurement Contracts Code.

The transposition is only partial, since it only concerns the contracting authorities specified in article 2 of the Public Procurement Contracts Code (i.e. the state and its public institutions other than those having a commercial and industrial character and regional authorities and local public authorities) if they fall within the scope of the Directive. In fact, the notion of contracting entities as per the Public Procurement Contracts Code is not exactly the same as that used in Directive 2004/17/EC, which specifies that contracting entities are public corporations or private organisations that operate utilities networks.

The Public Procurement Contracts Code only applies to the state and its public institutions, whereas Directive 2004/17/EC applies to a wide range of entities: the state, regional or local authorities, bodies governed by public law, associations formed by one or several such authorities or one or several of such bodies governed by public law. Yet in an annex, it also refers to a list of private companies that operate utilities networks including EDF and GDF.

43.12 Competition law

43.12.1 Merger control

43.12.1.1 Application to outsourcing agreements

Outsourcing agreements may lead to the creation of a concentration within the meaning of the merger rules in several circumstances:

(a) if the agreement causes a transfer of assets and/or employees likely to be considered as being a part of a company, that is, transfer of elements sufficient to have an economic activity and a market presence (providing a service for the customer and also for third parties);
(b) if the agreement involves the creation of a joint venture which performs all of the functions of an autonomous economic entity on a lasting basis;
(c) if the agreement involves the control of the management and financial resources of the contracting party, over the long term;
(d) in exceptional circumstances, if the agreement creates an economic dependency.

Outsourcing agreements do not often lead to a concentration, as they do not often lead to one of the circumstances above.

However, French authorities have had the opportunity to examine transactions in connection with outsourcing activities on few occasions.[9] In particular, a number of companies, which internally manufactured the products that they sold under their trademarks, decided to outsource the manufacture of their products. As a consequence, they sold their production assets (production site, employees dedicated to the production activity) to a third company, and entered into an outsourcing agreement appointing the latter to meet their needs.

It shall be noted that French authorities carry out analysis similar to that undertaken by the European Commission for the implementation of EC merger rules (*see* Chapter 29) in order to determine whether outsourcing agreements may lead to a concentration under French merger rules.

43.12.1.2 Thresholds

An acquisition, a merger, the setting up of a joint venture or any other lasting change of control over a company, may fall within the scope of the EU or the French merger control legislation if the applicable thresholds are met.

Pursuant to French merger rules set out in articles L. 430-1 to L. 430-10 of the Commercial Code, the acquisition of a company by another must be notified and authorised by the Competition Authority (that replaces the Ministry of Economy in this function as from March 2009), when it meets all three of the following conditions:

(a) the combined aggregate worldwide turnover, taxes excluded, of all the concerned undertakings exceeds €150 million;
(b) the aggregate turnover, taxes excluded, carried out in France by at least two of the undertakings concerned exceeds €50 million; and
(c) the concentration does not fall within the scope of the EC Merger Control Regulation.

9 Letter of the Ministry of the Economy on 29 December 2003 Famar/Aventis: acquisition of a production site of Aventis group, by a pharmaceutical group (Famar/Marinopulos) which the activity consists in offering outsourcing services to pharmaceutical and cosmetic companies (development of products, logistics, production packaging and distribution of products). Letter of the Ministry of the economy on 12 April 2003, case C2006-23 Favera/ Pfizer: acquisition by Favera of assets from Pfizer (2 production sites); the transfer of assets came with an outsourcing agreement between the parties according to which Favera should manufacture drugs on Pfizer's behalf.

43.12.1.3 Duty to notify or obtain approval

A concentration can be subject either:

(a) to a prior notification to, and approval by, the European Commission, if the EC Merger Control Regulation applies (i.e. if the EU thresholds are met); or
(b) to a prior approval by the French government if the EC Merger Control Regulation does not apply *and* the French thresholds are met.

Neither the size of the transaction nor its impact on competition are taken into account while analysing the obligation to notify. This becomes relevant only in the assessment of the situation once notified. The notification obligation is only triggered by the turnover thresholds of the companies involved in the transaction. Thus, even a transaction, which has no impact on competition, must be notified if the turnover of the companies involved meets the above conditions.

If the conditions are met, the Competition Authority must be notified of the transaction, which may not be implemented prior to clearance.

It is possible to notify an intended transaction, i.e. before the conclusion of the purchase agreement provided that a letter of intent has been signed or a memorandum of understanding (*accord de principe*) has been entered into.

43.12.1.4 Duty of the Competition Authority to respond

The Competition Authority must examine the operation within five to eight weeks after the receipt of the complete notification.

Where the Competition Authority has not rendered any decision within five weeks (or possibly eight weeks if commitments are to be made), the concentration is deemed authorised.

At the end of the period, the Competition Authority may find that the operation is authorised subject to, as the case may be, compliance with the commitments they have entered into.

When they consider that the operation is likely to affect competition and that the commitments are not a sufficient remedy, the Competition Authority will decide to examine more deeply the criteria and the consequences of the operation. The Competition Authority may either authorise the concentration, with or without commitments, or prohibit the concentration.

43.12.1.5 Fines

Fines may be imposed where:

(a) the concentration is put into effect without notification;
(b) the concentration is put into effect before a decision is received from the Competition Authority; and
(c) the notification is not complete or the parties supply incorrect information.

The Competition Authority may also impose periodic penalty payments on the parties to compel them to notify unless they restore the *status quo ante*.

43.12.2 Prohibited anti-competitive agreements

Article L. 420-1 of the French Commercial Code prohibits agreements that have the object or effect of preventing, restructuring or distorting competition in the market. Just as under EU competition law, infringements to those rules may lead the French competition authorities to impose on the companies involved fines of up to 10 per cent of the global turnover of the group to which the company concerned belongs. In case of serious infringements (in particular market shares, bid-rigging, concerted bids), a criminal procedure may follow and lead to penalties of up to €75,000 and four years' imprisonment for any individual having a personal, fraudulent and determining part in the prohibited practice.

Analysis under French competition rules of the exclusivity and non-competition provisions that outsourcing agreements may include is similar to that undertaken by the EU competition authorities (*see* Chapter 29).

43.13 Other relevant laws and best practice

It should be noted that various professional standards exist in France in relation to outsourcing. These standards are not compulsory, but constitute good practice guides. The following standards may be relevant for outsourcing agreements:

(a) ISO 9000 December 2000 Quality Management Systems; Fundamentals and Vocabulary;
(b) ISO 9001 December 2001 Quality Management Systems; Requirements;
(c) AFNOR Z67-801-1 Facilities Management Specifications;
(d) AFNOR Z67-801-2 Facilities Management Implementation of Services;
(e) Security Techniques ISO 27001 (Information Security Management Systems) and ISO 27002;
(f) Charter for the use of the knowledge base systems of the *Association Française de l'Audit et du Conseil Informatique* (French audit and information technology consulting association ("AFAI"));
(g) Charte Cigref-Syntec Informatique (Infogérance et TMA) (facilities management and third-party applications maintenance).

43.14 Summary

In France, outsourcing is viewed as a strategic means of improving the flexibility of a company.

However, the legal constraints upon outsourcing are far from negligible, particularly those relating to labour law and data protection. Notably, the various employment implications of outsourcing may be a source of complexity and are sometimes considered as an obstacle to outsourcing. Nevertheless, these can be managed provided that both parties are aware of all relevant employment issues and consider them early on in the process. It is particularly important to inform the employees, who will be transferred, early enough in order to avoid some blocking situations (e.g. with protected employees) and to facilitate the negotiation of the collective benefits which will apply to them.

Chapter 44

Netherlands

Serge Zwanen
Partner
Loyens & Loeff N.V.

44.1 Outline

Parts 1 to 11 of this Guide describe the key business issues relevant for outsourcing agreements. They also describe the key legal issues under English law. This chapter describes the specific legal and business issues which affect outsourcing arrangements in the Netherlands.

44.2 Background to outsourcing in the Netherlands[1]

44.2.1 History of outsourcing

Although not always known by that name, outsourcing has been practised in the Netherlands since the 1980s. Already at that time many customers outsourced in-house services (such as cleaning, catering and IT services) to suppliers.

However, outsourcing only expanded in the Netherlands around the millennium, following the trends which were developing in the US and the UK. Although the market expected this growth, outsourcing in the Netherlands has not yet developed into the phenomenon that it is in the US and the UK. There are several reasons for this, including:

(a) there are fewer financial institutions in the Netherlands;
(b) customers have been reluctant to outsource activities; and
(c) the public sector in the Netherlands has not embraced outsourcing yet.

Since 2006, there has been a slight "turn around" in outsourcing deals as customers unwind their outsourcing transactions in order to bring them back in-house. The decision to bring services back in-house has been motivated by various factors including:

1 Companies like Gartner and Morgan Chambers regularly publish research reports on outsourcing developments in the Netherlands. For more information *see* the websites of these companies (www.gartner.com and www.morgan-chambers.com).

(a) the failure to achieve anticipated cost savings;
(b) the need for more contract management time (and thus costs) in managing outsourcing arrangements than expected; and
(c) poor performance by the supplier.

Nevertheless, research companies like Morgan Chambers still believe that outsourcing is here to stay and will continue to grow in the Netherlands. It may well be that the credit crunch will result in a significant growth in outsourcing transactions, as it will force customers to cut costs and to focus on their core business.

44.2.2 Reasons for outsourcing

Cost cutting is still one of the most important drivers for outsourcing transactions in the Netherlands. Other important reasons for customers in the Netherlands to outsource services are to:

(a) focus on core business;
(b) improve their services; and
(c) gain access to new technology and products.

44.2.3 Industry sectors affected by outsourcing

Outsourcing transactions in the Netherlands occur in many types of industries, but there has been growth in outsourcing particularly in the financial services, the utilities and the telecoms industries. The largest outsourcing transactions have taken place in the financial services sector. As already mentioned, the Dutch public sector has been hesitant to outsource services to a supplier.

44.2.4 Near-shore and offshore outsourcing

Outsourcing transactions in the Netherlands include near-shore transactions to, for instance Hungary, the Czech Republic and Poland. Customers in the Netherlands also offshore their services to India and China.

44.3 People issues – ARD

44.3.1 Background

In general, the same people issues will be relevant for outsourcing projects in the Netherlands as in the UK, as described in Chapter 27. This should come as no surprise since both TUPE and the Dutch equivalent "NL TUPE" are a result of the implementation of the EU Directive, ARD.

In the Netherlands, ARD was originally implemented in 1981 in articles 7:662–7:667 of the Dutch Civil Code ("DCC"). These provisions were amended in 2002 when, amongst other changes, civil servants were excluded from NL TUPE. NL TUPE is also included in article 14a of the Collective Labour Agreement Act and article 2a of the Collective Labour Agreements Declaration of Generally Binding and Non-Binding Status Act, which states that collective labour agreements will be obligatory in certain sectors or industries.

44.3.2 Application of NL TUPE

As in the UK, NL TUPE includes rules governing employees in the event of a transfer, in whole or in part, of an identifiable economic business or undertaking. Unlike in the UK, there is no express reference in NL TUPE to the application of NL TUPE to contracting out, contracting in and re-tendering. NL TUPE will apply in general to contracting out and contracting in situations if and insofar as the contracting out or contracting in will involve a transfer, in whole or in part, of an identifiable economic business or undertaking. Whether or not "an identifiable economic business" is transferred will be decided by the actual facts and circumstances at hand. In practice, outsourcing transactions will usually meet the criteria for "a transfer of an identifiable economic business" and, as a consequence, NL TUPE will be applicable to most outsourcing transactions.

In a recent case, the "Heineken case", the applicability of NL TUPE was challenged. The case was brought in 2006 and, at the time of writing, was pending. In this instance, the facts were that catering staff were formally employed by a Heineken personnel entity. That Heineken entity seconded these catering staff to other Heineken companies. When a Heineken company, which made use of the seconded catering staff, decided to outsource its catering activities to a supplier, that Heineken company claimed that NL TUPE did not apply since the catering staff involved were not formally employed by that Heineken company. The trade unions challenged this view. In a summary proceeding, the court initially shared the view of Heineken. However, the District Court took the view that NL TUPE applied to this transaction. This decision was subsequently appealed. At the time of writing, the outcome of this appeal was pending since the Court of Appeal referred the case to the ECJ for consideration of the question of how ADR must be applied in the relevant situation.

44.3.3 Effect of NL TUPE - employees transfer

As in TUPE, NL TUPE means that employees employed by a customer will be automatically transferred to the supplier upon the transfer of the services to the supplier.

44.3.4 Effect of NL TUPE - rights, powers, duties and liabilities transfer

Chapter 27 generally applies to the Netherlands as well as the UK with regard to the transfer of rights. However, pension scheme rights will not automatically transfer. For pensions issues, refer to 44.4 below.

Unlike in the UK, NL TUPE provides that a transferred employee will have one year from the date of the transfer to seek compensation for liabilities accrued prior to the transfer from both the supplier and the customer.

44.3.5 Effect of NL TUPE - dismissals automatically unfair

With regard to dismissals relating to the transfer of business, NL TUPE is basically the same as TUPE. In the event of such a dismissal, an employee in the Netherlands will have two months to challenge the validity of the dismissal.

44.3.6 Effect of NL TUPE - duty to consult

Under the Works Council Act, companies which employ more than 50 people are obliged to install a works council. The works council represents the interests of employees and must be informed by or consulted by the management board in relation to certain material decisions. If an outsourcing transaction falls within the scope of NL TUPE, the works councils of both the customer and the supplier, if any, must be consulted prior to the envisaged transaction. If no works council is in place, individual employees must be informed (NL TUPE article 7:665a DCC).

If trade unions have been established in the industry in which the outsourcing transaction takes place, those trade unions must be informed of the anticipated transaction. If a works council is in place as well, the works council and the applicable trade unions will usually combine forces to enable the works council to provide its advice to the management board on the envisaged transaction.

Unlike in the UK (*see* Chapter 27) there are no remedies under Dutch law for employees if a customer or supplier does not meet its consultation duties. However, if the works council consultation is late or non-existent, it may result in a delay because the works council will have the right to challenge the transaction before the Dutch courts.

44.4 Pensions issues

44.4.1 Transfer of pension commitments in the Netherlands

Dutch law provides for far-reaching consequences relating to the transfer of pension commitments in the event of a transfer of a business. The consequences for pension commitments are outlined below. It is assumed that the pension commitments are insured either with a company pension fund or with an insurance company and that no mandatory industry-wide pension fund is applicable.

44.4.2 Transfer of pension commitments

Until 2002, Dutch law stated simply that the pension commitments granted by the customer did not transfer by law to the supplier. As a result, the supplier was not obliged to continue offering the pension scheme provided by the customer.

However, on 1 July 2002 new regulations were implemented regarding pension commitments in the event of a transfer of a business. These new regulations make a distinction between three situations which might exist before the transfer of a business:

(a) the customer provides a pension scheme but the supplier does not provide a pension scheme;

(b) the customer does not provide a pension scheme but the supplier does provide a pension scheme to its current employees;

(c) both customer and supplier provide a pension scheme.

The implications of these distinctions are described below.

In the situation described at point (a) above, the supplier will be obliged to continue the pension commitment provided by the customer after the transfer. The supplier must take into account the years of service accumulated by the transferred employees with the customer. The supplier may be liable to pay for back-service for prior years of service.

The supplier should be aware that its current employees may have the right to claim participation in the same pension scheme as the transferred employees. The fact that the supplier is obliged to continue the pension commitment does not mean that any future alteration of the pension commitment/pension scheme is excluded. As long as the supplier obtains the consent of the employees (and their representatives) alteration is possible.

In the situation described at point (b) above, the new regulations stipulate that the supplier will be obliged to provide its pension scheme to the transferred employees. However, the pension commitments will only become effective as of the date of transfer and will not include the employees' previous years of service with the customer.

In the situation described at point (c) above, in the event that both customer and supplier provide a pension scheme, the pension commitments provided by the customer will be transferred to the supplier (as under situation (a)) *unless* the supplier decides to grant the transferred employees the same pension rights as it grants its other employees. In other words, the supplier will have a choice between the two pension schemes. It is acknowledged that the pension scheme of the supplier might be less favourable than the pension scheme of the customer. However, the Dutch law accepts this possibility. This situation must be the subject of discussion with the employees and their representatives.

44.4.3 Insurance for pension commitments and transfer

According to the Dutch Pension Act, an employee is obliged to insure a pension commitment with either an insurance company or a company pension fund (or an industry-wide pension fund).

In the event of the transfer of a business which falls within the scope of NL TUPE, the insurance rights against the insurance company or pension fund will not transfer automatically. A contract between an insurance company and the customer will only transfer to the supplier with the consent of the insurance company. If the customer is no longer affiliated to the group of companies for whom the company pension fund has been established, the company pension fund may decide that the group of employees who are employed with the supplier can no longer participate in the fund as of the date of transfer or from a certain period after this date. As a consequence, the supplier can be confronted with a situation that, on the one hand, it is obliged to continue providing the pension commitment from the customer but, on the other hand, the supplier must look for a new pension insurer (insurance company or pension fund) or might have to accept new (and possibly more expensive) conditions.

44.5 Contract law

44.5.1 Liability and risk

Chapter 30 describes various ways of dealing with liability arising under outsourcing agreements governed by UK law. In the Netherlands, the most common way of dealing with legal liability is for the supplier to be liable for breach of contract except when its failure is due to a force majeure event (*see* 30.1.1 point (a)).

44.5.2 Force majeure

Article 6:75 Dutch Civil Code states that a breach cannot be attributed to a party if that breach is not caused by its fault nor is for the account of that party based on the law, a legal act or generally accepted principles. With this general wording "force majeure" is incorporated in the Dutch Civil Code.

Which events are deemed to be force majeure events cannot be derived from the above-mentioned wording of article 6:75 Dutch Civil Code. Which events the parties deem to be force majeure events is therefore a matter for negotiation between the parties. In practice, parties often define what they consider to be a force majeure event as well as what they do not consider to amount to a force majeure event.

If a force majeure event occurs, under Dutch law a party will not be forced to perform its obligations under the contract and therefore will not be liable for any damages the other party might suffer. Usually, outsourcing agreements contain a clause which entitles a party, faced with another party invoking force majeure, to terminate the contract if the force majeure event is not over within a certain period of time. 30 to 90 days is generally accepted as a fair period of time. Termination on this basis will then trigger a negotiated exit clause.

Parties should consider the impact of any force majeure event on their respective businesses, as described in Chapter 30 at 30.5 and 30.7. They should address which risks caused by a force majeure event might be mitigated. Which party should manage which specific risks will depend upon the specific circumstances and no general guidance can be given.

44.5.3 Liability for damages if one party is unable to invoke force majeure

Under Dutch law, a party which has not fulfilled its contractual obligations will in principle be liable for all damages suffered by the other party. Articles 6:95 and 6:96 Dutch Civil Code make clear that damages include losses suffered and loss of profits but also:

(a) reasonable costs to prevent or limit damages;
(b) reasonable costs to determine liability and damages; and
(c) reasonable costs made to claim damages outside of court. (This includes reasonable lawyers' costs for advice and writing letters to the party which is in breach.)

Note that the above is not an exhaustive list.

The rule that a party has a general obligation to mitigate its damages provides a qualification to the entitlement for damages. A further qualification is provided by the rule that it is only possible to claim damages which have a close connection with the event which caused the other party's liability (article 6:98 Dutch Civil Code).

44.5.4 Indemnity

Indemnities as described in 30.14 are also common in outsourcing contracts in the Netherlands. Indemnities are often given to cover matters like breaches of intellectual property rights and liabilities for employees who are transferring from the customer to the supplier. Suppliers generally want to limit their liability under indemnities in the same way that they want to cap their general liability to the customer (*see* 44.6). However, in negotiations, the supplier generally accepts that specific indemnities are not capped or at least have a different (higher) cap than the liability cap for general liability.

44.6 Limitations of liability

44.6.1 Limiting liability

As in the UK, parties generally agree to limit their liability under outsourcing agreements. Since this is a matter for negotiation, it is difficult to generalise about what is usually agreed by parties. The possible limitations described in Chapter 31 are also used in Dutch outsourcing agreements and the relevant factors for deciding the cap, as described in Chapter 31, also apply.

Parties negotiating outsourcing contracts, and especially customers, should be aware of the fact that contracts frequently provide for a difference between liability for direct damages and liability for indirect damages. This difference is mostly used to exclude liability for indirect damages. Indirect damages are sometimes referred to as consequential damages.

Although this distinction is widely accepted in practice, parties should be aware that under Dutch law the terms "direct damage", "indirect damage" and "consequential damage" have no legal meaning. As noted above, a party suffering damages will in general be able to claim all kinds of damages (articles 6:95 and 6:96 Dutch Civil Code). If the parties want to use these terms, they will need to clearly define what they consider to be direct damages or indirect/consequential damages (*see* Chapter 31).

In relation to limiting liability, it is also to be noted that, with a few specific qualifications, it is not possible to exclude liability for willful intent and/or gross negligence.[2]

44.6.2 Enforceability

If liability clauses are negotiated by the parties, then they will usually be enforceable in the form agreed. The Dutch courts have the ability to strike down clauses which conflict with the

2 In Dutch: "*opzet en grove schuld*".

principles of "reasonableness and fairness" laid down in the Dutch Civil Code (6:248 Dutch Civil Code). However, a Dutch court will not usually rely upon these principles to overturn a negotiated liability clause, especially not if the contract (and thus the liability clause) have been negotiated by parties who have been advised by legal counsel.

44.6.3 Limitation of liability by the customer

Although in practice discussions regarding the limitation of liability focus on limitations of the supplier's liability, the customer should consider carefully whether it also needs the benefit of a limitation of liability clause.

44.7 Data protection

44.7.1 General

In the Netherlands, the Data Protection Directive was implemented by the Dutch Data Protection Act (Wet bescherming persoonsgegevens; "the Act"). Since the Act is the implementing tool for the Data Protection Directive, Dutch law on data protection resembles UK law (as described in Chapter 32) to a large extent.

The Dutch supervisory authority is the Dutch Data Protection Authority (College bescherming persoonsgegevens; "DDPA"), which is an independent public body.

The Act applies to the processing of personal data in the course of business by entities which are established or have an establishment in the Netherlands.

44.7.2 Processing data

According to the Act, the processing of personal data has to be prudent, proportional and in accordance with all laws and regulations. Furthermore, the processing of personal data must be necessary for one or more specific and legitimate purposes. In general, personal data may only be processed if such processing can be based on one of the grounds set forth in the Act. Without a justification based on one of these grounds, such processing is prohibited. For some types of personal data (such as personal data concerning a person's health) there is a specific prohibition on processing this data, unless one of the grounds applies.

One of the grounds for justification is the unambiguous consent of the data subject (*betrokkene*). The DDPA is of the opinion that, where data processing is based on consent, such consent has to be unambiguous and freely given (informed consent). In this respect, it is debatable whether "consent" can be given or assumed in an employer–employee relationship, which by its nature harbours an inequality of authority. In addition to that, it is important to note that a data subject may withdraw his consent at any time. Furthermore, the DDPA is of the opinion that consent is not unambiguous, freely given and informed when it is given only by agreeing to general terms and conditions.

A data controller is under an obligation to inform the data subject of its identity and the purpose of the data processing unless the data subject is already acquainted with this information.

Furthermore, a data controller has to notify the DDPA of the processing of personal data and the purpose unless such notification is exempted under the Exemption Decree (Vrijstellingsbesluit Wbp).

44.7.3 Transfer of data outside the EEA

The Act determines that personal data may only be transferred to a country outside the EEA if that third country has a "suitable level of protection". However, a transfer of personal data to a country without a "suitable level of protection" may take place on certain limited grounds. These grounds are:

(a) the data subject has given its unambiguous consent for such transfer;
(b) such transfer is necessary in the execution of an agreement to which the data subject is a party or for precontractual measures;
(c) such transfer is necessary in the conclusion or execution of an agreement to which the data subject is not a party, but in which it has an interest.
(d) such transfer is necessary to uphold heavy-weighing general interests or for the establishment, exercise or defence in law of any right;
(e) the transfer is necessary for upholding the vital interests of the data subject; or
(f) the transfer is made from a public register set up by law that is open to general consultation (e.g. a trade register or land register).

These grounds are interpreted restrictively.

If none of the grounds for exemption apply, the Act also allows for the provision of a permit for the transfer of data issued by the Minister of Justice. The DDPA advises the Minister of Justice in this respect.

44.7.4 Violation of the Dutch Data Protection Act

In the event of a violation of the Act, the DDPA has the authority to impose an administrative fine. In addition, the DDPA is empowered to impose an order for periodic penalty payments or to force the data controller to cease its violation of the Act. Some violations (e.g. violation of the obligation to notify the DDPA of the processing of personal data) are considered criminal offences. Furthermore, the data controller may be liable for the damages incurred by a data subject as a result of any violation of the Act. At the request of a data subject, the civil courts can order a data controller to cease certain activities which violate the Act. In spite of the above remedies, damage to reputation is considered the greatest risk associated with violating the Act.

44.7.5 Works Councils Act

Under the Dutch Works Councils Act (Wet op de ondernemingsraden), an employer must request prior approval from the works council for decisions proposed concerning the introduction, modification or withdrawal of certain regulations within the company affecting the position of employees (e.g. the decision to install cameras within the company). It is noteworthy that the Works Councils Act states that the works council has the right of approval regarding regulations governing the registration, handling of and the protection of the personal details of the company's employees.

44.8 Insolvency issues

There are two main types of insolvency proceedings under Dutch law: bankruptcy proceedings (*faillissement*) and suspension of payments proceedings (*surseance van betaling*). Both types are governed by the Dutch Bankruptcy Code (Faillissementswet) and are described below. Generally, the aim of bankruptcy proceedings is the liquidation of the debtor's assets for the benefit of the creditors, whereas a suspension of payments primarily serves to provide the debtor with temporary relief against creditors pressing for payment with a view to assisting the continuity of its business.

44.8.1 Bankruptcy

44.8.1.1 Criteria for and adjudication of bankruptcy

Under the Dutch Bankruptcy Code, a debtor (whether an individual or a company) who has ceased to pay his creditors may be declared bankrupt by a court order obtained at its application or at the request of one or more of its creditors. The basis for a bankruptcy ruling is that the debtor has at least two creditors (one of them being the filing creditor if the filing is involuntary) and that at least one of the two debts is currently due and payable. In addition, the bankruptcy order may, in exceptional cases, be issued at the request of the public prosecutor for reasons of public interest. Dutch insolvency law does not recognise the concept of "balance sheet insolvency" as exists in other jurisdictions; instead the test is whether a debtor has ceased to pay.

The court will declare the debtor bankrupt when it has been given proof that the debtor has ceased to pay his debts, or if the declaration was requested by a creditor, when shown the existence of his claim.

44.8.1.2 Consequences of bankruptcy and the bankruptcy trustee

At the time the bankruptcy is declared, a trustee (curator) and a bankruptcy judge (*rechter commissaris*), whose main task is to supervise the actions of the trustee, are appointed by the court.

The most important effect of bankruptcy is that the debtor loses the right to dispose of and control its assets; instead, control is in the hands of the trustee. The bankruptcy estate includes the entire estate of the debtor at the time of the declaration of bankruptcy as well as any assets that the debtor acquires during the bankruptcy. All attachments (*beslagen*) made by specific creditors against the debtor's assets are automatically lifted after a bankruptcy. In principle, secured creditors (such as mortgage holders) are not affected by a bankruptcy.

The primary task of the trustee is to liquidate the assets of the debtor in order to (partially) satisfy its creditors. Creditors are invited to file their claims with the trustee. Claims will then be paid in order of preference. Unless all creditors can be fully satisfied, or a composition plan (*akkoord*) is put in place, as a result of the bankruptcy the debtor company will cease to exist.

44.8.2 Suspension of payments

44.8.2.1 Criteria for suspension of payments

Pursuant to the Dutch Bankruptcy Code, a debtor which foresees that it will be unable to continue to pay its debts may apply for a suspension of payments. Suspension of payments can also be requested by a debtor which foresees that it will not be able to pay off debts which will become payable in the future.

Note that only the debtor can file for a suspension of payments and it is not possible for creditors or other third parties to request a suspension of payments for the company.

44.8.2.2 Consequences of suspension of payments/moratorium trustee

A provisional suspension is usually granted upon filing a request. At the time a suspension is granted, the court will appoint a member of the local bar as a moratorium trustee (*bewindvoerder*), and usually a bankruptcy judge. The creditors will be invited to file their claims with the moratorium trustee and, during a suspension of payments, the debtor will not be able to administer or dispose of his assets without the cooperation and authorisation of the moratorium trustee. The court will also set a date at which a hearing of the creditors will take place. At this hearing, a definite suspension of payments will be granted unless there are grounds for refusal. Given that a suspension provides the debtor temporary relief against pressing creditors, a suspension may be granted for a maximum period of 18 months and may be extended without limit at the request of the debtor for successive 18-month periods.

If a definite suspension is not granted by the court, or if the court refuses to grant an extension, the court may, and usually does, declare the debtor bankrupt.

The most important consequences of a suspension are that the debtor can no longer be forced to make payments that are due and that (in the event of a definite suspension of payments) attachments (*beslagen*) made by creditors on the assets of the debtor are automatically lifted. However, secured and privileged creditors (such as mortgage holders) may still exercise their rights. As a result, a debtor is effectively granted a period of relief in order to attempt to reorganise the business to ensure the continuation of the enterprise and ultimately the full satisfaction of the creditors.

44.8.2.3 Conversion into bankruptcy

In practice, a suspension often becomes a bankruptcy. For example, if the moratorium trustee finds that the estate is in a position where it is no longer desirable to maintain the suspension or if it is unlikely that the debtor will be able to pay his creditors in the future, the trustee is obliged to request the termination of the suspension. After the court has terminated the suspension, the court will usually declare the debtor bankrupt. As mentioned above, this procedure may mean that the management board of the company can effectively have the company declared bankrupt after all.

Note that in principle it is not possible for creditors to request the bankruptcy of a debtor during a suspension, other than in accordance with certain specific provisions in the rules governing the suspension of payments. A company in distress sometimes requests a suspension of payments to avoid being declared bankrupt at the request of its creditors.

44.8.2.4 Protection

In Chapter 26, means of protection are described. These means of protection are also commonly used in the Netherlands. In addition it is noteworthy that if a supplier's parent company publishes its annual accounts in which the annual accounts of the supplier are consolidated, that parent company is jointly and severally liable for the supplier's debts under article 2:403 Dutch Civil Code.

44.9 Financial services regulation

44.9.1 Outline

This section describes the rules and regulations regarding the outsourcing of activities by financial undertakings (*financiële ondernemingen*). It describes how the relevant directives have been implemented and if and to what extent the implementation differs from that in the UK (for the situation in the UK, *see* Chapter 33).

44.9.2 Definition of outsourcing

Outsourcing is defined in section 1:1 of the Act on the Financial Supervision (Wet op het financieel toezicht, the "AFS") as the issue of an instruction to a third party by a financial undertaking to carry out activities on behalf of that financial company:

(a) that form a part of or arise from the operation of its business or the provision of financial services; or
(b) that form a part of the essential operating processes in support thereof.

44.9.3 Dutch regulations regarding outsourcing

44.9.3.1 AFS

The AFS came into force on 1 January 2007. Before January 2007, the rules regarding outsourcing were laid down in various policy guidelines supplied by the Dutch supervisory authorities.

Sections 3:18 and 4:16 of the AFS contain the main rules regarding the outsourcing of activities by financial undertakings. Under Dutch law, financial undertakings include management companies, investment institutions, investment firms, custodians, clearing institutions, financial service providers, banks and insurance companies.

On the basis of these rules, if a financial undertaking wishes to outsource part of its activities to a third party, it must ensure that the third party complies with the relevant rules applicable to the outsourced services.

A financial undertaking may not outsource activities if this constitutes an obstacle to proper supervision by the Netherlands Authority of Financial Markets (the "AFM") or the Dutch Central Bank ("DCB").

Section 5:31 of the AFS contains the main rules applying to the outsourcing activities of operators on a regulated market. Operators should ensure that the third party complies with the rules applicable to the activities which are being outsourced.

44.9.3.2 DPR

The Decree prudential rules AFS (Besluit prudentiële regels, "DPR") contain specific rules regarding activities outsourced by financial undertakings, including (*inter alia*) banks, insurance companies and clearing institutions.

Sections 27 and 28 of the DPR contain restrictions on the acceptability of outsourcing activities. Pursuant to Section 27 (1) of the DPR, a financial undertaking must not outsource activities if this might hinder the adequate monitoring of the undertaking's compliance with the rules and regulations regarding prudential supervision. According to Section 27(2) of the DPR, a financial undertaking must not outsource the tasks and duties of persons who determine the day-to-day policy of that undertaking. Furthermore, a financial undertaking must not outsource activities if that would have a negative effect on the quality of its independent internal audit.

44.9.3.3 Bgfo

Sections 38 to 38e of the Decree on the supervision of the conduct of financial undertakings AFS (Besluit gedragstoezicht financiële ondernemingen Wft, "Bgfo") contain specific rules covering outsourcing by financial undertakings that are subject to supervision regarding market behaviour.

These restrictions include:

(a) a financial undertaking must not outsource activities if this may hinder the adequate supervision of the undertaking's compliance with the rules on market behaviour; and
(b) a management company must not outsource control over the investment policy of a collective investment scheme. According to Section 38a Bgfo, an investment firm must not outsource activities if this is detrimental to the quality of its independent internal audit procedure.

44.9.4 Implementation of MiFID in the Netherlands

MiFID was implemented in 1 November 2007, in the AFS and in the accompanying governmental decrees and further regulations.

With the implementation of MiFID, investment firms and regulated markets have to comply with more extensive requirements in the event that they outsource their activities. MiFID has introduced a number of new provisions in the Bgfo and has resulted in some minor changes in the AFS. MiFID is described in Chapter 33. The provisions of MiFID that have not been implemented in Dutch law are described briefly below.

MiFID makes a distinction between operational functions that are critical and important and operational functions that are not critical or important. Section 13 of the MiFID Implementing Directive states that an operational function shall be regarded as critical and important if a defect or failure in its performance would materially impair the continuing compliance of an investment firm with the conditions and obligations of its authorisation or its other obligations under MiFID, its financial performance, or the soundness or the continuity of its investment services and activities. However, this distinction has not been implemented in Dutch law.

Under Section 14(4) of the MiFID Implementing Directive, the investment firm and a service provider which are members of the same group may, for the purposes of complying with this

Section and Section 15, take into account the extent to which the investment firm controls the service provider or has the ability to influence its actions.

However, regardless of whether the outsourcing takes place within the group or outside the group of companies of which the investment firm forms part, Section 37 Bgfo contains a general prohibition regarding outsourcing of activities if this constitutes an obstacle to the proper supervision of the compliance with the rules on market behaviour.

44.9.5 Other provisions in the Netherlands; policy guidelines of the AFM

The AFM has published a consultation paper in connection with new policy guidelines for investment firms that outsource the management of individual assets of non-professional investors to a third party in a non-Member State. This consultation is a result of the MiFID Implementing Directive.

According to the guidelines, the AFM may not object to the outsourcing to a third party in a non-Member State if the investment firm can ensure that the following conditions are satisfied:

(a) the outsourcing firm must ensure that the investment firm itself and the third party comply with all legal requirements;
(b) the outsourcing firm must ensure that the third party has sufficient resources to comply with the legal requirements; and
(c) the outsourcing firm must ensure that the AFM has access to the data concerning the outsourced activities in order to supervise.

The policy guidelines are "principle based". The conditions under which the AFM will not object have been formulated as target regulations. This means that the outsourcing firm must prove that the firm itself or the third party satisfies these conditions. However, they are free to determine in what way they satisfy the conditions. The guidelines also contain suggestions by way of examples.

44.10 Public Procurement Directives

The Netherlands has implemented the Public Procurement Directive through the Public Procurements Decree (Besluit aanbestedingsregels voor overheidsopdrachten). The Decree entered into law on 1 January 2005 and applies to all contracts awarded on or after that date.

The Decree gives effect to all of the provisions of the Public Procurement Directive described in Chapter 34. Hardly any specific national rules or guidelines have been added and it could be considered a copy of the Public Procurement Directive.

A number of countries, such as the UK (*see* Chapter 35) have developed the concept of the Private Finance Initiative ("PFI"). The Dutch equivalent of a PFI contract is the Design, Build, Finance, Maintain and Operate ("DBFMO") contract. DBFMO contracts have been used on a limited scale by the Dutch government for construction projects including those relating to infrastructure and accommodation. At the time of writing, DBFMO contracts have not been used for IT or other services.

44.11 Utilities Directive

The Netherlands has implemented the Utilities Directive through the Utilities Procurements Decree (Besluit aanbestedingen speciale sectoren). The Decree entered into force on 1 January 2005 and applies to all contracts awarded on or after that date.

The Decree gives effect to all of the provisions of the Utilities Directive described in Chapter 37. Hardly any specific national rules or guidelines have been added to the Utilities Directive and it too could be considered to be a copy of the Utilities Directive.

44.12 Proposed reform of public procurement law and utilities procurement law

The Dutch Ministry of Economic Affairs (Ministerie van Economische Zaken) has been working on a legislative proposal for a Public Procurement Act (Aanbestedingswet) to replace the current Public Procurement Decree and the Utilities Procurement Decree. The Public Procurement Act was also intended to cover situations which are not provided for in the Procurement Directives, for example by introducing specific rules for Annex II B contracts, which are contracts which do not exceed the specified thresholds for the award of service concessions. Furthermore, the proposed Act was intended to give detailed guidance to contracting authorities with respect to selection and exclusion criteria. The Dutch Lower House had unanimously adopted the Public Procurement Act, but on 8 July 2008 it was rejected by the Dutch Upper House.

At the time of writing it is not clear whether, and if so when, the Dutch Ministry of Economic Affairs will submit a new draft of the Procurement Act to Parliament. If the Ministry submits a new draft, this might contain provisions beyond those in the previously rejected Act. In any event, any new Procurement Act will not enter into force before 2011.

44.13 Competition law

Competition law in the Netherlands is governed by the Competition Act 1997 ("Dutch Competition Act"; Mededingingswet), which entered into force on 1 January 1998. As in most European Community Member States, the Competition Act is closely modelled on the competition rules in the EC Treaty ("EC Treaty") and subsequent EC competition legislation. Therefore, most of the sections in Chapter 29 on EC competition law, and in particular the various EC block exemption regulations and Commission guidelines, also apply to Dutch national competition law.

The Competition Act prohibits agreements between undertakings, decisions by associations of undertakings, and concerted practices that have as their object or effect the prevention, restriction or distortion of competition in the Dutch market. The definition of "agreement" is identical to the definition under Article 81 EC Treaty. The Dutch Competition Act further prohibits the abuse of a dominant position. The focus of the merger control rules is whether a concentration will lead to a substantial lessening of competition, in particular through the creation of a dominant position that will significantly impede competition in the market or part thereof.

The Dutch Act is enforced by the Netherlands Competition Authority (Nederlandse Mededingingsautoriteit; "NMa"). The Board (Raad van Bestuur) of the NMa is the administrative authority (*bestuursorgaan*) responsible for making decisions under the Competition Act.

44.13.1 Merger control

Article 27 of the Dutch Competition Act defines the term "concentration" as follows:

"(1)

(a) the merger of two or more previously independent undertakings;
(b) the acquisition of direct or indirect control of an undertaking by:

1 one or more natural or legal persons already in control of at least one other undertaking; or
2 one or more undertakings, through the acquisition of a participating interest in capital or assets pursuant to an agreement, or by any other means;

(2) the creation of a joint undertaking which performs all the functions of an autonomous economic entity on a lasting basis, is a concentration within the meaning of section 1, paragraph b."

The Dutch merger control rules thus also apply to joint ventures and cooperative joint ventures which are full-function concentrations, as is the case under the current EC Merger Control Regulation. The notion of "control", for the purposes of determining whether a concentration falls within the meaning of article 27 of the Dutch Competition Act will arise, is explained in article 26 of the Dutch Competition Act.

"Control" is defined as "the possibility of exercising decisive influence on the activities of an undertaking on the basis of actual or legal circumstances".

A concentration is subject to a mandatory notification requirement to the NMa where:

(a) the total worldwide turnover of the undertakings involved equalled or exceeded €113.45 million in the preceding calendar year; and
(b) at least two of the undertakings involved separately achieved a turnover in the Netherlands of €30 million or more in the preceding calendar year.

The substantive test under the merger control rules is whether a concentration will lead to a substantial lessening of competition, in particular through the creation of a dominant position that will significantly impede competition on the Dutch market or a part thereof.[3] This is the same test that is applied in European competition law under the EC Merger Control Regulation.

Depending on the exact structure of the transaction, an outsourcing operation can constitute a concentration under Dutch law.

3 Article 41 Competition Act.

44.13.2 Prohibited anti-competitive agreements

Article 6 of the Competition Act prohibits agreements between undertakings, decisions by associations of undertakings, and concerted practices that have as their object or effect the prevention, restriction or distortion of competition on the Dutch market. Breaches of prohibitions are punishable with fines up to 10 per cent of turnover. Individuals who are involved in a breach of competition law may also be subject to fines. Legislative proposals for making individuals who are involved in a breach of competition law subject to imprisonment have been rejected.

44.13.3 Exclusivity and non-compete clauses

When assessing non-compete covenants, the NMa follows the guidelines laid down by the Commission in the Ancillary Restraints Notice (*see* also Chapter 29). In practice, the NMa will allow non-compete covenants for a period of two years if goodwill is transferred, and for a period of three years where both goodwill and know-how are transferred.

As to "agreements of minor importance", "individual exemptions" and "block exemptions", refer to the information in Chapter 29 which applies equally to the Netherlands.

Chapter 45

Italy

Gabriele Capecchi
Partner
Legance

45.1 Background to outsourcing in Italy

Since the 1970s, companies in Italy have increasingly looked to outsourcing both as customers and suppliers. Recent research shows that outsourcing is pivotal for most technological industries (particularly for those operating in the automotive and engineering sectors) as well as fashion companies. Outsourcing is also popular for a wide range of services, including IT services, real-estate and logistic services, HR support, marketing and customer care.

Customers and suppliers tend to develop networks of relationships, giving rise to local industrial districts ("*distretti industriali*") specialising in specific market sectors.

Most economists maintain that this particular type of industrial organisation gives Italian companies sufficient flexibility to face domestic and international market fluctuations, and the level of integration reached by some districts operating in the fashion, furniture, engineering or agricultural sectors is regarded as a model of success.

Foreign markets are becoming increasingly important to Italian suppliers, with Germany and France ranking high among the countries receiving Italian exports. Outside the European Union, Brazil, China, the US and Canada are some of Italy's most valuable commercial partners while eastern European and Far Eastern countries are gradually beginning to show interest in Italian suppliers.

When facing this economic environment, lawyers must examine outsourcing agreements with due care and attention.

45.2 People issues – ARD

45.2.1 Application of ARD/ICC

The Italian Supreme Court has recently described outsourcing as an ensemble of "various techniques, through which an enterprise terminates the direct management of one or more of its products or services activities, which are not part of its core business" (decision no. 21287/2007). The court added that outsourcing projects can involve the parties entering into a services contract or the customer transferring a portion of its business to the supplier.

In the second scenario, the customer's employees will be transferred along with the business and the employees' consent is not required. The employees will be protected by the provisions of ARD, which Italy has implemented by means of article 2112 of the Italian Civil Code ("ICC").

The parties involved in the transfer of a business (or part thereof) have contractual freedom to determine which assets, liabilities, receivables and contracts will be transferred. However, a business (or part thereof) must exhibit some "functional autonomy" for the purposes of Italian labour laws (article 2112, para. 5). This measure restricts the parties from creating artificial parts of businesses, with the exclusive purpose of transferring employees without their consent.

45.2.2 Consequences of application of ARD/ICC

In the event of a business transfer, a number of safeguards exist for the benefit of the employees, which are described below.

45.2.2.1 Continuity of employment

Whenever a business transfer takes place, the same conditions of employment that applied to the personnel employed in the transferred business will bind the transferee by operation of law. The employees who are transferred will retain any rights deriving from the employment agreements that are in force when the transfer takes place.

45.2.2.2 Rights of the transferred employees

The transferor and the transferee will be jointly liable for the employees' accrued and existing rights at the date of the transfer. However, subject to certain procedures, the employees may exempt the transferor from the obligations deriving from the employment relationships.

45.2.2.3 Economic and legal treatment

The transferee will be required to apply the economic and legal treatment set forth in the national, territorial and company collective agreements in force at the time of the transfer, until their expiration or unless they are replaced by other collective agreements applicable to the transferee at the same level (i.e. national, territorial or company level).

45.2.2.4 Termination of employment relationships as a consequence of the transfer

The transfer of a business is not per se a valid reason for terminating an employment relationship. However, employees whose employment conditions are materially affected as a result of the transfer may resign stating this cause within three months from the transfer date. In this case the business transfer will be regarded as the cause of resignation and, as a consequence, the resigning employees will be entitled to receive statutory termination payments (i.e. severance payments, compensation in lieu of unused holidays etc.), as well as a payment in lieu of the notice period they would have been entitled to in the case of dismissal.

45.2.2.5 Liability for salaries and social security payments

If the transferor and the transferee enter into an outsourcing agreement after the completion of the transfer, they will be subject to the general joint liability regime in relation to the payment of salaries and social security payments to the suppliers' employees (*see* 45.5 below).

45.3 Information and consultation

45.3.1 Recipients of the notice

Pursuant to article 47 of Law 428/90, whenever a business transfer is planned, and the business (or part thereof) to be transferred employs more than 15 employees, the transferor and the transferee will be required to give written notice of the transfer in advance, to:

(a) the works councils ("*Rappresentanze Sindacali Unitarie*" or "*Rappresentanze Sindacali Aziendali*") at the locations concerned; and
(b) the external unions that entered into the National Collective Agreement that applies to the companies concerned.

In the absence of a works council, the notice will only need to be sent to the external unions.

45.3.2 Timing of notice

The notice must be given at least 25 days prior to the earlier of:

(a) the date on which the contract for the transfer is executed; or
(b) the date on which the parties reach a binding agreement.

45.3.3 Contents of notice

The notice must contain the following information:

(a) the date, or the proposed date, of the transfer;
(b) the reasons for the transfer;
(c) the legal, economic and social impact upon the employees;
(d) any proposed measures which will affect the employees (e.g. possible reorganisation of the transferee's activity entailing a reduction in headcount etc.).

45.3.4 Consultation

If a written request is submitted by any of the addressees within seven days of receipt of the notice, the transferor and the transferee will be required to start a joint consultation procedure with them within the following seven days. The consultation will be considered complete 10 days after the start date, regardless of whether or not an agreement is reached.

45.3.5 Result of non-compliance

Should the parties fail to comply with the information and consultation requirements, this will amount to "anti-union conduct" pursuant to article 28 of Italian Law No. 300/70 and the trade unions may seek a court order against the employer in order to force it to comply with its information and consultation duties.

45.3.6 Application of information and consultation obligations

The information and consultation obligations in article 47 will also apply when the decision regarding the transfer of business is made by a separate entity exercising control over the transferor or the transferee. Should the controlling entity fail to provide the necessary information, this will not justify the transferor's or the transferee's failure to comply with the obligations.

45.3.7 Application of Directive 2002/14/EC

In this context, it is worth noting that Italy has recently implemented Directive 2002/14/EC by means of Legislative Decree 25/2007. The Directive creates a harmonised framework for informing and consulting employees across the European Community. The new Decree applies to employers with at least 50 employees.

45.3.8 Consequences of application of Directive 2002/14/EC

The Directive creates various information and consultation obligations, concerning, *inter alia*, any decisions that are likely to cause material changes to the organisation of a business's work. It is anticipated that the provisions of the Decree will be implemented by collective bargaining agreements, although they appear to be directly applicable and enforceable. In particular, information and consultation obligations will be directly enforceable in relation to the following matters:

(a) possible future developments of the employer's activities and of the general employment conditions within the company, particularly when there is a threat to jobs; and
(b) any company's decision which is likely to lead to substantial changes in the organisation of a business's work.

The scope of the new law is broad enough to catch any corporate transactions (in theory, including significant outsourcing agreements), which may cause substantial changes to the organisation of a business's work.

45.3.9 Remedies for breach of Directive 2002/14/EC

Any breach of these information and consultation obligations will be punishable by an administrative penalty ranging from €3,000 to €18,000 and it may be considered anti-union conduct, for the reasons indicated above.

45.4 People issues – other employment issues

45.4.1 Liability for salaries, social security and withholding tax

It is worth noting that Italy has a joint liability regime that applies to customers, suppliers and subcontractors in relation to the payment of salaries, social security and withholding tax to the employees of suppliers and subcontractors:

(a) customers will be jointly liable with the supplier, as well as with any subcontractor, for a period of two years after termination of the contract for payment of salaries and social security to the employees of the supplier (and of any subcontractor) (Legislative Decree 276/2003);

(b) suppliers will be jointly liable with their subcontractors for the payment of withholding tax, social security and mandatory charges to the employees of the subcontractor. The two-year limitation period relevant to customers does not apply (Law Decree 223/2006);

(c) according to article 1676 ICC, employees of the suppliers and subcontractors will be able to claim from the customer (or from the supplier when acting, in turn, as customer) payment of their salaries, to the extent that they are unpaid by their employer, up to an amount not exceeding the price still to be paid, at the time of the claim, by the customer to the supplier.

45.4.2 Indemnities

In the light of this regime, customers frequently insert specific indemnification clauses into their outsourcing agreements (and suppliers include them in their subcontracts). Under these clauses the supplier/subcontractor agrees to keep the customer/supplier indemnified against any costs or expenses that it may incur as a consequence of any breach committed by the supplier/subcontractors of any of the mandatory provisions relating to salaries, social and insurance payments, etc.

45.4.3 Other cooperation

The supplier/subcontractor will also be asked to provide the customer/supplier with detailed documentation from time to time, attesting to their regular compliance with the statutory obligations or to cooperate with the customer/supplier if there are labour disputes or investigations by the authorities. Although these clauses will not overcome the statutory joint liability regime, they will provide contractual protection for customer/supplier.

45.4.4 Guarantees

The customer/supplier may also request specific guarantees (e.g. bank or insurance guarantees) from the supplier/subcontractor that can be enforced in the event of any breach of the supplier/subcontractor's indemnity obligations.

45.4.5 Health and safety liability

If the supplier is expected to provide the services on-site at the customer's site, Decree 81/2008 ("Consolidated Code on protection of safety and health on workplaces") will:

(a) impose the duty on the customer and the supplier to cooperate in order to mitigate the potential risk of them interfering in each other's operations (e.g. by separating, whenever possible, the working areas of their teams or by informing their employees of any potential risks that may result from the activities of the other team); and

(b) make the customer jointly liable with the supplier and its subcontractors for all damages (excluding those relating to the specific risks characterising the activities of the supplier and its subcontractors) suffered by the employees of the supplier or its subcontractors, which are not indemnified by INAIL (the Italian agency for the insurance of injuries at work).

Although the letter of the law is not clear on this point, it is arguable that, in this kind of agreement, the supplier will have similar liability for the employees of its subcontractors.

Therefore, the customer (and supplier) will usually seek indemnities and guarantees from the supplier (and subcontractor respectively) to cover the above liabilities.

Outsourcing agreements which fall under the scope of Decree 81/2008 must:

(a) contain a technical attachment, which explains how the parties will deal with the risk of interference; and

(b) indicate, under pain of nullity of the entire agreement, the cost that has been allocated to address any safety issues.

It is worth mentioning that breaches of safety rules are frequently also subject to criminal sanctions.

45.5 Pensions issues

An objective of the provisions of article 2112 of the ICC, is that accrued public pension rights will not be jeopardised by the transfer of business. After the transfer, the employees will continue to belong to the public pension system, and the transferee, as the new employer, will be liable for the payment of the relevant social security charges.

In certain cases, transferred employees will also be able to participate in pension funds (supplementary to the public scheme), in accordance with the applicable national collective agreement, to which both the employer and the employees adhere. In this case, if the same national collective agreement is also applied by the transferee, any transferred employee will continue to take part in the same scheme (and the transferee will pay the relevant charges). However, if there is a change in the national collective agreement applicable to the employees as a consequence of the transfer, the contributions previously accrued will be transferred to the new fund, if any, indicated by the different national collective agreement applied by the transferee.

45.6 Contract law

45.6.1 Outsourcing agreements as service agreements

The ICC does not expressly refer to outsourcing agreements. However, it is generally accepted that complex outsourcing agreements for the provisions of goods or services will be governed by the same provisions that apply to service agreements ("*appalti*") (article 1655 et seq. ICC).

If the supplier is expected to provide its goods or services on an ongoing basis, the outsourcing agreement will also be covered by the provisions that govern supply agreements ("*contratti di somministrazione*") (article 1559 et seq. ICC).

45.6.2 Implications of the outsourcing contract being a service agreement – statutory guarantee

Article 1667 ICC states that a supplier will be liable for any defect in its work or products and that it will guarantee that its work or products will be free from any defect. This guarantee will not apply if the customer is aware that the supplier's work contains defects and it nevertheless accepts it, or if such defects could be easily detected (provided that the supplier does not intentionally hide them). In order to enforce the guarantee, the customer will have to report any defect within 60 days of the date on which it becomes aware of it. The guarantee will expire two years after the delivery of the work.

45.6.3 Remedies for breach of statutory guarantee

The statutory guarantee will entitle a customer to require the supplier to cure any defects at the supplier's expense or to receive a reduction in the price as well as compensation for damages, if the defects are the result of the supplier's gross negligence.

In the event of a material defect that results in the customer being unable to use the work in the manner anticipated, the customer will have the right to terminate the agreement. This means that the supplier will be obliged (in accordance with the general principles of contract law) to reimburse the customer for any fees paid or expenses incurred and to compensate the customer fully for any damages suffered.

45.6.4 Outsourcing agreements as agreements for specific projects, technical or technological know-how, models or prototypes

If a supplier provides services relating to projects, technical or technological know-how, models or prototypes *which have been specifically provided by the customer*, then outsourcing agreements will also be governed by Law 192/1998. This law has been enacted to protect "captive" suppliers (or customers) against abuse by dominant customers (or suppliers). The main rules introduced by this law, which apply to the narrow range of outsourcing agreements which fall within its scope, are:

(a) the outsourcing agreement must be in writing or it will be invalid;

(b) the technical specifications for the products or services, their prices and the terms of payment must be clearly set forth in the agreement (and, in principle, payment must be made within 60 days, subject to some exceptions);

(c) without the authorisation of the customer, the supplier must not subcontract more than 50 per cent of its work to third parties;

(d) the customer will retain any IP rights relating to the projects and the technical specifications contained in communications with the supplier and any communications must be treated as confidential by the supplier; and

(e) any dispute will be subject to mandatory mediation, and, in the event of the failure of the mediation process, to a mandatory fast-track arbitration procedure, to be completed, in principle, within 60 days.

45.6.5 Implication of outsourcing agreements being agreements for specific projects, technical or technological know-how, models or prototypes

In the case of those outsourcing agreements which fall within the scope of Law 192/1998, the supplier will be responsible for the proper performance and quality of those services that have been outsourced to it. The supplier will also be responsible for the assembling tasks delegated to the supplier, in accordance with the applicable contractual terms and best industry practice. However, the supplier will not be held liable for defects in the materials or equipment supplied by the customer, as long as the supplier gives prompt notice of these defects. Any provisions in an outsourcing agreement which contradict these principles will be null and void.

45.6.6 Performance impossible

According to the general principles of contract law, if a supervening event renders performance of the work impossible, the supplier will be released from liability (article 1463 ICC). If performance is only partially possible, the customer may ask for a proportional reduction in the fee or may terminate the agreement if it no longer has a valuable interest in the performance of the contract.

According to well-established case law, the impossibility to perform must stem from events that were unforeseeable at the time of the agreement's execution and that result in an objective impossibility (not a mere obstacle) to perform.

45.7 Limitations of liability

It is possible to set out limitations to liability in outsourcing agreements which do not fall within the scope of Law 192/1998. However, a supplier is unable to limit liability for wilful misconduct or gross negligence (article 1229 ICC).

In relation to those agreements which fall within the scope of Law 192/1998, any limitation of the supplier's liability for the proper functioning or quality of those parts that have been outsourced to it and for the assembling tasks delegated to the supplier is null and void.

45.8 Data protection

45.8.1 Implementation of the Directive into Italian law

Italy was one of the first EU Member States to implement the Personal Data Protection Directive through Law 675/1996. The Italian public body responsible for monitoring the application of this law is the "*Garante per la protezione dei dati personali*". Law 675/1996 has now been repealed by Legislative Decree 196/2003, the "Data Protection Code" ("*Codice in materia di protezione dei dati personali*"). The latter consolidates the provisions of Law 675/1996 and other pieces of legislation on the subject of data protection.

45.8.2 Outsourcing supplier as data processor

When looking at outsourcing agreements, the supplier may be defined as a "data processor" ("*responsabile del trattamento*") depending upon the specific content of its duties. A data processor will be responsible, on behalf of the data controller, for data processing.

Appointing a data processor is not mandatory and is not a strict requirement of the Data Protection Directive. However, the *Garante* suggests that if the customer-data controller assigns any tasks relating to data processing to the supplier then it is advisable for the customer to appoint the supplier as a data processor.[1]

From a practical viewpoint, if an outsourcing agreement imposes upon the supplier the obligation to share with the customer any element of its data processing activities then that agreement should specify clearly whether or not the supplier is appointed as a data processor.

45.8.3 Implications of the supplier being a data processor

If the customer appoints the supplier as a data processor then:

(a) the customer must select the supplier on the basis of its experience, skills and reliability and its thorough compliance with the applicable provisions regarding data processing and security matters;

(b) the customer must check the procedures which the supplier intends to employ to deal with data subjects' information rights, confidentiality and security;[2]

(c) in general, the duties assigned to the data processor must be detailed in writing by the data controller;

(d) the data processor must abide by the instructions given by the data controller when outsourcing data processing operations and the outsourcing agreement should specify the specific instructions which the supplier must follow;

(e) the data controller must supervise the data processor's activity (article 29, Data Protection Code). In this situation, it is advisable that the outsourcing agreement specifies clearly how the customer intends to monitor the data processing activities performed by the supplier, as well as the supplier's obligation to cooperate with the monitoring activities by the customer.

The same principles apply if the data controller is a public entity and entrusts external suppliers with the performance of tasks which fall under its remit.[3]

1 *See* the opinion on "Postel" or electronic mail services of 19 December 1998 and the resolution of 27 April 2007 regarding insurance services.

2 *See* the resolution of 15 November 2007 concerning the outsourcing of customer care, post-sale, booking and phone banking services and the Guidelines for Data Processing within the Framework of Clinical Drug Trials of 14 July 2008.

3 *See* the release of 15 October 2007.

45.8.4 Notifying data subjects

With a few exceptions, the customer must inform any data subject whose data is to be processed under the terms of an outsourcing agreement and obtain his consent for the processing and supply the data subjects with details of the external supplier.

45.9 Insolvency issues

Generally, Decree 267/1942 governs Italian insolvency issues.

45.9.1 Right of the non-insolvent party to terminate

45.9.1.1 Right to terminate under contract

In contrast to the law in jurisdictions which are more creditor-oriented than Italy, in the case of insolvency, pursuant to article 72, para. 6 of Decree 267/1942, termination rights exercisable by one party in the event of another party's insolvency will be rendered null and void. This means that, in case of the insolvency of one party, the non-insolvent party may terminate the agreement only if it is allowed to do so by the provisions of Decree 267/1942, notwithstanding any provision of the contract to the contrary.

45.9.1.2 Right to terminate under law

If the outsourcing agreement can be classified as a "service agreement" and the insolvent party is the supplier, the customer will be able to terminate the outsourcing agreement, if it can prove that it entered into the agreement strictly in reliance on the supplier's personal qualities (article 81, para. 2).

45.9.2 Right of liquidator to disclaim

As a rule, if one of the parties is insolvent, the liquidator appointed to liquidate the assets of that party, may decide, under certain circumstances, whether to keep the existing agreement in force or to disclaim it. Specific rules will apply, depending on the type of agreement (e.g. sale, lease, loan etc.). As noted above, outsourcing agreements may be classified as "service agreements" ("*appalti*") under para. 41.6. Where they also cover the ongoing provision of services or supply of products, the provisions that apply to "supply agreements" ("*contratti di somministrazione*") will govern them. This means that:

(a) if, upon the insolvency of one of the parties, the outsourcing agreement has not yet been performed, wholly or partly, by both parties, the liquidator may, with the approval of the creditors' committee, decide to keep it in force or to disclaim it (article 72, para. 1);

(b) if the outsourcing agreement can be classified as a "service agreement", this option must be exercised within 60 days from the declaration of insolvency and if the liquidator decides to keep the agreement in force, adequate guarantees must be provided (article 81, para. 1); and

(c) if the outsourcing agreement can be classified as a "supply agreement" and the liquidator decides to keep it in force, the liquidator must pay for the delivery of services that have already been performed (article 74).

45.10 Financial services regulation

45.10.1 Implementation of MiFID

Italy has implemented the provisions of MiFID by means of Legislative Decree 164/2007, which contained a number of amendments to the Consolidated Financial Act (Legislative Decree 58/1998).

Most of the fundamental principles introduced by MiFID in relation to outsourcing agreements regarding the financial sector were already contained in existing Italian legislation, especially those which referred to the specific regulations issued by Consob (the public authority responsible for regulating and supervising the securities market) and the Bank of Italy.

However, in accordance with the provisions in MiFID, Legislative Decree 164/2007 required Consob and the Bank of Italy to implement joint regulation governing the procedures that customers who are financial intermediaries should follow upon outsourcing important or essential operational functions, among other matters.

This joint regulation was issued in October 2007 (Bank of Italy's and Consob's Joint Regulation under article 6, para. 2-bis of the Consolidated Financial Act, 29 October 2007).

45.10.2 Definition of important or essential

According to the regulation, a function is considered important or essential if failure to perform it:

(a) may seriously prejudice the customer's ability to fulfil the conditions and obligations necessary for authorisation to carry out its activity, as well as any other obligations concerning investment services; or
(b) may seriously prejudice the financial results, the soundness or the business continuity of the customer.

45.10.3 Responsibilities of the customer

The customer will remain fully responsible for the activities it outsources to the supplier. In particular, the customer must ensure that:

(a) the outsourcing does not imply the assignment of corporate responsibilities;
(b) relationships with, and duties towards clients will not be prejudiced; and
(c) none of the conditions under which the customer received the necessary authorisation to carry out its activity will be changed or cancelled.

45.10.4 Obligations of customers

The customer must evaluate diligently and execute any outsourcing agreement. In particular, it must ensure that:

(a) the supplier has the professional skills, capacity and any necessary authorisation to perform its services diligently and professionally;
(b) the supplier performs the services efficiently. To ensure this, the customer must follow adequate evaluation criteria;
(c) the supplier monitors the performance of the services and the relevant risks;
(d) appropriate measures are adopted to address the risk of failure by the supplier;
(e) the customer has efficient internal systems to monitor the activities assigned to the supplier as well as to address the relevant risks;
(f) the supplier informs the customer of any situation that might prejudice its ability to duly perform the services;
(g) the customer is able to terminate the outsourcing agreement, if necessary, without prejudicing the business continuity and the quality of the services;
(h) the supplier cooperates with the relevant authorities;
(i) the customer, its auditors and the relevant authorities have access to any information concerning the outsourced services, as well as to the premises where the services are performed by the supplier;
(j) the supplier guarantees confidentiality in the interests of the customer and of its clients; and
(k) the customer and the supplier implement a disaster recovery plan.

The outsourcing agreement must clearly define and specify the rights and obligations listed above.

45.10.5 Outsourcing outside the EU of retail asset management services

If the customer is outsourcing retail asset management services and the supplier is located within the territory of a non-EU country, the customer must also ensure that:

(a) the supplier is authorised to perform retail asset management services in its own country and is subject to prudent supervision; and
(b) a cooperation agreement is in force between the Italian authorities and the authorities of the country where the supplier is based.

If these conditions are not met, the customer must inform the relevant Italian authorities and may only enter into the outsourcing agreement if the authorities do not raise any objection within 60 days of receiving notice.

45.11 Public Procurement and Utilities Directives

45.11.1 Implementation of the Directives

Legislative Decree 163/2006 (the "Public Procurement Code") governs public procurement and utilities.

In fact, the Public Procurement Code regulates contracts for public works, public supply contracts, public service contracts, and project financing for public works and also implements European Directives 2004/18/EC and 2004/17/EC which apply to the award of such contracts to entities operating in the water, energy, transport and postal service sectors.

The Public Procurement Code does not merely restate the Directives; it sets out all procedures governing award procedures regardless of their threshold.

Given that the provisions of the Directives are substantially in line with those of the Government Procurement Agreement ("GPA"), the Public Procurement Code ensures that the GPA will be complied with in Italy.

45.11.2 Application of the Public Procurement Code to concession agreements

The Public Procurement Code also applies to concession contracts awarded in relation to public works but not to service concessions (concessions contracts are similar to service agreements, the difference being that the supplier does not receive cash as valuable consideration, but is granted the right to manage the infrastructure for a period of time). However, the Public Procurement Code also applies the general principles of transparency, non-discrimination, equal treatment and proportionality to concession contracts.

45.11.3 Project financing for public works

In October 2008, the Public Procurement Code was amended and new provisions regarding project financing for public works were introduced. The previous provisions and regulations had been criticised for their complexity, which deterred many operators from entering this sector of the market. The October 2008 reforms provided for two alternative procedures (a third one may be triggered if the awarding entity fails to tender for public works that are eligible for private financing and that have been included in the relevant annual list): a single-phase and a double-phase procedure.

The purpose of the single-phase procedure is to concentrate, in one sequence, the different phases which the contractor selection procedure consisted of under the previous regime.

The double-phase procedure is divided into two phases:

(a) in the first phase, the awarding administration carries out a competitive procedure, aimed at selecting a preliminary project to be financed. At the end of the procedure, the promoter, who presented the project selected by the awarding administration, is admitted to the next phase;

(b) in the second phase, the awarding administration calls for a new tender procedure, on the basis of the promoter's approved preliminary project and the associated economic and contractual conditions. The promoter is entitled to exercise a pre-emption right within 45 days of being informed that a more favourable bid than its own has been received. The pre-emption right is conditional upon the promoter's agreement to bring the terms of its bid in line with those of the more favourable bid.

Finally, if a public administration fails to tender for public works that are eligible for private financing and that have been included in the relevant annual list, the prospective contractors, if any, may implement the third procedure (mentioned above), which is aimed at forcing the public entity to carry out an awards procedure.

45.12 Competition law

45.12.1 The antitrust law

The Italian antitrust regime was created by Law 287/1990. This Law introduced a full set of substantive and procedural rules regarding mergers and restrictive practices (i.e. agreements between undertakings and abuse of dominant positions). Law 287/1990 was expressly based on the *acquis communautaire* and, as a consequence, currently all of the principles (and guidelines) developed at EU level apply at domestic level, subject to EU law prevailing. In particular, only those mergers which do not meet the EU thresholds and which satisfy the conditions set forth in Law 287/90 have to be filed in Italy. Moreover, investigations of agreements between undertakings and abuses of dominant position are carried out in compliance with the provisions of EC Regulation no. 1 of 2003.

45.12.2 The competition authority

The *Autorità Garante della Concorrenza e del Mercato* is the Italian public authority responsible for monitoring the application of antitrust legislation.

45.12.3 Relevant breaches of competition law

With respect to outsourcing agreements, it is worth noting that Law 192/1998 (*see* 45.6.4 above) introduced a specific type of abuse: pursuant to article 9, a customer or a supplier is not allowed to abuse the economic dependence of a supplier or a customer, respectively. In this context, economic dependence is synonymous with economic "captivity": the supplier (or the customer) is so intensely dependent on the other party that it is unable to negotiate its contractual rights and obligations at arm's length.

Article 9 contains some examples of abuses: typically, an abuse may be the refusal to provide (or to acquire) services or products, the imposition of discriminatory or excessively severe contractual terms or the arbitrary interruption of commercial relationships.

45.12.4 Implications of breach of competition law

Contractual undertakings which are tainted by abuse are null and void and the aggrieved party may seek interim protective measures from the Court as well as payment of compensation for damage. In the case of abuses which may be prejudicial to fair competition, the *Autorità Garante* may issue "cease-and-desist" orders and apply fines, in compliance with Law 287/1990.

45.13 Summary – key issues

45.13.1 Consultation

Customers and suppliers entering into outsourcing agreements which involve the transfer of a business or material changes to the organisation of a business's work where employees affected by the outsourcing arrangement include those in Italy will need to consider the specific consultation provisions described in 45.4 above.

45.13.2 Indemnities for the salaries and social security payments of the supplier/subcontractor

Customers entering into outsourcing agreements where the supplier is in Italy will need to ensure that they include in their outsourcing agreements indemnities for any liability they have for the salaries and social security payments of the supplier's employees. Suppliers entering into subcontracts where the subcontractor is in Italy will need to ensure that they include similar indemnities in their subcontracts.

45.13.3 On-site services

Where the supplier is to provide the customer with services on site at the customer's premises, in Italy, the parties will need to have regard to any health and safety liability they may have under Decree 81/2008 and may want to include suitable indemnities. If the subcontractor is to provide the supplier with services on site at the supplier's premises in Italy, the parties will want to include similar terms in the subcontract.

45.13.4 Data protection

Under Italian law, the customer must decide whether or not to appoint the supplier as a data processor and the outsourcing agreement must specify clearly whether or not the supplier is appointed as a data processor and set out other arrangements relating to how data protection issues will be dealt with.

45.13.5 Insolvency

Under Italian law, termination rights exercisable by one party in the event of another party's insolvency will be rendered null and void.

45.13.6 Public Procurement and Utilities Directives

The Public Procurement Code extends the Public Procurement and Utilities Directives so that they govern all award procedures regardless of their threshold.

Chapter 46

Sweden

Jörgen Axelsson
Partner
Setterwalls

46.1 Background to outsourcing in Sweden

46.1.1 Types of services outsourced

Outsourcing as a phenomenon in Sweden began in the early 1980s and has since grown rapidly. Companies initially outsourced services such as sanitation services and real-estate caretaking and soon began to outsource support functions such as accounts, human resources and IT. During the past few years, services commonly outsourced have included design, research and development, installation, support and maintenance. The types of services that are being outsourced continually change and climb the value chain. Services that are not included in the company's core activity are commonly outsourced.

46.1.2 Popularity of outsourcing

According to an extensive survey of 243 Swedish and 943 Nordic corporations performed by the management consultants Accenture, Swedish companies use outsourcing of services to a lesser extent than their Nordic cousins. Approximately half of the Swedish corporations outsourced services. In Finland and Denmark, the eagerness to outsource is wide; 88 per cent of the companies asked in Finland and 75 per cent in Denmark outsource services. Swedes tend to outsource IT to a greater extent than whole business processes such as finance and accounting services, purchasing services and product development services. According to the survey results, Swedish companies have much to gain in terms of reducing costs and increasing quality through greater outsourcing. Outsourcing of whole business processes ("BPO") is predicted to increase dramatically in the future. A great deal of that which is outsourced is moved abroad to countries with cheaper labour ("offshoring").

46.1.3 Disadvantages of outsourcing

A study of 25 large corporations carried out by the accountancy firm Deloitte shows that 70 per cent of the companies who have outsourced services have had negative experiences, making them more cautious. One in four of the customers interviewed had brought the outsourced services back in-house as a result of the outsourcing arrangement not fulfilling the customer's expectations. Half of these customers did not gain the cost benefits of the outsourcing that they had expected. Common fears among executives preventing them from outsourcing are those of dependency on the supplier and losing control and knowledge from the organisation.

46.1.4 Advantages of outsourcing

However, there are obviously great advantages to be gained from outsourcing and customers are outsourcing more and more each year. Depending on the business objectives of the customer, different factors apply and outsourcing can be subject to both advantages and disadvantages. Employment costs and flexibility, product development and delivery speed factors are all important factors that influence the decision to outsource.

46.1.5 Reasons for outsourcing

Motives to outsource include the need to:

(a) cut costs;
(b) focus on core activities;
(c) access competence;
(d) move closer to the end market;
(e) free resources for other activities;
(f) compensate for a lack of in-house resources;
(g) increase efficiency, quality and service in a company;
(h) respond to operational control difficulties or a reduced need for investment in a particular area in the company;
(i) share risks;
(j) cut currency risks through offshoring or benefit from cost flexibility.

Other customers are influenced by the fact that their competitors in the market have outsourced.

Historically, cost cutting was the main motive for outsourcing. Today, factors like capability and capacity are becoming more important, particularly as services become more difficult to find on the local market or in house. In order to benefit from all of these factors, Swedish organisations are reaching out globally to a greater extent than ever before.

At the moment, the price of IT services is reducing, making it profitable for customers to outsource this type of service. Prices for Windows services are falling 10–15 per cent per year and the market price for storage per gigabyte is falling by 20 per cent per year. This is predicted to continue until 2011, according to the consultants Compass.

46.2 People issues

46.2.1 Acquired Rights Directive

Firstly, the general point of view is that the Acquired Rights Directive ("ARD") is applicable to outsourcing in Sweden. The Swedish regulations concerning the said Directive are generally applicable to both private and public businesses (and the Swedish regulations therefore cover a slightly wider range than the original Directive).

The ARD has been implemented in Sweden mainly through four paragraphs, two in the Employment Protection Act 1982 and two in the Co-Determination Act 1976. The regulations can be considered to contain three essential rules.

46.2.1.1 Transfer of employment relationship

Employment relationships will be transferred from the previous supplier to the new supplier as an effect of the outsourcing (*see* Section 6b Employment Protection Act).

46.2.1.2 Not a just reason to terminate employment relationship

Secondly, the transfer is not considered a just reason to terminate an employment relationship (*see* Section 7 Employment Protection Act). In Sweden the employer has to show "just cause" for the termination of an employment relationship. Redundancy or misconduct/personal reasons may amount to just cause. A transfer of business is not just cause for dismissal by either the former supplier or the new supplier. There is essentially, therefore, a prohibition on dismissal of personnel from the transferred business.

46.2.1.3 Application of collective bargaining terms of conditions

Thirdly, the new supplier is, during a transitional period of 12 months, required to apply the terms and conditions stated in any collective bargaining agreement that the transferred employees had agreed with the former employer (*see* Section 28 Co-Determination Act). Further, the Directive has been implemented such that the acquirer is required not only to take over the employment of transferred employees and apply the terms in a collective bargaining agreement, but also to observe existing, accrued vacation benefits and flexi time etc.

46.2.2 Other employment issues

46.2.2.1 Collective bargaining agreements

Collective bargaining agreements, the terms and conditions of which a new supplier/employer is required to observe, are very common in Sweden. More or less all large Swedish companies are bound by collective bargaining agreements, either directly in relation to trade unions or by membership in the national Employers' Association. Collective bargaining agreements apply for all employees, except top managers who are not covered by the Employment Protection Act 1982.

Swedish collective bargaining agreements include terms and conditions regarding working hours, leave, overtime compensation, vacation, salary, notice period and additional benefits such as pension plans and certain insurances.

46.2.2.2 Duty to negotiate

In addition to regulating applicable terms of employment, entering into a collective bargaining agreement also means that an employer is required to cooperate and negotiate with trade unions on a regular basis in accordance with the Co-Determination Act 1976 (that mainly applies in relation to employers that are bound by such agreements).

The requirement to negotiate can be a significant issue in relation to outsourcing. The Co-Determination Act not only states that the employer is required to inform and negotiate with the union on a regular basis, but also that the employer has a primary obligation to negotiate in certain circumstances. For instance, before the employer makes a decision on the transfer of the business (or part of the business) the employer has to initiate negotiation with applicable trade union(s). If the employer is bound by a collective bargaining agreement, the employer has to initiate negotiation with the union party to the collective bargaining agreement. Where the employer is not bound by any collective bargaining agreements, the employer is still required to initiate negotiation before a decision to transfer a business is made. In that case, the employer has to initiate negotiation with every union of which any of the employees is a member. An employer that does not initiate negotiation risks liability to pay damages to the applicable unions.

46.3 Pensions issues

Collective bargaining agreements often contain terms and conditions regarding pension benefits. The liability for pension insurances agreed in collective bargaining agreements is transferred from the previous employer to the new employer. However, in relation to pensions there is an exception to the obligation of the new supplier/employer to observe the terms and conditions of collective bargaining agreements. Pension benefits set forth in the individual employment agreement are not automatically transferred to the new employer. However, the employer and the employee are not prohibited from reaching an express agreement to transfer such benefits.

46.4 Contract law

46.4.1 General principles

According to general contract law in Sweden, businesses on equal terms are free to enter into contracts and freely decide terms and conditions. A contract term may be modified under the Swedish Contracts Act should it be found to be unreasonable or to have arisen from a questionable situation. Aside from those exceptions, the main rule is that terms and conditions shall be upheld and respected by the parties in order to avoid breach of contract.

46.4.2 Force majeure

Should a party be found to be in breach of contract, the usual consequence is "liability payment". Liability can be avoided despite a breach of contract in some cases. For example, it is common to free a party to an outsourcing agreement of liability where the failure to comply is the result of a force majeure event.

There is no statutory definition of force majeure or its implications on the duty to comply with the agreed terms and conditions in the Contracts Act. However, it is an accepted term in legal literature and case law. Should the parties leave out a clause on force majeure altogether, it is plausible that a court would find that it is an implied clause. Although force majeure is an accepted concept, it ought to be defined by the parties to a contract in order to expressly state the width of events to be included.

Depending on whether force majeure is defined with an exhaustive list or an exemplifying list, it will be more or less preferable to the supplier and customer. Should the list be unreasonable, it can, as any unreasonable condition, be attacked under the Contracts Act. Furthermore, unpleasant or expensive consequences are more likely to be palatable when the parties recognise that risks and responsibilities were allocated fairly. The benefits of an exhaustive list include the certainty achieved and the incentive to avoid circumstances that are not within the definition. The common solution in Scandinavia is a general definition consisting of a non-exhaustive list and a list of conditions which the party asserting the force majeure must satisfy in order to avoid liability (such as a notification requirement or a requirement to avoid the event and/or to take reasonable steps to overcome the event).

The contract should also state the effect, other than in relation to liability, that an impossibility to provide the agreed services shall have and whether or not the forfeited party shall have the right to terminate the agreement. Both parties may want to have the right to terminate in certain events, depending on the consequences inferred. If the supplier fails to perform services due to force majeure, although it may be free from liability, it may also miss out on expected payments and be forced to comply with a remedy plan. In such cases, termination may be seen as a more attractive option to the supplier.

46.5 Limitations of liability

As in many other countries, it is common for the supplier to require that its liability for breach of contract is limited to direct damages and to a maximum amount. It is common for the parties to insist on a higher liability limit for intellectual property rights infringement and breach of confidentiality clauses.

46.6 Data protection

46.6.1 Implementation of Data Protection Directive

The principal data protection legislation in Sweden is the Personal Data Act. This Act implements the Data Protection Directive adopted by the EU in 1995. Compliance with the Personal Data Act is supervised by the Swedish Data Inspection Board.

46.6.2 Basic principles

The basic starting point is that the responsibility for ensuring that personal data is conducted in a lawful manner rests with the person processing such data for his/her own purposes, i.e. the data controller. The data controller determined *how* and *why* the data is being processed and the data processor, performing the practical handling of the data, can be likened to a tool, solely acting on the controller's instructions.

The main function of the Personal Data Act is to protect against the violation of people's personal integrity by the processing of data. The Personal Data Act lists certain fundamental requirements concerning the processing of personal data.

46.6.3 Requirement for consent

One such requirement is that personal data may only be processed for specific, explicitly stated and justified purposes. Personal data may, with some exceptions, in principle only be processed if the registered person gives his consent. However, there are exceptions to this rule: if it is necessary in the exercise of official powers, when a work task of public importance is to be performed, in order to enable the controller of public data to fulfil a legal obligation or in order that a contract with the registered person may be performed.

46.6.4 Exclusions from the Act

The Act does not apply to the processing of personal data that forms part of a course of operation of a purely private nature, and does not contravene the constitutional provisions relating to freedom of press or freedom of expression or limit the principle of access to public information. Processing of personal data in unstructured material, for example running text, may take place as long as this processing does not entail a violation of the personal integrity of the persons whose data is registered. If another act or ordinance contains rules that deviate from the Personal Data Act, those other provisions apply instead.

46.6.5 Notification

The processing of personal data must be notified to the Data Inspection Board. However, this does not apply if the person who is responsible for the processing has appointed a personal data representative. A person who contravenes the Act may be liable to pay damages or be sentenced to a criminal penalty.

46.6.6 Sensitive personal data

Particularly stringent rules apply to the processing of personal data that is sensitive, for example concerning political views, sexual orientation or health. This also applies when data is transferred to other countries. The person whose personal data is processed must always be informed of the processing of data that concerns him.

46.6.7 Application to outsourcing

In an outsourcing relationship the party responsible for processing will usually be the customer, as the supplier will be processing data solely as part of the services and in accordance with the instructions from the customer. That is, the customer will be controlling the data and making the decisions as to how and why the data is processed, but the supplier may be doing the actual processing and thus acting as processor. In such cases, the customer will be the controller.

46.6.8 Application to processing in Sweden

The Personal Data Act applies to controllers established in Sweden. The Act is also applicable when a controller from a country outside the EU and EEA uses equipment, such as terminals, situated in Sweden for the processing of personal data. In such cases, the controller must appoint an agent established in Sweden who will be treated as a controller for the purposes of the Act.

46.7 Financial services regulation

46.7.1 Implementation of MiFID

The Markets in Financial Instruments Directive 2004/39/ec ("MiFID") has been implemented in Swedish legislation by the Securities Markets Act (2007:528), which replaced the Securities Operations Act (1991:1981) and the Securities Exchange and Clearing Operations Act (1992:543). The Implementation Regulation 1287/2006 is directly applicable in Sweden and the Implementing Directive 2006/73/EC has been implemented by the Swedish Financial Supervisory Authority ("FSA") in two regulations:

(a) Regulation regarding Securities Operations Business (fffs 2007:16); and
(b) Regulation regarding Operations on the Securities Market (ec 2007:17).

Several regulations and general guidelines issued by the FSA have either been rescinded or amended as a result of the MiFID implementation. MiFID was fully implemented in Sweden on 1 November 2007.

The Swedish legislature chose to make the wording of the new legislation as similar as possible to the wording used in MiFID. Several new words and expressions not previously used in Swedish financial legislation have been introduced as a result. Subsequently, a number of other legal Acts have been amended to reflect the "new" MiFID terminology in Swedish legislation.

MiFID has now been applicable in Sweden for some time and yet it is still to be seen how the FSA and the Swedish courts will enforce and apply the new legislation.

46.7.2 The FSA and authorisation

The FSA is the supervisory authority of companies operating in financial markets in Sweden. All companies offering financial services in Sweden must obtain authorisation issued by the FSA. Such authorisations are provided for a number of different types of securities operations. The securities companies carrying authorisation to conduct securities operations under the rescinded Securities Operations Act were automatically granted new "MiFID authorisations". These covered the same operations as the former authorisations, with new MiFID-compliant wording, when the current Securities Markets Act came into force on 1 November 2007. In addition, two new authorisations were introduced as a result of the implementation of MiFID in Sweden:

(a) investment advice to clients regarding financial instruments; and
(b) operations of multilateral trading facilities ("MTF").

Since the rescinded Securities Operations Act did not contain any equivalents to the above authorisations, companies providing investment advice or operating an MTF have been obliged to apply for such authorisations.

46.7.3 Classification of marketplaces

A partly new classification of marketplaces has also been introduced in Sweden as a consequence of the implementation of MiFID. Until the new Securities Markets Act came into force there were two different marketplaces in Sweden, an exchange marketplace and an authorised marketplace. The term "authorised marketplace" has no equivalent in the current Securities Markets Act. However, the term "exchange" still exists and refers to the legal entity operating a regulated market instead of, as previously, the marketplace itself. OMX and Nordic Growth Market ("NGM") currently operate regulated markets in Sweden.

As indicated above, an MTF constitutes a new kind of marketplace in Sweden which requires authorisation. Previously, a financial institution could act as an intermediary between buyers and sellers of financial instruments in a way comparable to an MTF without a specific marketplace authorisation. Today, such institutions have to apply for authorisation if they intend to operate an MTF. However, if the operations in question are not regarded as operations of an MTF, the activity is still likely to be subject to authorisation. The rationale is that the business activity includes the receipt and forwarding of transaction orders with regard to financial instruments, something that the Securities Markets Act considers is an operation subject to authorisation.

46.8 Public Procurement Directives

46.8.1 Implementation of the EU Directives

Public procurement annually amounts to approximately SEK 500 billion (approximately €51 billion), which equates to about 20 per cent of the Swedish annual gross domestic product. Public procurement in Sweden is governed by the two Public Procurement Acts which came into force on 1 January 2008: the Swedish Public Procurement Act and the Swedish Procurement Act on procurement of water, energy, transportation and postal services. They are based on the EC Public Procurement Directives, the Classical Directive and the Utilities Directive.

The Swedish Competition Authority is responsible for information on and supervision of public procurement.

As a Member State, Sweden is automatically compliant with the World Trade Organization's agreement on government procurement, after implementing the procurement directives.

46.8.2 Application

The Acts regulate almost all types of public procurement, meaning that contracting entities, such as local government agencies, county councils, government agencies as well as certain publicly-owned companies must comply with the Acts when they purchase, lease, rent or hire purchase supplies, services and public works. The contracting entity must choose which award procedure to apply. However, the rules are different for public procurement above and below a number of so-called threshold values, as is stated in the directives. It should be noted, however, that the telecommunications sector is not covered by the Swedish Procurement Acts.

46.8.3 Fundamental principles

The Swedish Acts on public procurement are based upon the following fundamental principles of EC and Swedish law.

46.8.3.1 Principle of non-discrimination

The principle of non-discrimination prohibits all discrimination based on nationality. No contracting entity may, for example, give preference to a local company simply because it is located in the municipality.

46.8.3.2 Principle of equal treatment

According to the principle of equal treatment, all suppliers must be treated equally. All suppliers involved in a procurement procedure must, for example, be given the same information at the same time.

46.8.3.3 Principle of transparency

According to the principle of transparency, the procurement process must be characterised by predictability and openness. In order to ensure equal conditions for tenderers, the contract document has to be clear and unambiguous and contain all of the requirements made of the items to be procured.

46.8.3.4 Principle of proportionality

The principle of proportionality states that qualification requirements and requirements regarding the subject matter of the contract must have a natural relation to the supplies, services or works which are being procured and not be disproportionate.

46.8.3.5 Principle of mutual recognition

The principle of mutual recognition means, among other things, that documents and certificates issued by the appropriate authorities in a Member State must be accepted in the other Member States.

46.8.4 PFI/PPP

There are very few PFI or PPP projects in Sweden, although these projects are believed to be coming. There are no special rules on the procurement of PFI or PPP projects. Instead, the contracting entity is obliged to apply the Swedish Public Procurement Act or the Swedish Procurement Act of water, energy, transportation and postal services.

46.9 Competition law

46.9.1 Implementation of EU law

The newly amended Swedish Competition Act (SFS 2008:579) ("2008 Competition Act") came into force on 1 November 2008, replacing the 1993 Competition Act (SFS 1993:20). The 2008 Competition Act is the most important Act regulating competition in Sweden. In addition to technical legal amendments, there were several different substantive changes to the 2008 Competition Act providing even further alignment with EC legislation. Overall, Sweden is highly influenced by EC legislation concerning national competition law. Almost all of the EC Block Exemption Regulations are implemented in Swedish legislation through different Acts referring to the EC Regulations. Swedish competition law is also influenced by EC legislation in other ways. When it comes to merger control for example, the notions and guidelines published by the European Commission are used to a large extent. Terms such as concentration and control do not differ from EC legislation and nor does the calculation of turnover.

46.9.2 Specific points relevant to Sweden

From a competition law point of view, there are no material differences in Swedish legislation compared to EC legislation which in the author's opinion would raise new issues in relation to outsourcing arrangements. However, there are some general points specific to Swedish competition law which may be worth highlighting.

According to the 2008 Competition Act a mandatory notification of a concentration is required if:

(a) the combined aggregate turnover in Sweden of the undertakings concerned in the preceding financial year exceeds SEK1 billion; and
(b) not less than two of the undertakings involved had a turnover in Sweden during the preceding financial year exceeding SEK200 million for each of the undertakings.

Furthermore, the 2008 Competition Act, provides that if criterion (a) above is fulfilled but the turnover does not exceed the threshold in criterion (b), the Competition Authority may, if special circumstances exist, order a party to a concentration to notify this. In this case the parties may also hand in a voluntary notification.

Sanctions against infringements of prohibited anti-competitive agreements are administrative fines of up to 10 per cent of the undertaking's turnover in the preceding financial year. The 2008 Competition Act introduces the possibility of imposing a trade prohibition (disqualification order) on business leaders engaging in unlawful collusion in cartels.

46.10 Summary

The current recession in the economy increases the need for cost cutting and it can be expected that companies will consider outsourcing parts of their business activities as a means of cutting costs. The present economic climate is therefore likely to increase the outsourcing market.

Large companies are already accelerating their use of offshore outsourcing, and this mega-trend can be presumed to expand further as a result of the present downturn in the economy.

It is speculated that new IT innovations, such as cloud computing are likely to change the face of IT outsourcing as well. Through cloud computing, companies will be able to rent platforms, for example Microsoft's Sharepoint, and by using services create applications. When services in the cloud make giants such as Microsoft, Google and Amazon into a new species of IT service suppliers, this will undoubtedly have consequences for existing IT service suppliers.

Chapter 47

Switzerland

Michele Bernasconi and Nicola Bernardoni
Bär & Karrer AG

47.1 Outline

This chapter describes the most important legal and business issues which affect outsourcing arrangements in Switzerland.

Switzerland is not part of the EU. However, it will be apparent that, in several areas, Switzerland has been influenced by legal developments within the EU and has introduced legislation which is similar to that in the EU.

47.2 Background to outsourcing in Switzerland

47.2.1 Outsourcing customers in Switzerland

47.2.1.1 Finance sector
In Switzerland, as in other countries, since the late 1980s there have been important developments in outsourcing solutions. It will certainly not come as any surprise that out of the various different industries, the finance sector has always provided the strongest driver for outsourcing service solutions. Two-thirds of banks in the Swiss banking sector are said to have outsourced their IT.

47.2.1.2 Telecommunications sector
The increase in outsourcing projects was also very strong in the middle of the 1990s, following the liberalisation of the telecom sector, which trigged important developments in ICT outsourcing in Switzerland. Telecom service providers have entered into outsourcing agreements with specialised energy and IT service providers for the development of their networks, their services and end-customer infrastructure.

47.2.1.3 Media sector
The media industry has been an important driver in recent years.

47.2.1.4 Logistics industry
There has also been an increase in outsourcing in the logistic industry of logistic services and office management applications.

47.2.2 Reasons for outsourcing

As in other markets, cost saving and performance enhancement, as well as a general aim to focus on the core business, have encouraged companies to outsource ICT services or other kinds of services.

47.2.3 Multisourcing

In the ICT sector, it seems that companies prefer to outsource only certain "layers" of services, such as the application management or desktop services. The vast majority of outsourcing deals have concerned computer centre operations and application management, while only about 50 per cent use IT outsourcing for electronic workplace solutions.[1]

47.2.4 Joint ventures

It is also interesting to note that in both the financial and the energy sectors, companies have set up joint venture vehicles with competitors to run outsourcing services for the respective holding companies.

47.2.5 Growth in outsourcing

ICT outsourcing revenues in Switzerland have continued to grow in recent years, from approximately CHF2.6 billion in 2006 to CHF2.75 billion in 2007 and CHF2.9 billion in 2008.[2] Outsourcing researchers forecast a slow-down in the growth of ICT outsourcing in the future.

In addition, a significant decrease has already been seen in offshore outsourcing. It remains unclear whether this reflects a simple structural adjustment phase or whether offshore outsourcing will continue to fall.

47.3 Employment issues

47.3.1 Transfer of employees

47.3.1.1 Transfer of a business or a business unit

Under Swiss law, if an employer transfers a business or a part of a business (a business unit) to a third party,[3] the employment relationship is transferred to such third party, including all rights

1 Based on a study of Active Sourcing AG, Zurich.

2 Compare study of MSM Research AG, Schaffhausen.

3 Article 333 CO applies to an outsourcing if the business or business unit to be transferred is a kind of self-contained organisational business division, clearly separable from other parts of the business. In this respect it is of essence that the business unit to be outsourced maintains an independent and distinct economic identity (organisation, business purpose and individual character), regardless of whether or not this unit is economically autonomous.

and obligations as of the date of the transfer, unless the employee declines the transfer (article 333 of the Swiss Code of Obligation ("CO")).[4]

Accordingly, in an outsourcing that involves the transfer of a business unit from the customer to the supplier, all employment relationships relating to the business unit are automatically transferred from the customer to the supplier.[5]

However, the former employer (customer) remains jointly and severally liable with the new employer (supplier) for certain claims (article 333 para. 3 CO). This applies in particular to:

(a) claims of the employees that become due prior to the transfer; and
(b) claims that arise prior to expiry of the period of ordinary termination of the employment relationship (*see* 47.3.2.1 below).

If the business activity to be outsourced does not qualify as a business or business unit, as defined in article 333 CO, the transfer of the employment agreements from the customer to the supplier requires the consent of each employee unless the circumstances or the employment agreements provide for the contrary (article 333 para. 4 CO).

47.3.1.2 Duty of information and consultation

Prior to the transfer, the customer must inform the employees' representative body or, in the absence of such body, the employees (article 333a para. 1 CO) of:

(a) the reason for the transfer; and,
(b) the legal, economic and social consequences of the transfer.

In addition, if the business transfer requires measures that have an effect on the employees, the employer has a duty to consult the employees' representative body or, in the absence of such body, the employees (article 333a para. 2 CO).[6]

47.3.2 Redundancies: termination of employment agreements/mass dismissals

47.3.2.1 Termination of employment agreements

In Switzerland, the termination of employment agreements depends on the type of agreement. A distinction is primarily made between:

(a) employment agreements for a definite duration, which end at the expiration of the time limit (article 334 CO); and

4 RS 220 (RS: *Recueil systématique du droit fédéral*, i.e. Classified Compilation of Federal Legislation).

5 Without the consent of the employees, the customer cannot terminate the employment agreements in connection with an outsourcing which involves the transfer of a business or business unit to the supplier and, at the same time, offer through the supplier, new employment agreements with different terms and conditions. This would circumvent the employees' protection rights under article 333 CO.

6 The consultation must take place before the decision on transfer is made. However, the employer is not obliged to follow or implement the suggestions made by the employees. Further information and consultation duties may also arise if the outsourcing involves a mass redundancy (*see* 47.3.2.2), or if provided by any separate agreement.

(b) employment agreements for an indefinite duration, which may be terminated by giving the contractual or, if there is none, the statutory notice period (article 335 CO).

The notice period and the formalities of the notice[7] are often specified in the employment agreement.[8] However, the duration of the notice period must be the same for both the employer and the employee (article 335a CO).[9]

Swiss employment law is quite liberal when it comes to terminating employment agreements. The reason for terminating the agreement does not have to be an "important reason".[10]

47.3.2.2 Mass dismissal

According to article 335d CO, termination for reasons unrelated to the employees as people qualifies as a mass dismissal if the number of redundancies within a time period of 30 days is:

(a) at least 10 employees in an establishment with 20–100 employees; or,
(b) at least 10 per cent of the employees in an establishment with 100–300 employees; or,
(c) at least 30 per cent of the employees in an establishment with more than 300 employees.

If the employer plans a mass dismissal, before it takes a definitive decision it has to:

(a) consult with the employees' representative body or, if there is none, all of the employees;[11] and
(b) inform the employees in writing of:
    (i) the reasons for the mass dismissal;
    (ii) the number of employees to be dismissed;
    (iii) the number of persons usually employed; and
    (iv) the time period within which the notification of the dismissal is to be given.[12]

---

7 For evidence purposes notice of termination is usually given in writing.
8 If the notice period is not specified in the agreement, the following applies:
    (a) during the trial period (which cannot exceed three months), seven days' notice is sufficient to terminate the agreement;
    (b) after the trial period, the agreement may be terminated at the end of a month:
        (i) with one month's notice during the first year of employment;
        (ii) with two months' notice from the second year through the ninth year;
        (iii) with three months' notice after the ninth year.
9 Usually agreements provide for a two- or three-month notice period for regular employees and for a six-month notice period for executive employees.
10 Upon request by the employee, the employer has to state in writing the reasons for terminating the agreement.
11 The employer has to give the employees reasonable time to at least make suggestions on how to avoid the dismissals or to limit the number of dismissals and to alleviate the consequences. Contrary to the majority of countries in the EU, Switzerland has no rules imposing the duty to offer a social plan to the dismissed employees. The Collective Labour Agreements, if applicable, normally provide for additional compensations or benefits payable to employees in connection with mass dismissal or closing down of a business, but their financial significance is regularly far more limited than in other European western countries.
12 A copy of the notification described above must also be sent to the Cantonal Labour Office.

However, there is no formal right of approval by the employees, the representative body or the Cantonal Labour Office.[13]

47.4 Pensions issues

Swiss law requires employers to set up or join a pension scheme for employees who meet certain minimum requirements. The pension scheme is independent from the employer's business.

Generally, when employees are transferred under article 333 CO (*see* 47.3.1.1 above), the employees' vested benefits under the transferor's pension scheme are transferred to the transferee's pension scheme. After the transfer, the employees' pension benefits are calculated according to the new scheme's regulations.

However, if the workforce that forms part of the transferor's pension scheme reduces substantially, the respective pension scheme must be partially liquidated. The employees will then have individual or collective claims to a portion of the non-committed funds (free reserves) in addition to their ordinary claims to the vested benefit.

47.5 Contract law

Swiss contract law does not contain specific provisions for outsourcing agreements. Outsourcing agreements belong to the numerous types of contracts that are developed in accordance with the principle of "freedom of contracts" and that are not regulated by statute (so-called "innominate contracts").

However, outsourcing agreements often incorporate or display several elements of the various statutorily regulated contracts, such as:

(a) the services contract (article 394 et seq. CO);
(b) the works contract (article 363 et seq. CO);
(c) the sales contract (article 184 et seq. CO);
(d) the simple partnership (article 530 et seq. CO); and
(e) rent (article 253 et seq. CO).

As a consequence, in the case of a dispute, a Swiss court will have to determine which statutorily regulated contract type should best be applied, directly or by analogy, taking into consideration the intention of the parties, the most prominent contractual type and the general principles of law.

---

13 If the employer does not comply with the requirements to consult with the employees, the termination would be considered abusive, even though it remains valid. This entails a liability of the employer to grant to the dismissed employees an indemnity of up to two months' salary. In addition, the employer would have to compensate the dismissed employees for damages related to the fact that the consultation procedure has not taken place. Further, non-compliance with the requirement to notify the Cantonal Labour Offices may result in a delay of the effective date of termination and in administrative sanctions according to cantonal labour regulations.

One of the key questions is whether the supplier will be liable in the event of failure to achieve a particular result (as per works law) or whether it should be liable for failure to perform its obligations without due care (as per services law). In other words, if the supplier promises the customer a certain result, works law will apply. Alternatively, where the supplier has only agreed to deliver certain services to the customer and not guaranteed the achievement of a particular result, services law will apply.

There is a general tendency for the courts to assume that the rules for works contracts will apply, particularly in the cases where the parties have agreed certain service levels. Sales contract law usually applies to the transfer of assets from the customer to the supplier in cases where the parties agree on the transfer of title. If this is not the case, the courts would be inclined to apply the provision of the rent or the lease.

In order to reduce the legal uncertainty as to the rules that the courts will apply, outsourcing agreements are usually drafted with very detailed provisions aimed at providing a comprehensive set of rules that shall apply in case of dispute. In this case, the courts will apply the rules in the contract and not attempt to decide which statutory contract type could apply.

47.6 Exclusion and limitation of liability

Under Swiss contract law, the parties are generally free to exclude or limit their liability, subject to the following mandatory limitations:

(a) the exclusion or limitation in advance of liability for unlawful intent or gross negligence is null and void (article 100 para. 1 CO);

(b) the exclusion or limitation in advance of liability for death or personal injury is null and void.

In addition, a waiver of liability for simple negligence agreed in advance may be considered null and void at the discretion of the judge if the party making the waiver was employed by the other party at the time of the agreement, or if the liability arises out of the conduct of a business that is carried out under an official licence (e.g. banks, insurance companies).

In principle, liability for auxiliary persons (e.g. employees or other persons helping the principal in performing a contractual obligation) may be limited or excluded in advance (article 101 para. 2 CO). However, if the party making the waiver was employed by the other party at the time of the agreement, or if the liability arises out of the conduct of a business that is carried out under an official licence, a waiver in advance is only possible for simple negligence (article 101 para. 3).

It is also a fundamental principle of Swiss contract law that liability for the obligations that constitute the essence of the contract (e.g. the duty of care under services law) cannot be excluded in full. Here it is assumed that an exclusion of liability would create a contradictory situation. Such restrictions are therefore unlawful and unenforceable.

Subject to the above restrictions, the customer and the supplier are free to negotiate any exclusions or limitations of liability (including caps, liquidated damages, direct damages etc.).

Excessively high liquidated damages (and also, therefore, under certain circumstances, excessively high service-level penalties) can be reduced at the discretion of the judge (article 163 para. 3 CO).

47.7 Data protection

47.7.1 Federal Act on Data Protection

In Switzerland, data protection is primarily governed by the Federal Act on Data Protection of 19 June 1992 ("FADP").[14] In contrast to most of the European countries, Swiss data protection law applies to the personal data of both natural persons and legal entities ("data subjects").

The processing of personal data must be done in good faith and must be proportionate. Data accuracy and data security must be ensured. Data subjects are protected from their personal data being processed in ways that do not comply with the law or with the purposes intended at the time of collection, unless data subjects approve such data processing or another statutory justification applies.

Stronger legal protection is provided for sensitive personal data[15] and personality profiles.[16] The disclosure of such data to third parties[17] without lawful justification (e.g. consent of the data subjects) is prohibited.

47.7.2 Outsourcing of personal data processing within Switzerland

Data processing may be outsourced, within Switzerland, to a third-party supplier under an outsourcing agreement,[18] provided that the supplier processes data only to the same extent as the customer was authorised to do and that no legal or contractual confidentiality obligations

14 RS 235.1. Outsourcing of personal data by banks, securities dealers and insurance companies is subject to stricter regulations (*see* 47.9).

15 The FADP classifies personal data as "sensitive personal data" if it relates to:

(a) religious, philosophical, political or trade union-related views or activities;
(b) health, the intimate sphere of the person or racial origin;
(c) social security files; or
(d) criminal or administrative proceedings and penalties.

Personal data within this definition will almost always relate to a natural person rather than a legal entity.

16 Personality profile is defined in the FADP as a collection of data that permits an assessment of essential characteristics of the personality of a natural person.

17 A third party is any entity other than the disclosing entity, irrespective of the existence of an economic link between the disclosing entity and the recipient entity. Companies within the same group (parent and sister companies or subsidiaries) are considered third parties and thus the sharing of personal data within a group is deemed to be a disclosure to third parties for the purposes of the FADP.

18 For outsourcing of personal data by banks and securities dealers additional requirements must be complied with (*see* 47.9.1.2).

prohibit the outsourcing. The customer must further ensure that the supplier will comply with the applicable data security standards.

Explicit consent[19] of the data subjects is required for the transfer of sensitive personal data or personality profiles.

47.7.3 Cross-border transfer of personal data

The transfer[20] of personal data out of Switzerland is subject to further restrictions.

47.7.3.1 Countries with an adequate level of data protection

In principle, personal data may not be transferred to countries which lack an adequate level of data protection. The website of the Federal Data Protection and Information Commissioner ("FDPIC") contains a list of the countries with adequate data protection legislation.[21]

47.7.3.2 Countries without an adequate level of data protection

In the absence of legislation that guarantees adequate protection, personal data may exceptionally be disclosed abroad if, amongst other reasons:

(a) the data subject has consented in the specific case;

(b) sufficient safeguards, in particular contractual clauses, ensure an adequate level of protection abroad; or

(c) disclosure is made within the same legal person or company or between legal persons or companies that are under the same management, provided those involved are subject to data protection rules that ensure an adequate level of protection.

The FDPIC must be informed[22] of the safeguards and the data protection rules referred to under points (b) and (c) above.

19 Implied consent is not sufficient.

20 This includes allowing personal data to be accessed from abroad.

21 The countries which have implemented the Directive 95/46/EC of the European Parliament and of the Council of 24 October 1995 on the protection of individuals with regard to the processing of personal data and on the free movement of such data (EU Directive) are considered to provide the required adequate level of data protection for personal data of individuals. However, the EU Directive, unlike the FADP, does not provide such protection for legal entities. Consequently EU countries which have not implemented protection for legal entities in their national data protection laws cannot be considered to provide an adequate level of data protection for the personal data of legal entities pursuant to the FADP. For non-EU countries, it is necessary to check on a case-by-case basis whether they provide an adequate level of data protection. Neither US federal law nor the laws of any US state are considered to provide an adequate level of data protection, even if the recipient has adhered to the safe-harbour rules of the US Department of Commerce. *See* FDPIC website at: www.edoeb.admin.ch.

22 Information to the FDPIC must be provided before the first transfer of data is made or, if that is not possible, immediately after the disclosure has occurred.

47.8 Insolvency issues

47.8.1 Outline

Swiss insolvency law is comprehensively regulated on a federal level by the Federal Act on Debt Enforcement and Bankruptcy ("FADEB").[23]

When a court opens bankruptcy proceedings against a debtor, all of the bankrupt's assets form an estate which may no longer be disposed of by the debtor. All claims against the bankrupt estate become due and the estate is realised. The proceeds are then distributed among the creditors, some of which may be granted priority. Each creditor receives a certificate of shortfall for the unrecovered portion of its claim.

47.8.2 Effects on debtor's assets

Upon the opening of the bankruptcy proceedings by a competent court, all seizable assets of the debtor at that time, irrespective of where they are situated, constitute the "bankruptcy estate" destined for the satisfaction of the creditors.

Assets situated with the debtor but belonging to a third party do not fall within the bankruptcy estate. Such assets have to be singled out, either directly by the bankruptcy administrator or, if the ownership is unclear, by way of judicial proceedings in which the third party claims its proprietary interests.

47.8.3 Effects on creditor's rights

As regards claims based on a contractual relationship, the opening of the bankruptcy proceeding has the consequence that all obligations of a debtor become due vis-à-vis the bankruptcy estate.[24]

With the exception of certain types of contracts, the contractual relationship itself does not automatically terminate with the opening of bankruptcy proceedings. However, filings for bankruptcy or composition proceedings are often considered to be sufficiently serious to justify immediate termination of the contract by the other party.[25]

---

23 RS 281.1. Separate laws apply to enforcement actions against countries and cantons as well as bankruptcy and composition proceedings against financial institutions and bankruptcies of insurance companies.

24 Claims which do not have as their object a sum of money are converted into monetary claims of a corresponding value.

25 If the agreement does not provide for an automatic termination in the event of the bankruptcy of a contractual party and there is no possibility of an immediate termination, the bankruptcy administration can choose whether to terminate the agreement or to insist on the performance of the contract. In the latter case, the creditor cannot rescind the agreement, but can only ask for a security in relation of the performance of his obligations, and the related claims will be regarded as a debt against the bankruptcy estate, which has the effect that such claims rank prior to those of the other creditors.

47.9 Financial services regulation

47.9.1 Outsourcing by banks and securities dealers

47.9.1.1 Banking secrecy

The Swiss banking secrecy law is set out in article 47 of the Federal Law on Banks and Savings Banks ("FLBSB").[26] The banking secrecy law applies to all banking institutions in Switzerland and protects customer-related data from disclosures to any third party.[27] Any disclosure of non-encrypted data to a supplier would breach banking secrecy law if the bank's customer has not given his prior consent.

47.9.1.2 Circular letter on the outsourcing of the Swiss Financial Market Supervisory Authority

Outsourcing of business activities from banks and securities dealers organised in accordance with Swiss law, including Swiss branches of foreign banks and securities dealers, must comply with certain requirements. These requirements are set out in the "Outsourcing of Business Areas" Circular Letter no. 2008/7 (issued on 20 November 2008 and effective as from 1 January 2009 (the "Circular") of the Swiss Financial Market Supervisory Authority ("FINMA").[28]

The purpose of the Circular is to set out the conditions and requirements for outsourcing arrangements in terms of the bank's duties as an appropriate organisation, banking secrecy and data protection. In principle, the outsourcing of every business area is possible without the approval of the FINMA, provided that the provisions of the FADP[29] and the requirements for secure outsourcing[30] are complied with and, in the case of offshore outsourcing, the required documentary support can be provided. If an enterprise cannot fulfil these requirements prior to the outsourcing agreement being signed, it must submit an application and justification to the FINMA for an individual exemption.

The Circular specifically addresses "significant" outsourcings, that is, the outsourcing of services

26 RS 952.0.

27 Entities belonging to the same group are – from a Swiss banking secrecy perspective – deemed to be a "third party" irrespective of existing corporate law and/or regulatory links.

28 With the entering into force of the Federal Act on the Swiss Financial Market Supervisory Authority on 1 January 2009, three supervisory bodies – the Federal Office of Private Insurance ("FOPI"), the Swiss Federal Banking Commission ("SFBC") and the Anti-Money Laundering Control Authority – merged into the Swiss Financial Market Supervisory Authority ("FINMA"). Even though circulars issued by the FINMA do not qualify as statutory law, they do have an enormous practical relevance as they lay down the principles and requirements imposed by the FINMA when exercising its supervisory powers. The Circular letter issued by the FINMA basically reflects the "old" Circular Letter no. 99/2 issued on 26 August 1999 by the Swiss Federal Banking Commission.

29 Customer-related data must be protected against access by unauthorised persons through appropriate technical and organisational measures.

30 The customer and the supplier shall develop and set out in the contract a security concept which will allow the customer to monitor compliance with the security requirements which the supplier has to fulfil and permit the continuation of the outsourced business area in case the supplier, for whatever reason, is not able to provide its services.

which can impact in particular on the identification, limitation and monitoring of market, credit, default, settlement, liquidity, image, operational and legal risks.[31]

According to the Circular, any activity, function or operation of a bank can be outsourced to a third-party supplier, provided that the bank does not outsource:

(a) the supervision, ultimate management and control by the board of directors as well as other central management tasks;
(b) decisions concerning the commencement and discontinuation of business relationships.

The Circular lays down the following general principles to be followed to satisfy the requirement of secure outsourcing:

(a) the determination of the business area to be outsourced;[32]
(b) the customer's responsibility vis-à-vis the supervisory authority;[33]
(c) the relevant security measures which will be taken by the parties to protect the customer's business operations;[34]
(d) compliance with business and banking secrecy and data protection laws;[35]
(e) an obligation of the bank to inform its customers about the outsourcing;[36]
(f) the right of the supervisory body and the customer to enjoy unrestricted audit and supervision over the supplier;[37]
(g) additional requirements for offshore outsourcing;[38]
(h) the requirement for a written contract.[39]

47.9.2 Outsourcing by insurance companies

47.9.2.1 Federal Act on Supervision of Insurance Companies

The Federal Act on Supervision of Insurance Companies of 17 December 2004 ("FASIC")[40]

---

31 Outsourcing examples that are applicable in the Circular and examples that are not applicable in the Circular are included in the appendix to the Circular.
32 In accordance with the goals pursued with the outsourcing, the precise requirements for the provision of services are to be laid down and documented.
33 The enterprise must carefully select, instruct and control the supplier.
34 The proper conduct of business operations must be capable of being ensured at all times. The customer and the supplier must ensure the confidentiality, availability and accuracy of the data in order to guarantee the appropriate protection of data.
35 The Swiss supplier shall be subject to business secrecy rules of the enterprise and as far as clients' data is known to it, the banking and professional secrecy rules of the outsourcing enterprise.
36 Clients whose data is transmitted to a supplier as a result of an outsourcing solution are to be informed of the outsourcing arrangement before their data is transmitted to a supplier. In case of an outsourcing abroad, clients must be informed by a separate detailed letter and given the possibility to terminate the relationship within a reasonable timeframe and without disadvantages if data is not transferred on anonymous basis.
37 The outsourcing enterprise and its internal and external auditors as well as the Banking Commission must at all times possess complete and unrestricted insight into and control of the outsourced business.
38 In the event of outsourcing abroad, an enterprise must be capable of demonstrating that the enterprise itself as well as its Banking or Stock Exchange Law auditors and the Banking Commission may assume and also legally enforce their rights to perform controls.
39 A written and clear contract is to be concluded between the enterprise and the supplier.
40 RS 961.01.

requires that significant outsourcing agreements are included in the business plan[41] that must be submitted to the Financial Market Supervisory Authority ("FINMA"), to obtain a licence to operate as an insurance company in Switzerland (article 4 para. 2 lit. j FASIC).[42] Subsequently, any amendment or new significant outsourcing agreement must be notified to the FINMA before it becomes effective. If no formal examination is commenced by the FINMA, the amendment is deemed to be approved (article 5 para. 2 FASIC).

FASIC also requires that the people entrusted with the administration and management of an insurance company must have a good reputation and thereby ensure the proper conduct of the insurance company's business operations (article 14 FASIC). The same requirements apply to a supplier being entrusted with core activities, functions or operations under an outsourcing agreement.

47.9.2.2 Explanatory notes to the business plan

The explanatory notes to the requirement to prepare a business plan, as issued by the Federal Office for Private Insurance (recently merged into the FINMA),[43] give further details of the restrictions on and requirements for an outsourcing arrangement by insurance companies.

In principle:

(a) the outsourcing of activities of an insurance undertaking may not endanger the interests of the insured parties nor be detrimental to supervision by the FINMA;
(b) when outsourcing tasks, article 47 para. 4 FASIC must be observed, according to which natural and legal persons assuming tasks of the insurance undertaking are also subject to the duty to provide information to the supervisory authority.[44]

An outsourcing agreement is subject to approval if the following conditions apply cumulatively:

(a) the outsourcing arrangement concerns principal functions[45] or processes of an insurance undertaking; and

41 Form J: "Contracts or other agreements by which principal functions are to be outsourced".

42 Outsourcing for purposes of article 4 para. 2 lit. j FASIC also includes the transfer of tasks between the Swiss branch of a foreign insurance undertaking and the foreign head office or other unit of the company.

43 Explanations on the business plan (issue 08/2007).

44 The insurance undertaking shall designate one internally responsible person for each outsourced area.

45 Principal functions for the purposes of article 4 para. 2 lit. j are those functions necessary for the effective operation of an insurance undertaking. Such functions are:

(a) Core functions:
  (i) production (product development, distribution, risk underwriting);
  (ii) administration of client base (administration of policies);
  (iii) claims settlement.

(b) Other principal functions:
  (i) accounting;
  (ii) asset investment/management;
  (iii) IT.

Outsourcing of principal functions is possible in the following circumstances:

(a) of the core functions set out in points (a)(i)–(iii), a maximum of two may be outsourced, provided that such outsourcing is sufficiently justified;

(b) the outsourcing is long term; and
(c) the service provider is granted entrepreneurial discretion in fulfilling its tasks.[46]

Direction, supervision and control by the board of directors, as well as key management responsibilities, may not be outsourced.[47]

47.10 Public procurement

47.10.1 Outline

In Switzerland, public procurement is regulated both at a federal and cantonal level. In addition, Switzerland is a signatory to several international treaties which deal with public procurement (the most important are the WTO Government Procurement Agreement and the Bilateral Agreements with the EC). Nevertheless, as Switzerland is not an EU member, the EC public procurement directives do not apply to outsourcing in Switzerland.

Swiss procurement regulations provide for a mandatory competitive tender if the price paid for the services provided by the external supplier exceeds a certain threshold.

47.10.2 Procurements of federal authorities

Public procurements of federal authorities are governed by the Federal Act on Public Procurement ("FAPP").[48]

For procurements of services exceeding CHF50,000 at least three suppliers must be invited to tender ("invitation procedure").

For procurements of services exceeding CHF248,950 a public call for tenders must be made.

(b) the other principal functions set out in points (b)(i)–(iii) may be outsourced;
(c) captives may outsource all principal functions set out in points (a) and (b) to specialist captive management companies;
(d) companies in run-off after renouncing a licence may outsource all principal functions set out in points (a) and (b) as long as this appears useful in a concrete individual case (e.g. if only a few contracts and claims remain to be processed).

46 This means in particular that a mere assignment relationship in which the customer insurance company maintains its right of instruction in detail cannot be deemed outsourcing. If, for instance, the processing of some claims is carried out by an external law office, this is not qualified as outsourcing of an entrepreneurial function.

47 The explanatory notes expressly mention the following exceptions:

(a) outsourcing of internal audit;
(b) outsourcing of the management of captive re-insurers to appropriately specialised captive management companies;
(c) outsourcing of certain control functions within an insurance group or insurance conglomerate subject to group supervision.

48 RS 172.056.1.

47.10.3 Procurements of cantonal and communal authorities

Public procurements of cantonal or communal authorities are regulated by the Inter-Cantonal Agreement on Public Procurement ("ICAPP")[49] and by the relevant cantonal public procurement laws of each canton.

According to the ICAPP, an invitation procedure must be followed for procurement of services exceeding CHF150,000, while a public call of tenders is necessary for procurement of services exceeding CHF250,000.

47.11 Competition law

47.11.1 Outline

The provisions of the Swiss competition law can be found in the Federal Act on Cartels and Other Restraints of Competition ("FACORC" or "Swiss Cartel Act").[50]

According to article 2 FACORC, the Swiss Cartel Act applies to private and public enterprises[51] that are party to cartels or to other agreements affecting competition, have market power or take part in concentrations of enterprises.

The Swiss Cartel Act applies to restrictive practices that have an effect in Switzerland, even if the respective practice originates in another country.

47.11.2 Merger control

47.11.2.1 Concentration of enterprises

"Concentrations of enterprises" are subject to the Swiss merger control. This term is defined in article 4 as:

(a) the merger of two or more enterprises previously independent of each other;
(b) any transaction whereby one or more enterprises acquire, in particular by the acquisition of an equity interest or conclusion of an agreement, direct or indirect control of one or more hitherto independent enterprises or of a part thereof (i.e. the acquisition of sole or joint control).

In practice, if an outsourcing transaction will qualify as concentration, it will in most cases constitute an acquisition of either sole or joint control over an enterprise or a part of it.

The decisive question is whether the outsourcing transaction does entail such an enterprise.

In assessing this, the Swiss authorities are very likely to follow the rules set out in para. 25 et seq. of the Jurisdictional Notice of the European Commission under Council Regulation (EC) No. 139/2004 on the control of concentrations between undertakings. A transfer of assets/staff

49 RS 172.06.5.
50 RS 251.
51 As provided in article 1 bis FACORC, the term "enterprises" shall mean all customers and suppliers of goods or services in the commercial process regardless of their legal or organisational form.

constitutes such an enterprise if the assets constitute a business with access to the market. This requires that the assets previously dedicated to in-house activities of the seller will enable the outsourcing service supplier to provide services not only to the outsourcing customer but also to third parties, either immediately or within a short period after the transfer. This will be the case if the transfer relates to an internal business unit or a subsidiary already engaged in the provision of services to third parties. If third parties are not yet supplied, the assets transferred in the case of manufacturing should contain production facilities, the product know-how (it is sufficient if the assets transferred allow the build-up of such capabilities in the near future) and, if there is no existing market access, the means for the purchaser to develop a market access within a short period of time (e.g. including existing contracts or brands). As regards the provision of services, the assets transferred should include the required know-how (e.g. the relevant personnel and intellectual property) and those facilities which allow market access (such as, e.g., marketing facilities).

47.11.2.2 Turnover thresholds

A concentration has to be notified to the Secretariat if it fulfils certain turnover thresholds. A notification has to be made if in the last financial year prior to the concentration (article 9 para. 1 FACORC):

(a) the enterprises concerned had a joint worldwide turnover of at least CHF2 billion or a turnover in Switzerland of at least CHF500 million; and
(b) at least two of the enterprises concerned reported turnover in Switzerland of at least CHF100 million each.

If one of the enterprises involved has previously been found to have a dominant position in a market in Switzerland and the concentration involves either that market or a market up or downstream from there, notification must be made regardless of the turnover of the enterprises involved.

47.11.2.3 Creation or strengthening of a dominant position

Upon notification, Swiss competition authorities will assess the nature of the enterprises involved and the structure of the relevant market in order to determine whether the concentration creates or strengthens a dominant position (article 10 FACORC). A concentration will be prohibited or only be permitted under conditions and obligations, if:

(a) it creates or strengthens a dominant position that may eliminate effective competition; and
(b) the competitive conditions are not improved in another market to such a degree that they outbalance the disadvantages of the dominant position.

47.11.3 Unlawful restrictions of competition

According to the Swiss Cartel Act, agreements that eliminate or significantly affect competition are prohibited unless they can be justified on grounds of economic efficiency.[52]

In general, outsourcings between non-competitors will not give rise to problems under competition law. In contrast, where the outsourcing transaction involves two competitors, it has to be assessed

52 Since 1 April 2004, parties that enter into agreements eliminating competition will be subject to financial penalties of up to 10 per cent of their turnover in Switzerland over the previous three years.

whether the outsourcing agreement significantly restricts competition and if it does, whether it is necessary to achieve efficiencies. Theoretically, it could be argued that outsourcing agreements constitute agreements on the limitation of output that presumptively eliminate effective competition according to article 5 para. 3 lit. b FACORC. However, there are good arguments that outsourcing agreements do not fall under the presumption of article 5 para. 3 lit. b CA.

47.11.4 Abuse of dominant position

As regards the provisions regarding the abuse of a dominant position, an outsourcing agreement concluded with a dominant service supplier by itself should not constitute an abuse of a dominant position.

47.12 Other relevant issues

47.12.1 Transfer of property

In Switzerland, different rules apply for the transfer of title of movable and immovable property. For immovable property the transfer requires:

(a) a contract in writing with public authentication (such authentication can only be made by notaries who have been so empowered under the applicable laws); and
(b) the registration in the real-estate register.

For movable property the transfer requires a (written or oral) contract and the transfer of the possession ("*traditio*"). It is noteworthy that, under Swiss law, an agreement to reserve ownership is operative only if it has been entered in the public register of the transferee's domicile, which is kept for this purpose by the bankruptcy office.

47.12.2 Taxation

If an outsourcing arrangement involves the sale of assets from the customer to the supplier, such transactions will be subject to the following taxes:[53]

(a) value added tax if the assets are transferred to a supplier within Switzerland. Under certain circumstances, where the transaction involves the sale of a self-contained part of a business, the transaction may be completed without triggering value added tax by using the notification procedure. The same may apply if an outsourcing involves a de-merger or a joint venture;[54]
(b) taxes on profits if the sales of assets gives rise to a profit (e.g. because of the realisation of hidden reserves).

De-mergers and the incorporation of joint venture companies are tax neutral for outsourcings provided that a self-contained business element is transferred and continues to operate unchanged.

53 Complex outsourcing projects should always be carefully reviewed for tax considerations by tax experts and/or submitted to the tax authorities (tax rulings) at an early stage.

54 If the companies are sufficiently closely connected after the transaction, they may be eligible for group taxation (intercompany turnover between the companies involved would not be subject to value added tax).

47.12.3 Dispute resolution

47.12.3.1 Arbitration

Switzerland, as both a neutral and international venue, has a longstanding tradition of international arbitration.[55] A number of chambers of commerce offer arbitration services for both international and domestic arbitration. These include the chambers of commerce of Zurich, Geneva, Basel, Bern, Vaud and Ticino, which in 2004 adopted the "Swiss Rules of International Arbitration" (essentially based on the UNCITRAL Arbitration Rules[56]).

International arbitrations are governed by Chapter 12 of the Federal Act on Private International Law ("FAPIL"),[57] which applies to all arbitration cases where the arbitral tribunal has its seat in Switzerland and at least one of the parties had no domicile or habitual residence in Switzerland at the time when the arbitration agreement was concluded.

Switzerland is a party to several arbitration conventions, including the Geneva Protocol of 24 September 1923 on Arbitration Clauses,[58] the Geneva Convention of 26 September 1927 on the Enforcement of Foreign Arbitral Awards[59] and the New York Convention of 10 June 1958 on the Recognition and Enforcement of Foreign Arbitral Awards.[60]

Arbitration regarding parties domiciled in Switzerland is governed by the Inter-cantonal Arbitration Convention of 27 March 1969.

47.12.3.2 State courts

While substantive law is mainly federal, the law of civil procedure is traditionally governed by cantonal law. At present each of the 26 Cantons has its own Code of Civil Procedure.[61]

---

55 The Chambers of Commerce of Zurich and Geneva are among the world's very first providers of international arbitration services. The first Arbitration Rules of the Zurich Chamber of Commerce were launched in 1911.

56 The Swiss Rules of International Arbitration are essentially based on the UNCITRAL Arbitration Rules. However, the parties to the arbitration are free to choose the rules governing the arbitral proceedings as well as the law governing the subject matter in dispute. In the absence of a choice of procedural rules, the arbitral tribunal sets up its own rules as far as necessary.

57 RS 291.

58 RS 0.277.11.

59 RS 0.277.111.

60 RS 0.277.12.

61 In addition to these, several federal laws also contain procedural rules and the Swiss Federal Court has developed unwritten civil procedure law concerning basic questions. The existence of these multiple sources of procedural law has been a source of legal uncertainty and led to considerable difficulties in practice. In March 2000, the Federal Constitution was revised and the jurisdiction in the field of civil procedure law transferred to the federal legislator in order to eliminate these inadequacies through a single, uniform federal civil procedure law. A draft of the Federal Code of Civil Procedure was presented by the Federal Council in 2006. However, the legislation process is far from being concluded (discussions in the Parliament, referendum) and the enactment of the new law in its final version is not expected before 2010. Notwithstanding the unification of the Civil procedure law, the organisation of the courts shall remain in the competence of the 26 cantons.

Each canton has several courts of primary jurisdiction (or "district courts" in larger cantons) and one court of appeal. Under given circumstances, the decision of the last cantonal instance may be brought before the Supreme Federal Court, which decides in last instance.

Four cantons (Zurich, Bern, Aargau and St Gallen) have commercial courts, which have often proven very qualified in dealing with complex commercial disputes.[62] In some cantons, specialised courts exist for labour and rent/lease disputes.

47.13 Summary

Apart from the financial and insurance sectors, where the regulators have developed and set out in guidelines certain criteria and requirements for an outsourcing of "significant" business activities, Swiss law does not include specific regulations on outsourcing. Outsourcing contracts are not statutory regulated contract types and therefore outsourcing agreements are typically drafted with very detailed provisions in order to provide for a comprehensive set of rules that reduces the risk of unexpected consequences in case of a dispute. As is the case in other countries, thoughtful drafting of an outsourcing agreement involves the contemplation of a number of statutory laws that might be applicable to an outsourcing project or may be relevant as it comes to its implementation: employment law, data protection law, competition law, just to mention a few examples. In this respect, Switzerland, not being a member of the EU, generally has its own set of laws that apply (although a number of laws often correspond to or are akin to EU regulations). Despite this peculiarity, the volume of outsourcing projects in recent years confirms Switzerland as being a well-respected venue for both domestic and international outsourcing agreements.

62 The expertise of full-time judges in the commercial courts is supplemented by so-called commercial judges drawn from business and industry, who are chosen for their specialised knowledge in their own field.

Chapter 48

Ireland

Anne-Marie Bohan
Partner
Matheson Ormsby Prentice

48.1 Background to outsourcing in Ireland

48.1.1 Overview of outsourcing in Ireland

Ireland has long been a beneficiary of the international outsourcing industry, with many customers, particularly in the financial services, pharmaceutical and IT sectors, outsourcing into Ireland. There has also been an increasingly significant level of outsourcing between Irish customers and suppliers, with the services traditionally concentrated in the contact centre, data centre management, systems development, IT support, facilities management, payroll and accounts management areas, across a broad range of industry sectors. In more recent years, there has also been an increase in the level and volume of offshore outsourcings by Irish customers, particularly to eastern Europe and India. However, Ireland has in turn become a "near-shore" centre for a number of international outsourcing suppliers.

48.1.2 Recent developments

While Ireland benefited from exceptional economic growth during the late 1990s and early 21st century (much of which was driven by foreign direct investment and outsourcing into Ireland), there was relatively little public or political focus on offshore outsourcing (although there were notable exceptions in relation to industries which were traditionally unionised). However, the more difficult economic climate prevailing in Ireland and globally at the time of writing has led to a marked increase in opposition to offshore outsourcing, with staff and unions seeking to propose alternative cost-cutting plans to management with a view to retaining jobs in Ireland (the negotiations between Aer Lingus management and employee representatives, which resulted in management shelving outsourcing proposals in favour of a cost-cutting package proposed by the trade unions is a case in point). This has had an inevitable knock-on effect on public and political perceptions of "outsourcing", in which the long-standing benefits to Ireland are sometimes overlooked.

48.1.3 Outlook

Overall, however, outsourcing continues to benefit from high levels of support from government and business, with many of the benefits which led to Ireland's success as an outsourcing destination, such as low corporate tax rates, the availability of a skilled and highly educated labour pool and cultural compatibility with industrialised nations, continuing to hold true (for example, Ireland is included in Gartner Inc.'s 2008 list of leading locations for offshore services). Increasing competition from eastern Europe, particularly on costs, represents a significant challenge, which has led to an increasing focus on Ireland as an outsourcing centre for higher-value operations and skilled labour.

48.1.4 Similarities between Ireland and the UK

Many of the legal issues identified in Parts 1 to 11 of this Guide, and the resulting business issues, are applicable to outsourcing in and from Ireland, which is unsurprising given the long common legal heritage of Ireland and England prior to 1922. Where there are differences which are relevant to outsourcing contracts, the main issues have been identified below.

48.2 People issues - ARD

48.2.1 Implementation of ARD in Ireland

The European Communities (Protection of Employees and Transfer of Undertakings) Regulations 2003 (the "ARD Regulations") implemented the ARD into Irish law. The ARD Regulations give employees certain rights when the whole or part of an undertaking or business is transferred from one employer (transferor) to another employer (transferee) as a result of a legal transfer or merger.

48.2.2 Application of the ARD Regulations to Outsourcing

Whether the ARD Regulations apply to an outsourcing contract will be a question of fact in each case, and will depend on factors such as whether there has been a transfer of assets (either tangible or intangible), or, in the case of an outsourcing to a supplier of a labour-intensive part of a business, whether there is a transfer of a significant part of the workforce (whether in terms of numbers or skills (which, in itself, may be described as an intangible asset)). Unlike the position in the UK, there is no automatic application of the ARD Regulations in the event of a "service provision change".

48.2.3 Effect of application of ARD Regulations

If the ARD Regulations apply, all employees who are wholly or mainly engaged in the business have the right to transfer their employment to the supplier, on their existing terms and conditions of employment, with their continuity of service intact. Where a customer outsources for the first time, if the ARD Regulations apply, the affected employees will therefore have the right to transfer to the supplier. Where a customer changes supplier, the ARD Regulations (if applicable) will normally operate as between the incoming and outgoing suppliers, and should not affect the customer directly (they may indirectly impact on the customer through the new supplier's charges for the services). However, where a customer terminates an outsourcing contract and brings the services back "in-house", then if the ARD Regulations apply, the customer would in such case be the transferee for ARD Regulations purposes. In each case, the issues identified in Chapter 27 in respect of identification and indemnification of risks will need to be considered.

48.2.4 Consultation obligations under the ARD Regulations

48.2.4.1 Duty to consult

The ARD Regulations impose a duty on both the customer (unless the transfer is between two suppliers on a change of supplier) and supplier(s) to inform their respective affected employees (by way of their representatives) of various matters in relation to the transfer and consult with them on any measures envisaged in relation to such employees, with a view to reaching an agreement. The ARD Regulations do not specify that an agreement must be reached on all issues, but simply require that the affected employees must be consulted with a view to reaching an agreement.

48.2.4.2 Information employees must receive

The information that the affected employees are entitled to receive includes the reasons for the transfer and the legal, social and economic implications of the transfer for them, and must be provided at least 30 days in advance of the transfer or, if this is not reasonably practicable, in good time prior to the transfer. If there are any measures envisaged with regard to the employees (i.e. if there are to be changes to their terms and conditions of employment which are, strictly speaking, prohibited by the ARD Regulations or if redundancies post-transfer are contemplated), then they are entitled to be consulted, again, 30 days prior to the transfer, or if this is not reasonably practicable, in good time prior to the transfer.

48.2.4.3 Penalty for non-provision of information to employees

If information provision and, where applicable, consultation does not take place, or is carried out improperly or late, the affected employees or their representatives are entitled to complain to the Rights Commissioners and an award of up to four weeks' gross remuneration per employee may be made. Any claim would transfer to the supplier where the ARD Regulations apply.

48.2.4.4 Information the customer must provide to the supplier

As an adjunct to the above, and subject always to compliance with data protection legislation, the customer (or transferring supplier, as relevant) must supply all "relevant" employment-related information to the supplier, including information in relation to any outstanding claims that the affected employees might have against the customer (or transferring supplier), to facilitate the supplier in complying with its obligations under the ARD Regulations. If this information is not provided and the supplier incurs liability as a result, it may be in a position to recover any losses against the customer (or transferring supplier).

48.2.4.5 No obligation on supplier to provide information to customer

In contrast, unless there are reasons envisaged in relation to the affected employees' employment, there is no equivalent obligation on the incoming supplier to provide information to the customer (or transferring supplier), although in practice, the supplier will commonly request the customer's assistance in disseminating any information about it to transferring employees in advance of the transfer.

48.2.5 Secondment arrangements

Under some outsourcing agreements, the parties have seconded employees from the customer to the supplier, rather than have the employees transfer directly. However, this type of arrangement entails a number of inherent risks. There is a risk that the customer and supplier would be held to be co-employers of the employees. In addition, such an arrangement can make it more difficult to deal with the employees on a daily basis. Finally, if assets are transferred as part of the outsourcing, there is a risk that the ARD Regulations would in any event be deemed to apply, with the result that the secondment arrangement would not prevent employees claiming that they had a right to transfer. As any provision in any agreement which tries to exclude or limit any provision of the ARD Regulations, or which is inconsistent with any of its provisions, is void, structuring the arrangement as a secondment would not preclude the application of the ARD Regulations.

48.2.6 Offshore outsourcings

Where an Irish customer is entering into an offshore outsourcing, then while the ARD Regulations will apply in principle to the outsourcing, the supplier will be under no legal obligation to comply with any of the requirements of the ARD Regulations, including the consultation obligations (although they may be required to comply with their own regulations which transpose ARD (if applicable)). The contractual provisions dealing with the implications of ARD, including any indemnifications and the allocation of risk and cost, will therefore be of even greater importance for the customer.

48.3 People issues – other employment issues

48.3.1 Redundancy

48.3.1.1 Permissible redundancies

Employees affected by an outsourcing agreement can only be dismissed in the case of genuine redundancy. The ARD Regulations permit dismissals for economic, technical or organisational ("ETO") reasons requiring changes in the workforce, which has been broadly defined in relevant case law as redundancy. However, dismissals that occur because of the transfer which are not genuine redundancies or are otherwise unlawful give rise to a risk of unfair dismissal and wrongful dismissal claims against the customer and/or supplier(s). Generally, post-transfer dismissals on ETO grounds are easier to justify than pre-transfer dismissals, as pre-transfer dismissals are more likely to be viewed as arising solely by reason of the transfer.

48.3.1.2 Refusal to transfer

The position of employees who refuse to transfer differs from that in the UK, in that a refusal to transfer is not a deemed resignation. In fact, a recent Employment Appeals Tribunal decision held that two employees who refused to transfer under the ARD Regulations were entitled to redundancy payments from the transferor (it is understood this case is under appeal).

48.3.1.3 *Statutory redundancy*

An employee's statutory redundancy payment will be calculated as two weeks' normal remuneration for each year of continuous and reckonable service, plus the equivalent of one week's normal weekly remuneration. One week's normal remuneration is capped at €600 per week or €31,200 per year. The employee must also be given payment in lieu of notice, any outstanding holidays, bonuses and commissions, and arrears of salary, if any, etc.

48.3.2 Collective redundancies

The Protection of Employment Act 1977 (the "1977 Act"), imposes additional obligations relating to informing and consulting employees' representatives and notifying the Minister for Enterprise, Trade and Employment of proposed collective redundancies. Collective redundancies arise where the numbers being made redundant in any 30-day period, for reasons unconnected with the individual employee, amount to 30 or more individuals, or if fewer, if the number is between approximately 10 per cent and 25 per cent of the workforce (depending on how many people are employed in the organisation). The 1977 Act may be relevant where an outsourcing is likely to result in substantial redundancies.

48.3.3 Unfair dismissals/wrongful dismissals

Where a dismissal arises by reason solely of an outsourcing agreement to which the ARD Regulations apply, or is not a genuine redundancy, then it will be deemed to be unfair, and the affected employee may be entitled to reinstatement, re-engagement or up to two years' gross remuneration. In contrast to unfair dismissal claims brought under the Unfair Dismissals Act 1977 and 2003, where a claim in respect of a dismissal is brought under the ARD Regulations, the affected employee need not have a minimum year's service and is not under any duty to mitigate loss.

An employee may also, in these circumstances, institute an action at common law and seek damages for wrongful dismissal. An employee can choose whether he wants to proceed by way of unfair dismissal or wrongful dismissal. However, wrongful dismissal claims are very rare in transfer of undertakings situations.

48.4 Pensions issues

48.4.1 Pensions issues under the ARD Regulations

48.4.1.1 *Scope of protection – Martin/Beckmann liabilities*

The ARD Regulations do not apply to employees' rights to old age, invalidity or survivor's benefits under company pensions schemes that fall outside the scope of the Social Welfare Acts 2005 to 2006. In essence, therefore, occupational pension scheme benefits will not transfer unless they fall with the Martin/Beckmann liabilities exception. In practice, Martin/Beckmann liabilities would only be expected to arise in public sector schemes or older defined benefit schemes. Risks associated with Martin/Beckmann liabilities are generally addressed in the outsourcing contract through appropriate indemnification provisions.

48.4.1.2 No minimum pension protection

There is currently no Irish law equivalent to the UK's minimum pension protection (outlined in Chapter 28). However, it is expected that this position will change in the medium term, based on an announcement by the Irish Government in 2007 that the issue of pensions rights under ARD would be addressed. Further confirmation of this was given when ARD-related pension issues were included in the 2008 National Pay Deal as one of the issues to be addressed and resolved. In the meantime, the absence of legislative requirements has not prevented the replication, or partial replication, of pension arrangements as a result of commercial negotiations in situations where the ARD Regulations apply, particularly in the public sector and in industries with strong union representation.

48.5 Contract law

48.5.1 General principles

For the most part, the principles of Irish contract law will be the same as those applying under the laws of England and Wales. Material differences, particularly with respect to liability issues, are identified in 48.5.2 and 48.7 below.

48.5.2 Privity of contract issues

48.5.2.1 No third-party beneficiary legislation

There is no Irish equivalent to the Contracts (Rights of Third Parties) Act 1999. Accordingly, the privity of contract rule continues to apply under Irish law.

48.5.2.2 Implication of privity rule

This means that obligations in an agreement that purport to apply to entities that are not a party to the agreement cannot be enforced against those entities, and similarly benefits that purport to be extended to such entities, cannot be enforced by such entities. This can have significant implications for outsourcing arrangements which purport to impose obligations on subcontractors or group companies of the supplier, or to confer benefits on affiliates or customers of the customer, or replacement suppliers.

48.5.2.3 Addressing privity issues

The issue in relation to imposition of obligations can be overcome by making the supplier prime contractor and fully liable for the acts and omissions of its subcontractors and agents. Overcoming the inability of third parties to the contract to enforce purported benefits is more difficult, as there has been no judicial analysis as yet of the various contractual provisions which have been used to attempt to circumvent this limitation (such as providing that the customer can enforce on behalf of the third party, or deeming third-party losses to be losses of the customer).

48.6 Limitations of liability

48.6.1 General approach to liability and limiting liability

In general, the approach to liability issues and limitation on liability provisions, both from a legal and a commercial perspective, will be the same in Ireland as the position outlined in Chapters 30 and 31 in respect of the UK. However, there has been an increasing trend for customers which are multinationals or subsidiaries of multinationals (particularly US multinationals) to seek to impose "US-style" risk allocation provisions in outsourcing contracts, with the customers seeking broad indemnification and unlimited liability under an increasing category of heads. This development is particularly marked in the financial services sector, and poses additional challenges for suppliers in an increasingly competitive market.

48.6.2 Liability under fund custody and administration arrangements

The somewhat unusual approach to liability under fund custody and administration agreements which has been identified in Chapter 30 mirrors the approach taken in the Irish funds industry. However, it remains to be seen whether recent events in the international financial markets, including the issues which have arisen as a direct result of the Lehman insolvency, will lead to a change in approach to liability issues under fund custody and administration agreements.

48.6.3 Sale of Goods Legislation

Under the Sale of Goods Act 1893 and the Sale of Goods and Supply of Services Act 1980 (collectively the "Sale of Goods Legislation"), certain terms are implied into every contract for the sale of goods or the supply of a service.

In the context of services contracts, the implied conditions include conditions that the services will be supplied with "due skill, care and diligence", that where materials are used they will be sound and reasonably fit for the purposes for which they are required, and that where goods are supplied they will be of merchantable quality. Where the agreement is between non-consumers, as would be the case in outsourcings, these implied terms may be excluded or varied by an express term of the contract, or by the course of dealing between the parties, or by usage, if the usage is such as to bind both parties to the contract. However, it is not possible to exclude the implied condition as to title.

48.6.4 Unfair contract terms

Unlike the position in the UK, the application of the Irish legislation which implemented the Unfair Terms in Consumer Contracts Directive[1] (namely the European Communities (Unfair Terms in Consumer Contracts) Regulations 1995) is limited to consumer contracts, and will therefore not be relevant to any outsourcing agreement.

1 Directive 93/13/EEC of 5 April 1993 on unfair terms in consumer contracts.

48.7 Data protection

48.7.1 Implementation of the Data Protection Directive in Ireland

48.7.1.1 Implementing legislation

The Data Protection Directive has been implemented in Ireland through the Data Protection Acts 1988 and 2003 (collectively the "DP Acts").

48.7.1.2 Data Protection Commissioner

The Data Protection Commissioner (the "DPC") is the supervisory authority for the purposes of monitoring the application of the Data Protection Directive in Ireland. The DPC is appointed by the Irish government but is independent in the exercise of his functions, which are essentially to uphold the rights of individuals under the DP Acts, and to enforce against data controllers the obligations specified in the DP Acts. The DPC also exercises certain functions arising from Ireland's membership of the EU, including acting as Ireland's representative on the Article 29 Working Party.

48.7.2 Application of the DP Acts

48.7.2.1 Scope of application

The DP Acts will apply to data controllers "established in Ireland" where data are processed in the context of that establishment, or if the data controller is established neither in Ireland nor in any other EEA state, it makes use of equipment in Ireland for processing the data (otherwise than for the purpose of transit through the territory of Ireland).

48.7.2.2 Meaning of "established in Ireland"

A data controller (not being an individual) will be "established in Ireland" for the purposes of the DP Acts if it is:

(a) an incorporated entity established under the laws of Ireland, i.e. a company established under the Companies Act 1963 to 2006;
(b) a partnership or other unincorporated association formed under the laws of Ireland; or
(c) an entity not falling under the above categories but which maintains in Ireland an office, branch or agency through which it carries on any activity, or a regular practice.

48.7.2.3 Meaning of "data controller"

Whether an entity is a data controller or data processor will be a question of fact in each case. In the majority of outsourcings, the supplier will be a processor acting on behalf of the customer (which will be the data controller).

While in principle all data controllers and data processors to whom the DP Acts apply are obliged to register with the DPC, in practice the obligation will only apply where a controller is not "exempted". Certain "prescribed" categories of data controller, which include financial services institutions and insurance companies, are obliged to register even if they would otherwise fall within the exempt categories.

48.7.3 Implications of the DP Acts for outsourcing

48.7.3.1 Applicable guidelines

The DPC has not issued any specific guidelines in relation to outsourcing of data processing functions, or of services which of necessity involve data processing. However, several of the more general guidelines which have been issued by the DPC, including in particular with respect to transfers abroad and sharing of information within the public and private sectors, will be of relevance in the context of outsourcings.

48.7.3.2 General compliance

Obviously, in entering into any outsourcing arrangement, the customer as a data controller will be obliged to remain in compliance with its general data protection obligations. This includes in respect of disclosure of personal data relating to employees, which will need to be managed so as to ensure compliance with both the DP Acts and the ARD Regulations.

48.7.3.3 Processing agreements

In addition, under the DP Acts, where a customer outsources services which involve processing of personal data, the customer will be obliged to put in place a written agreement with the supplier which specifies that the supplier will only act in relation to the personal data on the instructions of the customer and which sets out the necessary security measures that the supplier will implement. The customer must then ensure compliance with those security measures.

48.7.3.4 Supplier obligations as data processor

It should not be overlooked that the supplier, where it is a data processor, will be independently subject to the data protection security principle, and may be obliged to register with the DPC.

48.7.4 Data protection issues in offshore outsourcings

48.7.4.1 Prohibition on transfer

Under the DP Acts, personal data cannot be transferred from Ireland to a country or territory outside the EEA unless that country or territory ensures an "adequate level of protection" for personal data. While the DP Acts go on to set out a number of factors to be taken into account in determining whether there is an "adequate level of protection" in the jurisdiction in question, in practice, unless the European Commission or the DPC has indicated that it views a jurisdiction as affording an adequate level of protection, or the transfer falls under one of the exemptions specified in the DP Acts, the prohibition will apply.

48.7.4.2 Applicable exemptions

The exemptions in the DP Acts include the EC Model Contract Clauses and BCRs, and the comments in Chapter 38 in relation to these exemptions are equally valid in an Irish context. There is also the possibility under the DP Acts of having the DPC specifically approve a bespoke form of contract, although in order to obtain approval, the customer would need to be in a position to justify its decision not to use the EC Model Contract Clauses, and the bespoke contract should not result in a reduction in the level of protection afforded to data subjects.

48.7.4.3 Consent issues

While data subject consent is one of the exemptions under which transfers from Ireland to non-EEA jurisdictions will be permitted, the DPC has raised concerns where personal data is transferred outside the EEA based on consent, particularly where the transfer is systematic. The stated preference of the DPC would be reliance on the EC Model Contract Clauses and BCRs, and for the other exemptions to be relied on only where it is genuinely not practicable or feasible to rely on these.

48.7.4.4 Processor to processor transfers

It should also be noted that the EC Model Contract Clauses provide for transfers between controller and transfers from controllers to processors. However, they do not exempt transfers from processors to processors, which can give rise to issues where a supplier wishes to subcontract part of the outsourced services to a non-EEA subcontractor or where the outsourcing structure is an "offshore/onshore" or "onshore/offshore" model.

48.7.5 Enforcement

48.7.5.1 Powers of the DPC

The DPC is the body with primary responsibility for enforcement of the DP Acts, and has wide-ranging powers under the DP Acts. The DPC will investigate breaches or likely breaches of the DP Acts, either where an individual complains to him of a contravention (in which case the DPC is obliged to investigate, unless he is of the view that it is frivolous or vexatious), or the DPC is otherwise of the opinion that there has been a contravention. The DPC also has the power to carry out "privacy audits" to ensure compliance with the DP Acts or to identify any contraventions of the DP Acts.

48.7.5.2 Offences

Breaches of many of the provisions of the DP Acts are not, of themselves, offences. Rather, the offence arises from failure to comply with a notice issued by the DPC. Breach of the registration obligations, the carrying on of prescribed processing, provision of false or misleading information to the DPC, and unauthorised disclosure, in certain circumstances, are offences under the DP Acts.

48.7.5.3 DPC notices

The forms of notice which may be issued by the DPC include:

(a) enforcement notices, which are served where the DPC is of the opinion that a person has contravened or is contravening a provision of the DP Acts. This type of notice may require the person to take such steps as are specified in the notice within a specified time to comply with the provision concerned; and
(b) prohibition notices, which prohibit the transfer of personal data from Ireland to a place outside Ireland unless such a transfer is required or authorised by or under any enactment, or required by any convention or other instrument imposing an obligation on Ireland.

48.7.5.4 Statutory duty of care

In addition to the above, the DP Acts establish a statutory duty of care owed by both data controllers and data processors, in respect of the collection by them of personal data or their dealings with such data, towards the relevant data subjects.

48.7.5.5 Individual rights

Individuals also have indirect powers of enforcement of the provisions of the DP Acts, including the right to establish the existence of personal data, the right of access to personal data, a right of rectification or erasure of any personal data in relation to which there has been a contravention of the data protection principles, and the right of a data subject to object to processing of personal data which is likely to cause damage or distress. While primary responsibility for enforcement of the DP Acts rests with the DPC, individuals have further indirect enforcement rights through complaints to the DPC.

48.7.6 Security breaches

48.7.6.1 No express obligation to notify

In common with many other jurisdictions, there have been a number of high-profile data security breaches in Ireland in the recent past. While the DP Acts do not currently impose any obligation on controllers or processors to notify either the DPC or affected customers or individuals in the event of a security breach, the DPC is of the view that, even in the absence of an express obligation, notification is arguably required under data protection principles. The DPC's view is that, in any event, security breaches should be notified to both it and data subjects as a matter of best practice. Data controllers are in general heeding this advice, not least to minimise any adverse publicity arising from a security breach.

48.7.6.2 Mandatory reporting under consideration

In early October 2008, the Minister for Justice indicated that the introduction of mandatory reporting obligations, where personal data is lost or stolen, and which would apply to all state agencies and financial institutions, amongst others, is under consideration. It is envisaged that a broad consultation would be undertaken in advance of introducing legislative changes to effect such an obligation. As stated, mandatory reporting of security breaches is an approach which the DPC would favour.

It is also interesting to note that the draft Directive on Privacy and Electronic Communications, which is limited to privacy issues in the electronic communications sector, contains a notification obligation which will apply to communications sector organisations. The European Data Protection Supervisor has, not unsurprisingly, advocated that this approach be extended more generally to information society service providers, including to the "online" financial services sector.

48.8 Insolvency issues

48.8.1 Examinerships

48.8.1.1 Overview of examinerships

Under the Companies (Amendment) Act 1990, an examinership procedure was introduced into Irish law. Under the examinership procedure, the High Court can place a company under its protection to enable the court-appointed examiner to investigate the company's affairs and to report to the Court on its prospects of survival. If survival of the company can be achieved, the Court may sanction a scheme of arrangement which often involves the part payment of the company's creditors and which enables the company to continue in business.

48.8.1.2 Protection of the High Court

The availability of the examinership procedure could have implications for both customers and suppliers in the event that the other party to an outsourcing contract avails itself of the court protection afforded by the procedure, as upon the appointment of an examiner, the company is placed under the protection of the High Court. Court protection lasts for an initial period of 70 days but can be extended by the court for an additional 30 days. During the protection period, no proceedings can be instigated against a company in examinership. The examiner's main function is to propose a scheme of arrangement to the court, which, if approved by the court and a majority of creditors, becomes binding.

48.8.1.3 Reasonable prospect of survival

A court cannot appoint an examiner unless there is a reasonable prospect for the survival of the company and the whole or any part of its undertaking. Not only must there be a reasonable prospect of survival of the company but there must also be a reasonable prospect of the survival of the whole or any part of its undertaking as a going concern. If, for example, an examiner proposed to sell a company's business and assets then there would not be a reasonable prospect of the survival of the undertaking as a going concern.

48.8.1.4 Restrictions on proceedings against company in examinership

Once the company is placed under court protection, the creditors of the company are prevented from taking any action to enforce their security. In particular:

(a) no proceedings for the winding up of the company may be commenced or resolution for winding up passed and any resolution passed shall have no effect;
(b) no receiver shall be appointed and if appointed shall be unable to act; and
(c) where any claim against the company is secured, no action may be taken to realise the whole or any part of that security except with the consent of the examiner.

Furthermore, there is a general prohibition barring issuing all other proceedings against a company that is under the protection of the court (except with leave of the court).

48.8.1.5 Scheme of arrangement

Where a scheme of arrangement is approved by the court and a majority of the creditors, it will become binding on all creditors, including those who objected to the scheme, and will generally result in the creditors receiving only a proportion of the amounts due to them.

48.8.1.6 Implications for outsourcing agreements
The initiation of an examinership procedure in relation to one party to an outsourcing could therefore significantly restrict the ability of the other party to recover costs or damages. For these reasons, the appointment of an examiner to a customer or supplier would generally be treated as triggering a right to terminate (but not automatic termination, in the same way as the appointment of a liquidator or receiver would trigger a termination right), with a view to limiting any further exposure of the unaffected party.

48.9 Financial services regulation

48.9.1 Financial regulation in Ireland

The Irish Financial Services Regulatory Authority (the "Financial Regulator") is the body responsible for authorisation and regulation of credit and financial services institutions and insurance providers in Ireland.

48.9.2 Implementation of MiFID in Ireland

48.9.2.1 Implementing legislation
MiFID has been implemented in Ireland through the European Communities (Markets in Financial Instruments Directive) Regulations 2007, as amended (the "MiFID Regulations"). Some measures complementary to the MiFID Regulations, such as the imposition of significant penalties for conviction on indictment for major breaches of the MiFID Regulations, required the enactment of primary legislation and were introduced in the Markets in Financial Instruments and Miscellaneous Provisions Act 2007.

48.9.2.2 No "gold-plating"
The MiFID Regulations do not contain any "gold-plating" of MiFID, and are a direct transposition of the requirements of MiFID into Irish law. Therefore, the general comments in relation to MiFID in Chapter 33 apply equally in an Irish context.

48.9.2.3 Formalisation of practice
The introduction of MiFID into Irish law formalised and codified, for MiFID firms, what was already industry practice across a broad range of financial services and insurance outsourcings, as well as introducing an express requirement to document the outsourcing in greater detail than might have been the case prior to MiFID (particularly for intra-group outsourcings).

48.9.3 Implementation of CRD in Ireland

48.9.3.1 Implementing legislation
CRD has been implemented into Irish law through the European Communities (Capital Adequacy of Investment Firms) Regulations 2006 and European Communities (Capital Adequacy of Credit Institutions) Regulations 2006 (collectively the "CRD Regulations"). The Financial Regulator has also issued an administrative notice on the implementation of CRD, which, together with the CRD Regulations and CEBS CRD guidance, forms the basis of the transposition of CRD in

Ireland. The Financial Regulator's notice cross-refers to the CEBS guidance which, absent an explicit statement to the contrary in the Financial Regulator's notice, should be also regarded as applicable Financial Regulator guidance.

48.9.3.2 No "gold-plating"

As is the case with the implementation of MiFID, the CRD Regulations did not impose additional obligations on credit institutions and investment firms. Accordingly, the general comments in Chapter 33 will equally apply in an Irish context.

48.9.4 Financial Regulator approach to outsourcing

The Financial Regulator has not published any specific guidance on outsourcing. In practice, however, the Financial Regulator has applied, as relevant, the international and sector-specific outsourcing guidelines and criteria identified in Chapter 33 (namely those of the Joint Forum, IOSCO and CEBS), the outsourcing rules under MiFID, and the governance requirements under CRD. Even where not mandatory in the context of non-material outsourcings, the relevant guidelines and rules should nonetheless be taken into account in the context of non-material outsourcings. Material outsourcings must be notified to the Financial Regulator in advance.

48.9.5 General Irish provisions

48.9.5.1 Financial Regulator Consumer Protection Code

The Financial Regulator has not published general principles or regulations applicable to regulated firms which would be equivalent to the FSA Handbook. In August 2006, however, it published its Consumer Protection Code ("CPC"), which will be of relevance to an outsourcing by a regulated entity (with some exceptions, including firms providing MiFID services) of functions which might impact on the firm's interactions with its customers. It has also published an Assistance Paper on outsourcing which sets out the views of the Financial Regulator in relation to certain aspects of outsourcing, and which effectively tracks the provisions of MiFID relating to outsourcing.

48.9.5.2 CPC general principles

The CPC sets out a number of general principles to which all firms covered by the CPC must adhere in their dealings with customers and prospective customers (whether or not consumers) and *within the context of their authorisations*. These obligations include:

(a) having and employing effectively the resources and procedures, systems and control checks that are necessary for compliance with the CPC;
(b) full disclosure of relevant material information;
(c) speedy, efficient and fair error correction and complaints handling; and
(d) ensuring that any outsourced activity complies with the requirements of the CPC.

48.9.5.3 Meaning of "consumer"

The CPC also contains detailed provisions which apply where a CPC firm is dealing with "consumers" (which for the purposes of the CPC includes businesses other than incorporated bodies having an annual turnover (or being part of a group having an annual turnover) in excess of €3 million). In addition to the general principles outlined above, the provisions dealing with consumer records, and error and complaints handling, may be of potential relevance in the context of outsourcing arrangements.

48.9.6 Financial services issues in offshore outsourcings

48.9.6.1 No prohibition on offshore outsourcings
In principle, there is no prohibition on regulated entities entering into offshore outsourcing arrangements. Where an outsourcing involves an offshore jurisdiction, the Financial Regulator will focus closely on the confidentiality, security and business continuity arrangements which are implemented as part of the outsourcing.

48.9.6.2 Minimum activities for funds administrators
In the funds administration sector, the Financial Regulator has imposed the following set of minimum activities which must be undertaken in Ireland where the administration services are provided in respect of Irish funds:

(a) calculation of net asset value and dealing price, including the updating/confirmation of the prices of the underlying securities, and the calculation of income and expense accruals;
(b) maintenance and updating of all accounting records, that is, income, expenses, assets and liabilities, including preparation of semi-annual and annual accounts, undertaking of all detailed reconciliation;
(c) issue of dividends, and the reconciliation of all bank accounts, including those relating to dividends;
(d) maintenance and servicing of the unitholders' register including input, alteration and deletion of records, and the issue of unitholders' certificates or their equivalent;
(e) origination and retention of correspondence with unitholders; and
(f) retention of all the back-up documents underlying the books and records.

However, it should be noted that these conditions do not preclude overseas hardware and software facilities being availed of by Irish management companies/administrators/trustees by means of direct access. However, the substantive administration and control of the relevant fund must remain in Ireland.

The Financial Regulator has recently stated that it will undertake an internal review of the minimum activities with a view to a possible move from the current minimum activities regime to that of a control-based environment. Following the internal review, there is likely to be a formal consultation with industry before any changes are effected.

48.10 Public Procurement Directives

48.10.1 Implementation of the Public Procurement Directive in Ireland

48.10.1.1 Implementing legislation
Ireland has implemented the Public Procurement Directive in Ireland through the European

Communities (Award of Public Authorities' Contracts) Regulations 2006 (the "Public Procurement Regulations"). The Public Procurement Regulations came into force in Ireland on 22 June 2006 and apply to all public contracts above certain thresholds (other than those entered into by utilities, dealt with in 48.12 below) entered into on or after that date.

48.10.1.2 Effect of implementation

The Public Procurement Regulations give effect to all of the provisions of the Public Procurement Directives described in Chapter 34, including framework agreements, competitive dialogue and electronic auctions. The Public Procurement Regulations also provide for a standstill period, which is already in line with the Remedies Directive, although Ireland has opted for a 14-day standstill period.

48.10.2 Guidance for other public procurement contracts

48.10.2.1 National guidelines – the Green Book

Public contracts that fall below the thresholds in the Public Procurement Regulations are dealt with at national level. The relevant procedures have been codified in the Department of Finance Public Procurement Guidelines (the "Green Book").

48.10.2.2 Scope of application

The Green Book applies to all government departments and offices, local and regional authorities and state-sponsored bodies in the procurement of public building and civil engineering contracts, public supply contracts and public service contracts, as well as to the disposal of public property.

48.10.2.3 Guidance

It is important to note that the Green Book is only a guidance document and is not legally binding on public contracting authorities. Rather, it sets out the general principle that a procedure based on competitive tendering should be used for all government contracts, save in exceptional circumstances when the approval of the Department of Finance is required. Non-compliance with the Green Book may give rise to corporate governance issues for state bodies.

48.10.3 General principles

There is a dearth of sector-specific guidance for public sector projects (other than in relation to PPP projects as described below, and the use of generic technical specifications in the ICT sector). However, public sector bodies must ensure that all procurement, whether above or below the Public Procurement thresholds, complies with certain general principles derived from the EC Treaty, such as non-discrimination, equality of treatment, transparency, proportionality and mutual recognition.

48.10.4 PPP and PFI contracts

48.10.4.1 Guidance at national level

PFIs are a common form of PPP where the delivery of public services involves private sector investment in infrastructure. Many of the PPP contracts entered into in Ireland in the delivery of infrastructure projects share the characteristics of PFI contracts which are identified in Chapter 35. PFI specific guidance and best practice notes, akin to the UK HM Treasury guidance on the Standardisation of PFI Contracts, have not been published by the Irish authorities. However, the Guidelines for the Provision of Infrastructure and Capital Investments through Public Private Partnerships: Procedures for the Assessment, Approval, Audit and Procurement of Projects, deal with various forms of public procurement, including "design, build, finance, operate and, maintain" (or "DBFOM") contracts (with deferred annual or unitary payments), which would be the equivalent of PFIs as described. In addition, the National Development Finance Agency has published a template form of project agreement for accommodation PPPs, as well as a compendium of clauses for a DBFOM contract (available at www.ppp.gov.ie), which cross-refers in some instances to the UK HM Treasury guidelines.

48.10.4.2 International practice

The HM Treasury guidelines would generally be viewed as best practice for DBFOM contracts, and accordingly the approach to risk allocation and key issues such as termination, force majeure, liability, compensation and waiver of damages (other than for breaches of contract not covered by the payment mechanism) will largely mirror the approach in the UK.

48.10.4.3 Recent developments

Some forms of DBFOM contracts, which incorporate a "balloon payment" on completion of construction, prior to service commencement, together with a shorter concession period during which the services fees will be paid, are being seen as more attractive investments to third-party financing institutions in the current financial market. It is also anticipated that the current credit market difficulties may lead to increasing focus on the covenant of the financing parties in DBFOM projects.

48.11 Utilities Directive

48.11.1 Implementation of the Utilities Directive in Ireland

48.11.1.1 Implementing legislation

Ireland implemented the Utilities Procurement Directive into Irish law through the European Communities (Award of Contracts by Utility Undertakings) Regulations 2007 (the "Utilities Regulations"). The Utilities Regulations came into force in Ireland on 28 February 2007 and apply to all utilities contracts above certain thresholds entered into on or after that date.

48.11.1.2 Effect of implementation

The Utilities Regulations give effect to all of the provisions of the Utilities Directives described in Chapter 37, including framework agreements and electronic auctions. The Utilities Regulations also provide for a standstill period, which is in line with the Remedies Directive, although with Ireland having opted for a 14-day standstill period.

48.11.1.3 National Guidelines – the Green Book

The Green Book will apply to utilities contracts which fall below the thresholds in the Utilities Regulations where the utility is a public sector body covered by the Green Book.

48.12 Competition law

48.12.1 Merger control

48.12.1.1 Irish merger control

The EU merger control regime described in Chapter 29 may apply to outsourcings involving an Irish customer and/or supplier. Alternatively, the outsourcing may be subject to Irish merger control under Part 3 of the Competition Act 2002 (the "Competition Act 2002") (if the EU merger control regime applies, the Irish rules will not be applicable).

48.12.1.2 Meaning of "merger/acquisition"

Under the Competition Act 2002, a merger or acquisition will be deemed to have occurred if, *inter alia*, the result of the acquisition by one undertaking of the assets (including goodwill, or a substantial part of the assets) of a second undertaking is to place the first in a position to replace or substantially replace the second in the business (or the part of the business concerned, as appropriate) in which that undertaking was engaged immediately before the acquisition. Creation of a full-function joint venture (i.e. a joint venture created to perform, on an indefinite basis, all of the functions of an autonomous entity) will also constitute a merger or acquisition for Competition Act 2002 purposes, as would the direct or indirect acquisition by one or more undertakings of the whole (or a part) of another undertaking.

48.12.1.3 Notification thresholds

In order for the mandatory notification obligation under the Competition Act 2002 to apply, the transaction must meet the following thresholds in the most recent financial year:

(a) the worldwide turnover of each of two or more of the undertakings involved is not less than €40 million; and

(b) each of two or more of the undertakings involved "carry on business" in any part of the island of Ireland (i.e. Ireland and Northern Ireland); and

(c) any one of the undertakings involved has a turnover in Ireland (i.e. not including Northern Ireland) of not less than €40 million.

48.12.1.4 Notification is mandatory

No merger meeting the thresholds can come into effect prior to obtaining clearance from the Competition Authority or the merger benefits from "deemed clearance" (where the Competition Authority has failed to issue a determination within statutorily defined periods). Clearance will cover not only the merger itself, but any ancillary restrictions (i.e. those which are directly related and necessary to the implementation of the merger and which are expressly referred to in the notification).

48.12.1.5 Substantive test

The substantive test for assessment under the Competition Act 2002 is "whether the result of the merger or acquisition would be to substantially lessen competition in markets for goods or services" in Ireland. In guidance that the Competition Authority has published in relation to its application of this test, consumer welfare, and in particular likely price increases to consumers as a result of the merger, are emphasised. The Competition Authority has also been sceptical to date in relation to arguments based on efficiencies, although recent indications are that this is changing.

48.12.2 Prohibited anti-competitive agreements

48.12.2.1 Below-threshold mergers
Where mergers fall below the thresholds for mandatory notification, they may nonetheless give rise to competition issues under Sections 4 and 5 of the Competition Act 2002, which prohibit anti-competitive agreements and abuse of dominance respectively (equivalent at national level to Articles 81 and 82 of the EC Treaty). The Competition Act 2002 provides for a voluntary notification procedure in respect of mergers falling below the specified thresholds. The advantage of voluntary notification is that where a merger is cleared by the Competition Authority, it is immune from challenge under Sections 4 and 5. However, in practice, voluntary notification is quite rare.

48.12.2.2 Other anti-competitive agreements
Similarly, where an outsourcing does not fall within the definition of a merger for the purposes of the EC Merger Regulation or the Competition Act 2002, the agreement itself, or an element of it, might be restrictive of competition contrary to Sections 4 and 5 of the Competition Act 2002. Under the Competition Act 2002, the Competition Authority may adopt Declarations in respect of categories of agreements which meet the criteria for exemption under Section 4(5) of the Competition Act 2002 (equivalent to Block Exemptions). The Competition Authority has adopted a number of Declarations at national level. In other cases, the Competition Authority may follow guidance at EU level, in which case the discussion in Chapter 29 in relation to exemptions and Commission notices will be of relevance in an Irish context.

48.13 Other relevant laws and best practice

48.13.1 Dealing with disputes

48.13.1.1 ADR options
The various forms of ADR discussed in Chapter 11 are becoming increasingly common in commercial disputes in Ireland, although mini trials/executive tribunals and early neutral evaluation ("ENE") are still rare.

48.13.1.2 The Commercial Court
In the context of litigating any claims in the Irish courts, it is likely that any claim under an outsourcing agreement would be initiated before the High Court. Application may then be made to have the matter entered into the commercial list of the High Court (colloquially known as the "Commercial Court"). Entry into the Commercial Court is at the discretion of the judge, but is likely to be granted in any case involving a business contract dispute or dispute in relation to the provision of services where the value of the claim is over €1 million, or in any case where the judge in question considers the dispute an appropriate matter for resolution by the Commercial

Court. The major advantages of the Commercial Court are judges who specialise in commercial disputes, and speed, with cases before the Commercial Court taking on average 26 weeks from initiation to listing for hearing. The timelines in the High Court can otherwise be very lengthy.

48.13.2 Taxation

48.13.2.1 Complexity

As is the case in the UK, outsourcing arrangements can give rise to a variety of complex taxation issues, and expert taxation advice should be sought at the earliest opportunity to ensure that the taxation implications of the proposals do not undermine the business case for the outsourcing. A number of the more common Irish taxation issues are highlighted below in more detail.

48.13.2.2 Capital allowances

Where plant and equipment in respect of which capital allowances are available is transferred, the transfer can trigger a balancing charge or balancing allowance on the books of the customer, depending on the difference between the proceeds received on disposal and the tax written-down value as at the date of disposal.

48.13.2.3 Capital gains tax

In outsourcings to unrelated suppliers, any disposal of assets by a customer will constitute a disposal for Irish capital gains tax purposes. In general, therefore, the customer will be required to account for the tax on the chargeable gain that arises, while the supplier is deemed to acquire the asset at its market value at the date of acquisition. However, the taxation analysis can become considerably more complex depending on how the consideration is structured.

Transfers of intellectual property may give rise to either capital gains or corporation tax liabilities, depending on how the transfer and consideration are structured.

48.13.2.4 Corporation tax

There may be a loss of the benefit of losses carried forward where the outsourced activity is a separate business of the customer, as the customer can no longer be viewed as carrying on that activity. This issue will not arise where the outsourced activity was merely a function previously carried on internally within the customer as an inherent part of its overall business.

48.13.2.5 Stamp duty

Irish stamp duty can arise in connection with a number of aspects of outsourcing arrangements which involve the transfer of assets. Transfers of land or premises (real property) on commencement and/or on termination will give rise to a charge to stamp duty of up to 6 per cent of the value of the real property.

A transfer of other assets including, for example, goodwill of a business carried on in Ireland, will also result in a charge to Irish stamp duty, although plant and machinery and similar equipment will generally transfer by delivery and therefore stamp duty should not become an issue in such case. Finally, stamp duty will be applicable to assignments of contracts based on the value of the contract, whereas novations will attract a minimum stamp duty charge.

Since 2004, there has been no stamp duty on the transfer of intellectual property rights under Irish law.

48.13.2.6 Value Added Tax and Sales Tax

Notwithstanding the general principle that, if a supply of goods or services is liable to VAT, the consideration is deemed to be VAT inclusive unless stated to the contrary, the Value Added Tax Act 1972 (as amended) specifies that a supplier which issues a VAT invoice is entitled to recover the VAT.

In relation to termination payments, where these are paid as compensation of damages, they should be VAT exempt. However, predefined contractual termination charges may be subject to VAT. Secondments are also likely to trigger a VAT charge under Irish VAT rules. Otherwise, the broad VAT principles outlined elsewhere in this Guide are also of general application in Ireland.

48.14 Summary

To date, Ireland has, on balance, been a beneficiary of the increase in outsourcing, particularly in sectors such as financial services, pharmaceuticals and technology. While many of the benefits which led to Ireland's success as an outsourcing destination, including low corporate tax rates, the availability of a skilled and highly educated labour pool and cultural compatibility with industrialised nations, continue to hold true, Ireland is facing increasing competition from lower-cost jurisdictions, and particularly near-shore countries in eastern Europe who have sought to use similar tools to replicate Ireland's success. The challenge for the outsourcing industry in Ireland, particularly in a more difficult global economic environment, will be to retain controls on costs, while attracting more of the higher-value operations and skilled jobs. Based on its past experience as a global outsourcing destination, and the benign political and legal environments, it should be well positioned to meet these challenges.

Part Thirteen - Conclusion

Chapter 49

Conclusion - Outsourcing in a Recession

49.1 Outline

This chapter draws together all of the key lessons learned in the rest of the Guide and applies them to one particular situation that is of particular relevance in today's market – the challenges of outsourcing in a recession.

49.2 Past experience of outsourcing in a recession

In the last two recessions/downturns, customers were drawn to the prospect of outsourcing to cut costs. Research supports the conclusion that the 2009 recession will lead to similar behaviour. For example, in February 2009, a report by EquaTerra stated two key findings. First, it found that IT outsourcing is significantly increasing in popularity amongst major UK organisations with 63 per cent of 2008–09 study participants looking to outsource more (compared to 54 per cent in 2007). Second, it found that 69 per cent of the IT heads questioned stated that cost saving was the main driver for outsourcing IT.[1]

However, it is not unusual for customers to question whether it is possible in practice to achieve cost savings in a recession by outsourcing. In the recession of 1990 to 1992 and the recession of 2001 to 2003, many customers outsourced services hastily in an effort to cut costs but ultimately failed to achieve the desired levels of savings. In a case of what Linda Cohen (Gartner analyst) calls "convenient amnesia", IT leaders may forget all of the lessons they learned, rushing into bad outsourcing arrangements and chasing elusive benefits. "Everyone has a gun to their head right now", she says. "But the financial voodoo of outsourcing deals doesn't work."

---

1 The "Outsourcing Service Provider Performance and Satisfaction Study 2008" investigated over 400 outsourcing contracts (330 of the top 500 UK contracts) held by over 125 of the top IT spending organisations in the UK. The total annual value of the contracts included in this study was over £8 billion, accounting for approximately two-thirds of the total UK outsourcing market in terms of annual contract value. All commercial sectors were represented in the study, as was the public sector, including both central and local government organisations. *See*, for example, Deloitte's 2008 outsourcing survey, which found that nearly two-thirds (64 per cent) of the 300 senior executives questioned cited cost reduction as the main attraction of outsourcing. *See* also the statement by Eric Simonson, managing principal at Everest Research Institute, who said: "The decrease in outsourcing transaction activity is primarily on account of deferred spending by large financial firms. However, we expect outsourcing and offshoring activity in the financial sector to pick up during 2009."

Whether customers will achieve cost savings in practice depends upon the individual facts of each case. Customers need to prepare a detailed business case based on sound due diligence to investigate whether outsourcing is the right strategy for them. However, there are certain key success factors which customers need to take into account to achieve cost reductions in today's market. Section 49.3 describes these key success factors for customers.

49.3 The customer perspective

49.3.1 Supplier market

The customer will need to analyse the supplier market and supplier needs to identify the credible suppliers and increase the attractiveness of its offering to these suppliers and hence its bargaining power, in accordance with Chapter 2. This may include considering matters such as whether services should be aggregated or divided up and what the ideal term for the outsourcing agreement is.

49.3.2 Service requirements

The customer will need to have a detailed understanding of the services it will require. This is not simple and involves (as described in Chapters 7, 8 and 9):

(a) Current services – a thorough understanding of the services and levels of services currently being received by the customer – this will usually form a useful starting point from which to analyse future service requirements.

(b) Service needs not wants – an analysis of which of the current services are really required to support the customer's business in the future. This involves distinguishing between services which are essential for the customer to carry out its business and those which are desirable but not necessary. This is sometimes described as distinguishing between "wants" (which may be unaffordable luxuries in a recession) and actual "needs".

(c) Value for money – a comparison between the importance of the service to the customer's business and the cost of that specific service. If the service is already outsourced, this may involve the customer having a detailed breakdown of the charges so that it can understand which elements of the services are the most expensive.

(d) How services are being provided – an analysis of the manner in which the services are currently being provided, together with an understanding of which elements of the service solution are essential and which services could be provided in another manner, if necessary, for example off-site rather than on-site.

(e) Cost analysis – an investigation of the ways in which the service charges can be reduced without affecting critical elements of the services, either by changing the nature of the services or the manner in which they are delivered, for example by standardising the services. This investigation requires the customer to be open minded and flexible in considering creative suggestions so that it can make an informed decision as to what it requires. The process will usually involve "top down" decision making by senior stakeholders who will be required to make difficult decisions about what is really necessary for the business. These decisions will then need to be communicated to users so that they understand and buy into them.

(f) Sourcing options – a consideration of the various sourcing options. All of the above steps could, in theory, be carried out by the customer on its own, whether it is intending to outsource the services or not. However, if the customer is considering outsourcing, it will need to explore the above issues in collaboration with its current or potential outsourcing supplier to see what suggestions the supplier has for reducing the charges, for example by offshoring or by the customer accepting the supplier's standard service offering.

(g) Document the conclusion – lastly, if the customer decides to outsource its services, the documentation of the agreed services and service delivery methods, so that it is clear which specific services are included and which have been deliberately omitted from scope. This documentation must be carefully drafted as, if services are omitted in error, the supplier will not include them in its charges and the customer will have to pay extra for them, potentially undermining the business case for the outsourcing.

Some customers may feel that the above analysis is unnecessary, particularly bearing in mind recent research stating that some supplier margins have increased over recent years. They may feel that they can reduce costs merely by putting pressure on the supplier to reduce its charges. The problem with this approach is that, unless the customer has tied down the boundaries of the services clearly, the supplier may be tempted to carry out its own analysis (not very different from the type of analysis that it is suggested that the customer should carry out above). The supplier will then make unilateral decisions as to how to cuts costs and services, with the resulting impact upon the customer's business.

49.3.3 Risk allocation

The parties will need to have carried out sufficient due diligence to understand the risks that may undermine the success of the outsourcing project. They will need to agree a sensible and consistent approach to the allocation and mitigation of risk that represents good value for the customer and is manageable from the supplier's perspective.

49.3.4 Charging assumptions

In addition to evaluating its service requirements, the customer should carry out sufficient due diligence to ensure that outsourcing will result in cost reductions in practice (as described in Chapter 4). This includes, wherever possible, investigating all of the information necessary for the supplier to provide the customer with a firm price without either party having to take the risk that the charges are calculated on the basis of unsubstantiated charging assumptions, for example as to volumes of services required.

The customer will also need to be aware of the cost implications of the legal and commercial terms that the customer is proposing, including any provisions transferring risk to the supplier, as described in Chapters 18 and 28, so that the supplier will not feel that it needs to include a risk premium in its charges. This means that the customer must employ a cross-functional team comprised of procurement, finance, operational and legal experts who can work effectively together in furthering the joint goals of the organisation. The parties will also need to decide which party will take certain key financial risks, including:

(a) Inflation risk – will the charges be linked to a particular index or will the supplier build inflation into its charges? What will happen if the economy experiences a period of deflation?
(b) Currency risk – in what currency will the charges be payable?
(c) Change in law risk – for example, who takes the risk of future environmental taxes?

The above issues have taken on a new importance, particularly in the current climate of currency fluctuations.

49.3.5 Flexible arrangements

Ideally, the customer needs to balance short-term pressures to cut costs against longer-term needs (as described in Chapter 10). This means ensuring that the outsourcing arrangement is flexible and sets out how the parties will deal with potential changes to the arrangement, for example when the recession ends, the customer's business starts to expand and the volume of services increases. The customer will then be able to carry out sensitivity analyses for the key drivers and other scenarios which may affect the charges in the future, to ensure that it will continue to receive value for money.

49.3.6 Efficient procurement process

If the customer is under internal political pressure to take action to cut costs quickly, it cannot afford to cut corners in deciding upon its services requirements. One area where it may be able to speed up the process is by ensuring that its procurement process is as efficient as possible (as described in Chapter 5).

This will usually involve the customer effectively project managing the procurement, appointing a project manager and project team with sufficient availability to manage the procurement to realistic timescales in accordance with a well thought-through project plan.

The customer may want to make appropriate use of competitive tension between suppliers, (as described in Chapter 3), for example by carrying out e-auctions where appropriate. Although some customers believe that negotiating with more than one supplier will take more time, this is not always the case if negotiations are handled effectively.

In practice, one way that customers in a recession speed up the procurement process (rightly or wrongly) is by limiting the suppliers they negotiate with to the major suppliers in the particular area. This has the advantage of reducing the need to carry out extensive due diligence on supplier capabilities.

49.3.7 Governance

The customer should not attempt to save costs by reducing the resources allocated to manage the outsourcing agreement below those necessary to perform essential service management functions, including those described in Chapter 10, such as:

(a) operational management – monitoring the arrangement on an operational level, to ensure that defects are being dealt with and the service levels are being met; and

(b) strategic management – monitoring whether the customer's business objectives have changed and if so whether the outsourcing agreement needs to change, for example as the recession ends and the customer wants to take advantage of growth opportunities.

Service management also includes the following elements, which, in a recession, take on a particular importance and the customer must ensure that it does not cut costs in a manner which undermines its ability to carry out these roles:

(a) cost management – ensuring that services are not modified by users in a manner that undermines the cost savings and causes cost creep;
(b) continuing requirements analysis – carrying out the requirements analysis mentioned above on a continuing basis to ensure that the customer is aware of and agrees with the supplier what services are required from time to time to support its changing needs, the best way to provide them and any new ways of reducing their cost.

49.3.8 Whole outsourcing lifecycle

The customer will need to ensure that, on termination of the arrangement, there is a smooth transition to another supplier and that the costs of the transition are reasonable and are taken into account in its business case, as described in Chapters 23 to 25. Before it signs the outsourcing agreement, the customer will therefore need to consider the specific assistance it will require on and before termination and wherever possible agree these charges with the supplier in advance.

49.4 The supplier perspective

49.4.1 Non-traditional outsourcing models

Suppliers need to be able to respond to the customer's need to cut costs and speed up the procurement process. One way that they may be able to do this is to embrace the move towards non-traditional outsourcing models (including application service provider ("ASP"), utility computing, software on demand, software as a service ("SAAS") and business process utility ("BPU") models) under which commoditised IT or business process services are made available to the customer on a rental basis.

These usually involve the supplier initially accepting an element of investment and risk by investing in establishing the services. However, once the services have been set up, if sufficient customers can be attracted to use them they may offer cheaper services, which can be provided to the customer with a shorter lead time.

Where non-traditional outsourcing models are impractical, the supplier may still be able to assist the customer to move to more standardised service offerings or to carry out the requirements analysis mentioned above.

49.4.2 Service obligations

In any event, suppliers need to resist the temptation to sign agreements with customers before the services have been adequately scoped and to avoid any risk of accepting open-ended service obligations.

49.4.3 Governance

Suppliers should ensure that they have sufficient staff to manage the contract from their side and that they do not attempt to save costs at the expense of this vital function. Where outsourcing contracts are negotiated with narrow margins, they will need to ensure that they have sufficient up-to-date information about their costs and revenue to be able to ascertain on an ongoing basis whether the individual outsourcing contract is profitable. The supplier will also need to ensure that it is appropriately compensated on termination for investments it has made in the services.

49.5 The challenge of outsourcing in a recession

Satisfying the above factors is not easy. In addition, the parties must satisfy them against the background of a turbulent economic climate which may lead to short-termism and political uncertainty within the customer and supplier organisations resulting in the personal insecurity of the various stakeholders affected by the outsourcing arrangement.

Index

All indexing is to paragraph number